KEY INDICATORS

FOR ASIA AND THE PACIFIC

2016

47TH EDITION

50 YEARS

ADB

ASIAN DEVELOPMENT BANK

© 2016 Asian Development Bank
6 ADB Avenue, Mandaluyong City, 1550 Metro Manila, Philippines
Tel +63 2 632 4444; Fax +63 2 636 2444
www.adb.org

Some rights reserved. Published in 2016.
Printed in the Philippines.

ISBN 978-92-9257-629-5 (Print), 978-92-9257-630-1 (PDF)
Publication Stock No. FLS168387-2

Cataloging-In-Publication Data

Asian Development Bank.
        Key indicators for Asia and the Pacific 2016.
Mandaluyong City, Philippines: Asian Development Bank, 2016.

1. Economic indicators. 2. Financial indicators. 3. Social indicators. 4. Energy and environmental indicators.
5. Sustainable development goals. 6. Infrastructure indicators. 7. Governance indicators.
I. Asian Development Bank.

Foreword

The *Key Indicators for Asia and the Pacific 2016 (Key Indicators 2016)*, the 47th edition of this series, includes the latest available economic, financial, social, and environmental indicators for the 48 regional members of the Asian Development Bank (ADB). Part I presents the current status of economies of Asia and the Pacific with respect to the Sustainable Development Goals (SDGs) based on selected indicators. Part II comprises statistics on economic, financial, social, and environmental dimensions of development. In Part III, statistics generated by ADB on the participation of selected Asian economies in global value chains are showcased.

The SDGs were launched at the United Nations General Assembly in September 2015 as a universal plan of action for ending poverty, protecting the planet, and ensuring that all people enjoy peace and prosperity. They comprise 17 goals, 169 targets, and 230 indicators. Part I of this publication presents a snapshot of Asia and the Pacific by using data for selected SDG indicators. The discussion is organized into five themes—People, Planet, Prosperity, Peace, and Partnership—each of which presents a brief analysis of key trends for selected indicators highlighting the region's status with respect to the SDGs. The analyses suggest that although Asia and the Pacific had an impressive scorecard with respect to the Millennium Development Goals, much needs to be done to address various aspects of sustainable development. Part I also discusses the data gaps in official statistics for tracking the SDGs, and opportunities and challenges that "big data"—the data that arise from people's transactions with digital technologies—present in the compilation of official statistics.

Regional tables in Part II present statistical indicators across eight themes: People; Economy and Output; Money, Finance, and Prices; Globalization; Transport and Communications; Energy and Electricity; Environment; and Government and Governance. The data reinforce the message of Asia and the Pacific's growing importance in the world. The region now accounts for roughly 55% of the global population, 40% of global gross domestic product (in purchasing power parity terms), and about a third of the world's merchandise exports. However, this growing importance is accompanied by issues that need to be addressed. About 1.2 billion people in Asia and the Pacific are still living on less than $3.10 per day, a poverty line more typical of national poverty lines in low and middle income countries than the $1.90 per day poverty line meant to capture extreme poverty. The region now consumes two-fifths of the world's energy, continues to increase its emissions of greenhouse gases and other pollutants, and faces increasing traffic congestion and rising consumption of scarce resources.

In recognition of the importance of in-depth trade statistics, Part III presents a number of key statistics related to global value chains generated by ADB for selected economies of Asia and the Pacific. These statistics were first introduced in the 2015 edition of *Key Indicators*. In an economic environment increasingly characterized by globally distributed production processes, these measures complement the traditional trade statistics and capture the essence of cross-economy production arrangements. With trade in intermediate goods and services accounting for more than half of all international trade, these statistics will be useful for analysts seeking to illuminate policy and research issues.

The online version of this publication is complemented by a suite of country tables for our 48 regional member countries containing information on a wide range of statistical indicators on population, labor force, national accounts, production and price indexes, energy, money and banking, government finance, external trade, balance of payments, international reserves, exchange rates, and external indebtedness. This year, data on the labor force and national accounts have been updated to provide more disaggregated data across economic sectors consistent with the United Nations System of National Accounts 2008. Balance-of-payments data have also been updated in line with the sixth edition of the International Monetary Fund's Balance of Payments and International Investment Position Manual.

We appreciate the continued cooperation of our statistical partners in regional member countries and international agencies for providing us the most recent official data on a variety of indicators. We hope *Key Indicators* will remain a valuable resource for information on development issues and data for a wide variety of audiences, including policy makers, development practitioners, government officials, researchers, students, and the general public. As always, we welcome feedback from our users on both the content and structure of the publication (which can be e-mailed to keyindicators@adb.org).

Takehiko Nakao
President

Acknowledgments

The *Key Indicators for Asia and the Pacific 2016 (Key Indicators 2016)* was prepared by the Development Economics and Indicators Division (ERDI) of the Economic Research and Regional Cooperation Department (ERCD) of the Asian Development Bank (ADB), under the overall supervision of Rana Hasan.

Contributions from ERCD's statistical partners—regional members and international organizations—who shared their data for the statistical tables on the Sustainable Development Goals Indicators (Part I), regional tables (Part II), global value chains (Part III), and country tables are greatly appreciated. ADB resident missions in Afghanistan, Armenia, Azerbaijan, Bangladesh, Cambodia, the People's Republic of China, Georgia, India, Indonesia, Kazakhstan, the Kyrgyz Republic, the Lao People's Democratic Republic, Mongolia, Nepal, Pakistan, Papua New Guinea, Sri Lanka, Tajikistan, Thailand, Turkmenistan, Uzbekistan, and Viet Nam provided support in compiling the data from their respective countries. ADB's Japanese Representative Office, Pacific Liaison and Coordination Office, Philippines Country Office, Pacific Subregional Office, and Timor-Leste Resident Mission also provided help in data compilation. We also appreciate the continuing cooperation of the governments and other international agencies.

The statistical tables including the country tables were prepared by ERDI staff and consultants under the general guidance of Kaushal Joshi, Mahinthan Joseph Mariasingham, Arturo Martinez Jr., and Lakshman Nagraj Rao with the technical assistance of Pamela Lapitan, Melissa Pascua, and Eric Suan. The research team included Raymond Adofina, Kristine Faith Agtarap, Glenita Amoranto, Nalwino Billones, Eileen Capilit, Clemence Fatima Cruz, Mario Ilagan, Cindy Justo, Jude David Roque, Magnolia San Diego, Iva Sebastian, Orlee Velarde, and Priscille Villanueva. Proofreading of statistical tables was done with the assistance of Ma. Roselia Babalo, Aileen Gatson, and Oth Marulou Gagni. The analysis of Sustainable Development Goals indicators was prepared by Erniel Barrios, Arturo Martinez Jr., and Lakshman Nagraj Rao while analysis of regional trends was done by Kevin Donahue, Arturo Martinez Jr., and Lakshman Nagraj Rao. Kaushal Joshi, Mahinthan Joseph Mariasingham, Arturo Martinez Jr., and Lakshman Nagraj Rao reviewed the statistical tables and analytical reports. Zhigang Li and Mahinthan Joseph Mariasingham, in collaboration with Pamela Bayona, Carlos Vincent Chua, Paul Feliciano, Amador Foronda, Janine Elora Lazatin, Julieta Magallanes, Resi Olivares, and Irene Talam, produced statistical tables on global value chains. The global value chains data development project benefited considerably from the feedback provided by Valerie Mercer-Blackman, Niny Khor, Woori Lee, Zhi Wang, and Chenying Yang. Kae Sugawara copyedited the statistical tables and analytical write-up. Cherry Lynn Zafaralla proofread the publication.

Rhommell Rico designed the cover and graphics for the publication, led the typesetting process, and provided technical support for the preparation of all dissemination materials. Joe Mark Ganaban and Joseph Manglicmot assisted in typesetting. The Office of Information Systems and Technology staff provided database management and technology support, while the Logistics Management Unit of the Office of Administrative Services facilitated the timely and smooth production of the *Key Indicators 2016*. The publishing team of the Department of External Relations (DER) conducted overall compliance check. We also thank Erik Churchill and Karen Lane, assisted by the DER staff, for organizing the dissemination activities.

Juzhong Zhuang
Deputy Chief Economist and
Deputy Director General

Contents

Sustainable Development Goals – Boxes, Figures, and Table

PART II – Regional Trends and Tables

Energy and Electricity...**223**

Electricity

    Table 6.1:   Electricity Production and Sources...228

    Table 6.2:   Electric Power Consumption and Electrification 229

Energy

    Table 6.3:   Use of Energy 230

    Table 6.4:   Energy Production and Imports..231

    Table 6.5:   Retail Prices of Fuel Energy ($ per liter)...232

Environment **233**

Land

    Table 7.1:   Agriculture Land Use (% of land area) 240

Pollution

    Table 7.2:   Deforestation and Pollution...241

Freshwater

    Table 7.3:   Freshwater Resources 243

Government and Governance **244**

Government Finance

    Table 8.1:   Fiscal Balance (% of GDP)...251

    Table 8.2:   Tax Revenue (% of GDP) 252

    Table 8.3:   Total Government Revenue (% of GDP)...253

    Table 8.4:   Total Government Expenditure (% of GDP)..254

    Table 8.5:   Government Expenditure by Economic Activity (% of GDP)..255

Governance

    Table 8.6:   Doing Business Start-Up Indicators..256

    Table 8.7:   Corruption Perceptions Index 257

Regional Trends and Tables – Boxes, Figures, and Tables

    Box 1.1:   Demographic Trends in Asia and the Pacific, 1960–Present...97

    Box 2.1:   Economic Trends in Selected Economies of Asia and the Pacific, 1960–Present 131

    Box 3.1:   Difference between Consumer Price Index and Producer Price Index..........................160

    Box 7.1:   Trends in Carbon Dioxide Emissions, 1960–Present.. 238

    Figure 1.1:   Distribution of Population by Global Region, and by Economy in Asia

                and the Pacific, 2015 (%)... 91

    Figure 1.2:   Average Annual Population Growth Rate, 2000–2015 (%) 92

    Figure 1.3:   Population Pyramid by 5-year Age Groups, by Sex (millions)...93

    Figure 1.4:   Age Dependency Ratio 94

    Figure 1.5:   Largest Urban Agglomerations Ranked by Population, 2015 (%) 95

    Figure 1.6a: Human Development Index, 2014 96

    Figure 1.6b: Human Development Index Average Annual Growth, 2000–2014 (%).............................96

PART III – Global Value Chains

Tables

Statistical Partners

The preparation and publication of the *Key Indicators for Asia and the Pacific 2016* would not have been possible without the support, assistance, and cooperation of the partners in the regional members of the Asian Development Bank (ADB) and in international, private, and nongovernment organizations. These partners, who shared their data, knowledge, expertise, and other information, help provide ADB, policy makers, and other data users with a better understanding of the performance of countries around Asia and the Pacific region, so that better policies can be formulated to improve the quality of life of people in the region.

REGIONAL MEMBERS

Afghanistan	Central Statistics Organization (http://cso.gov.af/en)
	Da Afghanistan Bank (http://www.centralbank.gov.af)
	Ministry of Finance (http://mof.gov.af/en)
Armenia	Central Bank of Armenia (https://www.cba.am/en)
	National Statistical Service of the Republic of Armenia (http://www.armstat.am/en)
Australia	Australian Bureau of Statistics (http://www.abs.gov.au)
	Department of Industry, Innovation and Science (http://www.industry.gov.au)
	Reserve Bank of Australia (http://www.rba.gov.au)
Azerbaijan	Central Bank of the Republic of Azerbaijan (http://en.cbar.az)
	State Statistical Committee of the Republic of Azerbaijan (http://www.stat.gov.az)
Bangladesh	Bangladesh Bank (http://www.bb.org.bd)
	Bangladesh Bureau of Statistics (http://www.bbs.gov.bd)
	Ministry of Finance (http://www.mof.gov.bd/en)
Bhutan	Ministry of Finance (http://www.mof.gov.bt)
	Ministry of Labour and Human Resources (http://www.molhr.gov.bt)
	National Statistics Bureau (http://www.nsb.gov.bt)
	Royal Monetary Authority of Bhutan (http://www.rma.org.bt)
Brunei Darussalam	Autoriti Monetari Brunei Darussalam (http://www.ambd.gov.bn)
	Department of Economic Planning and Development (http://www.depd.gov.bn)
	Ministry of Finance (http://www.mof.gov.bn/)
Cambodia	Ministry of Economy and Finance (http://www.mef.gov.kh)
	National Bank of Cambodia (http://www.nbc.org.kh)
	National Institute of Statistics (http://www.nis.gov.kh)

China, People's Republic of	National Bureau of Statistics of China (http://www.stats.gov.cn/english) The People's Bank of China (http://www.pbc.gov.cn) State Administration of Foreign Exchange (http://www.safe.gov.cn)
Cook Islands	Cook Islands Statistics Office (http://www.mfem.gov.ck) Ministry of Finance and Economic Management (http://www.mfem.gov.ck)
Fiji	Fiji Bureau of Statistics (http://www.statsfiji.gov.fj) Reserve Bank of Fiji (www.rbf.gov.fj)
Georgia	Ministry of Finance of Georgia (http://www.mof.ge) National Bank of Georgia (http://www.nbg.gov.ge) National Statistics Office of Georgia (http://www.geostat.ge)
Hong Kong, China	Census and Statistics Department (http://www.censtatd.gov.hk) Hong Kong Monetary Authority (http://www.hkma.gov.hk)
India	Central Statistics Office (http://mospi.nic.in) Ministry of Finance (http://finmin.nic.in) Reserve Bank of India (http://www.rbi.org.in)
Indonesia	Bank Indonesia (http://www.bi.go.id/web) Badan Pusat Statistik-Statistics Indonesia (http://www.bps.go.id) Ministry of Energy and Mineral Resources (http://www.esdm.go.id) PT Pertamina (Persero) (http://www.barata.co.id)
Japan	Bank of Japan (http://www.boj.or.jp/en) Economic and Social Research Institute (http://www.esri.go.jp) Japan Customs (http://www.customs.go.jp/english/) Japan Statistics Bureau (http://www.stat.go.jp/english) Ministry of Economy, Trade and Industry (http://www.meti.go.jp) Ministry of Finance (http://www.mof.go.jp)
Kazakhstan	Committee of Statistics (COS) of the Ministry of National Economy of the Republic of Kazakhstan (formerly Agency on Statistics of the Republic of Kazakhstan) (http://www.stat.gov.kz) National Bank of Kazakhstan (http://www.nationalbank.kz)
Kiribati	Kiribati National Statistics Office (http://www.mfed.gov.ki)
Korea, Republic of	Bank of Korea (http://www.bok.or.kr/eng/engMain.action) Ministry of Strategy and Finance (http://english.mosf.go.kr) Statistics Korea (http://kostat.go.kr)

Kyrgyz Republic	National Bank of the Kyrgyz Republic (http://www.nbkr.kg)
	National Statistical Committee of the Kyrgyz Republic (http://www.stat.kg)
Lao People's Democratic Republic	Bank of the Lao PDR (http://www.bol.gov.la)
	Lao Statistics Bureau (http://www.lsb.gov.la)
	Ministry of Finance (http://www.mof.gov.la)
Malaysia	Bank Negara Malaysia (http://www.bnm.gov.my)
	Department of Statistics (http://www.statistics.gov.my)
	Ministry of Finance (http://www.treasury.gov.my)
Maldives	National Bureau of Statistics (http://statisticsmaldives.gov.mv/)
	Maldives Monetary Authority (http://www.mma.gov.mv)
	Ministry of Finance and Treasury (http://www.finance.gov.mv)
Marshall Islands	Economic Policy, Planning and Statistics Office (http://www.spc.int/prism/country/mh/stats)
Micronesia, Federated States of	Department of Finance and Administration (http://www.fsmpio.fm/Depts/Finance/finance.htm)
Mongolia	Bank of Mongolia (http://www.mongolbank.mn/eng)
	National Statistics Office of Mongolia (http://en.nso.mn)
Myanmar	Central Bank of Myanmar (http://www.cbm.gov.mm/)
	Central Statistical Organization (http://www.csostat.gov.mm)
Nauru	Ministry of Finance and Economic Planning (http://www.naurugov.nr)
	Nauru Bureau of Statistics (http://www.spc.int/prism/country/nr/stats)
Nepal	Central Bureau of Statistics (http://cbs.gov.np)
	Ministry of Finance (http://www.mof.gov.np)
	Nepal Rastra Bank (http://www.nrb.org.np)
New Zealand	Ministry of Business, Innovation and Employment (www.mbie.govt.nz)
	Reserve Bank of New Zealand (http://www.rbnz.govt.nz)
	Statistics New Zealand (http://www.stats.govt.nz)
Pakistan	Ministry of Finance, Revenue, Economic Affairs, Statistics and Privatization (http://www.ead.gov.pk)
	Ministry of Finance (http://www.finance.gov.pk)
	Pakistan Bureau of Statistics (http://www.pbs.gov.pk)
	State Bank of Pakistan (http://www.sbp.org.pk)

Palau	Bureau of Budget and Planning, Ministry of Finance (http://palaugov.org/executive-branch/ministries/finance/ budgetandplanning)
Papua New Guinea	Bank of Papua New Guinea (http://www.bankpng.gov.pg)
	Department of Treasury (http://www.treasury.gov.pg)
	National Statistical Office (http://www.nso.gov.pg)
Philippines	Bangko Sentral ng Pilipinas (http://www.bsp.gov.ph)
	Bureau of Local Government Finance (http://www.blgf.gov.ph)
	Bureau of the Treasury (http://www.treasury.gov.ph)
	Department of Budget and Management (http://www.dbm.gov.ph)
	Department of Energy (http://www.doe.gov.ph)
	Philippine Statistics Authority (http://www.psa.gov.ph)
Samoa	Samoa Bureau of Statistics (http://www.sbs.gov.ws)
	Central Bank of Samoa (http://www.cbs.gov.ws)
Singapore	Department of Statistics (http://www.singstat.gov.sg)
	International Enterprise Singapore (http://www.iesingapore.gov.sg)
	Ministry of Finance (http://www.mof.gov.sg)
	Ministry of Manpower (http://www.mom.gov.sg)
	Ministry of Trade and Industry (http://www.mti.gov.sg)
	Monetary Authority of Singapore (http://www.mas.gov.sg)
Solomon Islands	Central Bank of Solomon Islands (http://www.cbsi.com.sb)
	Solomon Islands National Statistics Office (http://www.statistics.gov.sb)
Sri Lanka	Central Bank of Sri Lanka (http://www.cbsl.gov.lk)
	Department of Census and Statistics (http://www.statistics.gov.lk)
Taipei,China	Central bank of Taipei,China (http://www.cbc.gov.tw)
	Directorate-General of Budget, Accounting and Statistics (http://eng.dgbas.gov.tw)
	Ministry of Economic Affairs (www.moea.gov.tw)
	Ministry of Finance (http://www.mof.gov.tw)
Tajikistan	National Bank of Tajikistan (http://www.nbt.tj)
	State Statistical Committee of the Republic of Tajikistan (http://www.stat.tj)
Thailand	Bank of Thailand (http://www.bot.or.th)
	Ministry of Finance (http://www2.mof.go.th)
	National Economic and Social Development Board (http://www.nesdb.go.th/nesdb_en)
	National Statistical Office (http://web.nso.go.th)
	Energy Policy and Planning Office, Ministry of Energy (www.eppo.go.th)

Timor-Leste	Central Bank of Timor-Leste (www.bancocentral.tl/en)
	Ministry of Finance (http://www.mof.gov.tl)
	General Directorate of Statistics (http://www.statistics.gov.tl)

Tonga	Ministry of Finance and National Planning (http://www.finance.gov.to)
	National Reserve Bank of Tonga (http://www.reservebank.to)
	Department of Statistics (http://www.spc.int/prism/tonga)

| Turkmenistan | Central Bank of Turkmenistan (www.cbt.tm/en) |
| | The State Committee of Turkmenistan on Statistics (http://www.stat.gov.tm) |

| Tuvalu | Central Statistics Division (http://www.spc.int/prism/tuvalu) |

Uzbekistan	Cabinet of Ministers (http://www.gov.uz/en/government)
	Central Bank of the Republic of Uzbekistan (http://www.cbu.uz)
	Ministry of Finance (http://www.mf.uz)
	State Committee of the Republic of Uzbekistan on Statistics (http://www.stat.uz)

Vanuatu	Department of Finance and Treasury (https://doft.gov.vu)
	Reserve Bank of Vanuatu (http://www.rbv.gov.vu)
	Vanuatu National Statistics Office (http://www.vnso.gov.vu)

Viet Nam	General Statistics Office (http://www.gso.gov.vn)
	Ministry of Finance (http://www.mof.gov.vn)
	State Bank of Viet Nam (http://www.sbv.gov.vn)

INTERNATIONAL, PRIVATE, AND NONGOVERNMENT ORGANIZATIONS

Association of Southeast Asian Nations
Australian Institute of Petroleum
CEIC Data
European Bank for Reconstruction and Development
Food and Agriculture Organization of the United Nations
Graduate School USA, Pacific and Virgin Islands Training Initiatives
The Institute of Energy Economics, Japan, The Oil Information Center
International Energy Agency
International Labour Organization
International Monetary Fund
International Telecommunication Union
Interstate Statistical Committee of the Commonwealth of Independent States
Joint United Nations Programme on HIV/AIDS
Organisation for Economic Co-operation and Development
Secretariat of the Pacific Community

Transparency International
UNESCO Institute for Statistics
United Nations Children's Fund
United Nations Department of Economic and Social Affairs
United Nations Development Programme
United Nations Economic Commission for Europe
United Nations Economic and Social Commission for Asia and the Pacific
United Nations Educational, Scientific and Cultural Organization
United Nations Environment Programme
United Nations Human Settlements Programme
United Nations Population Division
United Nations Statistics Division
United Nations World Tourism Organization
United States Census Bureau
United States Bureau of Economic Analysis
World Bank
World Health Organization
WHO/UNICEF Joint Monitoring Programme (JMP) for Water Supply and Sanitation
World Trade Organization

Guide for Users

The *Key Indicators for Asia and the Pacific 2016 (Key Indicators 2016)* has the following structure. The Highlights section presents key messages from various parts of the publication. Part I comprises the data tables on indicators for the Sustainable Development Goals (SDGs). The indicators are presented according to the United Nations SDG global indicator framework, which was endorsed by the United Nations Statistical Commission in March 2016. The *Key Indicators 2016* includes data on as many of the indicators that are as widely available as possible for Asia and the Pacific economies. Tables in Part I present relevant SDG targets and statistical indicators for which data are available. Furthermore, the last section of Part I discusses the data gaps in official statistics for tracking the SDGs and opportunities and challenges that "big data"—the data that arise from people's transactions with digital technologies—present in the compilation of official statistics.

Part II consists of 100 statistical tables grouped into eight themes: People; Economy and Output; Money, Finance, and Prices; Globalization; Transport and Communications; Energy and Electricity; Environment; and Government and Governance. Each theme is further divided into subtopics. Accompanying tables in Part II contain indicators related to a subtopic. Part II also presents discussion boxes that summarize some of the major social and economic transformations in Asia and the Pacific since 1960.

The SDGs and themes in Parts I and II start with a short commentary with charts and boxes describing the status by economies with respect to selected targets and key trends of selected indicators. The accompanying statistical tables are presented for 48 economies of the Asia and Pacific region that are members of the Asian Development Bank (ADB). The term "country," used interchangeably with economy, is not intended to make any judgment as to the legal or other status of any territory or area. The 48 economies have been broadly grouped into developing member countries and developed member countries aligned with the operational effectiveness of ADB's regional departments. The latter refer exclusively to the three economies of Australia, Japan, and New Zealand. Based on ADB's regional operations, the remaining 45 developing member countries are further grouped into five groups based on ADB's operational regions: Central and West Asia, East Asia, South Asia, Southeast Asia, and the Pacific. Economies are listed alphabetically per country group. The term "regional members" used in some tables refers to all 48 regional members of ADB, both developing and developed. Indicators are shown for the most recent year (usually 2015) or period for which data are available and, in most tables, for an earlier year or period (usually 2000). Part III contains select indicators for depicting Asia and the Pacific economies' participation in global value chains and their sector-specific comparative advantage in terms of exports.

Finally, Part IV defines the indicators in the SDGs and regional tables. The publication is also available on ADB's website at www.adb.org/ki-2016 with individual statistical tables of the 48 regional members.

Data for the SDG indicators, regional tables, and country tables are mainly obtained from two sources: ADB's statistical partners in regional members and international statistical agencies, particularly from the United Nations SDG Indicators Global Database. The indicators data presented in Part I are mainly from the SDG Indicators Global Database, a master set of data prepared by the Department of Economic and Social Affairs of the United Nations Secretariat and databases maintained by several international agencies who prepared one or more of the series of statistical indicators included in the SDG Indicators Global Database based in their area of expertise and as per their mandates.

Data produced and disseminated by international agencies are generally based on country data—data produced and disseminated by the country (including data adjusted by the country to meet international standards). However, it should be noted that national data may be compiled using national standards and practices and, as such, international agencies often adjust the data for international comparability. In such cases, data disseminated by the international agencies may differ from data from national sources. In other cases, when data for a specific year or set of years are not available or they are available from multiple national sources (surveys, administrative data sources, and other sources), or when there are data quality issues, the relevant international agency may estimate the data. Some indicators are regularly produced for the purpose of global monitoring by the designated agency and there are no corresponding data at the country level (e.g., population below $1.90 at 2011 purchasing power parity). In other cases, the differences between data from national and international agencies may be because most recent and/or revised data available at the country level are not yet available with the relevant international agency. Some data gaps are filled by supplementing or deriving data collected through sample surveys financed and carried out by international agencies. For example, many of the health indicators are estimated using data from the Multiple Indicator Cluster Surveys and Demographic and Health Surveys. ADB exercises due care and caution in collecting the data before publication. Nevertheless, data from international sources presented in this publication may differ from those available within countries. Thus, for a detailed description of how the indicators are compiled by the international agencies, readers may refer to the metadata available from databases of the individual international agencies or in the SDG Indicators Global Database website for metadata of SDG indicators. Comparable and standardized national data gathered through a robust data reporting mechanism of the international agencies should be the basis for all data in the global monitoring databases and global indicators should be produced in full consultation with national statistical agencies.

Data obtained from the regional members are comparable to the extent that the regional members follow standard statistical concepts, definitions, and estimation methods recommended by the United Nations and other applicable international agencies. Nevertheless, regional members invariably develop and use their own concepts, definitions, and estimation methodologies to suit their individual circumstances, and these may not necessarily comply with recommended international standards. Thus, even though attempts are made to present the data in a comparable and uniform format, they are subject to variations in the statistical methods used by regional members, such that full comparability of data may not be possible. These variations are reflected in the footnotes of the statistical tables or noted in the Data Issues and Comparability sections. Moreover, the aggregates for developing member countries and regional members shown in some tables are treated as approximations of the actual total or average, or growth rates, due to missing data from the primary source. No attempt has been made to impute the missing data.

The data published by ADB do not constitute any form of advice or recommendation. In case of any questions on the data, users of this publication are requested to make inquiries and seek advice from the appropriate data sources.

Fiscal Year

The data cutoff date for this issue is **September 2016**.

Twenty-four regional members have varying fiscal years not corresponding to the calendar year. Whenever the statistical series (for example, national accounts or government finance) are compiled on a fiscal year basis, these are presented under single-year captions corresponding to the period under which most of the fiscal year falls, as follows:

Regional Members	Fiscal Year	Year Caption
Afghanistan	21 December 2014–20 December 2015	2015
Cook Islands (after 1990)	1 July 2014–30 June 2015	2015
Brunei Darussalam (after 2002) Hong Kong, China India Japan Myanmar New Zealand Singapore	1 April 2015–31 March 2016	2015
Australia Bangladesh Bhutan Nauru Pakistan Samoa Tonga	1 July 2014–30 June 2015	2015
Nepal	16 July 2014–15 July 2015	2015
Lao People's Democratic Republic (after 1992) Marshall Islands Micronesia, Federated States of Palau Thailand	1 October 2014–30 September 2015	2015

Key Symbols

...	Data not available at cutoff date
–	Magnitude equals to zero
0 or 0.0	Magnitude is less than half of unit employed
*	Provisional/preliminary/estimate/budget figure
|	Marks break in series
>	Greater than
<	Less than
≥	Greater than or equal to
≤	Less than or equal to
na	Not applicable
%	Percent

Measurement Units

kg	kilogram
km	kilometer
kWh	kilowatt-hour
kt	kiloton
ktoe	kiloton of oil equivalent
m^3	cubic meter
mj	megajoule
teu	twenty-foot equivalent unit

Abbreviations

ADB	Asian Development Bank
ADB SDBS	Asian Development Bank Statistical Database System
ARGO	AutoRegression with GOogle search data
ASEAN	Association of Southeast Asian Nations
BOP	balance of payments
BPM5	Balance of Payments Manual, Fifth Edition
BPM6	Balance of Payments and International Investment Position Manual, Sixth Edition
CBS	Central Bureau of Statistics
CDR	call detail record
CIESIN	Center for International Earth Science Information Network
CIF	cost, insurance, and freight
CO_2	carbon dioxide
CPI	consumer price index
DHS	Demographic and Health Survey
DMC	developing member country
DMSP-OLS	Defense Meteorological Satellite Program Operational Linescan System

DOTS	Direction of Trade Statistics
EDGE	Evidence and Data for Gender Equality
ESCAP	Economic and Social Commission for Asia and the Pacific
FAO	Food and Agriculture Organization of the United Nations
FDI	foreign direct investment
FOB	free on board
FSM	Federated States of Micronesia
FVA	foreign value added
GCF	gross capital formation
GDP	gross domestic product
GFC	global financial crisis
GHG	greenhouse gas
GHO	Global Health Observatory
GNI	gross national income
GVC	global value chain
GWG	global working group
HDI	Human Development Index
IAEG-SDGs	UN Inter-agency and Expert Group on SDG Indicators
HIV	human immunodeficiency virus
IDA	International Development Association
IEA	International Energy Agency
ILO	International Labour Organization
IMF	International Monetary Fund
ITU	International Telecommunication Union
J-REIT	Japan's real estate investment trust
KILM	Key Indicators of the Labour Market
Lao PDR	Lao People's Democratic Republic
LCU	local currency unit
LFS	Labor Force Survey
LFS-PUF	Labor Force Survey public use file
LVC	local value chain
MDG	Millennium Development Goal
MMA	Maldives Monetary Authority
MOF	Ministry of Finance
MOLAR	Ministry of Labor and Human Resources
NBS	National Bureau of Statistics
NOAA	United States National Oceanic and Atmospheric Administration
NPL	nonperforming loan
NRB	Nepal Rastra Bank
NSB	National Statistics Bureau
NSO	National Statistics Office
ODA	official development assistance
OECD	Organisation for Economic Co-operation and Development
PLI	price level index

PPI	producer price index
PPP	purchasing power parity
PRISM	Pacific Regional Information System
RMA	Royal Monetary Authority
RMS	Results Measurement System
SAE	small area estimation
SDG	Sustainable Development Goal
SDSN	Sustainable Development Solutions Network
SNA	System of National Accounts
SPC	Secretariat of the Pacific Community
UNAIDS	Joint United Nations Programme on HIV/AIDS
UNCTAD	United Nations Conference on Trade and Development
UNDESA	United Nations Department of Economic and Social Affairs
UNDP	United Nations Development Programme
UNEP	United Nations Environment Programme
UNESCO	United Nations Educational, Scientific and Cultural Organization
UNFPA	United Nations Population Fund
UNHCR	United Nations High Commissioner for Refugees
UNICEF	United Nations Children's Fund
UNIDO	United Nations Industrial Development Organization
UNODC	United Nations Office on Drugs and Crime
UNSD	United Nations Statistics Division
US	United States
WDI	World Development Indicators
WHO	World Health Organization
WPP	World Population Prospects

Unless otherwise indicated, "$" refers to United States dollars.

HIGHLIGHTS

Part I. Sustainable Development Goals

The Millennium Development Goals (MDGs) had shaped development policies around the world with specific, time-bound, and quantifiable targets since they were launched in 2000. Through concerted efforts of the world community, significant gains had been made with respect to specific targets on poverty, education, gender equality, child mortality, maternal health, disease, the environment, and global partnerships. When the MDG agenda concluded in 2015 last year, there were 1.1 billion fewer people who lived below the poverty line of $1.25 (2005 purchasing power parity [PPP]) a day, more than 40 million fewer out-of-school children of primary school age, and almost 7 million fewer deaths among children under 5 years of age since 1990. Likewise, Asia and the Pacific had an impressive MDG scorecard. The region met the MDG target of reducing the proportion of people in extreme poverty by half, much ahead of the 2015 deadline. Furthermore, the region successfully reduced by half the proportion of people without access to safe drinking water and achieved gender parity in primary and secondary education.

While there is much cause for celebration, an unfinished agenda remains due to uneven progress across the goals and across countries, and the uneven opportunities for people to share in the benefits of development and progress. It is on this premise that the Sustainable Development Goals (SDGs), also known as the Global Goals, were launched in 2015. The SDGs present a universal call to action to build on the progress achieved through the MDGs by addressing social, economic, and environmental aspects of sustainable development and ensuring that nobody will be left behind.

The year 2015 is a milestone year for the SDGs as it serves as the baseline from which development performance of countries will be assessed. In particular, performance will be measured based on 17 goals, 169 targets, and 230 statistical indicators. The *Key Indicators 2016* compiles data for a subset of these indicators for which data are available for the economies of Asia and the Pacific. The discussion is organized into five themes—People; Planet; Prosperity; Peace; and Partnership.

People

- Asia and the Pacific met the MDG target of halving poverty between 1990 and 2015. Notwithstanding this significant reduction, 330 million people (or roughly 9.0% of the region's total population) are still living on less than $1.90 (2011 PPP) a day based on latest data. Approximately 1.2 billion people in Asia and the Pacific are below the poverty line of $3.10 (2011 PPP) a day.

- The opportunity to live a healthy life requires having access to essential health-care services before, during, and after birth. In 2015, Asia and the Pacific's neonatal mortality rate is estimated at 20 per 1,000 live births, down from 35 in 2000 while the under-5 mortality rate is estimated at 36 per 1,000 live births, down from 70 in 2000.

- The region has managed to reduce the prevalence of undernourishment over the years. In 11 developing member countries, the prevalence of undernourishment was reduced by at least 10 percentage points. However, latest data suggest that one in seven people in Asia and the Pacific today are still undernourished.

- Early childhood development is an important driver of sustainable development. According to latest available data for reporting economies, enrollment in preprimary education in Asia and the Pacific is estimated at approximately 60.0%

of preprimary school-aged children. Data also show marked improvements in participation in preprimary education in at least three-quarters of economies of Asia and the Pacific between 2000 and 2015.

- Women's representation in political and economic decision-making processes is a critical ingredient to fuel sustainable development. On average, approximately 15% of seats in national parliaments of economies in Asia and the Pacific are held by women. However, significant gender disparities still exist on many fronts in Asia and the Pacific. Data for reporting economies suggest that women in the region spend between 10% and 25% of their time doing unpaid domestic and care work while their male counterparts spend between 2% and 11% doing the same.

Planet

- More than 90% of the population in Asia and the Pacific has access to improved drinking water sources but about 0.3 billion people are still without access to improved drinking water sources. In addition, about 1.5 billion people lack access to safely managed sanitation services in the region.

- In a majority of the economies of Asia and the Pacific with available data, the proportion of urban population living in slums is at least one-third.

- In Asia and the Pacific, 32 out of 36 economies with available data have air pollution levels exceeding the maximum recommended air pollution level set by the World Health Organization.

- Among economies with available data in the region, only Australia, Fiji, Indonesia, Japan, Kiribati, the Republic of Korea, the Philippines, and Solomon Islands have expanded the coverage of marine protected area between 2000 and 2016.

- Forest cover in Asia and the Pacific's total land area is at least 22.2% based on latest data.

Prosperity

- In proportion to GDP, the share of the manufacturing sector has increased in 16 out of 48 member economies in the region between 2000 and 2015.

- In 11 out of 18 economies of Asia and the Pacific with available data for recent years, the average income of the bottom 40% grew faster than the average income of the general population.

- Based on latest data, about nine in 10 people have access to electricity in Asia and the Pacific. The proportion of the population with access to electricity is at least 95% in 22 economies but it is below 75% in 15 economies.

- In Asia and the Pacific, about seven in 10 adults have accounts in a bank or other financial institution based on latest available data.

- Air traffic movement in Asia and the Pacific has increased severalfold over the years. In 2015, roughly 1.2 billion air passengers traveled to and from the region.

Peace

- Asia and the Pacific has one of the lowest intentional homicide rates in the world, estimated at 2.5 for every 10,000 people.

- Birth registration is a primary step toward securing a person's recognition before the law. Absence of such formal documentation may limit a person's access to health care, education, or labor market services and consequently undermine the inclusiveness of institutions. Globally, about 230 million children under the age of 5 have not been registered with a civil authority. More than half are from Asia and the Pacific.

Partnership

- The majority of the economies of Asia and the Pacific have experienced a rise in remittances as a share of GDP since 2000.

- Debt service as a proportion of exports of goods and services declined between 2000 and 2015 by at least 0.2 percentage points in 23 economies in the region.

- In about half of the 35 economies for which data are available in Asia and the Pacific for 2015, national statistical plans are fully funded and under implementation.

Data Revolution for Sustainable Development Goals Monitoring

- As the development community embraces the Sustainable Development Agenda, there is a need to prepare for a "data revolution" where surveys, censuses, and administrative databases, which are commonly used to produce official statistics, are complemented by information from innovative and state-of-the-art data sources to inform societies in solving the world's development challenges. "Big data"—the data that arise from people's transactions with digital technologies—present a unique opportunity to enhance the relevance and timeliness of official statistics.

- The development community needs to continue tracking relevant initiatives that use big data to have a more nuanced understanding of the scalability of such initiatives. Furthermore, the development community needs to work closely with various stakeholders including the private sector and government, particularly the national statistical offices, in addressing issues surrounding data quality and methodology, development of skills needed to work with big data, technological requirements, and the legal framework for sharing of big data.

Part II. Region at a Glance

The Regional Trends and Tables part is grouped into eight themes, each of which has a brief analysis of key trends of selected indicators highlighting important recent developments in Asia and the Pacific. The discussion is organized into eight themes—People; Economy and Output; Money, Finance, and Prices; Globalization; Transport and Communications; Energy and Electricity; Environment; and Government and Governance.

People

- Asia and the Pacific is home to more than 4 billion people, accounting for nearly 55% of the world's population. The region's list of five most populous economies includes the People's Republic of China (1.4 billion), India (1.3 billion), Indonesia (225 million), Pakistan (197 million), and Bangladesh (158 million).

- The total population of Asia and the Pacific grew at an annual rate of 1.21% between 2000 and 2015. In most economies of the region, population growth rates are declining and the latest population projections by the United Nations indicate that the share of Asia and the Pacific in the global population will decline to 50% by 2050 from its present share of 55%.

- Populations are relatively young with less than 15% aged 65 or over in most economies of the region. However, with the fall in birth rates and slower population growth, population aging is imminent in the coming decades. Forecasts show that about 20% of the population could be 65 or over by 2050 in at least 13 member economies. In the region's developed economies, for instance, an aging population is already apparent. An aging population presents challenges for policy makers as it tends to lower labor force participation and increase the number of people who are economically inactive but require access to social services.

- About 45% of the population of Asia and the Pacific lives in urban areas. As migration from rural to urban areas is driven largely by greater employment opportunities in cities, as well as improved access to services such as health care and education, the urban population is expected to grow in the coming years. In particular, the region's urban population is expected to grow from 2.1 billion today to as much as 3.4 billion people by 2050.

- Measured by the Human Development Index (HDI), seven economies from the region (Australia; Japan; New Zealand; Hong Kong, China; the Republic of Korea; Singapore; and Taipei,China) were among the "Very High Human Development" tier based on latest data. On the other hand, Afghanistan, Myanmar, Nepal, Pakistan, Papua New Guinea, and Solomon Islands have the lowest HDI values in the region.

Economy and Output

- Asia and the Pacific generated two-fifths of global GDP (in purchasing power parity terms) in 2015. Three of the world's 10 largest economies are in the region: the People's Republic of China, India, and Japan. These three economies accounted for nearly 70% of the region's output.

- Since 2000, there has been considerable convergence of per capita GDP (in purchasing power parity terms) in Asia and the Pacific, although there are still remarkable disparities across economies. For instance, Singapore's per capita GDP (highest in the region) is 44 times that of Solomon Islands (lowest in the region).

- Between 2014 and 2015, growth of real GDP exceeded 3% in 21 out of 41 economies of Asia and the Pacific with available data. The list of economies with the fastest GDP growth include Cambodia, India, Myanmar, Palau, and Uzbekistan.

- In nearly three-quarters of the economies of Asia and the Pacific, the services sector accounts for more than 50% of GDP based on latest data available.

- Between 2000 and 2015, a majority of the economies of Asia and the Pacific have increased investment spending as a share of GDP. Government consumption expenditure has increased in almost half of the region's reporting economies while household consumption as a share of GDP declined in more than two-thirds of the economies with available data. Gross domestic saving relative to GDP has increased in more than half of the reporting economies.

Money, Finance, and Prices

- In 2015, consumer price inflation remained low in most economies of Asia and the Pacific due to low international food and fuel prices.

- In 2015, the money supply expanded in all reporting economies except Azerbaijan, Brunei Darussalam, and Mongolia.

- Between 2014 and 2015, the ratio of nonperforming loans to total gross loans declined in most economies of Asia and the Pacific for which data are available.

- Stock market performance was largely positive across Asia and the Pacific in 2015: the People's Republic of China, Japan, and Fiji had stock markets that were among the world's top performers in 2015.

- Two of the region's currencies (Hong Kong dollar and Maldives rufiyaa) appreciated against the

United States dollar in 2015, compared with eight in 2014.

Globalization

- The Asia and the Pacific remains the largest recipient region of foreign direct investment (FDI). In 2015, global FDI flows increased to $1.8 trillion while those of Asia and the Pacific surpassed $0.5 trillion.

- Asia and the Pacific accounts for a significant share of global trade (32.2%), slightly trailing Europe's 35.5% share.

- Total external debt of developing member economies in Asia and the Pacific increased from approximately $1.1 trillion in 2000 to $4.5 trillion based on latest data.

Transport and Communications

- The average railway density for all reporting member economies of Asia and the Pacific was estimated at 7 kilometers (km) per 1,000 square kilometers (km^2) in 2011, which exceeded Latin America and the Caribbean's average of approximately 5 km per 1,000 km^2, but was far less than Europe's average of 50 km per 1,000 km^2.

- Economies of Asia and the Pacific significantly upgraded the quality of their roads between 2004 and 2015. The share of Primary and Class I roads in highway networks in the region increased from 12.4% in 2004 to 31.8% in 2015.

- Air carrier departures increased between 2000 and 2015 in 30 out of 37 Asia and Pacific economies for which data are available, while the number of passengers carried increased in 35 out of 37 economies over the same period.

- Mobile phone subscription rates increased in every regional economy between 2000 and 2015 for which data are available, and by at least 10 times in more than two-thirds of these economies.

- Fixed broadband internet subscriptions increased in 45 out of 47 reporting economies between 2000 and 2015. However, approximately 58% of the region's population remains unconnected to the internet, which slightly exceeds the global average.

Energy and Electricity

- Asia and the Pacific's energy production and use are rapidly expanding along with economic growth. The region accounts for roughly 45% of global energy use according to latest available data.

- Since 2000, per capita electricity consumption rose by at least 50% in 20 out of 41 developing member economies.

- More than three-quarters of economies of Asia and the Pacific for which data are available increased their energy efficiency levels between 2000 and 2013.

- Across Asia and the Pacific, coal, oil, and natural gas are the predominant sources of electricity production; renewables and nuclear energy comprise a smaller share.

Environment

- The significant economic growth that Asia and the Pacific experienced over the years has led to increased emissions over the years. Over the past decade, the region's total greenhouse gas (GHG) emissions grew faster than the global average.

- More than one-third of Asia and the Pacific economies for which data are available experienced an increase in total forested land in 2013.

- Between 2000 and 2013, less than half of Asia and Pacific economies experienced an increase in the share of total land devoted to agriculture.

- While Asia and the Pacific accounts for more than half of the global population, the region accounts for less than a third of the world's internal renewable freshwater resources.

Government and Governance

- In 2015, a majority of the economies of Asia and the Pacific had fiscal deficits amounting to 1%–7% of their respective GDP.

- Total government revenue as a share to GDP increased by at least 1 percentage point in eight economies between 2014 and 2015. Tax revenue as a percentage of GDP, on the other hand, dropped in a majority of the economies of Asia and the Pacific.

- Government spending on health as a percentage of GDP has increased in about two-thirds of the region's economies since 2000.

- The (arithmetic) average number of days required to start a business in developing economies of Asia and the Pacific declined from 45 days in 2005 to 20 days in 2015. The (arithmetic) average cost of starting a business as a share of gross national income per capita among developing member economies went down from 41.4% in 2005 to 17.9% in 2015.

Part III. Global Value Chains

Advances made in information, communication, and transportation technology have enabled businesses to fragment and distribute production processes across the globe, giving rise to global value chains (GVCs). A very high proportion of international trade transpires within these GVCs rendering traditional measures inadequate in assessing the effects of these transactions on indicators such as employment, income, and GDP growth. To better understand the dynamics of modern trade, the Asian Development Bank is producing and analyzing a variety of sophisticated measures of value added and GVC participation.

- Between 2011 and 2015, GVC participation of many Asian economies decreased markedly, largely due to the global slowdown in intermediate and final products trade. Viet Nam was a notable exception to the trend with many of its principal industries getting increasingly integrated into international production networks.

- There is a tendency in many Asian economies to rely more heavily on domestic markets for growth. The uncertainty created by the 2008 global financial crisis followed by the increasing domestic demand for goods and services due to robust growth and rising domestic income seem to be responsible.

- Many economies, including the People's Republic of China, India, and Indonesia, localized additional stages of the production processes both upstream and downstream in the GVCs, thereby increasing

their domestic value added and income. These developments, related to both the intermediate and final products, also led to the decline in gross trade and value-added trade experienced internationally in recent years.

- Japan; the Republic of Korea; and Taipei,China offshored certain stages of the production processes in a number of industries to emerging economies in the region like Thailand and Viet Nam. With the exception of Japan, these economies and Malaysia had the highest GVC participation in Asia with the share of foreign value added in their exports exceeding 30% in many industries.

- Propelled by the expanding business processing, tourism, and transportation industries, the Philippines' services exports posted strong growth between 2011 and 2015. Its value-added share is over 90% in services exports, due to the highly localized nature of the production processes. The country's information and communication technology and finance services, although relatively small, have the potential to participate in GVCs.

- Relatively smaller economies like Bangladesh, Mongolia, and Sri Lanka participated only in a few GVCs, generally in the upstream or at the lower value-adding stages. However, between 2011 and 2015, these three countries expanded their domestic value-added share in overall exports by localizing certain higher value-adding activities in manufacturing.

PART I

Sustainable Development Goals Trends and Tables

Introduction to the Sustainable Development Goals Trends and Tables

The Millennium Development Goals (MDGs) provided a comprehensive framework for monitoring socioeconomic progress as they set forth specific, time-bound, and quantified targets for addressing extreme poverty in its many dimensions, while also promoting gender equality, education, and environmental sustainability. When the MDGs concluded in 2015, significant gains had been made in most parts of the world, particularly in Asia and the Pacific as documented in *Key Indicators 2015*. While there is much cause for celebration, there remains an unfinished agenda due to uneven progress across the goals and across countries, and the uneven opportunities for people to share the benefits of development and progress.

In September 2015, leaders of 193 member states of the United Nations (UN) convened at the UN General Assembly in New York to launch the Sustainable Development Goals (SDGs). Also known as the Global Goals, they present a universal plan of action to build on the progress achieved through the MDGs by addressing social, economic, and environmental aspects of sustainable development. Like the MDGs, the SDGs set forth quantifiable targets to be achieved by 2030 (with a 2015 baseline) for ending poverty, protecting the planet, and ensuring that all people enjoy peace and prosperity. The global indicator framework of the SDGs was approved during the 47th Session of the UN Statistical Commission in March 2016. Although it is still subject to further refinements and improvements as a wider array of analytical tools and innovative data sources emerge, we have a clearer picture of just how much data the world needs to help meet the Global Goals.

The approved global indicator framework of the SDGs consists of 17 goals, 169 targets, and 230 indicators. The current set of indicators is grouped into three tiers. Indicators classified in Tier 1 have a clear, established methodology and data are regularly collected by many countries. Tier 2 indicators, although they have an established methodology, are not regularly collected by many countries. Tier 3 indicators do not have an established estimation methodology and standards. Of the 230 indicators, approximately 40% have an established methodology and are regularly collected. This means that there is a huge task confronting national statistical systems to produce and compile such data. Given that the data requirements for monitoring progress and ensuring accountability toward realizing the 17 SDGs are numerous and can be a challenge for the statistical systems of both developing and developed countries, it is imperative to explore how we can capitalize on new data sources for compiling the SDG indicators.

Part I of *Key Indicators 2016* examines the status of economies of Asia and the Pacific on the SDG agenda using empirical data for selected indicators from the global indicator framework. The second section provides a brief description on how big data can be used to address some of the data gaps associated with SDG monitoring.

Section 1. Sustainable Development Goal Indicators in Asia and the Pacific

Integrating the economic, social, and environmental dimensions of sustainable development to so as to enable everyone to fully participate in the growth processes is one of the tasks enshrined in the SDGs. The SDGs set out a plan of action to create a better future for the people and its planet by promoting prosperity, peace, and partnership (Figure 1.1).

Figure 1.1: Five Ps of the Sustainable Development Goals

Source: Adapted from http://www.un.org/sustainabledevelopment/sustainable-development-goals/.

To ensure that all countries will keep track of the achievement of the SDGs, monitoring of these indicators is imperative. Monitoring should be based on a wide variety of indicators at a more regular frequency so that programs can be developed and fine-tuned to facilitate each country's achievement of the goals. The UN Inter-agency and Expert Group on SDG Indicators (IAEG-SDGs) has been working on an indicator system for the measurement of the SDGs and a core set of 230 indicators has already been developed. Accounting for national circumstances in individual countries, this will be complemented by indicators at the national and subnational levels as committed by member states. Some thematic indicators are also being developed.

The indicator system associated with the SDGs should necessarily be linked to the policy cycle that starts with policy formulation, followed by policy legitimation, policy implementation, policy evaluation, policy change, and back to the formulation of new policies (Hak, Janouskova, and Moldan 2016). In the policy evaluation stage, the role of indicators is very crucial to ensure that certain strategies are adequately aligned toward achievement of the goals.

Along the principle of "leave no one behind", data disaggregation is also an important facet of indicators that will be developed specifically for the vulnerable segments of society. Box 1.1 provides a brief description of the analytical techniques that can be used for disaggregating the SDG indicators.

Box 1.1: Analytical Techniques for Disaggregating the Indicators of the Sustainable Development Goals

The lack of disaggregated data is one of the main issues raised regarding the monitoring framework of the Millennium Development Goals (MDGs). Although the data collected for MDG monitoring allowed tracking of how countries fared in terms of different social and economic indicators relative to other countries, they did not reveal how inequalities within each country changed over the years. This provided limited empirical evidence on which segments of a country's population made significant progress or lagged behind in terms of the MDGs. From a policy perspective, this is problematic because there are limited data to guide the design of intervention programs meant to appropriately target the disadvantaged. In response to this concern, the 2030 Agenda for Sustainable Development has espoused the "leave no one behind" principle, which requires appropriate Sustainable Development Goal (SDG) indicators to be estimated for different subpopulation groups based on income class, gender, ethnicity, and geographic location, and other relevant dimensions.

Sample Poverty Map: Poverty Headcount Index in Indonesia, 2000

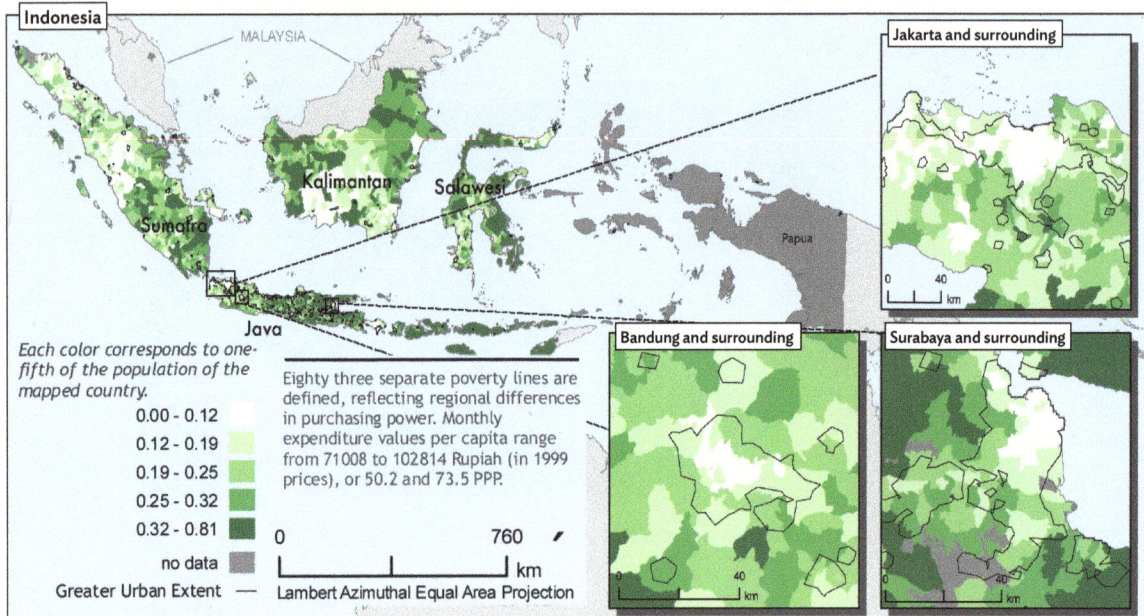

Sources: Center for International Earth Science Information Network (CIESIN), Columbia University. 2005. Poverty Head Index – Indonesia, Administrative Level 3: Subdistrict [Map]. Poverty Mapping Project: Small Area Estimates of Poverty and Inequality. Palisades, NY; NASA Socioeconomic Data and Applications Center (SEDAC). Small Area Estimates of Poverty and Inequality, v1 (1991–2002). http://dx.doi.org/10.7927/H49P2ZKM

Several strategies can be adopted to provide disaggregated SDG data and each technique entails varying levels of analytical rigor and data requirements. In the case of indicators estimated based on survey data, disaggregation requires that each subpopulation group for which estimates need to be provided is adequately represented in the survey. However, many of the national statistics offices from developing countries do not have adequate financial resources to employ sample sizes that are large enough to provide reliable estimates for different subpopulation groups. On the other hand, there are several small area estimation (SAE) techniques that "borrow strength" from other data sources that have wider coverage to be able to increase the effective sample size of surveys artificially. For example, the classic method proposed by Fay and Herriot (1979) uses optimal weighting strategies to combine survey and model-based estimates to improve the precision of their proposed estimator. Over time, more sophisticated SAE techniques have been developed. The methodology proposed by Elbers, Lanjouw, and Lanjouw (2003) is a good example of a more advanced SAE technique that is widely used in poverty mapping exercises. In general, the methodology entails regressing a certain income measure (e.g., household expenditure or income) on various correlates using survey data. The methodology requires that these correlates are available in both survey and census data. Out-of-sample prediction is then used to impute the chosen income measure by applying the estimated regression coefficients into the census data. Using the information on income imputed for each unit of the census, poverty measures can then be estimated for any desired level of disaggregation, although most of the initiatives have focused on disaggregating poverty numbers based on geographic location. Nevertheless, similar SAE techniques that are grounded on the same methodology may be employed to disaggregate other SDG indicators, provided that its data requirements are met.

continued.

Box 1.1: *(continued)*

Availability of Small Area Poverty Estimates in Asia and the Pacific

Country	Level of Disaggregation
Armenia	district
Azerbaijan	rayon (district)
Bangladesh	upazila (subdistrict)
Bhutan	subdistrict
Cambodia	commune
Fiji	tikina (district)
India	district
Indonesia	village
Nepal	district
Mongolia	soum (district)
Pakistan	district
Papua New Guinea	local-level government area
Philippines	city, municipality
Thailand	subdistrict
Viet Nam	district

Note: A number of studies on district-level poverty estimates for some of India's states were conducted in recent years.
The table above is not a comprehensive list of small area poverty estimates that are publicly available in Asia and the Pacific.
Sources: ADB compilation from international development organizations, national statistical agencies, and various sources.

However, there are several situations when it is more ideal to explore alternative methodologies to conventional SAE techniques for disaggregating the SDG indicators, e.g., reference period of the survey is far from that of the census (or other administrative records) or no conventional data collection tools exist. In such cases, big data and other new forms of data can be potentially tapped into to provide disaggregated estimates. For example, data on nighttime lights derived from satellite images can be used to provide geographically disaggregated measures of economic output. In an ongoing study undertaken by Glaeser et al. (2015), sophisticated computer algorithms are being used to process Google Street View images of houses to predict household income in New York City. A similar methodology could be explored to map wealth and poverty in other corners of the world where conventional poverty mapping tools are not available. On the other hand, a recent study by Marchetti, Guisti, and Pratesi (2016) makes use of Twitter-based emotion data (computed in the iHappy index) as a means of predicting the share of food consumption in a household's expenditure in Italy at the provincial level.

As seen above, there are several studies that have already shown that satellite images, data from everyday gadgets, social sites, and other high-throughput tools are high-density data that can be good predictors of various population traits. Since these types of data are usually high-density and available at very granular level, they can be considered promising data sources for SAE that can supplement the conventional data collected by national statistical agencies.

Sources:
C. Elbers, J. Lanjouw, and P. Lanjouw. 2003. Micro-level Estimation of Poverty and Inequality. *Econometrica* 71(1): 355–364.
R. Fay and R. Herriot. 1979. Estimates of Income for Small Places: An Application of James–Stein Procedures to Census Data. *Journal of American Statistical Association* 74 (1979): 269–277.
E. Glaeser, S. D. Kominers, M. Luca, and N. Naik. 2015. Big Data and Big Cities: The Promises and Limitations of Improved Measures for Urban Life. *NBER Working Paper* 21778. Cambridge MA: National Bureau of Economic Research (NBER).
S. Marchetti, C. Guisti, and M. Pratesi. 2016. The Use of Twitter Data to Improve Small Area Estimates of Households' Share of Food Consumption Expenditure in Italy. *AStA Wirtschafts- und Sozialstatistisches Archiv* 10(2): 79–93.

This section provides a summary of the selected SDG indicators that are widely available in ADB member countries. The data compiled here are mainly from the UN Department of Economic and Social Affairs, Statistics Division's SDG Indicators Global Database, i.e., the official SDG data repository, and data from international organizations and economy sources.

The SDG Indicators Global Database compiles data that are either directly produced by different international agencies based on their respective areas of expertise and mandates (e.g., proportion of population living below international poverty line estimated by The World Bank), data that are estimated from sample surveys which are financed and carried out by international agencies (e.g., health indicators that are estimated using data from the Multiple Indicator Cluster Surveys (MICS) and Demographic and Health Surveys (DHS)), unadjusted data that are compiled by international agencies based on what is directly produced by national statistical offices and other country sources, or data adjusted by international agencies based on what is directly produced by national statistical offices and other country sources. International agencies introduce statistical adjustments to facilitate data comparability across countries, impute estimates for years wherein data are not available, harmonize data when they are compiled from multiple national sources (e.g., surveys, administrative, and other sources) or address data quality issues. For detailed description of how international agencies compile their SDG-related data, readers may refer to the metadata available on the SDG Indicators Global Database's website.

Given the reasons cited above, the data compiled by national statistical agencies do not always match with the data compiled by international agencies. Hence, some of the data presented in this publication may differ from those available within countries.

The indicators are accompanied by a short analysis and supporting information presented in figures, boxes, and tables that are summarized according to the five themes: People, Planet, Prosperity, Peace, and Partnership. Most of the statistics presented in the tables and charts are usually presented for two data points between 2000 and 2015. In the succeeding discussion, these are occasionally referred to as the initial year (usually a year between 1998 and 2007 that is closest to 2000) and latest year (usually any year closest to 2015) depending on available data. There are also exceptions to this approach because the years for which data are available vary widely across countries. The 2015 figures shall serve as the baseline from which progress with respect to the SDGs can be assessed. However, there are instances when the latest estimates are even prior to 2010, indicating lack of timely data for monitoring the SDGs. The data for initial years allow us to gauge how countries have performed over the past 15 years and could be indicative of their future performance.

At the end of each section, issues in monitoring the goals and data gaps are briefly discussed to provide information to countries and other development partners on the amount of resources needed by statistical systems to produce and analyze the SDG indicators.

People

To end poverty and hunger, in all forms and dimensions, and to ensure that all human beings can fulfill their potential in dignity and equality and in a healthy environment.

Snapshots

- Between 2000 and 2013, approximately 707 million moved out of extreme poverty. However, around 330 million people in Asia and the Pacific still live in extreme poverty based on the $1.90 (2011 purchasing power parity) a day poverty line.

- Approximately one in seven people in Asia and the Pacific is undernourished.

- The prevalence of wasting among children under 5 years of age is relatively high in South Asia where five out of the six developing member countries (DMCs) have reported above 10% prevalence rates.

- Stunting affects more than 20% of children under 5 years of age in 18 DMCs as indicated by latest available data.

- Latest data suggest that there are 140 fewer maternal deaths per 100,000 births today in Asia and the Pacific than in 2000. On the other hand, the region's under-5 mortality rate is 36 per 1,000 live births.

- According to latest available data for reporting economies, enrollment in preprimary education in Asia and the Pacific is estimated at approximately 60.0% of preprimary school-aged children.

- Data for Asia and the Pacific show that as much as 33% of women aged 15 to 49 years have experienced physical violence from an intimate partner while 34% have experienced sexual violence.

- Lack of granular data on poverty, health and education remains to be a big challenge for targeting and monitoring progress of relevant SDGs for the region.

This section examines several indicators that underpin the first set of SDGs where data are available for ADB member countries. SDGs 1–5 are people-centered as they aim to create conditions that ensure the lasting protection of human dignity by eradicating extreme poverty and hunger and promoting health, well-being, quality education, and gender equality.

SDG 1: End Poverty in All Forms Everywhere

It is widely recognized that eradicating extreme poverty is one of the greatest challenges of this era.

While poverty is multidimensional, the lives of the extremely poor are commonly characterized by lack of income to buy one's basic needs.

Proportion of population below the international poverty line of $1.90 (2011 PPP) a day. Between 2002 and 2013, approximately 707 million people in Asia and the Pacific moved out of extreme poverty based on $1.90 a day poverty line. Amid this significant poverty reduction, the region is still home to around 330 million people who are living in extreme poverty, which is equivalent to about 9.0% of the region's total population according to the latest data available.

Extreme poverty in Asia and the Pacific has a remarkable spatial feature. For instance, the proportion of people who were living in extreme poverty is 16.1% in South Asia, while in East Asia, the proportion is estimated at only 1.8% of its population (Figure 2.1).

Proportion of population living below the national poverty line. Cost of living and preference for basic necessities vary significantly across the countries. National poverty lines capture these intercountry contextual differences. The goal is to reduce the proportion of people living below the national poverty line by at least half in 2030.

Figure 2.2 shows that the proportion of people living below the national poverty line dropped by more than 10 percentage points from 2000 to the latest year in 14 developing member countries (DMCs) with available data. However, in almost half (14 out of 30), the proportion of people living below their respective national poverty lines still exceed 20%.

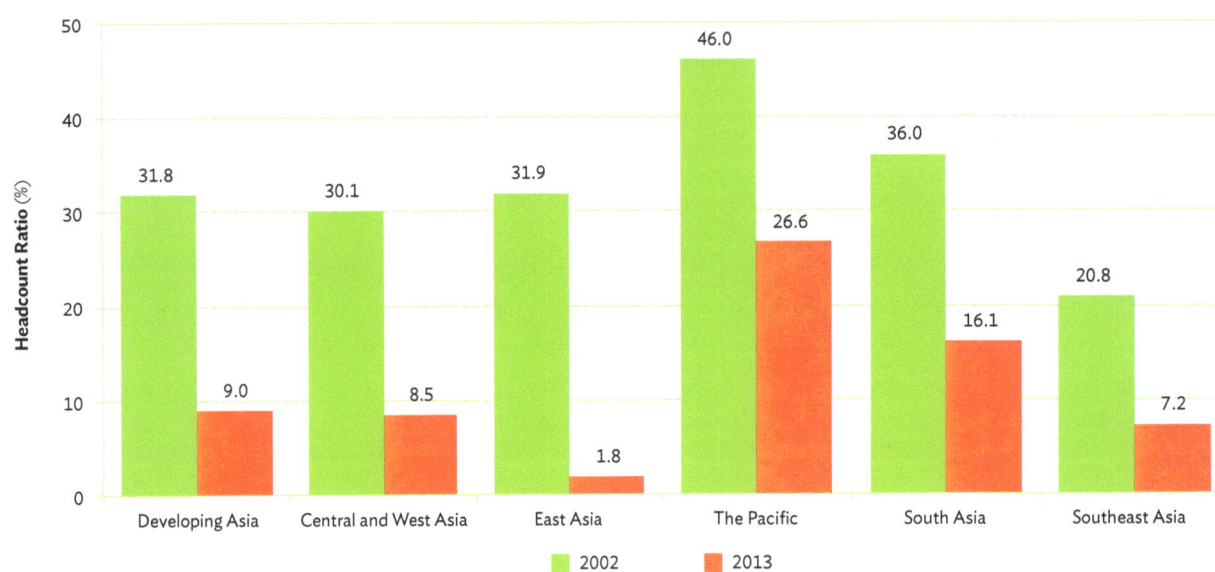

Figure 2.1: Proportion of Population below the $1.90 (2011 PPP) a Day Poverty Line, by Subregion

Source: ADB estimates using World Bank. PovcalNet Database. http://iresearch.worldbank.org/PovcalNet/home.aspx (accessed 4 October 2016).

Figure 2.2: Proportion of Population below the National Poverty Line

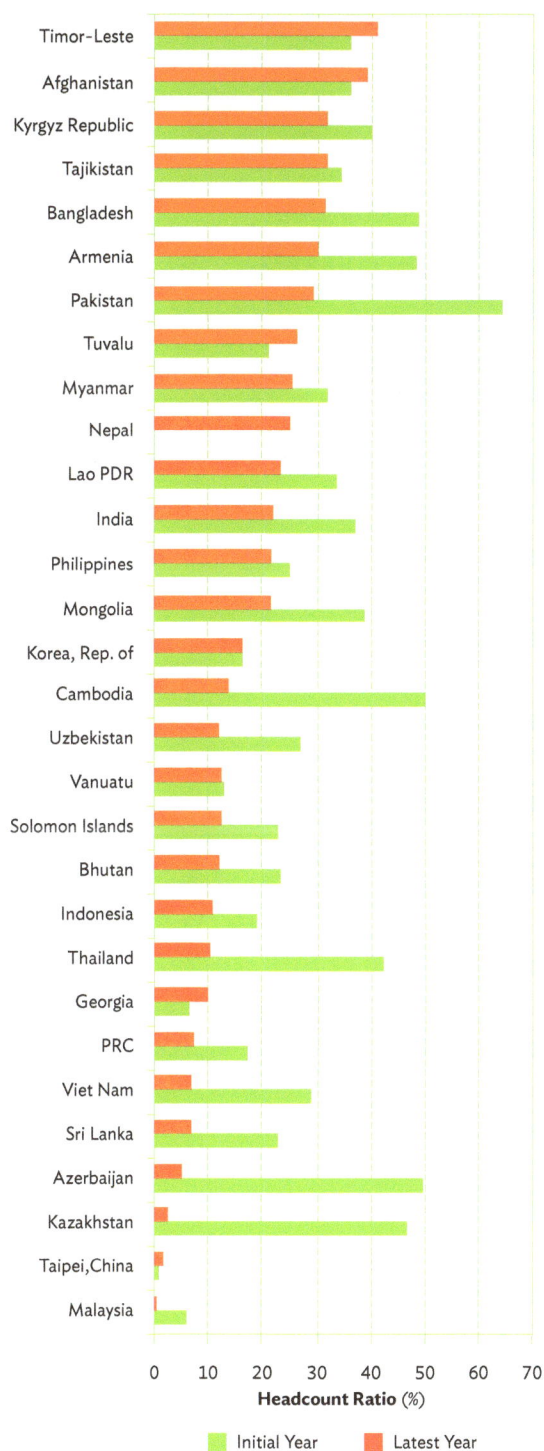

Timor-Leste
Afghanistan
Kyrgyz Republic
Tajikistan
Bangladesh
Armenia
Pakistan
Tuvalu
Myanmar
Nepal
Lao PDR
India
Philippines
Mongolia
Korea, Rep. of
Cambodia
Uzbekistan
Vanuatu
Solomon Islands
Bhutan
Indonesia
Thailand
Georgia
PRC
Viet Nam
Sri Lanka
Azerbaijan
Kazakhstan
Taipei,China
Malaysia

Headcount Ratio (%)

☐ Initial Year   ☐ Latest Year

Lao PDR = Lao People's Democratic Republic, PRC = People's Republic of China.
Notes: Only economies with recent estimates (2010 and later) are included.
Source: Table 2.1.

Equity and Other Issues

While official headline statistics suggest that substantial gains have been made toward the goal of reducing poverty at the national level, some segments of the population experienced slower development than others. For instance, available poverty estimates across Asia and the Pacific suggest that in most countries, the rural population is significantly more at risk of being poor than the urban population. Figure 2.3 shows how rural poverty rates compare to urban poverty rates in some of the region's most populous economies. On the other hand, data from some countries also confirm that working poverty rates vary according to gender and age. For instance, in Bangladesh, India, and Pakistan, the proportion of employed women living below the poverty line is higher than the working poverty rate among men. The situation is opposite in the Kyrgyz Republic and the Philippines, where the poverty rate among men is higher (Figure 2.4a). On the other hand, young workers aged 15–24 years in Cambodia, India, the Lao People's Democratic Republic (Lao PDR), Papua New Guinea, and Viet Nam have significantly higher poverty risk than workers who are 25 years and older (Figure 2.4b).

Reducing poverty for a wider segment of the population requires more efficient planning and more targeted intervention programs. In general, social assistance programs are designed to help the poorest segment of the population make ends meet and reduce the poverty risk among the economically vulnerable. Available statistics show that in some countries such as Georgia, Indonesia, the Philippines, Sri Lanka, and Viet Nam, social assistance programs are targeted to the vulnerable segments of the population since the proportion of people living in the bottom income quintile covered by social assistance programs is significantly higher than the proportion of the economies' total population receiving social assistance in each of these countries.

Figure 2.3: Proportion of Population below the $1.90 (2011 PPP) a Day Poverty Line in Selected Economies, by Location

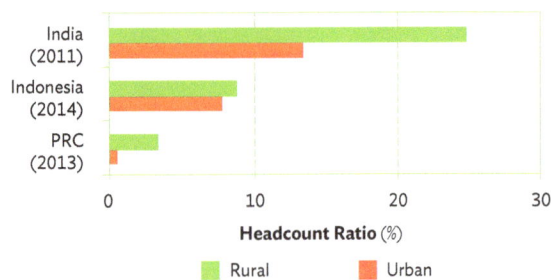

Headcount Ratio (%)

■ Rural   ■ Urban

PRC = People's Republic of China.
Source: World Bank. PovcalNet Database.
http://iresearch.worldbank.org/PovcalNet/home.aspx (accessed 4 October 2016).

Figure 2.4a: Incidence of Working Poor among Age 15 and Up in Selected Economies, by Sex
(%)

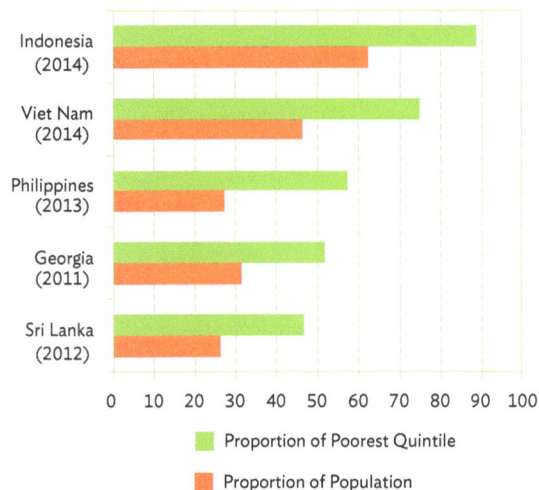

■ Female   ■ Male

Source: United Nations Statistics Division. Sustainable Development Goal Indicators Global Database. http://unstats.un.org/sdgs/indicators/database/ (accessed September 2016).

Figure 2.4b: Incidence of Working Poor among Age 15 and Up in Selected Economies, by Age Group
(%)

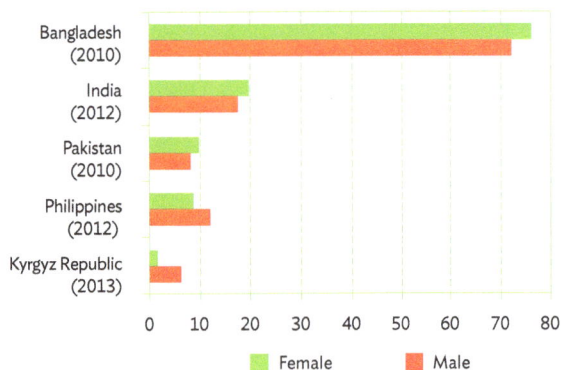

■ 15–24   ■ 25+

Lao PDR = Lao People's Democratic Republic.
Source: United Nations Statistics Division. Sustainable Development Goal Indicators Global Database. http://unstats.un.org/sdgs/indicators/database/ (accessed September 2016).

Figure 2.5: Proportion of Population Covered by Social Assistance Programs in Selected Economies
(%)

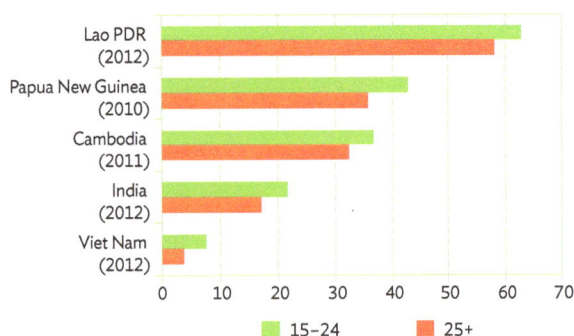

■ Proportion of Poorest Quintile
■ Proportion of Population

Source: United Nations Statistics Division. Sustainable Development Goal Indicators Global Database. http://unstats.un.org/sdgs/indicators/database/ (accessed September 2016).

Data Gaps

Targeting intervention programs requires correctly identifying the most vulnerable segments. For instance, those who have managed to exit poverty also have a higher risk of sliding back into it, with the effect of shocks, such as the loss of a job, death or sickness in the family, as well as harmful effects on livelihood of price volatilities, conflicts, and natural disasters. If the SDGs aim to totally eradicate poverty, there is a need to minimize the poverty risk for these people as well.

A finer granularity of data on poverty is required to identify the segments of the population with a higher risk of being trapped in poverty. However, movements into and out of poverty are not monitored, as household income and consumption surveys used to measure poverty are mostly cross-sectional surveys that do not utilize the same set of respondents over time. As such, conventional poverty measures are usually presented as cross-sectional snapshots of disadvantage. Box 2.1 underscores how poverty (as well as inequality) can be better examined when longitudinal data are available.

Monitoring to ensure that interventions result in the achievement of goals should be done more frequently. To accomplish this, more timely data on poverty are critical. In this case, model-based estimates can be considered for monitoring purposes. As an example, spatiotemporal models can be developed to account for the dynamic behavior of poverty indicators within the county. The spatial component will facilitate borrowing of information from similar countries or segments within the country for properly disaggregated space–time poverty measures. Disaggregation of data using spatiotemporal small area estimation can use administrative data or alternative data sources (e.g., images), among others, as auxiliary information. The use of information and communication technology tools for improved data capture and the application of big data such as the use of telecommunications for yielding small area estimates of poverty also appear to be promising means of getting poverty information faster for appropriate policy action.

Furthermore, there is a need to invest more in the collection of other indicators included in SDG 1. A quick assessment of data availability suggests that only a few of the SDG 1 indicators are regularly compiled in most countries in Asia and the Pacific. In addition, some indicators for social protection, mobilization of resources for poverty alleviation programs, and policy framework still need to be better formulated and measured more frequently to allow monitoring.

Box 2.1: Why the Sustainable Development Goal Era Necessitates Investing in Longitudinal Data

Social statistics on poverty and inequality are usually estimated using household surveys of living standards that collect data on income, consumption, and other indicators of well-being. In many developing countries, particularly in Asia and the Pacific, these surveys are conducted every 3–5 years using data from different samples of respondents. While cross-sectional surveys are useful for estimating the proportion of population who are poor during a specific survey period, they do not provide a comprehensive appraisal of the temporal dynamics of poverty.

To illustrate the limitations of cross-sectional data for poverty analysis, consider a hypothetical country with two classes of people: rich and poor. In the initial time period, 40% were rich and 60% were poor. Over time, all of the initially poor people became rich, while the initially rich slid down to poverty. From a cross-sectional perspective, we can say that there is a 20 percentage point reduction in poverty rate. While the poor were able to catch up, this development process with a complete reversal of classes may portray a very unstable distribution of economic opportunities.

Since panel data make it possible to distinguish the characteristics of people who stayed in poverty for a long time, or those who frequently move in and out of poverty from those who successfully made the transition into middle class status, and to locate where they are in the country, national governments can use the data to better determine the most effective interventions for a given population or geographical area. These inputs are vital to eradicating extreme poverty for all by 2030 (SDG 1).

The nuanced information provided by panel data are also vital to meeting other Sustainable Development Goals. Armed with panel data that can track factors and circumstances associated with the persistently marginalized, countries would be able to understand exactly when disadvantage begins to negatively affect households and when its impact becomes irreversible—and would therefore be in a better position to prevent inequality of opportunities instead of just managing its ill effects. Governments can use the same data to inform policy making on closing the income inequality gap. That way, they are also able to contribute to reducing inequality of opportunities within and among countries (SDG 10).

continued.

Box 2.1: *(continued)*

Although there is a clear need for panel data in light of the new SDGs, most of the long-running longitudinal data have been collected in industrialized countries simply because collecting such data is more costly and complicated. The systematic use of panel data can immensely help developing countries in Asia and the Pacific build a solid evidence base on which they can anchor policies and programs in support of the SDGs, but it will come at a price that they and all stakeholders must be willing to pay.

The good news is that longitudinal surveys are increasingly becoming available across Asia and the Pacific, and the family life surveys of Indonesia and Malaysia are some examples. However, because such initiatives have yet to be integrated in the official statistical systems of the aforementioned countries, they are not conducted regularly. But because panel surveys can build on the latest data from previous nationally representative cross-sectional household surveys, the start-up costs that may otherwise be prohibitive for many developing countries can already be reduced.

Notwithstanding the need for more funding and resources, it is important for national governments to acknowledge the potential of longitudinal panel data to better monitor our collective progress on the SDGs and foster sustainable and inclusive development, particularly when used together with cross-sectional and even big data.

SDG 2: End Hunger, Achieve Food Security and Improved Nutrition, and Promote Sustainable Agriculture

The United Nations Sustainable Development Goals Report 2016 estimates that globally, there are at least 790 million people who are undernourished. This implies that one in every nine persons is unable to put enough food on the table and is likely to go hungry. Since an undernourished person is exposed to various health risks and could render the person incapable of adequately achieving full potential, one of the Global Goals aims to end hunger and malnutrition by promoting sustainable agriculture and achieving food security by 2030.

Prevalence of undernourishment. Approximately one in seven people in Asia and the Pacific today are undernourished. Although the prevalence of undernourishment in majority of member countries is less than 10.0%, 14 economies have undernourishment rates exceeding 10.0%. Among the countries included in the analysis, Tajikistan has the highest incidence of undernourishment (33.2%), followed by Timor-Leste (26.9%) and Afghanistan (26.8%).

Figure 2.6 illustrates how the prevalence of undernourishment in economies of Asia and the Pacific has declined since 2000. The undernourishment rate declined by more than 10 percentage points in 11 DMCs: Afghanistan, Armenia, Azerbaijan, Cambodia, the Lao PDR, Mongolia, Myanmar, Nepal, Thailand, Timor-Leste, and Viet Nam.

Prevalence of wasting among children under 5 years of age. Wasting among children curtails their potential to be productive individuals later in their lives. More generally, wasting, undernourishment and diseases among children are typical roadblocks in their growth to become healthy adults in the future. The SDG target is to end malnutrition by 2030.

Table 2.2 shows that in nine out of the 31 DMCs with data for the latest year, the prevalence of wasting among children under 5 years of age exceeds 10%. Five of these nine DMCs are in South Asia where the prevalence of wasting is highest compared to other subregions. Bhutan is the only exception where the prevalence is relatively low at 5.9%. In East Asia, the prevalence of wasting is low, between 1.0% and 2.3%.

Figure 2.6: Prevalence of Undernourishment
(%)

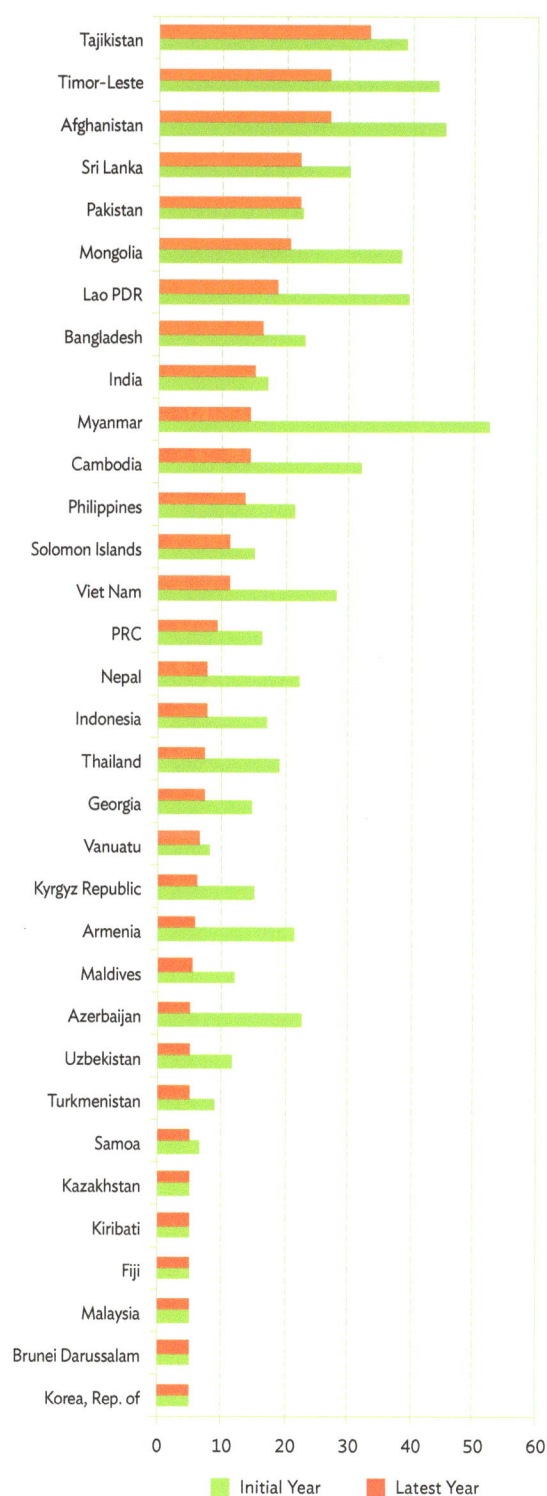

Initial Year   Latest Year

Lao PDR = Lao People's Democratic Republic, PRC = People's Republic of China.
Note: Latest year estimates for Azerbaijan, Uzbekistan, Turkmenistan, and Samoa are less than 5%. Initial and latest year estimates for Kazakhstan, Kiribati, Fiji, Malaysia, Brunei Darussalam, and the Republic of Korea are less than 5%.
Source: Table 2.2.

Prevalence of stunting among children under 5 years of age. Like wasting, stunting is a commonly used indicator of malnutrition among children. Statistics show that stunting affects more children than wasting. Table 2.2 shows that the prevalence of stunting among children under 5 years of age is higher compared to the prevalence of wasting for the same age group. In 18 economies with data for the latest year, at least two in 10 children under 5 years of age are stunted.

Although the prevalence of stunting among children under 5 years of age still exceeds 20% in the majority of the countries in Asia and the Pacific, it has declined in 17 economies since 2000 (Figure 2.7).

Prevalence of overweight children under 5 years of age. Unmanaged obesity among children can cause comparable health issues to stunting and wasting when they grow as adults later.

In eight out of the 28 member countries with data for the initial and latest years, the prevalence of overweight children under 5 years of age has fallen since 2000. However, the prevalence of overweight children under 5 years of age remains above 10% for nine DMCs. Table 2.2 provides the estimates for regional member economies.

Figure 2.7: Prevalence of Stunting Among Children under 5 Years of Age
(%)

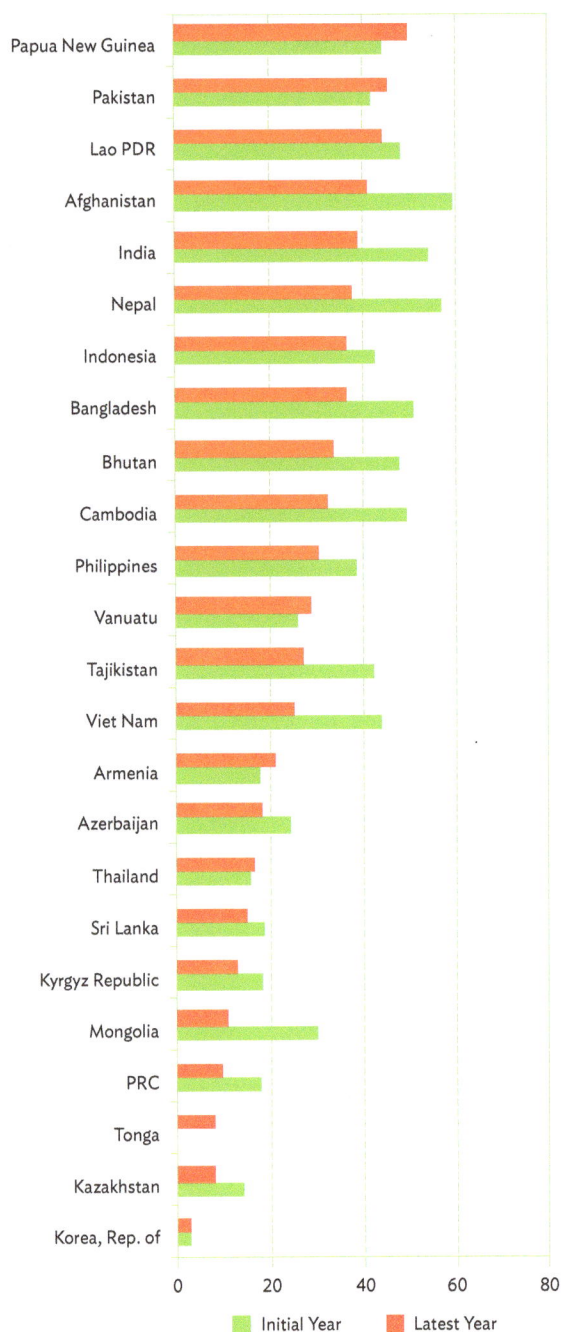

Lao PDR = Lao People's Democratic Republic, PRC = People's Republic of China.
Notes: Only economies with recent estimates (2010 and later) are included.
Source: Table 2.2.

Equity and Other Issues

Reducing hunger and sustaining the progress made during the MDG era is expected to be challenging for countries that are prone to frequent extreme weather events and natural disasters. Equity issues also exist within each country. For instance, boys have a higher risk of stunting than girls in most member economies in Asia and the Pacific (except for Mongolia, Sri Lanka, and Tajikistan). This gender disparity is more pronounced in Cambodia, the Kyrgyz Republic, the Lao PDR, Pakistan, and Papua New Guinea. (Figure 2.8). On the other hand, cases of overweight boys are more prevalent than those of overweight girls. Significant urban–rural disparities also exist with respect to various health-related indicators. In particular, stunting in rural areas is significantly higher in most economies with available data such as Bangladesh, Cambodia, India, Nepal, and Pakistan.

Figure 2.8: Prevalence of Stunting in Selected Economies, by Sex
(%)

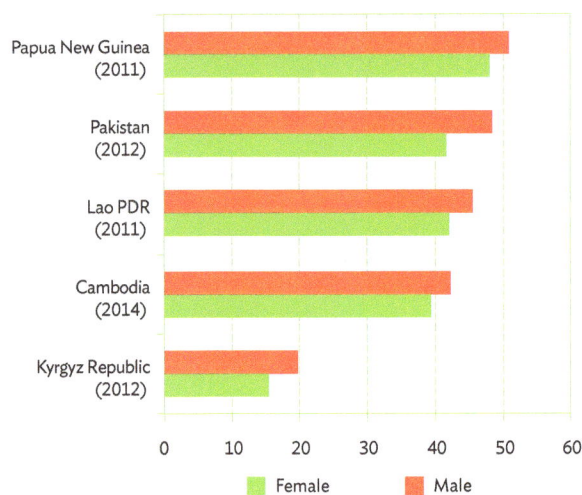

Lao PDR = Lao People's Democratic Republic.
Source: United Nations Statistics Division. Sustainable Development Goal Indicators Global Database. http://unstats.un.org/sdgs/indicators/database/ (accessed September 2016).

Data Gaps

Food security can be viewed in various dimensions including food availability, food accessibility, and food utilization. Food availability is achieved with sustainable agriculture or better bilateral agreements among nonproducing countries with producing countries. Food accessibility is enhanced with sustainable production and equitable and efficient distribution of food. Food utilization initially curbs hunger, and when sustained, can lead to improved nutrition for everybody. The goal traces the cycle of food production, food security, and nourishment. There are eight targets under SDG 2 but only five indicators are regularly collected in Asia and the Pacific. There are no specific indicators on food security and only a proxy indicator for sustainable agriculture.

While nutrition and hunger data up to 2015 are readily available, many targets do not have regularly collected data on relevant indicators. This prevents the generation of a more comprehensive food security analysis of the situation in the region.

Rural infrastructure serves multiple purposes of sharing results of research and development to pursue sustainable agricultural production, procurement of inputs to enhance productivity, delivery of produce to the consumers, and mobility of rural stakeholders to expand income generation beyond agriculture. All these issues eventually boil down to understanding the dynamic food security behavior of a country. Indicators on rural infrastructure further add to data gaps for SDG 2.

Assessing food security is difficult in the absence of indicators for vulnerable segments like the agricultural productivity of small-scale farmers. These segments may contribute at least to food security concerns among their family members. Absence of disaggregated figures could further exacerbate the food security threat among the marginalized segments of the population.

SDG 3: Ensure Healthy Lives and Promote Well-Being for All at All Ages

Proportion of births attended by skilled health personnel. Table 2.4 provides the estimates for all regional member economies. Although the proportion of births attended by skilled health personnel has increased in most parts of Asia and the Pacific in the last 15 years, births in some economies are still at high risk based on the latest data available. These include Timor-Leste (only 29.3% of births are attended by skilled health personnel), the Lao PDR (41.5%), Bangladesh (42.1%), Afghanistan (45.2%), India (52.3%), Pakistan (52.1%), Papua New Guinea (53.0%), and Nepal (55.6%).

Maternal mortality ratio per 100,000 live births. Maternal death results from a composite of factors including quality of pre- and postnatal care, quality of health facilities, skills of personnel during delivery, health status of women, and the general conditions of the well-being of women. The SDG target is to have a rate of lower than 70 maternal deaths per 100,000 live births by 2030.

Table 2.4 also provides the estimates of incidence of maternal death per 100,000 births for all regional member economies. As of 2015, the maternal mortality ratio is 123 per 100,000 live births in Asia and the Pacific. The highest ratios of maternal death were observed in the Pacific islands (191), followed by Central and West Asia (174), and South Asia (174). The ratios are relatively lower in Southeast Asia (110) and East Asia (27). The five countries in the region with highest prevalence of maternal deaths based on latest data are Afghanistan (396), Nepal (258), Papua New Guinea (215), Timor-Leste (215), and the Lao PDR (197).

Neonatal mortality rate per 1,000 live births. Neonatal death results from poor health condition of the mother and absence of an adequate health care system (including facilities and personnel). The SDG target is to reduce the neonatal mortality rate to at least as low as 12 per 1,000 live births.

As of 2015, DMCs with the highest neonatal mortality rates were Pakistan (46), Afghanistan (36), the Lao PDR (30), India (28), and Myanmar (26). Table 2.4 provides the estimates for regional member economies.

The neonatal mortality rate has been declining over the past 15 years. Among the developed member countries, neonatal mortality is down to three per 1,000 live births in New Zealand, two in Australia, and only one in Japan.

Under-5 mortality rate per 1,000 live births. Although the under-5 mortality rate in 2015 in Asia and the Pacific is estimated at 36 per 1,000 live births, many countries are already within the SDG target of 25 deaths per 1,000 live births. For instance, the under-5 mortality rates are already below 25 deaths per 1,000 live births in almost half of the member economies. In Southeast Asia, only Cambodia, Indonesia, the Lao PDR, Myanmar, and the Philippines have rates that exceed 25. At the subregional level, Central and West Asia has the highest under-5 mortality rate of 71 deaths per 1,000 live births. Lower rates are reported in the Pacific (51), South Asia (46), Southeast Asia (27), and East Asia (11). On the other hand, under-5 mortality rates are at least three times lower in the developed economies. Figure 2.9 also summarizes how under-5 mortality rates have changed since 2000.

Tuberculosis incidence rate per 100,000 population. The incidence of tuberculosis remains high in Asia and the Pacific. The economies with the highest incidence of tuberculosis include Timor-Leste (498), Kiribati (497), Papua New Guinea (417), Indonesia (399), and Cambodia (390). Nevertheless, the tuberculosis incidence rate has declined in all but 10 economies. In fact, the incidence of tuberculosis has dropped by at least 30 percentage points since 2000.

Figure 2.9: Under-5 Mortality Rates
(per 1,000 live births)

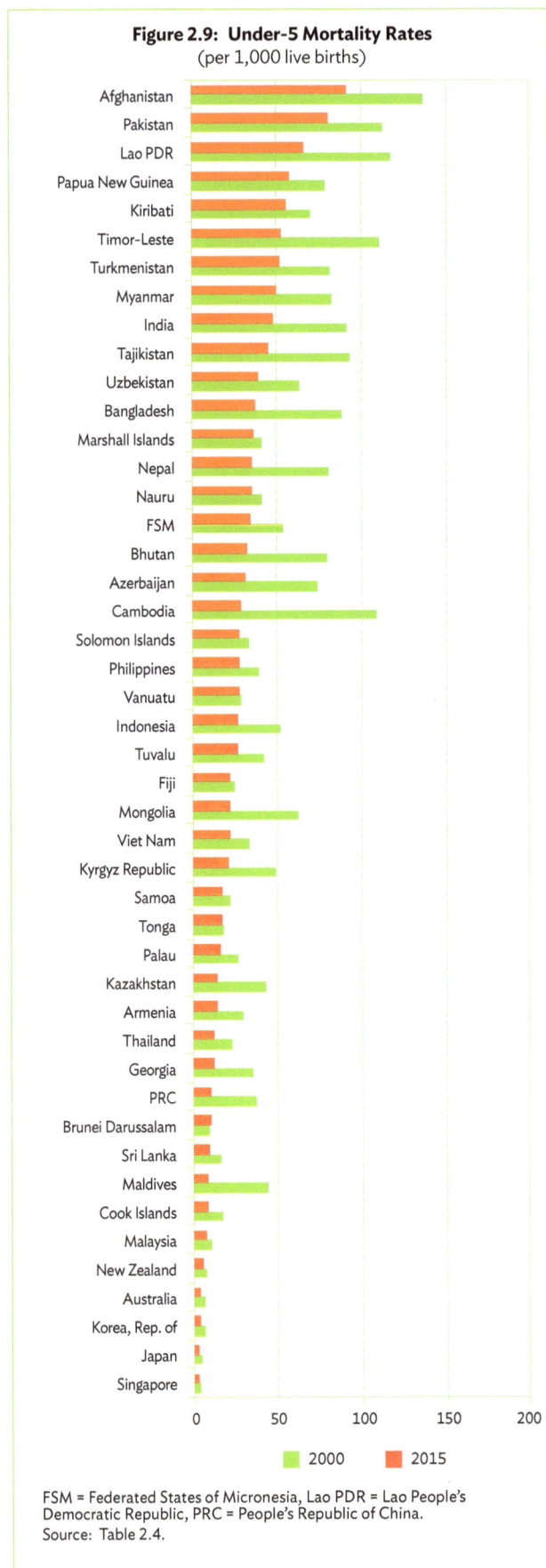

■ 2000   ■ 2015

FSM = Federated States of Micronesia, Lao PDR = Lao People's Democratic Republic, PRC = People's Republic of China.
Source: Table 2.4.

Number of new HIV infections per 1,000 uninfected population. The incidence of HIV in Asia and the Pacific varies throughout the region. Between 2000 and 2015, data show that new HIV infections are increasing in Central and West Asia, whereas in most parts of Southeast Asia (except for Indonesia and the Philippines), they are declining. In particular, incidence rates have significantly increased in Azerbaijan, Georgia, Indonesia, Kazakhstan, the Kyrgyz Republic, Pakistan, the Philippines, and Sri Lanka. On the other hand, substantial declines in the incidence of new HIV infections were observed in Cambodia, Malaysia, Myanmar, Nepal, Thailand, and Uzbekistan. As of 2015, HIV incidence per 1,000 uninfected population is highest in Papua New Guinea (0.36), Indonesia (0.29), Georgia (0.28), Myanmar (0.24), and Kazakhstan (0.21).

Mortality rate attributed to cardiovascular disease, cancer, diabetes, or chronic respiratory disease. Mortality rates attributed to these have fallen in all of Asia and the Pacific. During 2000–2012, the most significant reductions in death rates associated with these four main causes of noncommunicable disease were recorded in the Republic of Korea (–44.7%), the Maldives (–43.6%), Singapore (–36.2%), and New Zealand (–32.6%). In contrast, death rates have seen a rise in the Philippines (20.4%), Pakistan (5.1%), Turkmenistan (4.0%), Myanmar (3.1%), and Viet Nam (1.3%). As of 2012, the noncommunicable disease burden (i.e., from cardiovascular disease, cancer, diabetes, or chronic respiratory disease) in terms of mortality were highest in Turkmenistan (40.8%), Kazakhstan (33.9%), Mongolia (32.0%), Uzbekistan (31.0%), Fiji (30.8%), and Afghanistan (30.5%).

Equity and Other Issues

The increased mobilization of resources has paved the way to improved access to high-quality health-care services and, in turn, significant progress with regard to specific health-related targets of MDGs such as the reduction of incidence of HIV, tuberculosis, and child mortality. Nevertheless, improving the health outcomes of people remains an important goal and hence, still plays a key role in shaping sustainable development policies.

Within countries, progress has been uneven as some segments of the population still have higher risks of contracting preventable diseases primarily due to a lack of access to health care services. Hence, a more targeted and evidence-based policy intervention is needed for these vulnerable segments of society. Furthermore, efforts need to be intensified at the grassroots level, collective action needs to be fostered among stakeholders, and continuous funding remains vital especially in light of bringing more inclusive and equal health outcomes across regions and sectors.

On another note, some policy makers and stakeholders have criticized the MDGs for focusing attention and resources on the attainment of specific health-related goals at the expense of supporting broader health systems that are designed to address health issues in a more comprehensive fashion (WHO 2016). Learning from this "focusing problem" entails providing incentives to invest on broader-based health systems. Having a more integrated health system is also important as the prevailing demographic, epidemiological and health conditions within and across the region call for more integrated health systems. Systems thinking in health—that is, anchoring and achieving efficiency and effectiveness in health organization and governance, financing, physical and human resources, and service delivery—is essential to step up the ladder in achieving the health development goals, generate more responsive policies, and achieve more sustainable outcomes.

Data Gaps

There are 13 targets under SDG 3, but data for six indicators only are widely available for economies of Asia and the Pacific. In addition to model-based estimation, administrative data and person-generated databases (e.g., medical records, transaction history, and internet searches) can be explored to augment existing data. These can also be used in the construction of early warning devices for threats to health and well-being. Disaggregation (e.g., rural–urban, male–female, wealth) of various indicators are needed to tailor-fit various intervention strategies to the most vulnerable segments.

Even for epidemics, only the indicator of tuberculosis is collected regularly. There are no defined indicators yet or they are not regularly measured for many targets including mortality from noncommunicable diseases; substance abuse; mortality from accidents; access to sexual and reproductive healthcare; universal health coverage; mortality from hazardous chemicals; WHO framework on tobacco control; research and development for vaccines and medicines; health financing and recruitment of health personnel; and early warning, risk reduction, and management of national and global health risks. National health surveys for various years, health record databases, and even social media data repositories (e.g., Google Trends) can be used in the development of indicators for other targets following certain data mining algorithms.

SDG 4: Ensure Inclusive and Equitable Quality Education and Promote Lifelong Learning Opportunities for All

There is a wide consensus that the development of skills is an important driver of inclusive growth (ADB 2015). While a person should continuously expand his or her skill set throughout his or her lifetime, a strong foundation of skill development should start during childhood. SDG 4 emphasizes lifelong learning opportunities, implying not only access, but more importantly, the outcomes of all forms of trainings (formal education and otherwise).

Participation rate in organized learning (1 year before the official primary entry age). According to latest available data, the participation rate in preprimary education for regional members is approximately 60%. In addition, 58.1% of these countries have participation rates greater than 70.0%. Data have also shown marked improvements in at least three-fourths of regional members, from the earliest to the latest available year. Overall participation rates have improved vastly in the Lao People's Democratic Republic (from 9.5% to 50.4%), Pakistan (from 57.6% to 94.5%), Bangladesh (from 30.1% to 59.9%), Australia (from 52.5% to 80.3%), and Viet Nam (from 69.2% to 94.7%).

Access to preschools among many Southeast Asian countries is comparable to that of the developed member economies. Some economies still have very low preprimary education participation rate, including Azerbaijan, Cambodia, Myanmar, Samoa, and Tajikistan, where less than a third of children are enrolled in preprimary education. While good improvement has been made in access to preschool education in many economies during 2000–2015, programs should be closely monitored to ensure universal access to preschool education by 2030. Table 2.6 provides the estimates for regional member economies.

Trained teachers in preprimary education. While preprimary education is not part of formal education, training of preschool teachers is important because they play a big role in the development of children.

A significant number of teachers in preprimary education in some economies do not have the necessary teacher training. For instance, in Central and West Asia, specifically the Kyrgyz Republic, only 46.2% of preprimary teachers have formal training. In the case of Southeast Asia, 48.4% of the teachers in preprimary education in Myanmar and 64.4% in Brunei Darussalam have formal training. Among the Pacific countries, the proportions of teachers with training are lower in Solomon Islands (59.5%) and the Cook Islands (69.7%). While Nauru has a relatively higher proportion of teachers with training at 82.1%, Samoa, Tonga, and Vanuatu have already achieved 100%. Table 2.7 provides the estimates for regional member economies.

Percentage of trained teachers in primary education. Among member economies in Asia and the Pacific with available data, the lowest percentage of trained teachers in primary education can be found in Bangladesh (57.7%), Vanuatu (60.5%), and Solomon Islands (64.6%). On the other hand, countries with 100% trained teachers in primary education include Cambodia, Fiji, Kazakhstan, Mongolia, the Philippines, Tajikistan, Thailand, Uzbekistan, and Viet Nam. Table 2.7 provides the estimates for regional member economies.

Percentage of trained teachers in lower and upper secondary education. Although data on teacher training for lower and upper secondary education are not available for many economies, empirical evidence in economies with available data suggests that at least 60% of teachers in lower secondary and 34% in upper secondary education are trained. Nine of the 27 reporting economies recorded 100% trained teachers in either lower or upper secondary education—four are from the Pacific (Fiji, Papua New Guinea, Samoa, and Tuvalu); three from Southeast Asia (Cambodia, the Philippines,

and Viet Nam); and Mongolia from East Asia and Uzbekistan from Central and West Asia. The lowest percentages, however, were noted in Bangladesh (59.6%) for lower secondary and in Kiribati (33.6%) for upper secondary education. Table 2.7 provides the estimates for regional member economies.

Equity and Other Issues

Although there has been considerable progress in improving education outcomes of children around the world, particularly enrollment in basic education, through the MDGs, there are other equity issues that the SDGs may have to confront. In Thailand and Georgia, for instance, the latest data available suggest that the proportion of girls who have attained at least a minimum proficiency in mathematics is significantly higher than that of boys (Figure 2.10) while in a few economies like Australia, boys have better proficiency in mathematics than girls. While such a trend could be partly driven by differences in motivation to learn, there is merit in investigating whether there are other gender-differentiating factors at work that lead to boys and girls being unequally prepared for higher educational career.

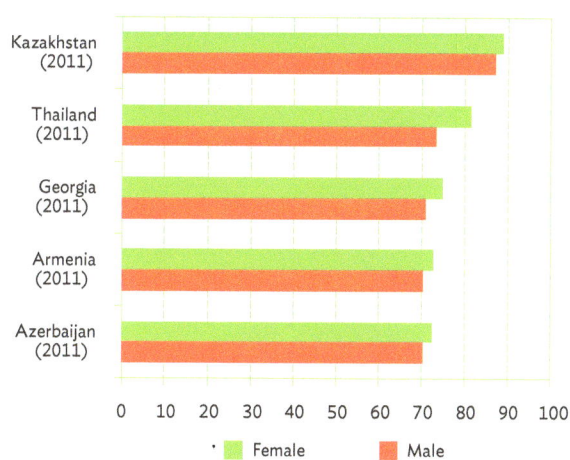

Figure 2.10: Proportion of Children at the End of Primary Achieving at Least a Minimum Proficiency Level in Mathematics in Selected Economies, by Sex (%)

Source: United Nations Statistics Division. Sustainable Development Goal Indicators Global Database. http://unstats.un.org/sdgs/indicators/database/ (accessed September 2016).

SDG 5: Achieve Gender Equality and Empower All Women and Girls

Gender equality and empowerment of women are culturally linked and among the most challenging discourse in development studies. Having recognized that women's representation in political and economic decision-making processes is a critical ingredient to fuel sustainable development, the SDGs remain committed in advancing gender equality.

Proportion of women aged 20–24 years who were married or in a union before age 15 and before age 18. Being married at a very young age may limit women's ability to optimize their potential and in turn could have adverse consequences on women's economic prospects. While available data suggest that the proportion of women who were married or in a union by the age of 15 is less than 5% in almost all member economies, in 19 out of 24 economies with available data, more than 10% of women aged 20–24 years were married or in a union before age 18.

Proportion of seats held by women in national parliaments. Table 2.8 shows the estimated proportion of seats in national parliaments held by women in economies of Asia and the Pacific. Among developed economies, Australia and New Zealand have relatively high proportion of national parliament seats held by women. On the other hand, about 9.5% of national parliament seats are held by women in Japan based on latest data. Among developing member economies, Timor-Leste (38.5%), Nepal (27.5%), Afghanistan (27.7%), the Philippines (27.2%), and Kazakhstan (26.2%) have the highest proportion of seats in national parliament that are held by women, while Solomon Islands (2.0%), Papua New Guinea (2.7%), and Sri Lanka (4.9%) have the lowest estimates.

Time spent on unpaid domestic and care work. There are differences in the amount of time men and women spend performing unpaid domestic and

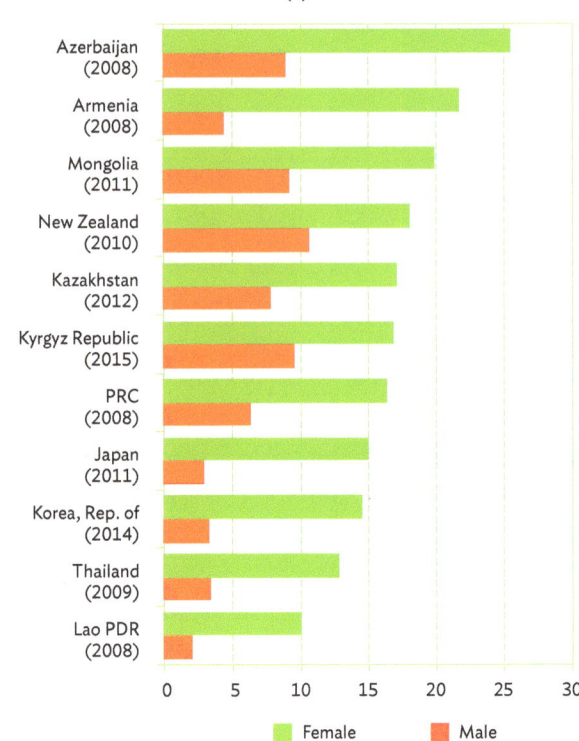

Figure 2.11: Time Spent on Unpaid Domestic and Care Work in Selected Economies, by Sex
(%)

Lao PDR = Lao People's Democratic Republic, PRC = People's Republic of China.
Note: Only economies with recent estimates (2008 and later) are included.
Source: United Nations Statistics Division. Sustainable Development Goal Indicators Global Database. http://unstats.un.org/sdgs/indicators/database/ (accessed September 2016).

care work. Based on available data, women in Asia and the Pacific spent anywhere between 10% and 25% of their time doing unpaid domestic and care work, while their male counterparts spent anywhere between 2% and 11% doing the same (Figure 2.11).

Percentage of women aged 15–49 years who have experienced physical or sexual violence by a current or former intimate partner in the previous 12 months. Empirical data suggest that in Asia and the Pacific, as much as 18.0% (Nepal) of women aged 15–49 years in some economies have experienced physical violence, while as much as 7.7% (Pakistan) experienced sexual violence by a partner. Figure 2.12a and Figure 2.12b presents the numbers for economies based on latest data available.

Data Gaps

Compared to MDG 3 that also aimed to promote gender equality and women empowerment, SDG 5 covers more areas such as elimination of violence against women and girls, addressing legal and cultural barriers that impose constraints on women's sexual and reproductive health, and the recognition of the value of unpaid and domestic work, among others. Despite these advances, significant data gaps exist. In particular, out of the 14 indicators in SDG 5, only four are classified as Tier 1. Most of the remaining indicators do not have established data collection standards, and thus, are not collected regularly. Nevertheless, there are ongoing initiatives to address such data gaps. Box 2.2 discusses one such initiative.

Figure 2.12a: Proportion of Women Aged 15–49 Years Who Have Experienced Physical Violence by a Current or Former Intimate Partner in the Previous 12 Months in Selected Economies
(%)

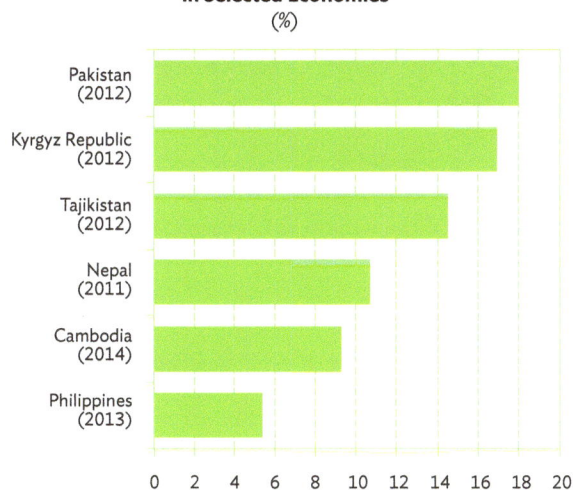

Note: Only economies with recent estimates (2010 and later) are included.
Source: United Nations. 2015. *The World's Women 2015: Trends and Statistics.* New York.

Figure 2.12b: Proportion of Women Aged 15–49 Years Who Have Experienced Sexual Violence by a Current or Former Intimate Partner in the Previous 12 Months in Selected Economies
(%)

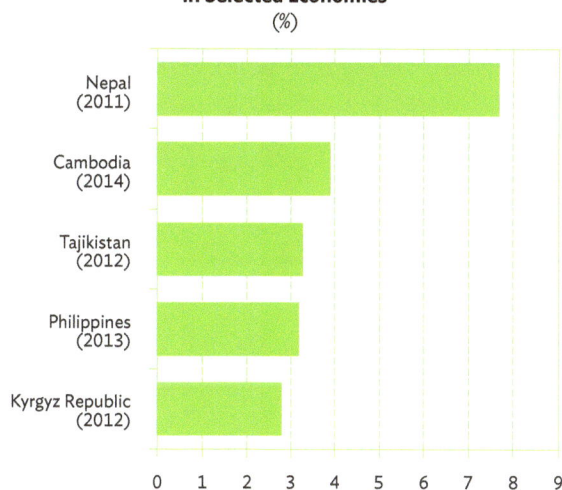

Note: Only economies with recent estimates (2010 and later) are included.
Source: United Nations. 2015. *The World's Women 2015: Trends and Statistics.* New York.

Box 2.2: Measuring Asset Ownership and Entrepreneurship from a Gender Perspective

Like the Millennium Development Goals (MDGs), the Sustainable Development Goals (SDGs) highlight the importance of having a global action to enhance statistics capacity to address the data requirements for monitoring progress in achieving socioeconomic development that is inclusive for both men and women. Although significant progress has been made in terms of providing gender-disaggregated data on educational and occupational outcomes, major gaps in the availability and quality of gender statistics remain in terms of access to economic resources. To capture the gender dimensions in this area, the United Nations Statistics Division (UNSD) and the UN Entity for Gender Equality and the Empowerment of Women, in collaboration with other development partners like the Asian Development Bank, have launched the Evidence and Data for Gender Equality (EDGE), a global initiative on gender statistics, which aims to establish standard definitions and data collection guidelines for producing timely and reliable sex-disaggregated data on entrepreneurship and asset ownership, along with other socioeconomic development outcomes.

As part of the EDGE initiative, the Survey on Measuring Asset Ownership and Entrepreneurship from a Gender Perspective has been designed to collect empirical evidence that facilitates a more nuanced understanding of the gender inequalities that exist in terms of access to economic resources. Moreover, it potentially addresses the information gap on the disaggregated data (i.e., information available by location, age, religion, ethnicity, education, and employment). Unlike the traditional method that collects data on assets at the household level, the EDGE survey employs a data collection approach at the individual level, consequently providing and highlighting an individual unit of analysis on ownership and rights. Particularly, it seeks to determine the ownership status of the individual members of the household (i.e., whether assets are owned exclusively or jointly); how these assets are acquired, including the value and use of these assets; who has the rights to bequeath and/or sell these assets; who primarily makes the decisions regarding their economic use; and who derives income from assets.

A household member may be classified as an asset owner in two ways. The first is when an interviewed household member reports himself or herself as an owner. This is termed the *self-assigned ownership approach*. The second way is when at least one of the interviewed household members reports another household member as an owner. This is termed the *most inclusive approach*. Between the two approaches, the most inclusive approach provides a broader definition of ownership as it considers the information provided by all respondents collectively. The former dwells on interviewing a specific member of the households and is strictly based on a respondent's reporting regarding themselves. For validity and to make it comparable with intra-household reporting and/or with nonrespondents' ownership of assets, two different sets of survey weights were used. Furthermore, while broad categories of assets are captured by the survey instruments, the distinctions between reported, documented, and economic types of ownership are also taken into account. This overall approach lends itself better than other surveys due to its uniqueness. The three types of ownership are recorded by asking the following questions: Which household members own this asset (*reported*)? Whose names are listed as owners on the ownership document of this asset (*documented*)? And, if this asset is to be sold, which members of this household would be involved in the decision to sell (*economic*)?

In addition to the different types of ownership, the EDGE survey also collects information on *exclusively* and *jointly owned* assets. Knowing whether an asset is exclusively owned by a person or jointly owned with someone else is important to our understanding of the social and economic dynamics that exist within the household.

While the novelty of the EDGE survey lies in collecting data on asset ownership at the individual level, it also presents several methodological challenges. In particular, individuals within the same household may have a varying perception of which assets are owned by every member. They may also have a different understanding of how the assets are owned. For example, consider a hypothetical household consisting of three members—A, B, and C. For simplicity, let us focus on a specific type of asset, say household dwelling. Box Table shows the data on type and form of ownership as reported by each household member. The rows correspond to the information reported by each household member while the columns represent how each member perceives the ownership status of the other members. Here, member A reports that he/she is the exclusive owner of the household's dwelling and, according to him/her, B and C would be involved in making a decision to sell the dwelling but they are neither reported nor documented owners. On the other hand, B thinks that he/she jointly owns the dwelling with A, while C reports that instead of B, it is he/she who co-owns the asset with A. If we follow the self-assigned approach in estimating the distribution of type and form of ownership, we will consider all the information as if they are all true. The task becomes more complicated if we are looking at different types of assets, say parcel of land. In particular, it is difficult to come up with an inventory or full list of all land parcels owned by all household members because it is not straightforward to know if each household member is referring to the same or different parcels of land during the interview. Another source of difficulty is the possibility that some assets are hidden from some household members.

continued.

Box 2.2: *(continued)*

Sample Evidence and Data for Gender Equality Survey Data on Ownership Status

Household Member	A	B	C
A	reported, documented, economic, exclusive	economic	economic
B	reported, documented, economic, jointly	reported, economic, jointly	reported, economic, jointly
C	reported, economic, jointly	economic	reported, economic, jointly

Since perception bias among respondents regarding reporting of assets, ownership status, and overlapping of reported assets among owners is possible, further studies that focus on the rigorous approaches of developing an inventory of assets are needed. The UNSD is currently preparing a set of guidelines on measuring asset ownership and entrepreneurship from a gender perspective to be presented at the UN Security Council next year. The guidelines will benefit from the rich experience of the pilot surveys in Georgia, Mongolia, and the Philippines where the Asian Development Bank and the countries' respective national statistics offices conducted the EDGE stand-alone pilot survey, as well as from other EDGE-related surveys carried in few other countries by other collaborating agencies.

Notes: The results from the three stand-alone pilot surveys in Georgia, Mongolia, and the Philippines under ADB's Regional Technical Assistance 8243 are being finalized at the time of writing.

Table 2.1:   **Selected Indicators for SDG 1 - Poverty**

By 2030, eradicate extreme poverty for all people everywhere, measured as people living below the international poverty line

By 2030, reduce at least by half the proportion of men, women, and children of all ages living in poverty in all its dimensions according to national definitions

Regional Member	1.1.1 Proportion of Population below the International Poverty Line[a] (%)		1.2.1 Proportion of Population Living below the National Poverty Line (%)	
	Initial Year	Latest Year	Initial Year	Latest Year
Developing Member Economies				
Central and West Asia				
Afghanistan	...	...	36.3 (2007)	39.1 (2014)
Armenia	19.3 (2001)	2.3 (2014)	48.3 (2001)	30.0 (2014)
Azerbaijan	2.7 (2001)	0.5 (2008)	49.6 (2001)	5.0 (2014)
Georgia	21.0 (2000)	9.8 (2014)	6.4[b] (2007)	10.1 (2015)
Kazakhstan	10.5 (2001)	0.0 (2013)	46.7 (2001)	2.7 (2015)
Kyrgyz Republic	42.2 (2000)	1.3 (2014)	39.9 (2006)	32.1 (2015)
Pakistan[c]	28.7 (2001)	6.1 (2013)	64.3 (2001)	29.5 (2013)
Tajikistan	54.4 (1999)	19.5 (2014)	34.3 (2013)	32.0 (2015)
Turkmenistan	42.3 (1998)	...	...	...
Uzbekistan	68.1 (2000)	66.8 (2003)	27.5 (2001)	12.8 (2015)
East Asia				
China, People's Rep. of	40.5[d] (1999)	1.9[d] (2013)	17.2[e] (2010)	7.2[e] (2014)
Hong Kong, China	...	...	...	...
Korea, Rep. of	...	...	16.5 (2012)	16.3 (2014)
Mongolia	10.6 (2002)	0.2 (2014)	38.8 (2010)	21.6 (2014)
Taipei,China	...	...	0.7[f] (2000)	1.5[f] (2014)
South Asia				
Bangladesh	33.7 (2000)	18.5 (2010)	48.9 (2000)	31.5 (2010)
Bhutan[g]	35.2 (2003)	2.2 (2012)	23.2 (2007)	12.0 (2012)
India[c]	38.2[d] (2004)	21.2[d] (2011)	37.2 (2004)	21.9 (2011)
Maldives[c]	10.0 (2002)	7.3 (2009)	23.0 (2002)	15.0[h] (2009)
Nepal[c]	46.1 (2003)	15.0 (2010)	...	25.2 (2010)
Sri Lanka[c]	8.3 (2002)	1.9 (2012)	22.7 (2002)	6.7 (2012)
Southeast Asia				
Brunei Darussalam	...	...	...	...
Cambodia	18.6 (2004)	2.2 (2012)	50.2 (2004)	14.0 (2014)
Indonesia	39.8[d] (2000)	8.3[d] (2014)	19.1[i] (2000)	10.9[j] (2016)
Lao PDR[c]	26.1 (2002)	16.7 (2012)	33.5 (2002)	23.2 (2012)
Malaysia	0.4 (2004)	0.3 (2009)	6.0 (2002)	0.6 (2014)
Myanmar	...	...	32.1 (2005)	25.6 (2010)
Philippines	18.4 (2000)	13.1 (2012)	24.9 (2003)	21.6 (2015)
Singapore	...	...	...	...
Thailand	2.6 (2000)	0.0 (2013)	42.3 (2000)	10.5 (2014)
Viet Nam[c]	38.8 (2002)	3.1 (2014)	28.9 (2002)	7.0 (2015)
The Pacific				
Cook Islands	...	...	...	28.4[k] (2006)
Fiji[c]	5.5 (2002)	4.1 (2008)	39.8[k] (2002)	35.2[k] (2008)
Kiribati	14.1 (2006)	...	21.8[k] (2006)	...
Marshall Islands	...	...	...	...
Micronesia, Fed. States of	11.4 (2005)	17.4 (2013)	27.9[k] (1998)	31.4[k] (2005)
Nauru	...	...	25.1[k] (2006)	...
Palau	...	...	24.9[k] (2006)	...
Papua New Guinea[c]	...	39.3 (2009)	...	39.9[l] (2009)
Samoa	...	0.8 (2008)	22.9 (2002)	26.9[k] (2008)
Solomon Islands[c]	45.6 (2005)	...	22.7[k] (2006)	12.7[k] (2013)
Timor-Leste	44.2 (2001)	46.8 (2007)	36.3[k] (2001)	41.8 (2014)
Tonga	2.8 (2001)	1.1 (2009)	16.2[k] (2001)	22.5[k] (2009)
Tuvalu[c]	...	2.7 (2010)	21.2[k] (2005)	26.3[k] (2010)
Vanuatu	...	15.4 (2010)	13.0[k] (2006)	12.7[k] (2010)
Developed Member Economies				
Australia	1.4 (2001)	0.7 (2010)	...	...
Japan	...	0.4 (2008)	...	...
New Zealand	...	...	...	...

... = data not available at cutoff date, 0.0 = magnitude is less than half of unit employed, Lao PDR = Lao People's Democratic Republic, SDG = Sustainable Development Goal.

a   Data are consumption-based, except for Australia, Japan, and Malaysia, which are income-based. The estimates are based on $1.90 (2011 purchasing power parity) a day poverty line.
b   Refers to registered poverty. For relative poverty or share of population under 60% of median consumption, the data are 24.6% for 2004 and 20.1% for 2015.
c   Household income and expenditure surveys for these economies were conducted in overlapping years. The table adopts the approach of the World Bank's World Development Indicators of using the initial year of the survey as the reference period for the poverty estimates.
d   Weighted average of rural and urban estimates.
e   Refers to rural areas only.
f   Refers to percentage of low-income population to total population.
g   Estimate for 2003 is based on data from the World Bank's PovcalNet database. An alternative estimate is from the United Nations Statistics Division's SDG Indicators Global Database, which is equal to 24.9% for the same year.
h   Refers to poverty estimate for 2009/10.
i   Reference period is February 2000.
j   Reference period is March 2016.
k   Data refer to percentage of population below the basic needs poverty line.
l   Refers to poverty headcount ratio using Papua New Guinea's upper poverty line.

Sources: World Bank. PovcalNet Database. http://iresearch.worldbank.org/PovcalNet/povDuplicateWB.aspx (accessed 4 October 2016); economy sources; United Nations. Sustainable Development Goals Indicators Global Database. http://unstats.un.org/sdgs/indicators/database/ (accessed 21 July 2016); World Bank. World Development Indicators. http://databank.worldbank.org/data/reports.aspx?source=world-development-indicators (accessed 26 April 2016).

End hunger, achieve food security and improved nutrition, and promote sustainable agriculture

Table 2.2:   **Selected Indicators for SDG 2 - Malnutrition**
By 2030, end all forms of malnutrition, including achieving by 2025, the internationally agreed targets on stunting and wasting in children under 5 years of age, and address the nutritional needs of adolescent girls, pregnant and lactating women and older persons

Regional Member	2.1.1 Prevalence of Undernourishment (%)		2.2.1 Prevalence of Stunting among Children under 5 Years of Age[a] (%)	
	Initial Year[b]	Latest Year[c]	Initial Year	Latest Year
Developing Member Economies				
Central and West Asia				
Afghanistan	45.2	26.8	59.3 (2004)	40.9 (2013)
Armenia	21.4	5.8	17.7 (2000)	20.8 (2010)
Azerbaijan	22.5	<5.0	24.1 (2000)	18.0 (2013)
Georgia	14.8	7.4	16.1 (1999)	11.3 (2009)
Kazakhstan	<5.0	<5.0	13.9 (1999)	8.0 (2015)
Kyrgyz Republic	15.2	6.0	18.1 (2006)	12.9 (2014)
Pakistan	22.4	22.0	41.5 (2001)	45.0 (2012)
Tajikistan	38.8	33.2	42.1 (2000)	26.8 (2012)
Turkmenistan	9.0	<5.0	28.1 (2000)	18.9 (2006)
Uzbekistan	11.5	<5.0	25.3 (2002)	19.6 (2006)
East Asia				
China, People's Rep. of	16.2	9.3	17.8 (2000)	9.4 (2010)
Hong Kong, China	...	...	...	...
Korea, Rep. of	<5.0	<5.0	2.5 (2003)	2.5 (2010)
Mongolia	38.2	20.5	29.8 (2000)	10.8 (2013)
Taipei,China	...	...	...	...
South Asia				
Bangladesh	23.1	16.4	50.8 (2000)	36.1 (2014)
Bhutan	...	...	47.7 (1999)	33.6 (2010)
India	17.0	15.2	54.2 (1999)	38.7 (2014)
Maldives	11.8	5.2	31.9 (2001)	20.3 (2009)
Nepal	22.2	7.8	57.1 (2001)	37.4 (2014)
Sri Lanka	29.9	22.0	18.4 (2000)	14.7 (2012)
Southeast Asia				
Brunei Darussalam	<5.0	<5.0	...	19.7 (2009)
Cambodia	32.0	14.2	49.2 (2000)	32.4 (2014)
Indonesia	17.2	7.6	42.4 (2000)	36.4 (2013)
Lao PDR	39.2	18.5	48.2 (2000)	43.8 (2011)
Malaysia	<5.0	<5.0	20.7 (1999)	17.2 (2006)
Myanmar	52.4	14.2	40.8 (2000)	35.1 (2009)
Philippines	21.3	13.5	38.3 (1998)	30.3 (2013)
Singapore	...	...	4.4 (2000)	...
Thailand	19.0	7.4	15.7 (2006)	16.3 (2012)
Viet Nam	28.1	11.0	43.4 (2000)	24.9 (2014)
The Pacific				
Cook Islands	...	...	...	...
Fiji	<5.0	<5.0	7.5 (2004)	...
Kiribati	<5.0	<5.0	...	...
Marshall Islands	...	...	...	...
Micronesia, Fed. States of	...	...	...	...
Nauru	...	...	24.0 (2007)	...
Palau	...	...	...	...
Papua New Guinea	...	...	43.9 (2005)	49.5 (2010)
Samoa	6.6	<5.0	6.4 (1999)	...
Solomon Islands	15.0	11.3	32.8 (2007)	...
Timor-Leste[d]	43.9	26.9	55.7 (2002)	57.7 (2009)
Tonga	...	...	...	8.1 (2012)
Tuvalu	...	...	10.0 (2007)	...
Vanuatu	8.1	6.4	25.9 (2007)	28.5 (2013)
Developed Member Economies				
Australia	<5.0	<5.0	2.0 (2007)	...
Japan	<5.0	<5.0	...	7.1 (2010)
New Zealand	<5.0	<5.0	...	...

(continued)

End hunger, achieve food security and improved nutrition, and promote sustainable agriculture

Table 2.2: **Selected Indicators for SDG 2 - Malnutrition** (*continued*)
By 2030, end all forms of malnutrition, including achieving by 2025, the internationally agreed targets on stunting and wasting in children under 5 years of age, and address the nutritional needs of adolescent girls, pregnant and lactating women and older persons

Regional Member	2.2.2.a Prevalence of Malnutrition (Wasting) among Children under 5 Years of Age[a] (%)		2.2.2.b Prevalence of Malnutrition (Overweight) among Children under 5 Years of Age[a] (%)	
	Initial Year	Latest Year	Initial Year	Latest Year
Developing Member Economies				
Central and West Asia				
Afghanistan	8.6 (2004)	9.5 (2013)	4.6 (2004)	5.4 (2013)
Armenia	2.5 (2000)	4.2 (2010)	16.0 (2000)	16.8 (2010)
Azerbaijan	9.0 (2000)	3.1 (2013)	6.2 (2000)	13.0 (2013)
Georgia	3.1 (1999)	1.6 (2009)	17.9 (1999)	19.9 (2009)
Kazakhstan	2.5 (1999)	3.1 (2015)	5.3 (1999)	9.3 (2015)
Kyrgyz Republic	3.4 (2006)	2.8 (2014)	10.7 (2006)	7.0 (2014)
Pakistan	14.2 (2001)	10.5 (2012)	4.8 (2001)	4.8 (2012)
Tajikistan	9.4 (2000)	9.9 (2012)	6.7 (2005)	6.6 (2012)
Turkmenistan	7.1 (2000)	7.2 (2006)	4.5 (2006)	...
Uzbekistan	8.9 (2002)	4.5 (2006)	11.1 (2002)	12.8 (2006)
East Asia				
China, People's Rep. of	2.5 (2000)	2.3 (2010)	3.4 (2000)	6.6 (2010)
Hong Kong, China	...	...	...	...
Korea, Rep. of	0.9 (2003)	1.2 (2010)	6.2 (2003)	7.3 (2010)
Mongolia	7.1 (2000)	1.0 (2013)	12.7 (2000)	10.5 (2013)
Taipei,China	...	...	...	...
South Asia				
Bangladesh	12.5 (2000)	14.3 (2014)	0.9 (2000)	1.4 (2014)
Bhutan	2.5 (1999)	5.9 (2010)	3.9 (1999)	7.6 (2010)
India	17.1 (1999)	15.1 (2014)	2.9 (1999)	1.9 (2006)
Maldives	13.4 (2001)	10.2 (2009)	3.9 (2001)	6.5 (2009)
Nepal	11.3 (2001)	11.3 (2014)	0.7 (2001)	2.1 (2014)
Sri Lanka	15.5 (2000)	21.4 (2012)	1.0 (2000)	0.6 (2012)
Southeast Asia				
Brunei Darussalam	...	2.9 (2009)	...	8.3 (2009)
Cambodia	16.9 (2000)	9.6 (2014)	4.0 (2000)	2.0 (2014)
Indonesia	5.5 (2000)	13.5 (2013)	1.5 (2000)	11.5 (2013)
Lao PDR	17.5 (2000)	6.4 (2011)	2.7 (2000)	2.0 (2011)
Malaysia	15.3 (1999)	...	5.5 (1999)	...
Myanmar	10.7 (2000)	7.9 (2009)	2.4 (2000)	2.6 (2009)
Philippines	8.0 (1998)	7.9 (2013)	1.9 (1998)	5.0 (2013)
Singapore	3.6 (2000)	...	2.6 (2000)	...
Thailand	4.7 (2006)	6.7 (2012)	8.0 (2006)	10.9 (2012)
Viet Nam	6.1 (2000)	6.8 (2014)	2.5 (2000)	3.5 (2014)
The Pacific				
Cook Islands	...	...	...	...
Fiji	6.3 (2004)	...	5.1 (2004)	...
Kiribati	...	...	...	...
Marshall Islands	...	...	...	...
Micronesia, Fed. States of	...	...	...	...
Nauru	1.0 (2007)	...	2.8 (2007)	...
Palau	...	...	...	...
Papua New Guinea	4.4 (2005)	14.3 (2010)	3.4 (2005)	13.8 (2010)
Samoa	1.3 (1999)	...	6.2 (1999)	...
Solomon Islands	4.3 (2007)	...	2.5 (2007)	...
Timor-Leste[d]	13.7 (2002)	18.9 (2009)	5.7 (2002)	5.8 (2009)
Tonga	...	5.2 (2012)	...	17.3 (2012)
Tuvalu	3.3 (2007)	...	...	6.3 (2007)
Vanuatu	5.9 (2007)	4.4 (2013)	4.7 (2007)	4.6 (2013)
Developed Member Economies				
Australia	– (2007)	...	7.7 (2007)	...
Japan	...	2.3 (2010)	...	1.5 (2010)
New Zealand	...	...	...	...

... = data not available at cutoff date, – = magnitude equals zero, 0.0 = magnitude is less than half of unit employed, Lao PDR = Lao People's Democratic Republic, SDG = Sustainable Development Goal.

a According to the World Health Organization, for some economies the estimates were adjusted where necessary to be nationally representative and to cover the age range 0–5 years, which might result in slight differences in prevalence from the survey results reported. Estimates for some economies are also "pending re-analysis." Details can be found in the "Notes" column of the joint child malnutrition dataset.
b Data refer to 3-year average for 1999–2001.
c Data refer to 3-year average for 2014–2016.
d For Timor-Leste, data are available for 2013 for indicators 2.2.1 (50.2%), 2.2.2a (11.0%), and 2.2.2b (1.5%) in the United Nations Statistics Division's SDG Database, but are pending re-analysis.

Sources: United Nations. Sustainable Development Goals Indicators Global Database. http://unstats.un.org/sdgs/indicators/database/ (accessed 21 July 2016); Food and Agriculture Organization of the United Nations. FAOSTAT. http://faostat3.fao.org/download/D/FS/E (accessed 16 August 2016); World Bank. World Development Indicators. http://databank.worldbank.org/data/reports.aspx?source=world-development-indicators (accessed 26 April 2016); World Health Organization. Joint Child Malnutrition Estimates – Levels and Trends (2016 Edition). http://www.who.int/nutgrowthdb/estimates2015/en/ (accessed 28 September 2016).

End hunger, achieve food security and improved nutrition, and promote sustainable agriculture

Table 2.3: **Selected Indicators for SDG 2 - Agricultural Investment**

By 2030, increase investment, including through enhanced international cooperation, in rural infrastructure, agricultural research and extension services, technology development and plant and livestock gene banks in order to enhance agricultural productive capacity in developing countries, in particular least developed countries

Regional Member	2.a.2 Total Official Flows (Official Development Assistance Plus Other Official Flows) to the Agriculture Sector	
	2000[a]	2014[b]
Developing Member Economies		
Central and West Asia		
Afghanistan	5.0	408.6
Armenia	15.4	17.2
Azerbaijan	81.3	38.4
Georgia	39.9	27.8
Kazakhstan	4.3	6.2
Kyrgyz Republic	89.1	16.1
Pakistan	67.9	351.4
Tajikistan	25.6	27.2
Turkmenistan	0.0	0.1
Uzbekistan	0.3	54.7
East Asia		
China, People's Rep. of	355.0	307.5
Hong Kong, China	...	...
Korea, Rep. of		...
Mongolia	4.4	20.5
Taipei,China	...	...
South Asia		
Bangladesh	389.8	349.8
Bhutan	6.4	13.4
India	251.5	1,013.3
Maldives	0.0	1.6
Nepal	83.8	87.3
Sri Lanka	56.7	51.5
Southeast Asia		
Brunei Darussalam	...	...
Cambodia	176.2	129.4
Indonesia	229.2	314.7
Lao PDR	31.1	74.8
Malaysia	9.7	3.4
Myanmar	2.1	78.9
Philippines	384.8	99.8
Singapore	...	...
Thailand	32.0	22.5
Viet Nam	121.0	278.3
The Pacific		
Cook Islands	0.0	0.3
Fiji	1.2	7.3
Kiribati	8.1	3.3
Marshall Islands	3.3	0.7
Micronesia, Fed. States of	9.8	0.9
Nauru	0.2 (2003)	0.9
Palau	0.2	0.6
Papua New Guinea	65.8	33.2
Samoa	3.0	2.3
Solomon Islands	3.9	7.2
Timor-Leste	9.9	32.2
Tonga	0.3	1.1
Tuvalu	7.4 (2001)	0.9
Vanuatu	4.3	4.6
Developed Member Economies		
Australia	...	...
Japan	...	...
New Zealand	...	...

... = data not available at cutoff date; 0.0 = magnitude is less than half of unit employed, Lao PDR = Lao People's Democratic Republic, SDG = Sustainable Development Goal.

a Data refer to commitments (constant 2014 $ million) except for Nauru, which refer to gross disbursements (constant 2014 $ million).
b Data refer to gross disbursements (constant 2014 $ million).

Source: United Nations. Sustainable Development Goals Indicators Global Database. http://unstats.un.org/sdgs/indicators/database/ (accessed 21 July 2016).

Table 2.4: **Selected Indicators for SDG 3 - Maternal and Child Health**
By 2030, reduce the global maternal mortality ratio to less than 70 per 100,000 live births

By 2030, end preventable deaths of newborns and children under 5 years of age, with all countries aiming to reduce neonatal mortality to at least as low as 12 per 1,000 live births and under-5 mortality to at least as low as 25 per 1,000 live births

Regional Member	3.1.1 Maternal Mortality Ratio (per 100,000 live births)[a]		3.1.2 Proportion of Births Attended by Skilled Health Personnel (%)		3.2.1 Under-5 Mortality Rate (per 1,000 live births)[a]		3.2.2 Neonatal Mortality Rate (per 1,000 live births)[a]	
	2000	2015	2000	2014	2000	2015	2000	2015
Developing Member Economies								
Central and West Asia	**365**	**174**			**106**	**71**	**52**	**37**
Afghanistan	1,100	396	14.3 (2003)	45.2	137	91	45	36
Armenia	40	25	96.8	99.5 (2010)	30	14	16	7
Azerbaijan	48	25	84.1	97.2 (2011)	74	32	33	18
Georgia	37	36	95.7	99.9	36	12	21	7
Kazakhstan	65	12	98.3	99.9 (2011)	44	14	20	7
Kyrgyz Republic	74	76	98.6	98.4	49	21	22	12
Pakistan	306	178	23.0 (2002)	52.1 (2013)	112	81	60	46
Tajikistan	68	32	71.1	87.4 (2012)	93	45	30	21
Turkmenistan	59	42	97.2	99.5 (2006)	82	51	31	23
Uzbekistan	34	36	95.6	99.9 (2006)	63	39	29	20
East Asia	**57**	**27**			**36**	**11**	**21**	**5**
China, People's Rep. of	58	27	96.6	99.9	37	11	21	6
Hong Kong, China	3 (2014)	2	100.0 (2005)	...	...	...	...	...
Korea, Rep. of	16	11	100.0 (2003)	...	6	3	2	2
Mongolia	161	44	96.6	98.9	63	22	26	11
Taipei,China	8	7 (2014)	...	...	...	...	...	...
South Asia	**377**	**174**			**90**	**46**	**44**	**27**
Bangladesh	399	176	13.9	42.1	88	38	43	23
Bhutan	423	148	23.7	74.6 (2012)	80	33	33	18
India	374	174	42.5	52.3 (2008)	91	48	45	28
Maldives	163	68	70.3 (2001)	95.5 (2012)	44	9	26	5
Nepal	548	258	11.9	55.6	81	36	39	22
Sri Lanka	57	30	96.0	98.6 (2007)	16	10	10	5
Southeast Asia	**199**	**110**			**49**	**27**	**21**	**13**
Brunei Darussalam	31	23	99.9 (2009)	99.7 (2013)	9	10	5	4
Cambodia	484	161	31.8	89.0	108	29	36	15
Indonesia	265	126	66.3 (2003)	87.4 (2013)	52	27	22	14
Lao PDR	546	197	19.4	41.5 (2012)	118	67	43	30
Malaysia	58	40	96.6	99.0	10	7	5	4
Myanmar	308	178	57.0 (2001)	70.6 (2010)	82	50	37	26
Philippines	124	114	59.8 (2003)	72.8 (2013)	40	28	17	13
Singapore	18	10	99.7 (2004)	...	4	3	2	1
Thailand	25	20	99.3	99.6 (2012)	23	12	13	7
Viet Nam	81	54	69.6	93.8	34	22	16	11
The Pacific	**346**	**191**			**73**	**51**	**28**	**22**
Cook Islands	...	...	98.0 (2001)	100.0 (2009)	17	8	9	4
Fiji	42	30	99.0	99.6 (2013)	25	22	14	10
Kiribati	166	90	63.0 (2005)	79.8 (2009)	71	56	29	24
Marshall Islands	...	...	86.2 (2007)	90.1 (2011)	41	36	19	17
Micronesia, Fed. States of	153	100	87.7 (2001)	100.0 (2009)	54	35	26	19
Nauru	...	...	97.4 (2007)	...	41	35	25	23
Palau	...	...	100.0 (2002)	100.0	27	16	15	9
Papua New Guinea	342	215	41.0	53.0 (2006)	79	57	30	25
Samoa	93	51	80.8 (2009)	82.5	22	18	12	10
Solomon Islands	214	114	85.5 (2007)	...	33	28	14	12
Timor-Leste	694	215	23.7 (2002)	29.3 (2010)	110	53	37	22
Tonga	97	124	95.3	97.9 (2012)	18	17	8	7
Tuvalu	...	...	100.0 (2002)	97.9 (2007)	43	27	25	18
Vanuatu	144	78	74.0 (2007)	89.4 (2013)	29	28	12	12
Developed Member Economies	**10**	**5**			**5**	**3**	**2**	**1**
Australia	9	6	100.0 (2003)	...	6	4	4	2
Japan	10	5	99.8 (2004)	...	5	3	2	1
New Zealand	12	11	96.6 (2001)	...	7	6	4	3
DEVELOPING MEMBER ECONOMIES	**269**	**125**			**71**	**36**	**35**	**20**
REGIONAL MEMBERS	**263**	**123**			**70**	**36**	**35**	**20**
WORLD	**341**	**216**			**76**	**43**	**31**	**19**

... = data not available at cutoff date, Lao PDR = Lao People's Democratic Republic, SDG = Sustainable Development Goal.

a Regional aggregates are weighted averages estimated using population of annual live births for the respective year headings. The data for under-five and neonatal deaths are from the UNICEF Global Databases. Aggregates are derived for reporting economies only. For maternal mortality ratio, aggregates for East Asia exclude Taipei,China.

Sources: For Indicator 3.1.1: World Health Organization. *Trends in Maternal Mortality: 1990 to 2015 Estimates by WHO, UNICEF, UNFPA, World Bank Group and the United Nations Population Division*; for Hong Kong, China: Centre for Health Protection. Official website: http://www.chp.gov.hk/en/data/4/10/27/110.html (accessed 28 September 2016) and for Taipei,China: *Directorate-General of Budget, Accounting, and Statistics.* http://eng.dgbas.gov.tw/public/data/dgbas03/bs2/yearbook_eng/y066.pdf. For Indicator 3.1.2: United Nations. Sustainable Development Goals Indicators Global Database. http://unstats.un.org/sdgs/indicators/database/ (accessed 21 July 2016) and World Development Indicators. http://databank.worldbank.org/data/reports.aspx?source=world-development-indicators (accessed 26 April 2016). For Indicators 3.2.1 and 3.2.2: United Nations International Children's Emergency Fund. Global Databases http://www.data.unicef.org (accessed 1 September 2016).

Table 2.5:   **Selected Indicators for SDG 3 - Communicable and Noncommunicable Diseases, Adolescent Birthrate, and Death Rates**

By 2030, end the epidemics of AIDS, tuberculosis, malaria and neglected tropical diseases and combat hepatitis, water-borne diseases and other communicable diseases

By 2030, reduce by one third premature mortality from noncommunicable diseases through prevention and treatment and promote mental health and well-being

Regional Member	3.3.1 Number of New HIV Infections (per 1,000 uninfected population)		3.3.2 Tuberculosis Incidence (per 100,000 population)		3.3.3 Incidence of Malaria (per 1,000 population)		3.4.1 Mortality Rate Attributed to Cardiovascular Disease, Cancer, Diabetes, or Chronic Respiratory Disease (%)	
	2000	2015	2000	2014	2000	2013	2000	2012
Developing Member Economies								
Central and West Asia								
Afghanistan	0.02	0.03	190	189	142.8	15.7	33.4	30.5
Armenia	0.12	0.14	61	45	...	...	31.5	29.7
Azerbaijan	0.05	0.12	681	77	17.9	–	32.0	23.3
Georgia	0.07	0.28	254	106	11.3	–	25.0	21.6
Kazakhstan	0.06	0.21	177	99	...	...	42.0	33.9
Kyrgyz Republic	0.05	0.16	244	142	6.7	–	34.2	28.6
Pakistan	0.01	0.09	275	270	43.3	12.8	19.5	20.5
Tajikistan	0.17	0.19	219	91	18.3	0.0	30.3	28.8
Turkmenistan	...	...	208	64	...	...	39.3	40.8
Uzbekistan	0.32	0.01	99	82	5.6	–	32.9	31.0
East Asia								
China, People's Rep. of	...	...	109	68	0.1	0.0	23.1	19.4
Hong Kong, China	...	...	110	74	...	...	...	...
Korea, Rep. of	...	...	80	86	2.8	0.2	16.9	9.3
Mongolia	–	0.02	253	170	...	...	39.6	32.0
Taipei,China	...	...	...	...	...	...	...	...
South Asia								
Bangladesh	–	0.01	225	227	364.9	68.7	18.7	17.5
Bhutan	...	...	402	164	27.5	0.1	23.8	20.5
India	...	...	216	167	40.4	23.7	28.7	26.3
Maldives			64	41	...	...	28.3	16.0
Nepal	0.32	0.05	163	158	10.8	1.2	26.0	21.6
Sri Lanka	0.01	0.03	66	65	107.0	–	23.4	17.6
Southeast Asia								
Brunei Darussalam	...	...	80	62	...	...	18.4	16.8
Cambodia	0.82	0.05	575	390	252.9	10.6	20.1	17.7
Indonesia	0.07	0.29	449	399	44.7	41.8	25.8	23.1
Lao PDR	...	...	330	189	101.1	29.8	29.2	24.2
Malaysia	0.55	0.17	78	103	16.3	3.2	25.0	19.6
Myanmar	0.84	0.24	411	369	60.4	45.0	23.6	24.4
Philippines	0.01	0.06	368	288	3.4	0.4	23.1	27.9
Singapore	...	...	52	49	...	...	16.5	10.5
Thailand	0.52	0.11	241	171	12.0	6.5	19.5	16.2
Viet Nam	0.34	0.16	197	140	9.3	0.9	17.2	17.4
The Pacific								
Cook Islands	...	...	7	12	...	...	...	...
Fiji	...	...	53	67	...	...	33.4	30.8
Kiribati	...	...	372	497	...	...	...	...
Marshall Islands	...	...	81	335	...	...	...	...
Micronesia, Fed. States of	...	...	279	195	...	...	...	...
Nauru	...	...	46	73	...	...	...	...
Palau	...	...	135	42	...	...	...	...
Papua New Guinea	0.87	0.36	418	417	270.3	185.1	28.4	26.4
Samoa	...	...	23	19	...	...	...	...
Solomon Islands	...	...	185	86	476.3	75.4	26.0	24.1
Timor-Leste	...	...	498 (2002)	498	336.7	89.7	29.9	23.8
Tonga	...	...	31	14	...	...	...	...
Tuvalu	...	...	357	190	...	...	...	...
Vanuatu	...	...	110	63	127.4	31.3	...	...
Developed Member Economies								
Australia	0.05	0.05	6	6	...	...	13.0	9.4
Japan	...	...	35	18	...	...	11.5	9.4
New Zealand	...	...	11	7	...	...	15.9	10.7

(continued)

Table 2.5: **Selected Indicators for SDG 3 - Communicable and Noncommunicable Diseases, Adolescent Birthrate, and Death Rates** (*continued*)

Regional Member	3.6.1 Death Rate due to Road Traffic Injuries (per 100,000 population)		3.7.2 Adolescent Birthrate (Aged 10–14 Years; Aged 15–19 Years) per 1,000 Women in That Age Group		3.9.1 Mortality Rate Attributed to Household and Ambient Air Pollution (per 100,000 population)		3.9.2 Mortality Rate Attributed to Unsafe Water, Unsafe Sanitation, and Lack of Hygiene (per 100,000 population)
	2000	2013	2000	2013	2000	2012	2012
Developing Member Economies							
Central and West Asia							
Afghanistan	15.7	15.5	146.0 (2003)	51.9 (2011)	…	113.0	34.6
Armenia	20.6	18.3	32.8	22.7	…	125.0	1.1
Azerbaijan	7.9	10.0	28.7	47.2	…	68.0	2.1
Georgia	10.5	11.8	39.9	41.5	…	292.0	0.2
Kazakhstan	14.1	24.2	31.1	36.4	…	93.0	1.2
Kyrgyz Republic	12.0	22.0	33.6	42.1	6.7	– (2013)	1.8
Pakistan	14.8	14.2	55.0 (2004)	44.0 (2011)	43.3	12.8 (2013)	20.7
Tajikistan	19.7	18.8	37.3	54.0 (2011)	18.3	0.0 (2013)	7.5
Turkmenistan	18.0	17.4	26.1	21.0 (2006)	…	73.0	5.8
Uzbekistan	9.7	11.2	20.9	29.5 (2010)	5.6	– (2013)	2.4
East Asia							
China, People's Rep. of	18.0	18.8	6.0	6.2 (2011)	…	163.0	0.4
Hong Kong, China	…	…	4.3	2.7	…	…	…
Korea, Rep. of	26.4	12.0	2.6	1.7	2.8	0.2 (2013)	0.2
Mongolia	18.7	21.0	27.6	26.7 (2014)	…	132.0	3.1
Taipei,China	…	…	…	…	…	…	…
South Asia							
Bangladesh	14.3	13.6	134.0	113.0	…	68.0	6.0
Bhutan	16.5	15.1	61.7	28.4 (2012)	…	60.0	7.1
India	16.3	16.6	51.0	28.1	…	130.0	27.4
Maldives	2.9	3.5	28.9	13.7 (2012)	…	21.0	0.6
Nepal	16.9	17.0	106.0 (2003)	71.0	10.8	1.2 (2013)	12.9
Sri Lanka	18.3	17.4	30.8	20.3 (2008)	107.0	– (2013)	3.4
Southeast Asia							
Brunei Darussalam	16.3	8.1	31.8	16.6 (2008)	…	0.2	–
Cambodia	17.8	17.4	52.0 (2003)	57.0	…	71.0	5.6
Indonesia	15.2	15.3	54.0	48.0 (2010)	…	84.0	3.7
Lao PDR	14.0	14.3	96.0	94.0 (2011)	101.1	29.8 (2013)	13.9
Malaysia	26.6	24.0	12.0	12.7 (2012)	16.3	3.2 (2013)	0.4
Myanmar	21.8	20.3	22.7	22.0	60.4	45.0 (2013)	10.5
Philippines	9.9	10.5	55.0 (2001)	57.0 (2012)	3.4	0.4 (2013)	5.1
Singapore	6.7	3.6	7.7	2.7	…	21.0	0.1
Thailand	37.7	36.2	33.1	60.0 (2012)	12.0	6.5 (2013)	1.9
Viet Nam	23.6	24.5	25.0	36.0	9.3	0.9 (2013)	2.0
The Pacific							
Cook Islands	5.6	24.2	47.0 (2001)	56.0 (2011)	…	10.0	…
Fiji	9.6	5.8	34.8 (2002)	27.5 (2008)	…	77.0	3.0
Kiribati	8.5	2.9	70.8	49.0 (2010)	…	48.0	15.9
Marshall Islands	17.3	5.7	71.9 (2002)	85.0 (2011)	…	26.0	7.6
Micronesia, Fed. States of	16.8	1.9	58.5	32.6 (2010)	…	41.0	9.7
Nauru	19.9	19.9	113.8	105.3 (2011)	…	2.9	…
Palau	15.6	4.8	25.9	27.0 (2010)	…	0.9	4.8
Papua New Guinea	17.3	16.8	70.0	65.0 (2004)	270.3	185.1 (2013)	12.4
Samoa	16.6	15.8	33.6 (2001)	39.2 (2011)	…	32.0	3.7
Solomon Islands	18.7	19.2	82.0	62.0 (2008)	476.3	75.4 (2013)	10.4
Timor-Leste	17.1	16.6	78.3 (2001)	51.0 (2008)	336.7	89.7 (2013)	10.3
Tonga	15.3	7.6	18.7	30.0 (2011)	…	30.0	4.8
Tuvalu	21.2	20.3	48.9	42.0 (2007)	…	18.0	…
Vanuatu	15.7	16.6	66.0 (2009)	78.0 (2011)	127.4	31.3 (2013)	7.3
Developed Member Economies							
Australia	9.5	5.4	17.8	14.2	…	0.4	0.0
Japan	12.3	4.7	5.4	4.4	…	24.0	0.1
New Zealand	12.1	6.0	27.9	19.1 (2014)	…	0.5	0.6

… = data not available at cutoff date, – = magnitude equals zero, 0.0 = magnitude is less than half of unit employed, Lao PDR = Lao People's Democratic Republic, SDG = Sustainable Development Goal.

Sources: United Nations. Sustainable Development Goals Indicators Global Database. http://unstats.un.org/sdgs/indicators/database/ (accessed 21 July 2016); World Health Organization. Global Health Observatory (GHO) data. http://www.who.int/gho (accessed September 2016).

Ensure inclusive and equitable quality education and promote lifelong learning opportunities for all

Table 2.6:   **Selected Indicators for SDG 4 - Early Childhood Education**
By 2030, ensure that all girls and boys have access to quality early childhood development, care and preprimary education so that they are ready for primary education

| Regional Member | 4.2.2 Participation Rate in Organized Learning (1 year before the official primary entry age)[a] (%) | | | | | |
| | 2000 | | | 2014 | | |
	Total	Female	Male	Total	Female	Male
Developing Member Economies						
Central and West Asia						
Afghanistan	...	...	...	...	...	...
Armenia	...	...	...	...	...	...
Azerbaijan	15.7	16.0	15.4	20.5	21.0	20.2
Georgia	50.0 (2004)	53.3 (2004)	47.0 (2004)	53.1 (2007)	57.1 (2007)	49.7 (2007)
Kazakhstan	75.7 (2001)	76.5 (2001)	74.8 (2001)	94.6 (2015)	100.0 (2015)	89.6 (2015)
Kyrgyz Republic	42.1	42.9	41.3	67.4	68.6	66.2
Pakistan	57.6 (2004)	56.1 (2004)	59.0 (2004)	94.5	88.5	100.0
Tajikistan	12.1	7.9	8.7	11.8 (2015)	11.1 (2015)	12.5 (2015)
Turkmenistan	...	...	...	...	...	...
Uzbekistan	36.6 (2008)	37.1 (2008)	36.1 (2008)	33.4 (2011)	33.8 (2011)	33.0 (2011)
East Asia						
China, People's Rep. of	...	...	...	...	...	...
Hong Kong, China	92.6 (2002)	93.5 (2002)	91.7 (2002)	99.2 (2011)	98.3 (2011)	100.0 (2011)
Korea, Rep. of	...	...	...	98.8 (2013)	98.8 (2013)	98.8 (2013)
Mongolia	50.4 (2000)	51.9 (2000)	49.0 (2000)	71.0 (2012)	71.2 (2012)	70.8 (2012)
Taipei,China	...	...	...	...	...	...
South Asia						
Bangladesh	30.1 (2009)	30.6 (2009)	29.6 (2009)	59.9 (2011)	59.6 (2011)	60.3 (2011)
Bhutan	4.6 (2000)	4.5 (2000)	4.7 (2000)	...	...	...
India	...	...	...	...	...	...
Maldives	69.5	70.0	69.1	80.2 (2007)	80.4 (2007)	80.0 (2007)
Nepal	77.9 (2011)	82.2 (2011)	73.9 (2011)	80.7 (2015)	80.6 (2015)	80.9 (2015)
Sri Lanka	...	...	...	...	...	...
Southeast Asia						
Brunei Darussalam	99.5 (2005)	99.1 (2005)	100.0 (2005)	99.6	100.0	99.3
Cambodia	12.9	13.1	12.7	32.7	31.6	33.6
Indonesia	79.2 (2005)	78.5 (2005)	80.0 (2005)	99.3	98.7	100.0
Lao PDR	9.5	9.8	9.1	50.4	51.1	49.8
Malaysia	77.2	...	...	95.9	...	...
Myanmar	5.0 (2006)	5.0 (2006)	5.1 (2006)	22.9	23.4	22.5
Philippines	24.0 (2001)	23.8 (2001)	24.1 (2001)	42.2 (2009)	43.0 (2009)	41.4 (2009)
Singapore	...	...	...	...	...	...
Thailand	99.1 (2006)	100.0 (2006)	98.2 (2006)	99.7 (2011)	99.4 (2011)	100.0 (2011)
Viet Nam	69.2	...	...	94.7 (2013)	...	...
The Pacific						
Cook Islands	98.4 (2013)	100.0 (2013)	96.8 (2013)	94.1	100.0	88.4
Fiji	48.6 (2004)	50.2 (2004)	47.1 (2004)	49.7 (2006)	50.6 (2006)	48.8 (2006)
Kiribati	...	...	...	...	...	...
Marshall Islands	62.1 (2002)	62.4 (2002)	61.9 (2002)	...	...	...
Micronesia, Fed. States of	...	...	...	...	...	...
Nauru	89.4 (2007)	78.5 (2007)	100.0 (2007)	71.2	82.3	61.6
Palau	...	...	...	90.8	81.1	100.0
Papua New Guinea	...	...	...	...	...	...
Samoa	39.0	43.5	34.9	29.5	32.2	27.1
Solomon Islands	...	...	...	...	...	...
Timor-Leste	58.5 (2013)	61.9 (2013)	55.3 (2013)	63.5	67.8	59.4
Tonga	...	...	...	...	...	...
Tuvalu	...	...	...	...	...	...
Vanuatu	...	...	...	...	...	...
Developed Member Economies						
Australia	52.5 (2001)	53.2 (2001)	51.9 (2001)	80.3 (2013)	80.4 (2013)	80.3 (2013)
Japan	97.3	...	...	95.7 (2013)	...	...
New Zealand	89.6	89.1	90.1	92.9	93.6	92.1

... = data not available at cutoff date, 0.0 = magnitude is less than half of unit employed, Lao PDR = Lao People's Democratic Republic, SDG = Sustainable Development Goal.

a   Covers participation in early childhood education and preprimary education.

Source: United Nations Educational, Scientific, and Cultural Organization Institute for Statistics. Data Centre. http://www.uis.unesco.org/datacentre/Pages/default.aspx (accessed August 2016).

Ensure inclusive and equitable quality education and promote lifelong learning opportunities for all

Table 2.7: **Selected Indicators for SDG 4 - Teacher Training and Supply**
By 2030, substantially increase the supply of qualified teachers, including through international cooperation for teacher training in developing countries, especially least developed countries and small island developing states

Regional Member	4.c.1.a Proportion of Teachers in Preprimary Education Who Have Received at Least the Minimum Organized Teacher Training (% of total teachers)		4.c.1.b Proportion of Teachers in Primary Education Who Have Received at Least the Minimum Organized Teacher Training (% of total teachers)	
	2000	2015	2000	2015
Developing Member Economies				
Central and West Asia				
Afghanistan	...	...	...	...
Armenia	97.1 (2002)	79.7 (2012)	66.7 (2004)	77.5 (2005)
Azerbaijan	79.2	85.2 (2014)	99.9	99.6 (2014)
Georgia	99.1	96.6 (2003)	94.7	94.6 (2009)
Kazakhstan	...	100.0 (2014)	100.0 (2014)	100.0
Kyrgyz Republic	32.1	46.2 (2011)	46.3	72.0 (2012)
Pakistan	...	...	78.0 (2004)	84.0 (2014)
Tajikistan	91.3 (2001)	100.0	81.6 (2001)	100.0
Turkmenistan	...	...	...	...
Uzbekistan	100.0 (2006)	100.0 (2011)	100.0 (2006)	100.0 (2011)
East Asia				
China, People's Rep. of	...	...	...	...
Hong Kong, China	...	...	87.5	96.4 (2014)
Korea, Rep. of	...	...	...	...
Mongolia	100.0	93.6 (2012)	100.0	100.0 (2014)
Taipei,China	...	...	...	...
South Asia				
Bangladesh	...	...	53.4 (2005)	57.7 (2011)
Bhutan	93.8	...	94.8	91.5 (2008)
India	...	...	...	...
Maldives	47.2	73.2 (2014)	66.5	86.1 (2014)
Nepal	72.7 (2008)	87.5	15.4 (2001)	94.4
Sri Lanka	...	...	82.1 (2010)	80.2 (2013)
Southeast Asia				
Brunei Darussalam	64.4 (2005)	64.38 (2014)	84.5 (2005)	87.4 (2014)
Cambodia	98.1 (2001)	100.0 (2014)	95.9 (2001)	100.0 (2014)
Indonesia	...	...	...	...
Lao PDR	83.1	90.6 (2014)	76.7	98.3 (2014)
Malaysia	98.6 (2011)	100.0 (2014)	97.9	98.6 (2014)
Myanmar	50.3 (2006)	48.4 (2014)	62.7	99.5 (2014)
Philippines	...	...	...	100.0 (2013)
Singapore	...	...	96.1 (2007)	94.3 (2009)
Thailand	...	...	...	100.0 (2014)
Viet Nam	50.5	97.8 (2014)	80.0	100.0 (2014)
The Pacific				
Cook Islands	60.9 (2005)	69.7 (2014)	79.2 (2007)	89.2 (2014)
Fiji	...	...	97.8 (2008)	100.0 (2012)
Kiribati	...	...	93.9 (2005)	85.4 (2008)
Marshall Islands	100.0 (2002)	...	...	...
Micronesia, Fed. States of	...	...	...	...
Nauru	77.5 (2006)	82.1 (2007)	...	74.2 (2007)
Palau	...	...	...	...
Papua New Guinea	...	...	...	...
Samoa	...	100.0 (2014)	...	...
Solomon Islands	61.3 (2011)	59.5 (2014)	58.0 (2010)	64.6 (2014)
Timor-Leste	...	...	...	...
Tonga	...	100.0 (2012)	99.6 (2013)	97.1 (2014)
Tuvalu	...	74.6 (2014)	...	...
Vanuatu	...	100.0 (2007)	100.0 (2007)	60.5 (2013)
Developed Member Economies				
Australia	...	...	...	...
Japan	...	...	...	...
New Zealand	...	...	...	...

(continued)

Table 2.7:   **Selected Indicators for SDG 4 - Teacher Training and Supply** *(continued)*
By 2030, substantially increase the supply of qualified teachers, including through international cooperation for teacher training in developing countries, especially least developed countries and small island developing states

Regional Member	4.c.1.c Proportion of Teachers in Lower Secondary Education Who Have Received at Least the Minimum Organized Teacher Training (% of total teachers)		4.c.1.d Proportion of Teachers in Upper Secondary Education Who Have Received at Least the Minimum Organized Teacher Training (% of total teachers)	
	2000	2015	2000	2015
Developing Member Economies				
Central and West Asia				
Afghanistan	...	...	...	...
Armenia	...	...	...	...
Azerbaijan	...	...	...	...
Georgia	76.8	94.6 (2009)	93.0	94.8 (2009)
Kazakhstan	...	...	...	...
Kyrgyz Republic	...	...	71.8 (2003)	84.6 (2010)
Pakistan	...	...	...	...
Tajikistan	94.0	...	93.6 (2002)	92.1 (2004)
Turkmenistan	...	...	...	...
Uzbekistan	...	...	100.0 (2006)	100.0 (2011)
East Asia				
China, People's Rep. of	...	...	...	...
Hong Kong, China	...	...	...	...
Korea, Rep. of	...	...	...	...
Mongolia	100.0	100.0 (2007)	100.0	100.0 (2006)
Taipei,China	...	...	...	...
South Asia				
Bangladesh	36.8	59.6 (2013)	22.4	56.2 (2013)
Bhutan	93.5 (2005)	90.2 (2008)	...	72.2 (2008)
India	...	...	...	...
Maldives	76.3	92.8 (2014)	54.3 (2002)	...
Nepal	32.6	80.6	28.5 (2002)	83.0
Sri Lanka	...	72.1 (2013)	...	82.1 (2011)
Southeast Asia				
Brunei Darussalam	...	94.0 (2014)	85.2 (2005)	87.8 (2013)
Cambodia	99.7 (2001)	100.0 (2014)	99.1 (2001)	99.8 (2007)
Indonesia	...	...	...	...
Lao PDR	98.5	99.5 (2014)	95.6	99.9 (2014)
Malaysia	...	...	...	...
Myanmar	62.1	93.2 (2014)	97.1	95.2 (2014)
Philippines	...	...	...	100.0 (2013)
Singapore	94.4 (2007)	91.6 (2009)	95.0 (2007)	91.7 (2009)
Thailand	...	...	...	...
Viet Nam	86.3	100.0 (2014)	...	...
The Pacific				
Cook Islands	...	...	96.7 (2005)	90.6 (2013)
Fiji	...	100.0 (2012)	94.8 (2008)	100.0 (2012)
Kiribati	83.6 (2005)	86.7 (2014)	43.1 (2005)	33.6 (2008)
Marshall Islands	...	...	...	...
Micronesia, Fed. States of	...	...	...	...
Nauru	...	...	...	36.4 (2007)
Palau	...	...	...	...
Papua New Guinea	...	...	...	100.0 (2012)
Samoa	...	...	71.9 (2009)	100.0 (2014)
Solomon Islands	...	70.8 (2010)	70.8 (2010)	84.6 (2013)
Timor-Leste	...	...	...	...
Tonga	...	...	...	65.1 (2013)
Tuvalu	...	...	...	100.0 (2013)
Vanuatu	...	66.7 (2013)	...	...
Developed Member Economies				
Australia	...	...	...	...
Japan	...	...	...	...
New Zealand	...	...	...	...

... = data not available at cutoff date, Lao PDR = Lao People's Democratic Republic, SDG = Sustainable Development Goal.

Sources: United Nations. Sustainable Development Goals Indicators Global Database. http://unstats.un.org/sdgs/indicators/database/ (accessed 21 July 2016); United Nations. Economic and Social Commission for Asia and the Pacific (ESCAP) Online Statistical Database http://www.unescap.org/statdb/DataExplorer.aspx (accessed 18 April 2016); World Bank. World Development Indicators. http://databank.worldbank.org/data/reports.aspx?source=world-development-indicators (accessed 26 April 2016).

Achieve gender equality and empower all women and girls

Table 2.8: **Selected Indicators for SDG 5 - Early Marriage and Women in Leadership**
Eliminate all harmful practices, such as child, early and forced marriage and female genital mutilation

Ensure women's full and effective participation and equal opportunities for leadership at all levels of decisionmaking in political, economic and public life

Regional Member	5.3.1 Proportion of Women Aged 20-24 Years Who Were Married or in a Union (%)				5.5.1 Proportion of Seats Held by Women in National Parliaments (%)	
	Before Age 15		Before Age 18		2000	2015
	Initial Year	Latest Year	Initial Year	Latest Year		
Developing Member Economies						
Central and West Asia						
Afghanistan	...	...	...	32.8 (2013)	27.3 (2005)	27.7
Armenia	...	– (2010)	...	7.2 (2010)	3.1	10.7
Azerbaijan	...	1.9 (2011)	...	11.0 (2011)	10.5 (2001)	16.9
Georgia	...	1.1 (2010)	...	14.0 (2010)	7.2	11.3
Kazakhstan	...	0.3 (2011)	...	6.1 (2011)	10.4	26.2
Kyrgyz Republic	...	0.9 (2014)	...	11.6 (2014)	2.3	19.2
Pakistan	...	2.8 (2013)	...	21.0 (2013)	21.1 (2002)	20.6
Tajikistan	...	0.1 (2012)	...	11.6 (2012)	15.0	19.0
Turkmenistan	0.6 (2006)	...	7.3 (2006)	...	26.0	25.8
Uzbekistan	0.3 (2006)	...	7.2 (2006)	...	7.2	16.0
East Asia						
China, People's Rep. of	...	...	...	...	21.8	23.6
Hong Kong, China	...	...	...	...	...	...
Korea, Rep. of	...	...	...	...	5.9	16.3
Mongolia	...	0.1 (2010)	...	4.7 (2010)	10.5	14.5
Taipei,China	...	...	...	...	...	...
South Asia						
Bangladesh	...	18.1 (2013)	...	52.3 (2013)	9.1	20.0
Bhutan	...	6.2 (2010)	...	25.8 (2010)	9.3	8.5
India	18.2 (2006)	...	47.4 (2006)	...	9.0	12.0
Maldives	...	0.3 (2009)	...	3.9 (2009)	6.0	5.9
Nepal	...	10.4 (2014)	...	36.6 (2014)	5.9	29.5
Sri Lanka	1.7 (2007)	...	11.8 (2007)	...	4.4 (2002)	4.9
Southeast Asia						
Brunei Darussalam	...	...	...	...	...	...
Cambodia	...	1.9 (2014)	...	18.5 (2014)	7.4	20.3
Indonesia	...	...	...	13.6 (2013)	8.0	17.1
Lao PDR	...	8.9 (2012)	...	35.4 (2012)	21.2	25.0
Malaysia	...	...	...	...	10.4	10.4
Myanmar	...	...	...	...	4.3 (2010)	12.7
Philippines	...	2.0 (2013)	...	15.0 (2013)	11.3	27.2
Singapore	...	...	...	...	4.3	23.9
Thailand	...	3.8 (2012)	...	22.1 (2012)	4.8	6.1
Viet Nam	...	0.9 (2014)	...	10.6 (2014)	26.0	24.3
The Pacific						
Cook Islands	...	...	...	...	...	...
Fiji	...	...	...	...	5.7 (2001)	16.0
Kiribati	...	2.8 (2009)	...	20.3 (2009)	4.9	8.7
Marshall Islands	5.6 (2007)	...	26.3 (2007)	...	3.0	9.1
Micronesia, Fed. States of	...	...	...	...	–	–
Nauru	1.9 (2007)	...	26.8 (2007)	...	– (2001)	5.3
Palau	...	...	...	...	–	–
Papua New Guinea	2.1 (2006)	...	21.3 (2006)	...	1.8	2.7
Samoa	...	0.7 (2014)	...	10.8 (2014)	8.2	6.1
Solomon Islands	3.1 (2007)	...	22.4 (2007)	...	2.0	2.0
Timor-Leste	...	3.0 (2009)	...	18.9 (2009)	26.1 (2003)	38.5
Tonga	...	0.3 (2012)	...	5.6 (2012)	–	–
Tuvalu	– (2007)	...	9.9 (2007)	...	–	6.7
Vanuatu	...	2.5 (2013)	...	21.4 (2013)	–	–
Developed Member Economies						
Australia	...	...	...	...	23.0	26.7
Japan	...	...	...	...	7.3	9.5
New Zealand	...	...	...	...	30.8	31.4

... = data not available at cutoff date, – = magnitude equals zero, Lao PDR = Lao People's Democratic Republic, SDG = Sustainable Development Goal.

Sources: United Nations. Sustainable Development Goals Indicators Global Database. http://unstats.un.org/sdgs/indicators/database/ (accessed April 2016); Inter-Parliamentary Union. Women in National Parliaments. http://www.ipu.org/wmn-e/classif-arc.htm (accessed September 2016).

Planet

To protect the planet from degradation, including through sustainable consumption and production, sustainably managing its natural resources and taking urgent action on climate change, so that it can support the needs of the present and future generations.

Snapshots

- More than nine out of every 10 people in Asia and the Pacific have access to improved drinking water sources while approximately two-thirds have access to improved sanitation.

- The freshwater extraction rate has increased in the majority of economies in the region since 2000.

- In Asia and the Pacific region, 32 out of 36 economies with available data have air pollution levels exceeding the maximum recommended air pollution level set by the World Health Organization.

- Seventeen out of the 46 reporting economies indicated an increase in their forest-covered area between 2000 and 2015.

Against a backdrop of continuing environmental challenges such as climate change, increased instances of natural disaster, and food and water insecurity around the world, the SDGs integrate environmental sustainability into one of the central pillars for eradication of poverty and achieving inclusive growth. In particular, SDGs 6, 11, 14, and 15 are planet-centered as they aim to ensure ecological integrity that can support the sustainable development of humankind. This section examines several indicators where data are available for relevant indicators.

SDG 6: Ensure Availability and Sustainable Management of Water and Sanitation for All

Water, sanitation, and complementary resources have remarkable linkage to the environment. In particular, inefficient usage of water causes stress on the limited resources available. Poor sanitation, on the other hand, threatens the health and well-being of people. The sixth goal seeks for a sustainable management of water and sanitation for all.

Proportion of population using safely managed drinking water services. About 93.3% of the population of Asia and the Pacific has access to improved drinking water sources based on latest data. However, in some countries like Afghanistan, Kiribati, Mongolia, and Papua New Guinea, about two-thirds or less of their population have access to improved drinking water sources. Nevertheless, access to improved drinking water sources has increased in most of the countries since 2000, particularly Afghanistan (82.8%), Cambodia (81.6%), the Lao People's Democratic Republic (Lao PDR) (66.4%), Timor-Leste (32.3%), Viet Nam (26.1%), Vanuatu (24.7%), Tajikistan (23.9%), Myanmar (21.1%), and Sri Lanka (20.0%). Figure 3.1 presents the estimates for economies of Asia and the Pacific.

Figure 3.1: Proportion of Population Using Safely Managed Drinking Water Services
(%)

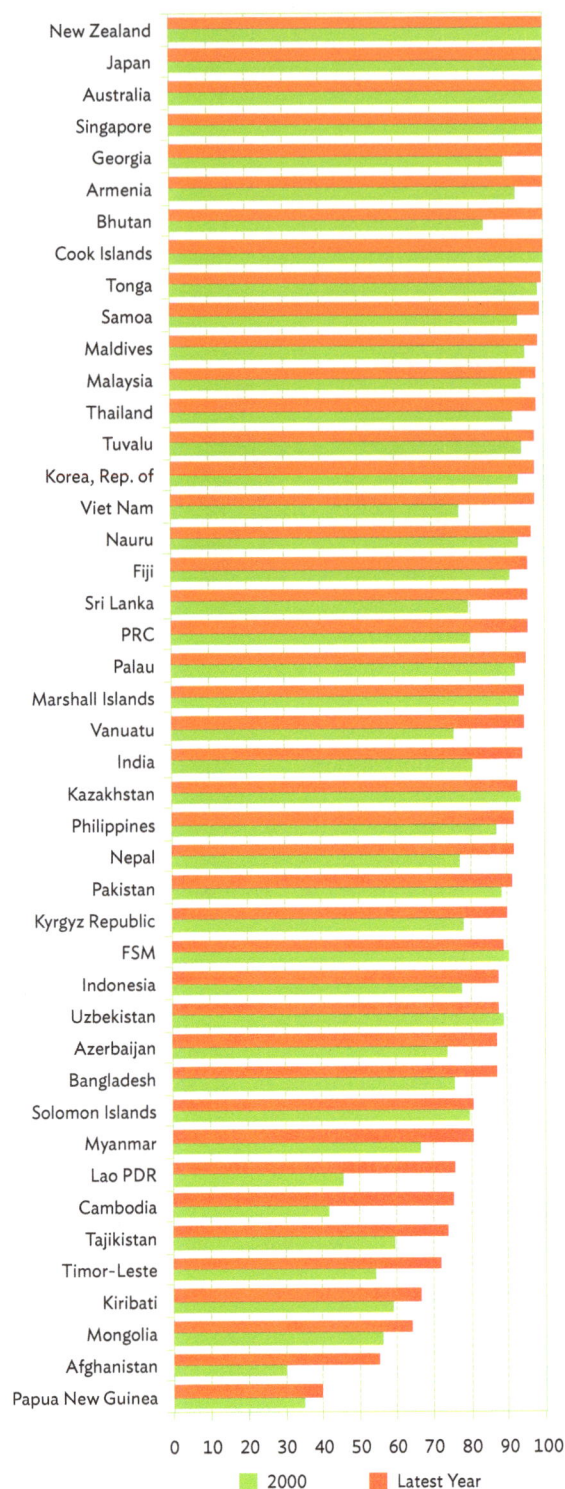

New Zealand, Japan, Australia, Singapore, Georgia, Armenia, Bhutan, Cook Islands, Tonga, Samoa, Maldives, Malaysia, Thailand, Tuvalu, Korea, Rep. of, Viet Nam, Nauru, Fiji, Sri Lanka, PRC, Palau, Marshall Islands, Vanuatu, India, Kazakhstan, Philippines, Nepal, Pakistan, Kyrgyz Republic, FSM, Indonesia, Uzbekistan, Azerbaijan, Bangladesh, Solomon Islands, Myanmar, Lao PDR, Cambodia, Tajikistan, Timor-Leste, Kiribati, Mongolia, Afghanistan, Papua New Guinea

0 10 20 30 40 50 60 70 80 90 100

■ 2000   ■ Latest Year

FSM = Federated States of Micronesia, Lao PDR = Lao People's Democratic Republic, PRC = People's Republic of China.
Note: Only economies with recent estimates (2010 and later) are included.
Source: Table 3.1.

Proportion of population using safely managed sanitation services. Less than two-thirds (63.8%) of Asia and the Pacific's population have access to improved sanitation. In East Asia, for instance, 77.2% of the population is covered by safely managed sanitation services; 72.2% in Southeast Asia; 68.5% in Central and West Asia; 42.8% in South Asia; and 31.7% in the Pacific islands. However, within these regions, there are countries where less than half of the population has access to safely managed sanitation services (Figure 3.2). These include Papua New Guinea (18.9%), Solomon Islands (29.8%), Afghanistan (31.9%), India (39.6%), Kiribati (39.7%), Timor-Leste (40.6%), Cambodia (42.4%), and Nepal (45.8%).

Level of water stress: Freshwater withdrawal as a proportion of available freshwater resources. Figure 3.3 presents the estimates of freshwater withdrawal as a proportion of available freshwater resources in reporting economies of Asia and the Pacific with data available for 2010 and onward. Armenia (37.9%), Azerbaijan (34.5%), and India (33.9%) recorded the highest levels of water stress in the region.

Table 3.1 shows the estimates for earlier years. Between and within regional disparities with respect to this indicator are also apparent in the data. For instance, among developed economies, Japan's 18.9% withdrawal rate is significantly higher than Australia's 3.9% and New Zealand's 1.6%. With the exception of Georgia, the withdrawal rate in Central and West Asian countries exceeds 18.0%. In East Asia, a high water withdrawal rate is reported for the Republic of Korea (41.9%) and the People's Republic of China (PRC) (21.2%). In South Asia, India has been withdrawing freshwater resources at a rate of 33.9% and Sri Lanka at 24.5%. On another note, the withdrawal rate in most Southeast Asian countries is at most 17.0%.

Figure 3.2: Proportion of Population Using Safely Managed Sanitation Services
(%)

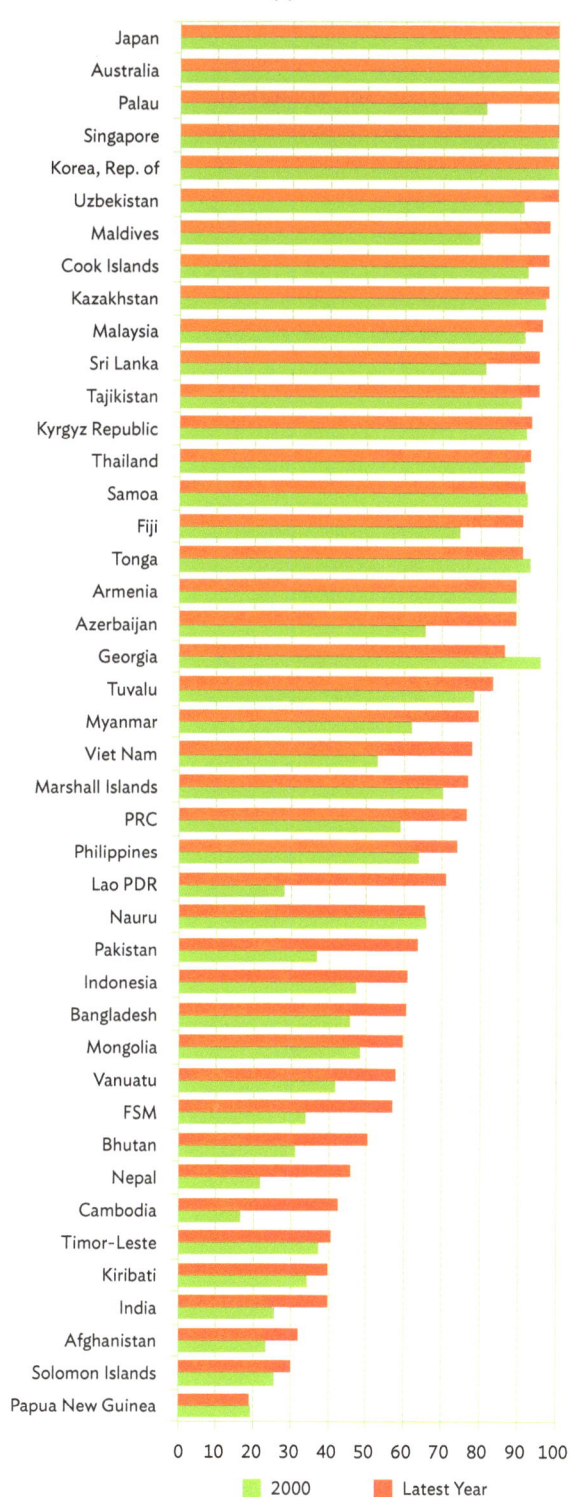

FSM = Federated States of Micronesia, Lao PDR = Lao People's Democratic Republic, PRC = People's Republic of China.
Note: Only economies with recent estimates (2010 and later) are included.
Source: Table 3.1.

Figure 3.3: Level of Water Stress: Freshwater Withdrawal as a Proportion of Available Freshwater Resources in Selected Economies
(%)

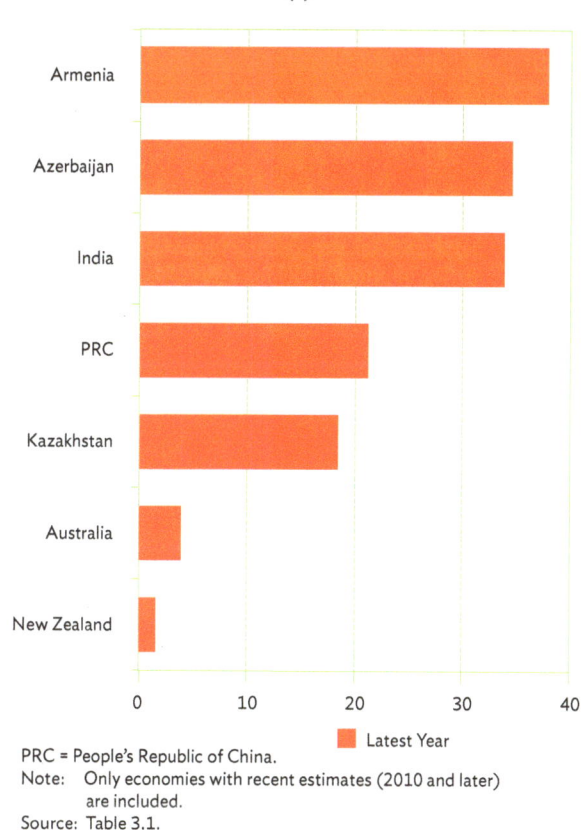

PRC = People's Republic of China.
Note: Only economies with recent estimates (2010 and later) are included.
Source: Table 3.1.

Equity and Other Issues

Improving access to clean water and sanitation facilities can have multiplier effects on many socioeconomic indicators like poverty, health, and productivity. However, some segments of the population still have a disproportionately lower access to these basic services. For instance, in Kiribati, Papua New Guinea, and Timor-Leste, there are significant urban–rural disparities in terms of the proportion of population using improved drinking water sources, while in Bhutan, Cambodia, and Solomon Islands, significant urban–rural disparities in terms of the proportion of people using safely managed sanitation exist (Figures 3.4a and 3.4b). The influx of migrants from rural areas may also lead to a significant strain on water and sanitation facilities of urban areas. People who lack access to clean water and sanitation facilities are exposed to higher risks of contracting diseases like cholera, typhoid, and hepatitis, and these health shocks may erode the savings of the affected people. Hence, there is an urgent need to identify the best cost-effective and environmentally sustainable practices of delivering safe water and sanitation services.

Figure 3.4a: Proportion of Population Using Improved Drinking Water Sources by Area in Selected Economies, 2015

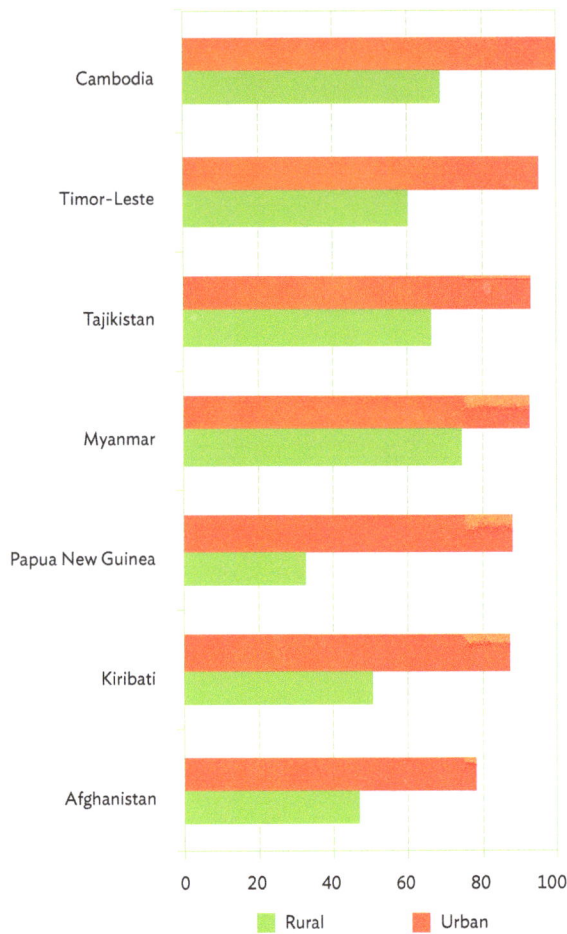

Figure 3.4b: Proportion of Population Using Safely Managed Sanitation Facilities by Area in Selected Economies, 2015

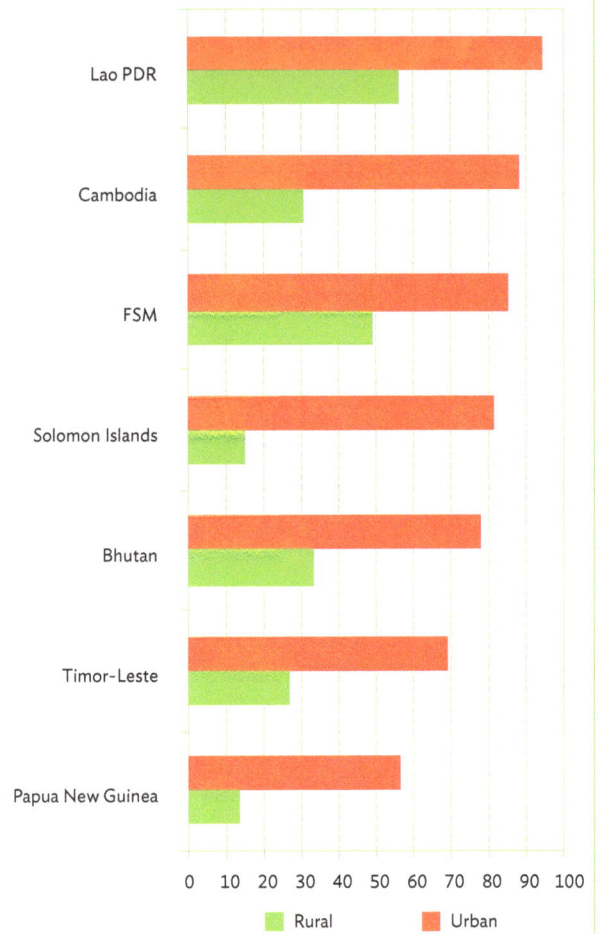

Source: United Nations Statistics Division. Sustainable Development Goal Indicators Global Database. http://unstats.un.org/sdgs/indicators/database/ (accessed August 2016).

FSM = Federated States of Micronesia, Lao PDR = Lao People's Democratic Republic
Source: United Nations Statistics Division. Sustainable Development Goal Indicators Global Database. http://unstats.un.org/sdgs/indicators/database/ (accessed August 2016).

Data Gaps

Sustainability of natural resources like water relies to a large extent on benchmark information that should serve as the basis of a regulatory framework for extraction. A comprehensive database of water resources that is updated regularly provides an indispensable instrument in the sustainable management not only of water but also its twin issue of sanitation.

In general, many of the targets under SDG 6 have no existing data collection system especially those related to water quality, efficiency of use, water resource management, and protection and restoration of water-related ecosystems. To complement the goal of strengthening the participation of local communities in improving water and sanitation management, a community-based reporting system of various indicators may be included in the package of programs intended to measure achievement of the targets under this goal.

SDG 11: Make Cities and Human Settlements Inclusive, Safe, Resilient and Sustainable

Housing and the environment are important dimensions of a person's well-being. Studies show that where a child grows up can have a strong impact on his or her long-term economic competitiveness. Given its key role as an enabler of economic prospects, housing and environmental investments should be linked to the development of economic policies.

Proportion of urban population living in slums, informal settlements or inadequate housing. In the majority of the reporting economies of Asia and the Pacific, at least a third of their respective urban population has inadequate housing. The highest numbers, based on latest data, are in Afghanistan (62.7%), Bangladesh (55.1%), Cambodia (55.1%), and Nepal (54.3%) (Figure 3.5). Nevertheless, there are indications that the proportion of people living in urban slums has decreased significantly. In Bangladesh, for instance, the percentage of people living in urban slums was 87.3% in 2000. Cambodia, Nepal, Mongolia, and Viet Nam have also made significant improvements on this front.

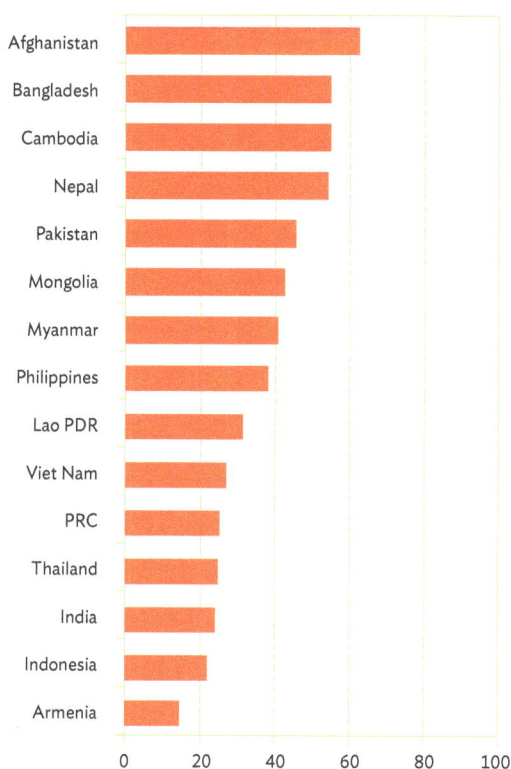

Figure 3.5: Proportion of Urban Population Living in Slums in Selected Economies, 2014

Lao PDR = Lao People's Democratic Republic, PRC = People's Republic of China.
Source: United Nations Statistics Division. Sustainable Development Goal Indicators Global Database. http://unstats.un.org/sdgs/indicators/database/ (accessed August 2016).

Average annual mean of particulate matter of 2.5 microns in diameter or smaller (PM2.5) concentration levels. Prolonged exposure to high levels of air pollution is a major risk to a person's health. Globally, millions of premature deaths are associated to ambient air pollution. The maximum safety standard air pollution level set by the World Health Organization (WHO) is 10 μg/m^3. However, available data for 36 economies of Asia and the Pacific suggest that 32 economies have air pollution levels exceeding 10 μg/m^3. Of these 32 economies, 21 economies have air pollution levels that are at least 2.5 times the WHO's threshold. The economies with air pollution levels that are below the maximum air pollution level set by the WHO include Australia, Brunei Darussalam, the Federated States of Micronesia, and New Zealand (Figure 3.6).

Equity and Other Issues

While cities and urban areas are expected to be the locus of developing economies' economic growth in the coming years, there are several issues that need to be addressed. For instance, the increasing concentration of urban population in capital cities may drive rural migrants to live in slums or other areas with slum-like conditions. On the other hand, secondary cities are also confronted with other challenges such as the lack of strong linkages to markets and poor infrastructure (UNDP 2013). If rapid urbanization is left unchecked, the number of people who are exposed to makeshift housing, fire hazards, poor sanitation, pollution, and crime may increase significantly.

Data Gaps

Pollution indicators are not regularly updated. In fact, they are not usually collected in many countries. Inclusiveness, safety, resilience, and sustainability of cities and human settlements are dependent on an efficient monitoring system that will ensure adequacy of mitigation programs and

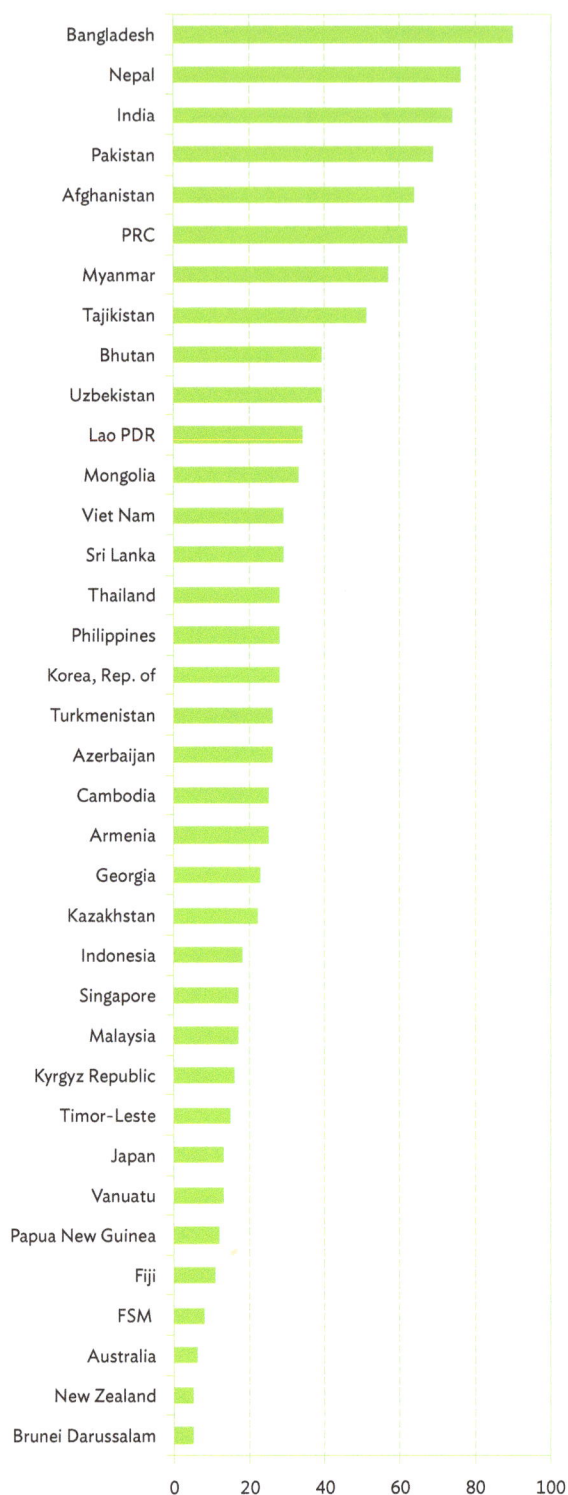

Figure 3.6: Average Annual Mean of Particulate Matter 2.5 Microns in Diameter or Smaller (PM2.5) Concentration Levels in Urban Areas (μg/m^3)

FSM = Federated States of Micronesia, Lao PDR = Lao People's Democratic Republic, PRC = People's Republic of China.
Source: Table 3.2.

policy regulations. For countries with lacking data, sustainability may be compromised, and worse, the damage could be unrepairable if detected only at an advanced stage.

SDG 14: Conserve and Sustainably Use the Oceans, Seas, and Marine Resources for Sustainable Development

Oceans and seas cover about three-quarters of the world's surface and their health is critical to ensure ecological balance. The role of oceans and seas cannot be undermined—not only in the provision of food, but also, more importantly, in weather and climate regulation, to ensure a state of equilibrium in various physical, chemical, and biological processes happening in marine waters. Furthermore, conservation and sustainable use of marine waters and resources are important for food and for equilibrium of weather systems originating from the seas.

Coverage of protected areas in relation to marine areas. To ensure sustainability of marine resources, conservation areas should be properly delineated to ensure diversity and continuously link the food chain in marine waters.

Table 3.2 presents the estimates of coverage of protected areas in relation to marine areas for economies with available data. The highest estimates were recorded in the Philippines (47.1%), New Zealand (44.4%), and Kiribati (36.4%). Among economies with available data in the region, only Indonesia, the Philippines, Australia, and Japan have expanded the coverage of marine protected areas between 2000 and 2016.

SDG 15: Protect, Restore and Promote Sustainable Use of Terrestrial Ecosystems, Sustainably Manage Forests, Combat Desertification, and Halt and Reverse Land Degradation and Halt Biodiversity Loss

Agriculture and other human activities have profound impact on terrestrial ecosystems resulting in certain processes like biodiversity loss, land degradation, or even desertification.

Forest area as a proportion of total land area. Forest area is a crucial foundation for maintenance of biodiversity, management of sustainable water sources, and even in mitigation of harmful consequences of extreme weather conditions.

Estimates based on the latest data suggest that about 22.2% of Asia and the Pacific's total land area is covered by forest. Forest cover in East Asia is estimated at 30.9% and in Southeast Asia at 28.6%. On the other hand, forest cover in Central and West Asia is estimated at 2.6%.

Figure 3.7 illustrates the forest cover for each country. The proportion of forest cover to total land area in developed economies of Asia and the Pacific ranges from as high as 68.5% in Japan to as low as 16.2% in Australia. Within Southeast Asia, the Lao PDR has the highest forest cover at 81.3% while Singapore has the lowest at 23.4%. In East Asia, the economies with the largest forest cover are the Republic of Korea and Taipei,China. In South Asia, except for Bangladesh and the Maldives, all economies have forest cover exceeding 23.0%. In Central and West Asia, however, all economies except Georgia have less than 20.0% land area covered with forest.

Figure 3.7: Proportion of Forest Area to Total Land Area, 2015
(%)

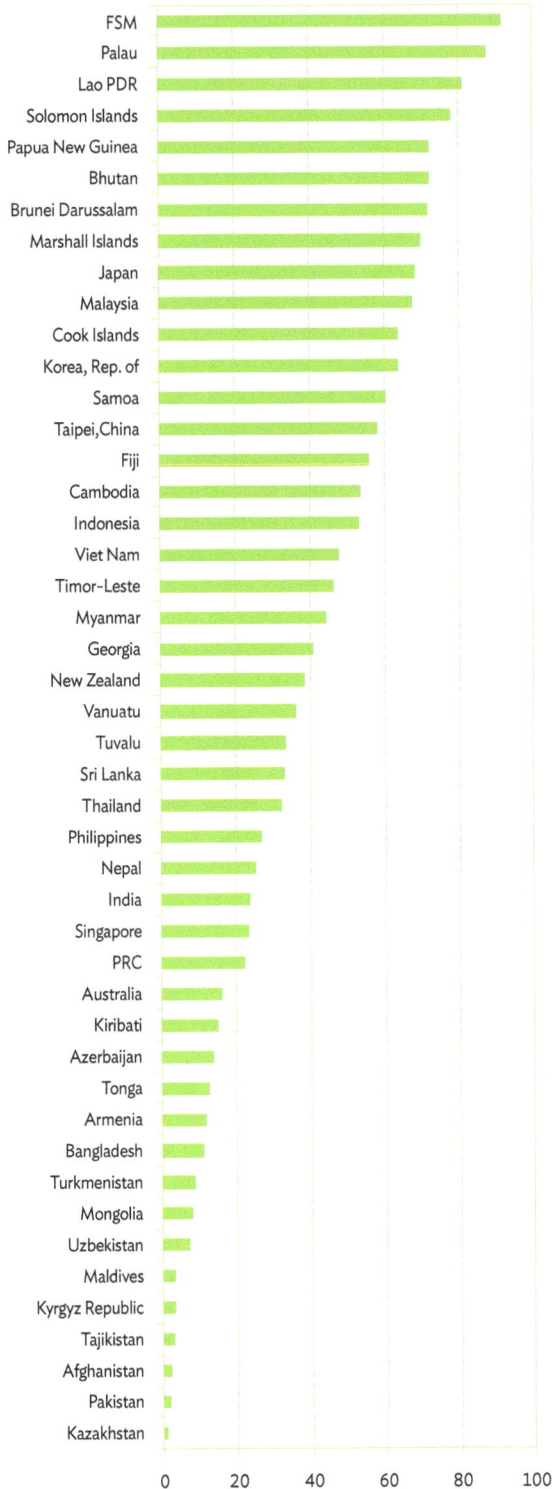

FSM	
Palau	
Lao PDR	
Solomon Islands	
Papua New Guinea	
Bhutan	
Brunei Darussalam	
Marshall Islands	
Japan	
Malaysia	
Cook Islands	
Korea, Rep. of	
Samoa	
Taipei,China	
Fiji	
Cambodia	
Indonesia	
Viet Nam	
Timor-Leste	
Myanmar	
Georgia	
New Zealand	
Vanuatu	
Tuvalu	
Sri Lanka	
Thailand	
Philippines	
Nepal	
India	
Singapore	
PRC	
Australia	
Kiribati	
Azerbaijan	
Tonga	
Armenia	
Bangladesh	
Turkmenistan	
Mongolia	
Uzbekistan	
Maldives	
Kyrgyz Republic	
Tajikistan	
Afghanistan	
Pakistan	
Kazakhstan	

FSM = Federated States of Micronesia, Lao PDR = Lao People's Democratic Republic, PRC = People's Republic of China.
Source: Table 3.2.

Data Gaps, Equity, and Other Issues

While data on forest cover is reasonably adequate, indicators for other targets under this goal to promote the implementation of sustainable management of all types of forests, combat desertification and restore degraded land and soil, reduce degradation of natural habitat, promote the fair and equitable sharing of the benefits from utilization of genetic resources, poaching, the impact of invasive alien species, resources for biodiversity, etc., are sparsely available. Lack of data or absence of framework of monitoring terrestrial ecosystem may endanger the ecological integrity of this ecosystem.

Ensure availability and sustainable management of water and sanitation for all

Table 3.1: Selected Indicators for SDG 6 - Water and Sanitation

By 2030, achieve universal and equitable access to safe and affordable drinking water for all

By 2030, achieve access to adequate and equitable sanitation and hygiene for all and end open defecation, paying special attention to the needs of women and girls and those in vulnerable situations

By 2030, substantially increase water-use efficiency across all sectors and ensure sustainable withdrawals and supply of freshwater to address water scarcity and substantially reduce the number of people suffering from water scarcity

Regional Member	6.1.1 Proportion of Population Using Safely Managed Drinking Water Services (%)		6.2.1 Proportion of Population Using Safely Managed Sanitation Services, Including a Hand-Washing Facility with Soap and Water (%)		6.4.2 Level of Water Stress: Freshwater Withdrawal as a Proportion of Available Freshwater Resources[a] (%)		6.a.1 Amount of Water- and Sanitation-Related Official Development Assistance That Is Part of a Government-Coordinated Spending Plan ($ million)	
	2000	2015	2000	2015	Initial Year	Latest Year	2000	2014
Developing Member Economies								
Central and West Asia								
Afghanistan	30.3	55.3	23.4	31.9	31.0 (2000)	...	4.9	66.9
Armenia	92.6	100.0	89.3	89.5	22.3 (2002)	37.9 (2012)	11.8	41.9
Azerbaijan	74.1	87.0	65.6	89.3	29.0 (2002)	34.5 (2012)	23.7	38.0
Georgia	89.3	100.0	95.7	86.3	2.9 (2005)	2.9 (2008)	0.8	61.5
Kazakhstan	93.8	92.9	96.8	97.5	17.2 (2002)	18.4 (2010)	8.1	0.0
Kyrgyz Republic	78.4	90.0	91.8	93.3	42.7 (2000)	32.6 (2006)	0.5	24.3
Pakistan	88.5	91.4	36.9	63.5	69.9 (2000)	74.4 (2008)	4.5	50.9
Tajikistan	59.6	73.8	90.4	95.0	53.2 (2000)	51.1 (2006)	4.3	30.3
Turkmenistan	59.6	60.4 (2006)	62.3	62.7 (2006)	100.6 (2000)	112.5 (2004)	0.0	0.3 (2011)
Uzbekistan	88.7	87.3 (2012)	90.9	100.0	110.0 (2001)	100.6 (2005)	2.4	95.6
East Asia								
China, People's Rep. of	80.3	95.5	58.8	76.5	19.5 (2005)	21.2 (2013)	584.5	164.9
Hong Kong, China	...	...	...	...	...	...	...	...
Korea, Rep. of	93.4	97.6 (2012)	100.0	100.0	41.8 (2002)	41.9 (2005)	...	...
Mongolia	56.3	64.4	48.2	59.7	1.6 (2006)	1.6 (2009)	0.3	18.4
Taipei,China	...	...	...	...	...	...	...	...
South Asia								
Bangladesh	76.0	86.9	45.4	60.6	2.9 (2008)	...	87.5	181.0
Bhutan	83.9	100.0	31.0	50.4	0.4 (2008)	...	0.2	5.1
India	80.6	94.1	25.6	39.6	31.9 (2000)	33.9 (2010)	182.8	398.9
Maldives	95.2	98.6	79.4	97.9	15.7 (2008)	...	0.6 (2001)	5.1
Nepal	77.1	91.6	21.7	45.8	4.5 (2000)	4.5 (2006)	67.4	73.2
Sri Lanka	79.7	95.6	81.2	95.1	24.6 (2000)	24.5 (2005)	34.2	126.8
Southeast Asia								
Brunei Darussalam	...	...	...	...	...	...	...	...
Cambodia	41.6	75.5	16.3	42.4	0.5 (2006)	...	1.9	43.2
Indonesia	77.9	87.4	47.1	60.8	3.7 (1990)	5.6 (2000)	92.6	87.7
Lao PDR	45.5	75.7	28.0	70.9	1.0 (2005)	...	42.1	31.0
Malaysia	94.1	98.2	91.2	96.0	1.6 (2000)	1.9 (2005)	394.6	68.3
Myanmar	66.6	80.6	61.9	79.6	2.8 (2000)	...	1.6	14.6
Philippines	87.1	91.8	63.8	73.9	16.5 (2006)	17.0 (2009)	22.1	15.4
Singapore	100.0	100.0	99.7	100.0	...	...	...	...
Thailand	91.9	97.8	91.3	93.0	13.1 (2007)	...	78.4	25.7
Viet Nam	77.4	97.6	52.9	78.0	9.3 (2005)	...	191.5	437.3
The Pacific								
Cook Islands	99.9	99.9	92.1	97.6	...	...	0.4	2.4
Fiji	90.7	95.7	74.6	91.1	0.3 (2000)	0.3 (2005)	0.5	4.1
Kiribati	58.9	66.9	34.2	39.7	...	...	0.7 (2001)	5.6
Marshall Islands	93.1	94.6	70.1	76.9	...	...	0.0 (2003)	1.1
Micronesia, Fed. States of	90.1	89.0	33.6	57.1	...	...	0.0 (2003)	1.8
Nauru	93.0	96.5	65.7	65.6	...	...	0.0 (2005)	0.1
Palau	92.2	95.3 (2011)	81.0	100.0	...	...	0.0 (2003)	0.6
Papua New Guinea	35.1	40.0	19.2	18.9	0.0 (2000)	0.0 (2005)	14.4	5.0
Samoa	93.3	99.0	92.2	91.5	...	...	0.3	15.2
Solomon Islands	79.7	80.8	25.5	29.8	...	...	2.4	5.1
Timor-Leste	54.3	71.9	37.4	40.6	14.3 (2004)	...	4.4	12.4
Tonga	98.6	99.6	93.0	91.0	...	...	10.4	1.6
Tuvalu	94.0	97.7	78.4	83.3 (2013)	...	...	0.6 (2002)	0.2
Vanuatu	75.8	94.5	41.7	57.9	...	...	0.6 (2003)	4.7
Developed Member Economies								
Australia	100.0	100.0	100.0	100.0	4.4 (2001)	3.9 (2013)	...	...
Japan	100.0	100.0	100.0	100.0	20.9 (2001)	18.9 (2009)	...	...
New Zealand	100.0	100.0	...	...	1.5 (2006)	1.6 (2010)	...	...

... = data not available at cutoff date, 0.0 = magnitude is less than half of unit employed, Lao PDR = Lao People's Democratic Republic, SDG = Sustainable Development Goal.

a   The UN's presentation for the indicator is for a range of years. For instance, 2002 refers to 1998–2002, 2007 refers to 2003–2007, and so on. The original source, AQUASTAT, gives the exact years pertaining to the specific figures. Hence, years indicated in the latter were reflected herein.

Sources: United Nations. Sustainable Development Goals Indicators Global Database. http://unstats.un.org/sdgs/indicators/database/ (accessed 21 July 2016); Food and Agriculture Organization of the United Nations. AQUASTAT. http://www.fao.org/nr/water/aquastat/main/index.stm (accessed August 2016); World Health Organization and United Nations Children's Fund (UNICEF). Joint Monitoring Programme for Water Supply and Sanitation. http://www.wssinfo.org/ (accessed August 2016); Organisation for Economic Co-operation and Development. Creditor Reporting System. http://stats.oecd.org/Index.aspx?DataSetCode=CRS1 (accessed August 2016).

Make cities and human settlements inclusive, safe, resilient, and sustainable

Conserve and sustainably use the oceans, seas, and marine resources for sustainable development

Protect, restore, and promote sustainable use of terrestrial ecosystems, sustainably manage forests, combat desertification, and halt and reverse land degradation, and halt biodiversity loss

Table 3.2: **Selected Indicators for SDGs 11, 14 and 15 - Air Quality; Forest, Marine Areas, and Terrestrial Ecosystems**

By 2030, reduce the adverse per capita environmental impact of cities, including by paying special attention to air quality and municipal and other waste management

By 2020, sustainably manage and protect marine and coastal ecosystems to avoid significant adverse impacts, including by strengthening their resilience, and take action for their restoration in order to achieve healthy and productive oceans

By 2020, conserve at least 10 per cent of coastal and marine areas, consistent with national and international law and based on the best available scientific information

By 2020, prohibit certain forms of fisheries subsidies which contribute to overcapacity and overfishing, eliminate subsidies that contribute to illegal, unreported and unregulated fishing and refrain from introducing new such subsidies, recognizing that appropriate and effective special and differential treatment for developing and least developed countries should be an integral part of the World Trade Organization fisheries subsidies negotiation

Regional Member	11.6.2 Average Annual Mean of Particulate Matter of 2.5 Microns in Diameter or Smaller (PM2.5) Concentration Levels in Urban Areas (μg/m3) (%)	14.5.1 Coverage of Protected Areas in Relation to Marine Areas (%)	
	2014	2000	2016
Developing Member Economies			
Central and West Asia			
Afghanistan	64.0	...	...
Armenia	25.0	...	...
Azerbaijan	26.0	...	...
Georgia	23.0	...	...
Kazakhstan	22.0	...	...
Kyrgyz Republic	16.0	...	...
Pakistan	69.0	–	–
Tajikistan	51.0	...	...
Turkmenistan	26.0	...	...
Uzbekistan	39.0	...	...
East Asia			
China, People's Rep. of	62.0	3.5	3.5
Hong Kong, China[a]	...	–	–
Korea, Rep. of	28.0	–	7.1
Mongolia	33.0	...	...
Taipei,China[b]	...	...	...
South Asia			
Bangladesh	90.0	33.3	33.3
Bhutan	39.0	...	...
India	74.0	4.2	4.2
Maldives	...	–	–
Nepal	76.0	...	...
Sri Lanka	29.0	–	–
Southeast Asia			
Brunei Darussalam	5.0	–	–
Cambodia	25.0	–	–
Indonesia	18.0	7.5	12.8
Lao PDR	34.0	...	...
Malaysia	17.0	–	–
Myanmar	57.0	–	–
Philippines	28.0	29.4	47.1
Singapore	17.0	–	–
Thailand	28.0	...	...
Viet Nam	29.0	7.7	7.7
The Pacific			
Cook Islands	...	–	–
Fiji	11.0	–	5.9
Kiribati	...	–	36.4
Marshall Islands	...	–	–
Micronesia, Fed. States of	8.0	–	–
Nauru	...	–	–
Palau	...	12.5	12.5
Papua New Guinea	12.0	–	–
Samoa	...	–	–
Solomon Islands	...	–	–
Timor-Leste	15.0	–	7.7
Tonga	...	–	–
Tuvalu	...	...	...
Vanuatu	13.0	–	–
Developed Member Economies			
Australia	6.0	29.4	33.6
Japan	13.0	32.6	34.8
New Zealand	5.0	44.4	44.4

(continued)

Make cities and human settlements inclusive, safe, resilient, and sustainable

Conserve and sustainably use the oceans, seas, and marine resources for sustainable development

Protect, restore, and promote sustainable use of terrestrial ecosystems, sustainably manage forests, combat desertification, and halt and reverse land degradation, and halt biodiversity loss

Table 3.2:   **Selected Indicators for SDGs 11, 14 and 15 - Air Quality; Forest, Marine Areas, and Terrestrial Ecosystems** (continued)

Regional Member	15.1.1 Forest Area as a Proportion of Total Land Area (%)		15.5.1 Red List Index	
	2000	2015	2000	2016
Developing Member Economies				
Central and West Asia				
Afghanistan	2.1	2.1	0.8	0.8
Armenia	11.8	11.8	0.9	0.8
Azerbaijan	10.6	13.8	0.9	0.9
Georgia	39.7	40.6	0.9	0.9
Kazakhstan	1.3	1.2	0.9	0.9
Kyrgyz Republic	4.5	3.3	1.0	1.0
Pakistan	2.7	1.9	0.9	0.9
Tajikistan	3.0	3.0	1.0	1.0
Turkmenistan	8.8	8.8	1.0	1.0
Uzbekistan	7.3	7.3	1.0	1.0
East Asia				
China, People's Rep. of	18.8	22.1	0.8	0.8
Hong Kong, China[a]	...	...	1.0	1.0
Korea, Rep. of	64.8	63.7	0.8	0.8
Mongolia	7.5	8.1	1.0	1.0
Taipei,China[b]	58.1	58.1 (2014)	...	...
South Asia				
Bangladesh	11.3	11.0	0.8	0.8
Bhutan	68.4	72.3	0.8	0.8
India	22.0	23.8	0.8	0.7
Maldives	3.3	3.3	0.9	0.9
Nepal	27.2	25.4	0.8	0.8
Sri Lanka	35.0	33.0	0.7	0.6
Southeast Asia				
Brunei Darussalam	75.3	72.1	0.9	0.8
Cambodia	65.4	53.6	0.9	0.8
Indonesia	57.8	53.0	0.8	0.8
Lao PDR	71.6	81.3	0.8	0.8
Malaysia	65.7	67.6	0.8	0.7
Myanmar	53.0	44.2	0.9	0.8
Philippines	23.6	27.0	0.7	0.7
Singapore	23.4	23.4	0.9	0.9
Thailand	33.3	32.1	0.9	0.8
Viet Nam	37.8	47.6	0.8	0.8
The Pacific				
Cook Islands	64.0	64.0	0.8	0.8
Fiji	53.7	55.7	0.7	0.7
Kiribati	15.0	15.0	0.8	0.8
Marshall Islands	70.2	70.2	0.9	0.8
Micronesia, Fed. States of	91.4	91.9	0.8	0.7
Nauru	–	–	0.8	0.8
Palau	86.1	87.6	0.9	0.8
Papua New Guinea	72.6	72.5	0.9	0.8
Samoa	60.4	60.4	0.8	0.8
Solomon Islands	81.0	78.1	0.8	0.8
Timor-Leste	57.4	46.1	0.9	0.9
Tonga	12.5	12.5	0.7	0.7
Tuvalu	33.3	33.3	0.9	0.8
Vanuatu	36.1	36.1	0.7	0.7
Developed Member Economies				
Australia	16.8	16.2	0.9	0.8
Japan	68.3	68.5	0.8	0.8
New Zealand	38.5	38.6	0.7	0.6

... = data not available at cutoff date, – = magnitude equals zero, Lao PDR = Lao People's Democratic Republic, SDG = Sustainable Development Goal.

a   The proportion of land area covered by forest in Hong Kong, China is included in the data of the People's Republic of China.
b   The proportion of land area covered by forest for Taipei,China does not include Kinmen County and Lienchiang County.

Sources: Food and Agriculture Organization of the United Nations; United Nations. Sustainable Development Goals Indicators Global Database. http://unstats.un.org/sdgs/indicators/database/ (accessed 21 July 2016); World Bank; for Taipei,China: economy source.

Prosperity

To ensure that all human beings can enjoy prosperous and fulfilling lives and that economic, social, and technological progress occurs in harmony with nature.

Snapshots

- In the majority of the economies of Asia and the Pacific, more than 80% of the population has access to electricity. However, at least 400 million people within the region did not have access to electricity in 2012.

- In some regional economies, there are still significant gender disparities in terms of employment prospects.

- In 11 out of 18 economies of Asia and the Pacific with available data for recent years, the average income of the bottom 40% grew faster than the average income of the general population.

As more people exit extreme poverty through the efforts galvanized by the international and national communities, there is a critical need to sustain the improvements on living standards of all. Hence, promoting shared prosperity is an important theme of the SDGs. In particular, SDGs 7, 8, 9, and 10 aim to provide everyone with prosperous and fulfilling lives. This section examines data for several indicators that focus on the equitable utilization of resources for the enhancement of people's living conditions.

SDG 7: Ensure Access to Affordable, Reliable, Sustainable and Modern Energy for All

Energy is a necessity for industrial development. It facilitates the accomplishment of household chores, delivers forms of entertainment and other household convenience, and, more generally, enhances the living conditions of the population.

Proportion of population with access to electricity. In 2012, about nine in 10 people had access to electricity in Asia and the Pacific. In 22 economies of the region (Armenia; Australia; Azerbaijan; the People's Republic of China (PRC); Georgia; Hong Kong, China; Indonesia; Japan; Kazakhstan; the Republic of Korea; the Kyrgyz Republic; Malaysia; the Maldives; New Zealand; Samoa; Singapore; Tajikistan; Thailand; Tonga; Turkmenistan; Uzbekistan; and Viet Nam), almost everyone (95%–100%) had access to electricity. On the other hand, about 87%–94% of the population in Mongolia, Pakistan, the Philippines, and Sri Lanka had electricity access, while at least one in every five people did not have access to electricity in 19 economies (Afghanistan, Bangladesh, Bhutan, Brunei Darussalam, Cambodia, the Federated States of Micronesia, Fiji, India, Kiribati, the Lao People's Democratic Republic (Lao PDR), the Marshall Islands, Myanmar, Nepal, Palau, Papua New Guinea, Solomon Islands, Timor-Leste, Tuvalu, and Vanuatu) In total, at least 400 million people within the region did not have access to electricity in 2012. Figure 4.1 presents the estimates for all reporting economies of Asia and the Pacific.

Figure 4.1: Proportion of Population with Access to Electricity, 2012
(%)

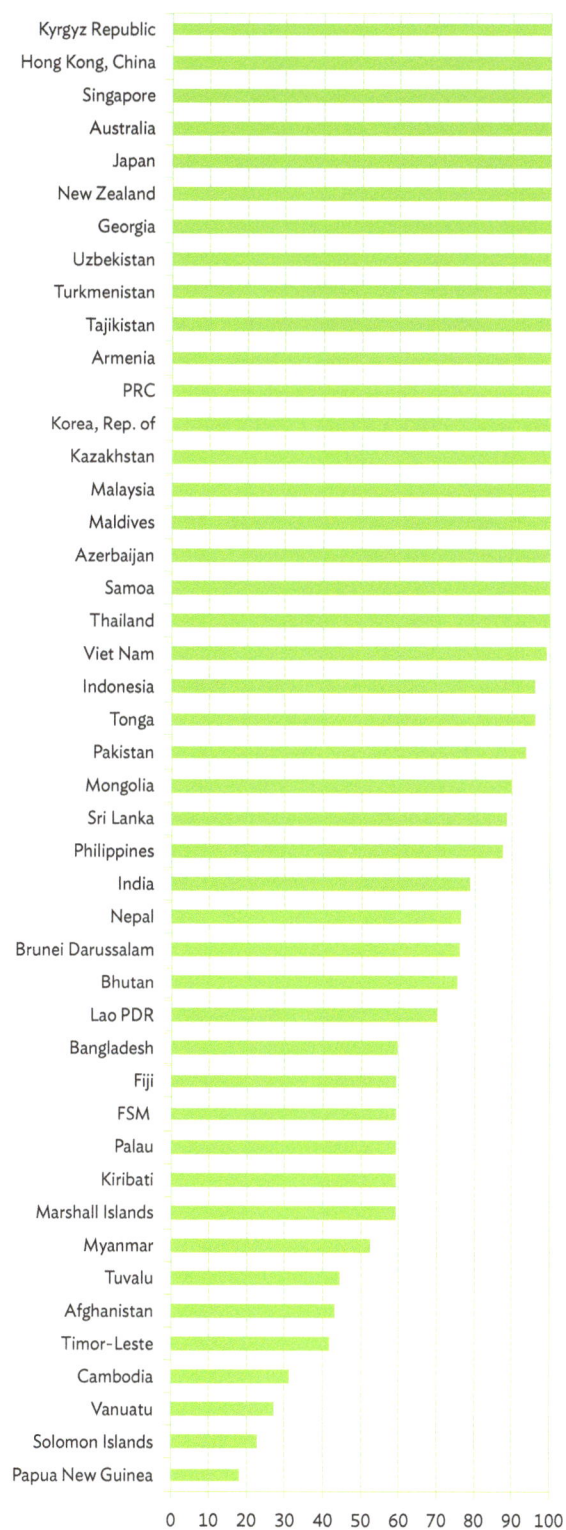

Kyrgyz Republic	
Hong Kong, China	
Singapore	
Australia	
Japan	
New Zealand	
Georgia	
Uzbekistan	
Turkmenistan	
Tajikistan	
Armenia	
PRC	
Korea, Rep. of	
Kazakhstan	
Malaysia	
Maldives	
Azerbaijan	
Samoa	
Thailand	
Viet Nam	
Indonesia	
Tonga	
Pakistan	
Mongolia	
Sri Lanka	
Philippines	
India	
Nepal	
Brunei Darussalam	
Bhutan	
Lao PDR	
Bangladesh	
Fiji	
FSM	
Palau	
Kiribati	
Marshall Islands	
Myanmar	
Tuvalu	
Afghanistan	
Timor-Leste	
Cambodia	
Vanuatu	
Solomon Islands	
Papua New Guinea	

0 10 20 30 40 50 60 70 80 90 100

FSM = Federated States of Micronesia, Lao PDR = Lao People's Democratic Republic, PRC = People's Republic of China.
Source: Table 4.1.

Renewable energy share in total final energy consumption. Some energy sources can be exhausted; others have negative repercussions on the environment. As scientists continue to search for various renewable energy sources, countries should increase outputs from commercially viable renewable sources. The target is to increase the share of renewable energy in the global energy mix significantly by 2030.

In Bhutan, the Lao PDR, and Nepal, over 80% of final energy consumption is already based on renewable sources. In other countries like Cambodia, Myanmar, Papua New Guinea, Solomon Islands, Sri Lanka, and Tajikistan, more than half of energy consumption is currently derived from renewable sources. However, in most countries, the share of renewable energy in total final energy consumption has decreased since 2000.

Energy intensity measured in terms of primary energy and GDP. Figure 4.2 shows the estimates of energy intensity for each country. At present, energy intensity levels are highest in Bhutan (11.8 megajoules per US dollar [MJ/$] constant 2011 purchasing power parity [PPP] GDP), Palau (11.3 MJ/$ 2011 PPP GDP), Papua New Guinea (10.5 MJ/$ 2011 PPP GDP), Turkmenistan (15.5 MJ/$ 2011 PPP GDP), and Uzbekistan (11.9 MJ/$ 2011 PPP GDP). In other developing economies, the energy intensity level ranges between 1.6 MJ/$ 2011 PPP GDP and 9.3 MJ/$ 2011 PPP GDP. On the other hand, the average intensity level in the three developed member countries is around 5 MJ/$ 2011 PPP GDP.

Data Gap, Equity, and Other Issues

The current data on certain indicators are not regularly updated. For other indicators, especially on research and development, resources allocated for the identification and development of clean and renewable sources need to be developed. Indicators on the expansion of infrastructure and upgrading of technology for the delivery of modern and sustainable energy services can be based, for example, on grid capacity and grid length per land area.

Figure 4.2: Energy Intensity Level of Primary Energy
(MJ/$ 2011 PPP GDP)

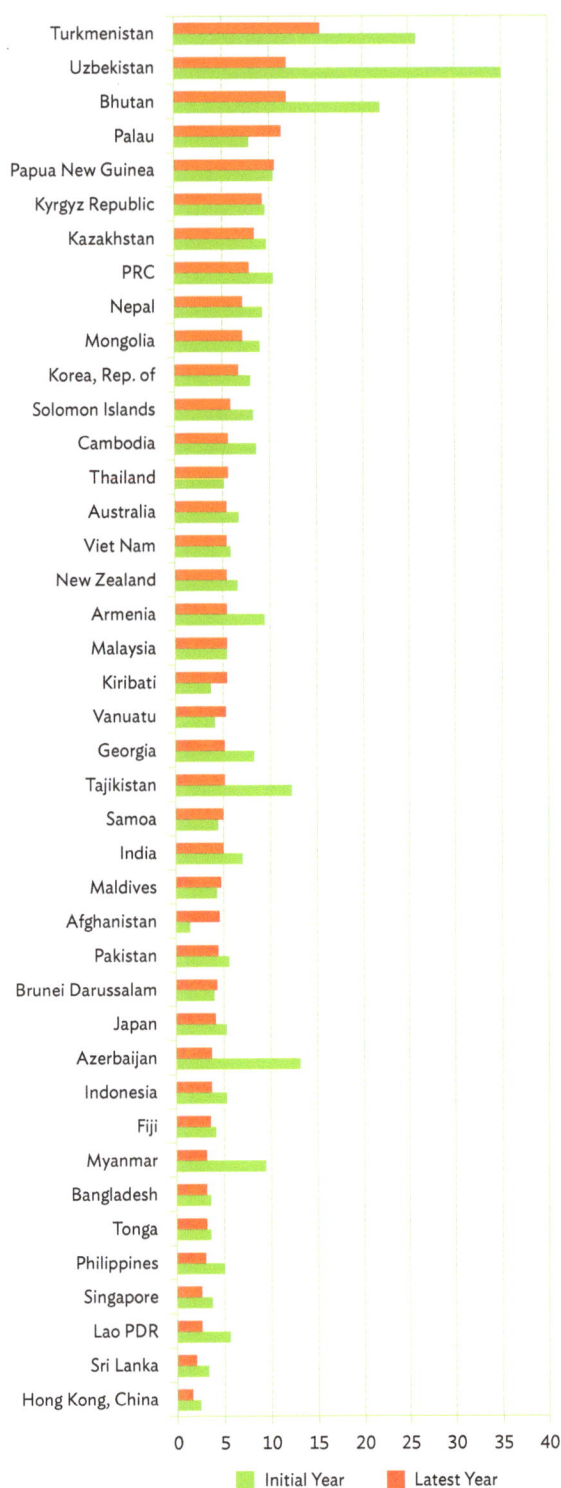

GDP = gross domestic product, Lao PDR = Lao People's Democratic Republic,
MJ = megajoule, PPP = purchasing power parity, PRC = People's Republic of China.
Notes: Initial year data is for 2000 except in Afghanistan, which is 2002. Latest year
varies between 2012 and 2013 across economies.
Source: Table 4.1.

SDG 8: Promote Sustained, Inclusive, and Sustainable Economic Growth, Full and Productive Employment and Decent Work for All

While economic growth is essential for a country's progress, its inclusivity is equally important since it will ensure that growth is fairly cascaded at the grassroots of society. Promoting full and productive employment and decent work for all is one of the main channels through which economic growth can be more inclusive for the lower echelons of society.

Annual growth rate of real GDP per capita. The target is to ensure that GDP per capita grows by at least 7% annually in the least developed countries, and at a level in accordance with national circumstances in other countries.[1]

In developing economies of Asia and the Pacific, the average annual growth rate in 2014 is estimated at 3.9%. Higher average growth can be observed in South Asia at 5.6%, followed by 4.3% in East Asia and 3.7% in Central and West Asia. Southeast Asia and the Pacific had an average growth of 3.4% and 2.4%, respectively. In 2014, the annual growth rate of GDP per capita in the majority of developing economies in the region ranged between –3.7% and 12.0%. On the other hand, the average annual growth rate of GDP per capita of the region's three developed economies rose by roughly 1.3%. Figure 4.3 presents the results for all reporting economies.

Higher growth of real GDP per employed person can also be seen in Turkmenistan (7.9%), Myanmar (6.8%), the PRC (6.7%), Sri Lanka (6.3%), and Uzbekistan (6.1%). These growth rates are much higher compared with those of the developed member countries Australia (2.1%), Japan (0.3%), and New Zealand (1.2%) (Table 4.2).

---

[1]   The estimates provided here are sourced from UN SDG Indicators Global Database. More updated estimates from economy sources are provided in Part II: Regional Trends and Tables.

Figure 4.3: Annual Growth Rate of Real GDP per Capita in constant 2005 $, 2013–2014
(%)

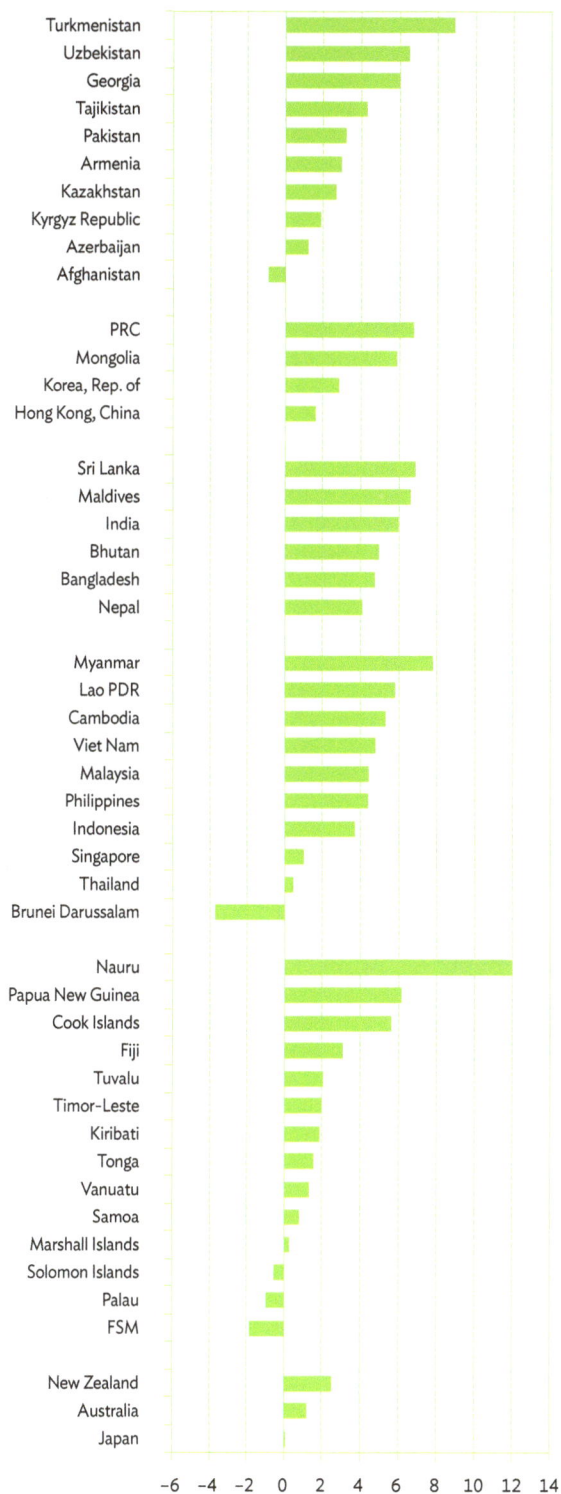

FSM = Federated States of Micronesia, GDP = gross domestic product,
Lao PDR = Lao People's Democratic Republic, PRC = People's Republic of China.
Source: Table 4.2

Unemployment rate. The target is to achieve full and productive employment and decent work for all by 2030.

Figure 4.4 shows the distribution of unemployment rates among the reporting member economies based on latest data. The highest unemployment rates are recorded in Kiribati (30.6%), Nauru (23.0%), Armenia (17.6%), Georgia (12.4%), and the Maldives (11.7%). On the other hand, the lowest unemployment rates are noted in Cambodia (0.1%), Myanmar (0.8%), Thailand (0.8%), Brunei Darussalam (1.7%), and Viet Nam (1.9%).

Figure 4.4: Unemployment Rate, 2014 or Nearest Year
(%)

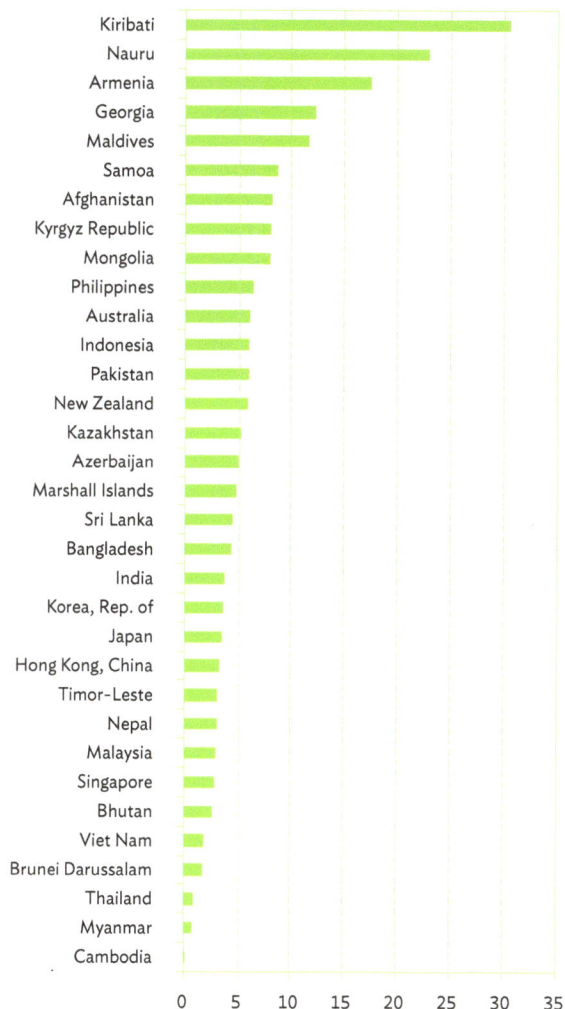

Note: Only economies with recent estimates (2010 and later) are included.
Source: Table 4.3.

Proportion of children aged 5–17 years engaged in child labor. The highest prevalence rates of child labor are observed in Nepal (37.4%), Afghanistan (29.4%), the Kyrgyz Republic (25.8%), and Cambodia (19.3%), while the lowest rates are noted in Bhutan (2.9%) and Armenia (3.9%) (Figure 4.5). Table 4.3 also presents estimates for earlier years.

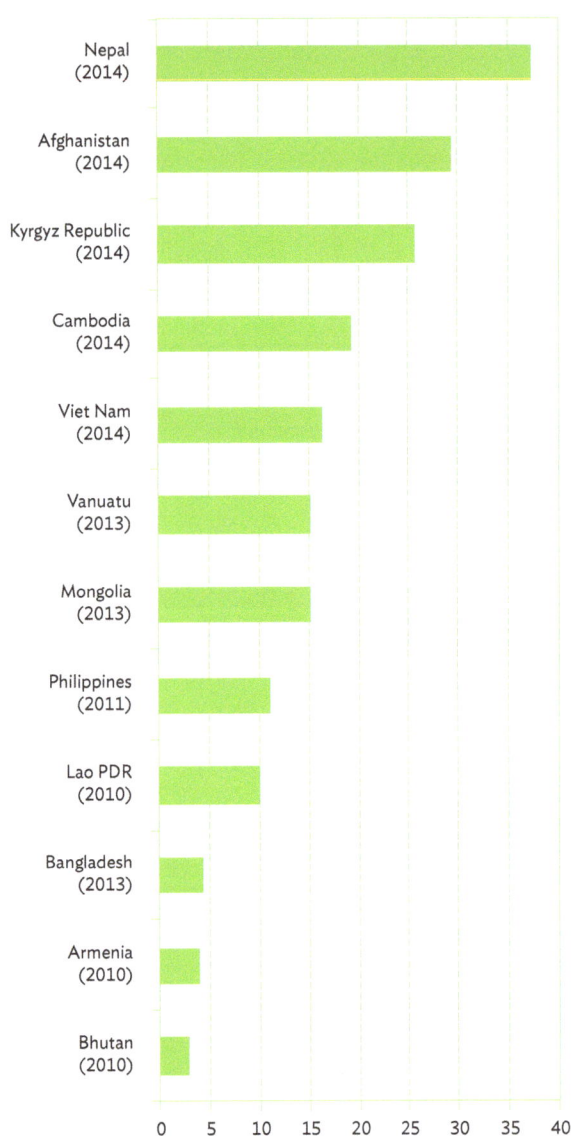

Figure 4.5: Proportion of Children Aged 5–17 Years Engaged in Child Labor in Selected Economies, Latest Year
(%)

Lao PDR = Lao People's Democratic Republic.
Note: Only economies with recent estimates (2010 and later) are included.
Source: Table 4.3.

Number of commercial bank branches and ATMs per 100,000 population. The number of commercial banks per 100,000 adults in developed member economies ranges between 29.1 and 34.1 based on latest available data. In developing economies of the region, the estimates range between 1.8 and 71.5. Some economies like Mongolia (71.5) and Uzbekistan (37.9) have a higher number of commercial banks per 100,000 adults compared with other economies. The numbers in Central and West Asia, South Asia, and Southeast Asia are generally lower compared with other regions.

Meanwhile, the number of ATMs per 100,000 adults in developed member economies ranges between 70.9 and 160.0 based on latest data available. In developing economies of the region, the estimates range between 1.0 and 280.8. Some economies like the Republic of Korea (280.0) and Thailand (111.3) have a higher number of ATMs per 100,000 adults compared with other economies.

Proportion of adults with an account at a bank or other financial institutions. Since 2011, the proportion of adults with an account in a bank or other financial institutions has grown by more than 8 percentage points in the majority of the member economies in Asia and the Pacific. Close to more than 90% of adults in East Asia have an account at a bank or other financial institutions, more than 50% in Southeast Asia and South Asia. The estimate is slightly lower for Central and West Asia where only 26% of adults have a bank account or one in other financial institutions.

Equity and Other Issues

Many member economies in the region confront the challenge of ensuring that there are enough good-quality and productive jobs for everyone. However, empirical data suggest that in many countries, women are still exposed to higher risks of unemployment. For instance, in Sri Lanka, the unemployment rate among women is higher by 17.0 percentage points than among men. In Nauru, the difference is 14.2 percentage points, and in Kiribati, 14.6 percentage points. On the other hand, the Maldives and Tajikistan exhibit higher unemployment rates among men. Furthermore, several countries need to work harder in reducing youth unemployment rates. For instance, Armenia, and Kiribati have significantly higher rates of unemployment in the 15–24 age group than in the group 25 years old and over.

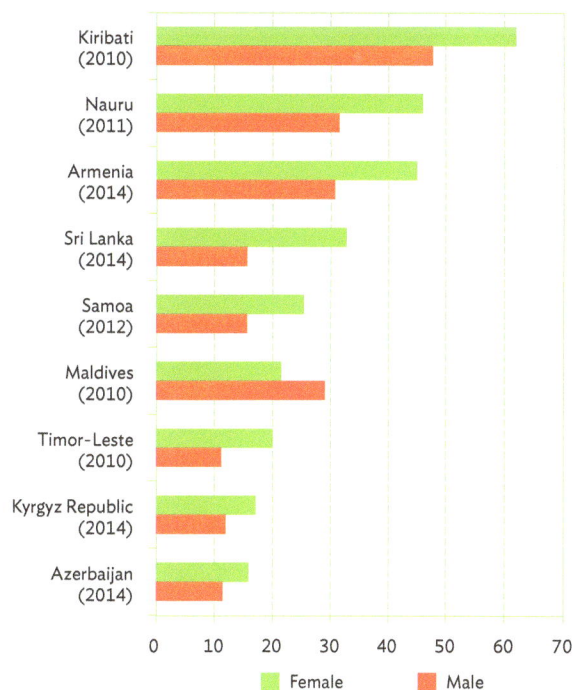

Figure 4.6: Unemployment Rate in Selected Economies, by Sex (%)

Source: United Nations Statistics Division. Sustainable Development Goal Indicators Global Database. http://unstats.un.org/sdgs/indicators/database/ (accessed September 2016).

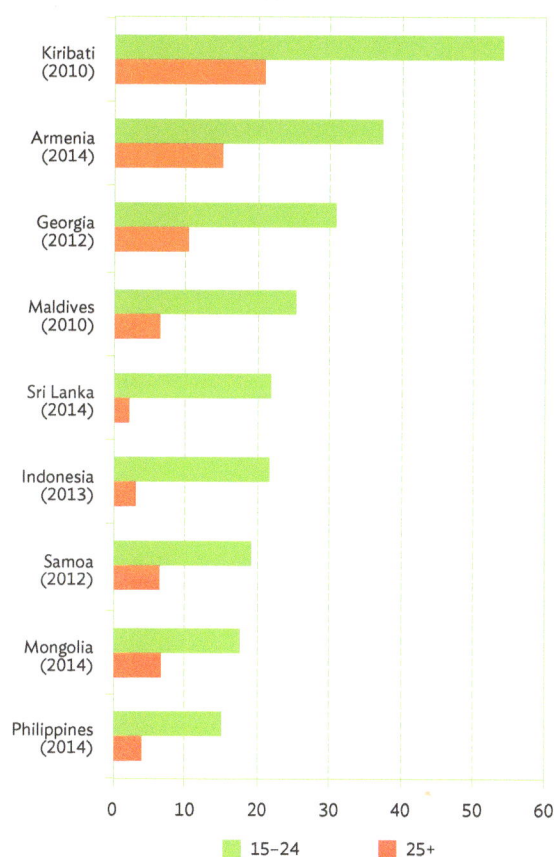

Figure 4.7: Unemployment Rate in Selected Economies, by Age Group (%)

Source: United Nations Statistics Division. Sustainable Development Goal Indicators Global Database. http://unstats.un.org/sdgs/indicators/database/ (accessed September 2016).

Data Gaps

Designing effective policies that promote inclusive growth requires finer granularity of data on GDP, employment rates, and other socioeconomic indicators. While most of the economic growth and employment indicators relevant to SDG 8 are widely available in many countries, they are usually presented at highly aggregated levels. In Part II, we provide examples on how nonconventional types of data, particularly satellite images, can be used to monitor progress with respect to SDG 8.

SDG 9: Build Resilient Infrastructure, Promote Inclusive and Sustainable Industrialization and Foster Innovation

Sustaining socioeconomic development and empowering societies hinge on channeling more investments to smart infrastructure. Smart infrastructure should be designed not only to make the delivery of basic services more efficient, but also to spur income-generating activities that result in an environment-friendly industrialization. To accomplish this, everyone should capitalize on the lessons from both developed and developing countries that have allocated a significant amount of resources on smart infrastructure-related research and development.

Air transport, passengers carried and freight volume. In 2014, a total of 1.1 billion air passengers traveled to and from Asia and the Pacific. Within the developing region, 543 million or 48.1% traveled to and from East Asia, 279.4 million or 24.7% in Southeast Asia, 91.5 million or 8.1% in South Asia, 18.9 million or 1.7% in Central and West Asia, and 4.3 million or less than 1% in the Pacific.

Freight volume by air transport in the region reached 18.1 billion metric tons (mt) in 2014, a 42.6% increase from 12.7 billion mt in 2000. East Asia accounts for 57.3% or 10.34 billion mt in 2014, the largest share in the region, followed by Southeast Asia with 19.8% and South Asia with 5.0% of the total freight volume transported by air. From 2000 to 2014, a significant increase in freight volume by air by more than 100% was observed in South Asia (154.7%) while it was almost doubled in Central and West Asia (95.6%) and East Asia (95.2%).

Manufacturing value added per capita. In the majority of regional member economies in 2015, the value added per capita in the manufacturing sector ranged between $8.71 and $9,292.02 at constant 2010 US dollars. Between 2000 and 2015, a significant increase in the value added per capita in the manufacturing sector can be seen in Myanmar (943%), the PRC (313%),

Viet Nam (252%), Cambodia (250%), Turkmenistan (226%), Georgia (212%), the Lao PDR (199%), Nauru (199%), Bangladesh (172%), and Bhutan (132%).

Manufacturing value added share in GDP. In proportion to GDP, the share of the manufacturing sector has increased in 16 of 48 member economies in the region between 2000 and 2015. A significant increase is observed in the following economies: 13.6 percentage points in Myanmar, 8.6 percentage points in Nauru, and 6.9 percentage points in Viet Nam. Currently, the relative share of the manufacturing sector to the total economic output is highest in the PRC (32.8%); the Republic of Korea (29.0%); Thailand (28.3%); Indonesia (24.6%); Malaysia (23.9%); Nauru (23.7%); Taipei,China (23.0%); the Philippines (22.5%); Myanmar (22.1%); and Viet Nam (20.3%).

Between 2000 and 2015, six economies from Central and West Asia recorded the biggest declines in the share of manufacturing sector to GDP—Afghanistan, Armenia, Azerbaijan, the Kyrgyz Republic, Tajikistan, and Uzbekistan—with a decrease ranging from 4.2 to 9.9 percentage points. Meanwhile, seven of 14 Pacific economies had the lowest shares of manufacturing value added to GDP—the Cook Islands, the Marshall Islands, the Federated States of Micronesia, Palau, Timor-Leste, Tuvalu, and Vanuatu—ranging from 0.2% to 4.0%.

Research and development expenditure as a proportion of GDP. Developed and other middle-to high-income economies of Asia and the Pacific top the list of regional economies with the highest research and development expenditure as a proportion of GDP (Figure 4.8). The list includes the Republic of Korea (4.3%), Japan (3.6%), Australia (2.2%), Singapore (2.2%), the PRC (2.0%), Malaysia (1.3%), and New Zealand (1.2%). In other economies, research and development expenditure is less than 1% of their respective GDP. Since 2000, there have been modest increases in Hong Kong, China; India; Nepal; Pakistan; and Thailand.

Figure 4.8: Research and Development Expenditure as a Proportion of GDP
(%)

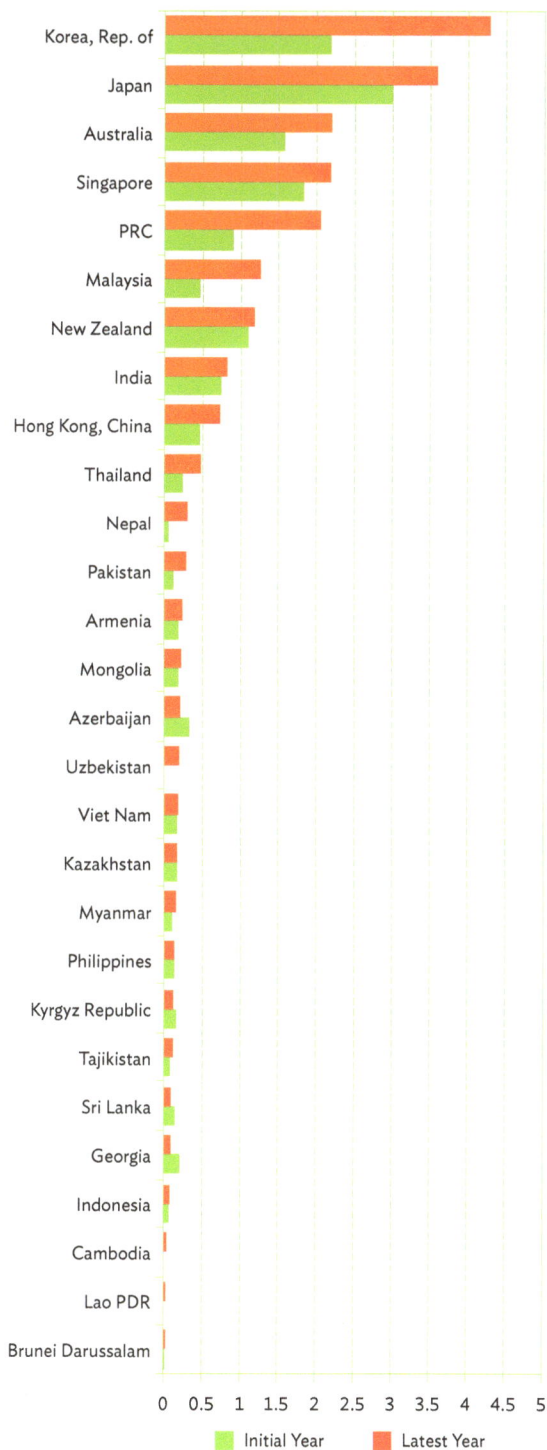

Lao PDR = Lao People's Democratic Republic, PRC = People's Republic of China.
Source: Table 4.7.

Data Gaps, Equity, and Other Issues

While there are signs that investments in smart infrastructure are generally improving in many countries, the availability of key infrastructure in some remote areas still compares unfavorably with that in capital cities and urban centers. In addition to initiating more infrastructure investments, governments can respond to this issue by providing an economic environment that will attract nongovernment players to be more active in ensuring that the economic benefits of infrastructure are accessible to everyone.

SDG 10: Reduce Inequality within and among Countries

Reducing high levels of social and economic inequalities could be beneficial for various reasons. For instance, with lower inequality and more equitable access to economic opportunities, it will be easier for people from lower echelons of society to fully realize their economic potential. With lower inequality, there is also presumably less risk of social conflict arising from some segments of the population being left out from enjoying the benefits of economic development. SDG 10 aims to arrest the potential threat to long-term social and economic development accompanying high inequality.

Annualized growth rates in average household income or expenditure per capita and average household income or expenditure per capita among the bottom 40% of the population. Figure 4.9 shows the estimates of growth rates of average household income or expenditure per capita for the entire population and for the bottom 40%. Between 2000 and 2015, the annualized growth rates in household income or expenditure per capita for the entire population were highest in Kazakhstan (8.9%), Cambodia (8.5%), Nepal (7.5%), the PRC (7.2%), Bhutan (6.5%), Viet Nam (6.2%), Thailand (4.8%),

Australia (4.4%), Pakistan (3.8%), Indonesia (3.8%), and India (3.2%). On the other hand, the annualized growth rates in household income or expenditure per capita among the bottom 40% of population were highest in the PRC (7.9%), Viet Nam (7.8%), Kazakhstan (7.6%), Bhutan (6.5%), Australia (4.7%), Nepal (4.1%), Cambodia (4.1%), Thailand (4.0%),

India (3.7%), and Indonesia (3.4%). Interestingly, the empirical data suggest that some economies that have experienced faster growth among the bottom 40% than the mean are those that have a slower reduction in poverty (Box Figure 4.1.1).

Equity and Other Issues

Not everyone benefits from economic growth equally. A high level of inequality indicates that the different segments of the population benefit from economic growth at different rates. There will be income convergence if the initially poor experience faster income growth than the rich. However, policy makers should be careful in implementing programs and interventions that are solely designed to minimize inequalities but disregard their impact on other SDGs such as poverty reduction. Box 4.1 discusses this issue by examining the performance of different countries with respect to SDGs 1 and 10.

Data Gaps

Although high and increasing inequality could threaten the sustainability of economic development, social and economic experts have long underscored the pitfalls of taking a normative negative perception about inequality. For instance, these experts argue that inequality arising from people having different skill sets and exerting different amounts of effort could be considered a positive type of inequality based on the principle of meritocracy. On the other hand, "bad" inequality refers to socioeconomic disparities that are driven by gender, race, parental background, and other uncontrollable circumstances that people are born into. Despite this distinction between "good" and "bad" inequality, conventional measures of inequality are essentially measures of total inequality, which is the sum of the good and bad components. A more thorough assessment of inequality can be done if inequality decomposition is also undertaken.

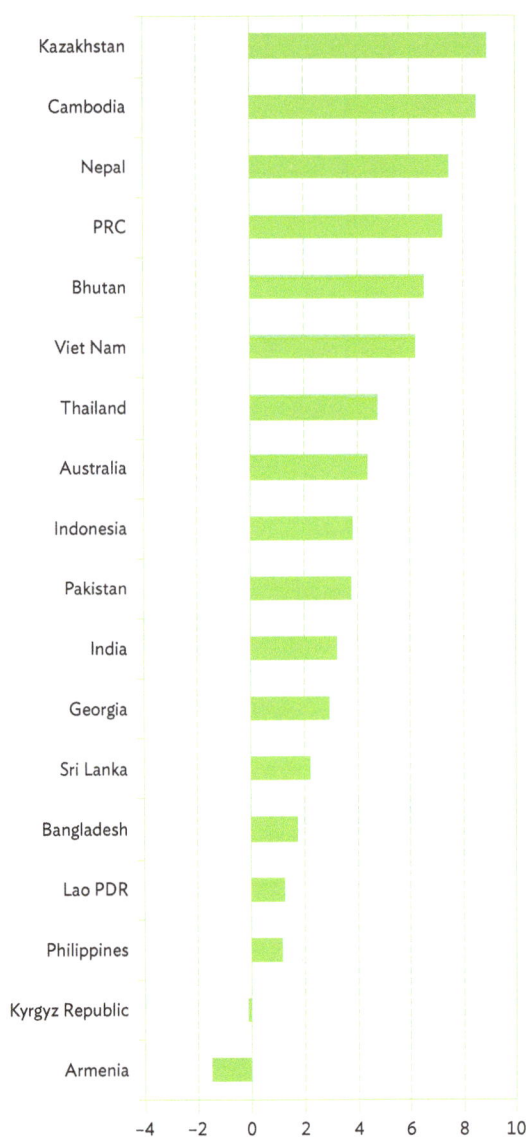

Figure 4.9: Growth Rates of Household Income or Expenditure per Capita among the Bottom 40% of the Population
(%)

Lao PDR = Lao People's Democratic Republic, PRC = People's Republic of China.
Source: Table 4.9.

Box 4.1: Complexities in the Inequality and Poverty Reduction Relationship

Asia and the Pacific has an impressive development scorecard: a massive reduction in poverty, an expansion in access to clean drinking water, and close to universal primary education. Where the region has not improved is reducing inequality.

The gap between the haves and have-nots within countries continues to widen, leading the United Nations to last year adopt Sustainable Development Goal (SDG) 10, which focuses on reducing inequalities within and among countries.

To monitor progress toward this goal, the SDGs track on the difference between the income growth of the bottom 40% of their population and the national average. This is founded on the assumption that fostering faster income growth for the bottom 40% relative to the national average will allow them to catch up with the rest and, thus, bring about a more equitable distribution of economic opportunities.

We analyzed data from the World Bank's PovcalNet database for 26 of ADB's developing member countries with sufficient data between 1990 and the present and found that there may be an elements of a trade-off between fighting poverty and reducing inequality.

Box Figure 4.1.1 describes the rate at which $1.90 (2011 PPP) and $3.10 (2011 PPP) a day poverty incidence have changed for 26 DMCs with available data. It also distinguishes between countries on the basis of whether the bottom 40% experienced higher income growth than average incomes or not. The former countries are labeled as having "equalizing" distribution, while the latter are labeled as having "nonequalizing" distribution. The data show that some of the fastest reduction in poverty were registered by countries with growing inequality as defined by the SDG 10 target. This pattern is consistent even if we use the $3.10 poverty line or other measures of inequality such as the Palma ratio.

Box Figure 4.1.1: Comparison of Change in Poverty Rates between Countries with Equalizing and Nonequalizing Distribution, 1990–Present

Panel A: Annualized Percentage Point Reduction in $1.90 Poverty Rate

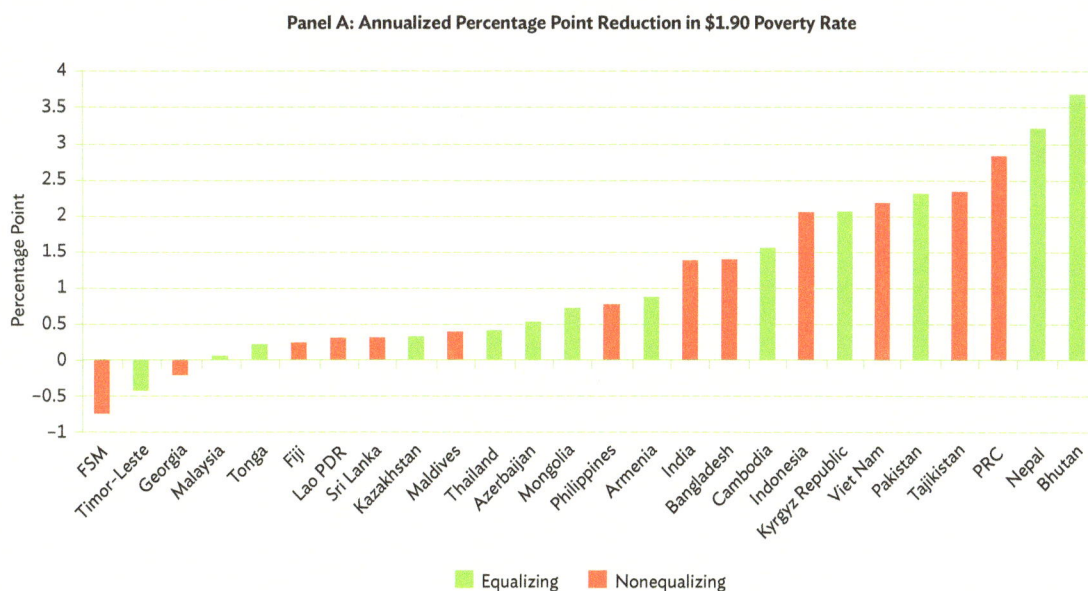

FSM = Federated States of Micronesia, Lao PDR = Lao People's Democratic Republic, PRC = People's Republic of China.
Notes: The y-axis corresponds to the annualized percentage point reduction in poverty rates. Positive values represent reduction in poverty over time while negative values represent increase in poverty over time.
Source: ADB estimates using World Bank. PovcalNet Database. http://iresearch.worldbank.org/PovcalNet/home.aspx. (accessed October 2016).

continued.

Box 4.1: *(continued)*

Panel B: Annualized Percentage Point Reduction in $3.10 Poverty Rate

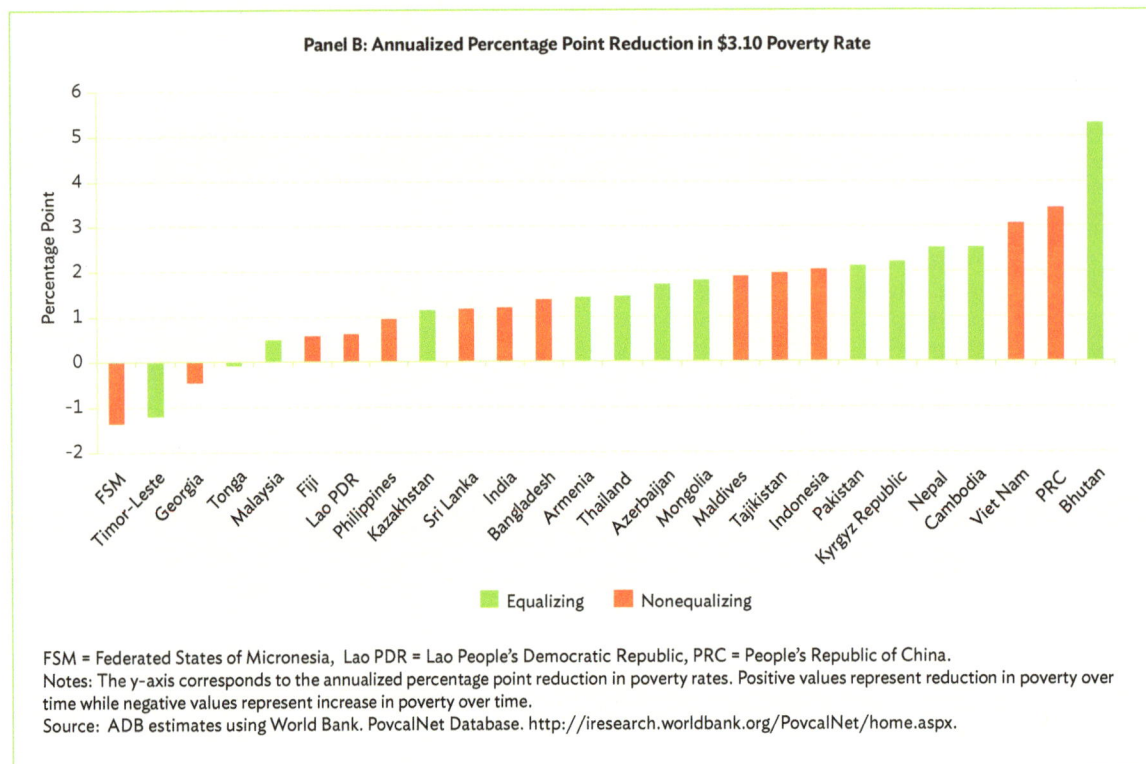

FSM = Federated States of Micronesia, Lao PDR = Lao People's Democratic Republic, PRC = People's Republic of China.
Notes: The y-axis corresponds to the annualized percentage point reduction in poverty rates. Positive values represent reduction in poverty over time while negative values represent increase in poverty over time.
Source: ADB estimates using World Bank. PovcalNet Database. http://iresearch.worldbank.org/PovcalNet/home.aspx.

In fact, countries with the highest average income growth (but higher levels of inequality) saw some of the largest reductions in poverty. Millions of people have been lifted out of poverty in countries like Bangladesh, the People's Republic of China (PRC), Indonesia, and Viet Nam because these developing member countries have posted remarkable average income growth rates. For instance, per capita income in the PRC has grown at an annual rate of 7% since the 1990s, while the annual growth rates for Viet Nam and Indonesia for the same period have been 6% and 3%, respectively.

Thus, assessments based solely on the distribution of income growth, without any regard for its impact on other SDGs such as putting an end to poverty (SDG 1) can be problematic. In some cases, it is conceivable that a naïve reliance on this SDG 10 target would even render countries with declining average income and declining income of the bottom 40% as "performers" simply because the average income growth declined faster compared to the income of the bottom 40%.

As we have seen in the cases of the PRC, India, Indonesia, and Viet Nam, countries can succeed in reducing poverty significantly for as long as their average income growth is also fast—even if the income of the upper 60% grew faster than that of the bottom 40%. On the other hand, in countries such as the Philippines where growth in the income of the upper 60% was not significantly faster relative to that of the bottom 40%, the average income—and the national poverty rates—hardly budged.

There is no question that inequality is an important development issue that needs to be addressed and must therefore be included in the SDGs. However, it is important to examine the interlinkages possible trade-offs between changes in poverty and inequality, without losing sight of other important dimensions of development such as increasing the poor's access to high-quality jobs, services, and infrastructure.

Ensure access to affordable, reliable, sustainable, and modern energy for all

Table 4.1:   **Selected Indicators for SDG 7 - Energy Efficiency and Modern, Renewable Energy Sources**
By 2030, ensure universal access to affordable, reliable and modern energy services

By 2030, increase substantially the share of renewable energy in the global energy mix

By 2030, double the global rate of improvement in energy efficiency

Regional Member	7.1.1 Proportion of Population with Access to Electricity (%)		7.2.1 Renewable Energy Share in the Total Final Energy Consumption (%)		7.3.1 Energy Intensity Measured in Terms of Primary Energy and GDP (MJ/$ 2011 PPP GDP)	
	2000	2012	2000	2012	2000	2013
Developing Member Economies						
Central and West Asia						
Afghanistan	37.5	43.0	59.5	10.8 (2011)	1.4 (2002)	4.6 (2012)
Armenia	98.0	100.0	7.2	6.6	9.4	5.4
Azerbaijan	96.0	100.0	2.1	2.9	13.2	3.7
Georgia	99.9	100.0	47.3	28.7	8.3	5.2
Kazakhstan	97.0	100.0	2.5	1.4	9.7	8.4
Kyrgyz Republic	100.0	100.0	35.2	22.5	9.6	9.3
Pakistan	79.5	93.6	50.4	45.5	5.5	4.4
Tajikistan	99.0	100.0	62.4	58.0	12.3	5.2
Turkmenistan	99.6	100.0	–	–	25.9	15.5
Uzbekistan	99.7	100.0	1.2	2.4	35.0	11.9
East Asia						
China, People's Rep. of	98.0	100.0	29.2	18.4	10.5	7.9
Hong Kong, China	100.0	100.0	0.6	1.1	2.5	1.6
Korea, Rep. of	98.0	100.0	0.7	1.6	8.1	6.7
Mongolia	82.7	89.8	5.7	3.2	9.0	7.1
Taipei,China	...	...	...	...	...	...
South Asia						
Bangladesh	32.0	59.6	59.4	38.3	3.5	3.2
Bhutan	68.5	75.6	95.5	90.0 (2011)	21.9	11.8 (2012)
India	62.3	78.7	52.4	39.0	7.0	5.0
Maldives	96.4	100.0	9.3	3.2 (2011)	4.3	4.7 (2012)
Nepal	72.8	76.3	88.3	84.7	9.3	7.1
Sri Lanka	80.7	88.7	64.2	60.9	3.3	2.0
Southeast Asia						
Brunei Darussalam	69.4	76.2	–	0.0	4.0	4.4
Cambodia	16.6	31.1	81.1	72.6	8.5	5.6
Indonesia	87.6	96.0	45.2	37.1	5.3	3.7
Lao PDR	46.3	70.0	91.2	86.5 (2011)	5.7	2.6 (2012)
Malaysia	96.4	100.0	8.2	6.8	5.5	5.4
Myanmar	47.0	52.4	80.2	78.7	9.4	3.2 (2012)
Philippines	71.3	87.5	34.9	29.4	5.1	3.0
Singapore	100.0	100.0	0.3	0.5	3.8	2.6
Thailand	82.5	100.0	22.0	23.0	5.2	5.6
Viet Nam	89.1	99.0	58.0	35.6	5.8	5.5
The Pacific						
Cook Islands	...	...	...	...	...	...
Fiji	52.5	59.3	13.4	12.2 (2011)	4.2	3.7 (2012)
Kiribati	52.5	59.3	11.1	2.9 (2011)	3.8	5.4 (2012)
Marshall Islands	52.5	59.3	...	...	...	...
Micronesia, Fed. States of	52.5	59.3	...	...	...	...
Nauru	...	...	...	...	...	...
Palau	52.5	59.3	3.3 (2001)	2.7 (2011)	7.8	11.3 (2012)
Papua New Guinea	11.0	18.1	66.4	53.4 (2011)	10.4	10.5 (2012)
Samoa	89.4	100.0	49.5	23.2 (2011)	4.4	5.0 (2012)
Solomon Islands	15.7	22.8	86.9	67.2 (2011)	8.3	5.9 (2012)
Timor-Leste	34.5	41.6	52.8 (2002)	38.3 (2010)	...	...
Tonga	85.8	95.9	2.5	1.1 (2011)	3.6	3.1 (2012)
Tuvalu	37.5	44.6	...	...	...	...
Vanuatu	19.1	27.1	68.8	34.2 (2011)	4.2	5.3 (2012)
Developed Member Economies						
Australia	100.0	100.0	8.4	8.4	6.7	5.5
Japan	100.0	100.0	3.9	4.5	5.3	4.2
New Zealand	100.0	100.0	28.9	30.8	6.6	5.5

... = data not available at cutoff date, – = magnitude equals zero, 0.0 = magnitude is less than half of unit employed, GDP = gross domestic product, Lao PDR = Lao People's Democratic Republic, MJ = megajoule, PPP = purchasing power parity, SDG = Sustainable Development Goal.

Sources: For Indicators 7.1.1 and 7.2.1: United Nations. Sustainable Development Goals Indicators Global Database. http://unstats.un.org/sdgs/indicators/database/ (accessed 21 July 2016). For Indicator 7.3.1: For economies whose latest year estimates are for 2013, ADB estimates using the International Energy Agency's energy balances data and the World Bank's GDP data; for the rest: United Nations. Sustainable Development Goals Indicators Global Database. http://unstats.un.org/sdgs/indicators/database/ (accessed 21 July 2016).

Promote sustained, inclusive and sustainable economic growth, full and productive employment, and decent work for all

Table 4.2: **Selected Indicators for SDG 8 - Economic Growth per Capita**
Sustain per capita economic growth in accordance with national circumstances and, in particular, at least 7 per cent gross domestic product growth per annum in the least developed countries

Regional Member	8.1.1 Annual Growth Rate of Real GDP per Capita at Constant 2005 $ (%)		8.2.1 Annual Growth Rate of Real GDP per Employed Person (%)	
	2000	2014	2000	2015
Developing Member Economies				
Central and West Asia				
Afghanistan	−8.7	−0.9	...	...
Armenia	6.5	3.0	7.6	−0.4
Azerbaijan	10.1	1.2	6.7	1.4
Georgia	3.1	6.0	−3.9	4.3
Kazakhstan	10.6	2.7	8.2	1.0
Kyrgyz Republic	4.1	1.9	5.2	2.1
Pakistan	1.9	3.2	4.5	1.2
Tajikistan	6.8	4.3	7.7	2.6
Turkmenistan	4.3	8.9	7.9	7.9
Uzbekistan	2.6	6.5	2.7	6.1
East Asia				
China, People's Rep. of	7.8	6.8	7.9	6.7
Hong Kong, China	6.2	1.6	4.9	1.6
Korea, Rep. of	8.2	2.8	4.4	1.5
Mongolia	0.2	5.9	...	...
Taipei,China	...	...	...	...
South Asia				
Bangladesh	3.9	4.8	1.9	3.7
Bhutan	5.7	5.0	...	...
India	2.2	6.0	3.0	4.2
Maldives	2.5	6.6	...	...
Nepal	4.2	4.1	...	...
Sri Lanka	5.3	6.9	2.2	6.3
Southeast Asia				
Brunei Darussalam	0.8	−3.7	...	...
Cambodia	6.4	5.3	5.6	5.5
Indonesia	3.5	3.7	3.7	3.3
Lao PDR	4.1	5.8	...	...
Malaysia	6.4	4.5	3.4	2.3
Myanmar	12.4	7.8	10.6	6.8
Philippines	2.2	4.4	6.7	4.0
Singapore	6.2	1.0	5.1	1.2
Thailand	3.3	0.5	2.4	2.8
Viet Nam	5.6	4.8	2.2	4.8
The Pacific				
Cook Islands	13.8	5.6	...	...
Fiji	−2.3	3.1	...	...
Kiribati	10.1	1.9	...	...
Marshall Islands	5.0	0.3	...	...
Micronesia, Fed. States of	5.0	−1.9	...	...
Nauru	−6.8	12.0	...	...
Palau	−1.3	−1.0	...	...
Papua New Guinea	−4.9	6.2	...	...
Samoa	6.6	0.8	...	...
Solomon Islands	−16.5	−0.5	...	...
Timor-Leste	12.8	2.0	...	...
Tonga	2.6	1.6	...	...
Tuvalu	12.8	2.1	...	...
Vanuatu	3.1	1.3	...	...
Developed Member Economies				
Australia	0.9	1.2	0.7	2.1
Japan	2.1	0.1	3.0	0.3
New Zealand	1.7	2.5	2.5	1.2

... = data not available at cutoff date, GDP = gross domestic product, Lao PDR = Lao People's Democratic Republic, SDG = Sustainable Development Goal.

Source: United Nations. Sustainable Development Goals Indicators Global Database. http://unstats.un.org/sdgs/indicators/database/ (accessed 21 July 2016).

Promote sustained, inclusive and sustainable economic growth, full and productive employment, and decent work for all

Table 4.3:   **Selected Indicators for SDG 8 - Unemployment, Youth Participation in Education and Work, and Child Labor**

By 2030, achieve full and productive employment and decent work for all women and men, including for young people and persons with disabilities, and equal pay for work of equal value

By 2020, substantially reduce the proportion of youth not in employment, education or training

Regional Member	8.5.2 Unemployment Rate, by Sex (%)					
	2000			2014		
	Total	Female	Male	Total	Female	Male
Developing Member Economies						
Central and West Asia						
Afghanistan	...	...	...	8.2 (2011)	16.5 (2011)	6.4 (2011)
Armenia	16.4 (2008)	18.6 (2008)	14.4 (2008)	17.6	19.5	15.8
Azerbaijan	11.8	12.7	10.9	4.9	5.8	4.0
Georgia	10.8	10.5	11.1	12.4	10.5	14.0
Kazakhstan	10.4 (2001)	12.0 (2001)	8.9 (2001)	5.2 (2013)	5.9 (2013)	4.6 (2013)
Kyrgyz Republic	12.6 (2002)	14.3 (2002)	11.2 (2002)	8.1	9.5	7.0
Pakistan	7.2	15.8	5.5	5.9 (2015)	9.0 (2015)	5.0 (2015)
Tajikistan	...	...	...	11.5 (2009)	10.5 (2009)	12.3 (2009)
Turkmenistan	...	...	...	...	...	...
Uzbekistan	...	...	...	...	...	...
East Asia						
China, People's Rep. of	...	...	...	...	...	...
Hong Kong, China	4.9	4.0	5.6	3.3 (2015)	3.1 (2015)	3.4 (2015)
Korea, Rep. of	4.4	3.6	5.0	3.6 (2015)	3.6 (2015)	3.7 (2015)
Mongolia	6.2 (2002)	6.2 (2002)	6.2 (2002)	7.9	7.3	8.5
Taipei,China	...	...	...	...	...	...
South Asia						
Bangladesh	3.3	3.3	3.2	4.3 (2013)	7.2 (2013)	3.0 (2013)
Bhutan	1.9 (2001)	3.2 (2001)	1.3 (2001)	2.6	3.5	1.9
India	4.3	4.3	4.3	3.6 (2012)	4.2 (2012)	3.4 (2012)
Maldives	14.4 (2006)	23.8 (2006)	7.9 (2006)	11.7 (2010)	13.8 (2010)	10.4 (2010)
Nepal	2.1 (2008)	2.0 (2008)	2.3 (2008)	3.0	3.4	2.6
Sri Lanka	7.7	11.4	5.9	4.4	7.3	2.9
Southeast Asia						
Brunei Darussalam	...	...	...	1.7 (2011)	2.4 (2011)	1.3 (2011)
Cambodia	2.5	2.8	2.1	0.1	0.1	0.1
Indonesia	6.1	6.7	5.7	5.9	6.3	5.8
Lao PDR	1.4 (2005)	1.4 (2005)	1.3 (2005)	...	...	...
Malaysia	3.0	3.1	3.0	2.9	3.2	2.7
Myanmar	...	...	...	0.8 (2015)	0.9 (2015)	0.7 (2015)
Philippines	11.2	11.5	11.0	6.3 (2015)	5.8 (2015)	6.6 (2015)
Singapore	3.7	3.5	3.9	2.8	3.0	2.6
Thailand	2.4	2.3	2.4	0.8	0.8	0.9
Viet Nam	2.3	2.1	2.4	1.9	1.8	1.9
The Pacific						
Cook Islands	...	...	...	...	...	...
Fiji	4.7 (2004)	6.0 (2004)	4.1 (2004)	8.6 (2007)	12.9 (2007)	6.4 (2007)
Kiribati	14.7 (2005)	18.2 (2005)	12.3 (2005)	30.6 (2010)	34.1 (2010)	27.6 (2010)
Marshall Islands	...	...	...	4.7 (2011)	4.5 (2011)	4.9 (2011)
Micronesia, Fed. States of	...	...	...	...	...	...
Nauru	22.8 (2002)	29.7 (2002)	17.0 (2002)	23.0 (2011)	25.5 (2011)	21.4 (2011)
Palau	...	...	...	...	...	...
Papua New Guinea	2.9	1.3	4.3	...	...	...
Samoa	5.0 (2001)	6.2 (2001)	4.4 (2001)	8.7 (2012)	10.3 (2012)	7.8 (2012)
Solomon Islands	...	...	...	...	...	...
Timor-Leste	9.9 (2001)	13.7 (2001)	8.0 (2001)	3.1 (2010)	4.8 (2010)	2.8 (2010)
Tonga	5.2 (2003)	7.4 (2003)	3.6 (2003)	...	...	...
Tuvalu	6.5 (2002)	8.6 (2002)	4.9 (2002)	...	...	...
Vanuatu	...	...	...	5.5 (2009)	6.2 (2009)	4.9 (2009)
Developed Member Economies						
Australia	6.3	6.1	6.5	6.1 (2015)	6.1 (2015)	6.1 (2015)
Japan	4.7	4.5	4.9	3.4 (2015)	3.1 (2015)	3.6 (2015)
New Zealand	6.1	6.0	6.3	5.8 (2015)	6.3 (2015)	5.3 (2015)

Promote sustained, inclusive and sustainable economic growth, full and productive employment, and decent work for all

Table 4.3: **Selected Indicators for SDG 8 - Unemployment, Youth Participation in Education and Work, and Child Labor** (continued)

Regional Member	8.6.1 Proportion of Youth (Aged 15–24 Years) Not in Education, Employment, or Training (%)		8.7.1 Proportion of Children Aged 5–17 Years Engaged in Child Labor (%)	
	2000	2014	2000	2014
Developing Member Economies				
Central and West Asia				
Afghanistan	...	...	...	29.4
Armenia	42.1 (2011)	40.9 (2013)	...	3.9 (2010)
Azerbaijan	19.5 (2005)	...	6.5 (2007)	...
Georgia	...	...	18.4 (2005)	...
Kazakhstan	...	...	2.2 (2006)	...
Kyrgyz Republic	10.6 (2007)	21.2 (2013)	...	25.8
Pakistan	...	...	...	...
Tajikistan	38.2 (2007)	...	10.0 (2005)	...
Turkmenistan	...	...	...	...
Uzbekistan	...	...	...	...
East Asia				
China, People's Rep. of	...	...	...	...
Hong Kong, China	7.4 (2009)	6.6 (2013)	...	...
Korea, Rep. of	18.5 (2008)	18.8 (2011)	...	...
Mongolia	18.5 (2006)	1.5 (2013)	...	15.2 (2013)
Taipei,China	...	...	...	...
South Asia				
Bangladesh	31.5 (2002)	40.3 (2013)	...	4.3 (2013)
Bhutan	...	...	...	2.9 (2010)
India	26.1 (2004)	27.2 (2010)	11.8 (2006)	...
Maldives	...	56.4 (2010)	...	...
Nepal	...	9.2 (2013)	...	37.4
Sri Lanka	22.9 (2010)	0.5 (2012)	...	2.5 (2009)
Southeast Asia				
Brunei Darussalam	...	...	...	...
Cambodia	21.1 (1998)	7.8 (2012)	...	19.3
Indonesia	29.6 (2008)	24.1 (2013)	...	6.9 (2009)
Lao PDR	...	...	...	10.1 (2010)
Malaysia	0.9 (2012)	1.1 (2013)	...	...
Myanmar	...	...	...	...
Philippines	24.7 (2009)	24.8 (2012)	...	11.1 (2011)
Singapore	16.9 (2009)	18.9 (2010)	...	...
Thailand	13.7 (2009)	13.8	8.3 (2006)	...
Viet Nam	11.3 (2012)	9.3 (2013)	...	16.4
The Pacific				
Cook Islands	...	...	...	...
Fiji	...	...	...	...
Kiribati	...	...	...	...
Marshall Islands	...	...	...	...
Micronesia, Fed. States of	...	...	...	...
Nauru	...	...	...	...
Palau	...	...	...	...
Papua New Guinea	...	...	...	...
Samoa	...	38.2 (2012)	...	...
Solomon Islands	...	...	...	...
Timor-Leste	...	...	4.2 (2002)	...
Tonga	...	...	...	...
Tuvalu	...	...	...	...
Vanuatu	...	...	...	15.2 (2013)
Developed Member Economies				
Australia	10.1 (2002)	9.8 (2012)	...	...
Japan	4.4 (2009)	3.9 (2013)	...	...
New Zealand	11.6 (2004)	11.9 (2013)	...	...

... = data not available at cutoff date, Lao PDR = Lao People's Democratic Republic, SDG = Sustainable Development Goal.

Sources: International Labour Organization. Key Indicators of the Labour Market (KILM) 2015. 9th Edition, Table 10c. http://www.ilo.org/global/statistics-and-databases/WCMS_424979/lang--en/index.htm (accessed 17 September 2016); United Nations. Sustainable Development Goals Indicators Global Database. http://unstats.un.org/sdgs/indicators/database/ (accessed 21 July 2016).

Promote sustained, inclusive and sustainable economic growth, full and productive employment, and decent work for all

Table 4.4:   **Selected Indicators for SDG 8 - Access to Banking, Insurance, and Financial Services**
Strengthen the capacity of domestic financial institutions to encourage and expand access to banking, insurance and financial services for all

Increase Aid for Trade support for developing countries, in particular least developed countries, including through the Enhanced Integrated Framework for Trade-Related Technical Assistance to Least Developed Countries

| Regional Member | 8.10.1 Number of Commercial Bank Branches and ATMs per 100,000 adults | | | | 8.10.2 Proportion of Adults (15 Years and Older) with an Account at a Bank or Other Financial Institution or with a Mobile-Money-Service Provider (%) | | 8.a.1 Aid for Trade Commitments and Disbursements (constant $ million)[a] | |
| | Commercial Bank Branches | | ATMs | | | | | |
	2004	2015	2004	2015	2011	2014	2006	2014
Developing Member Economies								
Central and West Asia							4,357	9,989
Afghanistan	0.4	2.4	0.0	1.0	14.4	12.2	2,167	2,195
Armenia	10.8	21.7 (2014)	3.0	56.7 (2014)	18.6	21.8	382	446
Azerbaijan	6.5	10.7 (2014)	17.0 (2006)	35.1 (2014)	18.5	30.7	160	187
Georgia	9.3	...	1.9	56.8	39.8	47.5	513	514
Kazakhstan	3.7	3.0	10.0	71.6	47.5	59.0	80	72
Kyrgyz Republic	5.1	7.9 (2014)	0.6	24.8 (2014)	6.0	20.9	146	439
Pakistan	7.7	9.7 (2014)	0.8	7.5 (2014)	13.1	10.4	688	4,735
Tajikistan	5.0	6.5 (2013)	0.6 (2005)	10.4 (2013)	3.6	16.0	126	303
Turkmenistan	...	...	...	...	0.7	2.2	2	13
Uzbekistan	38.8	37.9	1.0	10.7	24.9	45.2	92	1,085
East Asia							1,516	829
China, People's Rep. of	...	8.0 (2014)	9.6 (2006)	54.4 (2014)	75.6	83.6	1,323	586
Hong Kong, China	23.5	22.7 (2014)	...	49.7 (2011)	92.9	97.1	...	...
Korea, Rep. of	16.8	17.1	208.3	280.8	94.8	95.7	...	...
Mongolia	40.0	71.5 (2014)	...	58.6 (2014)	81.2	93.7	193	243
Taipei,China	...	...	...	...	...	...	...	...
South Asia							4,586	12,618
Bangladesh	6.9	8.2 (2014)	0.1	9.3 (2014)	39.8	34.5	903	2,790
Bhutan	14.4	15.5 (2014)	0.5	22.2 (2014)	...	38.9	48	151
India	9.0	12.8 (2014)	2.3 (2005)	17.8 (2014)	40.5	58.6	2,684	7,317
Maldives	10.3	12.1 (2014)	7.4	26.9 (2014)	...	...	3	72
Nepal	2.6	8.4 (2014)	...	8.8 (2014)	32.6	41.1	350	975
Sri Lanka	8.7	18.6 (2014)	9.2 (2007)	17.0 (2014)	76.5	85.4	598	1,314
Southeast Asia							5,239	9,696
Brunei Darussalam	21.2	20.7	35.3	78.6	...	...	...	...
Cambodia	2.3 (2006)	5.7 (2014)	0.0 (2005)	10.9 (2014)	5.6	15.3	318	985
Indonesia	5.2	11.0 (2014)	8.6	49.5 (2014)	26.0	45.3	1,647	1,185
Lao PDR	...	2.9 (2014)	...	19.9 (2014)	31.2	...	247	470
Malaysia	14.1	10.9	27.2	52.1	77.1	84.1	62	14
Myanmar	1.8	3.3 (2014)	...	1.6 (2014)	...	27.0	34	1,113
Philippines	8.2	8.7 (2014)	10.3	23.4 (2014)	37.1	37.1	412	444
Singapore	11.7	9.4 (2014)	47.9	59.5 (2014)	99.3	96.5	...	...
Thailand	7.8	12.6 (2014)	19.9	111.3 (2014)	78.5	82.3	320	419
Viet Nam	...	3.9 (2014)	1.4	23.8 (2014)	29.5	39.5	2,199	5,067
The Pacific							559	1,257
Cook Islands	...	...	...	...	...	...	1	34
Fiji	9.3	12.2 (2014)	19.0	44.5 (2014)	...	...	22	28
Kiribati	...	5.7 (2013)	...	14.3 (2013)	...	...	11	65
Marshall Islands	12.0	17.7 (2014)	3.0 (2007)	5.9 (2014)	...	...	2	11
Micronesia, Fed. States of	12.3	14.7 (2014)	3.1	14.7 (2014)	...	...	22	80
Nauru	...	...	...	...	...	...	23	4
Palau	...	...	31.2 (2007)	47.6	...	...	9	5
Papua New Guinea	1.9	1.8 (2014)	3.8 (2006)	8.2 (2014)	...	...	238	492
Samoa	17.6	21.7	12.1	41.7	...	...	12	110
Solomon Islands	7.5	4.1	1.5	11.9	...	...	75	155
Timor-Leste	1.2	5.0 (2014)	...	5.3 (2014)	...	...	46	111
Tonga	24.1	21.2 (2013)	22.5	27.2 (2013)	...	...	9	50
Tuvalu	...	...	...	...	...	...	8	53
Vanuatu	19.6	22.6 (2014)	4.9	34.8 (2014)	...	...	78	57
Developed Member Economies								
Australia	30.7	29.1 (2014)	133.8	160.0 (2014)	99.7	99.2	...	...
Japan	34.6	34.1	124.3	127.6	96.4	97.5	...	...
New Zealand	35.0	29.6	59.1	70.9	99.4	99.9	...	...

... = data not available at cutoff date, 0.0 = magnitude is less than half of unit employed, ATMs = automated teller machines, Lao PDR = Lao People's Democratic Republic, SDG = Sustainable Development Goal.

a   Sum of total official flows commitments for Aid for Trade (by recipient) and total official flows disbursed for Aid for Trade (by recipient).

Sources: For Indicator 8.10.1: International Monetary Fund. IMF Financial Access Survey Database. http://data.imf.org/?sk=E5DCAB7E-A5CA-4892-A6EA-598B5463A34C (accessed 31 August 2016). For Indicators 8.10.2 and 8.a.1: United Nations. Sustainable Development Goals Indicators Global Database. http://unstats.un.org/sdgs/indicators/database/ (accessed 21 July 2016).

Build resilient infrastructure, promote inclusive and sustainable industrialization, and foster innovation

Table 4.5: **Selected Indicators for SDG 9 - Air Transport Passenger and Freight Volumes**
Develop quality, reliable, sustainable and resilient infrastructure, including regional and transborder infrastructure, to support economic development and human well-being, with a focus on affordable and equitable access for all

Regional Member	9.1.2 Freight Volume, by Air Transport (thousand metric tons)		9.1.2 Passenger Volume, by Air Transport (number of passengers)	
	2000	2014	2000	2014
Developing Member Economies				
Central and West Asia				
Afghanistan	10,514.0	134,368.0	149,705.0	2,144,208.9
Armenia	3,830.0	3,227.8 (2010)	298,232.0	704,753.0 (2010)
Azerbaijan	40,600.0	10,318.4	545,800.0	1,770,192.0
Georgia	1,100.0	208.6	117,521.0	196,589.0
Kazakhstan	5,011.0	16,184.5	461,283.0	4,918,574.1
Kyrgyz Republic	2,229.0	111.7	240,954.0	712,285.9
Pakistan	100,609.0	165,305.0	5,293,541.0	5,559,595.5
Tajikistan	1,274.0	153.0	168,006.0	312,685.8
Turkmenistan	4,960.0	995.9	1,283,780.0	57,281.4
Uzbekistan	19,570.0	40,235.7	1,744,510.0	2,545,935.0
East Asia				
China, People's Rep. of	1,884,521.0	5,907,105.9	61,891,807.0	390,878,784.0
Hong Kong, China	1,330,362.0	2,167,753.1	14,377,973.0	37,455,220.0
Korea, Rep. of	2,106,801.0	2,311,971.4	34,331,368.0	59,067,351.2
Mongolia	3,029.0	6,699.9	253,917.0	683,225.2
Taipei,China	1,338.2	2,221.7	48,407,000.0	55,357,000.0
South Asia				
Bangladesh	40,178.0	98,425.9	1,331,369.0	3,116,217.4
Bhutan	2,069.0 (2005)	768.7	34,425.0	302,158.1
India	244,208.0	686,779.4	17,303,059.0	82,751,554.9
Maldives	6,839.0	224.0 (2005)	315,108.0	81,945.0 (2005)
Nepal	9,136.0	10,954.8	643,332.0	517,541.9
Sri Lanka	55,365.0	114,208.1	1,755,567.0	4,756,137.6
Southeast Asia				
Brunei Darussalam	29,177.0 (2000)	21,225.7	863,547.0	1,087,699.8
Cambodia	5,408.0 (2005)	2,836.6	168,810.0 (2005)	1,089,788.3
Indonesia	181,432.0	747,177.4	9,916,365.0	94,504,086.1
Lao PDR	1,369.0	1,331.3	210,847.0	1,310,119.9
Malaysia	447,003.0	630,537.7	16,560,793.0	47,555,552.8
Myanmar	1,625.0	4,146.7	437,600.0	1,272,290.3
Philippines	143,122.0	165,326.5	5,756,288.0	30,932,992.8
Singapore	2,014,269.0	1,137,149.0	16,704,341.0	32,883,396.8
Thailand	512,489.0	649,035.0	17,392,091.0	44,039,176.2
Viet Nam	45,992.0	225,333.4	2,877,894.0	24,703,605.2
The Pacific				
Cook Islands	2,455.4 (2010)	3,548.0	77,557.6 (2010)	87,303.0
Fiji	18,678.0	28,658.0	586,043.0	1,248,767.9
Kiribati	...	...	...	...
Marshall Islands	206.0	297.0 (2005)	16,109.0	25,789.0 (2005)
Micronesia, Fed. States of	...	...	...	...
Nauru	799.0	4,757.0	160,587.0	34,576.8
Palau	...	...	...	...
Papua New Guinea	14,027.0	16,932.8	1,099,772.0	2,074,021.3
Samoa	1,198.0	53.8	164,142.0	76,946.4
Solomon Islands	582.0	1,044.9	75,262.0	330,451.6
Timor-Leste	...	...	...	...
Tonga	0.0	0.0 (2004)	51,615.0	75,416.0 (2004)
Tuvalu	...	...	...	...
Vanuatu	977.0	1,356.9	101,503.0	320,226.6
Developed Member Economies				
Australia	433,393.0	316,076.1	32,577,569.0	67,686,801.2
Japan	2,855,581.0	2,325,844.0	109,123,312.0	110,544,000.0
New Zealand	130,155.0	168,163.6	10,781,314.0	15,050,502.2

... = data not available at cutoff date, 0.0 = magnitude is less than half of unit employed, Lao PDR = Lao People's Democratic Republic, SDG = Sustainable Development Goal.

Sources:　United Nations. Sustainable Development Goals Indicators Global Database. http://unstats.un.org/sdgs/indicators/database/ (accessed 21 July 2016); for Taipei,China: Directorate-General of Budget, Accounting and Statistics. 2015. *Statistical Yearbook 2014.* Nantou City.

Sustainable Development Goals

Build resilient infrastructure, promote inclusive and sustainable industrialization, and foster innovation

Table 4.6:   **Selected Indicators for SDG 9 - Growth in Manufacturing**[a]
Promote inclusive and sustainable industrialization and, by 2030, significantly raise industry's share of employment and gross domestic product, in line with national circumstances, and double its share in least developed countries

Regional Member	9.2.1.a Manufacturing Value Added Share in GDP (%)		9.2.1.b Manufacturing Value Added per Capita (at constant 2010 $)		9.2.2 Manufacturing Employment as a Proportion of Total Employment (%)	
	2000	2015	2000	2015	2000	2013
Developing Member Economies						
Central and West Asia						
Afghanistan	17.2	11.2	45.1	75.2	20.9	18.0
Armenia	15.3	11.1	210.3	421.3	8.8	8.3
Azerbaijan	9.6	5.3	158.2	330.9	4.6	5.0
Georgia	9.5	11.7	127.2	396.8	5.9	4.4
Kazakhstan	13.0	10.3	594.1	1,150.4	7.6	6.4
Kyrgyz Republic	23.2	14.6	149.9	151.9	9.1	7.0
Pakistan	10.1	12.6	80.8	145.9	12.5	13.0
Tajikistan	27.2	17.3	114.0	147.3	6.3	3.8
Turkmenistan	12.8	14.1	300.2	980.0	17.3	21.8
Uzbekistan	25.3	18.4	204.3	355.2	16.9	16.9
East Asia						
China, People's Rep. of	28.6	32.8	490.6	2,025.3	12.2	11.9
Hong Kong, China	3.8	1.4	841.0	503.7	10.4	3.6
Korea, Rep. of	22.7	29.0	3,511.6	7,400.2	20.3	16.7
Mongolia	5.5	5.0	76.3	175.3	5.6	6.0
Taipei,China	24.6	23.0	3,613.2	4,725.2	…	…
South Asia						
Bangladesh	13.7	18.7	67.0	181.9	7.0	12.2
Bhutan	7.6	7.9	92.3	213.8	3.2	6.0
India	13.3	12.7	103.8	227.2	10.5	12.1
Maldives	5.3	3.0	225.8	275.4	21.8	9.7
Nepal	8.1	5.5	38.4	38.8	6.0	6.4
Sri Lanka	20.1	18.0	318.0	583.2	16.2	17.5
Southeast Asia						
Brunei Darussalam	14.1	12.5	4,574.0	3,832.1	5.3	5.2
Cambodia	11.5	16.9	49.0	171.6	7.0	10.7
Indonesia	26.7	24.6	543.7	898.1	13.0	13.3
Lao PDR	8.1	10.9	50.9	152.2	1.6	1.8
Malaysia	27.0	23.9	1,817.9	2,490.9	22.5	16.8
Myanmar	8.5	22.1	23.3	243.1	8.6	10.6
Philippines	23.7	22.5	381.9	587.8	10.0	8.3
Singapore	20.4	18.9	6,949.3	9,292.0	21.0	13.2
Thailand	28.6	28.3	994.8	1,628.0	13.6	13.9
Viet Nam	13.4	20.3	95.2	335.2	9.2	14.0
The Pacific						
Cook Islands	3.5	3.1	444.6	406.4	…	…
Fiji	12.8	12.1	439.1	500.0	8.3	8.5
Kiribati	5.0	5.1	90.5	83.1	…	…
Marshall Islands	1.9	1.7	48.2	60.7	…	…
Micronesia, Fed. States of	1.8	0.4 (2014)	…	…	…	…
Nauru	15.1	23.7	859.6	2,569.8	…	…
Palau	3.2	1.4	325.1	160.3	…	…
Papua New Guinea	5.8	5.7	70.2	111.3	1.1	1.1
Samoa	13.5	7.0	345.4	232.0	…	…
Solomon Islands	4.9	7.2	52.5	104.7	8.7	6.6
Timor-Leste	2.0	0.2	16.8	8.7	3.1	6.7
Tonga	7.1	6.3	234.8	234.6	…	…
Tuvalu	0.8	1.0	25.4	37.9	…	…
Vanuatu	4.1	4.0	117.3	113.5	…	…
Developed Member Economies						
Australia	9.4	6.1	4,642.7	3,797.6	11.8	7.7
Japan	17.5	18.8	7,082.9	8,382.3	14.3	16.0
New Zealand	14.0	10.5	4,109.8	3,803.2	14.1	9.9

… = data not available at cutoff date, GDP = gross domestic product, Lao PDR = Lao People's Democratic Republic, SDG = Sustainable Development Goal.

a   United Nations Statistics Division data used for indicators 9.2.1.a and 9.2.1.b were computed from the GDP, manufacturing value added, and population data published by the United Nations Industrial Development Organization (UNIDO) in the International Yearbook of Industrial Statistics. (http://www.unido.org/publications/flagship-publications/international-yearbook-of-industrial-statistics.html).

Sources: United Nations. Sustainable Development Goals Indicators Global Database. http://unstats.un.org/sdgs/indicators/database/ (accessed 21 July 2016); World Bank. World Development Indicators. http://databank.worldbank.org/data/reports.aspx?source=world-development-indicators (accessed 26 April 2016).

Build resilient infrastructure, promote inclusive and sustainable industrialization, and foster innovation

Table 4.7: **Selected Indicators for SDG 9 - Research and Development**
Enhance scientific research, upgrade the technological capabilities of industrial sectors in all countries, in particular developing countries, including, by 2030, encouraging innovation and substantially increasing the number of research and development workers per 1 million people and public and private research and development spending

Regional Member	9.5.1 Research and Expenditure as a Proportion of GDP (%)		9.5.2 Researchers (Full-Time Equivalent) (per million inhabitants)	
	2000	2014	Initial Year	Latest Year
Developing Member Economies				
Central and West Asia				
Afghanistan	...	...	...	...
Armenia	0.18	0.24 a	...	...
Azerbaijan	0.34	0.21	...	...
Georgia	0.22	0.10 b	562 (2013)	585 b (2014)
Kazakhstan	0.18	0.17 (2013)	405 (2007)	734 (2013)
Kyrgyz Republic	0.16	0.13	...	...
Pakistan	0.13	0.29 c (2013)	83 (2005)	167 c (2013)
Tajikistan	0.09 (2001)	0.12 (2013)	...	...
Turkmenistan	...	...	...	...
Uzbekistan	...	0.20	...	534 d (2011)
East Asia				
China, People's Rep. of	0.90	2.05	547 (2000)	1,113 (2014)
Hong Kong, China	0.46	0.73 (2013)	1,139 (2000)	3,136 (2013)
Korea, Rep. of	2.18	4.29	2,345 (2000)	6,899 (2014)
Mongolia	0.19	0.23 a	...	...
Taipei,China	...	...	...	...
South Asia				
Bangladesh	...	...	...	...
Bhutan	...	...	...	...
India	0.74	0.82 (2011)	110 (2000)	157 (2010)
Maldives	...	...	...	...
Nepal	0.05 (2008)	0.30 (2010)	61 (2002)	...
Sri Lanka	0.14	0.10 (2013)	135 (2000)	111 (2013)
Southeast Asia				
Brunei Darussalam	0.02 (2002)	0.04 (2004)	288 (2002)	286 (2004)
Cambodia	0.05 (2002)		18 (2002)	
Indonesia	0.07 e	0.08 (2013)	213 (2000)	90 (2009)
Lao PDR	0.04 (2002)	...	16 (2002)	...
Malaysia	0.47	1.26	274 (2000)	2,052 (2014)
Myanmar	0.11	0.16 (2002)	12 (2001)	17 (2002)
Philippines	0.14 (2002)	0.14 (2013)	71 (2003)	221 (2013)
Singapore	1.82	2.19	4,245 (2000)	6,665 (2013)
Thailand	0.24	0.48	279 (2001)	974 (2014)
Viet Nam	0.18 (2002)	0.19 (2011)	114 (2002)	...
The Pacific				
Cook Islands	...	...	...	...
Fiji	...	...	...	...
Kiribati	...	...	...	...
Marshall Islands	...	...	...	...
Micronesia, Fed. States of	...	...	...	...
Nauru	...	...	...	...
Palau	...	...	...	...
Papua New Guinea	...	...	...	...
Samoa	...	...	...	...
Solomon Islands	...	...	...	...
Timor-Leste	...	...	...	...
Tonga	...	...	...	...
Tuvalu	...	...	...	...
Vanuatu	...	...	...	...
Developed Member Economies				
Australia	1.58	2.20 f (2013)	3,454 (2000)	4,531 (2010)
Japan	3.00	3.58	5,151 (2000)	5,386 (2014)
New Zealand	1.10 (2001)	1.17 (2013)	2,644 (2001)	4,009 (2013)

... = data not available at cutoff date, GDP = gross domestic product, Lao PDR = Lao People's Democratic Republic, SDG = Sustainable Development Goal.

a Partial data only.
b Higher education only.
c Excluding business enterprise and private nonprofit.
d Overestimated or based on overestimated data.
e Partial data taken from a regional publication.
f National estimation or based on national estimation.

Source: United Nations Educational, Scientific and Cultural Organization Institute for Statistics. Data Centre. http://www.uis.unesco.org/DataCentre/Pages/default.aspx (accessed August 2016).

Build resilient infrastructure, promote inclusive and sustainable industrialization, and foster innovation

Table 4.8: **Selected Indicators for SDG 9 - Official International Support and Value Added of Medium and High-Tech Industry**
Facilitate sustainable and resilient infrastructure development in developing countries through enhanced financial, technological and technical support to African countries, least developed countries, landlocked developing countries and small island developing States

Support domestic technology development, research and innovation in developing countries, including by ensuring a conducive policy environment for, inter alia, industrial diversification and value addition to commodities

Regional Member	9.a.1 Total Official Flows for Infrastructure (constant 2014 $ million)		9.b.1 Proportion of Medium and High-Tech Industry Value Added in Total Value Added[c] (%)	
	2000[a]	2014[b]	2000	2013
Developing Member Economies	**11,916.9**	**21,144.3**		
Central and West Asia	**1,243.6**	**5,724.8**		
Afghanistan	0.4	556.1	...	...
Armenia	136.6	207.1	0.1	0.0
Azerbaijan	23.3	504.4	0.2	0.1
Georgia	144.0	367.4	0.2	0.2
Kazakhstan	244.2	1,274.9	0.1	0.2
Kyrgyz Republic	98.4	144.5	0.1	0.0
Pakistan	526.5	2,180.9	0.3	0.3
Tajikistan	17.7	155.9	0.0	0.0
Turkmenistan	1.8	23.8	...	...
Uzbekistan	50.8	309.8	...	...
East Asia	**2,592.5**	**2,340.5**		
China, People's Rep. of	2,467.6	2,131.2	0.4	0.4
Hong Kong, China	...	...	0.4	0.3
Korea, Rep. of	...	...	0.6	0.6
Mongolia	124.9	209.3	0.0	0.1
Taipei,China	...	...	...	...
South Asia	**4,273.6**	**6,272.9**		
Bangladesh	701.9	1,041.1	0.2	0.1
Bhutan	34.0	71.3	...	...
India	3,313.7	4,352.7	0.4	0.4
Maldives	13.0	4.2	...	...
Nepal	124.9	220.7	0.1	0.1
Sri Lanka	86.1	582.9	0.1	0.1
Southeast Asia	**3,517.3**	**6,318.8**		
Brunei Darussalam	...	...	0.0	0.0
Cambodia	48.0	212.6	–	–
Indonesia	120.1	1,305.6	0.4	0.4
Lao PDR	79.9	71.4	...	...
Malaysia	575.8	10.7	0.5	0.4
Myanmar	0.0	104.9	...	...
Philippines	813.0	526.6	0.4	0.4
Singapore	...	...	0.8	0.8
Thailand	705.6	400.4	0.4	0.4
Viet Nam	1,175.0	3,686.6	0.2	0.3
The Pacific	**290.1**	**487.4**		
Cook Islands	1.1	13.5	...	...
Fiji	0.2	10.0	0.1	0.1
Kiribati	1.7	38.6	...	...
Marshall Islands	3.1	38.4	...	...
Micronesia, Fed. States of	4.8	6.2	...	...
Nauru	0.0 (2002)	1.5	...	...
Palau	0.2	3.6	...	...
Papua New Guinea	245.6	196.8	0.1	0.1
Samoa	3.2	26.7	...	...
Solomon Islands	10.4	30.2	...	...
Timor-Leste	2.9	52.9	...	...
Tonga	5.6	29.3	0.2	0.2
Tuvalu	0.1 (2002)	16.6	...	...
Vanuatu	11.2	23.0	...	...
Developed Member Economies	**...**	**...**		
Australia	...	...	0.3	0.3
Japan	...	...	0.5	0.6
New Zealand	...	...	0.1	0.2

... = data not available at cutoff date, – = magnitude equals zero, 0.0 = magnitude is less than half of unit employed, Lao PDR = Lao People's Democratic Republic, SDG = Sustainable Development Goal.

a   Commitments.
b   Gross disbursements.
c   Estimates are modeled by the United Nations Statistics Division.

Source: United Nations. Sustainable Development Goals Indicators Global Database. http://unstats.un.org/sdgs/indicators/database/ (accessed July 2016).

Sustainable Development Goals

Table 4.9: **Selected Indicators for SDG 10 - Household Income and Consumption Growth**
By 2030, progressively achieve and sustain income growth of the bottom 40 percent of the population at a rate higher than the national average

Regional Member	10.1.1.a Growth Rates of Household Expenditure or Income per Capita among the Bottom 40% of the Population[a] (%)	10.1.1.b Growth Rates of Household Expenditure or Income per Capita[a] (%)
Developing Member Economies		
Central and West Asia		
Afghanistan	...	...
Armenia	–1.5 (2008–2013)	–1.1 (2008–2013)
Azerbaijan	...	...
Georgia	2.9 (2008–2013)	2.6 (2008–2013)
Kazakhstan	8.9 (2009–2013)	7.6 (2009–2013)
Kyrgyz Republic	–0.1 (2008–2012)	–2.4 (2008–2012)
Pakistan	3.8 (2004–2010)	2.7 (2004–2010)
Tajikistan	...	...
Turkmenistan	...	...
Uzbekistan	...	...
East Asia		
China, People's Rep. of	7.2 (2005–2010)	7.9 (2005–2010)
Hong Kong, China	...	...
Korea, Rep. of	...	...
Mongolia	...	...
Taipei,China	...	...
South Asia		
Bangladesh	1.7 (2005–2010)	1.4 (2005–2010)
Bhutan	6.5 (2007–2012)	6.5 (2007–2012)
India	3.2 (2004–2011)	3.7 (2004–2011)
Maldives	...	...
Nepal	7.5 (2003–2010)	4.1 (2003–2010)
Sri Lanka	2.2 (2006–2012)	1.7 (2006–2012)
Southeast Asia		
Brunei Darussalam	...	...
Cambodia	8.5 (2007–2012)	4.1 (2007–2012)
Indonesia	3.8 (2011–2014)	3.4 (2011–2014)
Lao PDR	1.2 (2007–2012)	2.0 (2007–2012)
Malaysia	...	...
Myanmar		
Philippines	1.1 (2006–2012)	0.4 (2006–2012)
Singapore	...	...
Thailand	4.8 (2008–2012)	3.9 (2008–2012)
Viet Nam	6.2 (2004–2010)	7.8 (2004–2010)
The Pacific		
Cook Islands	...	...
Fiji	...	...
Kiribati	...	...
Marshall Islands	...	...
Micronesia, Fed. States of	...	...
Nauru	...	...
Palau	...	...
Papua New Guinea	...	...
Samoa	...	...
Solomon Islands	...	...
Timor-Leste	...	...
Tonga	...	...
Tuvalu	...	...
Vanuatu	...	...
Developed Member Economies		
Australia	4.4 (2003–2010)	4.7 (2003–2010)
Japan	...	...
New Zealand	...	...

... = data not available at cutoff date, Lao PDR = Lao People's Democratic Republic, SDG = Sustainable Development Goal.

a Based on real mean per capita consumption or income measured at purchasing power parity (PPP) using PovcalNet (http://iresearch.worldbank.org/PovcalNet). Data for Bangladesh, Cambodia, and the Lao PDR are expressed in 2005 PPP terms, while the data for the rest of the reporting member economies are expressed in 2011 PPP terms. Data reported are based on consumption, except for Australia, which collects income data.

Source: World Bank. Global Database of Shared Prosperity. http://www.worldbank.org/en/topic/poverty/brief/global-database-of-shared-prosperity (accessed 26 August 2016).

Peace

To foster peaceful, just, and inclusive societies which are free from fear and violence. There can be no sustainable development without peace and no peace without sustainable development.

Snapshots

- Globally, approximately 5.3 people per 100,000 population are victims of intentional homicide. The intentional homicide rate of 2.5 for every 100,000 people in Asia and the Pacific is one of the lowest around the world.

- The proportion of births registered with a civil authority are 100% among developed economies and nearly 100% in most economies of Central and West Asia. High proportions exceeding 90% are also noted in South Asia's Bhutan and the Maldives. In Southeast Asia, more than two-thirds of the births are registered with a civil authority, while in the Pacific, Kiribati, the Marshall Islands, and Tonga have birth registration rates that exceed 90%.

Armed conflict and violence could have a long-lasting disruptive impact on the lives of people. For instance, current estimates suggest that roughly 50 million people are displaced by violence and armed conflict around the world (UNHCR 2014). The Sustainable Development Agenda recognizes that peace is an important pillar of sustainable development. Hence, SDG 16 aims to promote peace and arrest endless cycles of violence by strengthening institutions' capacity to uphold political stability and the rule of law. This section examines several indicators that underpin SDG 16 where data are available for ADB member economies.

SDG 16: Promote Peaceful and Inclusive Societies for Sustainable Development, Provide Access to Justice for All and Build Effective, Accountable, and Inclusive Institutions at All Levels

Number of victims of intentional homicide per 100,000 population. Globally, approximately 5.3 people per 100,000 population are victims of intentional homicide. The intentional homicide rate of 2.5 for every 100,000 people in Asia and the Pacific

is one of the lowest around the world.[2] In South Asia, the incidence of victims of intentional homicide is lower than five per 100,000 people in all economies. Some of the economies with the lowest incidence (less than one per 100,000 population) of victims of intentional homicide are also in the region including Brunei Darussalam; the People's Republic of China (PRC); Hong Kong, China; Indonesia; Japan; the Republic of Korea; the Maldives; New Zealand; and Singapore (Figure 5.1). Some of the highest incidences, however, are also in the region. These include Tuvalu (20.3), Papua New Guinea (10.8), the Philippines (9.9), Pakistan (7.8), Mongolia (7.5), Kiribati (7.5), Kazakhstan (7.4), the Lao People's Democratic Republic (Lao PDR) (7.1), and Afghanistan (6.6).

Proportion of children under 5 years of age whose birth have been registered with a civil authority. According to the metadata of UNSD's SDG Indicators Global Database, birth registration is a primary step toward securing a person's recognition before the law. Absence of such formal documentation may limit a

---

2   The regional aggregate is population-weighted average estimated using number of victims of intentional homicide per 100,000 population. The data for population are from the United Nations Office of Drugs and Crime and United Nations Department of Economic and Social Affairs Population Division's World Population Prospects: The 2015 Revision.

Figure 5.1: Number of Victims of Intentional Homicide per 100,000 Population, Latest Year

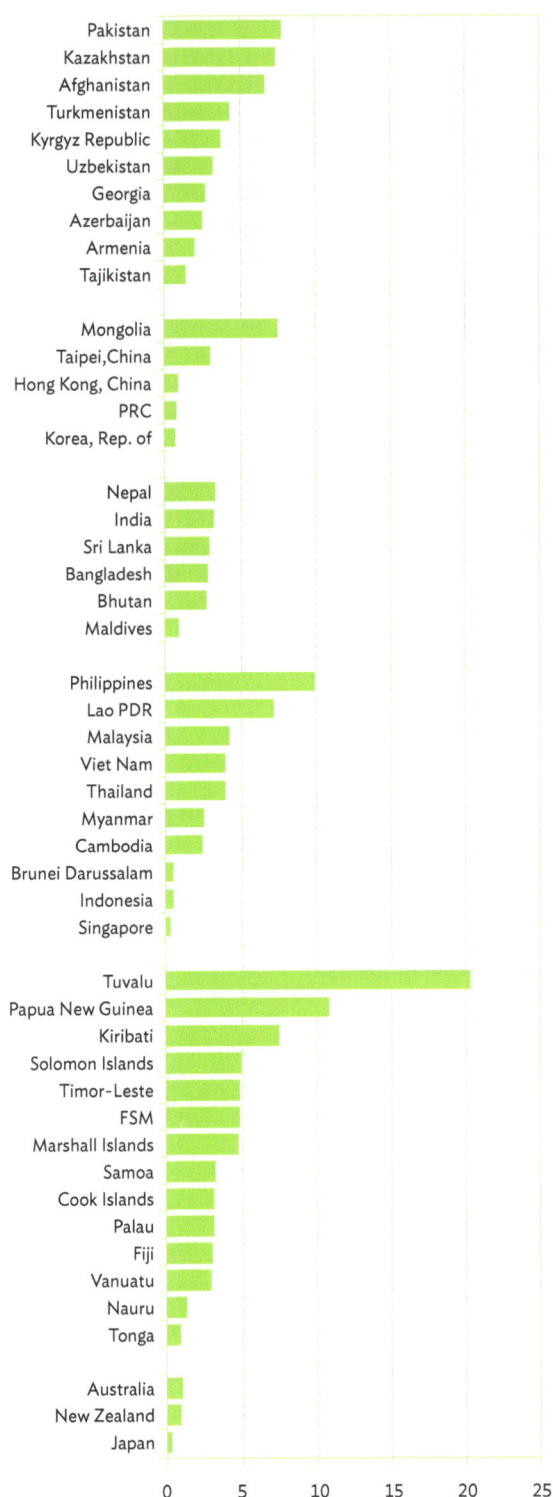

FSM = Federated States of Micronesia, Lao PDR = Lao People's Democratic Republic, PRC = People's Republic of China.
Source: Table 5.1.

person's access to health care, education, or labor market services and, consequently, undermine the inclusiveness of institutions. In recognition of this important role, one of the targets under SDG 16 is to provide a legal identity for all, including birth registration.

Figure 5.2 presents the estimates of the proportion of children under 5 years of age whose births have been registered with a civil authority for economies with data for 2010 or later years. Birth registration rates are 100% among developed economies, and nearly 100% in Central and West Asian economies (except Afghanistan). Among South Asian economies, the Maldives and Bhutan have birth registration rates that exceed 90%. In Southeast Asia, the Philippines, Thailand, and Viet Nam have birth registration rates that also exceed 90%. A high birth registration rate is also recorded in Tonga of the Pacific. Table 5.1 presents estimates for earlier years.

Proportion of population subjected to physical, psychological, or sexual violence in the previous 12 months. Figure 5.3 shows the incidence of sexual violence per 100,000 population based on latest data for each economy in Asia and the Pacific. The Maldives (163.2), Australia (87.5), and New Zealand (83.2) have the highest incidence. Economies with the lowest incidence (less than 2 per 100,000 population) are Myanmar (0.7), the Kyrgyz Republic (1.3), Thailand (1.8), and the Philippines (1.9).

Equity and Other Issues

Armed conflict and violence lead to a multitude of domestic problems. For instance, in a number of conflict-ridden countries, it is almost impossible to reduce extreme poverty significantly without arresting the endless cycles of armed violence and insecurity. However, these are not purely domestic issues as they transcend the borders of conflict-affected countries. Hence, it is important for conflict-unaffected countries to actively participate in addressing the root causes of violence and insecurity. Additionally, they should also actively facilitate multilateral action to ensure that the world's most marginalized segments have equal access to justice and security.

Figure 5.2: Proportion of Children under 5 Years of Age Whose Births Have Been Registered with a Civil Authority, Latest Year
(%)

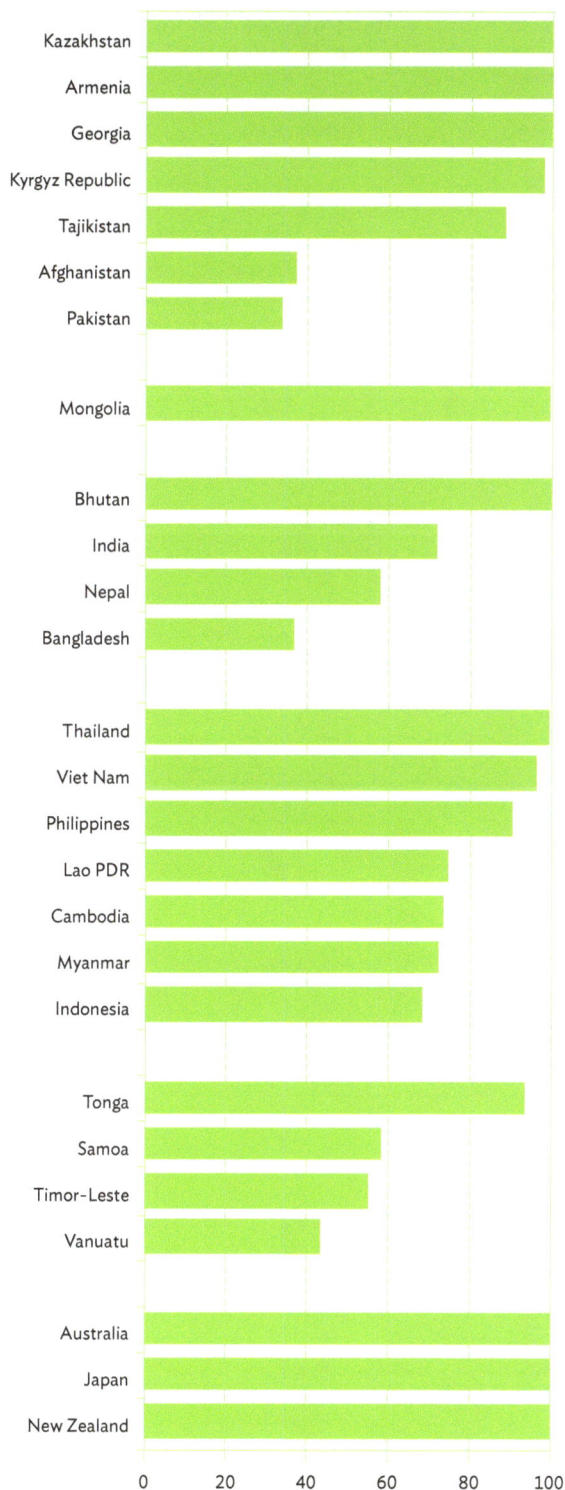

Lao PDR = Lao People's Democratic Republic.
Note: Only economies with recent estimates (2010 and later) are included.
Source: Table 5.1.

Figure 5.3: Incidence of Sexual Violence (based on number of police-recorded offences) at the National Level, Latest Year
(per 100,000 population)

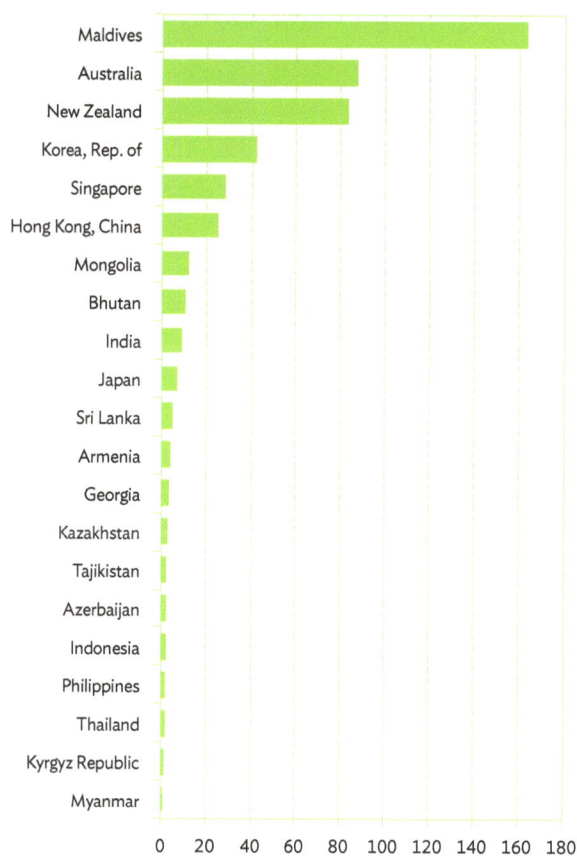

Notes: Only economies with recent estimates (2010 and later) are included. "Sexual violence" means rape and sexual assault, including sexual offences against children. Data supplied by countries may not exactly reflect the definition provided by United Nations Office of Drugs and and Crime (UNODC).
Source: UNODC. Homicide Database. https://data.unodc.org/ (accessed 11 October 2016).

Data Gaps

Data needed to monitor the progress with respect to SDG 16 are very sparse and are not collected regularly. While national governments and specialized intergovernmental institutions have important roles in addressing such data gaps, nongovernment institutions such as civil society organizations and research institutes could play a key role in providing supplementary data (SDSN 2016).

Promote peaceful and inclusive societies for sustainable development, provide access to justice for all, and build effective, accountable, and inclusive institutions at all levels

Table 5.1: **Selected Indicators for SDG 16 - Crime and Birth Registration**
Significantly reduce all forms of violence and related death rates everywhere

By 2030, provide legal identity for all, including birth registration

Regional Member	16.1.1 Number of Victims of Intentional Homicide (per 100,000 population)		16.9.1 Proportion of Children under 5 Years of Age Whose Births Have Been Registered with a Civil Authority (%)	
	2000	2012	2006	2014
Developing Member Economies				
Central and West Asia				
Afghanistan	4.1 (2009)	6.6	6.0 (2003)	37.4 (2011)
Armenia	2.7 (2004)	2.0 (2013)	96.0 (2005)	99.6 (2010)
Azerbaijan	2.8	2.5 (2014)	93.6	…
Georgia	5.0	2.7 (2014)	92.0 (2005)	99.6 (2013)
Kazakhstan	15.5	7.4 (2013)	99.0	99.7 (2011)
Kyrgyz Republic	8.7	3.7 (2014)	95.7	97.7
Pakistan	6.4	7.8	26.6 (2007)	33.6 (2013)
Tajikistan	3.1 (2006)	1.4 (2013)	88.0 (2005)	88.4 (2012)
Turkmenistan	…	4.3	95.5	…
Uzbekistan	…	3.2	99.9	…
East Asia				
China, People's Rep. of	2.0 (2002)	0.8	…	…
Hong Kong, China	0.6	0.9 (2013)	…	…
Korea, Rep. of	0.9 (2011)	0.7 (2014)	…	…
Mongolia	13.9 (2003)	7.5 (2014)	98.0 (2005)	99.3 (2013)
Taipei,China	5.1	3.0 (2011)	…	…
South Asia				
Bangladesh	2.5	2.8 (2014)	10.0	37.0 (2013)
Bhutan	2.0 (2008)	2.7 (2014)	…	99.9 (2010)
India	4.5	3.2 (2014)	41.1	71.9
Maldives	0.1 (2007)	0.9 (2013)	73.0 (2000)	92.5 (2009)
Nepal	2.7	3.3	35.0	58.1
Sri Lanka	6.8 (2003)	2.9 (2013)	97.2	…
Southeast Asia				
Brunei Darussalam	0.9 (2003)	0.5 (2013)	…	…
Cambodia	3.3 (2001)	2.4	66.4 (2005)	73.3
Indonesia	1.0	0.5 (2014)	55.0 (2002)	68.5 (2013)
Lao PDR	…	7.1	72.0	74.8 (2012)
Malaysia	2.2 (2001)	4.3	…	…
Myanmar	2.1 (2001)	2.5	64.9 (2003)	72.4 (2010)
Philippines[a]	7.4	9.9 (2014)	83.0 (2000)	90.2 (2010)
Singapore	0.9	0.3 (2014)	…	…
Thailand	8.2	3.9 (2014)	99.5	99.4 (2012)
Viet Nam	1.2 (2001)	4.0	92.7 (2005)	96.1
The Pacific				
Cook Islands	…	3.1	…	…
Fiji	2.6 (2007)	3.0	…	…
Kiribati	7.1 (2008)	7.5	92.0 (2008)	93.5 (2009)
Marshall Islands	…	4.7	…	95.9 (2007)
Micronesia, Fed. States of	…	4.8	…	…
Nauru	…	1.3	82.6 (2007)	…
Palau	…	3.1	…	…
Papua New Guinea	8.7	10.8	…	…
Samoa	8.7 (2009)	3.2 (2013)	47.7 (2009)	58.6
Solomon Islands	4.4 (2004)	4.9	80.0 (2007)	…
Timor-Leste	2.4 (2004)	4.9	53.0 (2003)	55.2 (2010)
Tonga	1.0	1.0	…	93.4 (2012)
Tuvalu	– (2002)	20.3	49.9 (2007)	…
Vanuatu	…	2.9	43.0 (2007)	43.4 (2013)
Developed Member Economies				
Australia	1.9	1.0 (2014)	100.0 (2012)	100.0 (2015)
Japan	0.6 (2003)	0.3 (2014)	100.0 (2012)	100.0 (2015)
New Zealand	1.3	0.9 (2014)	100.0 (2012)	100.0 (2015)

… = data not available at cutoff date, – = magnitude equals zero, Lao PDR = Lao People's Democratic Republic, SDG = Sustainable Development Goal.

a   In 2009, the Philippine National Police implemented a new crime reporting system wherein crime data for 2009 were set as the baseline for future research, study, and comparison. Thus, crime statistics in 2009 cannot be compared with those data obtained in the previous years (2008 and earlier) since the parameters were no longer the same.

Sources: For Indicator 16.1.1: For initial year and economies not available in United Nations (UN) SDG Indicators Global Database, data from United Nations Office of Drugs and Crime. Homicide Database. https://data.unodc.org/ (accessed 19 August 2016); for latest year, data from United Nations. Sustainable Development Goals Indicators Global Database. http://unstats.un.org/sdgs/indicators/database/ (accessed 21 July 2016). For Indicator 16.9.1: For initial year and economies not available in UN SDG Indicators Global Database, World Bank. World Development Indicators. http://databank.worldbank.org/data/reports.aspx?source=world-development-indicators (accessed 19 August 2016); for latest year, data from United Nations. Sustainable Development Goals Indicators Global Database. http://unstats.un.org/sdgs/indicators/database/ (accessed 21 July 2016).

Partnership

To mobilize the means required to implement this agenda through a revitalized Global Partnership for Sustainable Development, based on a spirit of strengthened global solidarity, focused in particular on the needs of the poorest and most vulnerable and with the participation of all countries, all stakeholders, and all people.

Snapshots

- The majority of the member economies experienced higher volumes of remittances in proportion to total GDP over the past 15 years, while 27 economies had an increase that exceeds 0.05 percentage points per year.

- Debt service as a proportion of exports of goods and services declined between 2000 and 2015 in 23 economies including India, Kazakhstan, the Kyrgyz Republic, and Papua New Guinea.

- Within Asia and the Pacific, the highest net official development assistance in 2014 were provided to Afghanistan, Viet Nam, Pakistan, India, and Bangladesh.

- In 19 out of 35 economies for which data are available in Asia and the Pacific, national statistical plans are fully funded and under implementation.

Attaining the SDGs by 2030 requires a strong commitment to global partnership and cooperation among all players. For low-income economies, official development assistance (ODA) will continue to be a major resource given their limited capacities to raise public resources domestically. Furthermore, ODA could be catalytic in crowding in other sources and building capacities. This section presents available data on ODA and other indicators of SDG 17 for ADB regional member economies.

SDG 17: Strengthen the Means of Implementation and Revitalize the Global Partnership for Sustainable Development

Volume of remittances as a proportion of total GDP. Latest data available show that the volume of remittances as a proportion of total GDP is highest in Nepal (32.2%), Tajikistan (28.8%), Tonga (26.3%), the Kyrgyz Republic (25.7%), and Samoa (17.6%) (Figure 6.1). The largest increase within the 15-year period (anytime between 2000 and 2015) was noted

in Nepal (2.0 percentage points per year), followed by Tajikistan (1.7 percentage points per year), and the Kyrgyz Republic (1.7 percentage points per year). On the other hand, the volume of remittances in proportion to GDP declined in Australia, Cambodia, Kazakhstan, Kiribati, the Republic of Korea, the Marshall Islands, New Zealand, Papua New Guinea, Thailand, Tonga, Tuvalu, and Vanuatu. Among the top 10 economies with data in 2014 or 2015, three economies registered a reduction in the volume of remittances: Tuvalu by 1.3 percentage points per year, the Marshall Islands by 0.36 percentage points per year, and Tonga by 0.4 percentage points per year.

Debt service as a proportion of exports of goods and services. Figure 6.2 shows the distribution of debt service relative to exports of goods and services. In the majority of the economies with available data, the numbers show that the proportion of debt service declined in the past 15 years. The annual reduction exceeded 0.5 percentage points in India, Kazakhstan, the Kyrgyz Republic, and Papua New Guinea. On the

Figure 6.1: Volume of Remittances as a Proportion of Total Gross Domestic Product (%)

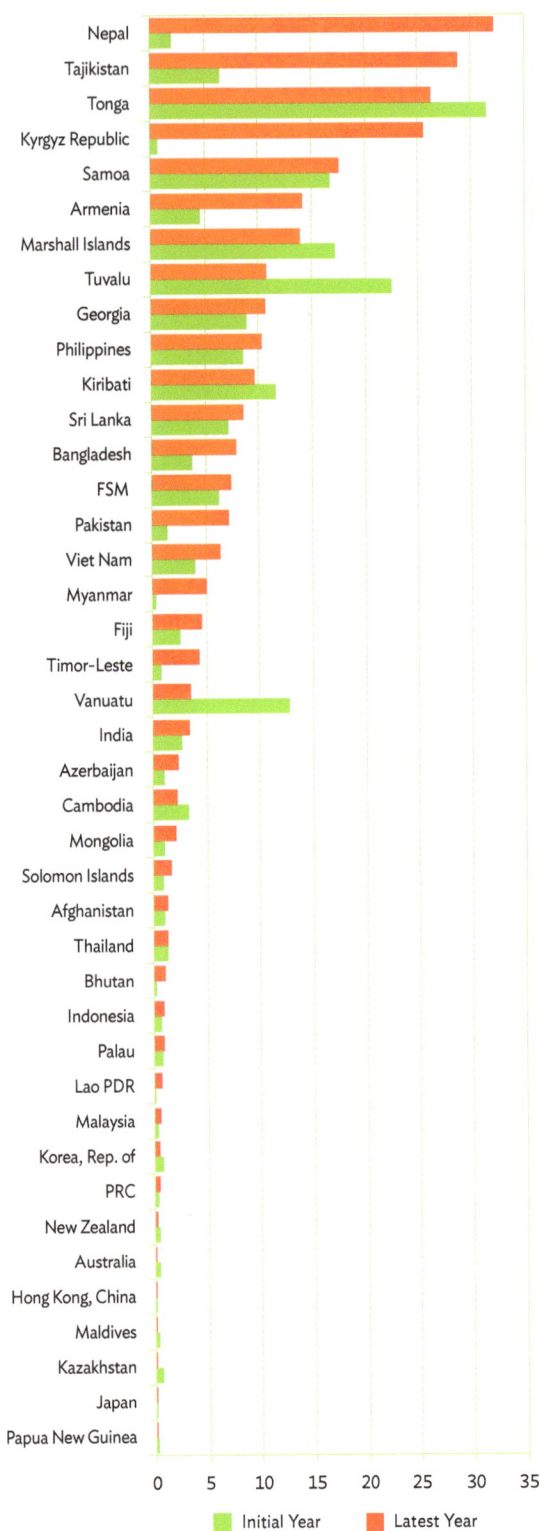

Figure 6.2: Debt Service (% of exports of goods and services)

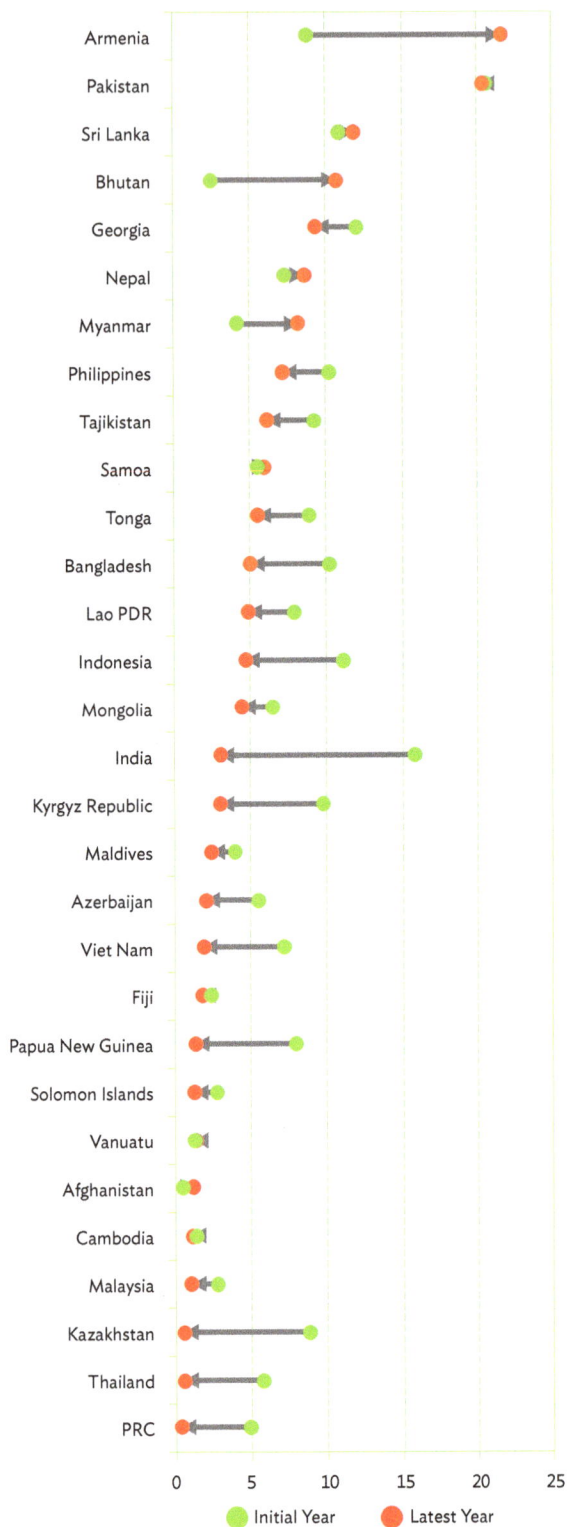

FSM = Federated States of Micronesia, Lao PDR = Lao People's Democratic Republic, PRC = People's Republic of China.
Source: Table 6.1.

Lao PDR = Lao People's Democratic Republic, PRC = People's Republic of China.
Source: Table 6.1.

other hand, it increased by more than 0.5 percentage points per year in Armenia and Bhutan. The five economies with highest proportion of debt service as a proportion of exports are Armenia (21.6%), Pakistan (20.3%), Sri Lanka (11.9%), Bhutan (10.7%), and Georgia (9.4%).

Net official development assistance. Within Asia and the Pacific, the highest net official development assistance in 2014 were provided to Afghanistan, Viet Nam, Pakistan, India and Bangladesh.[3]

Availability of National Statistical Plan. National statistical plans provide a strategy for an integrated development of a national statistical system. In about half of the 35 economies for which data are available from UNSD's SDG Indicators Global Database for 2015, national statistical plans were fully funded and under implementation. For a few economies, no such plan existed in 2015 while for others, national statistical plans have either expired or were awaiting adoption. Table 6.3 summarizes the availability of national statistical plans in economies of Asia and the Pacific based on latest data available.

Equity and Other Issues

While ODA flows from developed to developing countries comprised the majority of the development assistance flows during the MDG era, ODA flows between developing countries are likely to increase in the coming years. This type of ODA flow could play a key role in crafting better public policies for social inclusion that are contextualized to developing economies. Nevertheless, the sustainable development agenda still needs to be financed from a more innovative and diverse range of sources combining public, private, and joint financing that raise funds both internally and externally.

Data Gaps

Indicators for various targets under the theme of partnership are not available; when they are, they are sparse and not regularly updated. Difficulty in monitoring progress with respect to SDG 17 may also arise due to the lack of quantitative targets in some areas.

---

3   Details are provided in Regional Table 4.16.

Strengthen the means of implementation and revitalize the Global Partnership for Sustainable Development

Table 6.1: **Selected Indicators for SDG 17 - Development Financing**
Mobilize additional financial resources for developing countries from multiple sources

Assist developing countries in attaining long-term debt sustainability through coordinated policies aimed at fostering debt financing, debt relief and debt restructuring, as appropriate, and address the external debt of highly indebted poor countries to reduce debt distress

Regional Member	17.3.2 Volume of Remittances in US Dollars (as a proportion of total GDP)		17.4.1 Debt Service (as a proportion of exports of goods and services)	
	2000	Latest Year	2000	2013
Developing Member Economies				
Central and West Asia				
Afghanistan	1.0 (2008)	1.3 (2014)	0.5 (2005)	1.2
Armenia	4.6	14.1 (2015)	8.8	21.6
Azerbaijan	1.1	2.4 (2015)	5.5	2.1
Georgia	9.0	10.6 (2015)	12.1	9.4
Kazakhstan	0.7	0.1 (2014)	8.8	0.6
Kyrgyz Republic	0.7	25.7 (2015)	9.8	3.0
Pakistan	1.5	7.2 (2015)	20.8	20.3
Tajikistan	6.4 (2002)	28.8 (2015)	9.2 (2002)	6.2 (2012)
Turkmenistan	...	...	...	...
Uzbekistan	...	...	...	...
East Asia				
China, People's Rep. of	0.4	0.4 (2015)	4.9	0.3
Hong Kong, China	0.1	0.1 (2015)	...	...
Korea, Rep. of	0.9	0.5 (2015)	...	...
Mongolia	1.1	2.1 (2014)	6.5	4.5
Taipei,China	...	...	...	...
South Asia				
Bangladesh	3.7	7.9 (2015)	10.2	5.1
Bhutan	0.3 (2006)	1.0 (2015)	2.5 (2006)	10.7
India	2.7	3.4 (2014)	15.8	3.1
Maldives	0.4	0.1 (2015)	4.0	2.5
Nepal	2.0	32.2 (2015)	7.3	8.6
Sri Lanka	7.1	8.5 (2015)	10.9	11.9
Southeast Asia				
Brunei Darussalam	...	...	...	...
Cambodia	3.3	2.2 (2014)	1.4	1.1
Indonesia	0.7	1.0 (2014)	11.1	4.7
Lao PDR	0.0	0.8 (2015)	7.9	4.9
Malaysia	0.4	0.6 (2015)	2.8	1.1
Myanmar	0.4 (2012)	5.0 (2015)	4.2	8.2
Philippines	8.6	10.3 (2015)	10.2	7.2
Singapore	...	...	...	...
Thailand	1.3	1.3 (2015)	5.8	0.5
Viet Nam	4.0	6.3 (2011)	7.2	1.9
The Pacific				
Cook Islands	...	...	...	...
Fiji	2.6	4.6 (2014)	2.4	1.8
Kiribati	11.6 (2006)	9.6 (2014)	...	...
Marshall Islands	17.2 (2005)	14.0 (2014)	...	...
Micronesia, Fed. States of	6.3 (2009)	7.3 (2014)	...	...
Nauru	...	...	...	...
Palau	0.8 (2005)	0.9 (2014)	...	...
Papua New Guinea	0.2	0.1 (2014)	8.0	1.4 (2012)
Samoa	16.7	17.6 (2014)	5.5 (2004)	6.1
Solomon Islands	1.0	1.6 (2015)	2.8	1.3
Timor-Leste	0.8 (2006)	4.4 (2015)	...	...
Tonga	31.5 (2001)	26.3 (2014)	8.9 (2001)	5.6 (2012)
Tuvalu	22.6 (2005)	10.7 (2014)	...	...
Vanuatu	12.7	3.5 (2014)	1.4	1.2
Developed Member Economies				
Australia	0.5	0.2 (2015)	...	...
Japan	0.0	0.1 (2015)	...	...
New Zealand	0.5	0.2 (2015)	...	...

... = data not available at cutoff date, 0.0 = magnitude is less than half of unit employed, Lao PDR = Lao People's Democratic Republic, SDG = Sustainable Development Goal.

Sources: United Nations. Sustainable Development Goals Indicators Global Database. http://unstats.un.org/sdgs/indicators/database/ (accessed 21 July 2016); World Bank. World Development Indicators. http://databank.worldbank.org/data/reports.aspx?source=world-development-indicators (accessed 3 September 2016).

Strengthen the means of implementation and revitalize the Global Partnership for Sustainable Development

Table 6.2:   **Selected Indicators for SDG 17 - Access to Technology and Data Communications**
Fully operationalize the technology bank and science, technology and innovation capacity-building mechanism for least developed countries by 2017 and enhance the use of enabling technology, in particular information and communications technology

Regional Member	17.6.2 Fixed Internet Broadband Subscriptions per 1,000 Inhabitants[a]	
	Initial Year	2015
Developing Member Economies		
Central and West Asia		
Afghanistan	0.01 (2004)	0.05
Armenia	0.00 (2001)	95.78
Azerbaijan	0.12 (2002)	197.60
Georgia	0.09 (2001)	146.35
Kazakhstan	0.07 (2003)	130.49
Kyrgyz Republic	0.01 (2002)	37.06
Pakistan	0.09 (2005)	9.53
Tajikistan	0.00 (2003)	0.70
Turkmenistan	0.02 (2008)	0.56
Uzbekistan	0.11 (2003)	35.66
East Asia		
China, People's Rep. of	0.02 (2000)	185.61
Hong Kong, China	65.02 (2000)	319.36
Korea, Rep. of	84.17 (2000)	402.50
Mongolia	0.02 (2001)	71.17
Taipei,China	10.44 (2000)	242.60
South Asia		
Bangladesh	0.30 (2007)	24.10
Bhutan	2.98 (2008)	35.55
India	0.05 (2001)	13.35
Maldives	0.67 (2002)	64.74
Nepal	0.04 (2006)	10.64
Sri Lanka	0.02 (2001)	31.00
Southeast Asia		
Brunei Darussalam	5.59 (2001)	79.95
Cambodia	0.00 (2002)	5.33
Indonesia	0.02 (2000)	10.89
Lao PDR	0.00 (2003)	5.19
Malaysia	0.17 (2001)	89.50
Myanmar	0.00 (2005)	3.50
Philippines	0.13 (2001)	33.99
Singapore	17.61 (2000)	264.50
Thailand	0.03 (2001)	92.42
Viet Nam	0.01 (2002)	81.38
The Pacific		
Cook Islands	– (2001)	130.90 (2013)
Fiji	8.51 (2005)	14.26
Kiribati	3.56 (2005)	1.11
Marshall Islands	24.39 (2013)	18.87
Micronesia, Fed. States of	0.06 (2003)	31.37
Nauru	...	94.76 (2010)
Palau	3.74 (2004)	57.49
Papua New Guinea	0.46 (2008)	1.97
Samoa	0.18 (2004)	11.00
Solomon Islands	0.44 (2004)	2.43
Timor-Leste	0.01 (2003)	0.88
Tonga	0.11 (2002)	18.89
Tuvalu	5.18 (2004)	100.85
Vanuatu	0.08 (2003)	16.28
Developed Member Economies		
Australia	6.30 (2001)	278.52
Japan	6.80 (2000)	304.87
New Zealand	1.21 (2000)	315.46

... = data not available at cutoff date, 0.00 = magnitude is less than half of unit employed, – = magnitude equals zero, Lao PDR = Lao People's Democratic Republic, SDG = Sustainable Development Goal.

a   The original indicator refers to "Fixed Internet Broadband Subscriptions per 100 Inhabitants".

Sources: United Nations. Sustainable Development Goals Indicators Global Database. http://unstats.un.org/sdgs/indicators/database/ (accessed 21 July 2016); International Telecommunication Union. World Telecommunication/ICT Indicators Database. http://www.itu.int/en/ITU-D/Statistics/Pages/stat/default.aspx (accessed 6 June 2016).

Strengthen the means of implementation and revitalize the Global Partnership for Sustainable Development

Table 6.3:   **Selected Indicators for SDG 17 - Availability of National Statistical Plan**
Enhance capacity-building support to developing countries, including for least developed countries and small island developing States, to increase significantly the availability of high-quality, timely and reliable data disaggregated by income, gender, age, race, ethnicity, migratory status, disability, geographic location, and other characteristics relevant in national contexts

Regional Member	17.18.3 Availability of National Statistical Plan
Developing Member Economies	
Central and West Asia	
Afghanistan	A (2015)
Armenia	A (2015)
Azerbaijan	A (2011)
Georgia	D (2015)
Kazakhstan	...
Kyrgyz Republic	D (2015)
Pakistan	B (2015)
Tajikistan	A (2015)
Turkmenistan	D (2015)
Uzbekistan	E (2015)
East Asia	
China, People's Rep. of	D (2012)
Hong Kong, China	...
Korea, Rep. of	...
Mongolia	A (2015)
Taipei,China	...
South Asia	
Bangladesh	A (2015)
Bhutan	D (2015)
India	A (2015)
Maldives	A (2015)
Nepal	A (2015)
Sri Lanka	A (2015)
Southeast Asia	
Brunei Darussalam	...
Cambodia	A (2015)
Indonesia	D (2015)
Lao PDR	A (2015)
Malaysia	...
Myanmar	E (2015)
Philippines	A (2015)
Singapore	...
Thailand	A (2012)
Viet Nam	A (2015)
The Pacific	
Cook Islands	...
Fiji	E (2015)
Kiribati	A (2015)
Marshall Islands	D (2015)
Micronesia, Fed. States of	D (2015)
Nauru	...
Palau	...
Papua New Guinea	E (2015)
Samoa	A (2015)
Solomon Islands	E (2015)
Timor-Leste	A (2015)
Tonga	D (2015)
Tuvalu	E (2015)
Vanuatu	A (2015)
Developed Member Economies	
Australia	...
Japan	...
New Zealand	...

... = data not available at cutoff date, Lao PDR = Lao People's Democratic Republic, SDG = Sustainable Development Goal.

A   National statistical plan is fully funded and under implementation
B   National statistical plans are completed and awaiting adoption
C   National statistical plans are expired or without a plan and are currently designing or planning
D   National statistical plans are expired
E   National statistical plans do not exist

Sources: United Nations. Sustainable Development Goals Indicators Global Database. http://unstats.un.org/sdgs/indicators/database/ (accessed 22 October 2016).

Section 2. The Role of Big Data in Official Statistics and Sustainable Development Monitoring

Introduction

Data can be considered the lifeblood of evidence-based policy making. The proliferation of new types of data in the form of satellite and other digital images, digital records, machine-generated data, social media data, internet-compiled data, and consumer databases provide an unprecedented opportunity for a more holistic, inclusive, and highly energized era of networked problem solving where everyone is engaged in the decision-making process (Sachs 2012). As we embrace the Sustainable Development Agenda, there is a need to prepare for a "data revolution" where surveys, censuses, and administrative databases that are commonly used to produce official statistics are complemented by information from innovative and state-of-the-art data sources to inform societies in solving the world's sustainable development challenges.

The data revolution requires seamlessly integrating the data compiled by national statistical systems with the information collected by other data producers from public and private institutions. Hence, it may require modifying some aspects of how these data producers operate their core business. In the case of national statistical systems, the main challenge is to build their capacity to engage with big data. On the other hand, the challenge for private actors who already have the technical know-how to analyze big data is twofold. First, private data producers need to find a balance between protecting their interests and treating data as a public good while safeguarding its confidentiality. Second, they also need to adhere to a common statistical framework to ensure the quality and comparability of the data that they produce.

This section briefly examines the opportunities and challenges that big data present to our society. More specifically, it provides some insights on how we can navigate our way through so that we can leverage big data to compile official statistics and monitor the Sustainable Development Goals (SDGs).

What Is Big Data?

Big data generally refer to the type of data arising from people's digital transactions with computers, social media, mobile phones, photos, satellite images, sensors, and other types of digital technology. There are three main sources of big data: human-sourced information, process-mediated data, and machine-generated data. The human-sourced information includes data coming from social networks, personal documents, search engines, videos, mobile data content, user-generated maps, and e-mail, among others. Process-mediated data are those coming from traditional business systems, e.g., produced by public agencies (including medical records); and those that are produced by business (commercial transactions, banking records, e-commerce, credit cards, and loyalty cards). Machine-generated data may include fixed sensors (home, weather, traffic, scientific, security, and surveillance) and mobile sensors (mobile phone location, data from computer systems like logs and weblogs). In all of these contexts, big data are characterized in terms of five Vs: volume, velocity, variety, veracity, and variability.

Compilation of big data has been growing at a very fast pace; in fact, it is bounded by the storage capacities of various entities that collect the data. However, with the continuous development of new information technology and the dramatic increase of devices at the periphery of the network including embedded sensors, smartphones, and tablet computers, data extraction and storage capacity are becoming less of a constraint in the compilation of big data (Villars, Eastwood, and Olofson 2011). Similarly, big data analytics is flourishing. In fact, the existing literature offers a wide array of analytical tools such as regularized regression, model selection and validation, classification, and dimension reduction that can be used for examining big data (Wu and Kumar 2009).

The term "Big Data," on the other hand, refers to a wider ecosystem that includes various actors who play different roles in the generation, storage, retrieval, analytics, and usage of big data. Although the private sector has been the major user of big data, big data are expected to play a more significant role in complementing the traditional data sources for official statistics in the coming years. Hence, it is important for all players to understand the potential benefits as well as the constraints in using these new data sources. The following section discusses this issue.

Big Data and Official Statistics

There are several specific examples that showcase how big data can be useful for compiling official statistics. For instance, Statistics Netherlands uses location data through mobile phones to generate proxy measures for daytime population and tourism statistics. In addition, they use data from social media messages to develop a proxy indicator of consumer confidence. They also calculate inflation based on price information extracted from the web.[4] Furthermore, Statistics Netherlands uses traffic loop detection data in measuring the volume of vehicles and traffic density.[5] On the other hand, the Australian Bureau of Statistics has been examining the possible applications of big data in the development of sampling frames or registers, full or partial data substitution, imputation of missing data items, and data validation (Tam and Clarke 2015). There are various activities using big data and official statistics in Asia and the Pacific as well. For instance, web scrapping data is used in the development of price statistics (including price indexes) in the People's Republic of China (PRC), Japan, and the Republic of Korea. On the other hand, crowd-sourced data are used in decisions on infrastructure investments in the Philippines and in managing urban growth in Sri Lanka. Call detail records (CDRs) from mobile phones are used in monitoring daily migration in the Republic of Korea. CDR data are

---

4   For details, please see Struijs, Braaksma, and Daas (2014).
5   For details, please see Daas et al. (2015).

Table 7.1: Data List of Big Data-Related Initiatives in Asia and the Pacific

Economy	Institute or Department	Big Data Project
Australia	UN - Global Pulse	Estimating migration flows using online search data
Bangladesh	World Bank Group	Predicting vulnerability to flooding and enhancing resilience using big data
China, People's Rep. of	National Bureau of Statistics	Using web scraping price data for price index of e-commerce
		Crop survey by farmland: using satellite and aerial remote sensing to help estimate agricultural statistics
		Comparison of data of interbank transactions with retail sales: credit card data for use in verifying retail sales
		Application of big data for highway and waterway transport statistics
		Online price changes of means of production
		Big data enterprise statistical indicator
	World Bank Group	Using big data analytics to discover patterns of medical insurance utilization for medical cost monitoring in the People's Republic of China
	UNDP and Baidu	Using big data to support e-waste management in the People's Republic of China
Japan	Ministry of Internal Affairs and Communications	Web scraping and scanner data for price statistics
Korea, Rep. of	Statistics Korea	Online price index
		Daily migration of population: using mobile call detail record data for daily migration data
India	World Bank Group	Tracking light from the sky version 2.0 or monitoring rural electrification from space
		Real-time forecasting of skills demand and supply: analytics of big data from Babajob in India
	UN - Global Pulse	Understanding immunization awareness and sentiment through analysis of social media and news content
Indonesia	World Bank Group	Big data for freight transport and logistics policy making
		Using mobile phone data for national, subnational, and geo-coded average prices
		Using big data to predict student achievement in low-income school settings
	UN - Global Pulse	Understanding public perceptions of immunization using social media
		Mining citizen feedback data for enhanced local government decision making
	ILO and UN Global Pulse Lab Jakarta	Using social media to track workplace discrimination against women in Indonesia
Pakistan	World Bank Group	Using high-resolution satellite imagery and detection algorithms to better track poverty in Pakistan
Philippines	World Bank Group	OpenRoads Philippines: improved real-time decision making of infrastructure investments for the Philippines by linking geospatial road network data with rich geo-tagged social data collected through mobile phones
Singapore	Department of Statistics	Integrated environment system (IES): using environmental sensing systems and data analytics for real-time environmental information
		Population estimates: using administrative data from many sources for population estimates
Sri Lanka	World Bank Group	Enabling up-to-date and accurate authoritative country mapping with crowdsourced geospatial data
	LIRNEasia	Potential of mobile network big data as a tool in Colombo's transportation and urban planning
Viet Nam	World Bank Group	Using big data to predict student achievement in low-income school settings

ILO = International Labour Organization, UN = United Nations, UNDP = United Nations Development Programme.

Sources: United Nations Global Working Group on Big Data Project Inventory; United Nations Economic and Social Commission for Asia and the Pacific.

also used in price monitoring and in freight and logistics decision-making in Indonesia. Satellite imagery and remote sensing images are used in crop estimates in the PRC, in poverty tracking in Pakistan, in monitoring rural electrification in India, and monitoring pollution levels in Singapore. Box 7.1 provides another example of how data from satellite images, particularly nighttime lights, can be used to develop proxy measures for different types of social and economic indicators. In summary, there are numerous ongoing initiatives that explore the potential uses, limitations, and constraints in using big data in the generation of official statistics. To further advance these initiatives and explore the other frontiers of big data, the United Nations (UN) created a Global Working Group (GWG) on Big Data for Official Statistics in collaboration between the World Bank and the UN Statistics Division. Currently, the GWG maintains a detailed catalog of big data-related projects that are relevant for different types of official statistics through its GWG Big Data Inventory.

Box 7.1: Using Nighttime Lights to Measure Social and Economic Indicators

Data on nighttime lights is a good example of a novel source of information that is increasingly being used in ongoing studies that showcase the application of big data for monitoring the Sustainable Development Goals (SDGs).

Box Figure 7.1: Nighttime Lights of the World

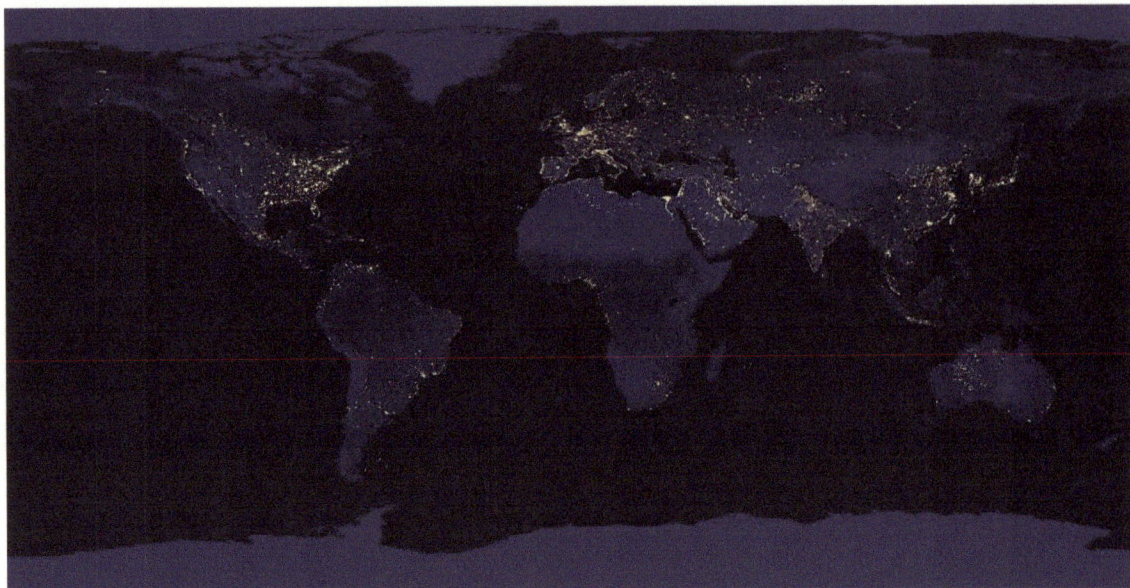

Source: National Aeronautics and Space Administration.

What are Nighttime Lights?

The Defense Meteorological Satellite Program Operational Linescan System of the United States National Oceanic and Atmospheric Administration collects satellite images of nighttime lights of every corner of the world within the 65° south and north latitude between 8:30 p.m. and 10 p.m. local time. Each pixel of an image represents a square kilometer of ground area, while a digital number ranging from 0 to 63 is used to gauge the intensity of the lights. The raw data are reprocessed to remove the noise caused by cloud cover, snow, and ephemeral lights caused by fire. Compiled annual data are available through the National Geophysical Data Center's website from http://ngdc.noaa.gov/eog/index.html.

Deriving Proxy Measures of Socioeconomic Indicators Using Data on Nighttime Lights

In principle, nighttime light is an important input in many economic production and consumption activities such as transportation of goods and people, outdoor lighting, illumination of houses and buildings, and consumption of mass media (Pinkovskiy and Sala-i-Martin 2015). Hence, it is not surprising to note that several studies find that nighttime lights or luminosity data correlate well with measures of economic activity such as gross domestic product (GDP) as well as other non-GDP-based socioeconomic indicators of population size, employment, and poverty (e.g., Chen and Nordhaus 2010, 2011; Gosh et al. 2010; Pinkovskiy and Sala-i-Martin 2015).

Box Figure 7.2: Correlation between Provincial Poverty Rates and Nighttime Lights Index Values

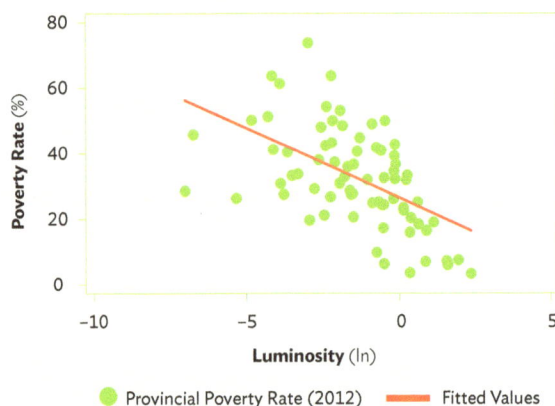

Provincial Poverty Rate (2012)   Fitted Values

Source: ADB estimates based on poverty numbers compiled by the Philippine Statistics Authority and nighttime lights data.

continued.

Box 7.1: *(continued)*

Access to nighttime lights data allows countries with weak statistical systems to impute the indicators identified above at regular time intervals. In addition, data on nighttime lights are also potentially useful for spatial analysis, as they allow for estimation at disaggregated levels since each pixel represents a sufficiently small area. For example, Lo (2001) concluded that nighttime light data produced reasonably accurate estimates of urban population at the provincial, country, and city levels in the People's Republic of China. Nighttime luminosity data also serve as a validation tool when socioeconomic indicators that are supposed to correlate well with each other manifest inconsistent trends. For example, Pinkovskiy and Sala-i-Martin (2015) argue that nighttime luminosity data are an effective validation tool when survey-based estimates of income conflict with GDP-based measures. According to the authors, "the strength of the correlation between nighttime lights and measured income is directly related to the strength of the correlation between the given income measurement and the true income it is trying to measure."

Box Figure 7.3: Images of Nighttime Lights in the Philippines, 2000 and 2013

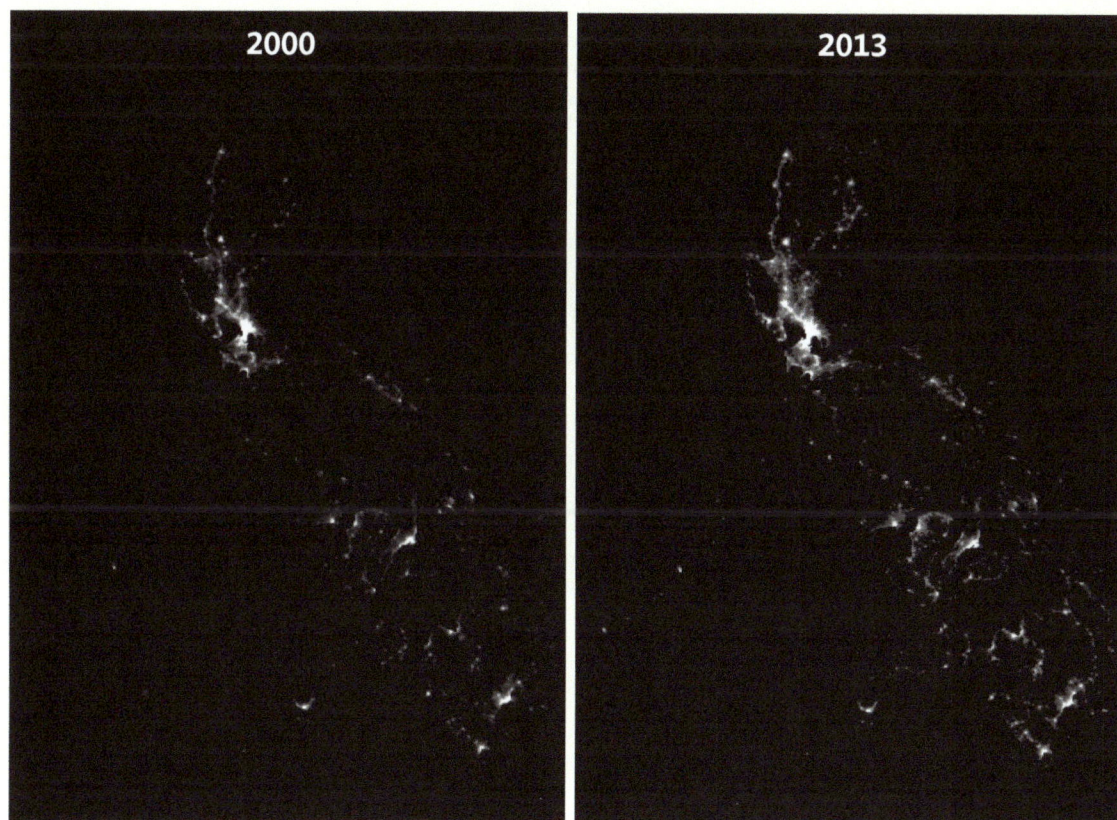

Source: ADB calculations based on data downloaded from National Oceanic and Atmospheric Administration. Version 4 DMSP-OLS Nighttime Lights Time Series. http://ngdc.noaa.gov/eog/dmsp/downloadV4composites.html (accessed 18 January 2016).

In an ongoing study, staff of the Economic Research and Regional Cooperation Department of the Asian Development Bank are exploring the feasibility of using nighttime lights data to measure the impact of infrastructure projects. To accomplish this, the authors are analyzing the increase in the illumination values within a 5-, 10-, and 15-kilometer radius surrounding the areas of a randomly selected set of road projects before, during, and after project implementation. Preliminary results suggest that the increase in the luminosity of areas with road projects was significantly higher than the observed increase in the illumination values of a preselected control group consisting of "similar" areas that did not have a road project during the same reference time period. Measures of GDP, poverty, and unemployment can then be estimated before and after project implementation by using the correlation between these measures and the illumination values.

continued.

Box 7.1: *(continued)*

Despite the advantages of using nighttime light data to derive proxy measures of conventional socioeconomic indicators, this approach is not without limitations. For example, since old satellites are replaced by new ones, there might be inconsistent readings from year to year. In addition, since the distribution of illumination values is right-censored, it is not possible to estimate economic growth or temporal changes in other socioeconomic measures for an area that has already reached the maximum digital number value of 63. Nevertheless, examining the relationship between nighttime lights and socioeconomic indicators serves as a good building block for policy in terms of using novel data sources to complement traditional sources that are used to compile official statistics.

Sources:

X. Chen and W. Nordhaus. 2010. The Value of Luminosity Data as a Proxy for Economic Statistics. *NBER Working Paper* 16317. Cambridge MA: National Bureau of Economic Research (NBER).

———. 2011. Using Luminosity Data as a Proxy for Economic Statistics. *Proceedings of the National Academy of Sciences of the United States of America* 108(21): 8589–8594.

T. Ghosh, R. L. Powell, C. D. Elvidge, K. E. Baugh, P. C. Sutton, and S. Anderson. 2010. Shedding Light on the Global Distribution of Economic Activity. *The Open Geography Journal* 3: 148–161.

C. P. Lo. 2001. Modeling the Population of China Using DMSP Operational Linescan System Nighttime Data. *Photogrammetric Engineering & Remote Sensing* 67: 1037–1047.

M. Pinkovskiy and X. Sala-i-Martin. 2015. Lights, Camera, … Income!: Estimating Poverty Using National Accounts, Survey Means, and Lights. *NBER Working Paper* 19831. Cambridge MA: National Bureau of Economic Research (NBER).

Although most of the studies that examine the viability of using big data to enhance official statistics compilation provide encouraging results, there are various issues that need to be considered before a decision to fully scale up such initiatives can be made. First, there should be a careful consideration of cost implications and sustainability of statistical outputs. Second, self-selection bias and representativeness are issues that need to be tackled when using several types of big data such as crowd-sourced and web scraped data since many people are still not connected to the internet. Third, there is also a need to work for codification and production of a metadata system to support the use of big data in official statistics (Ploug 2013). On this front, the UN Statistics Division is leading the development of classification and standards toward the formal definition of concepts related to big data for international comparability. In addition, there are several research areas that need to be examined further. In particular, big data analytics require new statistical methods that can allow inferences that are not heavily dependent on the conventional notion of statistical significance. Big data analytics should also provide analytical tools that tackle inherent features of big data such as heterogeneity, noise accumulation, spurious correlation, and incidental endogeneity.

In addition to these challenges, there is also a need to address institutional barriers to the use of big data for compilation of official statistics. For instance, specific guidelines on sharing of private sector data holdings need to be carefully developed and examined in close consultation with the public sector, particularly the national statistics offices. Furthermore, there is a need to develop the capacity of national statistics offices in the use of big data and continuous development of new methods that will facilitate the efficient integration of big data into the national statistical systems.

Big Data and Sustainable Development Goals

The previous section has touched on the various applications of big data for official statistics in general. This section summarizes how we can leverage big data for monitoring the SDGs in particular.

It focuses on three themes in which big data can play an important role in addressing the data gaps in the SDGs: disaggregation, timeliness, and development of proxy indicators.

As pointed out earlier, the *"leave no one behind"* principle that the SDGs espouse requires the statistical indicators to be broken down or disaggregated by subpopulation groups. However, the existing data collection mechanism even for Tier 1 indicators do not usually allow such disaggregation. Hence, there is a need to explore how new data sources could complement conventional data collection strategies in methodologically robust ways to facilitate disaggregation. Big data can potentially provide a more granular social and geospatial breakdown and reduce the cost of collecting such data. For instance, CDR and process-mediated data can complement official statistics in providing a finer disaggregation of poverty indicators. With an appropriate data mining algorithm, gender and time–location indicators can be generated from these databases and can be used subsequently as auxiliary information in the estimation of poverty incidence and other indicators at various disaggregation levels. Similarly, mobile technology can also be used to oversample marginalized groups that are harder to reach through conventional data collection methods.

Complementing the conventional data sources used to compile the SDG indicators with big data can also potentially improve the timeliness of the release of the statistics. Even with Tier 1 indicators, regular updating has been a challenge due to the frequency of surveys and censuses. Several types of big data like those generated from traditional business systems can complement official statistics as indicators of themes under prosperity. Model-based estimation with big data as exogenous factors can be used in updating indicators between business survey and/ or census years. Similar modeling approaches can be used in the establishment of early warning systems to monitor progress toward the achievement of SDG targets on a more regular basis (e.g., annually). As an example, Google Trends data are used in predicting influenza prevalence (Yang, Santillana, and Kou 2015). A similar method may also be useful in predicting HIV or tuberculosis prevalence rates to complement the scarce data available among the countries in the region.

Big data are expected to play a key role in developing proxy measures for SDG indicators classified as Tier 3. For instance, the use of fixed censor data (weather) may be explored for the development of some indicators for SDG 13 (climate action) in combination with global weather indicators such as El Niño Southern Oscillation data. Similarly, mobile censor data can be mined for latent indicators that can be used to monitor SDG 12 (responsible consumption and production). In particular, data from different sources can be combined in the generation of indexes wherein the process associated with the targets can be viewed to be the latent factors from various indicators available. These latent factors can be extracted through principal components analysis or sparse principal components analysis.

Summary

This section has identified several applications of big data in compiling official statistics and SDG indicators. Overall, the results are encouraging and highlight that big data's applications are wide-ranging. Nevertheless, there are some important lessons that are worth pointing out. "Big Data" is not a panacea to all data gaps that exist in official statistics and SDG indicators. In fact, big data are not always the right data because, in some cases, they can even introduce additional sources of bias and spurious correlations that could yield misleading conclusions. Secondly, sophisticated technology and data mining algorithms are not sufficient to fully understand the results from analysis of big data. It requires an effective combination of sectoral expertise and distinct hardware and software capabilities.

As the development community increasingly recognizes the advantages of using big data to enhance the relevance and timeliness of official statistics, it should also make a conscious effort to address issues surrounding data quality and methodology, development of skills needed to work with big data, technological requirements, and the legal framework for sharing and principles of use of big data. To accomplish this, the development community needs to continue tracking relevant initiatives using big data so that we can have a more nuanced understanding on the scalability of such initiatives. Furthermore, the development community needs to work closely with various stakeholders including the private sector and government, particularly the national statistics bureaus.

References

Asian Development Bank. 2015. *Key Indicators for Asia and the Pacific 2015*. Manila.

P. Daas, M. Puts, B. Buelens, and P. van den Hurk. 2015. Big Data as a Source of Official Statistics *Journal of Official Statistics* 31(2): 249–262.

T. Hak, S. Janouskova, and B. Moldan. 2016. Sustainable Development Goals: A Need for Relevant Indicators. *Ecological Indicators* 60: 565–573.

N. Ploug. 2013. New Forms of Data for Official Statistics. In Proceedings of the 59th World Statistics Congress of the International Statistical Institute, 25–30 August, Hong Kong, China. The Hague, Netherlands: International Statistical Institute.

J. Sachs. 2012. From Millennium Development Goals to Sustainable Development Goals. *The Lancet* 379: 2206–2211.

P. Struijs, B. Braaksma, and P. Daas. 2014. Official Statistics and Big Data. *Big Data and Society*, April-June 2014: 1–6.

Sustainable Development Solutions Network (SDSN). 2016. Measuring Peaceful, Just and Inclusive Societies: SDG16 Data Initiative.

S. Tam and F. Clarke. 2015. Big Data, Official Statistics and Some Initiatives by the Australian Bureau of Statistics. *International Statistical Review* 83(3): 436–448.

United Nations Development Programme (UNDP). 2013. *Strategy Paper: Sustainable and Inclusive Urbanization in Asia Pacific*. New York.

United Nations High Commissioner for Refugees (UNHCR). 2014. Global Trends 2013. Geneva.

R. Villars, M. Eastwood, and C. Olofson. 2011. Big Data: What It Is and Why You Should Care. IDC White Paper. Framingham, MA: International Data Corporation.

World Health Organization (WHO). 2015. *Health in 2015: From MDGs to SDGs*. Geneva.

X. Wu and V. Kumar. 2009. Top 10 Data Mining Algorithms. New York: Chapman and Hall/CRC Press.

S. Yang, M. Santillana, and S. Kou. 2015. Accurate Estimation of Influenza Epidemics Using Google Search Data via ARGO. Proceedings of the National Academy of Sciences 112: 14473–14478.

PART II
Regional Trends and Tables

Introduction to the Regional Trends and Tables

The 2016 issue of *Key Indicators for Asia and the Pacific* contains 100 statistical tables summarizing regional trends in social, economic, and environmental developments in Asian Development Bank (ADB) member economies in Asia and the Pacific. The statistical tables are grouped into eight themes: People, Economy, and Output; Money, Finance, and Prices; Globalization; Transport and Communications; Energy and Electricity; Environment; and Government and Governance.

Each theme has an accompanying brief analysis of key trends of selected indicators highlighting important recent developments in several subtopics. The data patterns are summarized by charts and figures that compare indicators for ADB member economies for the latest year available (e.g., 2015). Often, indicators for the latest year are also compared with the previous year (e.g., 2015 and 2014) or with an earlier year (e.g., 2015 and 2000) in order to identify regional, subregional, and economy-level trends.

People highlights demographic trends in terms of the size and growth of the population; birth, death, and fertility rates; age dependency ratios; international migration, urbanization, employment; health and education resources. The section also contains statistics on poverty and inequality, including the Gini coefficient, which measures the distribution of income in an economy, and the Human Development Index, which combines a range of economic and social statistics into an index reflecting the overall level of well-being in each economy. Important aspects of this theme are also covered in the earlier analysis of data for the Sustainable Development Goal Theme: People, which seeks to eradicate extreme poverty and other forms of socioeconomic disadvantage.

Economy and Output contains tables on gross domestic product (GDP) levels and growth; related statistics taken from the national accounts such as gross national income, value added, consumption expenditure, capital formation, exports and imports, and gross domestic saving; and production indicators. This theme compares the relative size of economies both within the region and in the world as a whole using data on GDP in purchasing power parity terms. This section also discusses how economies' GDP shares of agriculture, industry, and services have changed since 2000, and which economies are consuming more and which are investing more in capital for future growth.

Money, Finance, and Prices gives the latest statistics on inflation and other monetary and financial statistics. These include data on money supply, interest rates, bank lending, official exchange rates, and stock markets. The discussion for this theme focuses on the modest consumer price inflation in most Asia and the Pacific economies due to low international food and fuel prices, depreciation of most regional currencies against the US dollar in 2014–2015, trends in nonperforming bank loans and stock market performance.

Globalization focuses on external trade, balance of payments, international reserves, capital flows, external indebtedness, and tourism. The expansion of intraregional and interregional trade is an important aspect of globalization, as are international movements of labor and capital. This theme discusses trends in merchandise exports and imports; the increasing importance of services exports in some regional economies; remittances from migrant workers, which are significant sources of income for many economies in the region; net official loans and grants; and net private capital flows. More detailed statistical tables on global value chains are provided in Part III.

Transport and Communications covers statistics on road and rail networks, air carrier departures, container port traffic, and motor vehicle injuries and fatalities. This theme also includes statistics on mobile and fixed telephone subscriptions, and broadband internet penetration rates. The discussion covers the upgrading of road networks and expansion of rail networks across the region, increases in both vehicle ownership and road fatalities, and the surge in mobile telephone and broadband internet subscriptions.

Energy and Electricity comprises statistics on energy productivity, supplies and uses of primary energy, and electricity consumption and generation. The discussion focuses on trends in demand for energy, including a growing reliance on coal for generating electricity among the region's top producers, increasing dependence on energy imports among the region's top consumers, gains in energy efficiency in most economies and the persistence of fossil fuel subsidies in some economies, and the rapidly rising rates of electricity generation across the region that are accompanying industrialization and household electrification.

Environment includes indicators related to land use, forest resources, and air and water pollution. The discussion covers greenhouse gas emissions, particularly the contribution of agriculture to such emissions; deforestation; and freshwater resources. The earlier discussion of data for Sustainable Development Goal Theme: Planet also covers some of the indicators presented in this theme.

Government and Governance contains statistics on governments' tax revenue; fiscal balances; and expenditure on health and education services, and on social security and welfare. It also includes statistics on the time and cost required to register a new business in each economy, as well as the latest global rankings for Transparency International's Corruption Perceptions Index. The discussion focuses on regional trends in fiscal performance, government spending priorities, and tax revenue; reductions in the time and cost associated with starting a business; and the persistence of corruption.

In celebration of ADB's 50th anniversary in 2016, the publication also provides discussion boxes to present statistics that summarize some major social and economic transformations in Asia and the Pacific over the past 50 years. For this purpose, statistical trends on selected statistical indicators that have sufficiently long data series based on a consistent methodology are discussed.

People

Snapshots

- Asia and the Pacific comprises 55% of the world's population and is home to the two most populous economies in the world, the People's Republic of China and India.

- Between 2000 and 2015, the total population of the regional member economies grew at an annual rate of 1.21%.

- The region's aging population may impact labor force participation rates and present budgetary challenges for policy makers in the decades ahead.

- In about half of the economies in Asia and the Pacific, the majority of the population lives in urban areas.

- According to the United Nations Development Programme's Human Development Index, the quality of life has improved in most of the region's economies since 2000, albeit to varying degrees.

Key Trends

Asia and the Pacific comprises more than half of the world's total population. The combined populations of the 48 regional economies reached 4.05 billion in 2015, accounting for 55.1% of the world's population. The region with the next largest share of the global population was Africa at 16.1%, followed by Europe (11.1%), North America (7.8%), South America (5.7%), West Asia (3.3%), and the rest of the world (0.9%). South Asia surpassed East Asia to become the most populous within Asia and the Pacific, comprising 36.8% of the total in 2015. East Asia accounted for 36.0% of the region's total population in the same year, followed by Southeast Asia (15.5%), Central and West Asia (7.5%), and the Pacific (0.3%). Meanwhile, the developed economies of Australia, Japan, and New Zealand accounted for a combined 3.8% of the region's total (Table 1.1).

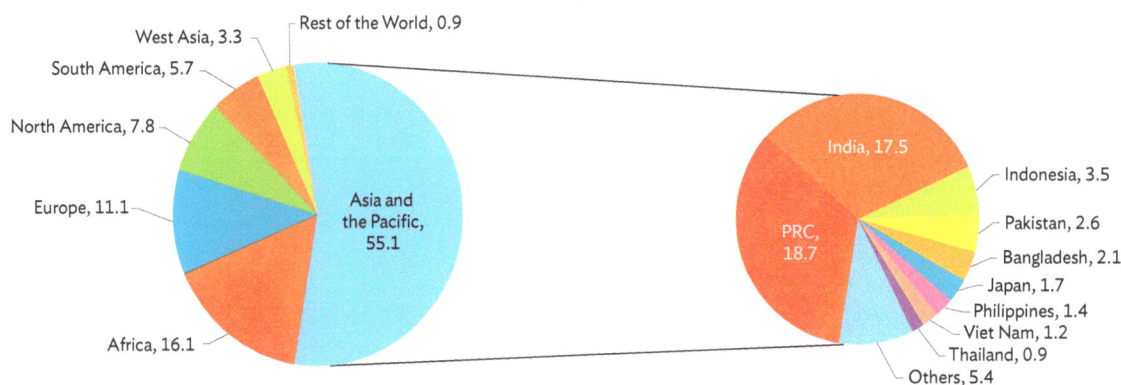

Figure 1.1: Distribution of Population by Global Region, and by Economy in Asia and the Pacific, 2015
(%)

West Asia, 3.3
Rest of the World, 0.9
South America, 5.7
North America, 7.8
Europe, 11.1
Asia and the Pacific, 55.1
Africa, 16.1

India, 17.5
Indonesia, 3.5
Pakistan, 2.6
Bangladesh, 2.1
PRC, 18.7
Japan, 1.7
Philippines, 1.4
Viet Nam, 1.2
Thailand, 0.9
Others, 5.4

PRC = People's Republic of China.
Note: The aggregate for the West Asia region was adjusted to exclude Armenia, Azerbaijan, and Georgia, which are included in the total for Asia and the Pacific.
Source: Table 1.1.

Asia and the Pacific is home to the two most populous economies in the world, the People's Republic of China (PRC) (1.4 billion) and India (1.3 billion), which accounted for 18.7% and 17.5% of the world's population in 2015, respectively (Figure 1.1). The region's next three most populous economies in 2015 are Indonesia (225 million), Pakistan (197 million), and Bangladesh (158 million) (Table 1.1).

The United Nations projects that the world population will reach 9.73 billion in 2050, of which 4.8 billion (49.4%) will reside in the member economies within Asia and the Pacific.[1]

Between 2000 and 2015, the total population of the regional member economies grew at an annual rate of 1.21%. Figure 1.2 shows the average annual population growth rate of each economy in the region for 2000–2015. The high-income and upper-middle-income economies of East Asia experienced relatively low average growth rates of less than 1.0%. In Central and West Asia, Afghanistan, Pakistan, and Tajikistan each had growth of at least 2.0% during the review period, while economies like Armenia had either very low or negative population growth rates. The most populous economy in the Pacific, Papua New Guinea, also had its highest population growth rate at 3.1%, while the Marshall Islands and Palau had negative growth rates. In Southeast Asia, every country except Thailand and Myanmar had an average annual population growth rate higher than 1.0% during the review period. Among ADB's developed members, Japan's population growth rate was barely positive at 0.02%.

Between 2000 and 2015, Asia and the Pacific's population expanded at an average annual rate of 1.21%. This compares with average annual population growth rates of 2.54% for Africa, 0.22% for Europe, 1.06% for North America, 1.22% for South America, 2.29% for West Asia, and 0.58% for the rest of the world.[2]

---

[1]   These figures are based on United Nations' estimates for ADB regional member countries, which include Australia, Japan, and New Zealand (UNDESA 2015).

[2]   Footnote 1.

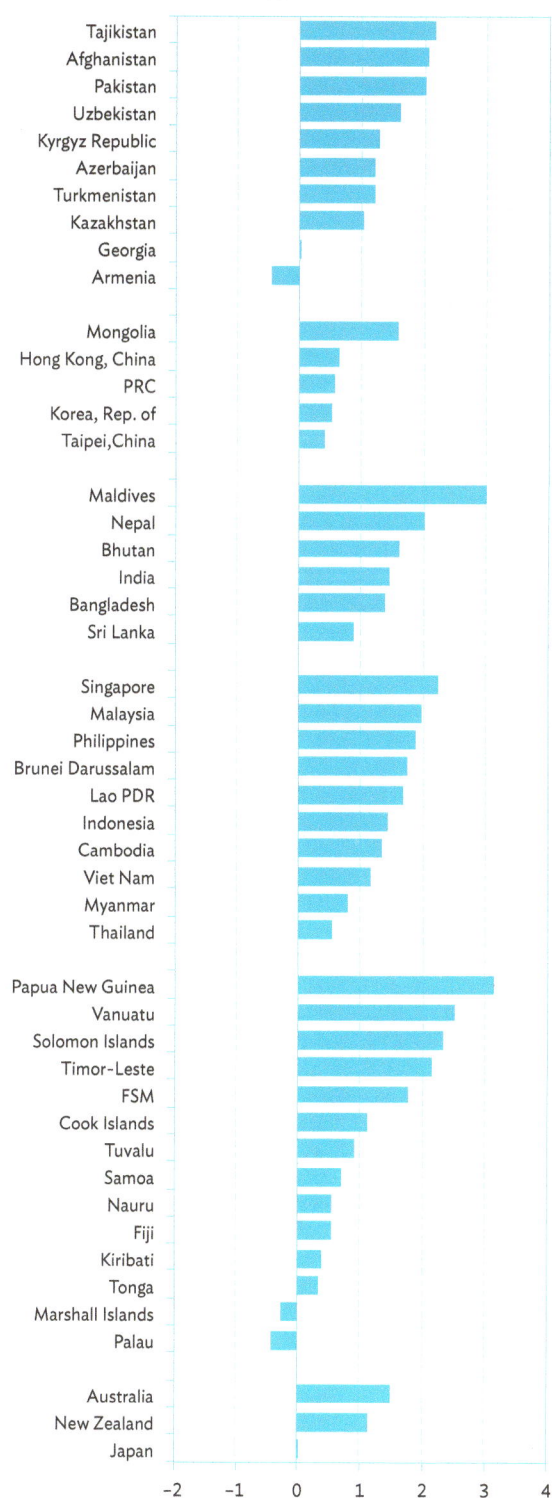

Figure 1.2: Average Annual Population Growth Rate, 2000–2015
(%)

FSM = Federated States of Micronesia, Lao PDR = Lao People's Democratic Republic, PRC = People's Republic of China.
Source: Table 1.1.

Regional Trends and Tables

Asia and the Pacific's aging population may present challenges for policy makers in the decades ahead. Increased life expectancy and decreased fertility rates will continue to have a major impact on the composition of the region's population structure. Figure 1.3 presents population pyramids for the region for 2000, 2015, and 2050. Each bar corresponds to the estimated population size of a specific gender and age group, with the blue and red bars representing the male and female population in 2015, respectively. The blue line corresponds to the estimated population size in 2000, while the black line corresponds to the estimated population size in 2050. The pattern shown in the figure suggests that a larger proportion of the region's population will comprise persons over the age of 65 in 2050. By 2050, for the first time in history, there will be roughly as many people in Asia over the age of 65 as under the age of 15 (Smith and Majmundar 2012). Prior to that, however, economies with a relatively young age structure should benefit from a rising share of the

working-age population in their total population, and therefore enjoy a declining dependency ratio. Figure 1.4 shows how the dependency ratio of each regional member economy has changed between 2000 and 2015. Except in Sri Lanka, dependency ratios dropped in all developing member economies during the review period. On the other hand, Sri Lanka and developed members (Australia, Japan, and New Zealand) observed increasing dependency ratios. In developed member economies, longer life expectancy and declining fertility rates are leading to an increase in the share of the population aged 65 years and above (Smith and Majmundar 2012). The increase in Sri Lanka's dependency ratio may be due to fertility rates in earlier years that were below the regional average as a result of decades of separatist conflict that ended in 2009 (Table 1.12). In general, an increasing dependency ratio driven by an aging population presents governments with fiscal challenges, including lower tax revenues from a relatively

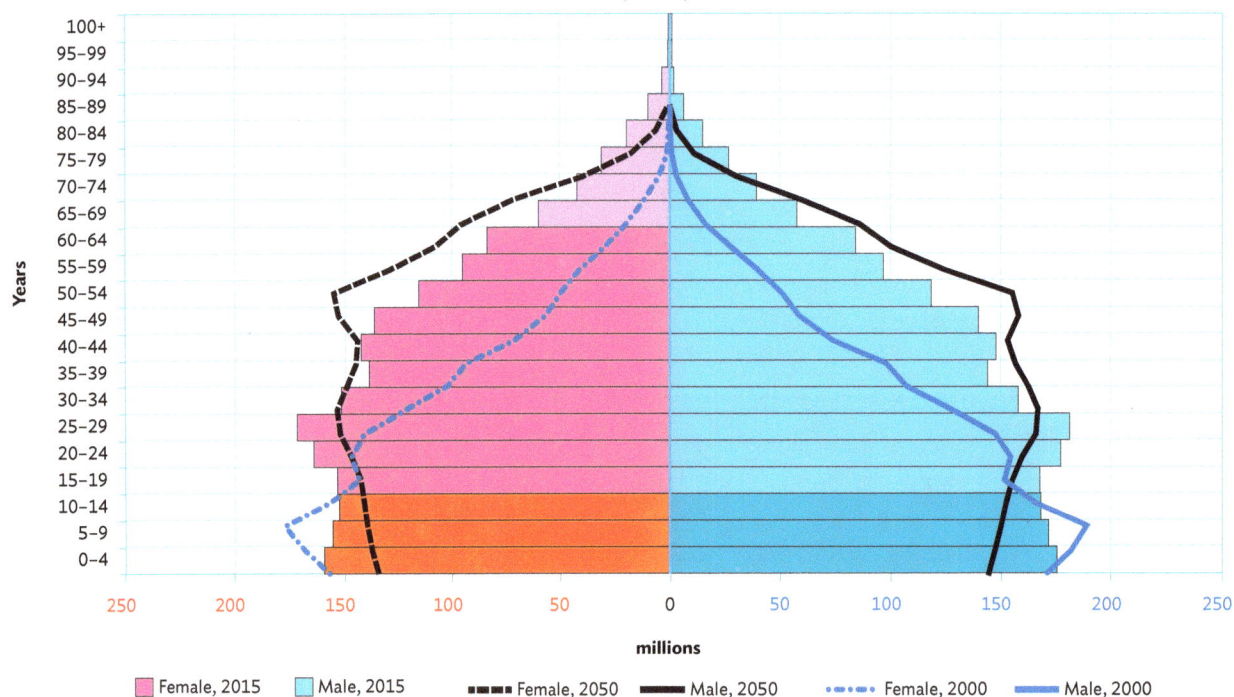

Figure 1.3: Population Pyramid by 5-year Age Groups in Asia and the Pacific, by Sex
(million)

Source: United Nations Department of Economic and Social Affairs, Population Division. 2016. World Population Prospects: The 2015 Revision. https://esa.un.org/undp/wpp

Figure 1.4: Age Dependency Ratio

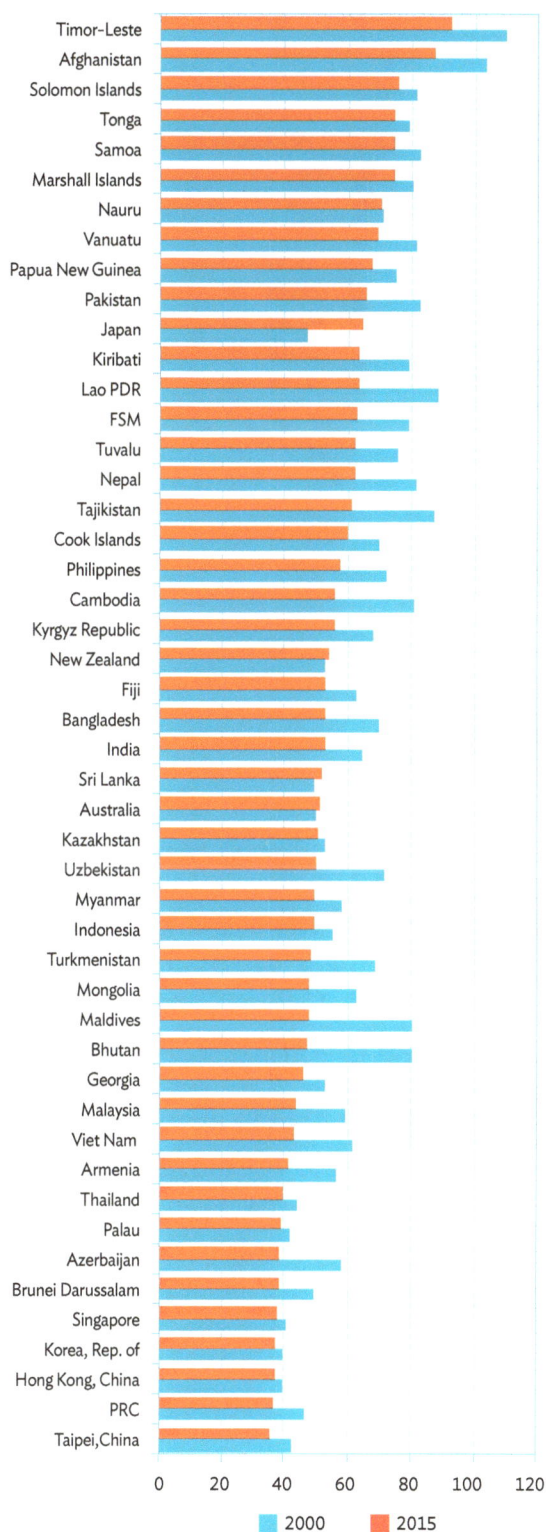

FSM = Federated States of Micronesia, Lao PDR = Lao People's Democratic Republic, PRC = People's Republic of China.
Note: For Taipei,China, the latest available year is 2014.
Source: Table 1.4.

smaller working-age population and increased health care spending for the elderly, and is also likely to reduce productive capacity and lead to lower long-term economic growth (Pettinger 2012).

In about half of the economies in Asia and the Pacific, the majority of the population lives in urban areas. Based on latest data, about 45% of the total population of the regional member economies live in urban areas. Compared to other regions of the world, the percentage of Asia and the Pacific's urban population is significantly lower than that of Europe (73.6%), Latin America and the Caribbean (79.8%), and North America (81.6%) and is just slightly higher than that of Africa (40.4%) (UNDESA 2014). Nevertheless, Asia and the Pacific was still home to 16 of the world's 30 largest cities in 2015 (Figure 1.5).

The proportion of the urban population in regional members grew by 9 percentage points between 2000 and 2015. Furthermore, the urban population's share of the total population increased in seven of the 10 economies in Central and West Asia, all five economies in East Asia, all six economies in South Asia, eight of the 10 economies in Southeast Asia, 11 of the 14 economies of the Pacific, and all three developed economies (Table 1.2).[3]

As migration from rural to urban areas is driven largely by greater employment opportunities in cities, as well as improved access to services such as health care and education (Amare et al. 2012), urban population is expected to grow in the coming years. In particular, the world's urban population is forecast to expand from about 4.0 billion in 2015 to 6.3 billion in 2050, with Asia and the Pacific continuing to account for roughly half of the world's urban population through 2050 (Amare et al. 2012).

3   No change in the urbanization rate was observed during the review period in the region's three economies that were fully urbanized in 2000: Hong Kong, China; Nauru; and Singapore.

Figure 1.5: Largest Urban Agglomerations Ranked by Population, 2015 (%)

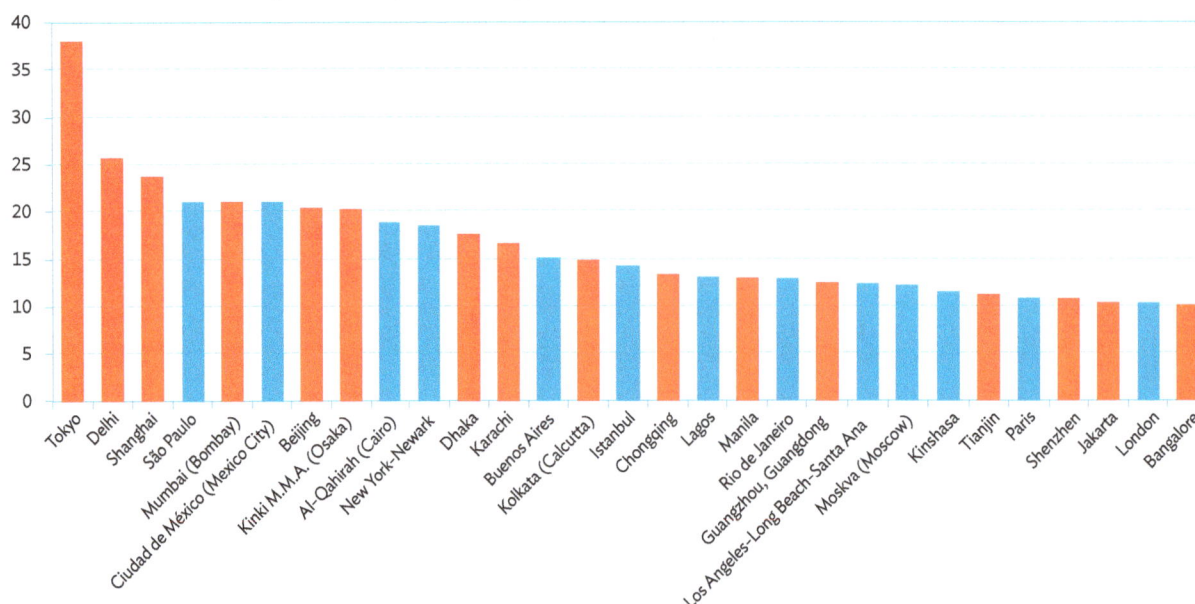

Note: Urban agglomeration refers to urban areas with population exceeding 10 million.
Source: United Nations Department of Economic and Social Affairs, Population Division. 2014. World Urbanization Prospects: The 2014 Revision. https://esa.un.org/undp/wup (accessed 29 August 2016).

Changes in labor force participation rates were mixed across the region between 2000 and 2015. About 70% of the economies in Central and West Asia and in South Asia and 50% in Southeast Asia had rising labor force participation rates during the review period, while about 60% of the economies in East Asia and about 70% of economies in the Pacific saw declines (Table 1.5). Among developed member economies, Australia and New Zealand experienced increases in their labor force participation rates while Japan saw a decline.

The unemployment rate declined between 2000 and 2015 in nearly 60% of the region's economies. The unemployment rate declined most steeply in Kazakhstan (8.0 percentage points), Azerbaijan (6.8 percentage points), the Federated States of Micronesia (5.8 percentage points), and the Philippines (4.9 percentage points) (Table 1.6). Notably, the unemployment rate declined during the review period in seven Southeast Asian economies for which data are available, possibly resulting from

the base effect of persistently high unemployment in the aftermath of the 1997/98 Asian financial crisis.

The quality of life, as measured by the Human Development Index (HDI), has improved in most of the region's economies since 2000, albeit to varying degrees.[4] Figure 1.6a shows the HDI values for each of the region's economies in 2014. The region's developed member economies including Australia, Japan, and New Zealand as well as high-income economies like Hong Kong, China; the Republic of Korea; and Singapore were in the HDI's top tier in 2014. On the other hand, Afghanistan, Myanmar, Nepal, Pakistan, Papua New Guinea, and Solomon Islands have the lowest HDI values in the region.

---

4   The Human Development Index (HDI) is calculated by the United Nations Development Programme for 188 economies worldwide. It covers three important aspects of welfare: life expectancy at birth, the average of mean years of schooling and expected years of schooling, and per capita gross national income.

Figure 1.6a: Human Development Index, 2014

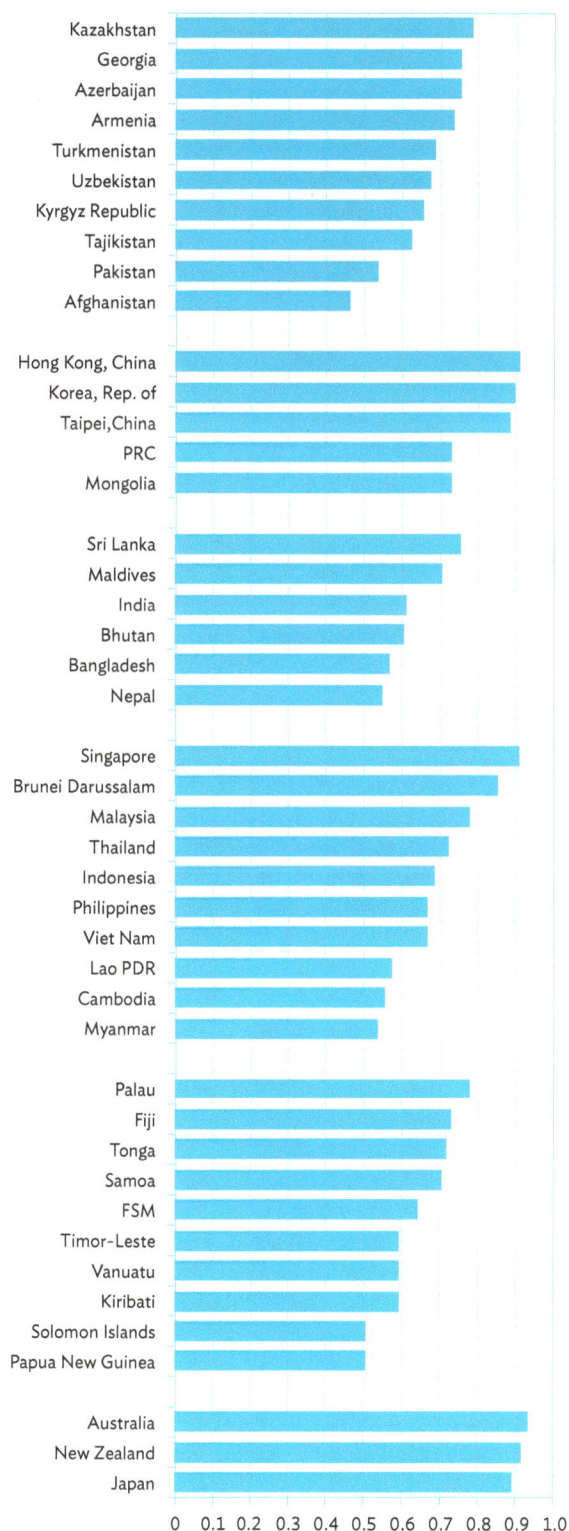

FSM = Federated States of Micronesia, Lao PDR = Lao People's Democratic Republic, PRC = People's Republic of China.
Note: For Taipei,China, data are obtained from the Directorate-General of Budget, Accounting, and Statistics.
Source: Table 1.10.

Figure 1.6b shows the average annual increase in the HDI of those economies with available data for 2000–2014. Trends from the chart reveal that, within each subregion, the economies with the lowest 2014 HDI also had the highest HDI average annual growth, with respect to the period covered. This was the case for Afghanistan and Pakistan in Central and West Asia, the PRC and Mongolia in East Asia, Bangladesh and Nepal in South Asia, Cambodia and Myanmar in Southeast Asia, and Papua New Guinea in the Pacific.

Figure 1.6b: Human Development Index Average Annual Growth, 2000–2014 (%)

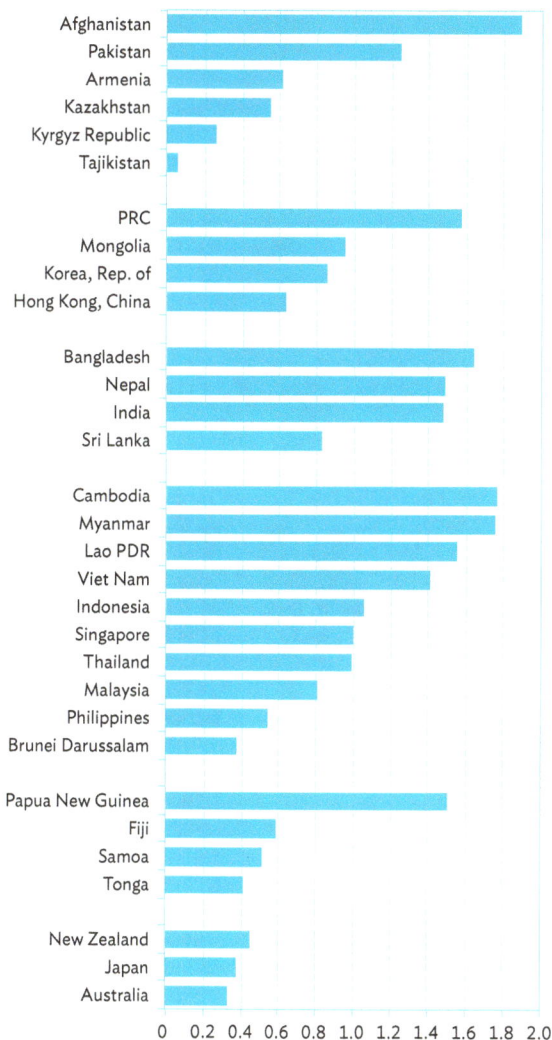

Lao PDR = Lao People's Democratic Republic, PRC = People's Republic of China.
Source: Table 1.10.

Box 1.1: Demographic Trends in Asia and the Pacific, 1960–Present

From 1.6 billion people in 1960, the population of the (current) regional member economies in Asia and the Pacific has grown to 4.0 billion based on 2015 figures. Since 1960, the region's population has grown at an average annual rate of 1.7% and is forecasted to grow by at least 0.35% per year until 2040 (Box Figure 1.1.1). By 2040, the population of Asia and the Pacific, in general, is anticipated to be three times what it was in 1960 (UNDESA 2015).[a]

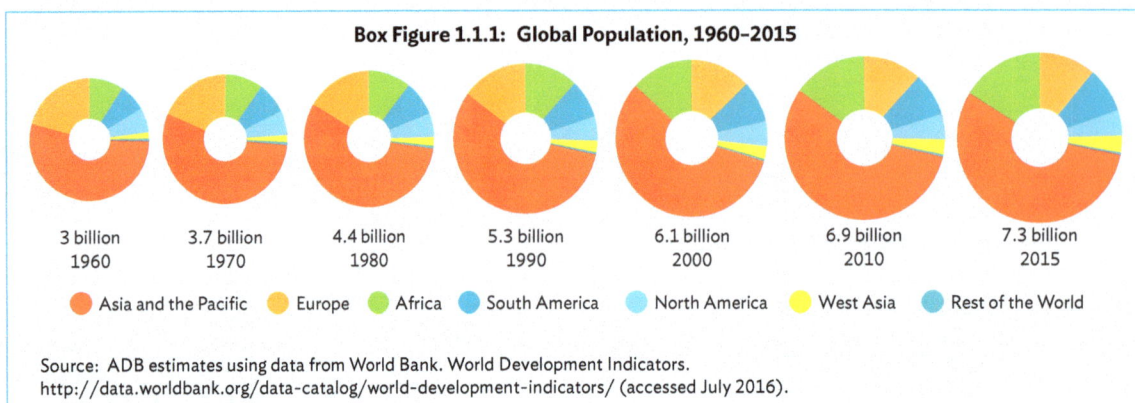

Box Figure 1.1.1: Global Population, 1960–2015

| 3 billion 1960 | 3.7 billion 1970 | 4.4 billion 1980 | 5.3 billion 1990 | 6.1 billion 2000 | 6.9 billion 2010 | 7.3 billion 2015 |

● Asia and the Pacific   ● Europe   ● Africa   ● South America   ● North America   ● West Asia   ● Rest of the World

Source: ADB estimates using data from World Bank. World Development Indicators. http://data.worldbank.org/data-catalog/world-development-indicators/ (accessed July 2016).

The population of both the People's Republic of China (PRC) and India surpassed the 1 billion mark. The PRC's population reached 1 billion people in 1982, while India attained the same milestone in 1998 (UNPD 2015). Since 1960, the PRC's population has grown at an annual rate of 1.32% while India's population expanded by 1.96% annually. Latest estimates suggest that the combined population of these two economies accounts for approximately 66.1% of the current population in the region, down by 2.6 percentage points from its 68.7% share in 1960. At present, the share of Asia and the Pacific of the world's total population is 55.1%; the slight decline in the region's global population share since 2000 is partially the result of the declining birth rate in the PRC and Africa's rising population.

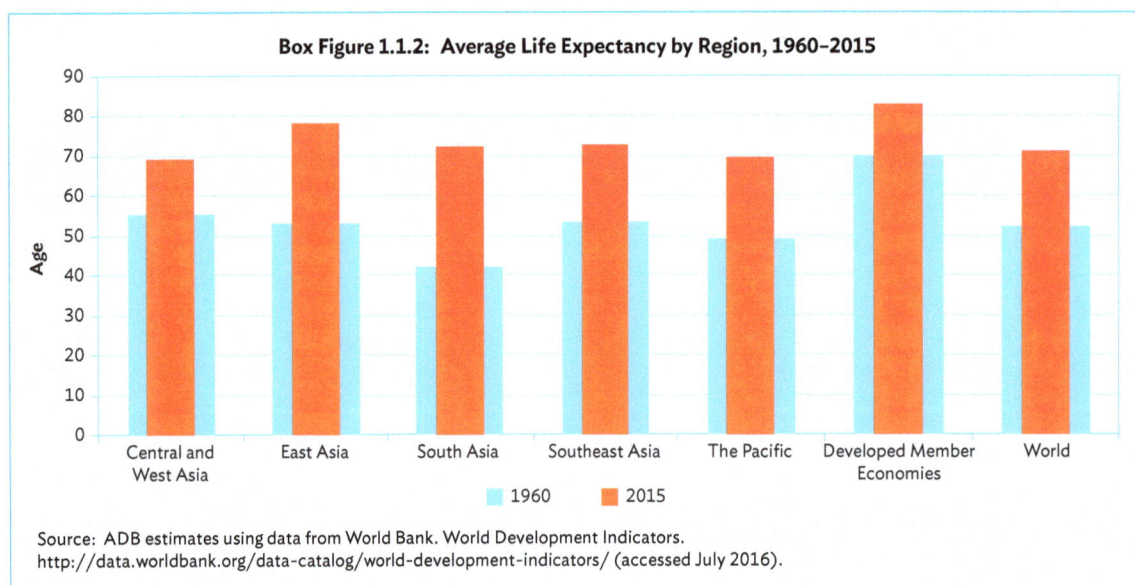

Box Figure 1.1.2: Average Life Expectancy by Region, 1960–2015

□ 1960   ■ 2015

Source: ADB estimates using data from World Bank. World Development Indicators. http://data.worldbank.org/data-catalog/world-development-indicators/ (accessed July 2016).

a   The numbers are based on 2015 revision medium-variant projections.

continued.

Box 1.1: *(continued)*

Today, a newborn in Asia and the Pacific is expected to live for 71 years, 25 years longer than his or her counterpart born in the 1960s. Since the 1960s, new generations of Asians have lived longer than their forbearers. Furthermore, the region is home to some of the economies with the highest average life expectancy in the world such as Japan; Hong Kong, China; Singapore; and Australia. In fact, Japan and Hong Kong, China have consistently been among the Asia and the Pacific's top five in terms of average life expectancy since 1960; Singapore, on the other hand, first joined this group in 1976. In 2014, life expectancy in Hong Kong, China; Japan; and Singapore was 84.0, 83.6, and 82.6 years, respectively. In the region's developing economies, average life expectancy increased from 45 years in 1960 to 70 years at present.

According to the Global Burden of Disease Study 2013, gains in life expectancy in Asia and the Pacific since 1960 have been in line with global developments, which include, among others, reduced deaths from infectious diseases, lower rates of cardiovascular disease deaths in high-income countries, and lower rates of childhood deaths in low-income countries.

The dependency ratio in Asia and the Pacific has declined by almost 40% over the past 50 years. Some parts of the region have experienced a steady decline in its dependency ratio and most economies even exceeded the rate of decline (26.8%) in the world average between 1960 and 2015. Azerbaijan; Brunei Darussalam; the PRC; Hong Kong, China; the Republic of Korea; Malaysia; Singapore; and Thailand have experienced the highest rates of decline since 1960 exceeding 50%. The dependency ratio in Asia and the Pacific, estimated at 76.3 people per 100 persons in 1960 has dropped to 46.9 people per 100 persons. Furthermore, the region had the lowest age dependency ratio in 2015 among all other regions in the World (Box Table 1.1).

Dependency Ratio by Region, 1960–2015
(per 100 working-age population)

Regions	1960	1980	2000	2015
Africa	85.1	91.6	84.7	79.1
Asia and the Pacific	76.3	72.2	56.1	46.9
Europe	56.7	54.0	48.4	50.0
South America	85.7	78.7	60.1	50.0
North America	66.9	51.2	50.1	50.5
West Asia	86.6	91.7	71.5	51.5
World	73.6	71.5	58.7	52.3

Sources: ADB estimates using data from World Bank. World Development Indicators. http://data.worldbank.org/data-catalog/world-development-indicators/ (accessed July 2016); for 2000 and 2015 world figures: Table 1.4.

More than half of the world's population is currently living in urban areas, and Asia and the Pacific accounts for 48.4% of the total urban population. In 2007, for the first time ever, majority (50.1%) of the world's population resided in urban areas and this is expected to reach 56.2% in 2020 and 66.4% in 2050 (UNDESA 2014). Currently, about 2.14 billion people, or 48.3% of the region's total population, live in urban areas.

The degree of urbanization varies within the region. For instance, from having one of the lowest urban population shares in 1960 at 16.9%, East Asia is one of the most urbanized areas in the region with 56.8% of its population living in urban areas based on latest data. This is primarily driven by the PRC's increasing urban population. Southeast Asia also experienced significant urbanization, increasing the share of its urban population from 18.6% in 1960 to 47.7% in 2015. Indonesia also contributed to this trend as its urban population grew significantly over the past 5 decades. On the other hand, the other subregions experienced modest gains. In the Pacific, for instance, the urban population is estimated at 20.3% of its total population.

In the Global Burden of Disease Study 2013, in absolute terms, Asia and the Pacific's urban population first exceeded 1 billion in 1990 and was approximately 1.87 billion in 2015, with an additional 1 billion urban dwellers expected to be added by 2040. The PRC had the largest urban population in the region, with roughly 779 million people living in urban areas. This was followed by India and Indonesia, with 419 million and 137 million urban residents, respectively.

continued.

Box 1.1: *(continued)*

While urbanization plays a role in poverty reduction by providing more economic opportunities, urbanization can also lead to the proliferation of slums and informal sector jobs, deteriorating living conditions, and increasing risks due to climate change (Mathur 2013). Managing urbanization in Asia and the Pacific will require promoting inclusive growth that impacts the lives of the urban poor and the application of green solutions such as linking megacities with satellite cities via train, light rail, or metro rather than highways; and conserving resources and improving energy efficiency through the use of renewables and "smart" grids (ADB 2012).

Box Figure 1.1.3: Urbanization Rate by Region, 1960–2015
(%)

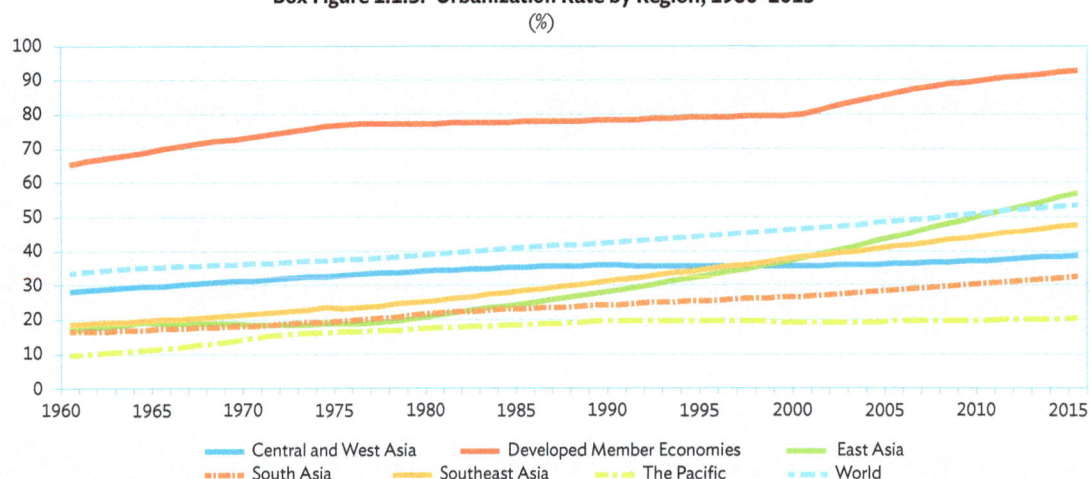

Source: ADB estimates using data from World Bank. World Development Indicators.
http://data.worldbank.org/data-catalog/world-development-indicators/ (accessed July 2016).

Sources:

Asian Development Bank (ADB). 2012. *Key Indicators for Asia and the Pacific 2012: Special Chapter on Green Urbanization in Asia.* Manila.

Global, Regional, and National Age–Sex Specific All-Cause and Cause-Specific Mortality for 240 Causes of Death, 1990–2013: A Systematic Analysis for the Global Burden of Disease Study 2013. *The Lancet* 385 (9963): 117–171. http://www.thelancet.com/pdfs/journals/lancet/PIIS0140-6736(14)61682-2.pdf

O.P. Mathur. 2013. *Urban Poverty in Asia*. Manila: Asian Development Bank.

United Nations Department of Economic and Social Affairs (UNDESA), Population Division. 2014. World Urbanization Prospects. https://esa.un.org/unpd/wup/ (accessed 3 September 2016).

_____ 2015. World Population Prospects. https://esa.un.org/unpd/wpp/ (accessed 3 September 2016).

World Bank. 2016. World Development Indicators. http://data.worldbank.org/data-catalog/world-development-indicators/ (accessed July 2016).

Data Issues and Comparability

Demographic data are either based on vital registration records or on censuses and surveys. In many developing member economies, vital registration records are incomplete and therefore cannot be used for statistical purposes. In most economies, population censuses are conducted every 10 years. For this reason, the growth rates are probably more reliable than the levels. The United Nations Department of Economic and Social Affairs' Population Division used future trends on fertility, mortality, and international migration to project population numbers until 2100. The medium-fertility variant used assumes fertility rates above 2.1 children per woman in 2005–2010.

Statistics on the urban population are compiled according to each economy's national definition, as there is no agreed international standard for defining an urban area. National estimates are used for urban ratios. If national estimates are not available, data from the *World Urbanization Prospects* are used.

Data on numbers of physicians and health resources are compiled by the World Health Organization, while data on pupils, teachers, and education resources are compiled by the UNESCO Institute for Statistics from country sources.

Household surveys are the best source for labor force data but these surveys are not carried out in all economies. Some rely on census data supplemented by enterprise surveys and unemployment registration records. Unemployment registration records are often incomplete and may refer only to formal employment, while a breakdown by economic activities also may not be available.

The statistics on the number of people living with HIV are estimates based on methods and on parameters developed by the UNAIDS Reference Group on HIV/AIDS Estimates, Modelling, and Projections. The estimates are presented together with ranges, called "plausibility bounds," where the wider the bound, the greater the uncertainty surrounding an estimate.

References

M. Amare, L. Hohfeld, S. Jitsuchon, and H. Waibe. 2012. Rural–Urban Migration and Employment Quality: A Case Study from Thailand. *ADB Economics Working Paper Series*. No. 209. Manila: Asian Development Bank.

T. Pettinger. 2012. Implications of Higher Dependency Ratio. EconomicsHelp.org. http://www.economicshelp.org/blog/5066/economics/implications-of-higher-dependency-ratio-2/.

J. P. Smith and M. Majmundar, eds. 2012. *Aging in Asia: Findings from New and Emerging Data Initiatives*. Washington, DC: National Academies Press.

United Nations Department of Economic and Social Affairs (UNDESA), Population Division. 2014. *World Urbanization Prospects: The 2014 Revision*. https://esa.un.org/unpd/wup/

———. 2015. *World Population Prospects: The 2015 Revision*. https://esa.un.org/unpd/wpp/

Table 1.1: **Midyear Population**

Regional Member	Population (million)				Population Growth Rates (%)			
	2000	**2005**	**2010**	**2015**	**2000**	**2005**	**2010**	**2015**
Developing Member Economies								
Central and West Asia	**231.7**	**251.6**	**279.0**	**305.3**	**1.8**	**1.0**	**2.0**	**1.8**
Afghanistan[a]	21.0	23.6	26.0	28.6	1.4	1.5	2.0	1.8
Armenia	3.2	3.1	3.0	3.0	−0.3	−0.6	−0.7	−0.3
Azerbaijan	8.1	8.5	9.1	9.7	1.1	1.2	1.2	1.2
Georgia[a, d]	4.4	4.3	4.4	3.7	−0.8	0.1	1.2	...
Kazakhstan	14.9	15.1	16.3	17.5	−0.3	0.9	1.4	1.5
Kyrgyz Republic[a]	4.9	5.1	5.4	5.9	1.4	1.2	0.3	2.1
Pakistan	140.0	154.0	173.5	191.7	2.3	1.9	2.1	1.9
Tajikistan	6.2	6.9	7.6	8.6	2.1	2.1	2.2	2.4
Turkmenistan	4.5	4.7	5.0	5.4	1.2	1.1	1.3	1.3
Uzbekistan	24.7	26.2	28.6	31.3	1.4	1.2	2.9	1.8
East Asia	**1,345.7**	**1,387.8**	**1,423.2**	**1,459.0**	**0.8**	**0.6**	**0.5**	**0.5**
China, People's Rep. of[a]	1,267.4	1,307.6	1,340.9	1,374.6	0.8	0.6	0.5	0.5
Hong Kong, China	6.7	6.8	7.0	7.3	0.9	0.4	0.7	0.9
Korea, Rep. of	47.0	48.1	49.4	50.6	0.8	0.2	0.5	0.4
Mongolia	2.4	2.5	2.7	3.0	1.3	1.1	1.8	2.2
Taipei,China	22.2	22.7	23.1	23.5	0.8	0.4	0.3	0.3
South Asia	**1,189.6**	**1,290.5**	**1,382.6**	**1,491.0**	**1.6**	**1.5**	**1.4**	**1.3**
Bangladesh	129.3	138.6	148.6	157.9	1.4	1.5	1.4	1.3
Bhutan	0.6	0.6	0.7	0.8	1.3	1.3	1.8	1.6
India[a]	1,019.0	1,106.0	1,186.0	1,283.0	1.8	1.5	1.4	1.2
Maldives	0.3	0.3	0.4	0.5	1.5	3.3	2.3	3.7
Nepal	21.0	25.3	26.3	28.0	3.0	2.3	1.4	1.4
Sri Lanka	19.4	19.6	20.7	21.0	1.3	0.9	1.0	0.9
Southeast Asia	**515.4**	**550.1**	**589.7**	**626.1**	**1.5**	**1.3**	**1.9**	**1.3**
Brunei Darussalam	0.3	0.4	0.4	0.4	2.5	1.8	1.8	1.3
Cambodia	12.5	13.3	14.1	15.1	1.3	1.3	1.3	1.3
Indonesia	206.3	219.9	238.5	255.2	1.2	1.3	2.7	1.3
Lao PDR	5.1	5.6	6.0	6.5	2.0	2.0	1.5	1.4
Malaysia	23.5	26.0	28.6	31.0	2.5	2.1	1.8	1.3
Myanmar[a]	47.7	50.0	51.7	52.5	1.2	0.8	0.7	0.9
Philippines	76.8	84.7	92.3	101.0	2.3	1.9	1.7	1.7
Singapore	4.0	4.3	5.1	5.5	1.7	2.4	1.8	1.2
Thailand	62.2	64.1	65.9	67.2	1.1	0.6	0.6	0.3
Viet Nam	77.1	81.9	86.9	91.7	1.4	1.2	1.1	1.1
The Pacific[b]	**8.0**	**9.1**	**10.4**	**11.8**	**3.6**	**2.6**	**2.7**	**2.7**
Cook Islands	18.0	21.5	23.7	18.8	9.1	5.9	4.9	1.1
Fiji	802.0	827.0	850.7	869.5	0.6	0.7	0.6	0.4
Kiribati[a]	84.5	92.5	103.1	109.7	1.7	1.8	2.1	1.3
Marshall Islands	51.2	51.2	52.9	54.0	0.8	1.4	1.2	0.4
Micronesia, Fed. States of[a]	107.0	105.6	102.8	102.3	0.2	−0.3	−0.5	0.2
Nauru	10.1	9.5	9.7	10.9	1.0	−2.2	1.9	2.0
Palau	18.9	19.8	18.3	17.6	0.3	0.8	−1.9	1.2
Papua New Guinea	5,190.8	6,051.7	7,055.4	8,225.6	3.3	3.1	3.1	3.1
Samoa	175.1	178.7	186.4	193.5	0.9	0.3	0.8	0.8
Solomon Islands	418.6	470.1	528.0	592.9	2.3	2.3	2.3	2.3
Timor-Leste	779.0	945.4	1,066.4	1,245.0	1.2	1.8	2.7	2.7
Tonga	99.1	101.2	102.8	104.0	0.4	0.4	0.2	0.2
Tuvalu	9.5	10.3	11.1	10.8	1.3	3.1	0.5	0.2
Vanuatu	191.7	217.8	245.4	277.5	2.7	2.6	2.7	2.4
Developed Member Economies	**149.7**	**152.1**	**154.5**	**155.3**	**0.2**	**0.2**	**0.3**	**0.2**
Australia	19.0	20.2	22.0	23.8	1.2	1.2	1.6	1.4
Japan	126.8	127.8	128.1	127.0	0.2	0.0	0.0	−0.1
New Zealand	3.9	4.1	4.4	4.6	0.6	1.1	1.1	1.9
DEVELOPING MEMBER ECONOMIES[c]	**3,290.4**	**3,489.1**	**3,684.9**	**3,893.8**	**1.3**	**1.1**	**1.2**	**1.0**
REGIONAL MEMBERS[c]	**3,440.1**	**3,641.2**	**3,839.3**	**4,048.6**	**1.2**	**1.0**	**1.1**	**1.0**
WORLD	**6,126.6**	**6,519.6**	**6,929.7**	**7,349.5**	**1.3**	**1.2**	**1.2**	**1.2**

0.0 = magnitude is less than half of unit employed, Lao PDR = Lao People's Democratic Republic.

a Population figures refer to 1 January for Georgia and the Kyrgyz Republic, 1 May for Afghanistan, 30 September for the Federated States of Micronesia, 1 October for India and Myanmar, 7 November for Kiribati, and 31 December for the People's Republic of China.
b Population figures for the Pacific developing member economies are in thousands, while the regional total for the Pacific are in millions.
c For reporting economies only.
d Population estimates for 2015 are based on the 2014 census. Data for earlier years are yet to be revised by GeoStat.

Sources: Economy sources; United Nations Population Division, Department of Economic and Social Affairs. World Population Prospects, the 2015 Revision. https://esa.un.org/unpd/wpp/ (accessed August 2016).

Table 1.2:   **Migration and Urbanization**

Regional Member	Net International Migration Rate[a] (per 1,000 population)			Urban Population (as % of total population)			
	2000–2005	2005–2010	2010–2015	2000	2005	2010	2015
Developing Member Economies							
Central and West Asia							
Afghanistan	7.3	–5.2	3.1	20.0	20.3	21.9	23.4
Armenia	–9.5	–9.1	–0.7	64.8	64.0	63.5	63.6
Azerbaijan	0.3	–2.2	–0.3	51.1	52.5	53.0	53.1
Georgia	–13.4	–13.3	–14.4	52.0	52.2	53.0	57.2
Kazakhstan	0.6	–0.4	1.9	56.5	57.1	54.5	56.8
Kyrgyz Republic	–6.9	–2.9	–4.0	34.7	34.8	34.1	33.7
Pakistan	–1.2	–1.6	–1.2	33.9	34.0	36.3	39.2
Tajikistan	–3.0	–1.8	–2.9	26.6	26.4	26.4	26.4
Turkmenistan	–5.0	–2.3	–1.0	45.9	47.0	48.4	50.0
Uzbekistan	–3.6	–2.2	–1.4	37.2	36.1	51.4	50.7
East Asia							
China, People's Rep. of	–0.3	–0.3	–0.3	36.2	43.0	50.0	56.1
Hong Kong, China	–1.2	1.3	4.2	100.0	100.0	100.0	100.0
Korea, Rep. of	1.0	1.7	1.2	79.6	81.3	81.9	82.5
Mongolia	–1.2	–1.1	–1.1	56.6	61.9	69.2	68.6
Taipei,China[b]	...	...	...	55.8	57.7	59.3	60.9
South Asia							
Bangladesh	–2.5	–4.8	–2.8	23.1	24.2	25.9	34.2
Bhutan	11.5	4.9	2.7	21.0	30.9	34.8	38.9
India	–0.4	–0.5	–0.4	27.7	28.8	29.9	31.0
Maldives	–0.1	–0.0	–0.0	27.0	35.0 (2006)	40.5	...
Nepal	–7.5	–7.8	–2.7	14.1	14.6	16.6	18.5
Sri Lanka	–4.7	–5.2	–4.7	14.6 (2001)	15.1	18.2 (2012)	19.2
Southeast Asia							
Brunei Darussalam	1.3	1.3	1.0	71.2	73.5	75.5	77.2
Cambodia	–0.6	–4.3	–2.0	16.0 (2001)	17.7	20.0	20.7
Indonesia	–0.8	–1.0	–0.6	42.0	45.9	49.9	53.7
Lao PDR	–6.3	–3.9	–3.6	22.0	27.4	33.1	38.6
Malaysia	4.0	4.8	3.1	62.9	66.5	71.0	74.3
Myanmar	–5.6	–5.8	–1.8	27.0	28.9	31.4	29.2
Philippines	–2.7	–4.1	–1.4	48.0	46.6	45.3	44.4
Singapore	20.7	18.8	14.9	100.0	100.0	100.0	100.0
Thailand	3.4	–2.6	0.3	31.1	32.5	42.0	44.5 (2013)
Viet Nam	–1.9	–2.0	–0.4	24.2	27.1	30.5	33.9
The Pacific							
Cook Islands	...	...	...	66.9	71.9	73.5	74.5
Fiji	–15.1	–6.8	–6.6	47.9	49.9	51.8	53.7
Kiribati	–4.6	–1.2	–4.0	47.5	49.1	54.1	57.1
Marshall Islands	...	...	...	68.4	69.9	71.3	72.7
Micronesia, Fed. States of	–24.1	–23.1	–15.7	22.3	22.3	22.3	22.4
Nauru	...	...	...	100.0	100.0	100.0	100.0
Palau	...	...	...	70.0	77.7	83.4	87.1
Papua New Guinea	–	–	–	13.2	13.1	13.0	13.0
Samoa	–17.7	–16.8	–13.4	22.0	21.2	20.1	19.1
Solomon Islands	–2.2	–4.8	–4.3	15.8	17.8	20.0	22.3
Timor-Leste	0.0	–20.5	–8.9	24.3	26.3	29.5	32.8
Tonga	–16.4	–16.0	–15.4	23.0	23.2	23.4	23.7
Tuvalu	...	...	...	46.0	49.7	54.8	59.7
Vanuatu	–0.5	1.0	0.5	21.7	23.1	24.6	26.1
Developed Member Economies							
Australia	5.8	10.7	8.9	87.2	88.0	88.7	89.4
Japan	1.0	0.7	0.6	78.6	86.0	90.5	93.5
New Zealand	6.7	2.9	0.3	85.7	86.1	86.2	86.4

... = data not available at cutoff date, 0.0 = magnitude is less than half of unit employed, Lao PDR = Lao People's Democratic Republic.

a   Refers to annual average.
b   For urban population, refers to localities of 100,000 or more inhabitants.

Sources: Economy sources; United Nations Population Division, Department of Economic and Social Affairs. World Urbanization Prospects, the 2014 Revision – Data Query. https://esa.un.org/unpd/wup/DataQuery/ (accessed August 2016).

Table 1.3 **Population Aged 0–14 Years and Aged 15–64 Years**[a]
(% of total population)

Regional Member	Aged 0–14 Years				Aged 15–64 Years			
	2000	2005	2010	2015	2000	2005	2010	2015
Developing Member Economies								
Central and West Asia								
Afghanistan	48.6	47.6	47.6	44.0	49.2	50.2	50.1	53.5
Armenia	25.9	21.9	20.5	18.4	64.1	66.5	68.9	70.8
Azerbaijan	31.1	26.0	22.7	21.9	63.3	67.6	71.3	72.5
Georgia	21.9	18.3	16.9	17.3	65.6	67.0	68.8	68.6
Kazakhstan	27.6	24.6	24.2	26.7	65.5	67.7	69.0	66.5
Kyrgyz Republic	35.0	31.1	30.0	31.4	59.6	63.3	65.5	64.4
Pakistan	41.1	38.2	36.2	35.0	54.8	57.6	59.4	60.5
Tajikistan	42.9	38.4	35.5	34.8	53.6	57.9	61.1	62.2
Turkmenistan	36.3	32.7	29.2	28.2	59.4	62.7	66.6	67.6
Uzbekistan	36.8	32.1	29.1	28.5	58.5	62.8	66.2	66.8
East Asia								
China, People's Rep. of	25.1	20.1	17.4	17.2	68.3	72.4	74.3	73.2
Hong Kong, China	17.2	14.1	12.1	12.0	71.8	73.7	75.0	73.0
Korea, Rep. of	21.0	18.5	16.2	14.0	71.7	72.3	72.7	72.9
Mongolia	34.8	28.9	27.0	28.2	61.5	67.3	69.2	67.7
Taipei,China	21.1	18.7	15.6	14.0 (2014)	70.3	71.6	73.6	74.0 (2014)
South Asia								
Bangladesh	37.1	34.5	32.1	29.4	59.1	61.3	63.2	65.6
Bhutan	40.6	34.1	30.1	26.9	55.6	61.8	65.4	68.1
India	34.7	32.8	30.9	28.8	60.9	62.4	64.0	65.6
Maldives	40.7	33.5	28.7	27.5	55.6	62.0	66.4	67.8
Nepal	41.0	39.8	37.2	32.7	55.2	55.8	57.9	61.8
Sri Lanka	26.8	25.6	25.4	24.6	67.0	67.6	67.2	66.1
Southeast Asia								
Brunei Darussalam	30.5	27.7	25.3	23.1	67.1	69.3	71.2	72.5
Cambodia	41.6	37.1	33.3	31.6	55.3	59.5	62.9	64.3
Indonesia	30.7	29.9	28.9	27.7	64.6	65.3	66.2	67.1
Lao PDR	43.3	40.5	37.0	34.8	53.1	55.8	59.3	61.4
Malaysia	33.3	30.1	27.3	24.5	62.8	65.5	67.8	69.6
Myanmar	31.9	30.7	29.8	27.6	63.3	64.4	65.2	67.1
Philippines	38.5	37.1	33.6	31.9	58.3	59.5	62.2	63.5
Singapore	21.5	19.1	17.3	15.5	71.2	72.6	73.6	72.8
Thailand	24.0	22.2	19.2	17.7	69.5	70.1	71.9	71.8
Viet Nam	31.7	27.2	23.7	23.1	61.9	66.3	69.8	70.2
The Pacific								
Cook Islands	34.7	31.4	28.0	27.8	59.1	61.3	64.0	62.6
Fiji	35.0	30.5	29.0	28.7	61.5	65.4	66.2	65.4
Kiribati	40.6	37.0	35.2	35.2	55.9	59.5	61.3	61.3
Marshall Islands	42.3	41.3	41.8	39.8	55.5	56.5	55.9	57.5
Micronesia, Fed. States of	40.3	38.8	36.9	34.1	56.0	57.2	59.3	61.6
Nauru	40.1	37.1	35.6	39.5	58.6	61.2	63.1	58.8
Palau	23.9	24.1	20.5	19.7	70.7	70.2	73.7	72.1
Papua New Guinea	40.2	39.9	39.0	37.1	57.3	57.5	58.3	59.8
Samoa	40.7	39.6	38.3	37.3	54.8	55.6	56.7	57.5
Solomon Islands	41.9	41.3	40.7	39.5	55.3	55.7	56.0	57.1
Timor-Leste	50.0	48.2	41.3	42.4	47.7	49.2	54.5	52.0
Tonga	38.3	38.0	37.4	36.8	56.0	55.9	56.7	57.4
Tuvalu	37.1	34.3	32.0	32.7	57.0	60.1	62.7	61.7
Vanuatu	41.5	39.7	38.2	36.5	55.2	57.0	57.9	59.3
Developed Member Economies								
Australia	20.8	19.8	19.0	18.7	66.8	67.3	67.5	66.3
Japan	14.6	13.8	13.3	12.9	68.2	66.3	63.8	60.8
New Zealand	22.7	21.6	20.5	20.2	65.5	66.4	66.5	64.9
DEVELOPING MEMBER ECONOMIES[b]	**30.7**	**27.7**	**25.6**	**24.6**	**63.9**	**66.4**	**68.0**	**68.3**
REGIONAL MEMBERS[b]	**30.0**	**27.2**	**25.2**	**24.2**	**64.1**	**66.4**	**67.9**	**68.1**
WORLD	**30.2**	**28.0**	**26.7**	**26.1**	**63.0**	**64.7**	**65.7**	**65.7**

Lao PDR = Lao People's Democratic Republic.

a From 2011 onward, the United Nations Population Division projected the country's population based on the medium-fertility variant where fertility is above 2.1 children per woman in the 2005–2010 censuses.
b For reporting economies only.

Sources: United Nations Department of Economic and Social Affairs, Population Division. World Population Prospects, The 2015 Revision. https://esa.un.org/unpd/wpp/ (accessed June 2016); for the Cook Islands, Kiribati, the Marshall Islands, Nauru, Palau, and Tuvalu: Statistics for Development Division. http://sdd.spc.int/en/ (accessed June 2015); for Taipei,China: Directorate-General of Budget, Accounting and Statistics. Monthly Bulletin of Statistics. http://eng.dgbas.gov.tw/mp.asp?mp=2 (accessed August 2016).

Table 1.4:   **Population Aged 65 Years and Over and Age Dependency Ratio**

Regional Member	Aged 65 Years and Over (% of total population)				Age Dependency Ratio			
	2000	2005	2010	2015[a]	2000	2005	2010	2015[a]
Developing Member Economies								
Central and West Asia	**4.5**	**4.7**	**4.6**	**4.6**	**77.8**	**69.9**	**64.9**	**62.5**
Afghanistan	2.2	2.2	2.3	2.5	103.3	99.1	99.5	87.0
Armenia	10.0	11.6	10.5	10.8	55.9	50.4	45.1	41.3
Azerbaijan	5.6	6.4	5.9	5.6	57.9	48.0	40.2	38.0
Georgia	12.5	14.6	14.3	14.0	52.5	49.1	45.4	45.7
Kazakhstan	6.8	7.7	6.8	6.7	52.6	47.7	44.9	50.3
Kyrgyz Republic	5.5	5.6	4.5	4.2	67.9	57.9	52.6	55.3
Pakistan	4.1	4.3	4.4	4.5	82.5	73.7	68.4	65.3
Tajikistan	3.5	3.7	3.3	3.0	86.7	72.7	63.5	60.9
Turkmenistan	4.3	4.6	4.1	4.2	68.4	59.4	50.0	47.9
Uzbekistan	4.7	5.1	4.7	4.7	70.9	59.2	51.0	49.7
East Asia	**6.7**	**7.6**	**8.4**	**9.7**	**46.1**	**38.1**	**34.7**	**36.6**
China, People's Rep. of	6.7	7.5	8.2	9.6	46.4	38.1	34.5	36.6
Hong Kong, China	11.0	12.2	12.9	15.1	39.3	35.7	33.3	37.0
Korea, Rep. of	7.3	9.2	11.1	13.1	39.5	38.4	37.6	37.2
Mongolia	3.7	3.7	3.8	4.0	62.5	48.5	44.4	47.6
Taipei,China	8.6	9.7	10.7	12.0 (2014)	42.3	39.7	35.8	35.1 (2014)
South Asia	**4.4**	**4.7**	**5.1**	**5.6**	**64.9**	**60.6**	**56.6**	**52.6**
Bangladesh	3.8	4.3	4.7	5.0	69.2	63.2	58.3	52.5
Bhutan	3.8	4.1	4.5	5.1	79.9	61.7	52.9	46.9
India	4.4	4.8	5.1	5.6	64.3	60.2	56.3	52.4
Maldives	3.7	4.5	4.9	4.7	79.9	61.3	50.6	47.4
Nepal	3.8	4.4	5.0	5.5	81.1	79.2	72.8	61.8
Sri Lanka	6.2	6.9	7.3	9.3	49.2	48.0	48.7	51.2
Southeast Asia	**4.9**	**5.2**	**5.5**	**5.9**	**57.8**	**54.1**	**50.0**	**48.1**
Brunei Darussalam	2.4	3.0	3.5	4.4	49.1	44.3	40.4	38.0
Cambodia	3.1	3.4	3.7	4.1	80.8	67.9	58.9	55.6
Indonesia	4.7	4.8	4.9	5.2	54.8	53.2	51.1	49.0
Lao PDR	3.6	3.7	3.7	3.8	88.3	79.1	68.5	62.8
Malaysia	3.8	4.4	4.9	5.9	59.1	52.7	47.4	43.6
Myanmar	4.8	4.9	5.0	5.4	57.9	55.3	53.4	49.1
Philippines	3.2	3.4	4.2	4.6	71.6	68.1	60.7	57.6
Singapore	7.3	8.2	9.0	11.7	40.4	37.7	35.8	37.4
Thailand	6.6	7.7	8.9	10.5	44.0	42.6	39.1	39.2
Viet Nam	6.4	6.6	6.5	6.7	61.5	50.9	43.3	42.5
The Pacific	**2.7**	**2.9**	**3.3**	**3.7**	**77.0**	**74.8**	**71.1**	**68.7**
Cook Islands	6.2	7.3	8.0	9.6	69.3	63.1	56.2	59.8
Fiji	3.4	4.1	4.8	5.8	62.5	53.0	51.1	52.8
Kiribati	3.6	3.5	3.5	3.5	79.0	68.0	63.1	63.2
Marshall Islands	2.1	2.2	2.3	2.7	80.0	76.9	78.8	74.0
Micronesia, Fed. States of	3.7	4.0	3.8	4.4	78.7	74.8	68.8	62.4
Nauru	1.3	1.7	1.3	1.7	70.7	63.4	58.5	70.0
Palau	5.4	5.7	5.8	8.2	41.4	42.5	35.7	38.7
Papua New Guinea	2.5	2.6	2.8	3.0	74.5	73.9	71.6	67.1
Samoa	4.5	4.8	5.1	5.2	82.5	79.9	76.4	74.0
Solomon Islands	2.8	3.0	3.3	3.4	81.0	79.5	78.6	75.1
Timor-Leste	2.3	2.6	4.3	5.6	109.6	103.4	83.6	92.3
Tonga	5.7	6.0	5.9	5.9	78.7	78.8	76.3	74.3
Tuvalu	5.9	5.6	5.3	5.6	75.4	66.5	59.5	61.9
Vanuatu	3.3	3.3	3.9	4.2	81.2	75.4	72.9	68.7
Developed Member Economies	**16.4**	**18.7**	**21.3**	**24.3**	**47.2**	**50.4**	**55.3**	**61.9**
Australia	12.4	12.9	13.5	15.0	49.7	48.6	48.2	50.9
Japan	17.2	19.8	22.9	26.3	46.6	50.7	56.8	64.5
New Zealand	11.8	12.0	13.0	14.9	52.7	50.6	50.4	54.0
DEVELOPING MEMBER ECONOMIES[b]	**5.4**	**5.9**	**6.4**	**7.1**	**56.5**	**50.6**	**47.0**	**46.3**
REGIONAL MEMBERS[b]	**5.9**	**6.4**	**7.0**	**7.7**	**56.1**	**50.6**	**47.4**	**46.9**
WORLD	**6.8**	**7.3**	**7.6**	**8.3**	**58.7**	**54.6**	**52.3**	**52.3**

Lao PDR = Lao People's Democratic Republic.

a   From 2011, the United Nations Population Division projected the country's population based on the medium-fertility variant where fertility is above 2.1 children per woman in 2005–2010 censuses.

b   For reporting economies only.

Sources: United Nations Department of Economic and Social Affairs, Population Division. World Population Prospects, The 2015 Revision. https://esa.un.org/unpd/wpp/ (accessed June 2016); for Cook Islands, Kiribati, the Marshall Islands, Nauru, Palau, and Tuvalu: Pacific Community, Statistics for Development Division. http://sdd.spc.int/en/ (accessed June 2015); for Taipei,China: Directorate-General of Budget, Accounting and Statistics. Monthly Bulletin of Statistics. http://eng.dgbas.gov.tw/mp.asp?mp=2 (accessed August 2016).

Table 1.5:   **Labor Force Participation Rate**
(%)

Regional Member	2000	2005	2010	2011	2012	2013	2014	2015
Developing Member Economies								
Central and West Asia								
Afghanistan[a]	50.6	51.7	51.3	51.5	51.7	52.1	52.4	52.5
Armenia	61.4	57.7	61.2	63.0	62.7	63.4	63.1	62.5
Azerbaijan	77.6	68.4	64.8	64.5	64.5	64.6	65.1	65.4
Georgia	65.2	64.0	64.2	65.2	66.9	66.2	66.5	67.8
Kazakhstan	66.0	69.4	71.2	71.6	71.7	71.7	70.7	71.1
Kyrgyz Republic	64.9	64.9	64.1	64.8	64.2	62.5	62.7	62.9
Pakistan	42.8	43.7	45.9	45.7	45.7	45.7	45.5	45.2
Tajikistan	56.3	55.0	50.3	49.4	48.9	48.6	47.8	48.0
Turkmenistan[b]	60.5	60.5	60.6	60.9	61.2	61.5	61.8	62.0
Uzbekistan	59.0	59.2	60.6	60.9	61.1	61.4	61.6	61.8
East Asia								
China, People's Rep. of[c]	77.5	73.5	70.9	70.9	70.9	71.0	71.0	70.9
Hong Kong, China	61.4	60.9	59.6	60.1	60.5	61.2	61.1	61.2
Korea, Rep. of	61.2	62.0	61.0	61.1	61.3	61.5	62.4	62.6
Mongolia	62.9	63.5	61.6	62.5	63.5	61.9	62.1	61.5
Taipei,China	57.7	57.8	58.1	58.2	58.4	58.4	58.5	58.7
South Asia								
Bangladesh	54.9	58.5 (2006)	59.3	...	...	57.1	...	...
Bhutan	56.5 (2001)	60.4	68.6	67.4	64.4	65.3	62.6	63.1
India[d]	37.6	39.2	37.4 (2009)	...	...	...	...	...
Maldives[e]	54.3	62.4	65.7	66.2	66.6	67.1	67.6	68.0
Nepal	85.8	84.6	83.4	83.3	83.2	83.1	83.0	83.0
Sri Lanka	50.3	49.3	48.6	53.0	52.6	53.8	53.3	53.8
Southeast Asia								
Brunei Darussalam	67.9 (2001)	...	...	68.9	...	...	65.6	...
Cambodia	65.2	74.6 (2004)	87.0	87.5	84.2	83.0	82.6	...
Indonesia	67.8	66.8	67.7	66.8	67.8	66.8	66.6	65.8
Lao PDR	79.9 (2001)	66.6	...	...	...	...	...	...
Malaysia	65.4	63.3	63.7	64.5	65.6	67.3	67.6	67.9
Myanmar[f]	63.6 (2001)	65.0	66.1	66.0	66.3	66.9	67.0	64.7
Philippines	64.9	65.1	64.1	64.6	64.2	63.9	64.6	63.7
Singapore[g]	63.2	63.0	66.2	66.1	66.6	66.7	67.0	68.3
Thailand	71.5	72.5	72.3	71.7	71.8	71.1	70.3	69.8
Viet Nam	49.6	52.5	77.4	77.0	76.8	77.5	77.5	77.8
The Pacific								
Cook Islands	69.0 (2001)	70.2 (2006)	...	71.0	...	...	...	...
Fiji	57.4	56.2	54.9	54.8	54.7	54.6	54.4	54.3
Kiribati	80.9	63.6	59.3	...	...	...	...	...
Marshall Islands	...	...	...	...	...	...	...	...
Micronesia, Fed. States of	58.6	...	57.3	...	...	...	...	...
Nauru	...	...	...	...	...	...	...	...
Palau	67.5	69.1	...	...	68.1	...	...	77.4
Papua New Guinea	72.2	72.9	71.7	71.3	70.8	70.6	70.3	70.3
Samoa	50.6 (2001)	49.8 (2006)	...	41.3	...	...	...	...
Solomon Islands	...	...	62.7 (2009)	...	...	...	...	...
Timor-Leste	56.0 (2001)	60.2 (2004)	41.7	...	...	30.6	...	...
Tonga	...	...	...	...	...	...	...	...
Tuvalu	58.2 (2002)	...	...	...	59.4	...	...	...
Vanuatu	77.0	73.6	71.0	71.1	71.1	71.1	71.0	71.0
Developed Member Economies								
Australia	63.1	64.4	65.4	65.4	65.1	64.9	64.7	64.9
Japan	62.4	60.4	59.6	59.3	59.1	59.3	59.4	59.6
New Zealand	65.2	67.7	68.0	68.3	68.0	68.2	68.9	69.0

... = data not available at cutoff date, Lao PDR = Lao People's Democratic Republic.

a Includes the population aged 10–59 years.
b The labor force data series includes individuals that are not registered.
c Refers to persons engaged in social labor and receiving remuneration payment or earning business income.
d Figures are computed using data on total labor force and total population.
e Data for 2000 refer to persons 12 years old and over and for 2006 onward to persons 15 years old and over. Figures include local population only.
f Data for 2014 are sourced from the results of the Population and Housing Census 2014 and may not be comparable to data from previous years.
g Refers to Singapore residents only.

Sources: Economy sources; International Labour Organization. Key Indicators of the Labour Market Online. 9th Edition. http://www.ilo.org/kilm (accessed June 2016); for Kiribati, Nauru, and Tuvalu: Secretariat of the Pacific Community. National Minimum Development Indicator Database. http://www.spc.int/nmdi/ (accessed June 2016).

Labor Force and Employment

Table 1.6: **Unemployment Rate**
(%)

Regional Member	2000	2005	2010	2011	2012	2013	2014	2015
Developing Member Economies								
Central and West Asia								
Afghanistan[a]	3.4 (2001)	3.4 (2004)	...	...	...	...	...	...
Armenia	11.7	8.2	19.0	18.4	17.3	16.2	17.6	18.5
Azerbaijan	11.8	7.3	5.6	5.4	5.2	5.0	4.9	5.0
Georgia	10.3	13.8	16.3	15.1	15.0	14.6	12.4	12.0
Kazakhstan	12.9	8.1	5.8	5.4	5.2	5.2	5.0	5.0
Kyrgyz Republic	7.5	8.1	8.6	8.5	8.4	8.3	8.0	7.6
Pakistan	7.8	7.7	5.6	5.9	5.9	6.2	6.0	5.9
Tajikistan	2.7	1.9	2.1	2.3	2.4	2.3	2.4	2.3
Turkmenistan[b]	10.3	10.4	10.4	10.3	10.3	10.2	10.1	10.0
Uzbekistan	0.4	0.3	0.1	0.1	0.1	0.0	0.0	...
East Asia								
China, People's Rep. of[c]	3.1	4.2	4.1	4.1	4.1	4.1	4.1	4.1
Hong Kong, China	4.9	5.6	4.3	3.4	3.3	3.4	3.3	3.3
Korea, Rep. of	4.4	3.7	3.7	3.4	3.2	3.1	3.5	3.6
Mongolia	4.6	3.3	9.9	7.7	8.2	7.9	7.9	7.5
Taipei,China	3.0	4.1	5.2	4.4	4.2	4.2	4.0	3.8
South Asia								
Bangladesh	4.3	4.2 (2006)	4.5	...	...	4.3	...	...
Bhutan	...	3.1	3.3	3.1	2.1	2.9	2.6	2.5
India[d]	2.7	3.1	2.5 (2009)	...	...	...	...	...
Maldives[e]	2.0	5.5 (2006)	11.7	...	...	...	5.2	...
Nepal	2.1	2.8	2.6	3.5	2.6	3.3	3.1	3.1
Sri Lanka	7.6	7.4	4.9	4.2	4.0	4.4	4.3	4.7
Southeast Asia								
Brunei Darussalam	7.2 (2001)	...	...	9.3	...	...	6.9	...
Cambodia	2.5	...	0.4	0.2	0.2	0.3	0.2	...
Indonesia	6.1	11.2	7.1	7.5	6.1	6.2	5.9	6.2
Lao PDR	5.0 (2001)	1.4	33.0	...	...	...	...	...
Malaysia	3.0	3.5	3.3	3.1	3.0	3.1	2.9	3.1
Myanmar[f]	4.0 (2001)	4.0	4.0	4.0	4.0	4.0	3.9	0.8
Philippines	11.2	7.8	7.4	7.0	7.0	7.1	6.6	6.3
Singapore[g]	4.4	4.2	2.8	2.7	2.6	2.6	2.6	2.6
Thailand	3.6	1.8	1.0	0.7	0.7	0.7	0.8	0.9
Viet Nam	2.3	4.7	2.7	2.0	1.8	1.7	1.9	2.1
The Pacific								
Cook Islands	13.1 (2001)	8.9 (2006)	...	8.2	...	...	...	...
Fiji	7.8	4.6	8.9	9.0	9.0	9.4	8.3	7.7
Kiribati	1.6	6.1	30.6	...	...	...	...	...
Marshall Islands	30.9	30.9	...	3.2	32.6	...	...	...
Micronesia, Fed. States of	22.0	...	16.2	...	...	...	...	...
Nauru	22.7 (2002)	...	...	22.9	...	...	...	...
Palau	2.3	4.2	...	...	4.1	...	...	...
Papua New Guinea	...	...	...	1.4	...	...	...	...
Samoa	4.9 (2001)	...	...	5.7	...	...	...	...
Solomon Islands	...	...	6.3 (2009)	...	...	...	...	...
Timor-Leste	...	7.2 (2004)	3.6	...	...	11.0	...	...
Tonga	...	...	...	6.4	...	...	...	...
Tuvalu	6.5 (2002)	6.5	...	...	39.6	...	...	...
Vanuatu	5.3	5.1	4.3	4.3	4.3	4.3	4.5	4.3
Developed Member Economies								
Australia	6.3	5.0	5.2	5.1	5.2	5.7	6.1	6.1
Japan	4.7	4.4	5.1	4.6	4.3	4.0	3.6	3.4
New Zealand	6.1	3.8	6.5	6.5	6.9	6.2	5.8	5.8

... = data not available at cutoff date, – = magnitude equals zero, 0.0 = magnitude is less than half of unit employed, Lao PDR = Lao People's Democratic Republic.

a Includes the population aged 10–59 years.
b The labor force data series includes individuals that are not registered.
c Refers to persons engaged in social labor and receiving remuneration payment or earning business income.
d Figures are computed using data on total labor force and total population.
e Data for 2000 refer to persons 12 years old and over and for 2006 onward to persons 15 years old and over. Figures include local population only.
f Data for 2014 are sourced from the results of the Population and Housing Census 2014 and may not be comparable to data from previous years.
g Refers to Singapore residents only.

Sources: Economy sources; International Labour Organization. Key Indicators of the Labour Market Online. 9th Edition. http://www.ilo.org/kilm (accessed June 2016); for the Cook Islands, Kiribati, the Marshall Islands, Nauru, Palau, Papua New Guinea, Samoa, Solomon Islands, Tonga, and Tuvalu: Secretariat of the Pacific Community. National Minimum Development Indicator Database. http://www.spc.int/nmdi/ (accessed June 2016).

Table 1.7: **Unemployment Rate Among 15–24-Year-Olds**
(%)

Regional Member	Total		Female		Male	
	2000	2015	2000	2015	2000	2015
Developing Member Economies						
Central and West Asia						
Afghanistan	21.2	19.9	20.3	20.8	21.3	19.7
Armenia	36.1	37.2	40.5	42.9	31.4	32.5
Azerbaijan	28.0	14.3	28.9	15.9	27.1	12.8
Georgia	20.9	29.8	20.3	32.1	21.4	28.6
Kazakhstan	14.1	5.1	15.5	5.9	12.9	4.4
Kyrgyz Republic	13.7	14.6	15.4	17.7	12.4	12.8
Pakistan	13.4	10.7	29.5	14.4	11.2	9.6
Tajikistan	18.6	16.8	13.4	13.9	22.3	18.6
Turkmenistan	19.3	19.5	20.3	20.7	18.7	18.8
Uzbekistan	19.9	19.8	21.4	21.5	19.0	18.8
East Asia						
China, People's Rep. of	10.1	12.1	8.5	11.1	11.5	12.8
Hong Kong, China	11.1	9.5	10.4	8.3	11.8	10.8
Korea, Rep. of	10.8	10.4	8.7	9.6	13.0	11.3
Mongolia	10.7	14.7	11.0	15.9	10.5	13.9
Taipei,China	7.1	11.5	6.0	11.0	7.9	11.9
South Asia						
Bangladesh	9.3	11.6	9.0	12.1	9.6	11.3
Bhutan	4.4	9.2	5.0	9.9	3.9	8.5
India	9.9	9.7	10.1	10.2	9.9	9.6
Maldives	24.4	27.9	23.1	25.4	25.2	29.9
Nepal	3.4	5.1	2.8	4.0	4.0	6.3
Sri Lanka	24.0	20.2	31.2	29.3	20.2	15.3
Southeast Asia						
Brunei Darussalam	8.6	5.7	9.4	6.4	8.0	5.3
Cambodia	3.8	0.8	2.8	0.6	5.0	1.0
Indonesia	18.1	19.3	18.4	21.0	18.0	18.3
Lao PDR	4.3	4.0	3.4	3.1	5.5	5.1
Malaysia	8.5	10.4	8.5	11.6	8.5	9.6
Myanmar	13.3	12.1	14.3	13.2	12.1	11.0
Philippines	23.0	15.7	25.6	17.5	21.5	14.6
Singapore	6.2	7.3	7.6	9.3	4.7	5.5
Thailand	6.9	4.7	6.3	5.5	7.4	4.2
Viet Nam	4.6	5.3	4.4	5.8	4.8	4.8
The Pacific						
Cook Islands	19.9 (2006)	15.5 (2011)	20.4 (2006)	15.3 (2011)	19.4 (2006)	15.6 (2011)
Fiji	17.0	18.2	22.4	23.9	14.0	14.8
Kiribati	...	54.0 (2010)	...	61.8 (2010)	...	47.6 (2010)
Marshall Islands	62.6 (1999)	50.0 (2011)	67.0 (1999)	50.0 (2011)	59.8 (1999)	50.0 (2011)
Micronesia, Fed. States of	...	11.3 (2010)	...	10.4 (2010)	...	12.2 (2010)
Nauru	58.2 (2006)	45.5 (2011)	65.9 (2006)	54.4 (2011)	51.7 (2006)	40.7 (2011)
Palau	11.9 (2005)	...	10.5 (2005)	...	12.8 (2005)	...
Papua New Guinea	5.8	6.7	6.3	7.1	5.3	6.2
Samoa	9.5	14.1	12.4	18.7	8.3	12.4
Solomon Islands	...	...	...	...	...	...
Timor-Leste	15.9	15.7	19.6	21.6	13.3	12.3
Tonga	11.4	11.7	14.6	14.6	9.6	9.7
Tuvalu	...	63.7 (2012)	...	...	...	...
Vanuatu	9.7	8.8	10.1	9.4	9.3	8.3
Developed Member Economies						
Australia[a]	12.2	13.5	11.5	12.5	13.0	14.5
Japan[b]	8.7	5.3	7.4	5.2	9.9	5.4
New Zealand[c]	13.6	14.4	12.4	14.8	14.7	14.1

... = data not available at cutoff date, Lao PDR = Lao People's Democratic Republic.

a Excludes Jervis Bay Territory.
b Data are averages of monthly estimates.
c Excludes Chatham Islands, Antarctic Territory, and other minor offshore islands.

Sources: International Labour Organization. *Key Indicators of the Labour Market*. 9th Edition. http://www.ilo.org/kilm (accessed June 2016); The Secretariat of the Pacific Community. 2004. *Pacific Islands Regional Millennium Development Goals Report*. Noumea, New Caledonia; Secretariat of the Pacific Community. National Minimum Development Indicator Database (v2.0). http://www.spc.int/nmdi/ (accessed August 2016).

Labor Force and Employment

Table 1.8:   **Employment in Agriculture, Industry, and Services**[a]
(% of total employment)

Regional Member	Agriculture			
	2000	2005	2010	2015
Developing Member Economies				
Central and West Asia				
Afghanistan	69.6 (2001)	69.6 (2004)	...	...
Armenia	44.4	46.2	38.6	35.3
Azerbaijan	39.1	38.7	38.2	36.4
Georgia	52.8 (2001)	54.3	52.2	48.6
Kazakhstan	31.4	31.9	28.3	18.0
Kyrgyz Republic	53.1	38.5	31.2	29.3
Pakistan	48.4	43.0	45.1	42.3
Tajikistan	65.0	67.5	65.9	64.9
Turkmenistan[b]	47.6	48.2 (2004)	...	...
Uzbekistan	34.4	29.1	26.8	27.7
East Asia				
China, People's Rep. of[c]	50.0	44.8	36.7	28.3
Hong Kong, China	0.3	0.3	0.0	0.0
Korea, Rep. of	10.6	7.9	6.6	5.2
Mongolia	48.6	39.9	33.5	28.5
Taipei,China	7.5 (2001)	5.9	5.2	5.0
South Asia				
Bangladesh	50.8	48.1 (2006)	47.5	77.6 (2013)
Bhutan	46.5 (2001)	43.6	59.4	58.0
India	59.9	56.1	53.2 (2009)	...
Maldives[d]	13.7	15.9 (2007)	4.3	10.4 (2014)
Nepal	...	...	65.6 (2011)	...
Sri Lanka[e]	36.0	32.8	32.5	28.5 (2014)
Southeast Asia				
Brunei Darussalam	...	...	...	...
Cambodia	73.7	60.3	72.3	64.3 (2014)
Indonesia	45.3	44.0	38.3	32.9
Lao PDR	82.7 (2001)	76.3	72.2	...
Malaysia	16.7	14.6	13.6	12.5
Myanmar	...	...	...	...
Philippines	37.1	35.7	33.2	29.2
Singapore[f]	0.1	0.1	0.2	0.1
Thailand	44.2	38.6	38.2	32.3
Viet Nam	65.1	55.1	49.5	44.0
The Pacific				
Cook Islands	7.2 (2001)	4.9 (2006)	4.3 (2011)	...
Fiji	1.5	1.1	1.7	1.9 (2014)
Kiribati[g]	...	2.7	22.1	...
Marshall Islands	20.5	...	11.0	...
Micronesia, Fed. States of	52.2	...	...	...
Nauru	...	...	...	...
Palau	7.1	7.8	...	...
Papua New Guinea	...	...	...	...
Samoa	39.9 (2001)	35.4 (2006)	37.0 (2011)	...
Solomon Islands	...	...	41.5 (2009)	...
Timor-Leste	...	...	51.0	40.5 (2013)
Tonga	...	27.9 (2006)	...	...
Tuvalu	...	...	...	...
Vanuatu	...	...	...	...
Developed Member Economies				
Australia	4.8	3.6	3.2	2.6
Japan	5.1	4.4	4.0	3.6
New Zealand	8.8	6.9	6.7	6.1

(continued)

Table 1.8: **Employment in Agriculture, Industry, and Services** (continued)
(% of total employment)

Regional Member	Industry			
	2000	2005	2010	2015
Developing Member Economies				
Central and West Asia				
Afghanistan	6.2 (2001)	6.2 (2004)	...	...
Armenia	20.6	15.9	17.4	15.9
Azerbaijan	12.1	12.4	13.7	14.1
Georgia[h]	5.8 (2001)	3.8	6.5	6.7
Kazakhstan	18.2	17.9	18.7	20.6
Kyrgyz Republic	10.5	17.6	21.1	20.9
Pakistan	11.6	13.8	13.4	15.5
Tajikistan	9.1	8.7	7.9	6.7
Turkmenistan[b]	13.0	13.8 (2004)	...	...
Uzbekistan	12.7	13.2	13.2	22.3
East Asia				
China, People's Rep. of[c]	22.5	23.8	28.7	29.3
Hong Kong, China	19.6	14.4	11.2	11.4
Korea, Rep. of	20.4	26.6	24.9	25.1
Mongolia	14.1	16.8	16.2	20.3
Taipei,China	36.6 (2001)	36.4	35.9	36.0
South Asia				
Bangladesh	13.1	14.6 (2006)	17.6	...
Bhutan	5.6 (2001)	17.2	6.6	9.6
India	16.3	18.8	21.5 (2009)	...
Maldives[d]	19.0	27.9 (2007)	9.4	18.8 (2014)
Nepal	...	...	9.8 (2011)	...
Sri Lanka[e]	23.6	25.4	24.6	26.5 (2014)
Southeast Asia				
Brunei Darussalam	...	...	...	...
Cambodia	7.0	9.7	9.2	9.0 (2014)
Indonesia	17.4	18.8	19.3	21.8
Lao PDR	8.7 (2001)	...	8.1	...
Malaysia	32.5	29.7	27.8	27.5
Myanmar	...	...	...	...
Philippines	16.2	15.4	15.0	16.2
Singapore[f]	25.7	21.7	21.8	17.2
Thailand	20.2	22.4	20.8	23.7
Viet Nam	13.1	17.6	21.0	22.7
The Pacific				
Cook Islands	6.0 (2001)	14.2 (2006)	11.7 (2011)	...
Fiji	30.8	30.8	23.9	25.5 (2014)
Kiribati[g]	...	3.2	16.1	...
Marshall Islands	7.8	...	0.7	...
Micronesia, Fed. States of	...	...	...	...
Nauru	...	...	...	...
Palau	0.7	2.6	...	...
Papua New Guinea	...	...	...	...
Samoa	19.7 (2001)	21.8 (2006)	12.2 (2011)	...
Solomon Islands	...	...	13.0 (2009)	...
Timor-Leste	...	...	8.8	12.7 (2013)
Tonga	...	27.8 (2006)	...	...
Tuvalu	...	...	...	...
Vanuatu	...	...	...	...
Developed Member Economies				
Australia	21.5	21.1	21.0	19.4
Japan	31.2	27.5	25.4	24.6
New Zealand	12.6	22.4	20.6	21.6

(continued)

Labor Force and Employment

Table 1.8:   **Employment in Agriculture, Industry, and Services** *(continued)*
(% of total employment)

Regional Member	Services			
	2000	**2005**	**2010**	**2015**
Developing Member Economies				
Central and West Asia				
Afghanistan	24.2 (2001)	24.2 (2004)	...	...
Armenia	35.0	37.8	44.0	48.8
Azerbaijan	48.7	48.8	48.1	49.6
Georgia^i	41.4 (2001)	41.9	41.3	44.7
Kazakhstan	50.5	50.2	53.0	61.4
Kyrgyz Republic	36.5	43.9	47.7	49.8
Pakistan	40.0	43.2	41.5	42.3
Tajikistan	26.0	23.9	26.3	28.4
Turkmenistan^b	39.4	38.0 (2004)	...	...
Uzbekistan	52.8	57.7	59.9	50.0
East Asia				
China, People's Rep. of^c	27.5	31.4	34.6	42.4
Hong Kong, China	79.8	85.1	88.8	88.1
Korea, Rep. of	69.0	65.4	68.5	69.7
Mongolia	37.2	43.3	50.2	51.3
Taipei,China	55.9 (2001)	57.7	58.8	59.0
South Asia				
Bangladesh	36.2	37.6 (2006)	35.3	22.4 (2013)
Bhutan	47.9 (2001)	39.2	33.7	32.4
India	23.7	25.1	25.3 (2009)	...
Maldives^d	67.3	56.2 (2007)	...	70.8 (2014)
Nepal	...	...	24.6 (2011)	...
Sri Lanka^e	40.3	41.8	42.9	45.0 (2014)
Southeast Asia				
Brunei Darussalam	...	...	...	...
Cambodia	19.3	30.0	18.6	26.6 (2014)
Indonesia	37.3	37.3	42.3	45.3
Lao PDR	8.6 (2001)	...	19.7	...
Malaysia	50.8	55.6	58.7	60.0
Myanmar	...	...	...	...
Philippines	46.7	48.1	51.8	54.6
Singapore^f	74.2	78.2	77.9	82.7
Thailand	35.6	39.0	41.0	44.0
Viet Nam	21.8	27.3	29.5	33.2
The Pacific				
Cook Islands	86.7 (2001)	80.9 (2006)	84.0 (2011)	...
Fiji	67.7	68.1	74.4	72.6 (2014)
Kiribati^g	...	30.7	61.8	...
Marshall Islands	72.3	...	88.2	...
Micronesia, Fed. States of	...	...	...	...
Nauru	...	...	...	...
Palau^j	92.2	89.6	...	...
Papua New Guinea	...	...	...	...
Samoa	40.4 (2001)	42.8 (2006)	50.9 (2011)	...
Solomon Islands	...	...	44.8 (2009)	...
Timor-Leste	...	...	39.8	46.7 (2013)
Tonga	...	44.3 (2006)	...	...
Tuvalu	...	...	...	...
Vanuatu	...	...	...	...
Developed Member Economies				
Australia	73.7	75.3	75.9	77.9
Japan	63.7	68.1	70.5	71.8
New Zealand	...	70.7	72.6	72.3

... = data not available at cutoff date, 0.0 = magnitude is less than half of unit employed, Lao PDR = Lao People's Democratic Republic.

a   Some values may not sum to 100 due to limitations in data availability.
b   The labor force data series includes individuals that are not registered.
c   Refers to persons engaged in social labor and receiving remuneration payment or earning business income.
d   Data for 2000 refer to persons 12 years old and over and for 2006 onward to persons 15 years old and over. Figures include local population only.
e   Some data may not add up because (i) data for 2005 and 2011–2013 cover all islands; (ii) data for 2003 exclude northern provinces; (iii) data for 2004 exclude Mullaitivu and Kilinochchi districts; and (iv) data for 2006–2010 and years before 2003 exclude northern and eastern provinces.
f   Refers to Singapore residents only.
g   Refers to cash work and unpaid village work. For 2005, employment figures by industry include only paid (cash work) workers.
h   Includes mining and quarrying; manufacturing; electricity, gas, steam, and air-conditioning supply; water supply; sewerage, waste management, and remediation activities.
i   Includes construction and service activities.
j   Includes electricity, gas, steam, and air-conditioning supply; water supply; sewerage, waste management, and remediation activities; construction; and service activities.

Source: Economy sources.

Table 1.9:   **Poverty and Inequality**

Regional Member	Proportion of Population below $1.90 (PPP) a Day (%)[a]		Proportion of Population below $3.10 (PPP) a Day (%)[a]	
	2000	Latest year	2000	Latest year
Developing Member Economies				
Central and West Asia				
Afghanistan	...	...	...	...
Armenia	19.3 (2001)	2.3 (2014)	53.1 (2001)	14.6 (2014)
Azerbaijan	2.7 (2001)	0.5 (2008)	16.3 (2001)	2.5 (2008)
Georgia	21.0	9.8 (2014)	45.1	25.3 (2014)
Kazakhstan	10.5 (2001)	0.0 (2013)	31.2 (2001)	0.3 (2013)
Kyrgyz Republic	42.2	1.3 (2014)	75.7	17.5 (2014)
Pakistan[b]	28.7 (2001)	6.1 (2013)	70.0 (2001)	36.9 (2013)
Tajikistan	54.4 (1999)	19.5 (2014)	86.1 (1999)	56.7 (2014)
Turkmenistan	42.3 (1998)	...	69.1 (1998)	...
Uzbekistan	68.1	66.8 (2003)	88.7	87.8 (2003)
East Asia				
China, People's Rep. of	40.5[c] (1999)	1.9 [c](2013)	67.2 [c](1999)	11.1[c](2013)
Hong Kong, China	...	...	...	...
Korea, Rep. of	...	...	...	...
Mongolia	10.6 (2002)	0.2 (2014)	33.6 (2002)	2.7 (2014)
Taipei,China	...	...	...	...
South Asia				
Bangladesh	33.7	18.5 (2010)	70.1	56.8 (2010)
Bhutan[d]	35.2 (2003)	2.2 (2012)	60.9 (2003)	13.3 (2012)
India[b]	38.2[c](2004)	21.2 [c](2011)	73.5 [c](2004)	58.0[c](2011)
Maldives[b]	10.0 (2002)	7.3 (2009)	36.5 (2002)	23.3 (2009)
Nepal[b]	46.1 (2003)	15.0 (2010)	73.8 (2003)	48.4 (2010)
Sri Lanka[b]	8.3 (2002)	1.9 (2012)	33.9 (2002)	14.6 (2012)
Southeast Asia				
Brunei Darussalam	...	...	...	...
Cambodia	18.6 (2004)	2.2 (2012)	53.3 (2004)	21.6 (2012)
Indonesia	39.8[c](2000)	8.3 [c](2014)	78.5 [c](2000)	36.4[c](2014)
Lao PDR[b]	26.1 (2002)	16.7 (2012)	61.7 (2002)	46.9 (2012)
Malaysia	0.4 (2004)	0.3 (2009)	2.3 (2004)	2.7 (2009)
Myanmar	...	...	...	...
Philippines	18.4	13.1 (2012)	43.1	37.6 (2012)
Singapore	...	...	...	...
Thailand	2.6	0.0 (2013)	17.0	0.9 (2013)
Viet Nam[b]	38.8 (2002)	3.1 (2014)	69.3 (2002)	12.0 (2014)
The Pacific				
Cook Islands	...	...	...	...
Fiji[b]	5.5 (2002)	4.1 (2008)	21.9 (2002)	18.5 (2008)
Kiribati	14.1 (2006)	...	34.7 (2006)	...
Marshall Islands	...	...	...	...
Micronesia, Fed. States of	11.4 (2005)	17.4 (2013)	28.5 (2005)	39.4 (2013)
Nauru	...	...	...	...
Palau	...	...	...	...
Papua New Guinea[b]	...	39.3 (2009)	...	64.7 (2009)
Samoa	...	0.8 (2008)	...	8.4 (2008)
Solomon Islands[b]	45.6 (2005)	...	69.3 (2005)	...
Timor-Leste	44.2 (2001)	46.8 (2007)	72.8 (2001)	80.0 (2007)
Tonga	2.8 (2001)	1.1 (2009)	7.6 (2001)	8.2 (2009)
Tuvalu[b]	...	2.7 (2010)	...	16.3 (2010)
Vanuatu	...	15.4 (2010)	...	38.8 (2010)
Developed Member Economies				
Australia	1.4 (2001)	0.7 (2010)	1.4 (2001)	1.0 (2010)
Japan	...	0.4 (2008)	...	0.7 (2008)
New Zealand	...	...	...	...

(continued)

Poverty Indicators

Table 1.9: **Poverty and Inequality** (continued)

Regional Member	Income Ratio of Highest 20% to Lowest 20%		Gini Coefficient	
	2000	Latest year	2000	Latest year
Developing Member Economies				
Central and West Asia				
Afghanistan	...	...	...	...
Armenia	5.7 (2001)	4.7 (2013)	0.354 (2001)	0.315 (2013)
Azerbaijan	6.0 (2001)	2.3 (2005)	0.365 (2001)	0.166 (2005)
Georgia	8.6	8.2 (2013)	0.405	0.400 (2013)
Kazakhstan	6.2 (2001)	3.7 (2013)	0.353 (2001)	0.264 (2013)
Kyrgyz Republic	4.7	3.9 (2012)	0.310	0.274 (2012)
Pakistan[b]	4.3 (2001)	4.1 (2010)	0.305 (2001)	0.296 (2010)
Tajikistan	5.2 (2003)	4.7 (2009)	0.327 (2003)	0.308 (2009)
Turkmenistan	6.2 (1993)	7.7 (1998)	0.354 (1993)	0.408 (1998)
Uzbekistan	6.1	5.8 (2003)	0.361	0.353 (2003)
East Asia				
China, People's Rep. of	8.9 (2002)	10.1 (2010)	0.426 (2002)	0.421 (2010)
Hong Kong, China	...	...	...	...
Korea, Rep. of	...	5.4 (2014)	0.307 (2012)	0.302 (2014)
Mongolia	5.4 (2002)	5.4 (2012)	0.329 (2002)	0.338 (2012)
Taipei,China	5.6	6.1 (2014)	0.326	0.336 (2014)
South Asia				
Bangladesh	4.9	4.7 (2010)	0.331	0.320 (2010)
Bhutan[d]	278.2 (2003)	6.8 (2012)	0.695 (2003)	0.387 (2012)
India[b]	4.9 (2004)	5.4 (2011)	0.334 (2004)	0.339 (2009)
Maldives[b]	46.6 (1998)	6.7 (2009)	0.627 (1998)	0.368 (2009)
Nepal[b]	7.7 (2003)	5.0 (2010)	0.433 (2003)	0.328 (2010)
Sri Lanka[b]	7.1 (2002)	6.4 (2012)	0.407 (2002)	0.386 (2012)
Southeast Asia				
Brunei Darussalam	...	...	...	...
Cambodia	5.6 (2004)	4.4 (2012)	0.355 (2004)	0.308 (2012)
Indonesia	4.2 (2002)	5.7 (2010)	0.297 (2002)	0.356 (2010)
Lao PDR[b]	5.4 (2002)	6.3 (2012)	0.347 (2002)	0.379 (2012)
Malaysia	11.0 (2004)	11.3 (2009)	0.461 (2004)	0.463 (2009)
Myanmar	...	...	...	...
Philippines	9.7	8.4 (2012)	0.462	0.430 (2012)
Singapore	...	...	...	...
Thailand	8.1	7.0 (2012)	0.428	0.393 (2012)
Viet Nam[b]	6.1 (2002)	7.0 (2012)	0.373 (2002)	0.387 (2012)
The Pacific				
Cook Islands	...	...	...	...
Fiji[b]	7.4 (2002)	8.2 (2008)	0.396 (2002)	0.428 (2008)
Kiribati	...	7.2 (2006)	...	0.376 (2006)
Marshall Islands	...	...	...	...
Micronesia, Fed. States of	39.5	...	0.612	...
Nauru	...	...	...	...
Palau	...	...	...	...
Papua New Guinea[b]	27.0 (1996)	10.4 (2009)	0.6 (1996)	0.439 (2009)
Samoa	...	7.9 (2008)	...	0.427 (2008)
Solomon Islands[b]	...	10.5 (2005)	...	0.461 (2005)
Timor-Leste	6.4 (2001)	4.6 (2007)	0.376 (2001)	0.316 (2007)
Tonga	...	6.9 (2009)	...	0.381 (2009)
Tuvalu[b]	...	...	...	...
Vanuatu	...	6.6 (2010)	...	0.372 (2010)
Developed Member Economies				
Australia	5.9 (2001)	5.9 (2010)	0.341 (2001)	0.349 (2010)
Japan	...	5.4 (2008)	...	0.321 (2008)
New Zealand	5.2 (2011)	5.3 (2012)	0.323 (2011)	0.333 (2012)

... = data not available at cutoff date, 0.0 = magnitude is less than half of unit employed, Lao PDR = Lao People's Democratic Republic, PPP = purchasing power parity.

a   Data are consumption-based, except for Australia, Japan, and Malaysia, which are income-based.

b   Household income surveys for either the initial and/or latest year were conducted in overlapping years. For consistency with the data in World Development Indicators database, the table above indicates the initial year of the survey as the reference year for the poverty estimates.

c   Values are weighted average of urban and rural populations.

d   Estimate for 2003 is based on data from the World Bank's PovcalNet database. An alternative estimate is from the United Nations Statistics Division's SDG Indicators Global Database, which is equal to 24.9% for the same year.

Sources: World Bank. PovcalNet Database Online. http://iresearch.worldbank.org/PovcalNet/index.htm (accessed October 2016); World Bank. World Development Indicators Online. http://data.worldbank.org/data-catalog/world-development-indicators (accessed June 2016); OECD Database on Income Distribution and Poverty. http://www.oecd.org/social/inequality-and-poverty.htm (accessed June 2016); for Taipei,China: Directorate-General of Budget, Accounting and Statistics. http://eng.dgbas.gov.tw/mp.asp?mp=2 (accessed September 2016); ADB estimates; economy sources.

Table 1.10: **Human Development Index**

Regional Member	2000	2005	2010	2011	2012	2013	2014	Rank in 2014[a]
Developing Member Economies								
Central and West Asia	**0.571**	**0.617**	**0.649**	**0.654**	**0.660**	**0.664**	**0.667**	
Afghanistan	0.334	0.399	0.448	0.456	0.463	0.464	0.465	171
Armenia	0.648	0.695	0.721	0.723	0.728	0.731	0.733	85
Azerbaijan	0.640	0.688	0.741	0.742	0.745	0.749	0.751	78
Georgia	0.672	0.711	0.735	0.740	0.747	0.750	0.754	76
Kazakhstan	0.679	0.746	0.766	0.772	0.778	0.785	0.788	56
Kyrgyz Republic	0.593	0.614	0.634	0.639	0.645	0.652	0.655	120
Pakistan	0.444	0.495	0.522	0.527	0.532	0.536	0.538	147
Tajikistan	0.535	0.579	0.608	0.612	0.617	0.621	0.624	129
Turkmenistan	...	...	0.666	0.671	0.677	0.682	0.688	109
Uzbekistan	0.594	0.625	0.655	0.661	0.668	0.672	0.675	114
East Asia	**0.706**	**0.773**	**0.810**	**0.816**	**0.822**	**0.826**	**0.829**	
China, People's Rep. of	0.588	0.641	0.699	0.707	0.718	0.723	0.727	90
Hong Kong, China	0.825	0.871	0.898	0.902	0.906	0.908	0.910	12
Korea, Rep. of	0.821	0.858	0.886	0.891	0.893	0.895	0.898	17
Mongolia	0.589	0.649	0.695	0.706	0.714	0.722	0.727	90
Taipei,China[b]	...	0.846	0.873	0.874	0.879	0.882	0.882	...
South Asia	**0.539**	**0.575**	**0.617**	**0.625**	**0.629**	**0.634**	**0.638**	
Bangladesh	0.468	0.505	0.546	0.559	0.563	0.567	0.570	142
Bhutan	...	...	...	...	...	...	...	132
India	0.496	0.539	0.586	0.597	0.600	0.604	0.609	130
Maldives	0.603	0.638	0.683	0.690	0.695	0.703	0.706	104
Nepal	0.451	0.480	0.531	0.536	0.540	0.543	0.548	145
Sri Lanka	0.679	0.712	0.738	0.743	0.749	0.752	0.757	73
Southeast Asia	**0.612**	**0.645**	**0.679**	**0.684**	**0.689**	**0.692**	**0.696**	
Brunei Darussalam	0.819	0.836	0.843	0.847	0.852	0.852	0.856	31
Cambodia	0.419	0.491	0.536	0.541	0.546	0.550	0.555	143
Indonesia	0.606	0.635	0.665	0.671	0.678	0.681	0.684	110
Lao PDR	0.462	0.501	0.539	0.552	0.562	0.570	0.575	141
Malaysia	0.723	0.731	0.769	0.772	0.774	0.777	0.779	62
Myanmar	0.425	0.478	0.520	0.524	0.528	0.531	0.536	148
Philippines	0.623	0.640	0.654	0.653	0.657	0.664	0.668	115
Singapore	0.819	0.841	0.897	0.903	0.905	0.909	0.912	11
Thailand	0.648	0.684	0.716	0.721	0.723	0.724	0.726	93
Viet Nam	0.575	0.616	0.653	0.657	0.660	0.663	0.666	116
The Pacific	**0.586**	**0.603**	**0.630**	**0.633**	**0.634**	**0.634**	**0.636**	
Cook Islands	...	...	...	...	...	...	...	...
Fiji	0.678	0.694	0.717	0.720	0.722	0.724	0.727	90
Kiribati	...	0.575	0.588	0.585	0.587	0.588	0.590	137
Marshall Islands	...	...	...	...	...	...	...	...
Micronesia, Fed. States of	0.603	0.622	0.638	0.640	0.641	0.639	0.640	123
Nauru	...	...	...	...	...	...	...	...
Palau	0.743	0.759	0.767	0.770	0.775	0.775	0.780	60
Papua New Guinea	0.424	0.452	0.493	0.497	0.501	0.503	0.505	158
Samoa	0.649	0.679	0.696	0.698	0.700	0.701	0.702	105
Solomon Islands	0.446	0.482	0.494	0.501	0.504	0.505	0.506	156
Timor-Leste	0.468	0.505	0.600	0.611	0.604	0.601	0.595	133
Tonga	0.671	0.693	0.713	0.716	0.717	0.716	0.717	100
Tuvalu	...	...	...	...	...	...	...	...
Vanuatu	...	0.572	0.589	0.590	0.590	0.592	0.594	134
Developed Member Economies	**0.876**	**0.894**	**0.905**	**0.908**	**0.910**	**0.912**	**0.913**	
Australia	0.898	0.912	0.927	0.930	0.932	0.933	0.935	2
Japan	0.857	0.874	0.884	0.886	0.888	0.890	0.891	20
New Zealand	0.874	0.895	0.905	0.907	0.909	0.911	0.913	9

... = data not available at cutoff date, Lao PDR = Lao People's Democratic Republic.

a Rank among the 188 countries classified in United Nations Development Programme's *Human Development Report 2015*.
b Obtained from statistics bureau of Taipei,China.

Sources: United Nations Development Programme. 2015. *Human Development Report 2015*. http://hdr.undp.org/en (accessed June 2016); for Taipei,China: Directorate-General of Budget, Accounting and Statistics. http://eng.stat.gov.tw/ct.asp?xItem=25280&ctNode=6032&mp=5 (accessed August 2016).

Social Indicators

Table 1.11:   **Life Expectancy at Birth**
              (years)

Regional Member	Both Sexes		Female		Male	
	2010	2014	2010	2014	2010	2014
Developing Member Economies						
Central and West Asia						
Afghanistan	59.0	60.4	60.2	61.6	57.8	59.2
Armenia	74.2	74.7	77.9	78.6	70.7	70.9
Azerbaijan	70.5	70.8	73.6	74.0	67.4	67.7
Georgia	74.0	74.7	77.7	78.4	70.5	71.2
Kazakhstan	68.3	71.6	73.3	75.9	63.5	67.1
Kyrgyz Republic	69.3	70.4	73.5	74.5	65.3	66.5
Pakistan	65.2	66.2	66.1	67.2	64.3	65.3
Tajikistan	68.6	69.6	72.0	73.2	65.3	66.2
Turkmenistan	65.0	65.6	69.3	69.9	60.9	61.5
Uzbekistan	67.9	68.3	71.3	71.8	64.6	65.0
East Asia						
China, People's Rep. of	75.0	75.8	76.6	77.3	73.5	74.3
Hong Kong, China	83.0	84.0	86.0	86.9	80.1	81.2
Korea, Rep. of	80.6	82.2	84.1	85.5	77.2	79.0
Mongolia	67.6	69.5	71.9	73.9	63.6	65.3
Taipei,China	79.2	79.9 (2013)	82.6	83.4 (2013)	76.1	76.9 (2013)
South Asia						
Bangladesh	70.1	71.6	71.2	72.9	69.0	70.4
Bhutan	67.9	69.5	68.2	69.7	67.6	69.2
India	66.5	68.0	67.7	69.5	65.4	66.6
Maldives	76.2	76.8	77.3	77.8	75.2	75.8
Nepal	68.0	69.6	69.4	71.1	66.6	68.2
Sri Lanka	74.3	74.8	77.9	78.2	70.9	71.5
Southeast Asia						
Brunei Darussalam	77.6	78.8	79.4	80.7	75.9	77.0
Cambodia	66.4	68.2	68.6	70.3	64.3	66.2
Indonesia	68.1	68.9	70.3	71.0	66.1	66.9
Lao PDR	64.3	66.1	65.7	67.5	63.0	64.8
Malaysia	74.2	74.7	76.5	77.1	71.9	72.4
Myanmar	64.9	65.9	67.0	68.0	62.9	63.9
Philippines	67.8	68.3	71.2	71.8	64.5	64.9
Singapore	81.5	82.6	84.0	84.9	79.2	80.5
Thailand	73.7	74.4	77.1	77.9	70.4	71.1
Viet Nam	75.0	75.6	80.0	80.5	70.2	71.0
The Pacific						
Cook Islands	74.5	75.4	77.4	78.3	71.7	72.6
Fiji	69.4	70.1	72.4	73.2	66.5	67.2
Kiribati	65.3	66.0	68.5	69.2	62.3	62.8
Marshall Islands	71.5	72.6	73.7	74.8	69.4	70.4
Micronesia, Fed. States of	68.6	69.1	69.5	70.1	67.8	68.1
Nauru	65.0	66.4	68.4	69.8	60.9	62.3
Palau	71.5	72.6	74.8	76.0	68.4	69.4
Papua New Guinea	62.0	62.6	64.1	64.8	59.9	60.5
Samoa	72.4	73.5	75.7	76.8	69.3	70.4
Solomon Islands	67.1	67.9	68.4	69.4	65.8	66.5
Timor-Leste	67.3	68.3	68.8	70.1	65.9	66.5
Tonga	72.2	72.8	75.2	75.8	69.3	69.9
Tuvalu	64.4	65.8	66.5	68.1	62.4	63.7
Vanuatu	70.8	71.9	72.9	74.0	68.9	69.9
Developed Member Economies						
Australia	81.7	82.3	84.0	84.3	79.5	80.3
Japan	82.8	83.6	86.3	86.8	79.6	80.5
New Zealand	80.7	81.4	82.7	83.3	78.8	79.6
WORLD	**70.5**	**71.5**	**72.6**	**73.6**	**68.4**	**69.4**

Lao PDR = Lao People's Democratic Republic.

Sources: World Bank. World Development Indicators Online. http://data.worldbank.org/data-catalog/world-development-indicators (accessed August 2016); for the
           Cook Islands, the Marshall Islands, Nauru, Palau, and Tuvalu: US Census Bureau Online. http://www.census.gov/ (accessed August 2016); for Taipei,China:
           Directorate-General of Budget, Accounting and Statistics. Social Indicators. http://eng.dgbas.gov.tw/mp.asp?mp=2 (accessed August 2016).

Table 1.12: **Births, Deaths, and Fertility Rates**

Regional Member	Crude Birth Rate (per 1,000 people)		Crude Death Rate (per 1,000 people)		Total Fertility Rate (births per woman)	
	2000	2014	2000	2014	2000	2014
Developing Member Economies						
Central and West Asia						
Afghanistan	48.3	34.2	12.1	8.2	7.5	4.8
Armenia	13.2	13.2	8.5	9.2	1.7	1.5
Azerbaijan	14.5	17.9	5.8	5.8	2.0	2.0
Georgia	12.0	13.5	10.0	11.5	1.6	1.8
Kazakhstan	14.7	23.1	10.1	7.6	1.8	2.7
Kyrgyz Republic	19.8	27.7	7.0	6.1	2.4	3.2
Pakistan	32.0	29.2	8.7	7.4	4.6	3.6
Tajikistan	30.6	30.6	7.8	5.6	4.0	3.5
Turkmenistan	23.7	21.1	7.7	7.8	2.8	2.3
Uzbekistan	21.4	23.3	5.5	4.9	2.6	2.2
East Asia						
China, People's Rep. of	14.0	12.4	6.5	7.2	1.4	1.6
Hong Kong, China	8.1	8.6	5.1	6.2	1.0	1.2
Korea, Rep. of	13.3	8.6	5.2	5.3	1.5	1.2
Mongolia	19.3	23.9	7.7	6.1	2.1	2.7
Taipei,China	13.8	9.0	5.7	7.0	1.7	1.2
South Asia						
Bangladesh	27.6	19.8	6.9	5.4	3.2	2.2
Bhutan	27.6	17.7	8.8	6.2	3.6	2.0
India	26.5	20.0	8.7	7.3	3.3	2.4
Maldives	22.8	21.2	4.7	3.8	2.9	2.1
Nepal	32.1	20.5	8.5	6.4	4.0	2.2
Sri Lanka	18.5	15.9	7.0	6.8	2.2	2.1
Southeast Asia						
Brunei Darussalam	21.9	16.0	3.0	3.0	2.3	1.9
Cambodia	28.1	24.1	9.4	6.1	3.8	2.6
Indonesia	21.5	20.0	7.3	7.2	2.5	2.5
Lao PDR	31.9	26.7	9.8	6.8	4.3	3.0
Malaysia	22.5	16.8	4.4	4.9	2.8	1.9
Myanmar	24.3	17.8	9.1	8.3	2.9	2.2
Philippines	29.6	23.6	6.2	6.7	3.8	3.0
Singapore	11.8	9.8	3.9	4.7	1.5 (1999)	1.3
Thailand	14.4	10.8	6.9	7.9	1.7	1.5
Viet Nam	17.5	17.2	5.5	5.8	2.0	2.0
The Pacific						
Cook Islands	23.1	14.7	6.3	7.8	3.2	2.3
Fiji	24.7	20.1	6.1	6.9	3.1	2.6
Kiribati	30.6	28.8	7.6	7.0	4.1	3.7
Marshall Islands	35.0	26.4	5.3	4.2	4.4	3.2
Micronesia, Fed. States of	29.9	23.5	6.3	6.2	4.3	3.2
Nauru	27.9	25.6	7.2	5.9	3.5	2.9
Palau	14.5	13.1 (2013)	6.5	11.0 (2013)	2.4 (1995)	2.0 (2005)
Papua New Guinea	34.8	28.5	9.1	7.7	4.5	3.8
Samoa	30.6	25.6	6.1	5.4	4.5	4.1
Solomon Islands	35.6	29.9	7.7	5.8	4.7	4.0
Timor-Leste	42.6	37.8	9.8	6.9	7.1	5.1
Tonga	28.3	24.8	6.3	6.0	4.3	3.7
Tuvalu	24.6	23.7	10.8	8.9	3.6	3.0
Vanuatu	32.4	26.5	6.2	4.7	4.4	3.3
Developed Member Economies						
Australia	13.0	12.9	6.7	6.5	1.8	1.9
Japan	9.4	8.0	7.7	10.0	1.4	1.4
New Zealand	14.7	12.7	6.9	6.9	2.0	1.9
WORLD	**21.6**	**19.3**	**8.5**	**7.7**	**2.7**	**2.5**

Lao PDR = Lao People's Democratic Republic.

Sources: World Bank. World Development Indicators Online. http://data.worldbank.org/data-catalog/world-development-indicators (accessed June 2016); for the Cook Islands, the Marshall Islands, Nauru, and Tuvalu: US Census Bureau Online. http://www.census.gov/ (accessed August 2016); for Taipei,China: Directorate-General of Budget, Accounting and Statistics. Social Indicators. http://eng.dgbas.gov.tw/mp.asp?mp=2 (accessed August 2016).

Table 1.13:   **Primary Education Completion Rate**[a]
(%)

Regional Member	Both Sexes		Female		Male	
	2000	2014	2000	2014	2000	2014
Developing Member Economies						
Central and West Asia						
Afghanistan	29.6 (1993)	...	15.1 (1993)	...	42.8 (1993)	...
Armenia	93.7 (2002)	100.1 (2008)	94.7 (2002)	106.1 (2008)	92.8 (2002)	95.4 (2008)
Azerbaijan	89.5	98.1	85.5	97.6	93.8	98.6
Georgia	98.1	116.5	97.9	116.9	98.4	116.0
Kazakhstan	92.7	113.0 (2015)	92.8	113.0 (2015)	92.7	113.0 (2015)
Kyrgyz Republic	93.5	105.0	92.9	104.4	94.1	105.6
Pakistan	64.5 (2005)	73.7	53.7 (2005)	67.0	74.7 (2005)	80.0
Tajikistan	91.3	99.6 (2015)	96.0 (2009)	99.4 (2015)	99.5 (2009)	99.7 (2015)
Turkmenistan	...		...		...	
Uzbekistan	94.4	95.7 (2011)	101.2 (2001)	94.8 (2011)	...	96.5 (2011)
East Asia						
China, People's Rep. of	91.9 (1997)	...	89.7 (1997)	...	94.0 (1997)	...
Hong Kong, China	94.2 (1996)	99.4	...	98.8	...	100.0
Korea, Rep. of	103.6	103.2 (2013)	104.1	102.8 (2013)	103.1	103.6 (2013)
Mongolia	87.0	109.9	89.3	108.2	84.6	111.4
Taipei,China	...	...	...	...	...	...
South Asia						
Bangladesh	64.4 (2005)	73.5 (2011)	66.9 (2005)	78.6 (2011)	62.0 (2005)	68.7 (2011)
Bhutan	51.0	97.0	47.3	102.8	54.5	91.4
India	71.8	96.2 (2013)	63.5	99.0 (2013)	79.3	93.7 (2013)
Maldives	177.7 (2001)	114.4 (2009)	183.6 (2001)	108.5 (2009)	172.0 (2001)	120.0 (2009)
Nepal	67.2	105.7 (2015)	57.2	111.2 (2015)	77.0	100.5 (2015)
Sri Lanka	107.3 (2001)	98.0	106.6 (2001)	96.9	107.9 (2001)	99.1
Southeast Asia						
Brunei Darussalam	116.0	100.6	113.0	100.3	118.7	100.8
Cambodia	51.1 (2001)	96.3	45.9 (2001)	96.3	56.1 (2001)	96.3
Indonesia	93.8 (2001)	102.9	94.2 (2001)	100.1	93.4 (2001)	105.6
Lao PDR	67.5	100.3	61.6	99.0	73.2	101.6
Malaysia	95.0 (1999)	102.4	...	...	...	...
Myanmar	76.5	85.1	74.2	86.0 (2010)	78.7	82.7 (2010)
Philippines	100.4 (2001)	101.0 (2013)	105.4 (2001)	105.0 (2013)	95.5 (2001)	97.3 (2013)
Singapore	...	...	...	...	...	...
Thailand	84.9	93.6	84.3	92.9	85.5	94.2
Viet Nam	99.0	106.2	96.6	108.3	101.3	104.3
The Pacific						
Cook Islands	87.9 (1999)	103.5	85.9 (1999)	104.9	89.8 (1999)	102.1
Fiji	95.0	102.9 (2013)	93.9	103.1 (2013)	96.0	102.8 (2013)
Kiribati	99.0	112.4	95.1	119.8	102.7	105.5
Marshall Islands	92.5 (1999)	99.8 (2011)	84.2 (1999)	103.9 (2011)	100.4 (1999)	95.9 (2011)
Micronesia, Fed. States of	...	...	...	...	...	...
Nauru	87.0 (2001)	112.4	90.1 (2001)	97.3	84.3 (2001)	128.3
Palau	104.5 (2004)	95.5	...	93.9	...	96.9
Papua New Guinea	55.1	78.6 (2012)	50.5	72.4 (2012)	59.5	84.4 (2012)
Samoa	94.0	100.5	95.5	98.1	92.7	102.8
Solomon Islands	72.5 (1994)	87.3	...	87.7	...	86.9
Timor-Leste	83.2 (2008)	98.4	82.7 (2008)	99.9	83.7 (2008)	96.9
Tonga	106.8 (2001)	110.9 (2013)	105.2 (2001)	106.4 (2013)	108.2 (2001)	115.1 (2013)
Tuvalu	101.7 (2001)	93.2	108.3 (2001)	98.1	96.1 (2001)	89.0
Vanuatu	92.1	93.8 (2013)	94.4	97.8 (2013)	89.9	90.2 (2013)
Developed Member Economies						
Australia	...	...	...	...	...	...
Japan	102.4	102.1 (2012)	102.3	102.0 (2012)	102.5	102.2 (2012)
New Zealand	...	...	...	...	...	...

... = data not available at cutoff date, Lao PDR = Lao People's Democratic Republic.

a The total number of new entrants in the last grade of primary education, irrespective of age, expressed as a percentage of the total population of the theoretical entrance age to the last grade of primary education.

Source: UNESCO Institute for Statistics. http://data.uis.unesco.org/Index.aspx (accessed August 2016).

Table 1.14: **Adult Literacy Rate**
(15 years and over, %)

Regional Member	Both Sexes		Female		Male	
	2000	**2015**	**2000**	**2015**	**2000**	**2015**
Developing Member Economies						
Central and West Asia						
Afghanistan	...	38.2	...	23.9	...	51.5
Armenia	99.4 (2001)	99.8	99.2 (2001)	99.7	99.7 (2001)	99.8
Azerbaijan	98.8 (1999)	99.8	98.2 (1999)	99.7	99.5 (1999)	99.9
Georgia	99.7 (2002)	99.8	99.6 (2002)	99.7	99.8 (2002)	99.8
Kazakhstan	99.5 (1999)	99.8	99.3 (1999)	99.8	99.8 (1999)	99.8
Kyrgyz Republic	98.7 (1999)	99.5	98.1 (1999)	99.4	99.3 (1999)	99.6
Pakistan	42.7 (1998)	56.4	29.0 (1998)	42.7	55.3 (1998)	69.6
Tajikistan	99.5	99.8	99.2	99.7	99.7	99.8
Turkmenistan	98.8 (1995)	99.7	98.3 (1995)	99.6	99.3 (1995)	99.8
Uzbekistan	98.6	100.0	98.1	100.0	99.2	100.0
East Asia						
China, People's Rep. of	90.9	96.4	86.5	94.5	95.1	98.2
Hong Kong, China	...	...	...	...	...	...
Korea, Rep. of	...	98.0 (2008)	...	97.6 (2008)	...	98.3 (2008)
Mongolia	97.8	98.4	97.5	98.6	98.0	98.2
Taipei,China	...	...	...	...	...	...
South Asia						
Bangladesh	47.5 (2001)	61.5	40.8 (2001)	58.3	53.9 (2001)	64.6
Bhutan	52.8 (2005)	63.9	38.7 (2005)	55.1	65.0 (2005)	71.1
India	61.0 (2001)	72.2	47.8 (2001)	63.0	73.4 (2001)	80.9
Maldives	96.3	99.3	96.4	98.9	96.2	99.8
Nepal	48.6 (2001)	64.7	34.9 (2001)	54.8	62.7 (2001)	75.8
Sri Lanka	90.7 (2001)	92.6	89.1 (2001)	91.7	92.3 (2001)	93.6
Southeast Asia						
Brunei Darussalam	92.7 (2001)	96.7	90.2 (2001)	95.4	95.2 (2001)	97.8
Cambodia	67.3 (1998)	78.3	57.0 (1998)	72.3	79.5 (1998)	85.0
Indonesia	90.4 (2004)	95.4	86.8 (2004)	93.8	94.0 (2004)	97.1
Lao PDR	69.6	79.9	58.5	72.8	81.4	87.2
Malaysia	88.7	94.6	85.4	93.1	92.0	96.2
Myanmar	89.9	93.1	86.4	91.2	93.9	95.2
Philippines	92.6	96.6	92.7	97.0	92.5	96.2
Singapore	92.5	96.8	88.6	95.0	96.6	98.6
Thailand	92.6	94.0	90.5	92.6	94.9	95.4
Viet Nam	90.2	94.5	86.6	92.8	93.9	96.3
The Pacific						
Cook Islands	...	...	...	...	...	...
Fiji	...	...	...	...	...	...
Kiribati	...	...	...	...	...	...
Marshall Islands	...	98.3	...	98.2	...	98.3
Micronesia, Fed. States of	...	...	...	...	...	...
Nauru	...	...	...	...	...	...
Palau	97.0 (2004)	99.5	96.5 (2004)	99.6	97.4 (2004)	99.5
Papua New Guinea	57.3	63.4	50.9	61.8	63.4	65.1
Samoa	98.5 (2004)	99.0	98.2 (2004)	99.1	98.8 (2004)	98.9
Solomon Islands	76.6 (1999)	...	69.0 (1999)	...	83.7 (1999)	...
Timor-Leste	37.6 (2001)	64.1	30.0 (2001)	59.5	45.3 (2001)	68.5
Tonga	98.9 (1996)	99.4	99.0 (1996)	99.4	98.8 (1996)	99.3
Tuvalu	...	...	...	...	...	...
Vanuatu	74.0 (1999)	85.1	...	83.7	...	86.5
Developed Member Economies						
Australia	...	...	...	...	...	...
Japan	...	...	...	...	...	...
New Zealand	...	...	...	...	...	...

... = data not available at cutoff date, Lao PDR = Lao People's Democratic Republic.

Source: UNESCO Institute for Statistics. http://www.uis.unesco.org/Pages/default.aspx (accessed September 2016).

Social Indicators

Table 1.15:   **Education Resources**

Regional Member	Primary Pupil–Teacher Ratio		Secondary Pupil–Teacher Ratio	
	2000	2015	2000	2015
Developing Member Economies				
Central and West Asia				
Afghanistan	42.3 (2006)	45.7 (2013)	31.6 (2007)	...
Armenia	20.3 (2001)	19.3 (2007)	...	...
Azerbaijan	18.7	12.6 (2014)	...	...
Georgia	16.8	9.1 (2014)	7.5	7.2 (2014)
Kazakhstan	18.7 (2001)	16.2	11.0 (2006)	7.5
Kyrgyz Republic	24.1	25.3 (2014)	13.3	11.3 (2014)
Pakistan	33.0	46.5 (2014)	24.2 (2003)	21.0 (2012)
Tajikistan	21.8	22.3	16.4	15.4 (2011)
Turkmenistan	...	...	...	...
Uzbekistan	21.4	15.6 (2011)	11.5	13.3 (2011)
East Asia				
China, People's Rep. of	22.2 (2001)	16.2 (2014)	17.1	14.3 (2014)
Hong Kong, China	21.5	13.8 (2014)	18.8 (2001)	13.6 (2014)
Korea, Rep. of	32.1	16.9 (2013)	21.0	15.6 (2013)
Mongolia	32.6	27.2 (2014)	19.9	13.7 (2014)
Taipei,China	19.0	12.7 (2014)	17.6	14.6 (2014)
South Asia				
Bangladesh	47.0 (2005)	40.2 (2011)	38.4	35.2 (2013)
Bhutan	41.1	26.7 (2014)	28.1 (2005)	14.3 (2014)
India	40.0	32.3 (2013)	33.6	30.8 (2013)
Maldives	22.7	12.0 (2014)	15.3	...
Nepal	38.0	23.1	30.2	28.6
Sri Lanka	26.3 (2001)	23.7 (2014)	17.3 (2011)	17.3 (2012)
Southeast Asia				
Brunei Darussalam	13.7	10.3 (2014)	10.9	9.1 (2014)
Cambodia	50.1	44.6 (2014)	18.5	28.9 (2007)
Indonesia	22.1	16.6 (2014)	14.6	15.5 (2014)
Lao PDR	30.1	25.2 (2014)	21.3	18.3 (2014)
Malaysia	19.6	11.4 (2014)	18.4	11.7 (2014)
Myanmar	32.8	27.6 (2014)	31.9	31.8 (2014)
Philippines	35.3	31.4 (2013)	36.4 (2001)	27.0 (2013)
Singapore	20.4 (2007)	17.4 (2009)	17.0 (2007)	14.9 (2009)
Thailand	20.8	15.4 (2014)	24.0 (2001)	19.9 (2011)
Viet Nam	29.5	19.2 (2014)	...	...
The Pacific				
Cook Islands	17.8	16.6 (2014)	13.9	13.9 (2014)
Fiji	28.1	28.0 (2012)	20.2	19.3 (2012)
Kiribati	31.7	26.4 (2014)	21.0 (2001)	17.4 (2008)
Marshall Islands	16.9 (2002)	...	16.7 (2002)	14.9 (2003)
Micronesia, Fed. States of	...	...	...	...
Nauru	21.5	39.5 (2014)	17.4	22.8 (2014)
Palau	15.7	...	15.1	...
Papua New Guinea	35.4	36.2 (2001)	...	27.4 (2012)
Samoa	24.0	30.2 (2010)	21.2	21.5 (2010)
Solomon Islands	19.9 (2010)	20.3 (2014)	10.1	25.9 (2012)
Timor-Leste	61.9 (2001)	31.4 (2011)	28.0 (2001)	24.3 (2011)
Tonga	22.1	21.9 (2014)	14.6	11.4 (2014)
Tuvalu	19.7	19.2 (2004)	...	...
Vanuatu	22.5	22.8 (2013)	24.7	15.1 (2001)
Developed Member Economies				
Australia	...	...	...	...
Japan	20.7	16.7 (2013)	14.0	11.7 (2012)
New Zealand	18.4	14.4 (2014)	15.5	14.0 (2014)

... = data not available at cutoff date, Lao PDR = Lao People's Democratic Republic.

Sources: UNESCO Institute for Statistics Data Centre Online. http://www.uis.unesco.org/Pages/default.aspx (accessed September 2016); for Taipei,China: Directorate-General of Budget, Accounting and Statistics. Monthly Bulletin of Statistics Online. http://eng.dgbas.gov.tw/mp.asp?mp=2 (accessed June 2016).

Table 1.16:   **Health Care Resources**
              (per 1,000 population)

Regional Member	Physicians		Hospital Beds	
	2000	2015	2000	2015
Developing Member Economies				
Central and West Asia				
Afghanistan	0.19 (2001)	0.27 (2013)	0.40 (2001)	0.50 (2012)
Armenia	2.99	2.70 (2013)	5.47	3.90 (2012)
Azerbaijan	3.61	3.40 (2013)	8.68	4.70 (2012)
Georgia	4.73	4.27 (2013)	4.77	2.60 (2012)
Kazakhstan	3.29	3.62 (2013)	7.19	7.20 (2012)
Kyrgyz Republic	2.82	1.97 (2013)	7.40	4.80 (2012)
Pakistan	0.64	0.83 (2010)	0.70 (2003)	0.60 (2012)
Tajikistan	2.22	1.92 (2013)	6.54	5.50 (2011)
Turkmenistan	4.18 (2002)	2.39 (2010)	4.90 (2004)	4.00 (2012)
Uzbekistan	2.95	2.53 (2013)	5.33	4.40 (2010)
East Asia				
China, People's Rep. of	1.25	1.94 (2012)	2.52	3.80 (2011)
Hong Kong, China	...	...	...	...
Korea, Rep. of	1.30	2.14 (2012)	6.10	10.30 (2009)
Mongolia	2.63 (2002)	2.84 (2011)	7.50 (2002)	6.80 (2012)
Taipei,China	1.50	2.10 (2014)	5.68	6.89 (2014)
South Asia				
Bangladesh	0.23 (2001)	0.36 (2011)	0.30 (2001)	0.60 (2011)
Bhutan	0.05 (2004)	0.26 (2012)	1.60 (2001)	1.80 (2012)
India	0.55	0.70 (2012)	0.69 (2002)	0.70 (2011)
Maldives	0.78	1.42 (2010)	1.70	4.30 (2009)
Nepal	0.05 (2001)	0.21 (2004)	0.20 (2001)	5.00 (2006)
Sri Lanka	0.43	0.68 (2010)	2.90	3.60 (2012)
Southeast Asia				
Brunei Darussalam	1.01	1.44 (2012)	2.60	2.80 (2012)
Cambodia	0.16	0.17 (2012)	0.60 (2001)	0.70 (2011)
Indonesia	0.16	0.20 (2012)	0.60 (2002)	0.90 (2012)
Lao PDR	0.29	0.18 (2012)	0.90 (2002)	1.50 (2012)
Malaysia	0.70	1.20 (2010)	1.80 (2001)	1.90 (2012)
Myanmar	0.30	0.61 (2012)	0.70	0.60 (2006)
Philippines	0.59	1.15 (2004)	1.00 (2001)	1.00 (2011)
Singapore	1.40 (2001)	1.95 (2013)	2.90 (2001)	2.00 (2011)
Thailand	0.37	0.39 (2010)	2.20	2.10 (2010)
Viet Nam	0.53 (2001)	1.19 (2013)	2.40 (2001)	2.00 (2010)
The Pacific				
Cook Islands	...	...	...	...
Fiji	0.45 (2003)	0.43 (2010)	2.10 (2004)	2.10 (2009)
Kiribati	0.23 (2004)	0.38 (2010)	1.50 (2004)	1.30 (2011)
Marshall Islands	0.47	0.44 (2010)	2.70 (2009)	2.70 (2010)
Micronesia, Fed. States of	0.60	0.18 (2010)	2.80	3.20 (2009)
Nauru	0.77 (2004)	0.71 (2010)	3.50 (2004)	5.00 (2010)
Palau	1.58	1.38 (2010)	5.90 (2006)	4.80 (2010)
Papua New Guinea	0.05	0.06 (2010)	...	...
Samoa	0.28 (2003)	0.48 (2010)	3.30	0.00 (2005)
Solomon Islands	0.13 (2003)	0.22 (2010)	2.20 (2003)	1.30 (2012)
Timor-Leste	0.00 (2001)	0.07 (2011)	5.90 (2010)	5.90 (2010)
Tonga	0.50	0.56 (2010)	3.20 (2001)	2.60 (2010)
Tuvalu	0.55 (2002)	1.09 (2010)	5.60 (2001)	5.60 (2001)
Vanuatu	0.14 (2004)	0.12 (2010)	3.10 (2001)	1.70 (2008)
Developed Member Economies				
Australia	2.50	3.27 (2011)	7.80	3.90 (2010)
Japan	2.01	2.30 (2010)	14.70	13.70 (2009)
New Zealand	2.20	2.74 (2010)	6.20 (2002)	2.30 (2011)

... = data not available at cutoff date, 0.00 = magnitude is less than half of unit employed, Lao PDR = Lao People's Democratic Republic.

Sources: World Bank. World Development Indicators Online. http://data.worldbank.org (accessed August 2016); for Taipei,China: Directorate-General of Budget, Accounting and Statistics. Monthly Bulletin of Statistics Online. http://eng.dgbas.gov.tw/mp.asp?mp=2 (accessed June 2016).

Table 1.17:   **Estimated Number of Adults Living with HIV**[a]
(15 years and over, thousand)

Regional Member	Adults		Women	
	2000	2015	2000	2015
Developing Member Economies				
Central and West Asia				
Afghanistan	1.8	6.7	0.5	1.9
Armenia	1.0	3.6	0.2	0.7
Azerbaijan	1.4	10.6	0.4	3.1
Georgia	1.9	9.6	0.7	2.1
Kazakhstan	4.0	22.9	0.6	7.1
Kyrgyz Republic	0.8	8.0	0.2	2.6
Pakistan	8.6	99.5	2.3	29.6
Tajikistan	5.0	15.8	2.1	5.4
Turkmenistan	...	...	...	...
Uzbekistan	20.3	32.1	4.5	9.7
East Asia				
China, People's Rep. of	...	...	...	...
Hong Kong, China	...	...	...	...
Korea, Rep. of	...	...	...	...
Mongolia	0.0	0.4	0.0	0.1
Taipei,China	...	...	...	...
South Asia				
Bangladesh	1.0	9.3	0.2	3.2
Bhutan	...	...	...	...
India	1,949.2	1,979.1	674.8	794.0
Maldives	...	...	...	...
Nepal	22.6	37.8	6.7	14.2
Sri Lanka	0.6	4.1	0.2	1.3
Southeast Asia				
Brunei Darussalam	...	...	...	...
Cambodia	114.5	70.1	45.1	37.0
Indonesia	41.5	675.5	9.3	246.9
Lao PDR	...	...	...	...
Malaysia	99.4	91.1	3.7	12.7
Myanmar	187.1	215.3	44.5	77.2
Philippines	2.6	42.1	0.9	4.5
Singapore	...	...	...	...
Thailand	616.0	434.0	176.5	179.7
Viet Nam	101.1	250.2	15.3	76.5
The Pacific				
Cook Islands	...	...	...	...
Fiji	...	...	...	...
Kiribati	...	...	...	...
Marshall Islands	...	...	...	...
Micronesia, Fed. States of	...	...	...	...
Nauru	...	...	...	...
Palau	...	...	...	...
Papua New Guinea	23.2	36.9	12.6	21.3
Samoa	...	...	...	...
Solomon Islands	...	...	...	...
Timor-Leste	...	...	...	...
Tonga	...	...	...	...
Tuvalu	...	...	...	...
Vanuatu	...	...	...	...
Developed Member Economies				
Australia	15.3	26.8	1.2	2.8
Japan	...	...	...	...
New Zealand	...	...	...	...

... = data not available at cutoff date, 0.0 = magnitude is less than half of unit employed, Lao PDR = Lao People's Democratic Republic.

a The modeled HIV estimates are calculated by UNAIDS using the Spectrum developed by the Futures Institute, and the Estimates and Projections Package (www.futuresinstitute.org).

Source: UNAIDS. AidsInfo Online Database. http://www.aidsinfoonline.org/devinfo/libraries/aspx/home.aspx (accessed June 2016).

Economy and Output

Snapshots

- The Asia and Pacific region's economic output accounts for two-fifths of the global gross domestic product (GDP) (in purchasing power parity terms) in 2015.

- Between 2014 and 2015, growth of real GDP exceeded 3% in 21 out of 41 economies of Asia and the Pacific with available data.

- In nearly three-quarters of the economies in the region, services sector accounts for more than 50% of GDP.

- Household consumption spending as a percentage of GDP has declined in more than two-thirds of the region's reporting economies while government consumption expenditure relative to GDP has increased in more than half of the region's reporting economies since 2000.

Key Trends

The Asia and the Pacific's economic output accounts for two-fifths of the global gross domestic product (GDP) (in purchasing power parity terms) in 2015. Figure 2.1 divides global GDP into seven regions. Each economy's GDP has been converted into a common currency using purchasing power parity (PPP) to eliminate differences in price levels. The Asia and Pacific region includes both developed and developing members. Estimates suggest that the share of GDP generated by the region rose to 40.5% in 2015, increasing nearly 11 percentage points between 2000 and 2015. Europe's share of global GDP fell 4.9 percentage points to 22.6% between 2000 and 2015, while North America's share fell 6.4 percentage points to 19.5%.

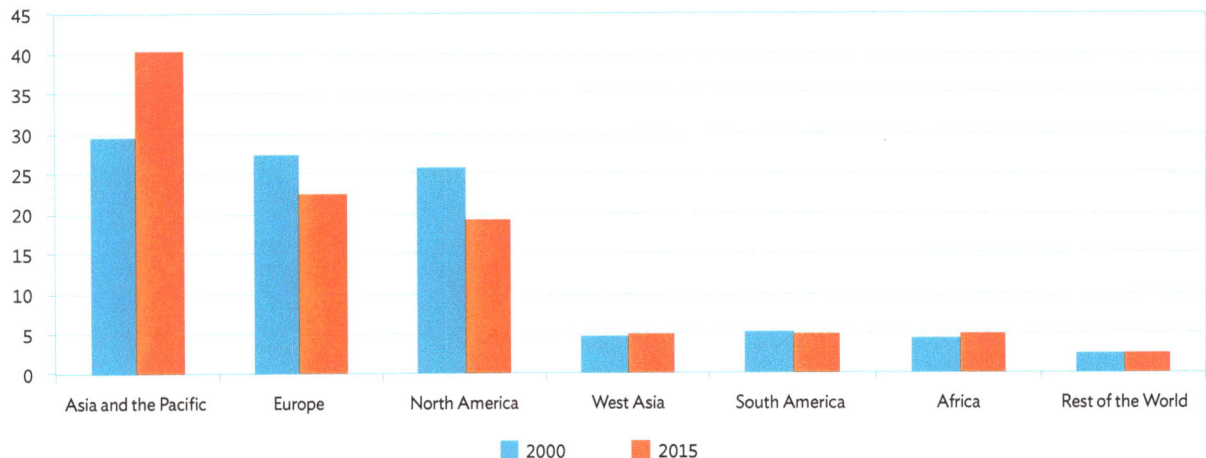

Figure 2.1: Distribution of Gross Domestic Product at Purchasing Power Parity: Asia and Pacific Region in the World Economy (%)

Sources: Derived from Table 2.1 and World Bank. World Development Indicators Online. http://data.worldbank.org/ (accessed September 2016).

Approximately 60% of Asia and the Pacific's total GDP in 2015 is accounted for by the People's Republic of China (PRC) and India. Figure 2.2 shows that the PRC contributed 42.0% of regional GDP and India 17.2%. India surpassed Japan in 2008 to become the region's second biggest economy in PPP-adjusted terms.[5]

Within Asia and the Pacific, there are significant differences in per capita GDP between economies. Figure 2.3 shows per capita GDP in PPP terms in index form for 35 reporting economies for 2000 and 2015. The average for all reporting economies in the region is equated to 100, which is represented by the red line. Economies with bars to the left of the vertical line had per capita GDP below that year's regional average, and those with bars to the right of the vertical line had per capita GDP above that year's regional average.

The PPP-adjusted per capita GDP in Singapore, which topped the list in 2015, was 44 times greater than that of Solomon Islands, at the bottom, and 7 times greater than the regional average.

In addition to Singapore, the per capita GDP of six other economies—Australia; Brunei Darussalam; Hong Kong, China; Japan; the Republic of Korea; and Taipei,China—was at least three times greater than the 2015 regional average. At the same time, seven economies had a per capita GDP in 2015, or the latest year for which data are available, which was less than half of the regional average.

Among the most populous developing members, only the PRC's per capita GDP in 2015 was higher than the regional average. Meanwhile, in Bangladesh, India, Indonesia, and Pakistan, per capita GDP was below the regional average. The PRC first exceeded the regional average in 2009, while Indonesia fell just below the regional average and has remained there since 2010.

Between 2014 and 2015, growth of real GDP exceeded 3% in 21 out of 41 economies of Asia and the Pacific with available data. Figure 2.4 shows the growth rates of real GDP for economies of Asia and the Pacific between 2013 and 2014, and between 2014 and 2015. Among the region's three

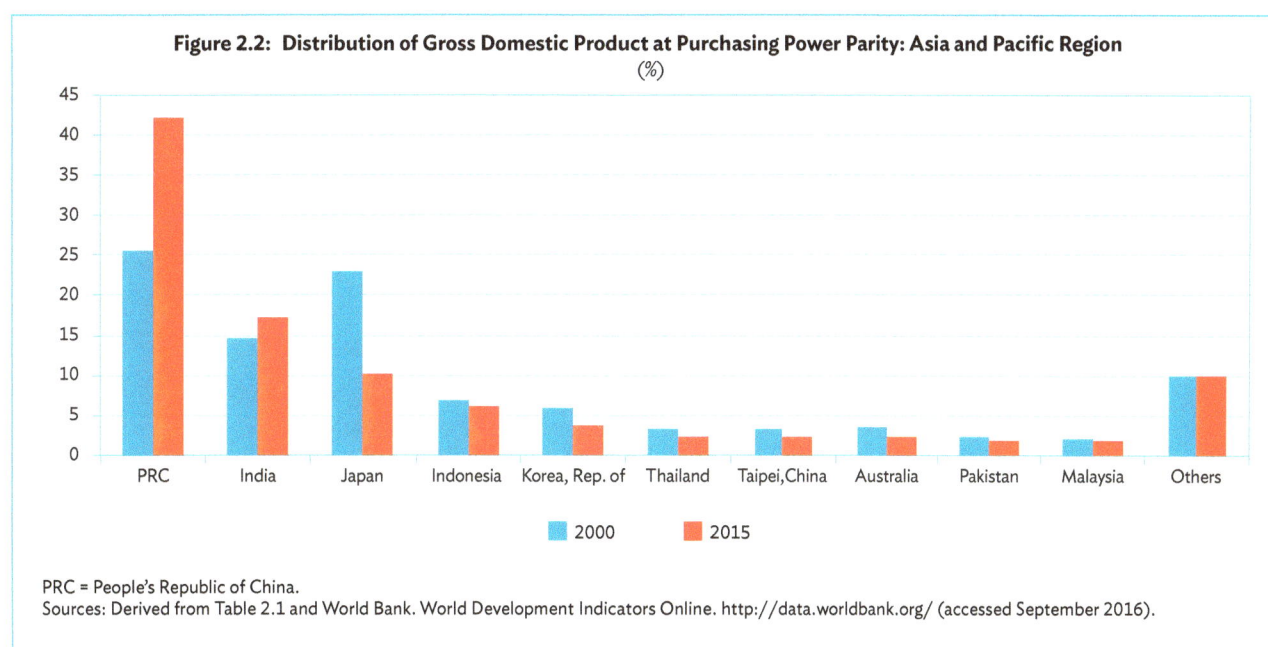

Figure 2.2: Distribution of Gross Domestic Product at Purchasing Power Parity: Asia and Pacific Region (%)

PRC = People's Republic of China.
Sources: Derived from Table 2.1 and World Bank. World Development Indicators Online. http://data.worldbank.org/ (accessed September 2016).

---

[5] Excluding the developed economies, the PRC and India accounted for approximately 70% of the GDP of developing economies in the region.

Figure 2.3: Indexes of per Capita Gross Domestic Product at Purchasing Power Parity
(regional average = 100)

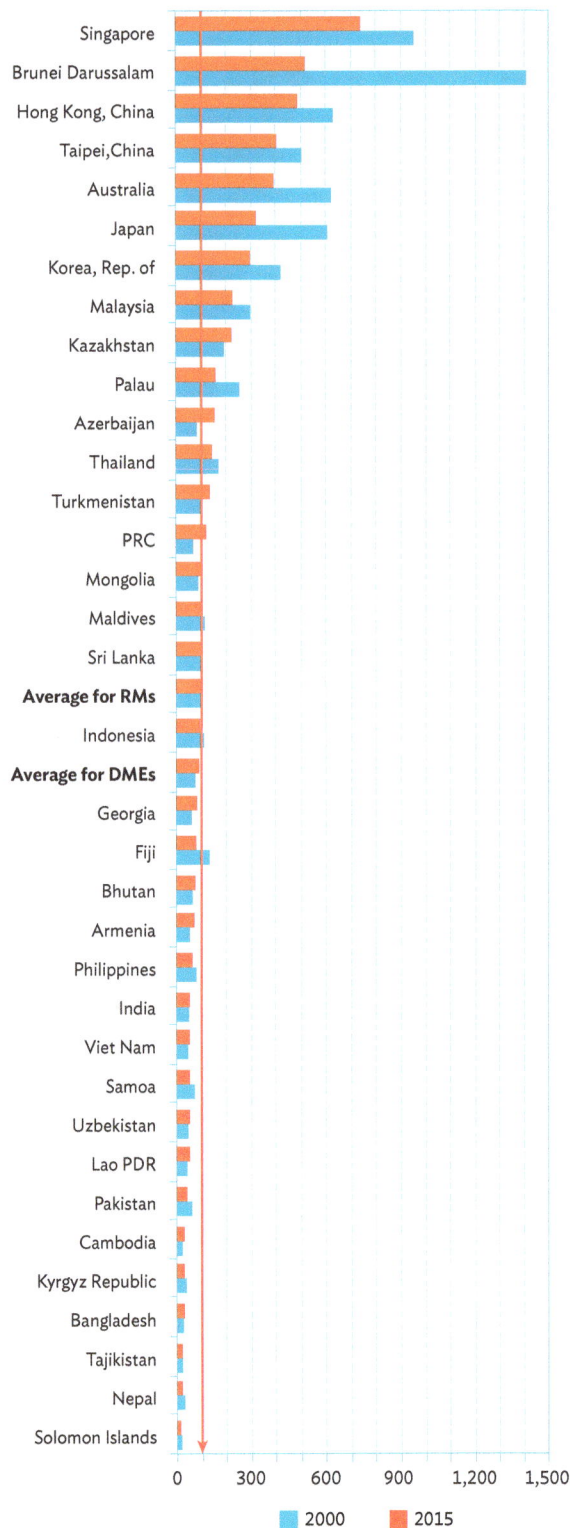

Singapore, Brunei Darussalam, Hong Kong, China, Taipei,China, Australia, Japan, Korea, Rep. of, Malaysia, Kazakhstan, Palau, Azerbaijan, Thailand, Turkmenistan, PRC, Mongolia, Maldives, Sri Lanka, Average for RMs, Indonesia, Average for DMEs, Georgia, Fiji, Bhutan, Armenia, Philippines, India, Viet Nam, Samoa, Uzbekistan, Lao PDR, Pakistan, Cambodia, Kyrgyz Republic, Bangladesh, Tajikistan, Nepal, Solomon Islands

0 300 600 900 1,200 1,500

■ 2000 ■ 2015

DME = developing member economy, Lao PDR = Lao People's Democratic Republic, PRC = People's Republic of China, RM = regional member.
Source: ADB estimates from Table 2.2.

developed economies, economic growth increased slightly in Japan between 2014 and 2015 (from –0.0% to 0.5%), while deceleration occurred both in Australia (from 2.5% to 2.3%) and New Zealand (from 3.6% to 2.4%). Overall, GDP growth accelerated only in less than a third of the region's economies in 2015.

India's economic growth accelerated to 7.6% in 2015 from 7.2% in the previous year, led by services on the supply side and private consumption on the demand side. In Indonesia, economic growth slowed down in 2015 from 5.0% to 4.8%, due to decelerated private consumption growth and in the Republic of Korea from 3.3% to 2.6% due to weak external demand.

Elsewhere in the region, seven Pacific economies recorded acceleration in economic growth—the Marshall Islands (from –0.9% to 0.6%), the Federated States of Micronesia (from –2.4% to 3.7%), Palau (from 4.3% to 9.4%), Samoa (from 1.9% to 2.8%), Solomon Islands (from 2.0% to 2.9%), Tonga (from 2.0% to 3.4%), and Tuvalu (from 2.2% to 3.6%).

Trade remains an important sector in many developing economies in Asia and the Pacific. In 13 out of 38 developing economies with relevant data, the total value of exports of goods and services in 2015, or the latest year for which data are available, exceeded 50% of GDP (Figure 2.5). In 26 out of the same 38 economies, total imports exceeded 30% of GDP in 2015. Singapore and Hong Kong, China were the only two economies in the region in which the values of imports and exports exceeded 100% of GDP. In the region's developed economies—Australia, Japan, and New Zealand—the ratios of exports to GDP and imports to GDP were less than 30% in all three cases. The region's trade dependence—as measured by the ratio of merchandise exports to GDP—remains constant at around 50% from 2000 to 2015.

Figure 2.4: Growth Rates of Real Gross Domestic Product
(%)

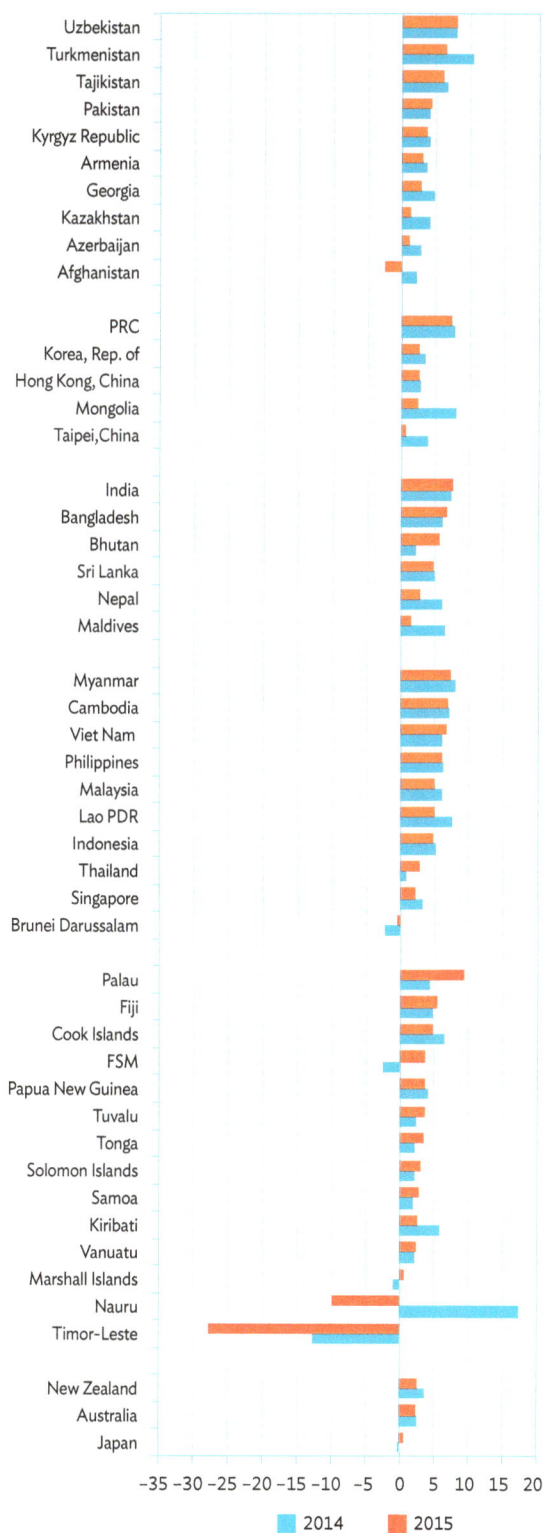

Uzbekistan
Turkmenistan
Tajikistan
Pakistan
Kyrgyz Republic
Armenia
Georgia
Kazakhstan
Azerbaijan
Afghanistan

PRC
Korea, Rep. of
Hong Kong, China
Mongolia
Taipei,China

India
Bangladesh
Bhutan
Sri Lanka
Nepal
Maldives

Myanmar
Cambodia
Viet Nam
Philippines
Malaysia
Lao PDR
Indonesia
Thailand
Singapore
Brunei Darussalam

Palau
Fiji
Cook Islands
FSM
Papua New Guinea
Tuvalu
Tonga
Solomon Islands
Samoa
Kiribati
Vanuatu
Marshall Islands
Nauru
Timor-Leste

New Zealand
Australia
Japan

−35 −30 −25 −20 −15 −10 −5 0   5 10 15 20

■ 2014   ■ 2015

FSM = Federated States of Micronesia, Lao PDR = Lao People's Democratic
Republic, PRC = People's Republic of China.
Source: Table 2.9.

Figure 2.5: Exports and Import of Goods and Services, 2015
(% of GDP)

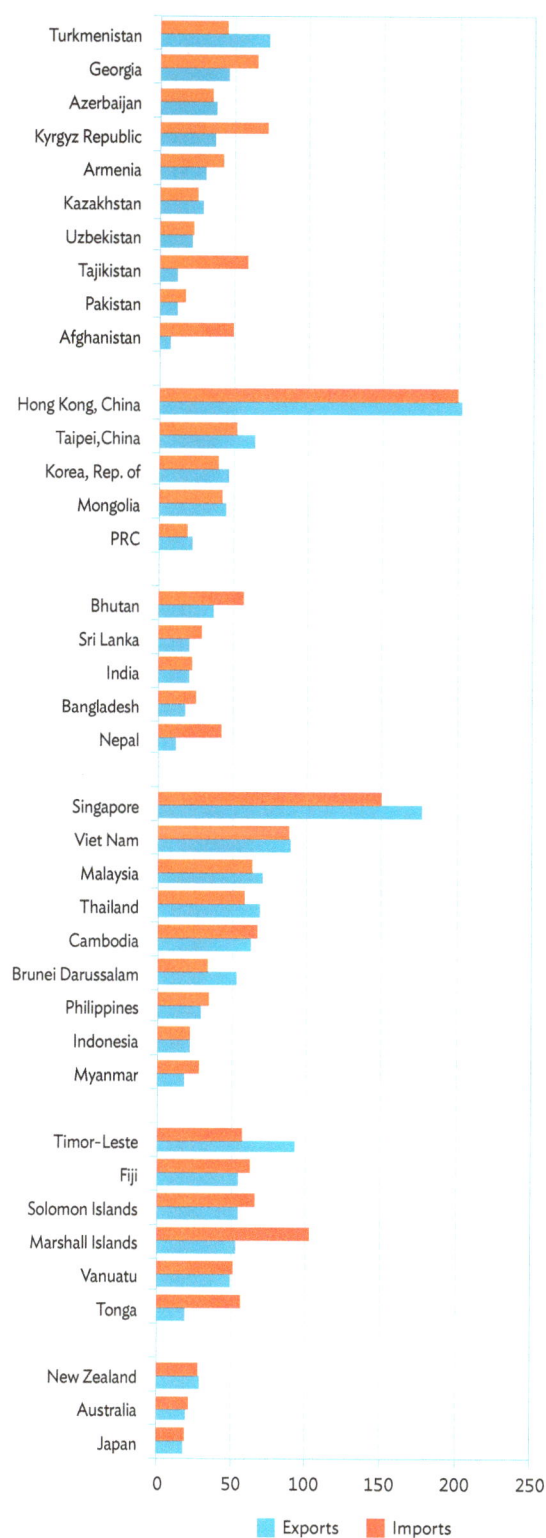

Turkmenistan
Georgia
Azerbaijan
Kyrgyz Republic
Armenia
Kazakhstan
Uzbekistan
Tajikistan
Pakistan
Afghanistan

Hong Kong, China
Taipei,China
Korea, Rep. of
Mongolia
PRC

Bhutan
Sri Lanka
India
Bangladesh
Nepal

Singapore
Viet Nam
Malaysia
Thailand
Cambodia
Brunei Darussalam
Philippines
Indonesia
Myanmar

Timor-Leste
Fiji
Solomon Islands
Marshall Islands
Vanuatu
Tonga

New Zealand
Australia
Japan

0   50   100 150 200 250

■ Exports   ■ Imports

GDP = gross domestic product, PRC = People's Republic of China.
Source: Table 2.7.

In nearly three-quarters of the economies of Asia and the Pacific, the services sector accounts for more than 50% of GDP. The percentage share of services to GDP increased in 39 out of 48 economies between 2000 and 2015, or the latest year for which data are available (Figure 2.6a). Rising incomes and migration to cities have generated demand for services such as communication, transportation, retailing, and health. Structural changes in economies and declining labor intensity in agriculture and manufacturing have channeled more workers into services, which are often labor-intensive.

The share of services in the PRC's GDP is estimated at 50.0% in 2015, while India's services' share of GDP is estimated at 53.2% during the same period. Economies in which services make the smallest contribution to GDP include most of Southeast Asia (notably Brunei Darussalam and Myanmar); several economies in Central and West Asia (notably Azerbaijan and Turkmenistan); and Bhutan, Cambodia, the Lao PDR, Nauru, and Timor-Leste.

In Hong Kong, China—where the economy is dominated by trade, finance, and tourism—services comprised a 92.7% share of GDP in 2014. In the region's developed member economies—Australia, Japan, and New Zealand—services comprised about 70% of GDP in 2015, or the latest year for which data are available.

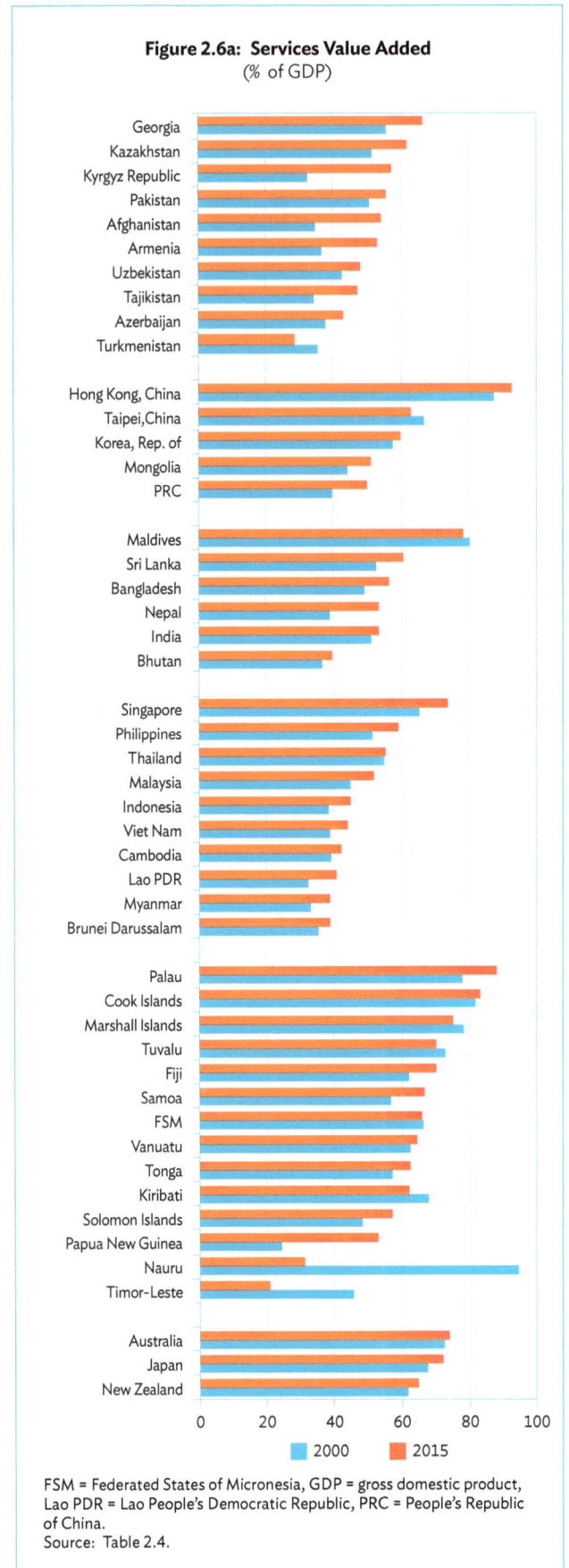

Figure 2.6a: Services Value Added
(% of GDP)

FSM = Federated States of Micronesia, GDP = gross domestic product, Lao PDR = Lao People's Democratic Republic, PRC = People's Republic of China.
Source: Table 2.4.

Between 2000 and 2015, or the latest year for which data are available, the share of agriculture in GDP fell in 40 economies of the region. As services continue to play a more significant role in most economies of Asia and the Pacific, the share of GDP generated by agriculture has generally declined. In 2000, the share of GDP generated by agriculture exceeded 25% in 17 economies of Asia and the Pacific. In 2015, only seven economies had agriculture value added as percentage of GDP that exceeded 25%. Figure 2.6b presents the estimates for all reporting economies in the region.

Between 2000 and 2015, the percentage share of industry to GDP increased in 21 out of 48 economies. Timor-Leste had the highest ratio of industry value added to GDP at 72.5% in 2015, up from 31.1% in 2000 (Figure 2.6c). Other notable increases during the period under review occurred in Nauru (from –1.8% to 66.2%), Myanmar (from 9.7% to 34.5%), and Turkmenistan (from 41.8% to 63.0%). The steepest declines occurred in Papua New Guinea (from 40.7% to 27.0%), Tajikistan (from 38.4% to 28.0%), and Armenia (from 38.3% to 28.2%).

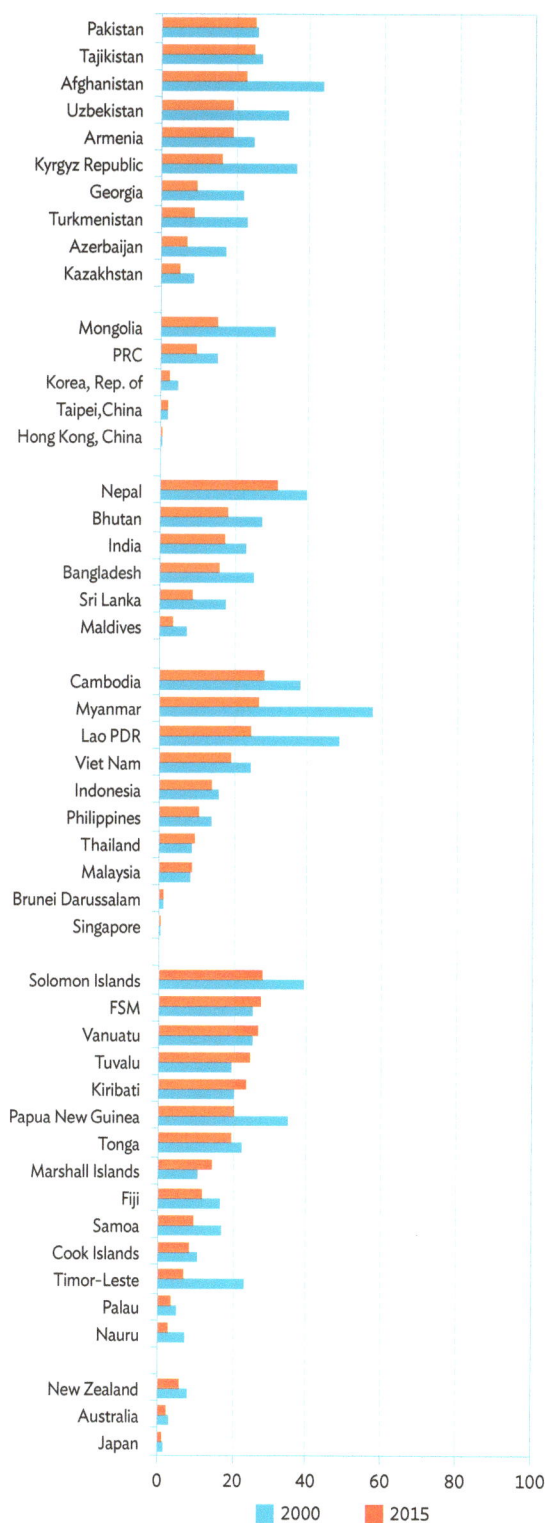

Figure 2.6b: Agriculture Value Added
(% of GDP)

FSM = Federated States of Micronesia, GDP = gross domestic product, Lao PDR = Lao People's Democratic Republic, PRC = People's Republic of China.
Source: Table 2.4.

Figure 2.6c: Industry Value Added
(% of GDP)

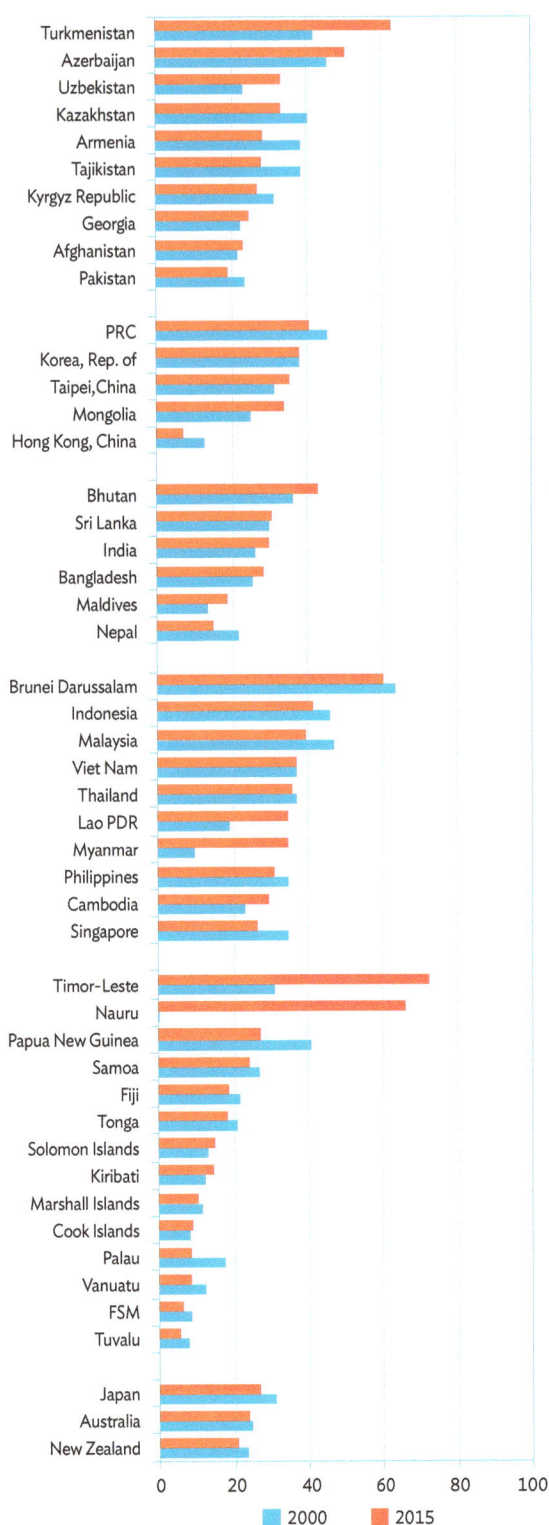

Turkmenistan
Azerbaijan
Uzbekistan
Kazakhstan
Armenia
Tajikistan
Kyrgyz Republic
Georgia
Afghanistan
Pakistan

PRC
Korea, Rep. of
Taipei,China
Mongolia
Hong Kong, China

Bhutan
Sri Lanka
India
Bangladesh
Maldives
Nepal

Brunei Darussalam
Indonesia
Malaysia
Viet Nam
Thailand
Lao PDR
Myanmar
Philippines
Cambodia
Singapore

Timor-Leste
Nauru
Papua New Guinea
Samoa
Fiji
Tonga
Solomon Islands
Kiribati
Marshall Islands
Cook Islands
Palau
Vanuatu
FSM
Tuvalu

Japan
Australia
New Zealand

0   20   40   60   80   100

■ 2000   ■ 2015

FSM = Federated States of Micronesia, GDP = gross domestic product,
Lao PDR = Lao People's Democratic Republic, PRC = People's Republic
of China.
Source: Table 2.4.

The majority of the economies of Asia and the Pacific have increased investment spending as a share of GDP since 2000. Figure 2.7a shows that gross capital formation as a percentage of GDP rose in three-quarters (27 out of 37) of reporting economies between 2000 and 2015, or the latest year for which data are available. Capital formation consists of fixed capital investment in construction, durable equipment, breeding stocks and orchards, and intellectual property products; and changes in inventories (European Commission et al. 2008). The economies with the highest levels of capital formation relative to GDP in 2015, or the latest year for which data are available, were Bhutan (57.7%), Turkmenistan (47.2%), and the PRC (44.9%). Except for Pakistan, which had the lowest share of gross capital formation to GDP at 15.1% in 2015, all reporting economies in South Asia and Central and West Asia, posted an increase in their share of gross domestic capital formation to GDP.

Other reporting economies with the lowest shares of gross domestic capital formation to GDP in 2015, or the latest year for which data are available, are Timor-Leste (15.2%), the Marshall Islands (16.3%), and Fiji (18.4%).

Figure 2.7a: Gross Capital Formation
(% of GDP)

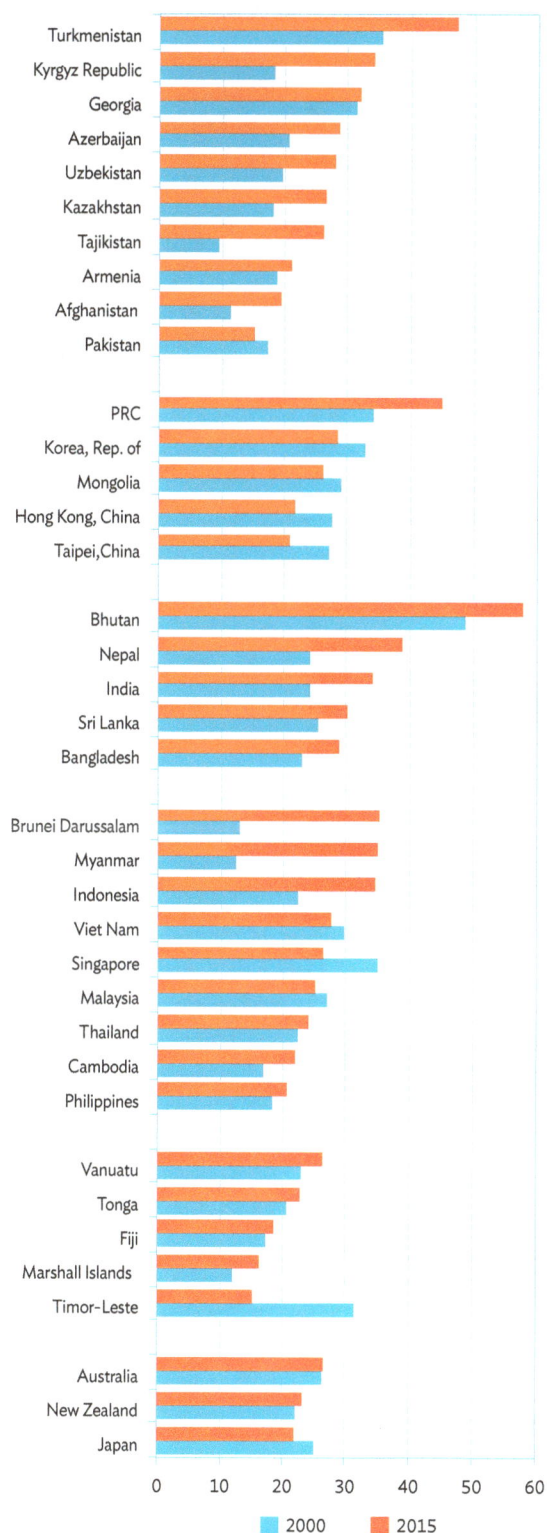

Turkmenistan
Kyrgyz Republic
Georgia
Azerbaijan
Uzbekistan
Kazakhstan
Tajikistan
Armenia
Afghanistan
Pakistan

PRC
Korea, Rep. of
Mongolia
Hong Kong, China
Taipei,China

Bhutan
Nepal
India
Sri Lanka
Bangladesh

Brunei Darussalam
Myanmar
Indonesia
Viet Nam
Singapore
Malaysia
Thailand
Cambodia
Philippines

Vanuatu
Tonga
Fiji
Marshall Islands
Timor-Leste

Australia
New Zealand
Japan

0   10   20   30   40   50   60

■ 2000   ■ 2015

GDP = gross domestic product, PRC = People's Republic of China.
Source: Table 2.6.

Household consumption spending as a percentage of GDP has declined in more than two-thirds of the region's reporting economies since 2000. Between 2000 and 2015, household consumption spending as a percentage of GDP dropped in 26 out of 38 economies with relevant data. Among the most populous developing economies, private consumption as a share of GDP fell between 2000 and 2015, or the latest year for which data are available, in the PRC from 47.1% to 39.1%, in India from 64.6% to 59.5%, and in Indonesia from 61.7% to 55.9% (Figure 2.7b). Tonga posted the highest level of household consumption as a share of GDP (101.9%), while Turkmenistan posted the lowest (15.1%). The Kyrgyz Republic posted the largest increase in private consumption as a share of GDP between 2000 and 2015 (22.5 percentage points).

Government consumption expenditure relative to GDP has increased in almost half of the region's reporting economies (19 out of 37) since 2000. In 2015, or the latest year for which data are available, government consumption expenditure as a share of GDP went up in 19 out of 37 economies. In five of six reporting economies of the Pacific including the Marshall Islands (50.9%), Solomon Islands (33.2%), Timor-Leste (22.7%), Fiji (20.3), and Tonga (19.4%), the share of government consumption expenditure relative to GDP exceeded that in every developing economy except Brunei Darussalam (25.1%) (Figure 2.7c). Meanwhile, the lowest ratios of government consumption expenditure as a share of GDP were in Bangladesh (5.4%), Cambodia (5.5%), and Viet Nam (6.3%). Among developed economies in Asia and the Pacific in 2015, the government consumption expenditure as a share of GDP is estimated at 20.4% in Japan, 18.0% in Australia, and 18.7% in New Zealand.

Figure 2.7b: Household Consumption Expenditure
(% of GDP)

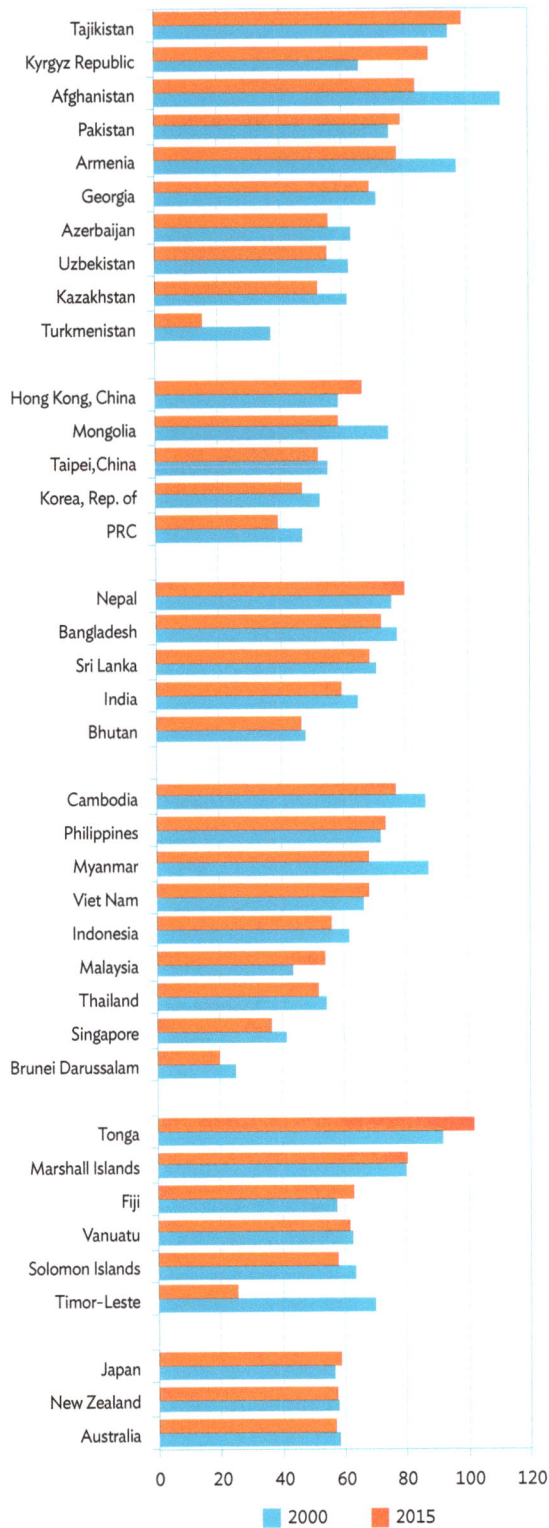

GDP = gross domestic product, PRC = People's Republic of China.
Source: Table 2.5.

Figure 2.7c: Government Consumption Expenditure
(% of GDP)

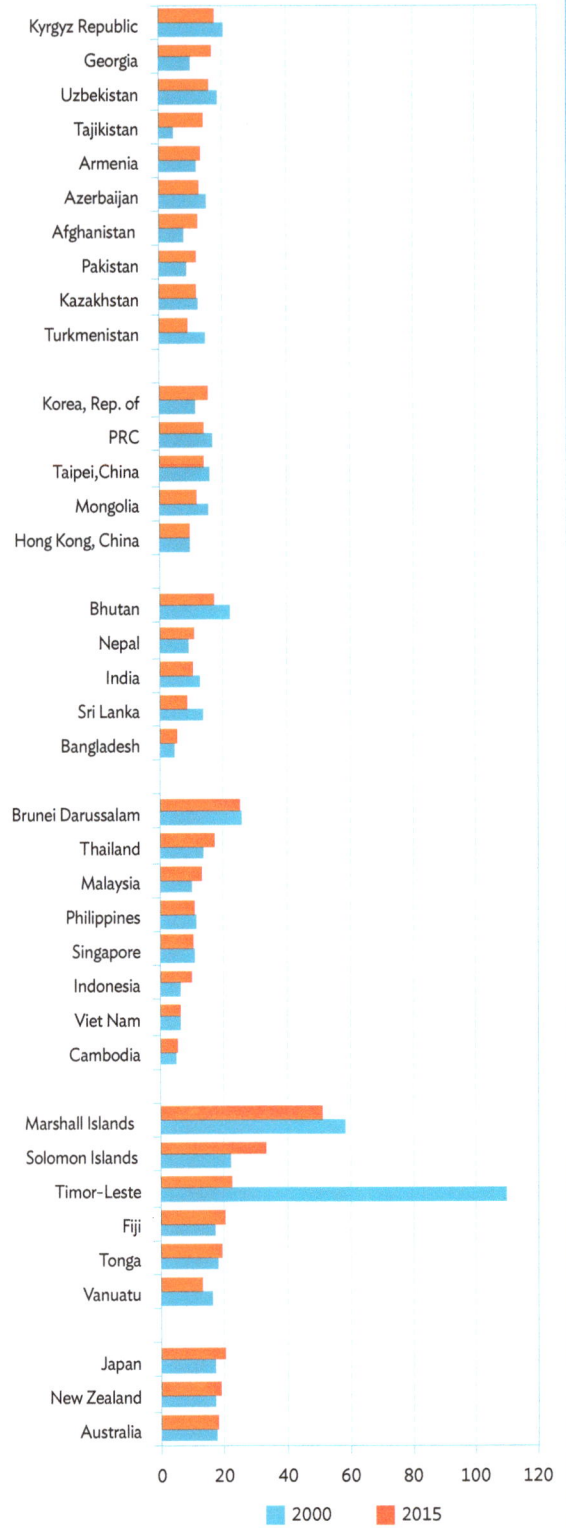

GDP = gross domestic product, PRC = People's Republic of China.
Source: Table 2.5.

Gross domestic saving as a share of GDP has increased in more than half of the economies in Asia and the Pacific since 2000. Between 2000 and 2015, gross domestic saving relative to GDP went up in 23 out of 37 regional economies with relevant data.

In 2015, or the most recent year for which data are available, Turkmenistan reported the highest ratio of domestic saving to GDP at 76.1%, while the Marshall Islands reported the lowest at −32.8% (Figure 2.7d). Turkmenistan also reported the biggest increase of 27.7 percentage points from 48.4%. On the other hand, Timor-Leste posted the biggest drop with a decline of 39.6 percentage points from 31.8% to −7.8%. Among reporting economies in East Asia, South Asia, and the developed economies, only Hong Kong, China; Japan; and Nepal, respectively, posted a decline in gross domestic saving as a percentage of GDP.

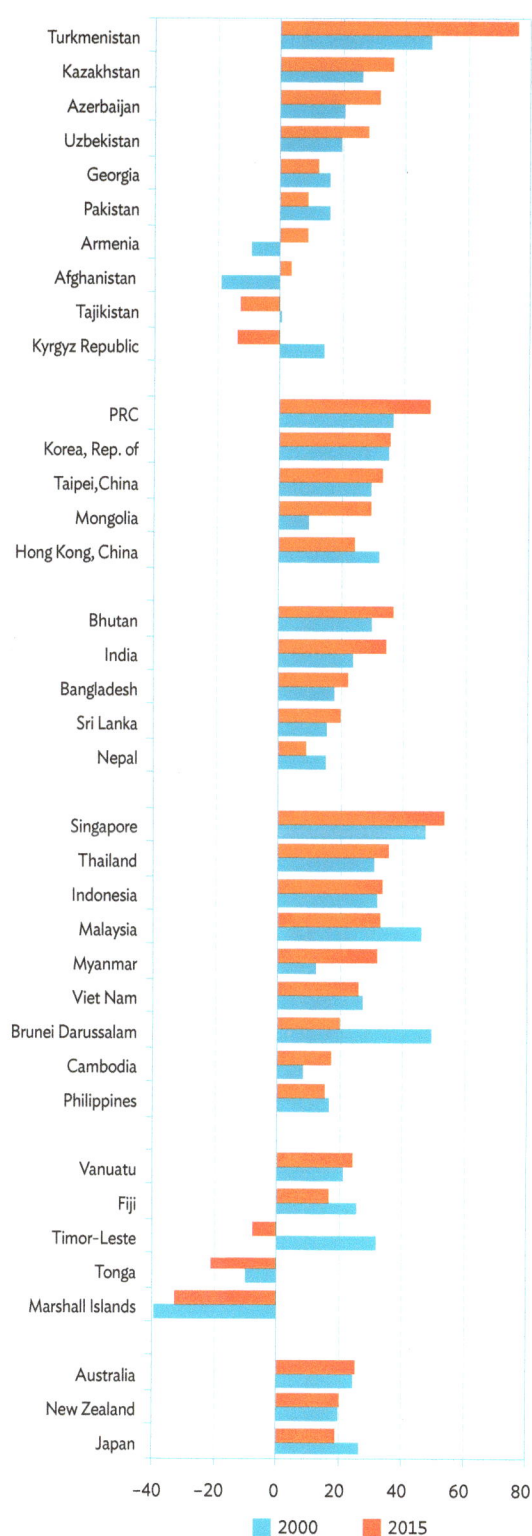

Figure 2.7d: Gross Domestic Saving
(% of GDP)

GDP = gross domestic product, PRC = People's Republic of China.
Source: Table 2.8.

Box 2.1: Economic Trends in Selected Economies of Asia and the Pacific, 1960–Present

Over the past 5 decades, Asia and the Pacific has experienced an increasing share of global gross domestic product (GDP).
The region's share of global GDP (expressed in constant 2010 United States [US] dollars) has increased from 12.7% in 1960 to 31.0% in 2015. Meanwhile, over the course of the past 5 decades, the region's share experienced a slight decline during 1995 to 2000 and a slight increase from 23.2% to 24.8% in 2005. This may be attributed to the Asian financial crisis in 1997 that resulted a slowdown in GDP growth for some Asian economies (Box Figure 2.1).

Box Figure 2.1: Asia and the Pacific's Share of Global Domestic Product, 1960–2015

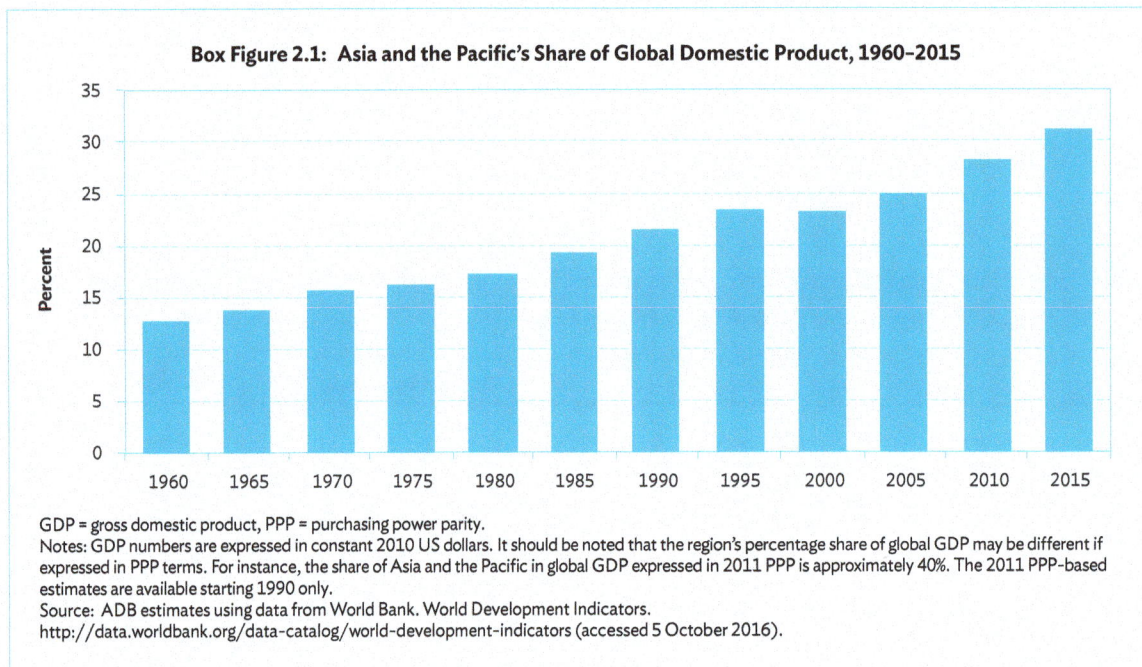

GDP = gross domestic product, PPP = purchasing power parity.
Notes: GDP numbers are expressed in constant 2010 US dollars. It should be noted that the region's percentage share of global GDP may be different if expressed in PPP terms. For instance, the share of Asia and the Pacific in global GDP expressed in 2011 PPP is approximately 40%. The 2011 PPP-based estimates are available starting 1990 only.
Source: ADB estimates using data from World Bank. World Development Indicators.
http://data.worldbank.org/data-catalog/world-development-indicators (accessed 5 October 2016).

Over time, Australia, the People's Republic of China (PRC), India, Japan, the Republic of Korea, and New Zealand have played important roles in driving the region's economic performance. Japan reestablished itself as an economic powerhouse to lead the region's economies into a period of growth and recovery in the decades following the Second World War. Japan's postwar economic expansion achieved an average annual GDP per capita growth of 9.1% throughout the 1960s before slowing markedly to 2.9% in the 1970s (Box Tables 2.2 and 2.3). In 1969, Japan's GDP of $1.89 trillion was more than twice as large as the combined output of Australia, the PRC, India, and the Republic of Korea.

The Republic of Korea was among the next wave of regional economies to enjoy similar economic success, expanding an average of 8.6% per year in the 1970s, by pursuing policies to boost production and the export of goods in sectors that Japanese industries had yielded in order to move to higher-value-added goods (Rodrik 2008).

The PRC's economic growth took off in the 1980s following the launch of domestic market reforms and an open trade policy in the late 1970s (Kau and Marsh 1993). The PRC's GDP per capita expanded at an average annual rate of 8.2% in the 1980s and 8.8% in the 1990s, before peaking at 9.6% in the 2000s.

India, which gradually pursued economic reforms that culminated in 1991 with the liberalization of its trade regime and the removal of most import licensing in the manufacturing sector, attained average annual GDP per capita growth of 5.1% in the 2000s and 6.0% in 2010–2015 (Sen 2008).

Australia experienced a dip in average annual GDP per capita growth between the 1960s and 1970s (from 2.8% to 1.7%). It then enjoyed relatively steady growth through out the 1980s, 1990s, and 2000s prior to another slowdown in 2010–2015, which was the result of moderating growth in its largest trading partner, the PRC (ADB 2016).

New Zealand has experienced relatively steady growth of 1.3%–1.5% in every decade since the 1960s, including 1.4% in 2010–2015.

continued.

Box 2.1: *(continued)*

Box Table 2.2: Gross Domestic Product of Selected Economies in Asia and the Pacific, 1960–2015
(2010 constant $, million)

Economy	1960s	1970s	1980s	1990s	2000s	2010–2015
Australia	303,582	424,667	590,318	814,595	1,119,653	1,301,251
China, People's Rep. of	154,662	313,672	792,927	2,050,825	5,459,247	8,797,998
India	200,368	265,398	460,913	806,012	1,549,482	2,367,206
Japan	1,889,639	2,814,916	4,312,785	4,980,754	5,251,308	5,669,563
Korea, Rep. of	55,997	151,966	344,979	652,418	1,027,729	1,266,580
New Zealand	...	69,283	84,539	111,125	144,602	167,575

... = data not available.
Notes: Last year of decade is the reference year. The gross domestic product numbers are expressed in constant 2010 US dollars.
Sources: ADB estimates using data from the World Bank. World Development Indicators Online. http://data.worldbank.org/ (accessed August 2016) and Organisation for Economic Co-operation and Development. National Accounts Statistics. http://www.oecd-ilibrary.org/economics/data/oecd-national-accounts-statistics_na-data-en (accessed August 2016).

Box Table 2.3: Average Annual Growth of Per Capita Gross Domestic Product of Selected Economies in Asia and the Pacific, 1960–2015
(%)

Economy	1960s	1970s	1980s	1990s	2000s	2010–2015
Australia	2.83	1.7	1.86	2.07	1.84	0.98
China, People's Rep. of	1.24	5.36	8.2	8.77	9.63	7.75
India	1.78	0.6	3.34	3.74	5.09	5.96
Japan	9.11	2.92	3.74	1.18	0.44	1.44
Korea, Rep. of	5.5	8.62	7.3	5.68	4.11	3.06
New Zealand	...	1.44	1.42	1.28	1.51	1.37

... = data not available.
Sources: ADB estimates using data from the World Bank. World Development Indicators Online. http://data.worldbank.org/ (accessed August 2016) and Organisation for Economic Co-operation and Development. National Accounts Statistics. http://www.oecd-ilibrary.org/economics/data/oecd-national-accounts-statistics_na-data-en (accessed August 2016).

Sources:

Asian Development Bank (ADB). 2016. *Asian Development Outlook 2016*. Manila.

M. Kau and S. Marsh. 1993. *China in the Era of Deng Xiaoping: A Decade of Reform*. New York: East Gate.

D. Rodrik. 2008. Normalizing Industrial Policy. *Working Paper* No. 3. Washington, DC: World Bank.

K. Sen. 2008. *Trade Policy, Inequality, and Performance in Indian Manufacturing*. New York: Routledge.

Data Issues and Comparability

Indicators in this theme are derived from national accounts compiled in accordance with the United Nations System of National Accounts (SNA). These indicators may not be fully consistent over time within a specific economy or across economies because of differences in their data compilation frameworks and changes in methodologies as national statistical offices gradually adopt the 2008 SNA framework. Furthermore, economies also have varying reference periods and price valuation methods. Some use the calendar year to compile national accounts while others use their fiscal year. Some economies with small statistical offices were not able to provide timely estimates.

References

European Commission, International Monetary Fund, Organisation for Economic Co-operation and Development, United Nations, and World Bank. 2009. System of National Accounts 2008. New York. http://unstats.un.org/unsd/nationalaccount/docs/SNA2008.pdf.

Table 2.1:   **Gross Domestic Product at Purchasing Power Parity**
(current international dollars, million)

Regional Member	2000	2005	2010	2011	2012	2013	2014	2015
Developing Member Economies								
Central and West Asia								
Afghanistan	...	26,954	46,549	51,634	58,333	63,079	65,497	64,558
Armenia	7,116	14,219	18,896	20,193	22,045	23,144	24,274	25,252
Azerbaijan	28,446	60,162	141,499	144,514	152,500	163,055	167,775	171,214
Georgia	11,445	18,312	25,902	28,346	30,701	32,259	34,305	35,610
Kazakhstan	122,353	225,094	334,937	366,465	390,384	419,759	444,147	453,981
Kyrgyz Republic	8,054	10,895	14,893	16,106	16,388	18,473	19,532	20,413
Pakistan	356,490	510,952	715,834	750,693	791,333	839,356	893,568	952,066
Tajikistan	6,163	10,990	16,539	17,287	18,934	20,675	22,416	23,980
Turkmenistan	18,749	27,498	48,601	58,014	65,641	73,516	82,420	85,199
Uzbekistan	48,288	70,587	117,120	131,147	144,434	159,046	171,863	187,668
East Asia								
China, People's Rep. of	3,681,134	6,588,188	12,358,726	13,810,256	15,154,696	16,585,177	18,082,915	19,524,345
Hong Kong, China	179,707	248,257	331,082	354,188	366,846	384,162	400,801	413,447
Korea, Rep. of	850,052	1,165,894	1,505,299	1,559,447	1,611,273	1,640,377	1,685,033	1,748,777
Mongolia	8,846	13,603	20,488	24,526	28,055	31,834	34,909	36,068
Taipei,China	480,625	657,933	893,930	947,053	984,435	1,022,476	1,080,093	1,097,915
South Asia								
Bangladesh	151,207	213,938	364,141	395,684	429,253	462,484	498,583	536,567
Bhutan	1,608	2,644	4,577	5,040	5,393	5,598	6,001	6,504
India	2,105,370	3,273,787	5,312,240	5,781,844	6,219,189	6,740,178	7,347,139	7,987,761
Maldives	...	2,282	3,781	4,195	4,379	4,659	5,043	5,556
Nepal	28,486	38,000	52,654	55,504	59,274	63,018	68,105	70,556
Sri Lanka	84,448	112,586	168,798	186,763	207,597	218,145	232,546	246,117
Southeast Asia								
Brunei Darussalam	19,587	24,379	30,717	32,480	33,804	33,739	29,852	25,013
Cambodia	13,260	23,268	35,370	38,652	42,222	45,580	50,275	54,352
Indonesia	973,477	1,377,638	2,003,952	2,171,519	2,344,875	2,515,534	2,685,309	2,842,241
Lao PDR	9,413	15,005	22,953	26,229	28,775	31,425	35,825	38,595
Malaysia	299,738	424,426	581,370	624,786	671,123	714,066	769,367	815,829
Myanmar	...	...	182,941	197,077	215,424	237,382	260,564	282,371
Philippines	261,127	367,107	513,962	543,769	590,802	642,578	693,559	742,260
Singapore	164,855	235,069	358,220	388,311	409,978	436,142	457,758	471,631
Thailand	458,573	671,429	887,632	913,511	997,611	1,041,268	1,067,028	1,107,790
Viet Nam	151,084	255,657	382,113	414,339	444,114	475,825	512,581	552,297
The Pacific								
Cook Islands	...	...	...	...	...	...	...	...
Fiji	4,530	5,707	6,562	6,493	6,721	7,196	7,822	8,167
Kiribati	118	144	169	176	188	211	224	...
Marshall Islands	124	156	181	184	193	201	198	...
Micronesia, Fed. States of	270	313	342	354	362	355	348	...
Nauru	...	...	...	...	...	...	...	...
Palau	207	263	249	267	280	278	295	325
Papua New Guinea	7,912	9,891	21,250	22,897	24,974	26,593	...	...
Samoa	532	797	1,020	1,099	1,082	1,096	1,148	1,164
Solomon Islands	371	686	952	988	1,008	1,129	1,097	1,142
Timor-Leste	1,152	4,550	9,014	11,558	12,541	10,653	8,135	...
Tonga	358	459	510	534	547	540	553	...
Tuvalu	23	26	31	34	35	36	37	...
Vanuatu	416	486	683	705	731	757	787	...
Developed Member Economies								
Australia	505,141	664,044	862,945	932,989	968,139	1,051,307	1,077,877	1,082,380
Japan	3,290,079	3,889,582	4,323,768	4,388,645	4,558,488	4,662,925	4,649,481	4,739,545
New Zealand	82,990	106,148	136,049	143,508	145,755	164,744	170,016	...
DEVELOPING MEMBER ECONOMIES[a]	**10,545,715**	**16,710,234**	**27,536,678**	**30,104,862**	**32,588,472**	**35,193,054**	**37,949,727**	**40,636,731**
REGIONAL MEMBERS[a]	**14,423,924**	**21,370,007**	**32,859,441**	**35,570,004**	**38,260,856**	**41,072,030**	**43,847,101**	**46,458,656**

... = data not available at cutoff date, Lao PDR = Lao People's Democratic Republic.

a   For reporting economies only.

Source: ADB estimates.

Table 2.2: **Gross Domestic Product per Capita at Purchasing Power Parity**
(current international dollars)

Regional Member	2000	2005	2010	2011	2012	2013	2014	2015
Developing Member Economies								
Central and West Asia								
Afghanistan	...	1,142	1,790	1,948	2,160	2,294	2,331	2,257
Armenia	2,209	4,519	6,206	6,669	7,290	7,658	8,054	8,404
Azerbaijan	3,523	7,078	15,628	15,754	16,415	17,309	17,599	17,742
Georgia	2,580	4,237	5,839	6,343	6,826	7,332	9,204	9,589
Kazakhstan	8,221	14,861	20,521	22,134	23,249	24,641	25,689	25,883
Kyrgyz Republic	1,648	2,117	2,749	2,940	2,952	3,262	3,381	3,463
Pakistan	2,547	3,319	4,126	4,239	4,379	4,553	4,753	4,966
Tajikistan	996	1,604	2,171	2,216	2,370	2,534	2,685	2,805
Turkmenistan	4,165	5,792	9,639	11,361	12,689	14,029	15,530	15,851
Uzbekistan	1,959	2,698	4,100	4,470	4,851	5,259	5,588	5,996
East Asia								
China, People's Rep. of	2,904	5,039	9,217	10,250	11,192	12,189	13,220	14,203
Hong Kong, China	26,963	36,438	47,135	50,086	51,274	53,449	55,346	56,592
Korea, Rep. of	18,083	24,220	30,465	31,327	32,223	32,664	33,417	34,549
Mongolia	3,704	5,363	7,481	8,802	9,880	10,981	11,781	11,916
Taipei,China	21,665	28,946	38,630	40,833	42,304	43,799	46,151	46,794
South Asia								
Bangladesh	1,169	1,544	2,450	2,643	2,831	3,009	3,200	3,398
Bhutan	2,702	4,164	6,577	7,116	7,483	7,637	8,053	8,591
India	2,066	2,960	4,479	4,739	5,036	5,388	5,799	6,226
Maldives	...	6,741	9,606	10,323	10,426	10,723	11,207	11,911
Nepal	1,354	1,502	2,006	2,095	2,207	2,316	2,469	2,524
Sri Lanka	4,362	5,731	8,164	8,949	10,164	10,600	11,196	11,739
Southeast Asia								
Brunei Darussalam	60,303	68,004	79,414	82,568	84,553	83,060	72,475	59,956
Cambodia	1,064	1,746	2,504	2,702	2,914	3,106	3,382	3,610
Indonesia	4,720	6,266	8,402	8,974	9,554	10,110	10,649	11,138
Lao PDR	1,850	2,669	3,799	4,279	4,628	4,982	5,598	5,945
Malaysia	12,760	16,295	20,336	21,498	22,742	23,637	25,143	26,317
Myanmar	...	...	3,536	3,781	4,100	4,480	5,061	5,384
Philippines	3,401	4,335	5,566	5,773	6,169	6,597	7,000	7,350
Singapore	40,928	55,105	70,562	74,910	77,174	80,779	83,690	85,209
Thailand	7,368	10,482	13,465	13,796	15,004	15,598	15,925	16,476
Viet Nam	1,959	3,121	4,396	4,717	5,003	5,304	5,650	6,022
The Pacific								
Cook Islands	...	...	...	...	...	...	...	...
Fiji	5,649	6,901	7,714	7,601	7,833	8,348	9,036	9,393
Kiribati	1,401	1,561	1,637	1,690	1,778	1,971	2,066	...
Marshall Islands	2,427	3,039	3,424	3,461	3,626	3,761	3,683	...
Micronesia, Fed. States of	2,526	2,967	3,327	3,452	3,543	3,475	3,406	...
Nauru	...	...	...	...	...	...	...	...
Palau	10,926	13,248	13,608	14,867	15,923	15,993	16,953	18,502
Papua New Guinea	1,524	1,634	3,012	3,147	3,329	3,438	...	...
Samoa	3,038	4,461	5,473	5,849	5,717	5,748	5,977	6,016
Solomon Islands	887	1,460	1,804	1,828	1,823	1,995	1,894	1,927
Timor-Leste	1,479	4,812	8,453	10,584	11,213	9,027	6,712	...
Tonga	3,614	4,534	4,958	5,178	5,293	5,213	5,330	...
Tuvalu	2,406	2,520	2,782	3,245	3,249	3,340	3,428	...
Vanuatu	2,171	2,234	2,782	2,801	2,830	2,861	2,905	...
Developed Member Economies								
Australia	26,546	32,911	39,168	41,763	42,596	45,477	45,944	45,505
Japan	25,938	30,441	33,761	34,335	35,736	36,618	36,572	37,332
New Zealand	21,512	25,677	31,271	32,735	33,065	37,087	37,700	...
DEVELOPING MEMBER ECONOMIES[a]	**3,274**	**4,859**	**7,474**	**8,048**	**8,627**	**9,221**	**9,869**	**10,466**
REGIONAL MEMBERS[a]	**4,279**	**5,951**	**8,560**	**9,132**	**9,730**	**10,342**	**10,960**	**11,518**

... = data not available at cutoff date, Lao PDR = Lao People's Democratic Republic.

a For reporting economies only.

Source: ADB estimates.

Table 2.3: **Gross National Income per Capita, Atlas Method**
(current $)

Regional Member	2000	2005	2010	2011	2012	2013	2014	2015
Developing Member Economies								
Central and West Asia								
Afghanistan	220	250	520	570	720	730	670	630
Armenia	660	1,520	3,370	3,420	3,760	3,930	4,020	3,880
Azerbaijan	610	1,270	5,370	5,530	6,290	7,350	7,600	6,560
Georgia	750	1,410	3,000	3,300	3,870	4,240	4,490	4,160
Kazakhstan	1,260	2,950	7,440	8,410	10,220	12,290	12,490	11,580
Kyrgyz Republic	280	450	850	880	1,040	1,220	1,260	1,170
Pakistan	490	740	1,080	1,150	1,260	1,360	1,400	1,440
Tajikistan	170	320	730	790	890	1,000	1,350	1,240
Turkmenistan	600	1,600	4,110	4,790	5,660	6,690	7,530	7,510
Uzbekistan	630	530	1,300	1,510	1,700	1,910	2,070	2,150
East Asia								
China, People's Rep. of	930	1,750	4,300	5,000	5,870	6,710	7,400	7,820
Hong Kong, China	26,930	28,890	33,620	35,690	36,320	38,520	40,320	41,000
Korea, Rep. of	10,750	17,800	21,320	22,610	24,630	25,860	26,970	27,440
Mongolia	470	900	2,000	2,600	3,670	4,370	4,260	3,830
Taipei,China	14,675	17,644	20,034	20,909	21,901	22,620	23,347	23,041
South Asia								
Bangladesh	420	540	780	870	950	1,010	1,080	1,190
Bhutan	780	1,220	1,990	2,170	2,320	2,340	2,370	2,370
India	450	730	1,260	1,400	1,500	1,520	1,560	1,590
Maldives	3,400	3,560	5,360	5,840	5,950	6,000	6,470	6,670
Nepal	230	310	540	610	690	720	730	730
Sri Lanka	880	1,220	2,430	2,860	3,360	3,490	3,650	3,800
Southeast Asia								
Brunei Darussalam	14,800	23,290	44,947	42,983	43,329	45,629	42,972	36,783
Cambodia	300	460	750	810	880	960	1,020	1,070
Indonesia	560	1,220	2,530	3,010	3,580	3,740	3,630	3,440
Lao PDR	280	460	1,000	1,120	1,300	1,490	1,640	1,730
Malaysia	3,420	5,250	8,280	9,080	10,200	10,850	11,120	10,570
Myanmar	...	...	...	...	...	...	1,280	...
Philippines	1,220	1,520	2,750	2,640	3,000	3,340	3,500	3,540
Singapore	23,670	28,370	44,790	48,530	51,300	54,470	55,330	52,090
Thailand	1,990	2,770	4,610	5,000	5,610	5,830	5,780	5,620
Viet Nam	400	680	1,270	1,390	1,550	1,740	1,900	1,980
The Pacific								
Cook Islands	5,545	8,475	9,790	12,997	15,060	16,207	17,167	16,735
Fiji	2,230	3,590	3,650	3,610	4,020	4,660	4,870	4,800
Kiribati	1,390	1,760	1,990	2,060	2,520	2,870	3,110	3,230
Marshall Islands	2,850	3,570	3,720	3,880	3,940	4,250	4,390	...
Micronesia, Fed. States of	2,210	2,550	2,870	3,050	3,220	3,280	3,200	...
Nauru	...	2,520	5,565	7,770	10,178	...	...	...
Palau	5,890	9,250	8,910	9,310	9,670	9,760	10,650	12,180
Papua New Guinea	620	700	1,270	1,520	1,820	2,040	2,240	...
Samoa	1,600	2,370	3,230	3,590	3,860	3,960	4,050	3,930
Solomon Islands	1,010	900	910	1,120	1,520	1,830	1,830	1,940
Timor-Leste	810	910	2,770	3,630	3,940	3,680	2,670	1,920
Tonga	2,030	2,500	3,550	3,830	4,210	4,300	4,260	...
Tuvalu	2,710	3,740	4,720	5,080	5,650	5,840	5,720	...
Vanuatu	1,430	1,780	2,690	2,860	2,950	3,200	3,160	...
Developed Member Economies								
Australia	21,110	30,310	46,530	50,130	59,810	65,500	64,620	60,070
Japan	34,980	39,140	41,980	45,190	47,830	46,340	41,900	36,680
New Zealand	14,070	25,520	29,340	31,850	36,440	39,170	41,370	40,080

... = data not available at cutoff date, Lao PDR = Lao People's Democratic Republic.

Sources: World Bank. World Development Indicators Online. http://data.worldbank.org (accessed 29 September 2016); ADB estimates using Atlas method based on economy sources for Brunei Darussalam (2010–2015); the Cook Islands (2000–2015); Nauru (2005–2012); and Taipei,China (2000–2015).

National Accounts

Table 2.4:   **Agriculture, Industry, and Services Value Added**
(% of GDP)[a]

Regional Member	Agriculture				Industry				Services			
	2000	2005	2010	2015	2000	2005	2010	2015	2000	2005	2010	2015
Developing Member Economies												
Central and West Asia												
Afghanistan	43.7 (2002)	35.2	28.8	22.9	21.7 (2002)	26.0	21.3	22.9	34.6 (2002)	38.8	49.8	54.2
Armenia	25.1	20.6	18.8	19.0	38.3	44.7	36.3	28.2	36.5	34.6	45.0	52.8
Azerbaijan	17.1	9.8	5.9	6.8	45.3	63.3	64.3	50.2	37.5	26.9	29.8	43.0
Georgia	21.9	16.7	8.4	9.2	22.4	26.8	22.2	24.5	55.7	56.5	69.4	66.3
Kazakhstan	8.6	6.6	4.7	5.0	40.1	39.2	41.9	33.2	51.3	54.2	53.4	61.8
Kyrgyz Republic	36.6	31.3	18.7	15.9	31.3	22.0	28.2	26.9	32.1	46.7	53.1	57.1
Pakistan	25.9	21.5	24.3	25.5	23.3	27.1	20.6	19.0	50.7	51.4	55.1	55.5
Tajikistan	27.3	23.8	21.8	25.0	38.4	30.7	27.9	28.0	34.3	45.6	50.3	47.1
Turkmenistan	22.9	18.8	14.5	8.5 (2014)	41.8	37.6	48.4	63.0 (2014)	35.2	43.6	37.0	28.6 (2014)
Uzbekistan	34.4	29.5	19.8	19.0 (2013)	23.1	29.1	33.4	33.2 (2013)	42.5	41.4	46.8	47.8 (2013)
East Asia												
China, People's Rep. of	15.0	12.1	9.9	9.3	45.6	47.0	46.4	40.7	39.5	40.9	43.7	50.0
Hong Kong, China	0.1	0.1	0.1	0.1 (2014)	12.6	8.7	7.0	7.2 (2014)	87.3	91.3	93.0	92.7 (2014)
Korea, Rep. of	4.4	3.1	2.5	2.3	38.1	37.5	38.3	38.0	57.5	59.4	59.3	59.7
Mongolia	30.9	22.1	13.1	14.8	25.0	36.2	37.0	34.1	44.1	41.7	50.0	51.1
Taipei,China[b]	2.0	1.6	1.6	1.8	31.3	32.3	33.8	35.4	66.7	66.1	64.6	62.8
South Asia												
Bangladesh	25.5	20.1	17.8	15.5	25.3	27.2	26.1	28.2	49.2	52.6	56.0	56.4
Bhutan	27.4	23.2	17.5	17.7 (2014)	36.0	37.3	44.6	42.9 (2014)	36.6	39.5	37.9	39.4 (2014)
India	23.0	18.8	18.2	17.0	26.0	28.1	27.2	29.7	51.0	53.1	54.6	53.2
Maldives	6.9 (2001)	7.5	4.1	3.4 (2014)	13.2 (2001)	14.8	14.9	18.5 (2014)	79.9 (2001)	77.7	81.0	78.1 (2014)
Nepal	39.6	35.2	35.4	31.8	21.5	17.1	15.1	14.9	38.9	47.7	49.5	53.3
Sri Lanka	17.6	11.8	9.5	8.7	29.9	30.2	29.7	30.7	52.5	58.0	60.9	60.6
Southeast Asia												
Brunei Darussalam	1.0	0.9	0.7	1.1	63.7	71.6	67.4	60.2	35.3	27.5	31.9	38.7
Cambodia	37.9	32.4	36.1	28.2	23.0	26.4	23.2	29.4	39.1	41.2	40.8	42.3
Indonesia	15.6	13.1	14.3	14.0	45.9	46.5	43.9	41.3	38.5	40.3	41.8	44.7
Lao PDR	48.5	36.7	30.6	24.8 (2014)	19.1	23.5	29.8	34.7 (2014)	32.4	39.8	39.6	40.5 (2014)
Malaysia	8.3	8.4	10.2	8.6	46.8	46.9	40.9	39.6	44.9	44.7	48.9	51.8
Myanmar	57.2	46.7	36.8	26.7	9.7	17.5	26.5	34.5	33.1	35.8	36.7	38.7
Philippines	14.0	12.7	12.3	10.3	34.5	33.8	32.6	30.8	51.5	53.5	55.1	58.9
Singapore	0.1	0.1	0.0	0.0	34.8	32.4	27.6	26.4	65.1	67.6	72.3	73.6
Thailand	8.5	9.2	10.5	9.1	36.8	38.6	40.0	35.7	54.7	52.2	49.4	55.1
Viet Nam	24.5	19.3	21.0	18.9	36.7	38.1	36.7	37.0	38.7	42.6	42.2	44.2
The Pacific												
Cook Islands	10.3	6.9	4.9	8.1	8.3	9.6	8.5	8.9	81.4	83.5	86.6	83.0
Fiji	16.5	14.1	11.0	11.5 (2014)	21.6	19.2	20.9	18.7 (2014)	61.9	66.8	68.1	69.9 (2014)
Kiribati	20.0	23.5	24.6	23.5 (2014)	12.2	7.5	10.3	14.6 (2014)	67.8	69.0	65.0	62.0 (2014)
Marshall Islands	10.4	9.2	15.6	14.3	11.4	9.2	11.6	10.6	78.2	81.6	72.9	75.1
Micronesia, Fed. States of	25.3	24.2	26.7	27.8	8.7	5.7	7.8	6.5	66.1	70.2	65.5	65.8
Nauru	7.2 (2004)	7.8	4.3	2.6 (2012)	-1.8 (2004)	-6.5	47.8	66.2 (2012)	94.6 (2004)	98.7	47.9	31.2 (2012)
Palau	4.8	4.3	4.5	3.4	17.4	16.6	10.8	8.7	77.8	79.1	84.7	87.9
Papua New Guinea	35.2	34.0	20.3	20.2 (2013)	40.7	44.3	33.6	27.0 (2013)	24.1	21.7	46.0	52.8 (2013)
Samoa	16.7	12.3	9.1	9.3	26.8	30.6	25.9	24.2	56.6	57.2	65.0	66.6
Solomon Islands	38.9 (2004)	32.8	30.4	28.0 (2014)	12.9 (2004)	9.6	13.3	15.0 (2014)	48.2 (2004)	57.6	56.3	57.0 (2014)
Timor-Leste[b]	23.3	7.4	4.5	6.7 (2014)	31.1	76.6	81.8	72.5 (2014)	45.7	16.0	13.7	20.8 (2014)
Tonga	22.2	20.0	18.2	19.4 (2014)	20.7	19.0	20.0	18.2 (2014)	57.1	61.0	61.8	62.4 (2014)
Tuvalu	19.4	21.6	27.6	24.5 (2012)	7.8	8.5	5.7	5.6 (2012)	72.8	69.9	66.7	70.0 (2012)
Vanuatu	25.4	24.1	21.9	26.8 (2014)	12.2	8.5	13.0	8.7 (2014)	62.3	67.4	65.0	64.5 (2014)
Developed Member Economies												
Australia	3.1	2.9	2.2	2.3	24.7	24.6	25.2	23.8	72.2	72.5	72.6	73.9
Japan	1.6	1.2	1.2	1.2 (2014)	31.1	28.1	27.5	26.9 (2014)	67.3	70.6	71.3	72.0 (2014)
New Zealand	7.8	4.5	6.6	5.6	23.6	23.9	21.2	21.1	61.8	64.3	64.4	64.9

... = data not available at cutoff date, 0.0 = magnitude is less than half of the unit employed, GDP = gross domestic product, Lao PDR = Lao People's Democratic Republic.

a   Computed as a share of GDP at current prices.
b   The treatment of oil production from 2000 onward reflects the 2008 System of National Accounts concepts on resident units.

Source: Economy sources.

Table 2.5: **Household and Government Consumption Expenditure** (% of GDP)[a]

Regional Member	Household Consumption				Government Consumption			
	2000	2005	2010	2015	2000	2005	2010	2015
Developing Member Economies								
Central and West Asia								
Afghanistan	111.2 (2002)	115.7	97.4	84.1	7.7 (2002)	10.0	14.0	12.3
Armenia	97.1	75.5	82.0	78.1	11.8	10.6	13.1	13.1
Azerbaijan	63.0	41.6	38.9	55.8	15.1	10.5	10.9	12.5
Georgia	71.1 (2003)	64.6	72.3	69.2	9.8 (2003)	17.3	21.1	16.5
Kazakhstan	61.9	49.9	45.4	52.2	12.1	11.2	10.8	11.6
Kyrgyz Republic	65.7	84.5	84.6	88.2	20.0	17.5	18.1	17.5
Pakistan	75.4	76.9	79.7	79.2	8.6	7.8	10.3	11.8
Tajikistan	94.6	81.1	84.7	98.8 (2014)	4.8	14.6	11.3	13.9 (2014)
Turkmenistan	37.1	46.6	5.1	15.1 (2012)	14.5	13.2	9.5	8.9 (2012)
Uzbekistan	61.9	46.7	49.0	55.2	18.7	17.6	15.8	15.9
East Asia								
China, People's Rep. of	47.1	40.5	35.7	39.1	16.8	14.2	13.1	14.1
Hong Kong, China	58.6	57.5	61.4	66.3	9.4	9.2	8.9	9.7
Korea, Rep. of	52.5	50.7	48.6	47.1	11.3	13.3	14.5	15.2
Mongolia	75.1	55.2	55.2	58.8	15.3	12.1	12.7	11.9
Taipei,China	55.1	56.1	53.1	52.3	15.7	15.3	14.9	13.9
South Asia								
Bangladesh	77.5	74.4	74.1	72.4	4.6	5.5	5.1	5.4
Bhutan	47.7	40.4	43.8	46.4 (2014)	21.9	21.9	20.0	16.9 (2014)
India	64.6	58.3	56.0	59.5	12.6	10.9	11.4	10.6
Maldives	...	...	...	...	...	...	...	...
Nepal	75.9	79.5	78.6	80.2	8.9	8.9	10.0	11.0
Sri Lanka	70.9	69.0	68.5	68.6	13.7	13.1	8.5	8.8
Southeast Asia								
Brunei Darussalam	24.8	22.5	14.7	19.8	25.8	18.4	22.2	25.1
Cambodia	86.7	84.3	81.3	77.1 (2014)	5.2	5.8	6.3	5.5 (2014)
Indonesia	61.7	64.4	56.2	55.9	6.5	8.1	9.0	9.8
Lao PDR	...	...	...	...	...	...	...	...
Malaysia	43.8	44.2	48.1	54.1	10.2	11.5	12.6	13.1
Myanmar[b]	87.7	86.9	67.3	68.2	...	...	...	...
Philippines	72.2	75.0	71.6	73.8	11.4	9.0	9.7	11.0
Singapore	41.5	39.1	35.5	36.7	10.7	10.2	10.2	10.4
Thailand	54.1	55.8	52.1	51.6	13.6	13.7	15.8	17.2
Viet Nam	66.5	65.5	66.6	68.0	6.4	5.5	6.0	6.3
The Pacific								
Cook Islands	...	...	...	...	...	...	...	...
Fiji	57.2	77.0	72.3	63.1 (2014)	17.3	15.9	15.0	20.3 (2014)
Kiribati	...	...	...	...	...	...	...	...
Marshall Islands	80.4 (2004)	79.8	83.0	80.7 (2013)	58.2 (2004)	58.1	53.8	50.9 (2013)
Micronesia, Fed. States of	...	...	...	...	...	...	...	...
Nauru	...	...	...	...	...	...	...	...
Palau	...	...	...	...	...	...	...	...
Papua New Guinea	44.6	48.0	...	...	16.6	16.1	...	...
Samoa	...	...	...	...	...	...	...	...
Solomon Islands	63.4 (2003)	63.2	60.2	58.0 (2014)	21.9 (2003)	45.7	40.8	33.2 (2014)
Timor-Leste[c]	69.9	22.1	14.3	25.3 (2014)	109.6	13.3	21.4	22.7 (2014)
Tonga	91.9	100.9	98.1	101.9 (2014)	18.2	15.5	18.1	19.4 (2014)
Tuvalu	...	...	...	...	...	...	...	...
Vanuatu	62.4	65.8	60.6	61.6 (2014)	16.4	13.2	17.5	13.2 (2014)
Developed Member Economies								
Australia	58.1	57.9	55.4	56.9	17.7	17.4	18.0	18.0
Japan	56.5	57.8	59.2	58.6	16.9	18.4	19.7	20.4
New Zealand	58.0	58.2	58.1	57.4	17.0	17.9	19.5	18.7

... = data not available at cutoff date, GDP = gross domestic product, Lao PDR = Lao People's Democratic Republic.

a Computed as a share of GDP at current prices.
b Data for household consumption include government consumption.
c The treatment of oil production from 2000 onward reflects the 2008 System of National Accounts concepts on resident units.

Source: Economy sources.

Table 2.6:   **Gross Capital Formation and Changes in Inventories**
(% of GDP)[a]

Regional Member	Change in Inventories				Gross Capital Formation			
	2000	2005	2010	2015	2000	2005	2010	2015
Developing Member Economies								
Central and West Asia								
Afghanistan	...	-12.4 (2008)	5.3	26.5	11.3 (2002)	21.8	17.5	19.4
Armenia	0.2	0.7	-0.6	0.0	18.6	30.5	32.9	21.0
Azerbaijan	-2.5	0.2	-0.1	0.1	20.7	41.5	18.1	28.7
Georgia	4.7 (2003)	5.4	2.3	3.6	31.3 (2003)	33.5	21.6	32.1
Kazakhstan	0.8	3.0	1.0	5.0	18.1	31.0	25.4	26.4
Kyrgyz Republic[b]	1.7	0.2	-0.7	-3.9	18.3	16.2	28.1	34.2
Pakistan	1.4	1.6	1.6	1.6	17.2	19.1	15.8	15.1
Tajikistan	2.0	0.5	-0.6	0.3 (2014)	9.4	11.6	23.8	26.2 (2014)
Turkmenistan[c]	...	...	...	...	35.4	22.9	52.9	47.2 (2012)
Uzbekistan	-4.4	4.5	-0.8	1.9	19.6	26.5	26.6	28.1
East Asia								
China, People's Rep. of	1.0	0.9	2.6	1.6	34.0	40.9	47.0	44.9
Hong Kong, China	1.1	-0.3	2.1	-1.0	27.6	21.1	23.9	21.7
Korea, Rep. of	1.3	1.3	1.5	-0.6	32.9	32.2	32.0	28.5
Mongolia	3.8	9.6	7.6	8.0	29.0	37.5	42.1	26.2
Taipei,China	0.9	0.3	1.3	0.1	27.2	24.5	25.0	20.8
South Asia								
Bangladesh[c]	...	...	...	...	23.0	24.5	26.2	28.9
Bhutan	-1.8	-0.0	0.5	-0.7 (2014)	48.7	52.0	61.7	57.7 (2014)
India	0.7	2.8	3.5	1.7	24.3	34.7	36.5	34.2 (2014)
Maldives	...	...	...	...	...	...	...	...
Nepal	5.0	6.5	16.1	11.0	24.3	26.5	38.3	38.8
Sri Lanka	0.6	2.8	5.9	3.5	25.4	26.1	30.4	30.1
Southeast Asia								
Brunei Darussalam	0.1	0.0	0.2	0.2	13.1	11.4	23.7	35.2
Cambodia	-1.4	-0.4	1.2	1.1 (2014)	16.9	18.5	17.4	22.0 (2014)
Indonesia	2.4	1.4	1.9	1.4	22.2	25.1	32.9	34.6
Lao PDR	...	...	...	...	...	...	...	...
Malaysia	1.6	0.1	1.0	-1.1	26.9	22.4	23.4	25.1
Myanmar	0.7	0.5	0.3	0.2	12.4	13.2	23.2	34.9
Philippines	-3.7	1.6	0.0	-0.9	18.4	21.6	20.5	20.6
Singapore	2.9	-1.7	1.7	0.8	34.9	21.4	27.9	26.3
Thailand	0.7	2.7	1.4	-0.8	22.3	30.4	25.4	24.1
Viet Nam	2.0	2.5	3.0	3.0	29.6	33.8	35.7	27.7
The Pacific								
Cook Islands	...	...	...	...	...	...	...	...
Fiji	1.9	1.4	2.9	...	17.3	21.0	18.7	18.4 (2014)
Kiribati	...	...	...	...	...	...	...	...
Marshall Islands	0.1 (2004)	0.2	0.1	0.3 (2013)	12.1 (2004)	12.5	36.2	16.3 (2013)
Micronesia, Fed. States of	...	...	...	...	...	...	...	...
Nauru	...	...	...	...	...	...	...	...
Palau	...	...	...	...	...	...	...	...
Papua New Guinea	1.5	1.0	...	...	21.9	17.5	...	...
Samoa	...	...	...	...	...	...	...	...
Solomon Islands	...	...	...	...	...	...	...	...
Timor-Leste[d]	-3.7	–	0.1	0.2 (2014)	31.3	5.0	11.3	15.2 (2014)
Tonga	0.5	0.3	0.5	0.3 (2014)	20.7	22.3	30.1	22.8 (2014)
Tuvalu	...	...	...	...	...	...	...	...
Vanuatu	0.5	0.7	0.8	0.7 (2014)	22.9	24.1	34.7	26.4 (2014)
Developed Member Economies								
Australia	0.3	0.4	-0.2	0.1	26.3	27.5	27.6	26.6
Japan	-0.1	0.1	-0.2	0.3	25.1	22.5	19.8	22.0
New Zealand	1.2	0.7	0.4	0.1	22.0	25.4	20.1	23.3

... = data not available at cutoff date, 0.0 or –0.0= magnitude is less than half of unit employed, – = magnitude equals zero, GDP = gross domestic product, Lao PDR = Lao People's Democratic Republic.

a   Computed as a share of GDP at current prices.
b   Changes in inventories is not included in gross capital formation.
c   Changes in inventories is included in gross capital formation.
d   The treatment of oil production from 2000 onward reflects the 2008 System of National Accounts concepts on resident units.

Source: Economy sources.

Table 2.7:   **Exports and Imports of Goods and Services**
(% of GDP)[a]

Regional Member	Exports of Goods and Services				Imports of Goods and Services			
	2000	**2005**	**2010**	**2015**	**2000**	**2005**	**2010**	**2015**
Developing Member Economies								
Central and West Asia								
Afghanistan	29.7 (2002)	26.0	9.8	7.0	59.8 (2002)	73.6	43.9	49.3
Armenia	23.4	28.8	20.8	29.8	50.5	43.2	45.3	42.0
Azerbaijan	40.2	62.9	54.3	37.8	38.4	52.9	20.7	34.8
Georgia	31.8 (2003)	33.7	35.0	45.0	46.4 (2003)	51.6	52.8	64.9
Kazakhstan	56.6	53.2	44.2	28.5	49.1	44.6	29.9	24.7
Kyrgyz Republic	41.8	38.3	51.6	36.2	47.6	56.8	81.7	72.2
Pakistan	13.4	15.7	13.5	10.9	14.7	19.6	19.4	17.1
Tajikistan	92.4	54.3	26.8	11.3 (2014)	100.2	72.8	59.0	58.5 (2014)
Turkmenistan	97.2	65.0	77.8	73.3 (2012)	82.4	47.8	45.3	44.4 (2012)
Uzbekistan	26.5	37.9	33.1	21.5 (2014)	26.7	28.7	24.5	22.1 (2014)
East Asia								
China, People's Rep. of	20.4 (1999)	...	26.5	22.4	17.6 (1999)	...	22.9	18.8
Hong Kong, China	141.8	194.7	219.4	201.6	137.4	182.4	213.5	199.3
Korea, Rep. of	35.0	36.8	49.4	45.9	32.9	34.4	46.2	38.9
Mongolia	54.0	58.8	46.7	44.9	67.9	63.6	56.7	42.0
Taipei,China	51.9	60.6	70.9	64.6	49.9	56.4	63.9	51.6
South Asia								
Bangladesh	14.0	16.6	16.0	17.3	19.2	23.0	21.8	24.8
Bhutan	29.4	38.2	42.5	36.3 (2014)	48.3	64.4	70.7	57.3 (2014)
India	12.8	19.3	22.0	19.9	13.7	22.0	26.3	22.5
Maldives	89.5	...	...	...	71.6	...	...	...
Nepal	23.3	14.6	9.6	11.7	32.4	29.5	36.4	41.7
Sri Lanka	38.2	32.3	19.6	20.5	48.4	41.3	26.8	28.0
Southeast Asia								
Brunei Darussalam	67.4	70.2	67.4	52.2	35.8	27.3	28.0	32.7
Cambodia	49.9	64.1	54.1	62.3 (2014)	61.7	72.7	59.5	66.6 (2014)
Indonesia	41.0	34.1	24.3	21.1	30.5	29.9	22.4	20.8
Lao PDR	...	...	...	...	...	...	...	...
Malaysia	119.8	112.9	86.9	70.9	100.6	91.0	71.0	63.3
Myanmar	0.5	0.2	19.6	17.4	0.6	0.1	15.1	27.9
Philippines	51.4	46.1	34.8	28.2	53.4	51.7	36.6	33.5
Singapore	189.2	226.1	199.3	176.5	176.9	196.3	172.8	149.6
Thailand	64.8	68.4	66.1	69.1	56.5	69.5	60.6	57.7
Viet Nam	55.0	63.7	72.0	89.8	57.5	67.0	80.2	89.0
The Pacific								
Cook Islands	...	...	...	...	...	...	...	...
Fiji	65.4	51.0	57.8	54.8 (2014)	70.5	63.9	63.9	62.8 (2014)
Kiribati	...	...	...	...	...	...	...	...
Marshall Islands	30.3 (2004)	32.2	38.9	52.6 (2013)	87.3 (2004)	93.7	112.5	102.8 (2013)
Micronesia, Fed. States of	...	...	...	...	...	...	...	...
Nauru	...	...	...	...	...	...	...	...
Palau	...	...	...	...	...	...	...	...
Papua New Guinea	66.2	74.5	...	...	49.2	56.1	...	...
Samoa	...	...	...	...	...	...	...	...
Solomon Islands	27.6 (2003)	33.3	47.6	54.4 (2014)	33.1 (2003)	52.7	79.0	66.2 (2014)
Timor-Leste[b]	28.4	81.5	93.9	92.7 (2014)	141.5	22.7	41.4	57.4 (2014)
Tonga	15.4	17.7	13.2	18.5 (2014)	46.8	57.8	57.9	56.5 (2014)
Tuvalu	...	...	...	...	...	...	...	...
Vanuatu	34.7	45.4	46.6	48.7 (2014)	43.7	54.8	52.7	51.1 (2014)
Developed Member Economies								
Australia	19.4	18.1	19.4	19.8	21.5	20.8	20.4	21.2
Japan	10.9	14.3	15.2	17.9	9.4	12.9	14.0	18.9
New Zealand	35.7	28.3	30.3	28.1	32.8	29.7	28.0	27.5

... = data not available at cutoff date, GDP = gross domestic product, Lao PDR = Lao People's Democratic Republic.

a Computed as a share of GDP at current prices.
b The treatment of oil production from 2000 onward reflects the 2008 System of National Accounts concepts on resident units.

Source: Economy sources.

Table 2.8:   **Gross Domestic Saving**
(% of GDP)[a]

Regional Member	2000	2005	2010	2011	2012	2013	2014	2015
Developing Member Economies								
Central and West Asia								
Afghanistan[b]	−18.8 (2002)	−25.8	−11.4	−3.7	3.8	7.8	7.1	3.6
Armenia	−8.9	14.0	4.9	3.4	1.9	0.9	2.4	8.8
Azerbaijan	20.4	47.5	49.8	52.6	50.0	47.8	43.7	31.7
Georgia	16.7 (2003)	15.7	3.8	7.6	9.3	11.8	12.3	12.3
Kazakhstan	26.0	38.9	43.8	49.9	45.8	42.0	40.6	36.2
Kyrgyz Republic	14.3	−2.1	−2.7	−1.6	−15.9	−15.6	−13.5	...
Pakistan	16.0	15.2	10.0	9.1	7.1	8.2	8.5	9.0
Tajikistan	0.6	4.3	4.0	−10.8	−13.5	−13.9	−12.7	...
Turkmenistan	48.4	40.2	85.4	83.1	76.1	...	...	...
Uzbekistan	19.4	32.7	35.2	34.3	32.6	31.0	30.1	28.1
East Asia								
China, People's Rep. of	36.4	46.4	50.6	49.4	49.2	49.1	49.0	48.4
Hong Kong, China	32.0	33.3	29.8	28.0	26.4	24.6	24.0	24.0
Korea, Rep. of	34.9	34.5	35.2	34.5	33.8	34.1	34.5	35.3
Mongolia	9.6	32.7	32.1	36.3	33.5	30.7	30.4	29.4
Taipei,China	29.4	29.1	31.7	30.4	28.8	30.7	31.5	33.2
South Asia								
Bangladesh	17.9	20.0	20.8	20.6	21.2	22.0	22.1	22.2
Bhutan	29.7	25.9	33.4	38.4	43.6	24.1	36.7	...
India[c]	23.7	33.4	33.7	34.3	...	...	...	...
Maldives	...	...	...	...	...	...	...	...
Nepal	15.2	11.6	11.5	14.0	11.0	10.6	11.9	8.8
Sri Lanka	15.4	17.9	16.8	14.0	14.7	18.1	19.8	...
Southeast Asia								
Brunei Darussalam	49.4	59.1	39.4	42.5	34.9	25.0	35.6	19.9
Cambodia	8.1	9.9	12.4	11.1	12.3	17.2	17.3	...
Indonesia	31.8	27.5	34.8	35.5	34.4	33.7	33.4	33.2
Lao PDR	...	...	...	...	...	...	...	...
Malaysia	46.1	44.3	39.3	38.8	36.5	34.5	34.3	32.7
Myanmar	12.3	13.1	32.7	37.0	36.6	33.8	32.6	31.8
Philippines	16.4	15.9	18.7	16.8	14.9	15.8	17.0	15.2
Singapore	47.2	51.2	54.3	54.2	53.4	53.4	53.4	53.2
Thailand	30.7	29.4	30.9	28.5	28.9	30.1	30.7	35.4
Viet Nam	27.1	29.0	27.4	27.7	29.6	28.4	27.9	25.7
The Pacific								
Cook Islands	...	...	...	...	...	...	...	...
Fiji	25.6	7.1	12.7	15.1	14.2	15.5	16.6	...
Kiribati	...	...	...	...	...	...	...	...
Marshall Islands	−39.9 (2004)	−39.3	−38.0	−37.3	−32.5	−32.8	...	...
Micronesia, Fed. States of	...	...	...	...	...	...	...	...
Nauru	...	...	...	...	...	...	...	...
Palau	...	...	...	...	...	...	...	...
Papua New Guinea	38.8	35.9	...	...	...	...	...	...
Samoa	...	...	...	...	...	...	...	...
Solomon Islands	...	...	...	...	...	...	...	...
Timor-Leste[d]	31.8	18.3	52.6	56.8	40.0	39.7	−7.8	...
Tonga	−10.0	−16.3	−16.1	−9.6	−12.8	−19.8	−21.3	...
Tuvalu	...	...	...	...	...	...	...	...
Vanuatu	21.2	13.9	27.0	21.5	20.9	23.3	24.0	...
Developed Member Economies								
Australia	24.3	24.7	26.6	28.2	28.2	27.2	26.7	25.2
Japan	26.3	23.6	20.7	19.4	19.0	18.4	18.8	...
New Zealand	19.7	17.6	17.3	17.3	17.4	19.8	20.2	...

... = data not available at cutoff date, GDP = gross domestic product, Lao PDR = Lao People's Democratic Republic.

a   Computed as a share of GDP at current prices.
b   Data for 2000 are estimates for 2002.
c   Refers to gross savings.
d   The treatment of oil production from 2000 onward reflects the 2008 System of National Accounts concepts on resident units.

Source: Economy sources.

Table 2.9: **Growth Rates of Real Gross Domestic Product**
(%)

Regional Member	2000	2005	2010	2011	2012	2013	2014	2015
Developing Member Economies								
Central and West Asia								
Afghanistan	8.2 (2003)	9.9	3.2	8.7	10.9	6.4	2.2	−2.4
Armenia	5.9	13.9	2.2	4.7	7.2	3.3	3.6	3.0
Azerbaijan	11.1	26.4	5.0	0.1	2.2	5.8	2.8	1.1
Georgia	2.9 (1999)	9.6	6.2	7.2	6.4	3.4	4.6	2.8
Kazakhstan	9.8	9.7	7.3	13.0	4.6	5.8	4.1	1.2
Kyrgyz Republic	5.4	−0.2	−0.5	6.0	−0.1	10.9	4.0	3.5
Pakistan	2.0 (2001)	9.0	2.6	3.6	3.8	3.7	4.0	4.2
Tajikistan	8.3	6.7	6.5	2.4	7.5	7.4	6.7	5.9
Turkmenistan	5.5	13.0	9.2	14.7	11.1	10.2	10.3	6.5
Uzbekistan	3.8	7.0	8.5	8.3	8.2	8.0	8.0	8.0
East Asia								
China, People's Rep. of	8.4	11.3	10.6	9.5	7.7	7.7	7.3	...
Hong Kong, China	7.7	7.4	6.8	4.8	1.7	3.1	2.7	2.4
Korea, Rep. of	8.9	3.9	6.5	3.7	2.3	2.9	3.3	2.6
Mongolia	1.1	7.3	−1.3 (2009)	17.3	12.3	11.6	7.9	2.3
Taipei,China	6.4	5.4	10.6	3.8	2.1	2.2	3.9	0.7
South Asia								
Bangladesh	6.0	6.0	5.6	6.5	6.5	6.0	6.1	6.6
Bhutan	6.9	7.1	11.7	7.9	5.1	2.1	5.5	...
India	3.8	9.3	10.3	6.7	5.6	6.6	7.2	7.6
Maldives	4.0	−8.1	7.2	8.7	2.5	4.7	6.5	1.5
Nepal	6.0	3.5	4.8	3.4	4.8	4.1	6.0	2.7
Sri Lanka	6.0	6.2	3.5 (2009)	8.4	9.1	3.4	4.9	4.8
Southeast Asia								
Brunei Darussalam	2.8	0.4	−1.8 (2009)	3.7	0.9	−2.1	−2.3	−0.6
Cambodia	8.4	13.3	6.0	7.1	7.3	7.4	7.1	6.9
Indonesia	4.9	5.7	6.2	6.2	6.0	5.6	5.0	4.8
Lao PDR	6.3	6.8	8.1	8.0	7.9	7.9	7.6	4.9
Malaysia	8.9	5.3	7.4	5.3	5.5	4.7	6.0	5.0
Myanmar	13.7	13.6	9.6	5.6	7.3	8.4	8.0	7.3
Philippines	4.4	4.8	7.6	3.7	6.7	7.1	6.2	5.9
Singapore	8.9	7.5	15.2	6.2	3.7	4.7	3.3	2.0
Thailand	4.5	4.2	7.5	0.8	7.2	2.7	0.8	2.8
Viet Nam	6.8	7.5	6.4	6.2	5.2	5.4	6.0	6.7
The Pacific								
Cook Islands	13.9	−1.1	−3.0	1.0	4.7	−1.4	6.3	4.8
Fiji	−1.7	−1.3	3.0	2.7	1.4	4.7	5.3	...
Kiribati	5.3	−0.2	−1.6	0.5	5.2	5.8	2.4	...
Marshall Islands	5.9	2.9	6.4	1.7	3.7	2.4	−0.9	0.6
Micronesia, Fed. States of	4.8	2.1	3.3	1.0	−1.7	−3.0	−2.4	3.7
Nauru	...	−9.8	20.1	14.2	20.2	15.4	17.5	−10.0
Palau	4.2	1.5	3.3	5.0	3.2	−2.4	4.3	9.4
Papua New Guinea	−2.5	3.9	11.2	3.4	4.0	3.6	...	...
Samoa	8.6	4.7	4.4	3.5	−2.3	0.5	1.9	2.8
Solomon Islands	−14.2	9.2	9.7	7.4	2.3	2.8	2.0	2.9
Timor-Leste[a]	2.3	52.7	−1.3	10.6	1.9	−12.8	−27.8	...
Tonga	−0.8	1.6	3.3	2.9	0.8	−3.1	2.0	3.4
Tuvalu	1.7	−3.9	−2.7	8.5	0.2	1.3	2.2	3.6
Vanuatu	5.9	5.3	1.6	1.2	1.8	2.0	2.3	...
Developed Member Economies								
Australia	3.9	3.2	2.0	2.4	3.6	2.4	2.5	2.3
Japan	2.3	1.3	4.7	−0.5	1.7	1.4	−0.0	0.5
New Zealand	2.8	3.4	1.4	2.5	2.3	2.7	3.6	2.4

... = data not available at cutoff date, 0.0 or −0.0 = magnitude is less than half of unit employed, Lao PDR = Lao People's Democratic Republic.

a   The treatment of oil production from 2000 onward reflects the 2008 System of National Accounts concepts on resident units.

Source: Economy sources.

National Accounts

Table 2.10:   **Growth Rates of Real Gross Domestic Product per Capita**
              (%)

Regional Member	2000	2005	2010	2011	2012	2013	2014	2015
Developing Member Economies								
Central and West Asia								
Afghanistan	6.3 (2003)	8.2	1.3	6.6	8.9	4.5	0.0	−4.1
Armenia	6.2	14.5	2.9	5.2	7.3	3.3	3.9	3.3
Azerbaijan	9.9	24.9	3.8	−1.2	0.9	4.5	1.4	−0.1
Georgia	3.7 (1999)	9.4	5.0	6.4	5.7	3.7	...	3.2
Kazakhstan	10.2	8.7	5.7	11.4	3.2	4.3	2.6	−0.2
Kyrgyz Republic	4.0	−1.4	−0.8	4.8	−1.4	8.7	2.0	1.4
Pakistan	0.1 (2001)	6.9	0.5	1.5	1.8	1.7	2.0	2.3
Tajikistan	6.1	4.5	4.2	−0.0	5.0	5.2	4.3	3.5
Turkmenistan	4.3	11.8	7.8	13.2	9.7	8.8	8.9	5.2
Uzbekistan	2.4	5.8	5.4	5.4	6.6	6.3	6.2	6.1
East Asia								
China, People's Rep. of	7.6	10.7	10.1	9.0	7.2	7.2	6.7	...
Hong Kong, China	6.7	6.9	6.0	4.1	0.5	2.6	1.9	1.5
Korea, Rep. of	8.0	3.7	6.0	2.9	1.8	2.5	2.9	2.2
Mongolia	−0.2	6.1	−3.0 (2009)	15.3	10.2	9.4	5.6	0.1
Taipei,China	5.6	5.0	10.3	3.6	1.7	1.9	3.7	0.4
South Asia								
Bangladesh	4.5	4.4	4.2	5.7	5.2	4.6	4.6	5.1
Bhutan	5.6	5.7	9.7	6.0	3.3	0.4	3.7	...
India	2.0	7.7	8.8	5.3	4.3	5.3	5.9	6.3
Maldives	2.4	−11.0	4.8	5.3	−0.8	1.2	2.8	−2.1
Nepal	2.9	1.2	3.4	2.0	3.3	2.7	4.5	1.4
Sri Lanka	4.6	5.3	2.4 (2009)	7.3	11.5	2.6	3.9	3.8
Southeast Asia								
Brunei Darussalam	0.3	−1.3	−3.1 (2009)	2.0	−0.7	−3.7	−3.7	−1.8
Cambodia	7.0	11.7	4.6	5.7	6.0	6.1	5.7	5.5
Indonesia	3.7	4.3	3.4	4.6	4.5	4.1	3.6	3.4
Lao PDR	4.2	4.7	6.6	6.5	6.4	6.4	6.0	3.4
Malaysia	6.2	3.2	5.5	3.6	3.9	2.3	4.6	3.6
Myanmar	12.4	12.7	8.9	4.8	6.4	7.5	7.0	5.3
Philippines	2.0	2.8	5.8	1.9	4.9	5.3	4.4	4.1
Singapore	7.0	5.0	13.2	4.0	1.1	3.0	1.9	0.8
Thailand	3.3	3.6	6.9	0.4	6.8	2.3	0.4	2.4
Viet Nam	5.3	6.3	5.3	5.1	4.1	4.3	4.9	5.5
The Pacific								
Cook Islands	4.4	−6.7	−7.5	24.0	3.6	3.4	6.3	3.7
Fiji	−2.3	−2.0	2.3	2.3	1.0	4.2	4.9	...
Kiribati	3.5	−2.0	−3.6	−0.8	3.9	4.5	1.1	...
Marshall Islands	5.1	1.5	5.1	1.2	3.3	2.0	−1.3	0.3
Micronesia, Fed. States of	4.6	2.3	3.8	1.4	−1.4	−2.9	−2.4	3.5
Nauru	...	−7.8	17.9	10.1	19.3	11.7	15.4	−11.7
Palau	2.7 (2001)	0.7	5.2	7.0	5.2	−1.2	4.3	8.1
Papua New Guinea	−5.5	0.8	7.8	0.3	0.9	0.5	...	...
Samoa	7.6	4.4	3.6	2.7	−3.0	−0.2	1.1	2.0
Solomon Islands	−16.2	6.8	7.2	4.9	−0.0	0.5	−0.3	0.6
Timor-Leste[a]	1.0 (2001)	50.0	−3.9	7.7	−0.8	−15.1	−29.7	...
Tonga	−1.2	1.1	3.1	2.6	0.6	−3.3	1.8	3.1
Tuvalu	1.3 (2001)	−6.7	−3.2	14.3	−1.4	1.1	2.1	3.4
Vanuatu	3.1	2.6	−1.0	−1.4	−0.8	−0.5	−0.1	...
Developed Member Economies								
Australia	2.7	2.0	0.4	1.0	1.9	0.7	1.0	0.9
Japan	2.1	1.3	4.7	−0.3	1.9	1.5	0.1	0.7
New Zealand	2.2	2.3	0.3	1.7	1.8	2.0	2.1	0.5

... = data not available at cutoff date, 0.0 or −0.0 = magnitude is less than half of unit employed, Lao PDR = Lao People's Democratic Republic.

a   The treatment of oil production from 2000 onward reflects the 2008 System of National Accounts concepts on resident units.

Source: ADB estimates using economy sources.

Table 2.11:   **Growth Rates of Agriculture Real Value Added**
(%)

Regional Member	2000	2005	2010	2011	2012	2013	2014	2015
Developing Member Economies								
Central and West Asia								
Afghanistan	3.4 (2003)	12.2	-18.0	4.7	3.3	8.3	3.7	-16.9
Armenia	-1.0	11.2	-16.0	14.0	9.5	7.6	6.1	13.2
Azerbaijan	12.1	6.7	-4.7	5.8	6.6	4.9	-2.6	6.6
Georgia	-7.7 (2004)	11.7	-4.2	8.5	-3.8	11.3	1.6	2.9
Kazakhstan	-3.2	7.1	-12.9	22.5	-17.4	11.2	1.3	4.1
Kyrgyz Republic	2.6	-4.2	-2.6	1.8	1.2	2.7	-0.5	6.2
Pakistan	-2.2 (2001)	6.5	0.2	2.0	3.6	2.7	2.7	2.9
Tajikistan	8.0 (2001)	2.8	6.8	0.4	9.5	7.7	9.2	3.2
Turkmenistan	-2.6	14.1	29.8	...	8.1	9.9	1.7	...
Uzbekistan	3.2	5.9	6.6	6.8	7.1	6.8	6.9	...
East Asia								
China, People's Rep. of	2.3	5.1	4.3	4.2	4.5	4.0	4.2	...
Hong Kong, China	0.3 (2001)	-0.2	3.9	0.8	-3.3	4.9	-6.0	-2.2
Korea, Rep. of	1.1	1.4	-4.3	-2.0	-0.9	3.1	3.6	-1.5
Mongolia	-16.3	11.3	3.6 (2009)	-0.3	21.1	19.2	13.7	10.7
Taipei,China	1.8	-3.9	2.3	4.5	-3.2	1.4	0.5	-3.9
South Asia								
Bangladesh	7.4	2.2	6.2	4.5	3.0	2.5	4.4	3.3
Bhutan	5.4	1.1	0.9	2.4	2.3	2.4	2.4	...
India	0.0	5.1	8.6	5.0	1.5	4.2	-0.2	1.2
Maldives	0.2	5.9	-0.9	1.1	0.0	5.1	0.2	-3.0
Nepal	4.9	3.5	2.0	4.5	4.6	1.1	4.5	0.8
Sri Lanka	2.3	1.8	3.2 (2009)	4.6	3.9	3.2	4.9	5.5
Southeast Asia								
Brunei Darussalam	6.6	1.3	5.7 (2009)	-2.6	8.1	-1.2	4.8	6.4
Cambodia	-1.2	15.7	4.0	3.1	4.3	1.6	0.3	0.2
Indonesia	1.9	2.7	3.0	3.9	4.6	4.2	4.2	4.0
Lao PDR	4.2	0.7	3.2	2.7	3.3	3.5	3.6	...
Malaysia	6.1	2.6	2.4	6.8	1.0	2.0	2.1	1.2
Myanmar	11.0	12.1	4.7	-0.7	1.7	3.6	2.8	3.4
Philippines	3.4	2.2	-0.2	2.6	2.8	1.2	1.7	0.1
Singapore	-4.8	7.1	2.4	2.1	3.6	14.5	1.9	-3.6
Thailand	6.8	-0.1	-0.5	6.3	2.7	0.8	0.7	-3.8
Viet Nam	4.6	4.2	0.5	4.2	2.9	2.6	3.4	2.4
The Pacific								
Cook Islands	0.1	-3.5	1.9	-6.7	14.9	3.9	8.7	-2.8
Fiji	-1.2	0.9	-2.6	8.2	-1.9	6.7	-0.3	...
Kiribati	-7.2	-7.4	-3.9	9.3	2.9	-0.2	3.7	...
Marshall Islands	22.6	-9.1	27.7	5.8	10.5	0.7	-1.1	-0.2
Micronesia, Fed. States of	7.1	4.4	1.2	1.3	-0.2	-3.0	5.0	6.2
Nauru	...	...	...	...	...	...	...	...
Palau	-2.1	7.0	-4.3	9.0	1.4	-9.5	-4.5	-4.7
Papua New Guinea	2.1	5.6	2.9	0.9	6.1	4.7	...	...
Samoa	8.1	2.4	-6.1	10.1	-12.6	8.9	1.1	5.6
Solomon Islands	-17.1	-1.8	14.8	2.3	-0.5	-0.8	7.1	...
Timor-Leste[a]	-0.1 (2001)	4.1	-2.9	-17.1	26.7	0.1	-2.6	...
Tonga	-2.5	-2.1	0.5	2.0	0.5	3.7	3.1	...
Tuvalu	-1.7 (2001)	0.9	14.4	0.4	-6.3	...	...	...
Vanuatu	4.3	2.3	4.8	6.1	2.2	4.8	4.2	...
Developed Member Economies								
Australia	6.5	4.2	-0.8	3.6	1.4	-0.6	0.7	1.8
Japan	2.0	1.0	-1.0	2.0	0.6	2.0	-2.3	...
New Zealand	3.6	5.2	-7.9	12.3	5.6	2.0	8.3	2.0

... = data not available at cutoff date, 0.0 = magnitude is less than half of unit employed, Lao PDR = Lao People's Democratic Republic.

a   The treatment of oil production from 2000 onward reflects the 2008 System of National Accounts concepts on resident units.

Source: Economy sources.

National Accounts

Table 2.12: **Growth Rates of Industry Real Value Added**
(%)

Regional Member	2000	2005	2010	2011	2012	2013	2014	2015
Developing Member Economies								
Central and West Asia								
Afghanistan	10.3 (2003)	13.0	6.3	9.8	7.8	4.5	2.4	4.5
Armenia	12.8	14.8	5.7	0.0	5.7	0.5	−2.3	3.7
Azerbaijan	5.7	43.6	4.5	−4.4	−1.1	4.4	0.4	−1.9
Georgia	−0.9 (1999)	9.6	8.2	9.2	9.6	2.4	4.6	3.3
Kazakhstan	15.3	10.7	9.5	2.9	1.8	3.1	1.5	−0.4
Kyrgyz Republic	8.8	−9.8	2.5	7.3	−11.4	30.2	5.7	1.4
Pakistan	4.1 (2001)	12.1	3.4	4.5	2.5	0.6	4.5	3.6
Tajikistan	15.6 (2001)	7.7	5.6	−15.1	−2.6	4.0	14.9	14.7
Turkmenistan	1.0	10.6	−1.0	...	10.7	8.0	11.6	...
Uzbekistan	1.8	5.3	4.4	4.5	6.5	8.8	6.6	...
East Asia								
China, People's Rep. of	9.4	12.1	12.7	10.7	8.2	7.9	7.2	...
Hong Kong, China	−3.2 (2001)	−3.0	8.0	9.5	4.7	1.6	7.6	1.0
Korea, Rep. of	11.0	4.7	10.4	4.5	1.9	3.3	3.1	1.7
Mongolia	1.5	4.2	−0.4 (2009)	8.8	14.8	14.6	12.7	8.8
Taipei,China	7.1	7.6	20.8	6.0	3.3	1.7	7.0	−0.9
South Asia								
Bangladesh	6.2	8.3	7.0	9.0	9.4	9.6	8.2	9.7
Bhutan	7.3	3.8	12.5	4.1	6.8	3.9	3.1	...
India	6.0	9.7	7.6	7.8	3.6	5.0	5.9	7.4
Maldives	−3.3	10.3	4.3	12.1	0.8	−7.6	12.9	26.4
Nepal	8.6	3.0	4.0	4.3	3.0	2.7	7.1	1.5
Sri Lanka	9.0	8.0	4.2 (2009)	9.3	9.0	4.1	3.5	3.0
Southeast Asia								
Brunei Darussalam	3.0	−1.8	−5.0 (2009)	3.2	−1.4	−5.6	−4.4	0.0
Cambodia	31.2	12.7	13.0	13.4	10.4	11.5	9.8	11.7
Indonesia	5.9	4.7	4.9	6.3	5.3	4.3	4.3	2.7
Lao PDR	9.3	10.6	17.5	14.6	11.4	9.7	7.3	...
Malaysia	13.6	3.6	8.4	2.5	4.9	3.6	6.0	5.1
Myanmar	21.3	19.9	18.6	10.2	8.0	11.4	12.1	8.7
Philippines	6.5	4.2	11.6	1.9	7.3	9.2	7.8	6.0
Singapore	11.3	8.0	23.9	7.0	2.3	2.5	2.8	−3.4
Thailand	4.0	4.9	10.6	−4.1	7.2	1.5	−0.2	1.2
Viet Nam	10.1	8.4	7.2	6.7	5.7	5.4	7.1	9.6
The Pacific								
Cook Islands	18.2	−6.3	−8.4	11.6	11.0	−6.3	−23.8	34.2
Fiji	−5.5	−6.7	6.5	2.0	−2.2	4.4	2.7	...
Kiribati	−6.4	6.7	2.5	−4.8	30.1	37.3	−1.4	...
Marshall Islands	−14.5	4.6	−4.8	0.8	2.8	7.9	−16.7	−1.6
Micronesia, Fed. States of	6.6	−3.0	17.9	11.8	−1.3	−19.5	−28.5	−7.5
Nauru	...	...	...	...	...	...	...	...
Palau	27.6	9.0	3.2	5.4	−4.4	−16.2	1.8	26.1
Papua New Guinea	−0.8	4.1	13.3	−5.4	−2.6	1.1	...	...
Samoa	14.4	4.7	10.1	2.4	−1.1	0.1	−1.9	0.9
Solomon Islands	−29.7	−3.1	15.4	38.2	−1.4	−2.0	−13.2	...
Timor-Leste[a]	−24.0 (2001)	73.4	−3.7	13.1	0.6	−16.9	−36.2	...
Tonga	−0.4	−2.8	11.6	5.5	1.2	−14.3	1.3	...
Tuvalu	5.5 (2001)	−18.7	−41.5	42.8	−26.1	...	...	...
Vanuatu	46.4	5.3	12.6	−19.4	−22.1	9.8	3.2	...
Developed Member Economies[b]								
Australia	...	...	...	...	...	...	...	...
Japan	...	...	...	...	...	...	...	...
New Zealand	...	...	...	...	...	...	...	...

... = data not available at cutoff date, 0.0 = magnitude is less than half of unit employed, Lao PDR = Lao People's Democratic Republic.

a   The treatment of oil production from 2000 onward reflects the 2008 System of National Accounts concepts on resident units.
b   National accounts are compiled using chain volume measures.

Source: Economy sources.

Table 2.13: **Growth Rates of Services Real Value Added**
(%)

Regional Member	2000	2005	2010	2011	2012	2013	2014	2015
Developing Member Economies								
Central and West Asia								
Afghanistan	10.4(2003)	5.4	18.1	10.3	16.0	6.4	2.2	1.3
Armenia	3.1	14.7	4.7	6.1	6.9	2.8	6.7	0.0
Azerbaijan	9.6	9.3	6.9	6.8	7.5	8.4	7.6	4.4
Georgia	1.4(1999)	6.5	8.2	5.8	5.9	3.6	4.5	2.9
Kazakhstan	8.4	10.4	6.0	4.8	10.4	6.9	5.7	2.4
Kyrgyz Republic	5.8	8.4	−1.3	6.7	6.3	4.8	4.6	3.7
Pakistan	3.1(2001)	8.5	3.2	3.9	4.4	5.1	4.4	5.0
Tajikistan	3.9(2001)	8.5	7.1	11.4	11.9	9.4	1.7	0.1
Turkmenistan	18.0	27.1	18.4	...	−10.9	−9.2	−13.2	...
Uzbekistan	5.4	7.6	11.2	11.7	9.7	7.9	7.6	...
East Asia								
China, People's Rep. of	9.7	12.3	9.7	9.4	8.0	8.2	7.9	...
Hong Kong, China	1.7(2001)	6.9	6.5	5.0	1.8	2.7	2.4	1.9
Korea, Rep. of	7.3	3.9	4.4	3.1	2.8	2.9	3.3	2.8
Mongolia	10.5	9.7	0.8(2009)	17.8	10.3	7.8	7.8	1.1
Taipei,China	6.5	4.1	6.3	3.1	1.3	2.3	2.9	0.5
South Asia								
Bangladesh	5.5	6.4	5.5	6.2	6.6	5.5	5.6	5.8
Bhutan	8.7	14.8	12.1	13.3	0.7	1.6	8.2	...
India	5.1	10.9	9.7	6.6	8.1	7.8	10.3	8.9
Maldives	5.4	−13.8	8.0	5.8	1.5	6.4	5.0	−0.8
Nepal	5.9	3.3	5.8	3.4	5.0	5.7	6.2	3.6
Sri Lanka	6.1	6.4	3.3(2009)	8.9	11.7	4.5	5.2	5.3
Southeast Asia								
Brunei Darussalam	2.5	4.1	2.1(2009)	4.9	5.5	4.7	1.0	−1.6
Cambodia	8.9	13.1	3.3	5.7	7.4	8.7	8.7	7.1
Indonesia	5.2	7.9	8.4	8.4	6.8	6.4	6.0	5.5
Lao PDR	6.9	9.9	7.0	8.1	9.2	9.7	9.4	...
Malaysia	6.0	7.3	7.4	7.2	6.6	6.0	6.7	5.2
Myanmar	13.4	13.1	9.5	8.5	12.0	10.3	9.1	9.1
Philippines	3.3	5.8	7.2	4.9	7.1	7.0	6.2	6.8
Singapore	7.7	7.4	11.2	6.6	4.3	6.3	3.7	3.5
Thailand	4.3	4.4	6.9	3.3	8.2	3.9	1.5	5.0
Viet Nam	5.3	8.6	−7.7	7.5	6.7	6.7	6.2	6.3
The Pacific								
Cook Islands	15.4	−0.3	−2.6	0.1	2.3	−0.6	9.6	2.0
Fiji	0.8	−17.0	2.9	2.0	3.0	4.5	6.9	...
Kiribati	1.7	4.6	−0.1	−1.6	2.0	2.6	0.4	...
Marshall Islands	6.3	3.2	3.5	1.5	1.8	1.4	2.5	2.3
Micronesia, Fed. States of	3.2	0.8	2.3	0.3	−1.7	−0.8	−1.2	2.7
Nauru	...	...	...	...	...	...	...	...
Palau	−2.0	−1.0	3.6	4.1	3.1	−1.2	5.6	8.2
Papua New Guinea	−12.7	3.6	14.0	11.9	4.8	4.4	...	...
Samoa	6.2	5.2	4.0	2.5	−0.9	−0.2	3.3	3.1
Solomon Islands	−5.7	23.8	6.4	2.5	5.3	7.2	3.6	...
Timor-Leste[a]	31.3(2001)	8.5	11.0	8.7	9.7	−0.9	3.9	...
Tonga	0.0	3.6	1.0	1.8	0.5	−0.5	1.6	...
Tuvalu	−0.5(2001)	−4.8	2.3	6.4	8.3	...	...	...
Vanuatu	2.2	6.6	3.0	3.2	4.4	0.1	2.4	...
Developed Member Economies[b]								
Australia	...	...	...	...	...	...	...	...
Japan	...	...	...	...	...	...	...	...
New Zealand	...	...	...	...	...	...	...	...

... = data not available at cutoff date, 0.0 = magnitude is less than half of unit employed, Lao PDR = Lao People's Democratic Republic.

a The treatment of oil production from 2000 onward reflects 2008 System of National Accounts concepts on resident units.
b National accounts are compiled using chain volume measures.

Source: Economy sources.

National Accounts

Table 2.14: **Growth Rates of Real Household Final Consumption**
(%)

Regional Member	2000	2005	2010	2011	2012	2013	2014	2015
Developing Member Economies								
Central and West Asia								
Afghanistan	...	...	...	...	...	...	...	...
Armenia	8.3	8.8	3.8	2.4	9.1	0.9	1.0	-7.9
Azerbaijan	10.0	13.2	10.8	8.4	8.4	8.6	8.1	8.5
Georgia	...	...	...	6.7	4.5	-0.1	3.2	...
Kazakhstan	1.2	10.7	11.5	10.9	10.9	21.3	1.8	1.1
Kyrgyz Republic	-5.0	8.3	2.7	9.3	11.2	8.0	3.0	-6.5
Pakistan	0.5 (2001)	12.9	2.2	4.6	5.0	2.1	5.4	3.6
Tajikistan	0.8 (2001)	20.6	10.5	24.2	15.0	9.3	1.8	...
Turkmenistan	-48.3	-15.2	-60.6	73.8	114.9	-31.7	26.8	...
Uzbekistan	...	...	...	...	...	...	...	...
East Asia								
China, People's Rep. of	...	...	...	...	...	...	...	...
Hong Kong, China	4.5	3.5	6.1	8.4	4.1	4.6	3.3	4.7
Korea, Rep. of	9.1	4.4	4.4	2.7	1.2	1.4	1.7	2.2
Mongolia	...	...	-2.5 (2009)	15.8	13.0	15.4	6.3	7.8
Taipei,China	5.1	3.3	3.8	3.3	1.8	2.4	3.0	2.6
South Asia								
Bangladesh	4.1	3.9	4.6	6.5	4.1	5.1	4.0	...
Bhutan	0.4	1.3	10.5	0.4	7.0	13.1	18.0	...
India	3.4	8.6	8.7	9.3	5.3	6.8	6.2	7.4
Maldives	3.2	...	...	...	...	...	...	...
Nepal	...	4.7	6.2	0.6	15.9	2.7	4.2	2.9
Sri Lanka	4.0	1.7	...	9.9	2.3	7.8	5.7	6.5
Southeast Asia								
Brunei Darussalam	-7.0	-0.6	5.0 (2009)	5.4	8.7	6.0	-3.1	4.5
Cambodia	4.9	12.3	9.7	10.4	6.4	4.0	4.5	...
Indonesia	1.6	4.0	4.7	5.1	5.5	5.4	5.2	5.0
Lao PDR	...	...	...	...	...	...	...	...
Malaysia	13.0	9.1	6.9	6.9	8.4	7.3	7.0	6.0
Myanmar[a]	4.3	14.6	2.6	6.1	8.1	11.9	6.8	5.0
Philippines	5.2	4.4	3.4	5.6	6.6	5.6	5.5	6.3
Singapore	14.7	3.4	5.9	4.3	3.5	3.1	2.2	4.5
Thailand	7.0	4.2	5.0	1.8	6.7	1.0	0.6	2.1
Viet Nam	3.1	5.8	8.2	4.1	4.9	5.2	6.1	9.3
The Pacific								
Cook Islands	...	...	...	...	...	...	...	...
Fiji	...	...	...	...	...	...	...	...
Kiribati	...	...	...	...	...	...	...	...
Marshall Islands	...	1.0	2.6	0.5	-1.5	2.1	...	...
Micronesia, Fed. States of	...	...	...	...	...	...	...	...
Nauru	...	...	...	...	...	...	...	...
Palau	...	...	...	...	...	...	...	...
Papua New Guinea	-28.5	9.8	...	...	...	...	...	...
Samoa	...	...	...	...	...	...	...	...
Solomon Islands	6.5 (2004)	9.3	8.7	3.9	3.8	4.2	4.6	...
Timor-Leste[b]	16.3 (2001)	-2.2	9.3	–	18.8	3.4	9.8	...
Tonga	...	...	...	...	...	...	...	...
Tuvalu	...	...	...	...	...	...	...	...
Vanuatu	...	2.4	2.6	3.0	3.0	3.5	3.9	...
Developed Member Economies								
Australia	4.1	4.5	2.3	3.8	2.6	1.6	2.6	2.7
Japan	0.4	1.5	2.8	0.3	2.3	1.7	-0.9	-1.2
New Zealand	1.3	5.2	2.2	2.9	1.8	2.9	2.6	2.3

... = data not available at cutoff date, – = magnitude equals zero, Lao PDR = Lao People's Democratic Republic.

a   Includes government consumption expenditure.
b   The treatment of oil production from 2000 onward reflects the 2008 System of National Accounts concepts on resident units.

Source: Economy sources.

Table 2.15: **Growth Rates of Real Government Consumption Expenditure**
(%)

Regional Member	2000	2005	2010	2011	2012	2013	2014	2015
Developing Member Economies								
Central and West Asia								
Afghanistan	...	...	...	...	...	...	...	...
Armenia	2.8	19.0	3.9	1.9	-1.4	7.6	-1.2	4.5
Azerbaijan	2.3	3.4	3.4	3.4	3.1	3.6	3.7	1.0
Georgia	...	...	...	1.0	7.3	4.3	11.2	...
Kazakhstan	15.0	10.8	2.7	11.3	13.2	1.7	9.8	3.8
Kyrgyz Republic	5.9	-2.7	-1.1	2.2	2.1	-0.4	-0.5	0.2
Pakistan	7.5	1.7	-0.6	0.0	7.3	10.1	1.5	16.0
Tajikistan	10.8 (2001)	0.4	0.9	7.8	2.1	2.3	7.6	...
Turkmenistan	28.0	17.9	5.8	10.1	8.0	13.9	8.9	...
Uzbekistan	...	...	...	...	...	...	...	...
East Asia								
China, People's Rep. of	...	...	...	...	...	...	...	...
Hong Kong, China	2.4	-2.6	3.4	2.5	3.6	2.7	3.0	3.4
Korea, Rep. of	0.9	4.5	3.8	2.2	3.4	3.3	3.0	3.4
Mongolia	...	8.9 (2006)	-5.5 (2009)	15.3	19.9	15.8	12.2	-7.8
Taipei,China	0.6	0.4	1.1	2.0	2.2	-0.8	3.6	-0.3
South Asia								
Bangladesh	0.9	7.7	6.8	6.7	3.1	5.8	7.9	...
Bhutan	0.0	2.8	7.5	3.6	-0.8	-10.1	2.4	...
India	1.4	8.9	5.8	6.9	0.5	0.4	12.8	2.2
Maldives	...	...	...	...	...	...	...	...
Nepal	...	1.2	1.3	13.1	15.9	-6.9	10.0	7.4
Sri Lanka	5.3	12.0	16.0 (2009)	-2.1	6.0	0.1	6.1	10.3
Southeast Asia								
Brunei Darussalam	7.7	-1.0	5.0 (2009)	5.3	0.4	3.6	1.9	-3.6
Cambodia	12.4	3.9	-6.2	7.8	4.7	6.3	2.4	...
Indonesia	-0.9	6.6	0.3	5.5	4.5	6.7	1.2	5.4
Lao PDR	...	...	...	...	...	...	...	...
Malaysia	1.6	6.5	3.4	14.2	5.4	5.8	4.3	4.4
Myanmar	...	...	...	...	...	...	...	...
Philippines	-1.0	2.1	4.0	2.1	15.5	5.0	3.3	7.8
Singapore	20.9	5.0	10.7	-3.1	-1.9	11.1	-0.1	6.6
Thailand	2.8	8.0	9.3	3.4	6.8	2.5	2.1	2.2
Viet Nam	5.0	8.2	12.3	7.1	7.2	7.3	7.0	7.0
The Pacific								
Cook Islands	...	...	...	...	...	...	...	...
Fiji	...	...	...	...	...	...	...	...
Kiribati	...	...	...	...	...	...	...	...
Marshall Islands	...	2.7	-0.7	1.2	5.5	1.7	...	...
Micronesia, Fed. States of	...	...	...	...	...	...	...	...
Nauru	...	...	...	...	...	...	...	...
Palau	14.4 (1999)	...	...	...	...	...	...	...
Papua New Guinea	3.7	1.1	...	...	...	...	...	...
Samoa	...	...	...	...	...	...	...	...
Solomon Islands	33.7 (2004)	80.6	10.0	-17.2	-9.0	14.7	8.7	...
Timor-Leste[a]	33.5 (2001)	-30.2	1.1	-5.0	7.3	-22.8	3.8	...
Tonga	...	...	...	...	...	...	...	...
Tuvalu	...	...	...	...	...	...	...	...
Vanuatu	...	-0.1	4.3	-0.8	-1.3	2.2	-3.7	...
Developed Member Economies								
Australia	3.2	3.2	1.8	3.4	3.9	0.6	1.4	1.3
Japan	4.6	0.8	1.9	1.2	1.7	1.9	0.1	1.2
New Zealand	0.9	7.2	1.9	1.8	-0.1	2.2	2.3	1.8

... = data not available at cutoff date, 0.0 = magnitude is less than half of unit employed, Lao PDR = Lao People's Democratic Republic.

a The treatment of oil production from 2000 onward reflects the 2008 System of National Accounts concepts on resident units.

Source: Economy sources.

National Accounts

Table 2.16:   **Growth Rates of Real Gross Capital Formation**
              (%)

Regional Member	2000	2005	2010	2011	2012	2013	2014	2015
Developing Member Economies								
Central and West Asia								
Afghanistan	...	...	...	...	...	...	...	...
Armenia	5.2	26.9	0.5	−5.2	0.5	−9.1	−3.0	−0.9
Azerbaijan	2.6	5.8	2.0	1.0	4.0	4.5	−1.7	−11.1
Georgia	...	...	...	28.0	19.1	−11.7	26.9	...
Kazakhstan	10.7	35.0	2.0	5.9	12.2	6.2	8.8	5.7
Kyrgyz Republic	22.1	13.7	−5.2	6.3	42.4	5.1	15.7	−10.2
Pakistan	4.9	12.9	−6.5	−6.7	2.5	2.8	2.8	13.1
Tajikistan	39.2 (2001)	2.6	7.5	13.3	−21.9	15.1	17.6	...
Turkmenistan	−6.0	12.4	24.0	12.6	1.0	18.3	8.7	...
Uzbekistan	...	...	...	...	...	...	...	...
East Asia								
China, People's Rep. of	...	...	...	...	...	...	...	...
Hong Kong, China	19.5	−0.8	11.1	2.3	3.3	3.0	1.5	−7.5
Korea, Rep. of	14.5	2.4	17.8	3.5	−2.3	−0.1	5.3	6.8
Mongolia	...	15.0 (2006)	−29.8 (2009)	62.8	17.4	1.4	−30.1	−27.7
Taipei,China	9.0	1.3	35.8	−5.7	−3.1	3.2	4.1	0.5
South Asia								
Bangladesh	7.3	10.7	8.6	9.6	10.6	5.4	9.9	...
Bhutan	26.5	−12.2	46.1	11.8	3.5	−35.7	38.3	...
India	−5.5	16.2	14.1	3.9	12.9	1.8	9.3	...
Maldives	...	...	...	...	...	...	...	...
Nepal	...	9.5	34.4	0.3	−21.6	20.7	22.8	7.9
Sri Lanka	8.7	9.4	2.0 (2009)	20.2	21.7	−8.8	7.2	4.9
Southeast Asia								
Brunei Darussalam	6.7 (2001)	0.5	−0.3 (2009)	37.0	28.8	11.9	−31.2	6.6
Cambodia	8.6	29.9	−18.6	9.8	6.2	25.0	8.8	...
Indonesia	12.9	12.4	8.8	7.9	11.0	2.8	5.5	3.3
Lao PDR	...	...	...	...	...	...	...	...
Malaysia	29.2	−2.5	25.3	4.5	18.3	4.9	2.6	6.4
Myanmar	11.3	29.8	34.6	33.1	13.6	12.3	13.3	14.5
Philippines	1.1	3.0	31.6	2.8	−4.3	27.9	5.2	15.1
Singapore	25.5	−0.5	24.4	4.0	13.9	3.7	−2.0	−6.2
Thailand	8.0	21.7	32.0	2.6	11.0	3.2	−12.5	4.3
Viet Nam	10.1	11.2	10.4	−6.8	2.4	5.5	8.9	9.0
The Pacific								
Cook Islands	...	...	...	...	...	...	...	...
Fiji	...	...	...	...	...	...	...	...
Kiribati	...	...	...	...	...	...	...	...
Marshall Islands	...	3.4	19.1	−51.8	−47.2	86.8	...	...
Micronesia, Fed. States of	...	...	...	...	...	...	...	...
Nauru	...	...	...	...	...	...	...	...
Palau	−23.1 (1999)	...	...	...	...	...	...	...
Papua New Guinea	36.8	−9.8	...	...	...	...	...	...
Samoa	...	...	...	...	...	...	...	...
Solomon Islands	−13.4 (2004)	71.1	88.7	−34.6	3.6	1.9	2.9	...
Timor-Leste[a]	6.1 (2001)	−2.5	−5.1	64.9	−16.8	−27.1	8.7	...
Tonga	...	...	...	...	...	...	...	...
Tuvalu	...	...	...	...	...	...	...	...
Vanuatu	...	7.8	−5.2	−15.2	−16.6	17.0	9.0	...
Developed Member Economies								
Australia	...	...	...	...	...	...	...	...
Japan	3.7	−0.3	4.5	0.1	4.5	1.4	2.4	2.9
New Zealand	−3.9	4.0	7.3	8.0	4.0	7.6	9.4	1.8

... = data not available at cutoff date, Lao PDR = Lao People's Democratic Republic.

a   The treatment of oil production from 2000 onward reflects the 2008 System of National Accounts concepts on resident units.

Source: Economy sources.

Table 2.17: **Growth Rates of Real Exports of Goods and Services**
(%)

Regional Member	2000	2005	2010	2011	2012	2013	2014	2015
Developing Member Economies								
Central and West Asia								
Afghanistan	...	...	...	...	...	...	...	...
Armenia	19.0	15.9	26.5	14.7	8.4	8.6	6.4	4.9
Azerbaijan	15.4	52.8	9.1	2.0	–4.9	2.1	–1.9	–0.1
Georgia	...	...	...	15.5	14.4	20.3	0.4	...
Kazakhstan	27.9	0.4	3.1	0.4	4.2	2.1	–2.5	–3.8
Kyrgyz Republic	10.5	–11.0	–11.7	15.7	–19.2	12.3	–6.2	–4.0
Pakistan	16.0	9.6	15.7	2.4	–15.0	13.6	–1.6	–2.6
Tajikistan	...	2.9	23.0	1.0	1.0	–10.0	–	...
Turkmenistan	82.7	19.2	13.9	10.1	9.0	13.2	9.1	...
Uzbekistan	...	...	...	...	...	...	...	...
East Asia								
China, People's Rep. of	...	...	...	...	...	...	...	...
Hong Kong, China	16.2	10.6	16.8	3.9	1.9	6.2	0.9	–1.5
Korea, Rep. of	17.2	7.8	12.7	15.1	5.1	4.3	2.0	–1.5
Mongolia	...	...	...	18.2	8.3	12.8	53.2	–4.0
Taipei,China	18.0	7.6	25.7	4.2	0.4	3.5	5.9	–0.2
South Asia								
Bangladesh	14.4	15.6	0.9	29.3	12.5	2.5	3.2	...
Bhutan	3.3	34.3	7.5	3.2	–2.4	3.9	–6.0	...
India	18.2	26.1	19.6	15.6	6.7	7.8	1.7	–5.2
Maldives	7.6	...	...	...	...	...	...	...
Nepal	...	–3.0	–10.4	–2.1	1.9	10.3	18.8	6.8
Sri Lanka	17.1	6.6	...	10.2	–0.2	6.6	4.3	4.7
Southeast Asia								
Brunei Darussalam	11.9	–1.3	...	–3.0	1.2	–5.7	0.9	–10.8
Cambodia	39.4	16.4	16.0	18.9	7.9	20.9	11.3	...
Indonesia	26.5	16.6	15.3	14.8	1.6	4.2	1.0	–2.0
Lao PDR	...	...	...	...	...	...	...	...
Malaysia	16.1	8.3	11.1	4.2	–1.7	0.3	5.0	0.6
Myanmar	79.3	3.6	10.9	–13.7	6.5	12.9	18.7	15.2
Philippines	13.7	5.0	21.0	–2.5	8.6	–1.0	11.7	9.0
Singapore	14.4	12.5	17.4	5.6	1.8	4.8	4.3	2.5
Thailand	15.8	7.8	14.1	9.2	5.0	2.7	0.2	0.2
Viet Nam	...	7.8	14.6	10.8	15.7	17.4	11.6	12.6
The Pacific								
Cook Islands	...	...	...	...	...	...	...	...
Fiji	...	...	...	...	...	...	...	...
Kiribati	...	...	...	...	...	...	...	...
Marshall Islands	...	–3.1	25.5	8.5	4.2	9.1	...	...
Micronesia, Fed. States of	...	...	...	...	...	...	...	...
Nauru	...	...	...	...	...	...	...	...
Palau	...	...	...	...	...	...	...	...
Papua New Guinea	7.1	6.8	...	...	...	...	...	...
Samoa	...	...	...	...	...	...	...	...
Solomon Islands	...	10.5	34.8	35.3	8.8	–6.8	–9.6	...
Timor-Leste	...	76.4	–7.0	7.2	10.7	–13.3	–25.1	...
Tonga	...	...	...	...	...	...	...	...
Tuvalu	...	...	...	...	...	...	...	...
Vanuatu	...	7.1	0.4	10.4	–1.2	3.9	–0.5	...
Developed Member Economies								
Australia	9.7	3.3	5.1	0.9	5.0	5.6	5.8	6.5
Japan	12.6	6.2	24.8	–0.4	–0.2	1.2	8.3	2.8
New Zealand	6.1	–0.4	2.8	2.3	3.0	0.0	4.2	5.0

... = data not available at cutoff date, 0.0 = magnitude is less than half of unit employed, Lao PDR = Lao People's Democratic Republic.

Source: Economy sources.

National Accounts

Table 2.18:   **Growth Rates of Real Imports of Goods and Services**
              (%)

Regional Member	2000	2005	2010	2011	2012	2013	2014	2015
Developing Member Economies								
Central and West Asia								
Afghanistan	...	...	...	...	...	...	...	...
Armenia	7.2	14.3	12.8	−1.4	−2.8	−2.1	−1.0	−15.1
Azerbaijan	17.3	19.8	12.4	1.5	−3.1	1.1	−2.1	−0.5
Georgia	...	...	...	17.9	15.6	2.9	11.1	...
Kazakhstan	28.0	12.1	2.9	2.8	22.6	6.6	−3.3	−0.2
Kyrgyz Republic	0.4	6.5	−6.9	14.9	12.4	4.1	1.6	−17.0
Pakistan	−2.3	40.5	4.3	−0.1	−3.1	1.8	0.2	−1.1
Tajikistan	...	16.5	8.0	1.2	1.2	1.1	1.0	...
Turkmenistan	4.1	−9.3	9.5	10.1	13.3	10.3	9.5	...
Uzbekistan	...	...	...	...	...	...	...	...
East Asia								
China, People's Rep. of	...	...	...	...	...	...	...	...
Hong Kong, China	16.4	8.0	17.4	4.6	2.9	6.6	1.0	−1.9
Korea, Rep. of	21.8	7.8	17.3	14.3	2.4	1.7	1.5	3.2
Mongolia	...	...	...	49.5	15.4	7.6	6.8	−16.6
Taipei,China	14.9	2.9	28.0	−0.5	−1.8	3.4	5.7	0.9
South Asia								
Bangladesh	10.2	19.1	0.7	29.2	10.5	1.2	1.2	...
Bhutan	4.2	13.0	28.7	6.0	−7.1	−1.8	−3.5	...
India	4.6	32.6	15.6	21.1	6.0	−8.2	0.8	−2.8
Maldives	−5.1	...	...	...	...	...	...	...
Nepal	...	6.9	28.3	−4.7	3.4	14.2	21.0	9.6
Sri Lanka	14.8	2.7	...	23.6	0.5	−1.5	9.6	10.6
Southeast Asia								
Brunei Darussalam	−6.2	10.2	...	33.7	20.6	14.5	−30.9	−11.7
Cambodia	30.6	17.3	10.3	16.3	8.1	24.5	10.1	...
Indonesia	25.9	17.8	17.3	15.0	8.0	1.9	2.2	−5.8
Lao PDR	...	...	...	...	...	...	...	...
Malaysia	24.4	8.9	15.6	6.3	2.9	1.7	4.0	1.2
Myanmar	−8.0	2.2	51.9	1.2	3.7	54.4	22.3	21.6
Philippines	11.8	3.3	22.5	−0.6	5.6	4.4	9.3	14.0
Singapore	20.1	11.5	16.2	4.0	3.0	4.5	3.9	2.1
Thailand	26.0	16.2	22.8	12.4	5.6	1.6	−5.3	−0.4
Viet Nam	...	5.9	13.7	4.1	9.1	17.3	12.8	18.1
The Pacific								
Cook Islands	...	...	...	...	...	...	...	...
Fiji	...	...	...	...	...	...	...	...
Kiribati	...	...	...	...	...	...	...	...
Marshall Islands	...	0.7	7.8	−21.5	0.7	10.1	...	...
Micronesia, Fed. States of	...	...	...	...	...	...	...	...
Nauru	...	...	...	...	...	...	...	...
Palau	...	...	...	...	...	...	...	...
Papua New Guinea	−4.7	4.7	...	...	...	...	...	...
Samoa	...	...	...	...	...	...	...	...
Solomon Islands	...	26.4	51.7	−6.4	3.8	−0.5	−0.6	...
Timor-Leste	...	−14.1	−10.9	8.1	23.0	−17.3	13.0	...
Tonga	...	...	...	...	...	...	...	...
Tuvalu	...	...	...	...	...	...	...	...
Vanuatu	...	2.9	−2.2	−1.9	0.8	6.5	0.2	...
Developed Member Economies								
Australia	12.1	12.4	6.4	10.3	11.6	0.6	−1.8	0.1
Japan	10.7	4.2	11.1	5.9	5.3	3.1	7.2	0.4
New Zealand	−1.1	4.9	11.5	6.6	1.3	8.1	7.4	1.9

... = data not available at cutoff date, Lao PDR = Lao People's Democratic Republic.

Source: Economy sources.

Table 2.19:   **Growth Rates of Agriculture Production Index**
             (%)

Regional Member	2000	2005	2010	2011	2012	2013
Developing Member Economies						
Central and West Asia						
Afghanistan	−16.2	8.7	−0.6	−4.4	10.7	−2.2
Armenia	−2.3	14.3	−12.5	10.6	6.7	4.6
Azerbaijan	8.8	13.7	−1.2	6.3	4.8	3.2
Georgia	−13.6	16.5	−6.7	7.5	−5.9	19.7
Kazakhstan	−7.6	7.5	−12.5	31.5	−22.5	15.1
Kyrgyz Republic	4.8	−3.8	3.7	2.3	−0.3	1.8
Pakistan	1.3	3.1	−2.0	5.0	−0.4	−18.7
Tajikistan	12.8	−5.7	3.8	8.0	11.3	6.4
Turkmenistan	7.9	12.1	0.7	−2.0	4.7	1.6
Uzbekistan	3.3	5.8	5.7	6.0	5.8	5.8
East Asia						
China, People's Rep. of	5.0	3.7	2.5	3.0	3.5	1.3
Hong Kong, China	2.4	13.5	0.0	6.7	6.3	–
Korea, Rep. of	1.0	0.6	−6.4	−2.6	1.7	3.0
Mongolia	−2.9	−8.3	−22.0	9.4	5.3	10.1
Taipei,China	2.2	−5.7	2.1	3.7	−1.7	0.3
South Asia						
Bangladesh	6.2	12.9	6.6	2.8	0.5	1.8
Bhutan	−23.1	26.7	6.0	16.5	−8.9	−3.2
India	−1.1	5.8	8.8	6.4	2.0	3.4
Maldives	5.3	−22.0	−8.0	−1.9	−6.0	−3.6
Nepal	5.1	2.0	1.1	7.2	15.3	−7.0
Sri Lanka	2.1	8.7	10.7	−3.7	2.9	11.1
Southeast Asia						
Brunei Darussalam	14.8	−25.7	5.5	6.4	3.5	8.7
Cambodia	2.2	26.9	8.6	15.3	2.4	4.0
Indonesia	3.4	2.7	2.6	3.3	6.7	1.0
Lao PDR	15.1	4.1	4.8	6.3	15.6	1.0
Malaysia	3.6	4.6	0.9	8.1	−0.4	1.8
Myanmar	9.4	6.0	2.2	0.3	−3.4	1.9
Philippines	3.6	2.8	−0.2	2.6	3.7	1.2
Singapore	−59.0	−22.7	0.5	9.5	3.9	6.6
Thailand	7.8	−2.0	−1.1	7.4	7.0	0.1
Viet Nam	3.8	3.8	3.1	4.5	7.4	1.0
The Pacific						
Cook Islands	0.6	2.5	3.2	−6.9	0.8	−0.5
Fiji	0.1	1.5	−5.4	12.7	−8.5	1.5
Kiribati	−5.3	0.9	1.1	−1.1	3.1	0.9
Marshall Islands	−74.9	15.2	−5.0	−44.5	0.8	5.0
Micronesia, Fed. States of	1.4	2.1	2.5	−4.7	5.8	2.7
Nauru	1.6	1.4	−0.7	−1.3	0.6	2.7
Palau	...	...	...	...	...	...
Papua New Guinea	3.0	1.9	−1.7	5.7	−1.0	0.8
Samoa	4.5	3.4	−0.7	0.2	7.7	−3.1
Solomon Islands	5.0	12.2	2.8	1.2	2.7	2.7
Timor-Leste	6.7	−1.6	−3.1	−11.9	16.2	−7.7
Tonga	−1.9	0.7	−2.9	−3.7	−0.5	0.9
Tuvalu	2.5	1.9	0.6	−5.6	1.1	2.1
Vanuatu	−4.6	0.9	27.2	−3.7	2.0	6.1
Developed Member Economies						
Australia	−1.9	8.7	−2.3	9.2	9.8	−0.4
Japan	−0.6	0.9	−2.7	−1.4	2.6	−0.3
New Zealand	7.1	−2.2	1.4	0.4	5.0	−1.4

... = data not available at cutoff date, – = magnitude is equal to zero, 0.0 = magnitude is less than half of unit employed, Lao PDR = Lao People's Democratic Republic.

Sources: Food and Agricultural Organization of the United Nations. FAOSTAT. http://faostat3.fao.org (accessed 5 August 2016); economy sources.

Table 2.20: **Growth Rates of Manufacturing Production Index**
(%)

Regional Member	2000	2005	2010	2011	2012	2013	2014	2015
Developing Member Economies								
Central and West Asia								
Afghanistan	...	...	...	...	...	...	...	...
Armenia	...	...	...	...	...	...	...	...
Azerbaijan	...	...	...	...	...	...	...	...
Georgia	...	...	...	...	...	...	...	...
Kazakhstan	17.3	15.9	15.1	...	–6.0	0.7	–0.8	–0.9
Kyrgyz Republic	...	...	...	...	...	...	...	...
Pakistan	...	18.2	4.7	...	1.2	4.1	4.0	3.2
Tajikistan	12.0	10.5	...	...	...	...	...	...
Turkmenistan	13.4	...	...	...	...	...	...	...
Uzbekistan	–	...	...	...	...	...	...	...
East Asia								
China, People's Rep. of	...	...	16.6	14.3	10.5	10.5	9.4	7.0
Hong Kong, China	–0.5	3.0	3.6	0.7	–0.8	0.1	–0.4	–1.5
Korea, Rep. of	17.2	6.3	16.7	6.0	1.4	0.7	0.3	–0.6
Mongolia	...	...	...	...	...	...	...	...
Taipei,China	–17.4	3.2	26.5	4.7	–0.3	0.6	6.6	–1.5
South Asia								
Bangladesh	4.9	8.5	6.3	16.9	10.8	11.6	9.2	...
Bhutan	...	...	...	...	...	...	...	...
India	5.3	10.3	9.0	3.0	1.3	–0.8	2.3	2.0
Maldives	...	...	...	...	...	...	...	...
Nepal	6.5	...	...	4.8	3.8	4.0	7.0	0.3
Sri Lanka	...	...	...	...	...	...	...	...
Southeast Asia								
Brunei Darussalam	...	...	...	...	...	...	...	...
Cambodia	48.8	...	...	...	...	...	...	...
Indonesia	3.6	1.3	4.8	4.1	4.1	6.0	4.8	4.8
Lao PDR	...	...	...	...	...	...	...	...
Malaysia	24.9	5.1	11.0	5.7	5.3	4.2	6.0	...
Myanmar	...	...	...	10.1	6.8	8.8	9.2	9.4
Philippines	...	2.1	23.3	1.0	7.7	14.0	7.4	2.3
Singapore	15.3	9.5	29.8	8.4	0.4	1.7	2.6	...
Thailand	6.9	5.0	14.2	–8.5	2.2	–3.2	–4.6	...
Viet Nam	...	...	...	...	...	2.0	1.0	...
The Pacific								
Cook Islands	...	...	...	...	...	...	...	...
Fiji	–5.6	...	7.6	3.9	–25.7	5.2	2.9	4.0
Kiribati	...	...	...	...	...	...	...	...
Marshall Islands	...	...	...	...	...	...	...	...
Micronesia, Fed. States of	...	...	...	...	...	...	...	...
Nauru	...	...	...	...	...	...	...	...
Palau	...	...	...	...	...	...	...	...
Papua New Guinea	...	...	...	...	...	...	...	...
Samoa[a]	2.8	–	15.2	3.6	7.7	3.2	...	...
Solomon Islands	...	...	...	...	...	...	...	...
Timor-Leste	...	...	...	...	...	...	...	...
Tonga	...	...	...	...	...	...	...	...
Tuvalu	...	...	...	...	...	...	...	...
Vanuatu	...	...	...	...	...	...	...	...
Developed Member Economies								
Australia	1.2	–0.9	0.6	–0.2	0.7	–3.3	–1.2	–1.5
Japan	5.7	1.3	15.6	–2.8	0.6	–0.8	2.1	–1.2
New Zealand	4.3	0.6	4.3	–0.7	1.2	1.4	2.1	1.5

... = data not available at cutoff date, – = magnitude equals zero, Lao PDR = Lao People's Democratic Republic.

a   Refers to volume indexes of industrial production.

Source: Economy sources.

Money, Finance, and Prices

Snapshots

- Consumer price inflation remained low in most economies in Asia and the Pacific in 2015 due to low international food and fuel prices.

- In 2015, the money supply expanded in all reporting economies except Azerbaijan, Brunei Darussalam, and Mongolia.

- The ratio of nonperforming loans to total gross loans declined between 2014 and 2015 in the majority of economies in the region for which data are available.

- Three economies in the region had stock markets that were among the world's top 10 performers in 2015.

- Only two of the region's currencies appreciated against the US dollar in 2015, compared with eight in 2014.

Key Trends

Consumer price inflation remained low in most economies in Asia and the Pacific in 2015. Figure 3.1a shows the estimates of inflation rates for economies of Asia and the Pacific for recent years. The data suggest that consumer price inflation remained low in majority of the economies in the region. In 2014, 22 out of 46 reporting economies had inflation rates below 3% and this number increased to 27 out of 46 in 2015. Almost half of the reporting economies had inflation rates below 3% in both years.

Eight economies experienced negative consumer price inflation in 2015: the Federated States of Micronesia (–0.2%); Taipei,China (–0.3%); Brunei Darussalam (–0.4%); Singapore (–0.5%); Solomon Islands (–0.6%); Thailand (–0.9%); Tonga (–1.0%); and the Marshall Islands (–2.2%). On the other hand, two of the four highest rates of inflation in 2015 were observed in economies in Central and West Asia: Kazakhstan (6.6%) and the Kyrgyz Republic (6.5%).

Among the region's three largest economies, consumer price inflation rate in the People's Republic of China (PRC) is estimated at 1.4% in 2015, in India at 4.9%, and in Japan at 0.8%.

On a subregional basis, consumer price inflation accelerated in three of the 10 Central and West Asian economies for which 2015 data are available (Armenia, Azerbaijan, and Georgia). South Asia also experienced relatively high inflation by regional standards, (unweighted) averaging 4.2% in 2015. With the exception of Mongolia, very low inflation rates have been observed in East Asia in recent years, including an (unweighted) average of only 1.2% in 2015. Economies in Southeast Asia and the Pacific posted inflation rates of 1.9% and 1.0%, respectively, in 2015.

Figure 3.1a: Inflation Rate
(annual % change)

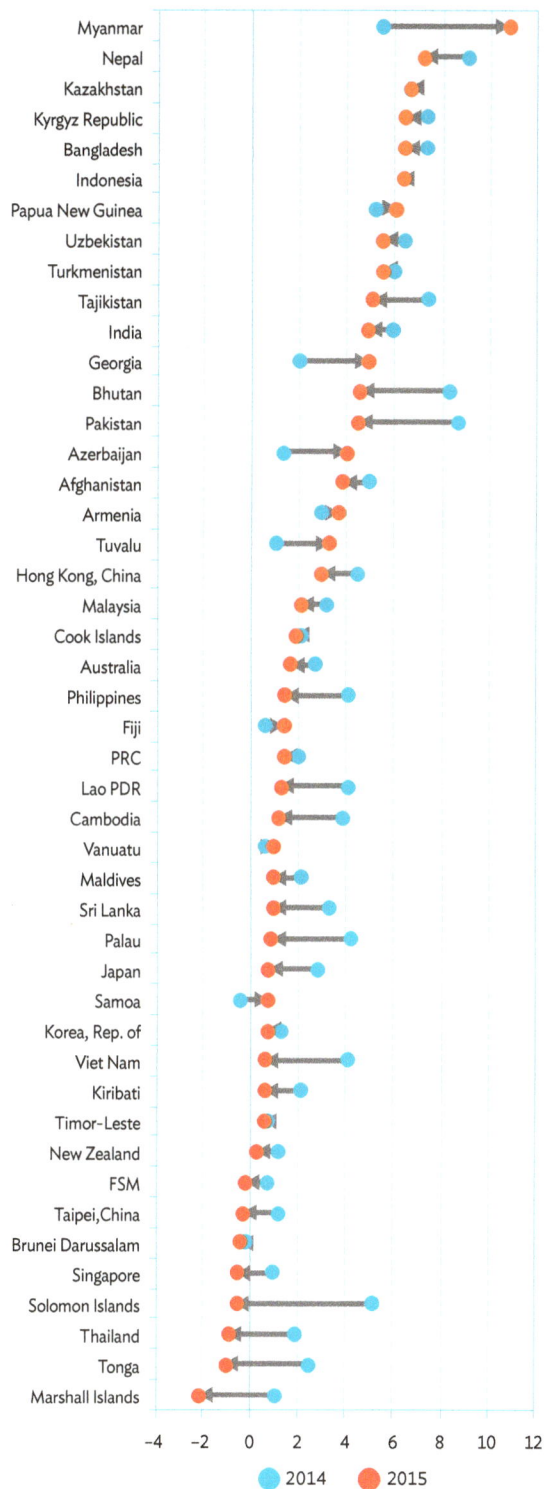

Figure 3.1b: Food Inflation Rate
(annual % change)

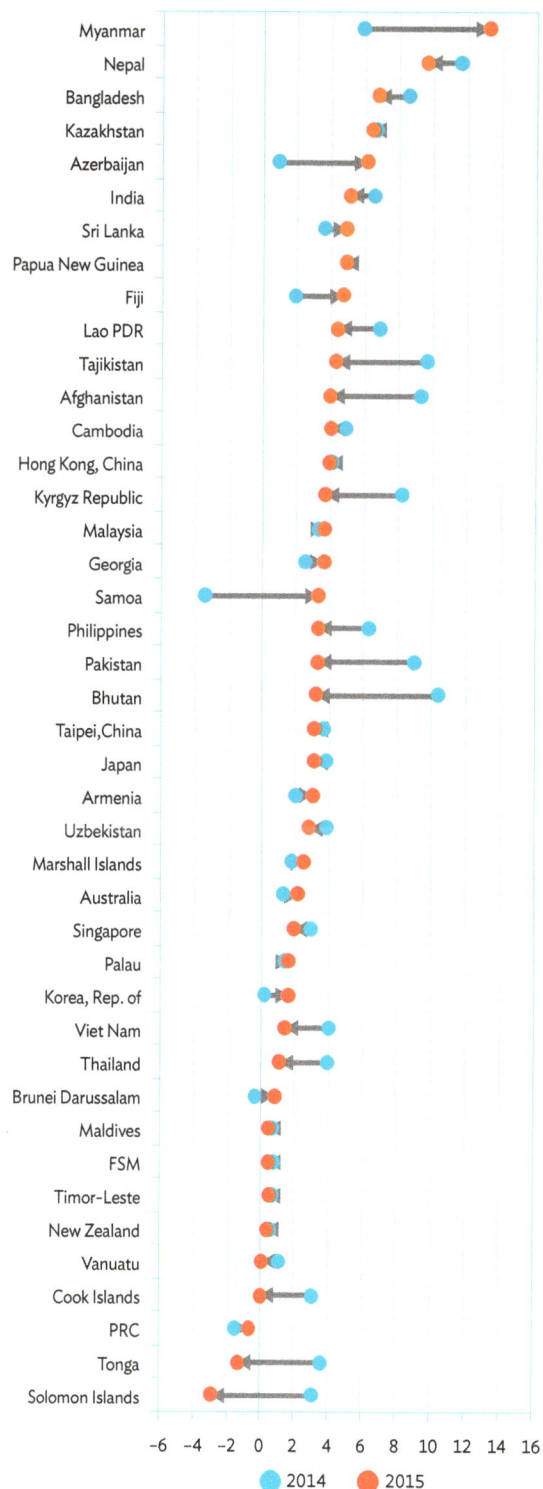

FSM = Federated States of Micronesia, Lao PDR = Lao People's Democratic
Republic, PRC = People's Republic of China.
Source: Table 3.1.

FSM = Federated States of Micronesia, Lao PDR = Lao People's Democratic
Republic, PRC = People's Republic of China.
Source: Table 3.2.

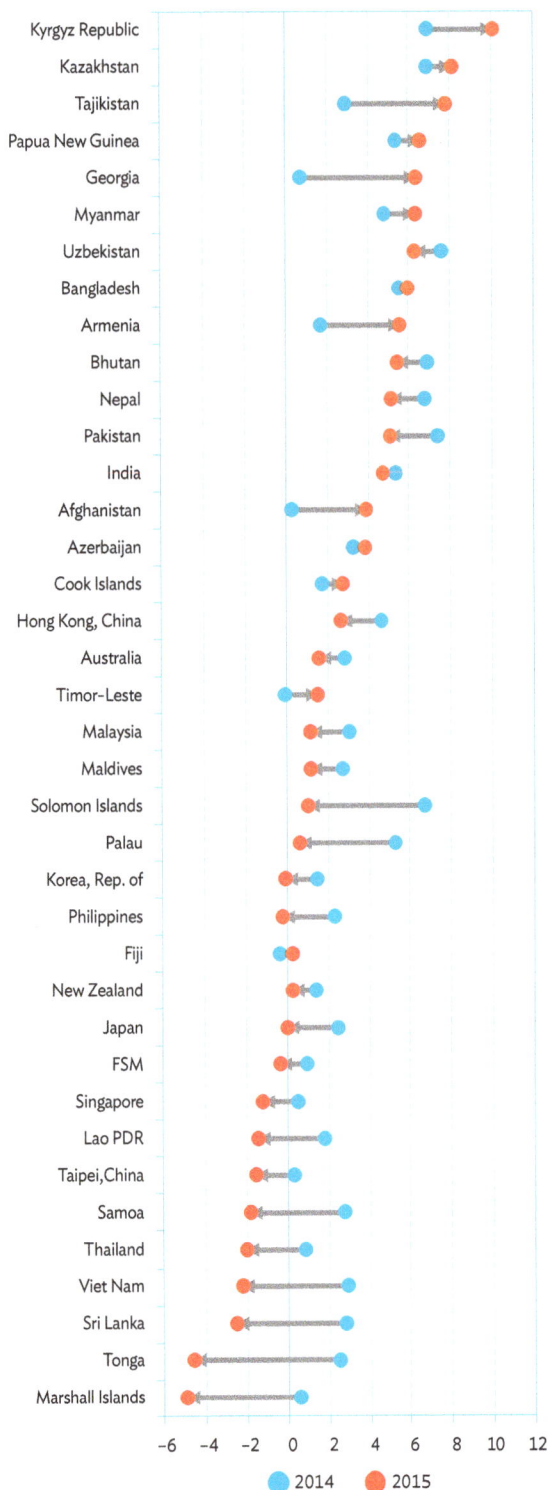

Figure 3.1c: Nonfood Inflation Rate
(annual % change)

2014   2015

FSM = Federated States of Micronesia, Lao PDR = Lao People's Democratic Republic.
Source: Table 3.3.

Wholesale and/or producer price deflation has been an emerging concern for some economies in Asia and the Pacific; lower investment and lower economic growth were seen as contributory factors to deflation. On a regional basis, wholesale and/or producer prices had a negative (unweighted) average growth rate of 2.6% in 2015 from a positive growth of 2.7% in 2014.

Further, 17 out of 24 economies for which data are available recorded negative wholesale and/or producer price inflation rates, with Azerbaijan (–30.6%) having the highest rate, followed by Kazakhstan (–20.5%); Singapore (–15.3%); Taipei,China (–8.8%); and the PRC (–5.2%). Meanwhile, the Kyrgyz Republic and Georgia were the only two regional economies to experience accelerated growth rates between 2014 and 2015, from 1.4% to 8.5%, and 2.8% to 7.4%, respectively.

While consumer price inflation was generally low but positive in 2015 across the region, producer price inflation was negative in the PRC and a number of other Asian economies such as Hong Kong, China; India; the Republic of Korea; Malaysia; the Philippines; Singapore; and Thailand. Box 3.1 discusses the potential reasons why consumer price index and producer price index produce different trends.

The money supply expanded in 2015 in all reporting economies except for Azerbaijan, Brunei Darussalam, and Mongolia. The (unweighted) average rate of expansion in the money supply in 2015 for all economies for which data was available was 10.8% (Figure 3.2). Three countries in Central and West Asia experienced increases in the growth rate of their money supply—Kazakhstan (23.8 percentage points), the Kyrgyz Republic (11.9 percentage points), and Tajikistan (11.6 percentage points)—while Mongolia recorded the lowest decline.

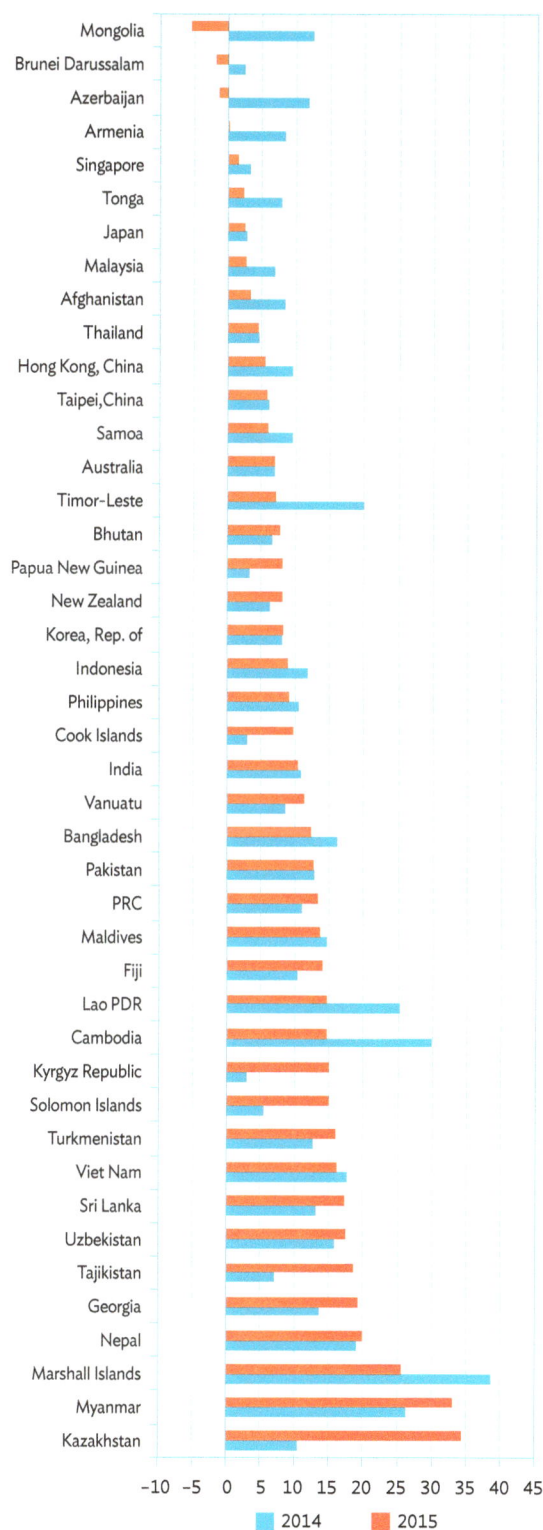

Figure 3.2: Growth in Money Supply
(%)

Lao PDR = Lao People's Democratic Republic, PRC = People's Republic of China.
Source: Table 3.6.

Economies in Asia and the Pacific have increased their reliance on credit since 2000, the impacts of the global financial crisis notwithstanding. The amount of credit available in the banking sector increased in 34 of 40 regional economies between 2000 (or the first year for which data are available) and 2015 (or the latest year for which data are available) (Figure 3.3). Bhutan led all economies during the period, with the amount of domestic credit provided by the banking sector as a percentage of GDP increasing from 2.9% in 2000 to 54.3% in 2015, followed by increases in domestic credit in Cambodia (from 6.4% to 53.9%) and Mongolia (from 9.0% to 69.3%) (Table 3.10).

In 2015 or the latest year for which data are available, Japan (376.6%) had the highest domestic credit-to-GDP ratio among all regional economies, followed by Hong Kong, China (211.5%) and the PRC (196.9%). The Federated States of Micronesia (–26.2%) and Timor-Leste (–9.0%) had negative domestic credit-to-GDP ratios in 2015 or the latest year for which data are available, while Afghanistan's ratio was barely positive (0.4%).

The ratio of nonperforming loans (NPLs) to total gross loans declined between 2014 and 2015 in most economies in the region for which data are available. The simple average of the NPL-to-total gross loans ratio of 30 regional economies with available data slightly declined from 5.0% in 2014 to 4.9% in 2015 (Figure 3.4). The most significant decline was observed in Kazakhstan (4.4 percentage points). Other noteworthy declines occurred in Brunei Darussalam (3.5 percentage points), the Maldives (3.4 percentage points), and Samoa (3.0 percentage points).

The economies with the highest NPL-to-gross loans ratios at the end of the review period were Tajikistan (19.1%), the Maldives (14.1%), and

Figure 3.3: Domestic Credit Provided by the Banking Sector
(% of GDP)

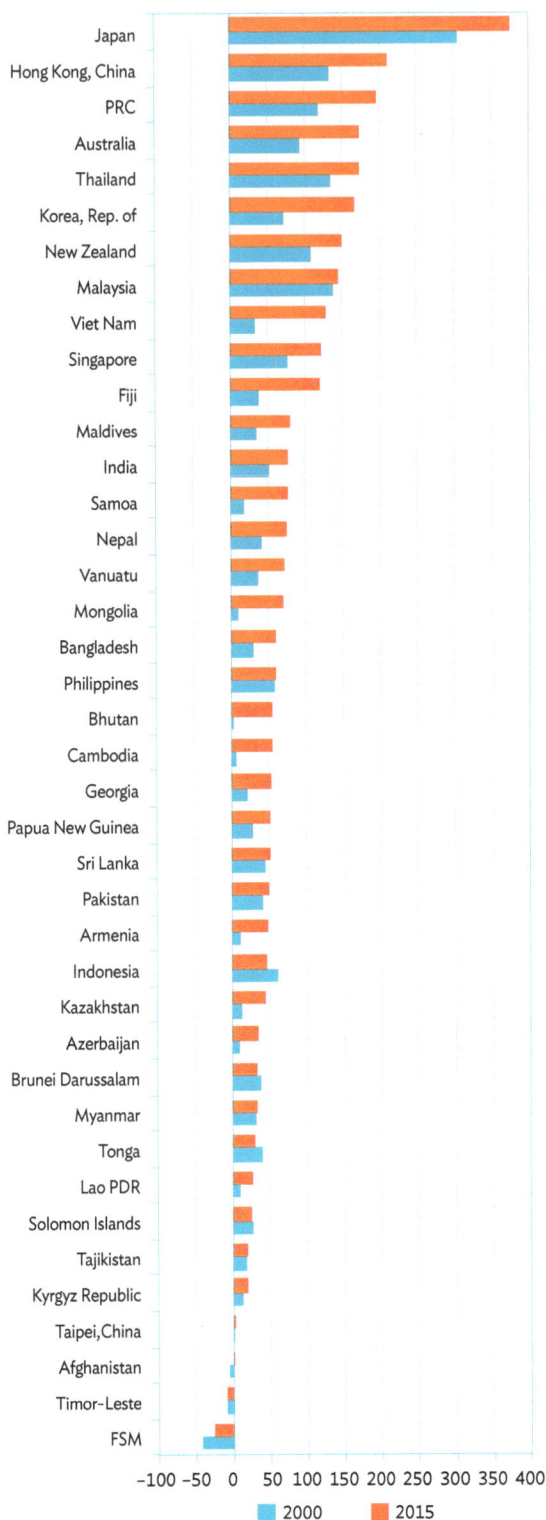

Japan
Hong Kong, China
PRC
Australia
Thailand
Korea, Rep. of
New Zealand
Malaysia
Viet Nam
Singapore
Fiji
Maldives
India
Samoa
Nepal
Vanuatu
Mongolia
Bangladesh
Philippines
Bhutan
Cambodia
Georgia
Papua New Guinea
Sri Lanka
Pakistan
Armenia
Indonesia
Kazakhstan
Azerbaijan
Brunei Darussalam
Myanmar
Tonga
Lao PDR
Solomon Islands
Tajikistan
Kyrgyz Republic
Taipei,China
Afghanistan
Timor-Leste
FSM

-100 -50 0 50 100 150 200 250 300 350 400

■ 2000   ■ 2015

FSM = Federated States of Micronesia, GDP = gross domestic product,
Lao PDR = Lao People's Democratic Republic, PRC = People's Republic
of China.
Source: Table 3.10.

Afghanistan (12.3%). Those with the lowest NPL-to-gross loans ratios at the end of the review period were Turkmenistan (0.0%); Taipei,China (0.2%); and Brunei Darussalam and Uzbekistan (0.4% each).

Figure 3.4: Nonperforming Bank Loans
(% of total gross loans)

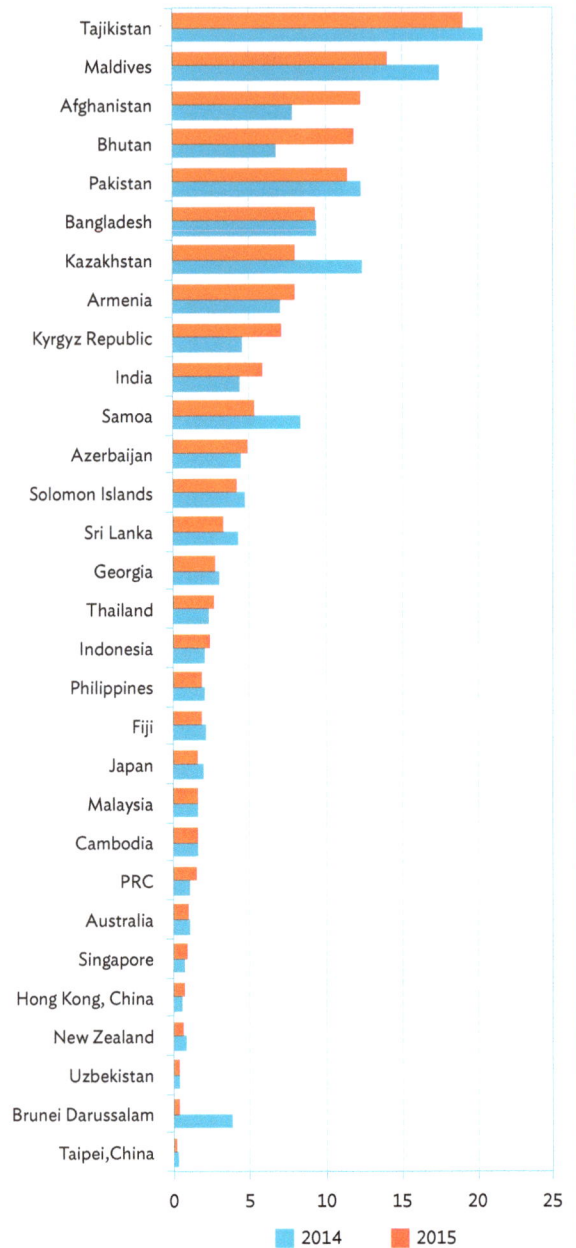

Tajikistan
Maldives
Afghanistan
Bhutan
Pakistan
Bangladesh
Kazakhstan
Armenia
Kyrgyz Republic
India
Samoa
Azerbaijan
Solomon Islands
Sri Lanka
Georgia
Thailand
Indonesia
Philippines
Fiji
Japan
Malaysia
Cambodia
PRC
Australia
Singapore
Hong Kong, China
New Zealand
Uzbekistan
Brunei Darussalam
Taipei,China

0   5   10   15   20   25

■ 2014   ■ 2015

PRC = People's Republic of China.
Sources: World Bank. World Development Indicators Online.
http://data.worldbank.org/ (accessed 12 August 2016); and for Taipei,China:
economy sources.

Three economies in the region had stock markets that were among the world's top 10 performers in 2015. Despite midyear volatility, gains in the stock market in the PRC in 2015 of more than 60% were the second largest in the world, trailing only Venezuela (Figure 3.5a) (ADB 2016). Japan and Fiji ranked eighth and ninth in the world, respectively, in terms of increases in stock market indexes in 2015.

Along with the PRC, Japan, and Fiji, the top stock market performers within the region included Pakistan; New Zealand; India; the Maldives; Sri Lanka; the Philippines; and Hong Kong, China (Figure 3.5b).

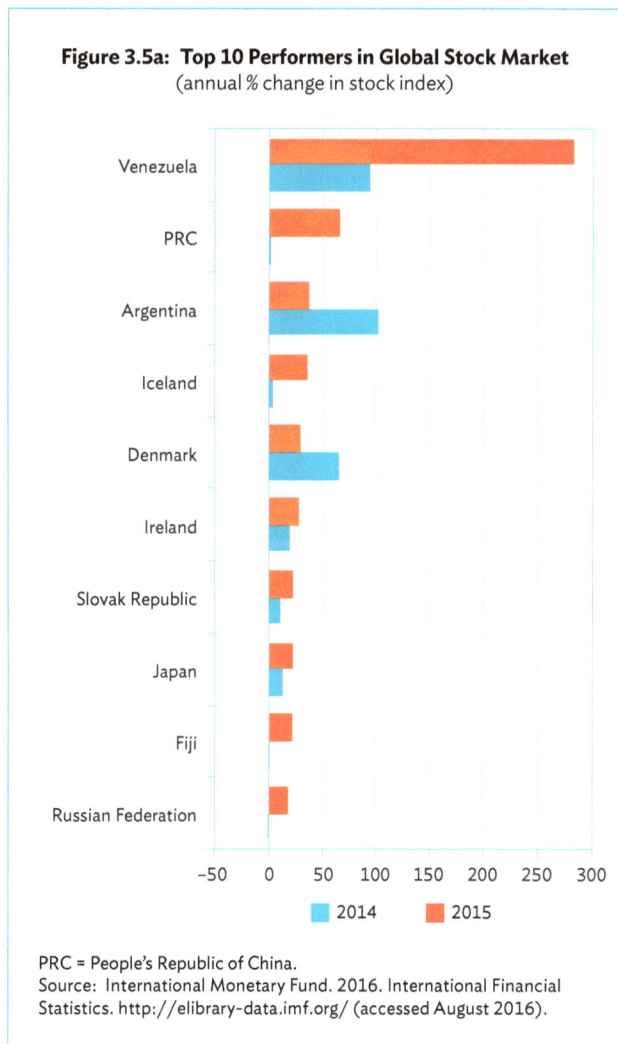

Figure 3.5a: Top 10 Performers in Global Stock Market
(annual % change in stock index)

PRC = People's Republic of China.
Source: International Monetary Fund. 2016. International Financial Statistics. http://elibrary-data.imf.org/ (accessed August 2016).

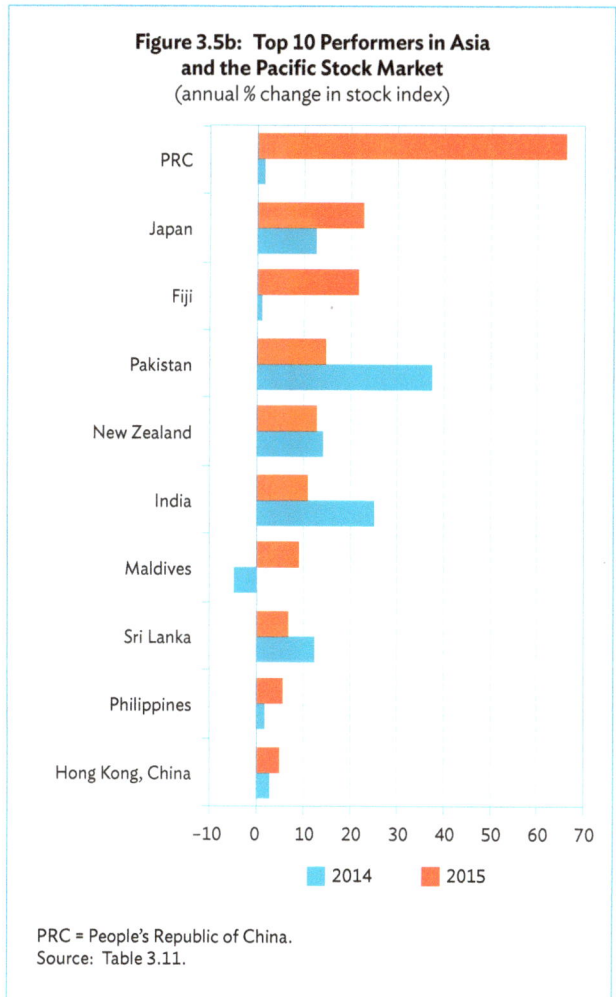

Figure 3.5b: Top 10 Performers in Asia and the Pacific Stock Market
(annual % change in stock index)

PRC = People's Republic of China.
Source: Table 3.11.

Regional Trends and Tables

Only two of the region's currencies appreciated against the US dollar in 2015, compared with eight in 2014. The modest recovery in the United States, where GDP growth continues to outpace economic gains in other advanced economies, and the Federal Reserve's long-anticipated raising of the target range for the federal funds rate in December 2015 contributed to a strengthening of the US dollar against most regional currencies in 2015 (Figure 3.6). The only exceptions to this trend were the Hong Kong dollar and the rufiyaa (Maldives), which marginally appreciated by 0.03% and 0.09%, respectively. (Both currencies adhere to a dollar-pegged exchange rate regime.)

The currencies of Central and West Asia were particularly hard-hit in 2015 as a result of plunging petroleum prices, recession in the Russian Federation, and weakness in other trading partner economies (ADB 2016). In 2015, the manat (Azerbaijan) depreciated by 30.6% against the US dollar, the lari (Georgia) by 28.5%, and the somoni (Tajikistan) by 24.8%.

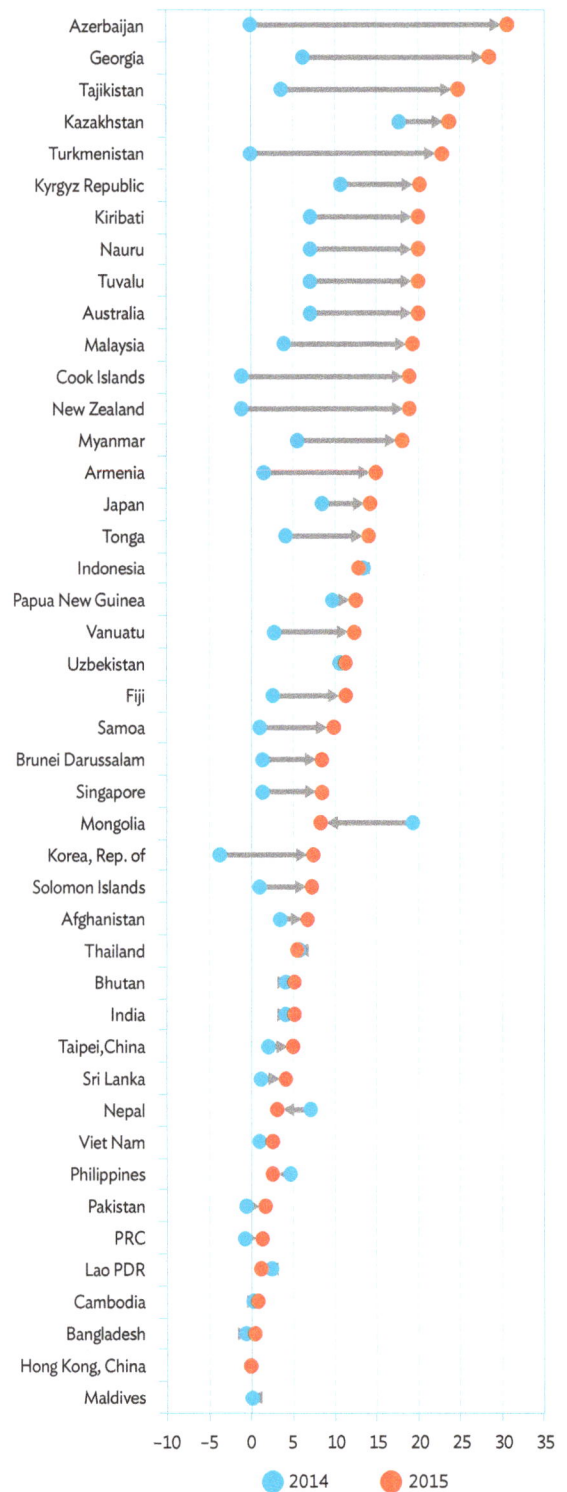

Figure 3.6: Dollar Exchange Rates
(annual % change)

Lao PDR = Lao People's Democratic Republic, PRC = People's Republic of China.
Source: Table 3.13.

Box 3.1: Difference between Consumer Price Index and Producer Price Index

The producer price index (PPI) and the consumer price index (CPI) are two distinct measures of inflation that serve a different purpose. Simply put, the PPI measures the average cost for a typical producer and is commonly used to deflate revenue streams to allow measurement of output growth in real terms. On the other hand, CPI measures the average cost of goods and services bought by a typical consumer and is useful to adjust income and expenditure streams to account for temporal changes in cost of living.

Each price index is calculated based on varying baskets of goods and services (Box Figure 3.1.1). In particular, the PPI is calculated based on all marketable outputs sold by domestic producers while the CPI basket includes items that are commonly consumed by an average individual, including imported goods and services. The PPI includes intermediate goods and services that are domestically produced but excludes imported goods and services.

Box Figure 3.1.1: Conceptual Differences between Producer and Consumer Price Indexes

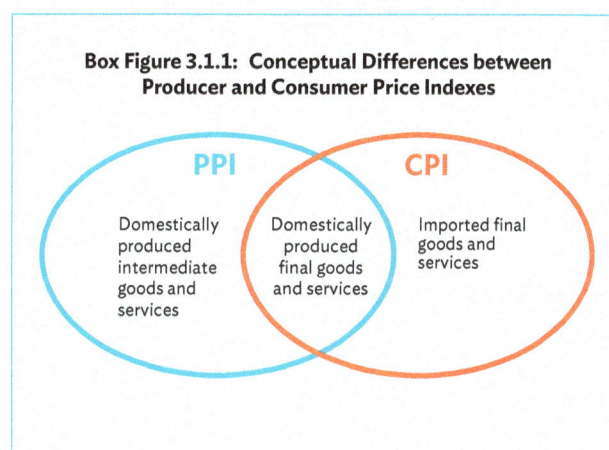

PPI

CPI

Domestically produced intermediate goods and services

Domestically produced final goods and services

Imported final goods and services

The types of prices used in index calculation also differ between the PPI and CPI. The PPI is calculated based on the revenue received by the producers; and since sales and excise taxes do not represent revenue to the producer, they are not included in the calculation of the PPI. On the other hand, sales and excise taxes are included in the calculation of CPI because they directly impact the consumers by having to pay higher prices for the goods and services. Thus, significant changes in consumer taxation may cause the two price indexes to move into different directions. In addition to taxes, CPI also implicitly includes costs of transporting goods from producers to consumers. Additionally, price markups used to cover the costs of doing business between wholesalers and retailers are also incorporated in the calculation of CPI (McCormack 2013).

Another source of difference between the PPI and CPI is the set of weights used in calculations. In particular, the weights used for the computation of the PPI are typically based on gross output figures as reported in either a census or survey of establishments or industries. On the other hand, commodity items included in the CPI basket are weighted based on their corresponding expenditure shares as reported in household consumption surveys. Differences in the timing of these censuses and surveys may also lead to different updating periods for the PPI and CPI. For instance, in some countries, censuses or surveys of establishments are conducted more frequently than household consumption surveys; hence, the PPIs have more frequent updates. In other countries, the situation is the opposite and CPIs are updated more frequently.

Although a priori we should not expect the PPI and CPI to exhibit the same trends due to standard technical differences in basket composition, weighting, and timing of price collection, empirical evidence suggests that the two generally moved in lockstep until the late 1990s only diverging by the 2000s (Han, Wei, and Xie, forthcoming). In the case of Asia, an ongoing study of Han et al. shows that inflation estimates in the People's Republic of China, the Republic of Korea, India, Singapore, Thailand, the Philippines, and Malaysia show CPI numbers moving upward while PPI estimates are going down (Box Figure 3.1.2). The concept of global value chains provides an instructive analytical lens to understand the growing divergence between CPI and PPI movements. When globalization was less intense and economies were relatively less open until the 1990s, the firms conducted their entire production process in the same location. Since the value chains were domestically concentrated, producer and consumer prices moved in tandem. Over time, trade liberalization, cheaper shipping costs, and other technological advances have reshaped how firms make products and distribute them across the globe. The global value chains have created opportunities for firms to become more efficient by conducting various stages

continued.

Box 3.1: *(continued)*

of their production process in locations where they can exploit relative costs and factor endowments. Nowadays, it is uncommon to see goods and services being produced entirely in a single location. Since multiple stages of production are happening at different locations and, hence, there is an increasing share of consumer goods and services that are imported, the basket for calculating CPI overlaps less with the basket for the PPI. In principle, this partially explains the weaker correlation between PPI and CPI movements. Nevertheless, the issue of diverging inflation trends based on the two indexes remains an important policy concern for some countries. Addressing this issue has been the topic of ongoing research.

Box Figure 3.1.2: Inflation Trends in Recent Years, Consumer Price Index versus Producer Price Index

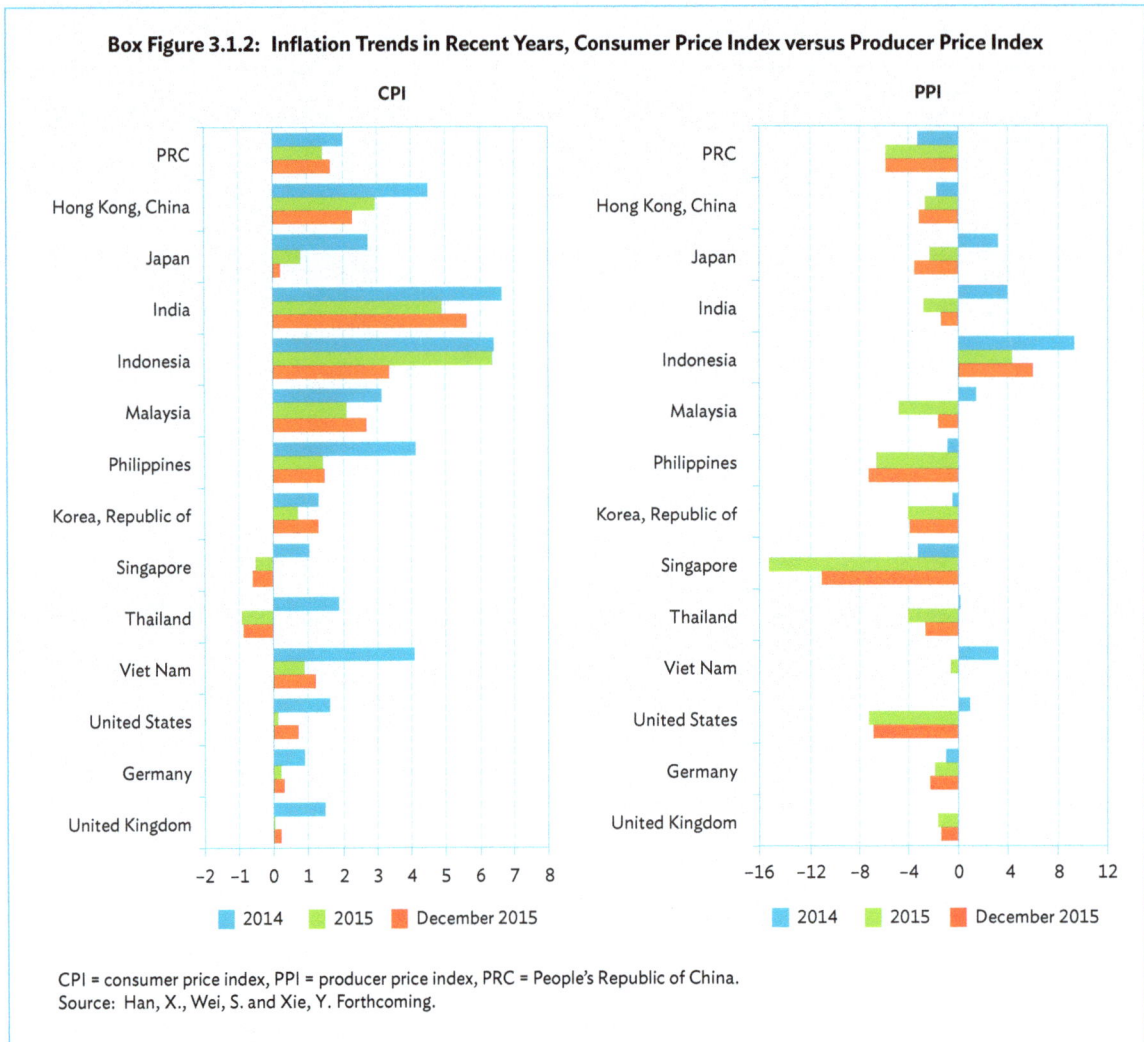

CPI = consumer price index, PPI = producer price index, PRC = People's Republic of China.
Source: Han, X., Wei, S. and Xie, Y. Forthcoming.

Sources:

Han, X., Wei, S. and Xie, Y. Forthcoming. Divergence between CPI and PPI as Inflation Gauges: The Role of Global Value Chains.
McCormack, K. 2013. How Does the Producer Price Index Differ from the Consumer Price Index? Ireland Central Statistics Office, Information Notice. http://www.cso.ie/en/media/csoie/surveysandmethodologies/surveys/prices/documents/PPI_differ_CPI1.pdf

Data Issues and Comparability

Some economies need to meet international reporting standards and classifications on the compilation of monetary and financial statistics, as detailed by the International Monetary Fund on its Dissemination Standards Bulletin Board.

The CPI coverage differs from economy to economy. Sometimes the basket of goods and services in the index is outdated or represents only urban areas or the capital city. Other price measurements, such as the wholesale price index and the PPI, are not available in the Pacific economies and it is recommended that they make an effort to compile these indexes.

Broad money supply in most economies relates to M2. However, 12 of the 43 economies that have data report M3, which is broader than M2 as it also includes less liquid financial assets, thereby posing limits to comparability.

The methodology in compiling or measuring banks' average deposit and lending rates also varies for each economy. Some economies use the central bank policy rate while others use commercial bank rates.

References

Asian Development Bank (ADB). 2016. *Asian Development Outlook 2016*. Manila.

Bank of Japan. Outline of Monetary Policy. https://www.boj.or.jp/en/mopo/outline/qqe.htm/
———. Purchases of ETFs and J-REITs. http://www3.boj.or.jp/market/en/menu_etf.htm

International Monetary Fund (IMF). 2016. *World Economic Outlook: Too Slow for Too Long*. Washington, DC.

———. Dissemination Standards Bulletin Board. http://dsbb.imf.org/Pages/SDDS/StatMethod.aspx

United Nations Economic and Social Commission for Asia and the Pacific (ESCAP). 2016. *Economic and Social Survey of Asia and the Pacific 2015 (Year-End Update) Report*. Bangkok.

Table 3.1: **Growth Rates of Consumer Price Index**[a]
(%)

Regional Member	2000	2005	2010	2011	2012	2013	2014	2015
Developing Member Economies								
Central and West Asia								
Afghanistan	...	11.9	−4.5	13.7	8.4	6.4	4.9	3.8
Armenia	−0.8	0.6	8.2	7.7	2.6	5.8	3.0	3.7
Azerbaijan	1.5 (2001)	8.3 (2006)	5.7	7.8	1.1	2.4	1.4	4.0
Georgia	4.6	6.2	11.2	2.0	−1.4	2.4	2.0	4.9
Kazakhstan	13.2	7.6	7.1	8.3	5.1	5.8	6.7	6.6
Kyrgyz Republic	18.7	4.3	8.0	16.6	2.8	6.6	7.5	6.5
Pakistan	3.6	9.2	10.1	13.7	11.0	7.4	8.6	4.5
Tajikistan	60.6	7.1	9.8	9.3	6.4	3.7	7.4	5.1
Turkmenistan	8.3	10.7	4.4	5.3	5.3	6.8	6.0	5.5
Uzbekistan	24.9	7.8	7.6	7.3	7.2	7.0	6.4	5.5
East Asia								
China, People's Rep. of	0.4	1.8	3.3	5.4	2.6	2.6	2.0	1.4
Hong Kong, China	−3.7	0.8	2.3	5.3	4.1	4.4	4.5	3.0
Korea, Rep. of[b]	2.3	2.8	2.9	4.0	2.2	1.3	1.3	0.7
Mongolia	6.2 (2001)	4.8 (2006)	7.6 (2009)	8.9	14.0	12.5	10.5	...
Taipei,China	1.3	2.3	1.0	1.4	1.9	0.8	1.2	−0.3
South Asia								
Bangladesh	2.8	6.5	7.3	10.9	8.7	6.8	7.3	6.4
Bhutan	4.0	5.3	7.0	8.8	10.9	8.8	8.3	4.5
India	3.7	4.2	10.4	...	9.9	9.4	5.9	4.9
Maldives	−1.2	1.3	6.2	11.3	12.5	2.3	2.1	1.0
Nepal	3.3	4.5	9.6	9.6	8.3	9.9	9.1	7.2
Sri Lanka[c]	6.2	11.0	6.2	6.7	7.5	6.9	3.2	0.9
Southeast Asia								
Brunei Darussalam	1.2	1.1	0.4	0.1	0.2	0.3	−0.2	−0.4
Cambodia[c]	−0.8	5.8	4.0	5.4	2.9	2.9	3.9	1.2
Indonesia[d]	9.3	10.5	5.1	5.4	4.3	7.0	6.4	6.4
Lao PDR	7.7 (2001)	7.2	6.0	7.6	4.3	6.4	4.1	1.3
Malaysia	1.5	2.9	1.7	3.2	1.6	2.1	3.2	2.1
Myanmar	−0.2	9.4	7.7	5.0	1.5	5.5	5.5	10.8
Philippines	6.7	6.5	3.8	4.6	3.2	3.0	4.1	1.4
Singapore	1.3	0.5	2.8	5.2	4.6	2.4	1.0	−0.5
Thailand	1.6	4.5	3.3	3.8	3.0	2.2	1.9	−0.9
Viet Nam	−1.6	8.3	10.0	18.6	9.2	6.6	4.1	0.6
The Pacific								
Cook Islands	3.2	2.5	−0.3	2.2	3.0	1.9	2.1	1.9
Fiji	1.1	2.3	3.7	7.3	3.4	2.9	0.6	1.4
Kiribati[c]	0.4	−0.3	−3.9	1.5	−3.0	−1.5	2.1	0.6
Marshall Islands[c]	0.9	3.5	1.8	5.4	4.3	1.9	1.1	−2.2
Micronesia, Fed. States of	1.8	4.1	3.7	4.1	6.3	2.2	0.7	−0.2
Nauru	2.3	9.8	−4.6	−0.8	−0.8	−2.1	...	...
Palau	−1.7 (2001)	3.9	1.4	4.7	3.6	3.4	4.2	0.9
Papua New Guinea	15.6	1.8	6.0	4.4	4.6	5.0	5.2	6.0
Samoa	0.9	1.9	0.8	5.2	2.1	0.6	−0.5	0.7
Solomon Islands[c]	7.1	7.2	1.0	7.4	5.9	5.4	5.2	−0.6
Timor-Leste	...	1.5	9.2	15.4	4.4	...	0.7	0.6
Tonga	6.3	8.7	3.6	6.3	1.1	0.8	2.5	−1.0
Tuvalu	1.5 (2001)	3.2	−1.9	0.5	1.4	2.0	1.1	3.3
Vanuatu	2.5	0.8	2.9	1.0	1.4	1.4	0.6	1.0
Developed Member Economies								
Australia	2.4	2.4	2.3	3.1	2.3	2.3	2.7	1.7
Japan	−0.7	−0.3	−0.7	−0.3	0.0	0.3	2.8	0.8
New Zealand	2.6	3.0	2.3	4.0	1.1	1.1	1.2	0.3

... = data not available at cutoff date, 0.0 = magnitude is less than half of unit employed, Lao PDR = Lao People's Democratic Republic.

a Unless otherwise indicated, data refer to the whole country.

b Data refer to all cities.

c Data refer to capital city.

d For 2000–2002, data refer to consumer price index for 43 cities; for 2003–2007, 45 cities; for 2008–2013, 66 cities; and for 2014–2015, 82 cities.

Source: Economy sources.

Table 3.2: **Growth Rates of Food Consumer Price Index**[a]
(%)

Regional Member	2000	2005	2010	2011	2012	2013	2014	2015
Developing Member Economies								
Central and West Asia								
Afghanistan	...	9.1	-9.1	13.9	7.0	5.3	9.2	4.0
Armenia	-2.2	0.7	8.6	11.2	2.3	5.8	2.2	3.0
Azerbaijan	2.7 (2001)	11.9 (2006)	7.2	10.4	0.9	2.2	1.0	6.1
Georgia	7.5	8.3	23.1	0.6	-4.1	6.3	2.7	3.6
Kazakhstan	16.0	8.1	6.2	11.9	4.5	4.3	6.6	6.4
Kyrgyz Republic	...	7.0	6.5	25.0	-4.1	5.3	8.2	3.7
Pakistan	2.2	12.5	12.9	18.0	11.0	7.1	9.0	3.3
Tajikistan	66.3	8.3	13.4	10.3	5.6	3.2	9.7	4.3
Turkmenistan	...	...	...	...	...	...	...	...
Uzbekistan	18.9	6.7	4.8	3.5	5.1	4.9	3.9	2.8
East Asia								
China, People's Rep. of	1.7	-6.4	6.5	4.3	-6.2	-0.2	-1.5	-0.7
Hong Kong, China	-2.2	1.7	2.3	7.1	5.8	4.4	4.2	3.9
Korea, Rep. of[b]	1.1	3.1	6.6	8.1	4.0	0.9	0.3	1.7
Mongolia	...	12.8 (2007)	1.7 (2009)	...	...	...	...	...
Taipei,China	0.4	7.3	0.6	2.3	4.2	1.3	3.7	3.1
South Asia								
Bangladesh	2.6	7.9	8.5	14.1	7.7	5.2	8.6	6.7
Bhutan	...	5.7	8.8	10.2	13.9	8.7	10.4	3.2
India	1.6	4.2	10.0	...	11.2	11.9	6.5	5.1
Maldives	-4.7	8.0	7.5	19.9	20.9	4.3	0.7	0.5
Nepal	0.5	4.0	15.1	14.7	7.7	9.6	11.6	9.6
Sri Lanka[c]	4.5	11.4	6.9	8.8	4.7	7.9	3.7	4.9
Southeast Asia								
Brunei Darussalam	–	0.5	1.0	-0.0	-0.0	0.1	-0.3	0.8
Cambodia[c]	-3.4	8.4	4.4	6.6	3.2	3.0	4.9	4.0
Indonesia[d]	2.7	10.0	9.4	6.9	5.7	9.3	...	7.6
Lao PDR	6.7 (2001)	7.7	7.7	10.2	5.5	12.0	6.9	4.4
Malaysia	2.1	3.7	2.5	4.8	2.7	3.6	3.4	3.6
Myanmar	-2.6	9.3	7.2	3.9	-1.5	6.0	5.9	13.2
Philippines	3.0	6.4	4.1	5.7	2.4	2.8	6.3	3.3
Singapore	0.5	1.3	1.4	3.0	2.3	2.1	2.9	1.9
Thailand	-1.1	5.0	5.3	8.0	4.9	3.4	3.9	1.1
Viet Nam	-3.9	11.3	10.7	26.5	8.1	2.7	4.0	1.5
The Pacific								
Cook Islands	3.4	1.1	2.9	2.3	3.1	2.6	3.1	0.0
Fiji	-3.2	1.7	4.1	10.6	4.3	3.5	1.9	4.7
Kiribati[c]	0.7	-4.8	-11.1	-0.8	-2.4	-0.6	...	...
Marshall Islands[c]	-0.8	0.3	-1.5	4.7	4.9	2.6	2.0	2.5
Micronesia, Fed. States of	1.1	3.4	2.2	2.6	4.5	2.6	0.8	0.5
Nauru	...	...	...	...	...	...	...	...
Palau	-2.4 (2001)	-1.5	1.8	4.8	4.4	3.2	1.5	1.7
Papua New Guinea	13.6	3.5	5.4	-1.0	-1.4	-0.9	4.9	4.8
Samoa	-0.1	0.3	-6.6	5.3	1.9	0.7	-3.4	3.4
Solomon Islands[c]	6.6	5.6	-2.6	4.8	4.4	2.6	3.1	-2.9
Timor-Leste	...	0.4	12.0	18.7	4.7	...	0.7	0.5
Tonga	0.4	6.0	3.0	6.6	1.5	1.8	3.6	-1.3
Tuvalu	5.3 (2001)	5.5	-5.9	0.8	0.2	...	...	...
Vanuatu	2.0	0.5	5.2	1.0	2.7	1.4	1.0	0.1
Developed Member Economies								
Australia	2.1	1.6	1.6	3.7	0.7	0.5	1.3	2.1
Japan	-1.9	-0.9	-0.3	-0.4	0.1	-0.1	3.8	3.1
New Zealand	1.4	1.5	1.3	4.9	-0.3	0.6	0.7	0.4

... = data not available at cutoff date, – = magnitude equals zero, 0.0 = magnitude is less than half of unit employed, Lao PDR = Lao People's Democratic Republic.

a   Coverage of food varies by economy. Unless otherwise indicated, data refer to the whole economy.
b   Refers to all cities.
c   Refers to capital city.
d   For 2000–2002, data refer to consumer price index for 43 cities; for 2003–2007, 45 cities; for 2008–2013, 66 cities; and for 2014–2015, 82 cities.

Sources: Economy sources; for the People's Republic of China: CEIC database (accessed September 2016).

Table 3.3: **Growth Rates of Nonfood Consumer Price Index**[a]
(%)

Regional Member	2000	2005	2010	2011	2012	2013	2014	2015
Developing Member Economies								
Central and West Asia								
Afghanistan	...	16.3	3.8	13.3	10.4	7.8	0.3	3.9
Armenia	3.0	0.5	9.6	3.4	4.6	4.6	1.7	5.6
Azerbaijan	0.2 (2001)	5.3 (2006)	2.3	2.6	1.0	0.8	3.2	3.8
Georgia	−0.8	3.6	5.0	1.0	−1.7	−1.6	0.7	6.4
Kazakhstan	11.5	6.3	6.4	5.4	4.3	3.1	6.9	8.1
Kyrgyz Republic	...	3.7	11.4	10.7	10.1	7.4	6.9	10.1
Pakistan	4.3	7.5	8.5	11.0	11.0	7.6	7.4	5.0
Tajikistan	44.2	2.7	5.5	7.2	6.7	6.1	2.9	7.8
Turkmenistan	...	...	...	...	...	...	...	...
Uzbekistan	36.6	6.9	5.3	8.3	4.9	5.5	7.6	6.3
East Asia								
China, People's Rep. of	...	...	...	...	...	...	...	...
Hong Kong, China	−4.1	0.5	2.2	4.6	3.4	4.3	4.6	2.6
Korea, Rep. of[b]	2.4	2.8	2.4	3.4	1.9	1.4	1.4	0.5
Mongolia	...	7.4 (2007)	12.5 (2009)	...	...	...	...	...
Taipei,China	1.6	0.5	1.1	1.1	1.1	0.6	0.3	−1.5
South Asia								
Bangladesh	3.0	4.3	5.4	4.2	10.2	9.2	5.5	6.0
Bhutan	...	5.1	6.1	8.1	9.3	8.7	6.9	5.4
India	7.2	4.6	11.2	...	8.8	7.3	5.4	4.7
Maldives	−0.2	−0.8	3.8	8.5	10.0	1.4	2.7	1.1
Nepal	6.9	5.1	4.9	5.4	9.0	10.0	6.8	5.2
Sri Lanka[c]	10.1	10.7	8.0	5.0	10.0	6.1	2.8	−2.5
Southeast Asia								
Brunei Darussalam	...	...	...	0.1	0.3	0.3	–	...
Cambodia[c]	1.2	3.9	3.8	4.5	2.7	2.0	2.7	...
Indonesia[d]	7.3	9.8	4.0	4.7	3.9	4.3	...	5.3
Lao PDR	8.8 (2001)	6.7	4.2	6.1	2.8	2.3	1.8	−1.4
Malaysia	1.3	2.7	1.4	2.5	1.3	1.6	3.0	1.2
Myanmar	...	9.4	8.8	7.3	7.4	4.6	4.8	6.3
Philippines	9.3	6.8	3.7	4.1	3.7	2.1	2.3	0.4
Singapore	1.7	0.2	3.2	5.9	5.2	2.4	0.5	−1.2
Thailand	3.2	4.3	2.1	1.3	1.9	1.5	0.8	−2.0
Viet Nam	−0.3 (2002)	5.6	9.1	13.3	8.4	4.6	2.9	−2.2
The Pacific								
Cook Islands	3.1	3.0	−1.6	2.1	2.9	1.5	1.7	2.7
Fiji	3.7	2.7	3.5	6.0	3.0	2.7	−0.3	0.3
Kiribati[c]	1.6	−1.9	2.8	4.8	−3.6	−2.3	...	...
Marshall Islands[c]	3.1	5.4	3.7	5.7	4.0	1.4	0.6	−4.9
Micronesia, Fed. States of	2.5	4.7	3.0	5.1	8.0	2.5	0.9	−0.3
Nauru	...	...	...	...	...	...	...	...
Palau	−1.6 (2001)	5.9	1.2	4.7	3.3	3.5	5.3	0.6
Papua New Guinea	17.0	0.6	6.5	7.8	8.0	8.0	5.4	6.6
Samoa	1.6	3.3	3.4	3.4	2.1	0.6	2.7	−1.8
Solomon Islands[c]	8.1	8.4	4.1	9.6	6.2	6.3	6.8	1.0
Timor-Leste	...	3.4	3.5	8.2	3.6	...	−0.1	1.5
Tonga	11.5	10.9	4.0	6.0	0.9	−0.1	2.5	−4.5
Tuvalu	2.5 (1998)	...	...	...	...	...	...	...
Vanuatu	...	...	...	...	...	...	...	...
Developed Member Economies								
Australia	0.6	2.1	2.1	2.6	2.6	2.6	2.8	1.6
Japan	−0.3	−0.1	−0.8	−0.3	−0.0	0.4	2.5	−0.0
New Zealand	2.9	3.4	2.5	3.9	1.3	1.3	1.4	0.3

... = data not available at cutoff date, – = magnitude equals zero, 0.0 = magnitude is less than half of unit employed, Lao PDR = Lao People's Democratic Republic.

a Coverage of food varies by economy. Unless otherwise indicated, data refer to the whole country.
b Refers to all cities.
c Refers to capital city.
d For 2000–2002, data refer to consumer price index for 43 cities; for 2003–2007, 45 cities; for 2008–2013, 66 cities; and for 2014–2015, 82 cities.

Sources: Economy sources; ADB estimates based on consumer price index weights from official sources.

Table 3.4: **Growth Rates of Wholesale and/or Producer Price Index**
(%)

Regional Member	2000	2005	2010	2011	2012	2013	2014	2015
Developing Member Economies								
Central and West Asia								
Afghanistan	...	...	...	...	...	...	...	...
Armenia	0.8	7.7	22.6	9.1	7.0	4.7	8.5	−0.8
Azerbaijan	3.3 (2001)	17.3	30.5	33.5	4.5	−3.9	−5.1	−30.6
Georgia	5.8	7.4	11.4	12.8	1.6	−1.9	2.8	7.4
Kazakhstan	38.0	23.7	25.2	27.2	3.5	−0.3	9.5	−20.5
Kyrgyz Republic	8.0 (1998)	...	22.8	22.0	5.3	−2.1	1.4	8.7
Pakistan	1.8	6.7	13.8	21.2	10.4	7.3	8.2	−0.3
Tajikistan	39.2	10.4	27.2	15.5	6.1	2.1	4.7	3.0
Turkmenistan	...	...	...	...	...	...	...	...
Uzbekistan	60.9	25.6	15.6	19.6	14.5	11.7	13.6	13.5
East Asia								
China, People's Rep. of	2.8	4.9	5.5	6.0	−1.7	−1.9	−1.9	−5.2
Hong Kong, China	0.2	0.8	6.0	8.3	0.1	−3.1	−1.7	−2.7
Korea, Rep. of	2.1	2.1	3.8	6.7	0.7	−1.6	−0.5	−4.0
Mongolia	...	...	...	...	...	...	...	...
Taipei,China	1.8	0.6	5.5	4.3	−1.2	−2.4	−0.6	−8.8
South Asia								
Bangladesh[a]	−0.4	3.4	...	...	...	...	...	...
Bhutan	...	...	...	...	...	...	...	...
India	7.2	4.5	9.6	8.9	7.4	6.0	2.0	−2.5
Maldives	−2.4 (2002)	4.6	3.9	...	...	0.3	2.1	−2.4
Nepal	1.4 (2001)	7.3	12.6	9.9	6.4	9.0	8.3	6.1
Sri Lanka	1.7	11.5	2.6	19.9	3.5	9.2	3.2	1.0
Southeast Asia								
Brunei Darussalam	...	...	...	...	...	...	...	...
Cambodia	...	...	...	...	...	...	...	...
Indonesia[b]	12.5	15.3	4.9	7.5	3.8	5.0	5.4	4.2
Lao PDR	...	...	...	...	...	...	...	...
Malaysia	3.1	5.8	5.6	9.6	0.1	−1.7	1.4	−4.8
Myanmar	...	...	...	...	...	...	...	...
Philippines	5.8	11.4	5.9	8.7	1.1	1.6	2.7	−3.9
Singapore	10.1	9.6	4.7	8.4	0.5	−2.7	−3.3	−15.3
Thailand	3.8	9.2	9.4	5.5	1.0	0.3	0.1	−4.1
Viet Nam	−0.2	4.4	12.6	18.4	3.4	5.2	3.3	−0.6
The Pacific								
Cook Islands	...	...	...	...	...	...	...	...
Fiji	...	...	...	...	...	...	...	...
Kiribati	...	...	...	...	...	...	...	...
Marshall Islands	...	...	...	...	...	...	...	...
Micronesia, Fed. States of	...	...	...	...	...	...	...	...
Nauru	...	...	...	...	...	...	...	...
Palau	...	...	...	...	...	...	...	...
Papua New Guinea	...	...	...	...	...	...	...	...
Samoa	...	...	...	...	...	...	...	...
Solomon Islands	...	...	...	...	...	...	...	...
Timor-Leste	...	...	...	...	...	...	...	...
Tonga	...	...	...	...	...	...	...	...
Tuvalu	...	...	...	...	...	...	...	...
Vanuatu	...	...	...	...	...	...	...	...
Developed Member Economies								
Australia	2.6	3.6	−0.1	2.8	2.0	1.2	2.1	1.0
Japan	0.0	1.6	−0.1	1.5	−0.9	1.3	1.1	−3.0
New Zealand	5.2	3.4	2.7	4.7	1.0	0.9	1.1	−1.3

... = data not available at cutoff date, 0.0 = magnitude is less than half of unit employed, Lao PDR = Lao People's Democratic Republic.

a For agricultural and industrial products only.
b Change of the wholesale price index for 2013 was estimated by rebasing January–October 2013 and 2012 data to 2005.

Source: Economy sources.

Table 3.5:   **Growth Rates of Gross Domestic Product Deflator**
(%)

Regional Member	2000	2005	2010	2011	2012	2013	2014	2015
Developing Member Economies								
Central and West Asia								
Afghanistan	9.8 (2003)	11.6	14.3	10.4	9.3	3.5	−1.1	5.0
Armenia	−1.4	3.2	7.8	4.3	5.4	3.4	2.3	1.2
Azerbaijan	12.5	16.1	13.6	22.5	2.9	−0.4	−1.3	−8.9
Georgia	8.4 (2004)	7.9	8.5	9.5	1.1	−0.8	3.8	5.8
Kazakhstan	17.4	17.9	19.6	19.1	4.7	8.9	5.6	−0.9
Kyrgyz Republic	27.2	7.1	10.0	22.5	8.7	3.2	8.4	2.2
Pakistan	2.7	7.0	10.9	19.6	6.0	7.0	6.9	3.6
Tajikistan	22.7	9.5	12.4	18.8	11.8	4.3	5.5	0.2
Turkmenistan	21.3	7.0	0.3	12.8	8.3	1.2	0.6	−4.9
Uzbekistan	47.1	21.4	16.5	16.6	15.0	14.3	12.0	8.6
East Asia								
China, People's Rep. of	2.0	3.8	6.7	8.1	2.4	2.2	0.8	...
Hong Kong, China	−3.4	−0.1	0.3	3.8	3.6	1.8	2.9	3.6
Korea, Rep. of	1.1	1.0	3.2	1.6	1.0	0.9	0.6	2.2
Mongolia	12.0	20.1	...	15.1	12.8	2.9	7.4	1.9
Taipei,China	−0.9	−1.5	−1.5	−2.3	0.5	1.5	1.7	3.0
South Asia								
Bangladesh	1.9	5.1	7.1	7.9	8.2	7.2	5.7	5.9
Bhutan	3.7	5.9	6.0	8.6	9.2	5.9	7.6	...
India	3.6	4.2	9.0	8.5	7.9	6.2	3.3	1.1
Maldives	2.1	1.4	0.9	10.6	5.5	6.0	3.0	8.5
Nepal	4.7	5.8	14.4	11.0	6.6	6.1	9.0	5.2
Sri Lanka	6.7	10.4	...	3.8	10.8	6.2	3.9	2.1
Southeast Asia								
Brunei Darussalam	29.0	18.8	5.3	20.2	1.2	−2.8	−1.9	−17.6
Cambodia	−3.1	6.1	3.1	3.4	1.3	1.0	3.1	1.2
Indonesia	9.6	14.3	8.2	7.5	3.8	5.0	5.4	4.2
Lao PDR	21.8	7.8	3.1	7.6	4.1	7.7	4.0	1.2
Malaysia	4.9	4.6	4.1	5.4	1.0	0.2	2.5	−0.4
Myanmar	2.5	19.2	7.0	10.3	3.1	4.4	4.2	3.9
Philippines	5.7	5.8	4.2	4.0	2.0	2.1	3.2	−0.6
Singapore	3.6	2.1	−0.0	1.1	0.7	−0.7	0.0	1.6
Thailand	1.3	4.8	4.7	3.7	1.9	1.6	1.0	0.3
Viet Nam	3.4	9.0	12.1	21.3	10.9	4.8	3.7	−0.2
The Pacific								
Cook Islands	2.2	−2.6	6.2	1.4	−1.7	0.0	−2.0	4.2
Fiji	−2.4	7.1	2.5	3.8	3.3	2.3	5.1	...
Kiribati	3.2	0.6	1.5	2.3	0.5	0.9	4.0	...
Marshall Islands	−3.0	2.0	1.4	3.1	3.3	0.8	−3.2	−2.6
Micronesia, Fed. States of	1.1	2.1	2.5	3.7	6.7	−0.1	3.1	−4.5
Nauru	...	1.6	−18.4	7.0	16.4	...	...	...
Palau	2.6 (2001)	8.7	−4.8	4.4	4.1	7.8	4.0	6.6
Papua New Guinea	13.1	7.9	9.2	6.5	0.1	3.3	...	...
Samoa	1.1	5.1	2.0	4.4	2.9	0.8	1.5	0.4
Solomon Islands	6.9	8.8	1.8	4.8	4.2	6.8	1.9	4.0
Timor-Leste	−40.1	9.6	27.5	26.4	11.8	−5.0	2.5	...
Tonga	7.4	6.7	3.7	5.8	2.2	0.6	1.1	−0.1
Tuvalu	5.9 (2001)	1.5	2.6	1.3	0.9	1.8	2.7	0.7
Vanuatu	2.4	0.4	2.6	3.1	0.4	2.7	2.0	...
Developed Member Economies								
Australia	2.6	3.8	1.0	6.1	2.1	−0.2	1.4	−0.6
Japan	−1.2	−1.3	−2.2	−1.9	−0.9	−0.6	1.7	2.0
New Zealand	3.0	2.1	3.7	2.1	−0.5	4.4	0.5	0.7

... = data not available at cutoff date, −0.0 or 0.0 = magnitude is less than half of unit employed, Lao PDR = Lao People's Democratic Republic.

Source: Economy sources.

Table 3.6:   **Growth Rates of Money Supply (M2)**
             (%)

Regional Member	2000	2005	2010	2011	2012	2013	2014	2015
Developing Member Economies								
Central and West Asia								
Afghanistan	31.5 (2003)	44.6	23.1	14.3	6.4	9.4	8.3	3.3
Armenia	36.5	27.7	11.8	23.7	19.5	14.8	8.3	0.1
Azerbaijan[a]	86.7	22.3	24.3	32.1	20.7	15.0	11.8	-1.3
Georgia[a]	39.6	27.9	30.1	14.5	11.4	24.5	13.8	19.3
Kazakhstan[a]	45.0	25.2	13.3	15.0	7.9	10.2	10.5	34.3
Kyrgyz Republic	12.1	9.9	21.1	14.9	23.8	22.8	3.0	14.9
Pakistan	9.4	19.8	13.0	16.8	13.4	16.6	12.8	12.7
Tajikistan	57.3	36.3	18.6	33.1	19.6	19.7	7.1	18.7
Turkmenistan[a]	94.6	5.6	74.2	52.1	32.8	21.3	12.7	16.0
Uzbekistan	37.1	54.2	52.4	32.3	29.2	22.5	15.8	17.5
East Asia								
China, People's Rep. of	12.3	16.5	19.7	17.3	14.4	13.6	11.0	13.3
Hong Kong, China	7.8	5.1	8.1	12.9	11.1	12.4	9.5	5.5
Korea, Rep. of	5.2	7.0	6.0	5.5	4.8	4.6	8.1	8.2
Mongolia	17.6	34.6	62.5	37.0	18.7	24.2	12.5	-5.5
Taipei,China	6.5	6.6	5.5	4.8	3.5	5.8	6.1	5.8
South Asia								
Bangladesh	18.6	16.7	22.4	21.3	17.4	16.7	16.1	12.4
Bhutan	16.1	10.7	30.1	20.2	-0.2	18.6	6.6	7.8
India[a]	16.8	17.0	16.1	13.5	13.6	13.4	10.9	10.5
Maldives	4.2	10.6	14.6	20.0	4.9	18.4	14.7	13.7
Nepal	21.8	8.3	14.1	28.0	22.7	16.4	19.1	19.9
Sri Lanka	12.9	19.1	18.0	20.9	18.3	18.0	13.1	17.2
Southeast Asia								
Brunei Darussalam	25.9	-4.5	4.8	10.0	0.9	2.2	2.5	-1.8
Cambodia	26.9	16.1	20.0	21.4	20.9	14.6	29.9	14.7
Indonesia	14.3	16.3	15.4	16.4	15.0	12.8	11.9	8.9
Lao PDR	45.9	8.2	39.5	28.7	31.0	17.0	25.2	14.7
Malaysia[a]	5.1	8.3	6.8	14.3	9.0	7.3	7.0	2.6
Myanmar	42.2	27.3	42.6	42.5	16.2	24.8	26.2	32.9
Philippines	4.8	16.4	10.4	7.0	9.4	33.5	10.5	9.1
Singapore	-2.0	6.2	8.6	10.0	7.2	4.3	3.3	1.5
Thailand	3.7	6.1	10.9	15.1	10.4	7.3	4.7	4.4
Viet Nam	56.2	29.7	33.3	12.1	18.5	18.8	17.7	16.2
The Pacific								
Cook Islands	4.8	-5.2	-2.8	-13.4	19.2	-25.6	3.0	9.6
Fiji[a]	-2.1	15.2	3.5	11.0	6.3	19.0	10.4	14.0
Kiribati	...	...	...	...	...	...	...	...
Marshall Islands	18.4	1.4	9.5	-1.2	-9.9	-10.1	38.7	25.6
Micronesia, Fed. States of	...	...	...	...	...	...	...	...
Nauru	...	...	...	...	...	...	...	...
Palau	...	...	...	...	...	...	...	...
Papua New Guinea[a]	5.4	29.5	11.4	16.1	11.0	6.7	3.4	8.0
Samoa	16.4	19.1	6.4	-6.1	-1.6	6.4	9.6	6.0
Solomon Islands[a]	0.4	46.1	13.3	25.8	17.4	12.4	5.5	15.0
Timor-Leste	155.5 (2001)	17.6	18.2	9.3	26.2	22.9	19.9	7.1
Tonga	8.3	12.1	5.1	2.7	-1.6	7.0	8.0	2.4
Tuvalu	...	...	...	...	...	...	...	...
Vanuatu	5.5	11.6	-6.0	1.3	-0.6	-5.6	8.5	11.4
Developed Member Economies								
Australia[a]	7.3	8.9	4.5	9.1	9.1	6.5	7.0	6.9
Japan[b]	1.9	0.4	1.9	2.6	2.2	3.4	2.8	2.5
New Zealand[a]	6.5	7.8	3.2	6.5	6.0	5.0	6.3	8.1

... = data not available at cutoff date, Lao PDR = Lao People's Democratic Republic.

a Refers to M3.
b For 2000, data refers to M2, otherwise M3.

Source: Economy sources.

Table 3.7:   **Money Supply (M2)**
(% of GDP)

Regional Member	2000	2005	2010	2011	2012	2013	2014	2015
Developing Member Economies								
Central and West Asia								
Afghanistan	11.0 (2002)	17.9	37.3	35.5	31.2	31.0	33.2	33.5
Armenia	14.7	16.3	26.3	29.8	31.6	33.9	34.7	36.9
Azerbaijan[a]	16.6	14.7	24.8	26.7	30.6	33.2	36.6	39.2
Georgia[a]	10.1	16.9	29.9	29.2	30.2	36.7	38.3	42.1
Kazakhstan[a]	15.3	27.2	38.9	33.2	32.7	31.3	31.4	42.1
Kyrgyz Republic	11.3	21.1	31.4	27.8	31.7	34.0	31.1	33.8
Pakistan	36.6	45.6	37.7	35.8	37.0	38.7	39.0	40.2
Tajikistan	8.2	15.5	18.1	19.7	19.6	21.0	19.9	22.3
Turkmenistan[a]	19.4	10.5	17.6	20.3	22.4	24.4	24.7	28.3
Uzbekistan	12.2	14.4	22.4	23.5	24.4	24.2	23.2	23.2
East Asia								
China, People's Rep. of	134.9	159.3	177.5	175.9	182.4	188.2	193.2	205.7
Hong Kong, China	272.9	310.1	401.7	416.5	439.4	470.4	487.6	484.7
Korea, Rep. of	111.4	111.1	131.2	131.4	133.3	134.4	139.8	144.2
Mongolia	21.1	37.5	48.0	48.7	45.6	49.3	47.9	43.4
Taipei,China	182.6	201.9	219.2	226.7	228.6	233.2	234.2	239.0
South Asia								
Bangladesh	31.5	40.9	45.5	48.1	49.0	50.3	52.1	52.0
Bhutan	50.8	50.9	57.6	59.1	51.4	56.4	53.0	52.2
India[a]	60.3	73.6	83.6	84.5	84.3	84.4	84.5	85.8
Maldives	41.1	47.0	53.4	53.3	51.7	55.1	57.6	59.5
Nepal	49.0	51.0	60.3	67.4	74.0	77.6	79.7	88.6
Sri Lanka	37.6	41.7	28.3	30.4	29.7	31.9	33.1	36.3
Southeast Asia								
Brunei Darussalam	93.6	57.8	67.3	59.4	58.7	63.0	67.4	80.8
Cambodia	13.0	19.5	41.4	45.4	50.5	53.3	62.7	66.5
Indonesia	53.2	43.4	36.0	36.7	38.4	39.1	39.5	39.4
Lao PDR	17.4	18.7	38.0	42.1	49.1	49.4	55.3	59.8
Malaysia[a]	128.6	123.8	132.2	136.2	139.3	142.5	140.4	137.7
Myanmar	32.7	21.6	23.6	28.9	30.3	33.4	37.5	44.7
Philippines	39.7	41.2	47.6	47.2	47.5	58.0	58.5	60.6
Singapore	103.4	103.6	125.0	128.1	131.5	132.0	132.0	129.3
Thailand	99.3	104.1	109.0	120.0	121.2	124.5	128.0	129.7
Viet Nam	50.5	75.6	129.3	112.4	114.1	122.8	131.5	143.6
The Pacific								
Cook Islands	42.0	44.0	62.6	53.0	61.4	46.3	45.8	46.0
Fiji[a]	42.4	58.9	67.6	66.9	67.6	74.1	73.9	78.9
Kiribati	...	...	...	...	...	...	...	...
Marshall Islands	64.8	69.3	81.1	76.4	64.3	55.9	80.9	103.7
Micronesia, Fed. States of	...	...	...	...	...	...	...	...
Nauru	...	...	...	...	...	...	...	...
Palau	...	...	...	...	...	...	...	...
Papua New Guinea[a]	31.2	33.6	34.1	35.9	38.3	38.1	...	...
Samoa	38.2	42.4	52.1	46.0	44.6	46.8	42.6	43.8
Solomon Islands[a]	31.7	40.5	44.0	47.2	50.1	51.0	50.5	50.7
Timor-Leste	4.5	4.1	6.9	5.4	6.0	8.9	14.4	...
Tonga	29.2	39.0	40.9	38.6	36.8	40.4	38.1	41.9
Tuvalu	...	...	...	...	...	...	...	...
Vanuatu	89.7	98.6	83.3	80.8	78.6	70.9	73.7	...
Developed Member Economies								
Australia[a]	65.4	73.6	94.8	95.1	98.2	102.3	105.2	110.6
Japan[b]	127.5	206.7	226.9	238.2	241.6	247.9	250.8	250.8
New Zealand[a]	87.8	98.7	110.5	112.2	116.3	115.3	118.2	123.1

... = data not available at cutoff date, GDP = gross domestic product, Lao PDR = Lao People's Democratic Republic.

a Refers to M3.
b For 2000, data refers to M2, otherwise M3.

Source: Economy sources.

Money and Finance

Table 3.8:   **Interest Rate on Savings and Time Deposits**
(% per annum, period averages)

Regional Member	Savings Deposits				Time Deposits[a]			
	2000	2005	2010	2015	2000	2005	2010	2015
Developing Member Economies								
Central and West Asia								
Afghanistan	...	...	...	...	...	...	...	...
Armenia	...	...	...	...	20.72	6.66	10.70	15.37
Azerbaijan[b]	...	...	...	...	10.40	9.38	10.70	8.22
Georgia	...	...	...	...	...	...	...	...
Kazakhstan	...	...	...	...	7.53	10.29	9.84	7.50
Kyrgyz Republic	...	...	...	...	28.07	9.78	11.47	10.65
Pakistan	5.75	1.24	5.02	4.69	7.37	4.21	7.21	5.88
Tajikistan[c]	5.28 (2002)	3.63	3.83	0.94	14.84 (2002)	20.16	17.78	15.57
Turkmenistan	...	...	...	...	...	...	...	...
Uzbekistan	...	...	...	...	...	...	...	...
East Asia								
China, People's Rep. of	0.99	0.72	0.36	0.35	2.25	2.25	2.33	2.06
Hong Kong, China	4.50	0.97	0.01	0.01	5.40	1.73	0.16	0.14
Korea, Rep. of	7.08	3.57	3.18	1.72	7.94	3.72	3.86	1.81
Mongolia	7.20	7.80	3.20	2.90	13.80	12.60	10.70	13.30
Taipei,China	3.50	0.55	0.24	0.31	4.98	1.77	1.03	1.32
South Asia								
Bangladesh	5.81	4.19	4.88	4.50	8.97	8.31	9.00	9.00
Bhutan[d]	6.00	4.50	4.75	5.30	9.50	6.50	6.75	6.75
India	4.00	3.50	3.50	4.00	7.10	5.32	7.50	7.80
Maldives	5.50	2.25	2.25	2.20	6.50	4.50	3.75	3.94
Nepal	5.25	3.38	7.00	2.91	6.88	3.63	8.13	6.52
Sri Lanka	8.40	5.00	5.00	5.00	15.00	9.00	8.50	7.25
Southeast Asia								
Brunei Darussalam	1.13 (2003)	1.01	0.47	0.34	1.69 (2003)	1.63	0.82	0.74
Cambodia	6.13	2.08	1.18	1.45	7.20	6.83	6.58	6.73
Indonesia	8.86	4.32	3.92	1.73	12.17	10.95	7.88	8.47
Lao PDR	...	...	...	...	...	...	...	...
Malaysia	2.72	1.41	0.94	1.06	4.24	3.70	2.81	3.31
Myanmar	...	...	...	...	...	...	...	...
Philippines[e]	7.40	3.80	1.60	0.71	10.50	6.00	2.07	3.13
Singapore	1.28	0.26	0.13	0.14	2.42	0.86	0.45	0.34
Thailand	2.50	1.88	0.50	0.47	3.50	3.00	1.55	1.40
Viet Nam	0.20	3.00	3.00	...	6.24	8.40	11.50	...
The Pacific								
Cook Islands	...	...	...	...	...	...	...	...
Fiji	...	...	...	...	...	...	...	...
Kiribati	...	...	...	...	...	...	...	...
Marshall Islands	...	...	...	...	...	...	...	...
Micronesia, Fed. States of	...	...	...	...	...	...	...	...
Nauru	...	...	...	...	...	...	...	...
Palau	...	...	...	...	...	...	...	...
Papua New Guinea	3.88	1.80	1.00	0.32 (2013)	9.38	1.30	4.80	2.02 (2013)
Samoa	3.00	2.75	0.88	1.00	7.35	6.38	2.25	2.90
Solomon Islands	...	...	...	...	...	...	...	...
Timor-Leste[c]	0.20 (2002)	0.75	0.75	0.75	- (2002)	1.28	1.33	1.01
Tonga[b, f]	3.15	3.36	1.51	2.46	4.22	5.60	3.60	2.95
Tuvalu	...	...	...	...	...	...	...	...
Vanuatu	...	...	...	...	...	...	...	...
Developed Member Economies								
Australia	5.10 (2004)	5.40	4.50	1.95	5.90	4.55	6.00	2.45
Japan[c, g]	0.09	0.01	0.04	0.02	0.24	0.03	0.10	0.06
New Zealand[b]	...	...	...	...	6.49	6.90	4.72	3.31

... = data not available at cutoff date, Lao PDR = Lao People's Democratic Republic.

a   Refers to interest rate on time deposits of over 12 months unless otherwise indicated.
b   Figures are derived simple averages of monthly rates for time deposits of 6 months.
c   For time deposits of 12 months.
d   For fixed deposits of 1 year to less than 3 years.
e   Refers to rates charged on interest-bearing deposits with maturities of over 1 year.
f   Figures refer to weighted averages.
g   Refers to time deposits from 12 months to less than 2 years. It is computed as the arithmetic average of the monthly figures.

Sources: Economy sources; for the People's Republic of China: CEIC database (accessed 10 October 2016).

Table 3.9: **Yield on Short-Term Treasury Bills and Lending Interest Rate**
(% per annum, period averages)

Regional Member	Yield on Short-Term Treasury Bills[a]				Lending Interest Rate			
	2000	2005	2010	2015	2000	2005	2010	2015
Developing Member Economies								
Central and West Asia								
Afghanistan	...	...	...	...		18.0 (2006)	15.7	15.0
Armenia	24.4	4.1	10.6	12.9	31.6	18.0	19.2	17.6
Azerbaijan	16.7	7.5	1.8	1.9 (2014)	19.7	17.0	20.7	17.5
Georgia	...	11.6	9.6	8.8	24.7	17.6	15.8	12.5
Kazakhstan	6.6	3.3	...	...	...	...	...	...
Kyrgyz Republic	70.7	6.8	11.1	13.5	51.9	26.6	23.1	24.2
Pakistan[b]	8.4	7.2	12.5	7.1	...	...	...	...
Tajikistan[c]	...	...	6.7	0.4 (2014)	25.6	23.3	23.4	25.8
Turkmenistan	...	...	...	...	...	...	...	...
Uzbekistan	...	...	...	...	...	...	...	...
East Asia								
China, People's Rep. of[d]	2.6	1.9	2.6	4.8 (2014)	5.9	5.6	5.8	4.4
Hong Kong, China	5.7	3.7	0.3	0.0	9.5	7.8	5.0	5.0
Korea, Rep. of[e]	7.1	3.6	2.7	1.8	8.5	5.6	5.5	3.5
Mongolia	...	13.7	...	...	37.0	30.6	20.1	19.6
Taipei,China[f]	...	1.3	0.3	0.4	7.7	3.8	2.7	2.8
South Asia								
Bangladesh	6.3	6.7	2.2	5.4	12.8	10.6	12.2	11.7
Bhutan[c]	7.3	3.5	2.0	0.1	16.0	14.0	14.0	13.8
India[g]	9.0	5.7	6.2	7.4	12.3	10.8	8.3	10.0
Maldives[h]	...	...	4.9	6.8	13.0	13.0	10.4	11.1
Nepal	5.3	2.2	6.8	0.5	9.5	8.1	8.0	...
Sri Lanka	14.0	9.0	8.6	6.7	16.2	10.8	10.2	7.0
Southeast Asia								
Brunei Darussalam	...	...	...	...	5.5	5.5	5.5	5.5
Cambodia	...	...	...	...	...	...	...	...
Indonesia	...	...	...	...	18.5	14.1	13.3	12.7
Lao PDR[i]	29.9	18.6	8.0	...	32.0	26.8	22.6	...
Malaysia	2.9	2.5	2.6	3.1	7.7	6.0	5.0	4.6
Myanmar	...	...	...	...	15.3	15.0	17.0	13.0
Philippines	9.9	6.1	3.5	1.7	10.9	10.2	7.7	5.6
Singapore	2.2	2.1	0.3	0.3 (2012)	5.8	5.3	5.4	5.4
Thailand[j]	...	2.7	1.4	1.6	7.8	5.8	5.9	6.6
Viet Nam[k]	5.4	6.1	11.1	4.2	10.6	11.0	13.1	7.1
The Pacific								
Cook Islands	...	...	...	...	...	...	...	...
Fiji	3.5	1.9	3.4	1.2	8.4	6.8	7.5	5.8
Kiribati	...	...	...	...	...	...	...	...
Marshall Islands	...	...	...	...	...	...	...	...
Micronesia, Fed. States of	...	...	...	...	15.3	16.4	15.1	15.9
Nauru	...	...	...	...	...	...	...	...
Palau	...	...	...	...	...	...	...	...
Papua New Guinea[l]	17.0	3.8	4.6	5.3	17.5	11.5	10.4	8.7
Samoa	...	...	...	...	11.4 (2002)	11.4	10.7	9.4
Solomon Islands	7.0	4.5	3.7	0.5	14.6	14.1	14.4	10.5
Timor-Leste	...	...	...	...	16.7 (2003)	16.7	11.0	13.5
Tonga	...	...	...	...	11.3	11.4	11.5	8.3
Tuvalu	...	...	...	...	...	...	...	...
Vanuatu	...	...	...	...	9.9	7.5	5.5	3.6
Developed Member Economies								
Australia[m]	6.0	...	4.4	3.5 (2012)	9.3	9.1	7.3	5.6
Japan	0.7	0.0	0.1	-0.0	2.1	1.7	1.6	1.2 (2014)
New Zealand[n]	6.4	6.5	2.8	3.0	7.8	7.8	6.3	5.8

... = data not available at cutoff date, 0.0 = magnitude is less than half of unit employed, Lao PDR = Lao People's Democratic Republic.

a Refers to 3-month Treasury bills, unless otherwise indicated.
b Refers to weighted average yield on 6-month Treasury securities.
c Refers to 91-day Treasury bills.
d Refers to 3-month Treasury bonds trading rate.
e Refers to 91-day certificates of deposit.
f Refers to base lending rates, but figures before 2003 are prime lending rates.
g Figures are for fiscal year ending March.

h Refers to rate on 28-day Treasury bills.
i Refers to weighted average auction rate for 6-month Treasury bills.
j Refers to government securities bills.
k Refers to average monthly yield on 360-day Treasury bills sold at auction.
l Refers to rate on 182-day Treasury bills.
m Refers to 90-day bank-accepted bills.
n Refers to financing bill rate.

Sources: International Monetary Fund. International Financial Statistics Online. http://data.imf.org/regular.aspx?key=60998122 (accessed August 2016); World Bank. World Development Indicators Online. http://data.worldbank.org/indicator/FR.INR.LEND (accessed August 2016); Organisation for Economic Co-operation and Development. Main Economic Indicators. http://dx.doi.org/10.1787/data-00043-en (accessed August 2016); economy sources.

Money and Finance

Table 3.10: **Domestic Credit Provided by Banking Sector and Bank Nonperfoming Loans**

Regional Member	Domestic Credit Provided by Banking Sector[a] (% of GDP)				Bank Nonperfoming Loans (% of total gross loans)			
	2000	2005	2010	2015	2000	2005	2010	2015
Developing Member Economies								
Central and West Asia								
Afghanistan	...	-4.8 (2006)	4.2	0.4	...	...	49.9	12.3
Armenia[b]	11.5	8.8	27.8	48.2	17.5	1.9	3.0	7.9
Azerbaijan	9.6	11.2	23.0	35.4	28.0 (2001)	7.2	4.7	4.9
Georgia[c]	21.5	21.5	33.2	52.6	11.6 (2001)	1.2	5.9	2.7
Kazakhstan[d]	12.3	39.0	45.4	44.9	11.9 (2002)	3.3	20.7	8.0
Kyrgyz Republic[e]	12.2	13.8	12.5	19.0	30.9	6.2 (2006)	15.8	7.1
Pakistan	41.6	46.5	46.2	48.8	19.5	9.0	14.7	11.4
Tajikistan[f]	17.9	13.0	7.6	20.2	...	11.3 (2006)	7.4	19.1
Turkmenistan	...	...	...	...	...	...	0.1	0.0 (2014)
Uzbekistan	...	...	...	...	...	3.0 (2006)	1.0	0.4
East Asia								
China, People's Rep. of[g]	119.0	133.6	143.6	196.9	22.4	8.6	1.1	1.5
Hong Kong, China[h]	134.0	139.8	195.4	211.5	7.3	1.4	0.8	0.7
Korea, Rep. of[i]	70.9	125.5	151.0	166.5	8.9	1.2	0.6	0.6 (2014)
Mongolia	9.0	26.6	25.9	69.3	...	...	...	...
Taipei,China	1.8	1.9	0.9	2.0 (2011)	5.3	2.2	0.6	0.2
South Asia								
Bangladesh[j]	30.2	47.7	57.4	59.7	34.9	13.2	5.8 (2011)	9.3
Bhutan	2.9	21.8	45.6	54.3	...	...	5.2	11.9
India	51.2	58.4	71.9	76.8	12.8	5.2	2.4	5.9
Maldives	34.8	48.8	85.6	80.1	...	...	20.9 (2012)	14.1
Nepal	40.8	42.2	67.4	75.1	...	...	...	...
Sri Lanka	43.7	43.6	35.4	50.5	15.0	9.6	3.8 (2011)	3.2
Southeast Asia								
Brunei Darussalam	38.6	10.4	25.1	33.4	...	...	6.9	0.4
Cambodia	6.4	7.2	22.7	53.9	...	...	3.1	1.6
Indonesia	60.7	46.2	34.2	46.7	34.4	7.3	2.5	2.4
Lao PDR	9.0	8.1	26.5	...	...	...	...	...
Malaysia[k]	138.4	117.7	123.3	144.8	15.4	9.4	3.4	1.6
Myanmar	31.2	24.6 (2004)	24.1 (2012)	32.1	...	...	...	...
Philippines[l]	58.3	47.2	49.2	59.2	24.0	10.0	3.4	1.9
Singapore[m]	76.7	61.2	80.8	121.1	3.4	3.8	1.4	0.9
Thailand	134.3	111.0	133.5	173.4	17.7	9.1	3.9	2.7
Viet Nam	32.6	65.4	124.7	128.3	...	2.2 (2008)	2.1	2.9 (2014)
The Pacific								
Cook Islands	...	...	...	...	...	...	...	...
Fiji	37.9	111.6	132.3	119.9	...	...	4.4	1.8
Kiribati	...	...	...	...	...	...	...	...
Marshall Islands	...	...	...	...	...	...	...	...
Micronesia, Fed. States of	-42.3	-24.6	-14.9	-26.2 (2014)	...	...	...	...
Nauru	...	...	...	...	...	...	...	...
Palau	...	...	...	...	...	...	...	...
Papua New Guinea	28.2	22.2	34.8	51.0 (2014)	...	...	...	...
Samoa	18.3	31.8	63.9	76.1	...	8.8 (2008)	10.9	5.3
Solomon Islands	26.5	29.4	27.2	24.3	...	...	9.3	4.1
Timor-Leste	-8.7 (2002)	-9.2	-23.7	-9.0	...	...	...	...
Tonga	38.8	48.9	40.3	29.5 (2014)	...	...	...	...
Tuvalu	...	...	...	...	...	...	...	...
Vanuatu	35.6	44.5	63.7	72.1 (2014)	...	...	...	...
Developed Member Economies								
Australia[n]	93.4	113.4	154.3	173.9	0.5	0.6	2.1	1.0
Japan[o]	304.7	320.3	332.0	376.6	5.3	1.8	2.5	1.6
New Zealand	108.0	126.4	150.7	...		0.3 (2007)	2.1	0.6

... = data not available at cutoff date, 0.0 = magnitude is less than half of unit employed, GDP = gross domestic product, Lao PDR = Lao People's Democratic Republic.

a Domestic credit provided by the banking sector as a share of GDP is a measure of banking sector depth and finance sector development in terms of size. Since the claims on the central government are a net item (claims on the central government minus central government deposits), this net figure may be negative, resulting in a negative figure of domestic credit provided by the banking sector.
b Includes loans that are overdue less than 90 days. Loans classified as loss, which are fully provisioned against, are held off-balance sheet.
c Loans with overdue principal or interest for 90 days or more.
d Beginning 2009, institutional coverage includes all banks except BTA Bank.
e Beginning 2007, loans are classified as substandard, doubtful, and loss.
f Nonperforming loans include overdue loans for 1+ days.
g Data from 2010 onward may not be strictly comparable with prior periods. For 2010, data were compiled using the cross-border, cross-sector consolidation basis for all domestically incorporated entities (CBCSDI) and from 2011 onward, the domestic consolidation (DC) basis. Basel III was introduced in 2013.
h Loans classified as substandard, doubtful, and loss; not necessarily linked to a 90-day criterion. Basel III was introduced in 2013.
i Loans classified as substandard, doubtful, and loss; not necessarily linked to a 90-day criterion.
j Basel II was implemented in 2009.
k Loans with principal and/or interest past over 180 days; credit card debt and bankers' acceptances past over 90 days; loans secured by cash and cash substitutes past 365 days. Basel III was introduced in 2013.
l Thirty days for loans payable in lump sum or payable in quarterly, semiannual, or annual installments; 90 days for loans payable in monthly installments; as soon as they are past due for loans payable in daily, weekly, or semimonthly installments. Series revised due to a new loan classification system introduced in 2009. Basel III was introduced in 2014.
m Other characteristics may be considered beyond the 90-day past due criterion to classify a loan as nonperforming. Basel III was introduced in 2013.
n Includes both impaired and past due items. Basel III was introduced in 2013.
o For nine major banks only. All data refer to the annual data ending March of the indicated calendar year.

Sources: World Bank. World Development Indicators Online. http://data.worldbank.org/ (accessed 12 August 2016); for Taipei,China: economy sources.

Table 3.11:   **Growth Rates of Stock Market Price Index**
(%)

Regional Member	2000	2005	2010	2011	2012	2013	2014	2015
Developing Member Economies								
Central and West Asia								
Afghanistan	...	...	...	...	...	...	...	...
Armenia	...	...	...	...	...	...	...	...
Azerbaijan	...	...	...	...	...	...	...	...
Georgia	...	...	...	...	...	...	...	...
Kazakhstan	...	...	...	...	...	...	...	...
Kyrgyz Republic	...	...	...	...	...	...	...	...
Pakistan	42.1	47.3	32.3	15.2	23.2	45.8	37.4	14.6
Tajikistan	...	...	...	...	...	...	...	...
Turkmenistan	...	...	...	...	...	...	...	...
Uzbekistan	...	...	...	...	...	...	...	...
East Asia								
China, People's Rep. of	37.3	-22.1	3.4	-5.7	-16.8	-1.1	1.5	66.0
Hong Kong, China	26.5	11.1	19.3	-0.3	-4.4	10.4	2.7	4.8
Korea, Rep. of	-8.7	28.5	23.6	12.6	-2.6	1.5	1.1	1.4
Mongolia	...	...	...	...	...	...	...	...
Taipei,China	5.7	1.0	23.1	2.6	-8.3	8.2	11.1	-0.4
South Asia								
Bangladesh	12.2	23.4	114.4	-10.4	-23.6	-9.8	15.0	-1.6
Bhutan	...	...	...	...	...	...	...	...
India	11.2	32.6	29.8	-2.6	-2.5	11.4	25.2	10.9
Maldives	...	51.8	-20.4	-22.9	-6.9	-5.3	-4.8	8.9
Nepal	...	...	...	...	...	...	...	...
Sri Lanka	-10.3	46.8	113.1	34.0	-22.2	10.3	12.5	6.7
Southeast Asia								
Brunei Darussalam	...	...	...	...	...	...	...	...
Cambodia	...	...	...	...	...	...	...	...
Indonesia	-9.1	35.0	53.9	21.0	10.0	11.8	7.2	-1.3
Lao PDR	...	...	...	...	...	...	...	...
Malaysia	21.4	6.4	27.1	9.7	6.5	8.7	5.5	-6.1
Myanmar	...	...	...	...	...	...	...	...
Philippines	-6.3	17.5	43.1	32.8	14.7	16.0	1.8	5.5
Singapore	5.0	16.2	27.4	0.8	0.6	7.6	1.2	-2.6
Thailand	-18.7	4.2	45.6	21.3	17.3	21.3	-0.2	0.2
Viet Nam	...	8.3	12.2	-11.1	-4.2	18.7	18.9	-0.6
The Pacific								
Cook Islands	...	...	...	...	...	...	...	...
Fiji	...	13.5	-11.7	-10.5	0.4	2.0	0.9	21.7
Kiribati	...	...	...	...	...	...	...	...
Marshall Islands	...	...	...	...	...	...	...	...
Micronesia, Fed. States of	...	...	...	...	...	...	...	...
Nauru	...	...	...	...	...	...	...	...
Palau	...	...	...	...	...	...	...	...
Papua New Guinea	...	52.5	26.2	3.2	-28.0	-15.3	-12.3	-6.3
Samoa	...	...	...	...	...	...	...	...
Solomon Islands	...	...	...	...	...	...	...	...
Timor-Leste	...	...	...	...	...	...	...	...
Tonga	...	...	...	...	...	...	...	...
Tuvalu	...	...	...	...	...	...	...	...
Vanuatu	...	...	...	...	...	...	...	...
Developed Member Economies								
Australia	1.7	17.6	-2.6	-14.5	14.6	15.1	1.1	-2.1
Japan	11.6	13.5	2.0	-7.2	-6.5	46.0	12.6	22.7
New Zealand	2.3	19.4	9.7	6.2	6.9	25.5	14.1	12.7

... = data not available at cutoff date, Lao PDR = Lao People's Democratic Republic.

Sources: International Monetary Fund. 2016. International Financial Statistics. http://elibrary-data.imf.org/ (accessed August 2016); and for Taipei,China: economy sources.

Money and Finance

Table 3.12:   **Stock Market Capitalization**[a]

Regional Member	Stock Market Capitalization ($ million)				Stock Market Capitalization (% of GDP)			
	2000	2005	2010	2015	2000	2005	2010	2015
Developing Member Economies								
Central and West Asia								
Afghanistan	...	...	...	...	...	...	...	...
Armenia	2 (2001)	43	145	132 (2012)	0.1 (2001)	0.9	1.6	1.2 (2012)
Azerbaijan	...	...	...	...	...	...	...	...
Georgia	24	355	1,060	943 (2012)	0.8	5.5	9.1	6.0 (2012)
Kazakhstan	1,289 (2002)	10,529	26,673	34,892	5.2 (2002)	18.4	18.0	18.9
Kyrgyz Republic	4	42	79	165 (2012)	0.3	1.7	1.6	2.5 (2012)
Pakistan	6,625	45,317	38,007	32,568 (2011)	9.0	41.4	21.4	15.2 (2011)
Tajikistan	...	...	...	...	...	...	...	...
Turkmenistan	...	...	...	...	...	...	...	...
Uzbekistan	32	37	715 (2006)	...	0.2	0.3	4.2 (2006)	...
East Asia								
China, People's Rep. of	512,979 (2003)	401,852	4,027,840	8,188,019	31.1 (2003)	17.7	66.7	75.4
Hong Kong, China	623,398	1,054,999	2,711,316	3,184,874	363.1	581.0	1,185.9	1,027.6
Korea, Rep. of	171,262	718,011	1,091,911	1,231,200	30.5	79.9	99.8	89.4
Mongolia	37	46	1,093	1,293 (2012)	3.2	1.8	15.2	10.5 (2012)
Taipei,China	262,295	485,825	752,335	767,898	79.1	129.3	168.6	146.8
South Asia								
Bangladesh	2,192	3,300	41,617	47,700 (2011)	4.1	4.8	36.1	37.1 (2011)
Bhutan	54	100	215	387	12.0	12.4	13.8	18.3
India	279,093 (2003)	553,074	1,631,830	1,516,217	45.1 (2003)	66.3	95.5	73.1
Maldives	...	...	...	...	...	...	...	...
Nepal	...	...	...	...	...	...	...	...
Sri Lanka	1,074	5,720	19,924	20,804	6.6	23.4	35.1	25.3
Southeast Asia								
Brunei Darussalam	...	...	...	...	...	...	...	...
Cambodia	...	...	...	...	...	...	...	...
Indonesia	26,813	81,428	360,388	353,271	16.2	28.5	47.7	41.0
Lao PDR	...	...	...	...	...	...	...	...
Malaysia	113,156	180,518	408,689	382,977	120.6	125.8	160.3	129.3
Myanmar	...	...	...	...	...	...	...	...
Philippines	25,981	39,799	157,321	238,820	32.1	38.6	78.8	81.8
Singapore	152,826	257,340	647,226	639,956	159.5	202.0	273.8	218.6
Thailand	29,217	123,885	277,732	348,798	23.1	65.4	81.5	88.2
Viet Nam	...	9,481 (2008)	30,115	51,877	...	9.6 (2008)	26.0	26.8
The Pacific								
Cook Islands	...	...	...	...	...	...	...	...
Fiji	244	587	419	452 (2012)	14.5	19.5	13.3	11.4 (2012)
Kiribati	...	...	...	...	...	...	...	...
Marshall Islands	...	...	...	...	...	...	...	...
Micronesia, Fed. States of	...	...	...	...	...	...	...	...
Nauru	...	...	...	...	...	...	...	...
Palau	...	...	...	...	...	...	...	...
Papua New Guinea	2,963 (2003)	6,138	11,027	12,592 (2011)	83.8 (2003)	126.1	113.5	97.8 (2011)
Samoa	...	...	...	...	...	...	...	...
Solomon Islands	...	...	...	...	...	...	...	...
Timor-Leste	...	...	...	...	...	...	...	...
Tonga	...	...	...	...	...	...	...	...
Tuvalu	...	...	...	...	...	...	...	...
Vanuatu	...	...	...	...	...	...	...	...
Developed Member Economies								
Australia	372,794	804,015	1,454,491	1,187,083	89.8	116.0	127.3	88.6
Japan	3,157,222	4,572,901	3,827,774	4,894,919	66.7	100.0	69.6	118.7
New Zealand	18,613	40,592	52,870 (2012)	74,351	35.4	35.4	29.9 (2012)	42.8

... = data not available at cutoff date, GDP = gross domestic product, Lao PDR = Lao People's Democratic Republic.

a   Stock market data were previously sourced from Standard & Poor's (S&P) until they discontinued their Global Stock Markets Factbook and database in April 2013. Time series were replaced in December 2015 with data from the World Federation of Exchanges and may differ from the previous S&P definitions and methodology.

Sources: World Bank. World Development Indicators Online. http://databank.worldbank.org/data (accessed 13 August 2016); ADB estimates using data from economy sources for Bhutan and Taipei,China.

Table 3.13: **Official Exchange Rate**

(local currency units per $, period averages)

Regional Member	2000	2005	2010	2011	2012	2013	2014	2015
Developing Member Economies								
Central and West Asia								
Afghanistan	47.36	49.49	46.45	46.75	50.92	55.38	57.25	61.14
Armenia	539.53	457.69	373.66	372.50	401.76	409.63	415.92	477.92
Azerbaijan	0.89	0.95	0.80	0.79	0.79	0.78	0.78	1.02
Georgia	1.98	1.81	1.78	1.69	1.65	1.66	1.77	2.27
Kazakhstan	142.13	132.88	147.36	146.62	149.11	152.13	179.19	221.73
Kyrgyz Republic	47.70	41.01	45.96	46.14	47.00	48.44	53.65	64.46
Pakistan	53.65	59.51	85.19	86.34	93.40	101.63	101.10	102.77
Tajikistan	2.08	3.12	4.38	4.61	4.74	4.76	4.94	6.16
Turkmenistan	1.04	1.26	2.85	2.85	2.85	2.85	2.85	3.50
Uzbekistan	236.61	1,106.10	1,578.42	1,706.61	1,897.56	2,097.20	2,319.55	2,583.54
East Asia								
China, People's Rep. of	8.28	8.19	6.77	6.46	6.31	6.20	6.14	6.23
Hong Kong, China	7.79	7.78	7.77	7.78	7.76	7.76	7.75	7.75
Korea, Rep. of	1,130.96	1,024.12	1,156.06	1,108.29	1,126.47	1,094.85	1,052.96	1,131.16
Mongolia	1,076.67	1,205.25	1,357.06	1,265.52	1,357.58	1,523.93	1,817.94	1,970.31
Taipei,China	31.23	32.17	31.64	29.46	29.61	29.77	30.37	31.90
South Asia								
Bangladesh	52.14	64.33	69.65	74.15	81.86	78.10	77.64	77.95
Bhutan	44.94	44.10	45.73	46.67	53.44	58.60	61.03	64.15
India	44.94	44.10	45.73	46.67	53.44	58.60	61.03	64.15
Maldives	11.77	12.80	12.80	14.60	15.36	15.37	15.38	15.37
Nepal	71.09	71.37	73.26	74.02	85.20	92.99	99.53	102.64
Sri Lanka	77.01	100.50	113.06	110.57	127.60	129.07	130.56	135.86
Southeast Asia								
Brunei Darussalam	1.72	1.66	1.36	1.26	1.25	1.25	1.27	1.37
Cambodia	3,840.75	4,092.50	4,184.92	4,058.50	4,033.00	4,027.25	4,037.50	4,067.75
Indonesia	8,421.78	9,704.74	9,090.43	8,770.43	9,386.63	10,461.24	11,865.21	13,389.41
Lao PDR[a]	7,887.64	10,655.17	8,258.77	8,030.06	8,007.76	7,860.14	8,048.96	8,147.91
Malaysia	3.80	3.79	3.22	3.06	3.09	3.15	3.27	3.91
Myanmar[b]	6.52	5.82	5.63	5.44	640.65	933.57	984.35	1,162.62
Philippines	44.19	55.09	45.11	43.31	42.23	42.45	44.40	45.50
Singapore	1.72	1.66	1.36	1.26	1.25	1.25	1.27	1.37
Thailand	40.11	40.22	31.69	30.49	31.08	30.73	32.48	34.25
Viet Nam	14,167.75	15,858.92	18,612.92	20,509.75	20,828.00	20,933.42	21,148.00	21,698.80
The Pacific								
Cook Islands	2.20	1.42	1.39	1.27	1.23	1.22	1.21	1.43
Fiji	2.13	1.69	1.92	1.79	1.79	1.84	1.89	2.10
Kiribati	1.72	1.31	1.09	0.97	0.97	1.04	1.11	1.33
Marshall Islands[c]	1.00	1.00	1.00	1.00	1.00	1.00	1.00	1.00
Micronesia, Fed. States of[c]	1.00	1.00	1.00	1.00	1.00	1.00	1.00	1.00
Nauru	1.72	1.31	1.09	0.97	0.97	1.04	1.11	1.33
Palau[c]	1.00	1.00	1.00	1.00	1.00	1.00	1.00	1.00
Papua New Guinea	2.78	3.10	2.72	2.37	2.08	2.24	2.46	2.77
Samoa	3.29	2.71	2.48	2.32	2.29	2.31	2.33	2.56
Solomon Islands	5.09	7.53	8.06	7.64	7.36	7.30	7.38	7.91
Timor-Leste[c]	1.00	1.00	1.00	1.00	1.00	1.00	1.00	1.00
Tonga	1.76	1.94	1.91	1.73	1.72	1.77	1.85	2.11
Tuvalu	1.72	1.31	1.09	0.97	0.97	1.04	1.11	1.33
Vanuatu	137.64	109.25	96.91	89.47	92.64	94.54	97.07	108.99
Developed Member Economies								
Australia	1.72	1.31	1.09	0.97	0.97	1.04	1.11	1.33
Japan	107.77	110.22	87.78	79.81	79.79	97.60	105.94	121.04
New Zealand	2.20	1.42	1.39	1.27	1.23	1.22	1.21	1.43

... = data not available at cutoff date, Lao PDR = Lao People's Democratic Republic.

a Simple averages of midpoint rates reported daily.
b Beginning 1 April 2012, the Central Bank of Myanmar adopted the managed float exchange rate regime for kyat vis-à-vis the US dollar.
c Unit of currency is the US dollar.

Sources: International Monetary Fund. May 2016. *International Financial Statistics* (CD-ROM). Washington, DC; for Turkmenistan: United Nations National Accounts Main Aggregates Database and Interstate Statistical Committee of the Commonwealth of Independent States; for Uzbekistan: economy source, United Nations National Accounts Main Aggregates Database, and Interstate Statistical Committee of the Commonwealth of Independent States; for Taipei,China: economy source.

Table 3.14: **Purchasing Power Parity Conversion Factor**[a]
(local currency units per $, period averages)

Regional Member	2000	2005	2010	2011	2012	2013	2014	2015
Developing Member Economies								
Central and West Asia								
Afghanistan	9.89 (2002)	12.16	16.04	17.36	18.62	18.97	18.46	19.20
Armenia	144.93	157.74	183.12	187.10	193.53	196.84	198.92	199.28
Azerbaijan	0.17	0.21	0.30	0.36	0.36	0.36	0.35	0.32
Georgia	0.53	0.63	0.80	0.86	0.85	0.83	0.85	0.89
Kazakhstan	21.25	33.72	65.13	80.17	82.47	88.35	91.76	90.04
Kyrgyz Republic	8.11	9.26	14.80	17.76	18.94	19.23	20.51	20.75
Pakistan	10.73	12.72	20.77	24.35	25.33	26.66	28.05	28.76
Tajikistan	0.29	0.66	1.49	1.74	1.91	1.96	2.03	2.02
Turkmenistan	...	...	...	...	...	...	...	...
Uzbekistan	67.42	225.59	532.69	600.58	678.02	759.92	848.62	913.15
East Asia								
China, People's Rep. of	2.71	2.82	3.31	3.51	3.52	3.55	3.52	3.47
Hong Kong, China	7.44	5.69	5.37	5.46	5.55	5.57	5.63	5.80
Korea, Rep. of	747.23	788.92	840.57	854.59	854.89	871.41	881.93	891.25
Mongolia	138.38	223.58	476.22	537.13	594.84	602.32	636.72	642.31
Taipei,China	21.54	18.38	15.79	15.11	14.92	14.90	14.90	15.20
South Asia								
Bangladesh	15.68	17.33	21.90	23.15	24.58	25.92	26.95	28.25
Bhutan	12.27	13.66	15.84	16.86	18.07	18.82	19.92	20.11
India	10.34	11.28	14.65	15.11	16.00	16.72	17.00	17.00
Maldives	6.83 (2001)	6.28	7.87	8.53	8.84	9.22	9.34	9.34
Nepal	13.32	15.51	22.65	24.63	25.77	26.90	28.85	30.05
Sri Lanka	15.24	21.79	38.00	38.65	42.06	43.97	44.93	45.44
Southeast Asia								
Brunei Darussalam	0.53	0.65	0.61	0.72	0.70	0.67	0.73	0.71
Cambodia	1,062.55	1,106.83	1,330.18	1,347.11	1,340.92	1,349.07	1,349.60	1,353.09
Indonesia	1,427.63	2,013.80	3,425.30	3,606.57	3,674.27	3,794.87	3,934.67	4,060.46
Lao PDR	1,372.34	1,929.15	2,426.42	2,467.75	2,527.46	2,691.26	2,639.72	2,601.83
Malaysia	1.19	1.28	1.41	1.46	1.45	1.43	1.44	1.42
Myanmar [b]	...	...	217.43	234.97	237.95	244.38	250.46	257.75
Philippines	13.71	15.47	17.52	17.85	17.88	17.96	18.23	17.93
Singapore	1.00	0.90	0.90	0.89	0.88	0.86	0.85	0.85
Thailand	11.06	11.34	12.17	12.37	12.38	12.39	12.31	12.22
Viet Nam	2,923.18	3,575.10	5,647.10	6,709.19	7,307.63	7,532.73	7,682.41	7,591.67
The Pacific								
Cook Islands	...	...	...	...	...	...	...	...
Fiji	0.79	0.88	0.92	1.04	1.06	1.07	1.09	1.12
Kiribati	0.98	0.96	0.99	0.96	0.93	0.92	0.92	0.93
Marshall Islands	...	...	...	...	...	...	...	...
Micronesia, Fed. States of	0.86	0.80	0.87	0.88	0.90	0.89	0.91	...
Nauru	...	...	...	1.00	...	...	...	...
Palau	0.72	0.74	0.74	0.75	0.76	0.82	0.85	0.88
Papua New Guinea	1.23	1.53	1.82	1.86	1.77	1.78	1.95	...
Samoa	1.43	1.48	1.66	1.66	1.70	1.70	1.67	1.70
Solomon Islands	3.91	4.66	5.87	6.37	6.66	6.53	6.98	7.18
Timor-Leste	0.39	0.41	0.47	0.52	0.54	0.53	0.51	0.50
Tonga	0.93	1.12	1.40	1.45	1.46	1.44	1.45	...
Tuvalu	1.04	1.11	1.12	1.11	1.10	1.10	1.12	...
Vanuatu	90.42	88.70	99.50	100.51	99.10	100.10	100.47	...
Developed Member Economies								
Australia	1.31	1.39	1.50	1.51	1.54	1.45	1.47	1.49
Japan	154.97	129.55	111.63	107.45	104.27	102.74	104.72	105.33
New Zealand	1.44	1.54	1.50	1.49	1.50	1.41	1.42	1.47

... = data not available at cutoff date, Lao PDR = Lao People's Democratic Republic.

a Purchasing power parity (PPP) figures are extrapolated from the 2011 International Comparison Program (ICP) benchmark estimates or imputed using a statistical model based on the 2011 ICP.
b Gross domestic product (GDP) deflators were smoothened by applying the implied inflation for each reference or base year using the 2005 level as the base. The smoothened series of the GDP deflator was used to extrapolate PPP for the other years.

Sources: World Bank. World Development Indicators Online. http://databank.worldbank.org/data/home.aspx (accessed 25 July 2016); ADB estimates using data from economy sources for Afghanistan; Myanmar; Nepal; Pakistan; Taipei,China; and Tajikistan; CEIC data; and US Bureau of Economic Analysis.

Table 3.15: **Price Level Indexes**
(PPPs to official exchange rates, period averages, United States = 100)

Regional Member	2000	2005	2010	2011	2012	2013	2014	2015
Developing Member Economies								
Central and West Asia								
Afghanistan	20.35 (2002)	24.57	34.54	37.13	36.57	34.26	32.25	31.40
Armenia	26.86	34.46	49.01	50.23	48.17	48.05	47.83	41.70
Azerbaijan	18.54	22.02	37.39	45.64	45.69	45.48	44.85	30.98
Georgia	26.72	35.01	44.93	50.92	51.62	50.03	48.13	39.22
Kazakhstan	14.95	25.38	44.20	54.68	55.31	58.08	51.21	40.61
Kyrgyz Republic	17.01	22.58	32.19	38.48	40.30	39.71	38.23	32.20
Pakistan	20.01	21.37	24.38	28.20	27.12	26.23	27.75	27.99
Tajikistan	13.96	21.04	34.12	37.73	40.31	41.14	41.21	32.75
Turkmenistan	...	...	...	...	...	...	...	...
Uzbekistan	28.49	20.39	33.75	35.19	35.73	36.23	36.59	35.34
East Asia								
China, People's Rep. of	32.74	34.43	48.87	54.25	55.83	57.22	57.24	55.66
Hong Kong, China	95.53	73.14	69.06	70.16	71.59	71.76	72.66	74.79
Korea, Rep. of	66.07	77.03	72.71	77.11	75.89	79.59	83.76	78.79
Mongolia	12.85	18.55	35.09	42.44	43.82	39.52	35.02	32.60
Taipei,China	68.97	57.14	49.92	51.29	50.38	50.04	49.08	47.65
South Asia								
Bangladesh	30.07	26.94	31.45	31.21	30.03	33.19	34.71	36.24
Bhutan	27.30	30.97	34.64	36.12	33.82	32.12	32.64	31.35
India	23.01	25.58	32.05	32.37	29.94	28.54	27.85	26.49
Maldives	55.73 (2001)	49.06	61.45	58.39	57.51	59.99	60.76	60.78
Nepal	18.74	21.73	30.92	33.27	30.24	28.92	28.98	29.28
Sri Lanka	19.80	21.68	33.61	34.96	32.97	34.07	34.41	33.45
Southeast Asia								
Brunei Darussalam	30.64	39.10	44.62	57.04	56.35	53.63	57.36	51.69
Cambodia	27.67	27.05	31.79	33.19	33.25	33.50	33.43	33.26
Indonesia	16.95	20.75	37.68	41.12	39.14	36.28	33.16	30.33
Lao PDR	17.40	18.11	29.38	30.73	31.56	34.24	32.80	31.93
Malaysia	31.29	33.82	43.86	47.69	46.85	45.27	43.94	36.32
Myanmar[a]	...	...	36.07	40.34	37.14	26.18	25.44	22.17
Philippines	31.03	28.08	38.83	41.22	42.33	42.30	41.07	39.40
Singapore	58.13	54.20	66.00	70.88	70.56	68.85	66.93	62.07
Thailand	27.56	28.20	38.41	40.57	39.82	40.32	37.89	35.67
Viet Nam	20.63	22.54	30.34	32.71	35.09	35.98	36.33	34.99
The Pacific								
Cook Islands	...	...	...	...	...	...	...	...
Fiji	37.04	52.23	47.86	58.13	59.18	58.31	57.93	53.20
Kiribati	57.02	73.54	90.84	99.19	96.23	88.78	83.14	69.51
Marshall Islands	...	...	...	...	...	...	...	...
Micronesia, Fed. States of	86.48	80.03	86.81	87.93	90.16	89.13	91.46	...
Nauru	...	...	...	...	...	...	...	...
Palau	72.08	73.67	73.86	74.92	76.39	82.25	85.16	88.31
Papua New Guinea	44.23	49.20	66.85	78.41	85.16	79.51	79.16	...
Samoa	43.43	54.47	66.67	71.65	73.95	73.42	71.80	66.50
Solomon Islands	76.93	61.84	72.85	83.43	90.51	89.37	94.67	90.67
Timor-Leste	38.79	40.66	47.41	51.68	54.29	52.95	51.33	50.22
Tonga	52.75	57.50	73.33	84.02	85.03	81.39	78.66	...
Tuvalu	60.07	84.47	102.59	114.49	113.83	106.25	101.27	...
Vanuatu	65.69	81.19	102.68	112.34	106.98	105.88	103.50	...
Developed Member Economies								
Australia	75.83	106.02	137.85	155.87	159.47	139.98	132.52	111.75
Japan	143.80	117.54	127.17	134.64	130.68	105.27	98.84	87.02
New Zealand	65.60	108.08	107.74	117.39	121.17	115.72	117.68	102.23

... = data not available at cutoff date, Lao PDR = Lao People's Democratic Republic, PPP = purchasing power parity.

a   The Central Bank of Myanmar devalued the local currency effective 1 April in 2012. To achieve a consistent price series, the exchange rate used for estimating the price level index in prior years was extrapolated using the pre-devaluation exchange rate series.

Sources: ADB estimates using economy sources, CEIC, US Bureau of Economic Analysis, and World Bank data.

Globalization

Snapshots

- Asia and the Pacific remains the largest foreign direct investment recipient region in the world.
- Asia and the Pacific trails only Europe among all regions as the world's export leader, accounting for nearly a third of global exports.
- Growth in remittances to developing member economies in US dollar terms fell from 4.6% in 2014 to 0.8% in 2015.
- Total external debt of developing member economies in Asia and the Pacific increased from approximately $1.1 trillion in 2000 to $4.5 trillion based on latest data.
- Total international tourist arrivals increased by more than 150% in member economies in Asia and the Pacific between 2000 and 2015.

Key Trends

Asia and the Pacific remains the largest foreign direct investment (FDI) recipient region in the world. Global FDI flows increased to $1.76 trillion in 2015, representing a 38% annual increase according to the latest World Investment Report published by the United Nations Conference on Trade and Development (UNCTAD). This is the highest level of FDI since the 2008–2009 global financial crisis, and the pick-up in cross-border mergers and acquisitions has been identified as the principal factor driving these trends.

Among the regions in the world, Asia and the Pacific has the highest share of total FDI flows. For instance, in developing Asia alone, FDI inflows surpassed $0.5 trillion in 2015 (UNCTAD 2016). The People's Republic of China (PRC); Hong Kong, China; and Singapore, which were the three largest recipients of FDI inflows in the region, were among the list of the 10 economies with the largest FDI inflows around the world, occupying the second, third, and eighth spots, respectively (Figure 4.1). The surging levels of FDI in Hong Kong, China were due to increased equity investment, which resulted in part from the major corporate restructuring of two of its

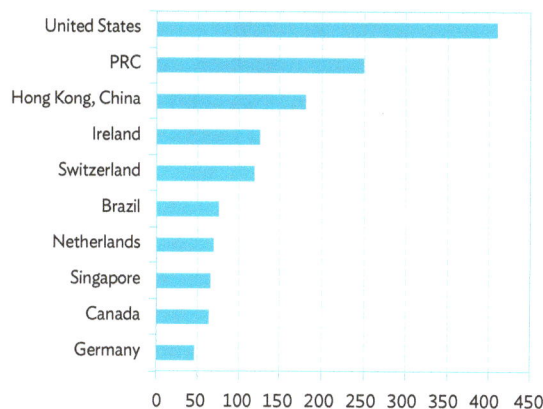

Figure 4.1: Top 10 Economies in Terms of Net Inflows of Foreign Direct Investments, 2015
($ billion)

PRC = People's Republic of China.
Source: World Bank. World Development Indicators Online. 2016.
http://data.worldbank.org/indicator/BX.KLT.DINV.CD.WD
(accessed October 2016).

largest conglomerates (UNCTAD 2016). They were closely followed by India, Australia, and Association of Southeast Asian Nations (ASEAN) member states (Figure 4.2). Sustained gross domestic product (GDP) growth in ASEAN is reflected in and fueled by relatively high levels of FDI, much of it coming from

Figure 4.2: Top 10 Economies in Asia and the Pacific in Terms of Net Inflows of Foreign Direct Investments, 2015
($ billion)

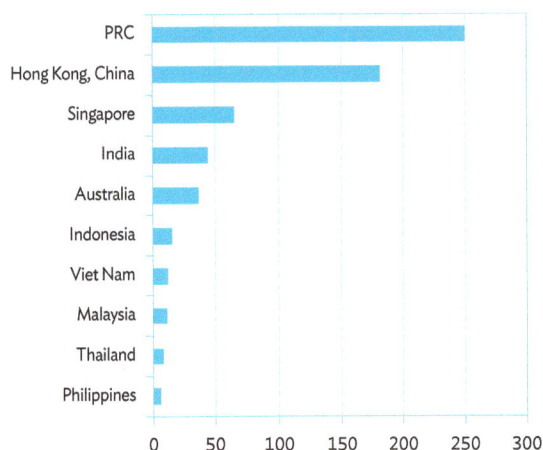

PRC = People's Republic of China.
Source: Table 4.6.

Figure 4.3: Net Inflows of Foreign Direct Investment
(% of GDP)

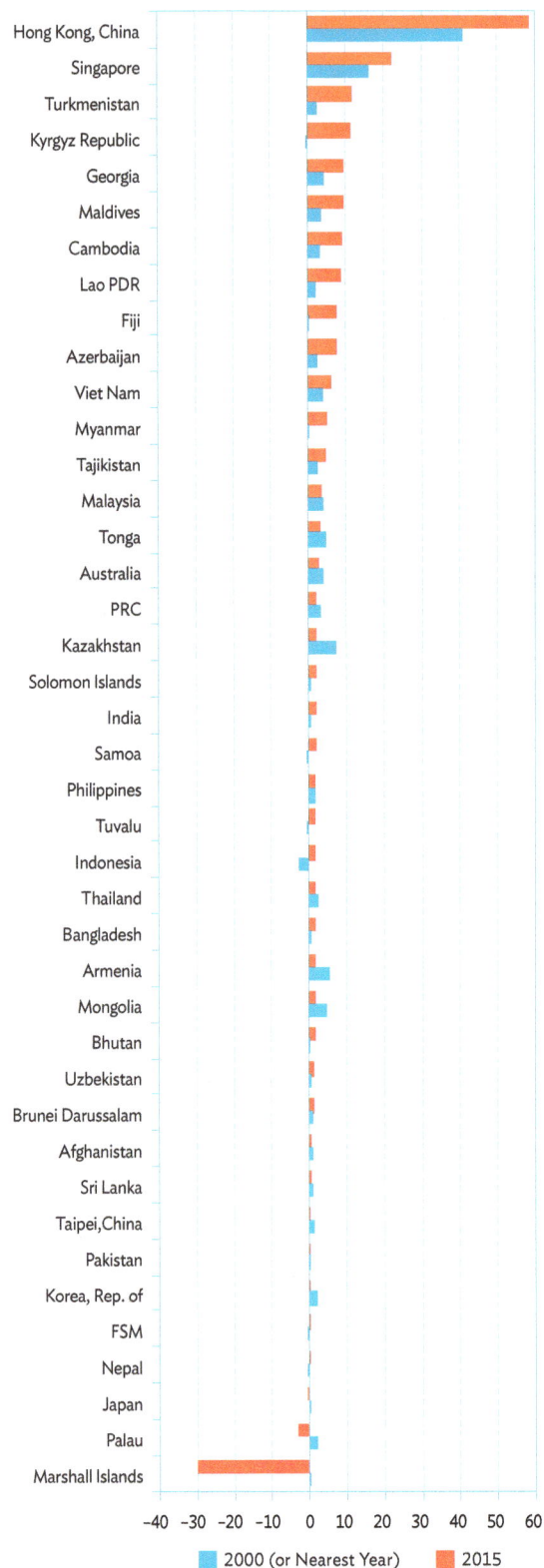

■ 2000 (or Nearest Year)   ■ 2015

FSM = Federated States of Micronesia, GDP = gross domestic product, Lao PDR = Lao People's Democratic Republic, PRC = People's Republic of China.
Source: Table 4.7.

the PRC and Japan (Vanham 2015). Interestingly, low-income economies in ASEAN have performed particularly well in terms of FDI in recent years. For example, FDI in Viet Nam continues to grow rapidly as multinational firms expand their electronics production facilities (ADB 2016).

In proportion to their respective gross domestic product (GDP), the six regional economies in 2015 with the highest levels of FDI were Hong Kong, China; Singapore; Turkmenistan; the Kyrgyz Republic; Georgia; and the Maldives (Figure 4.3). The placement of Singapore and Hong Kong, China atop this list is not surprising given their high levels of FDI in absolute terms.

Despite Asia's high levels of FDI in 2015 and taking into account the global and regional economic slowdown, UNCTAD predicts that FDI inflows to the region will decline by about 15% in 2016 (ADB 2016).

Asia and the Pacific trails only Europe among all regions as the world's export leader. Global trade declined sharply in the first half of 2015 before gradually picking up. For instance, preliminary estimates suggest that growth of global merchandise imports slowed from 3.0% in 2014 to 1.7% in 2015 (Constantinescu, Mattoo, and Ruta 2016).

Despite the sluggish trade growth in most regions in 2015, Asia and the Pacific still accounts for a significant share of global trade. For instance, the region had the second-highest regional share of the world's exports in 2015, accounting for 32.2%; Europe tops the list with 35.5% share (Figure 4.4). Within the region, the PRC is considered the largest exporter, accounting for 38.4% of the region's total exports, followed by Japan (10.5%) and the Republic of Korea (9.0%).

Overall, global trade growth has decelerated since the early 2000s, particularly since the 2008–2009 global financial crisis (Constantinescu, Mattoo, and Ruta 2016). Between 2000 and 2015, amid this secular trend of slowing global trade growth, Asia and the Pacific's share of global merchandise exports jumped from 23.0% to 32.2% (Table 4.13).

Growth in remittances to developing member economies in US dollar terms fell from 4.6% in 2014 to 0.8% in 2015. The slower growth rate in remittances in 2015 was mainly due to weakness in the global economy, low oil prices (which can dampen labor demand in the Middle East), the closure of money transfer operator accounts in accordance with anti-money-laundering laws, and depreciating currencies in remittance-source countries such as the Russian Federation (Global Knowledge Partnership on Migration and Development 2016).

Figure 4.4: Shares in Total World Exports, Regions of the World; and Major Exporters in the Asia and Pacific Region, 2015
(%)

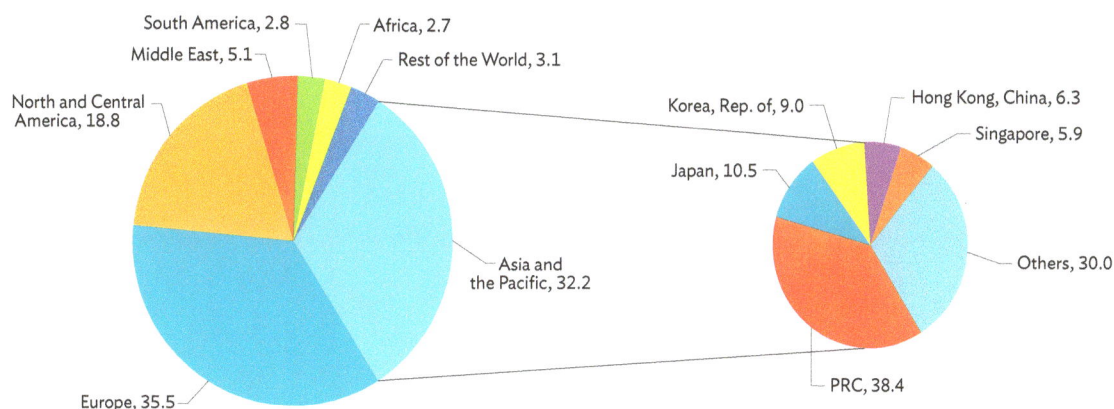

PRC = People's Republic of China.
Sources: International Monetary Fund. May 2016. *Direction of Trade Statistics* (CD-ROM). Washington, DC.; Table 4.13.

The aggregate level of remittances in Asia and the Pacific has increased significantly from about $39 billion in 2000 to more than $272 billion in 2015 (Table 4.4). India and the PRC were the two economies receiving the most remittances in the region in 2015 (Figure 4.5). The Philippines, with a much smaller population and GDP than either India or the PRC, received the third-largest amount of remittances in the region in 2015, followed by Pakistan and Bangladesh. In 2000, India was the largest recipient while the Philippines was the second-largest. The PRC barely registered among the top recipients of remittances in 2000.

In 2015, a number of the smaller economies in Central Asia—including Armenia, the Kyrgyz Republic, and Tajikistan—as well as Nepal, Samoa, and Tonga had the highest levels of remittances as a share of GDP (Table 4.5).

Total external debt of developing member economies in Asia and the Pacific increased from approximately $1.1 trillion in 2000 to $4.5 trillion based on latest data. Table 4.19 presents the estimates of external debt for developing member economies in Asia and the Pacific since 2000. Out of 40 reporting economies, external debt (in nominal terms) doubled in 28 economies since 2000. The largest percentage increase was noted in Mongolia, Kazakhstan, and Papua New Guinea, while modest increase was noted in Solomon Islands, Myanmar, and Palau. The Marshall Islands and Turkmenistan experienced declining external debt since 2000.

Figure 4.6 identifies six economies of Asia and the Pacific with the highest external debt as share of gross national income. Based on latest data, external debt in Hong Kong, China reached 414.8%, followed by Mongolia (186.2%), Papua New Guinea (147.6%), Bhutan (105.1%), the Kyrgyz Republic (101.1%), and the Lao People's Democratic Republic (95.9%). Table 4.20 presents the estimates for other developing member economies in the region.

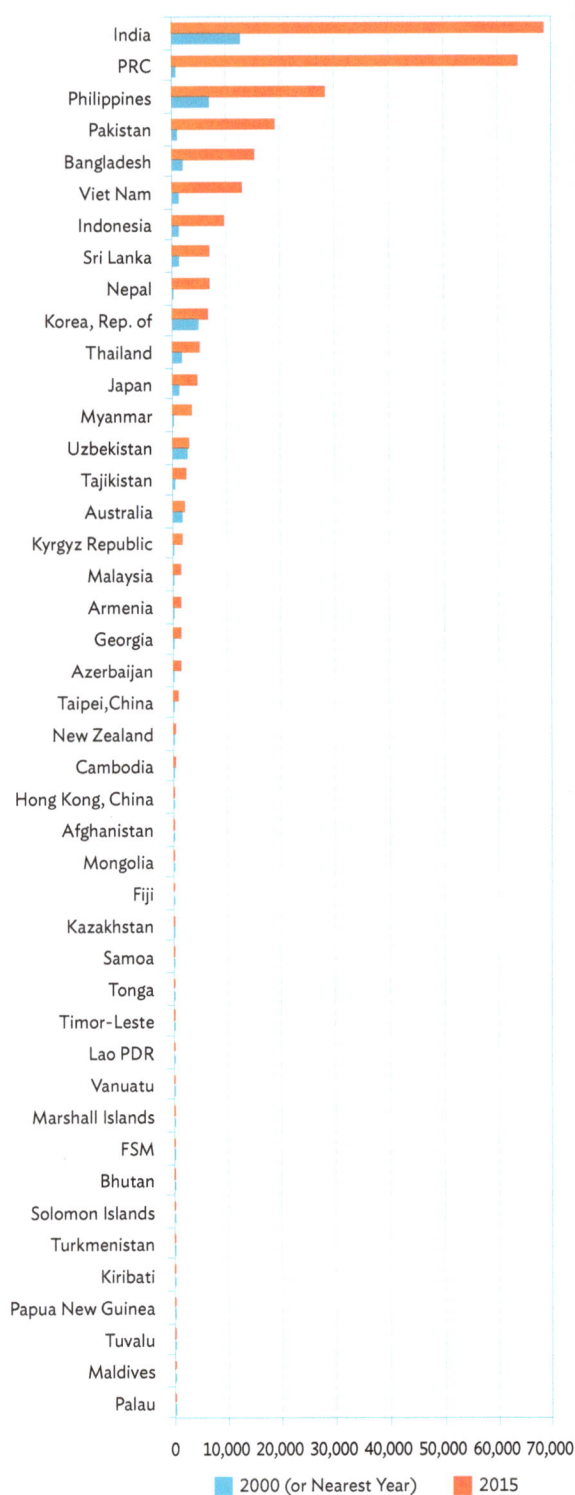

Figure 4.5: Worker's Remittances and Compensation of Employees Receipts
($ million)

FSM = Federated States of Micronesia, Lao PDR = Lao People's Democratic Republic, PRC = People's Republic of China.
Source: Table 4.4.

Figure 4.6: External Debt as Share of Gross National Income in Selected Economies
(%)

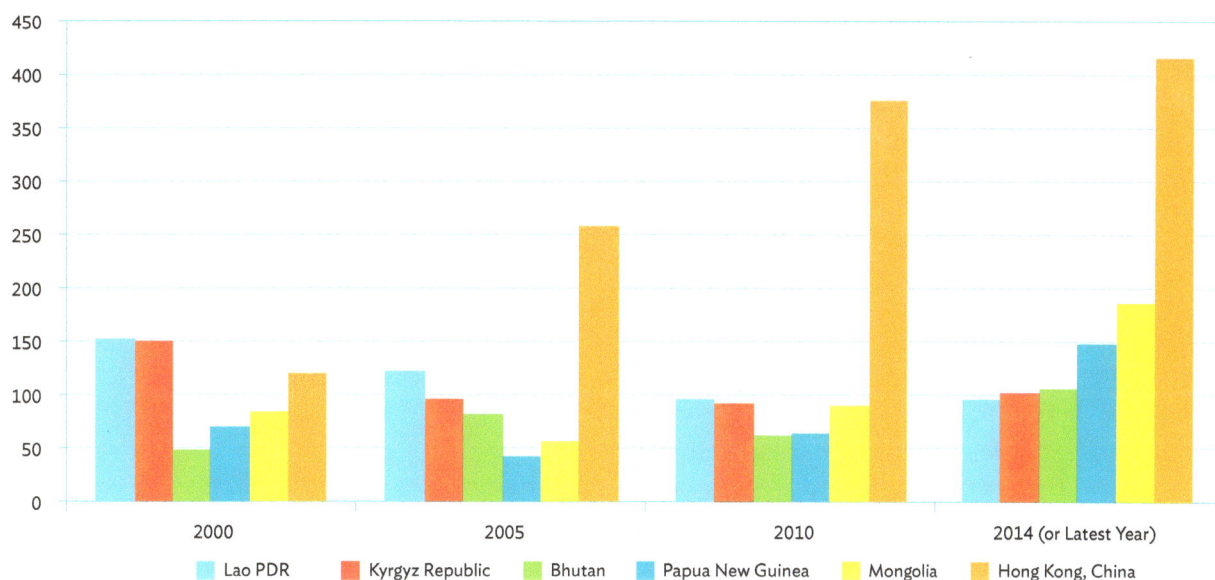

Lao PDR = Lao People's Democratic Republic.
Note: Latest year is 2015 for Hong Kong, China and 2013 for Papua New Guinea.
Source: Table 4.20.

Lending in the PRC drives much of Hong Kong, China's external debt. According to the Hong Kong Monetary Authority, state-owned enterprises account for more than 40% of lending made by Hong Kong, China banks in the PRC. A number of defaults on bond payments by state-owned enterprises in 2016 suggest that credit risks have risen for these banks exposed to lending in the PRC (DBS Group Research).

Total international tourist arrivals increased by more than 150% in Asia and the Pacific between 2000 and 2015. As international tourist arrivals surged across the region between 2000 and 2015, the PRC remained the region's top tourist destination in 2015 by a wide margin with 56.9 million such arrivals, up from 31.2 million in 2000 (Figure 4.7). Thailand was the second-most popular destination in 2015 with 29.8 million arrivals, up from 9.6 million (and the third spot) in 2000.

The three largest percentage increases in tourist arrivals between 2000 and 2015, or the latest year for which data are available, occurred in Central Asia (Armenia, the Kyrgyz Republic, and Tajikistan). All three countries experienced significant percentage gains in international tourist arrivals during the review period from a very low base. The next largest increase in international tourist arrivals in percentage terms between 2000 and 2015 was in Myanmar where a series of political, economic, and administrative reforms launched by the government in 2011 have resulted in expanded tourism (ADB 2016).

India enjoyed the highest average receipts per international tourist arrival in 2015 at $2,618. India was followed by Solomon Islands ($2,136) and the Maldives ($2,080) in terms of the highest average receipts per international tourist arrival in 2015, a figure that is tied to average length of stay, among other factors (Figure 4.8). Of the 22 economies for which data are available, 15 saw an increase between 2000 and 2015 in average tourism receipts per international arrival. In dollar terms, the PRC enjoyed the largest gain in average international tourism receipts per tourist arrival during the review period at $1,486, while Bhutan experienced the largest decline at $792 per international tourist arrival.

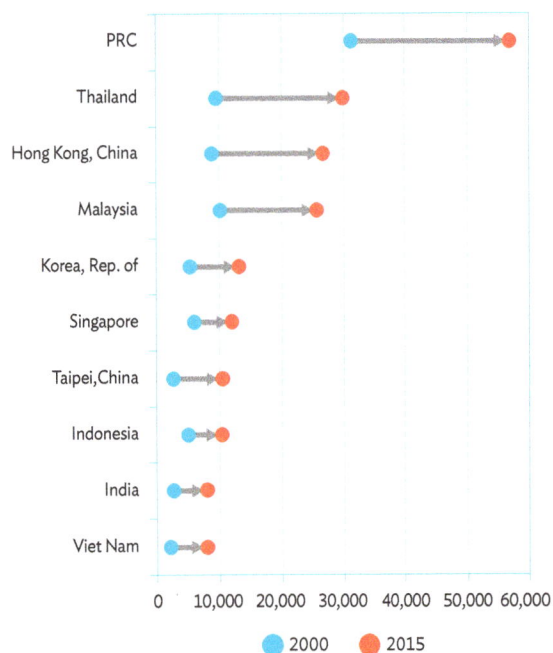

Figure 4.8: International Tourism Receipts per International Tourist Arrival ($)

Lao PDR = Lao People's Democratic Republic, PRC = People's Republic of China.
Sources: Table 4.23 and 4.24.

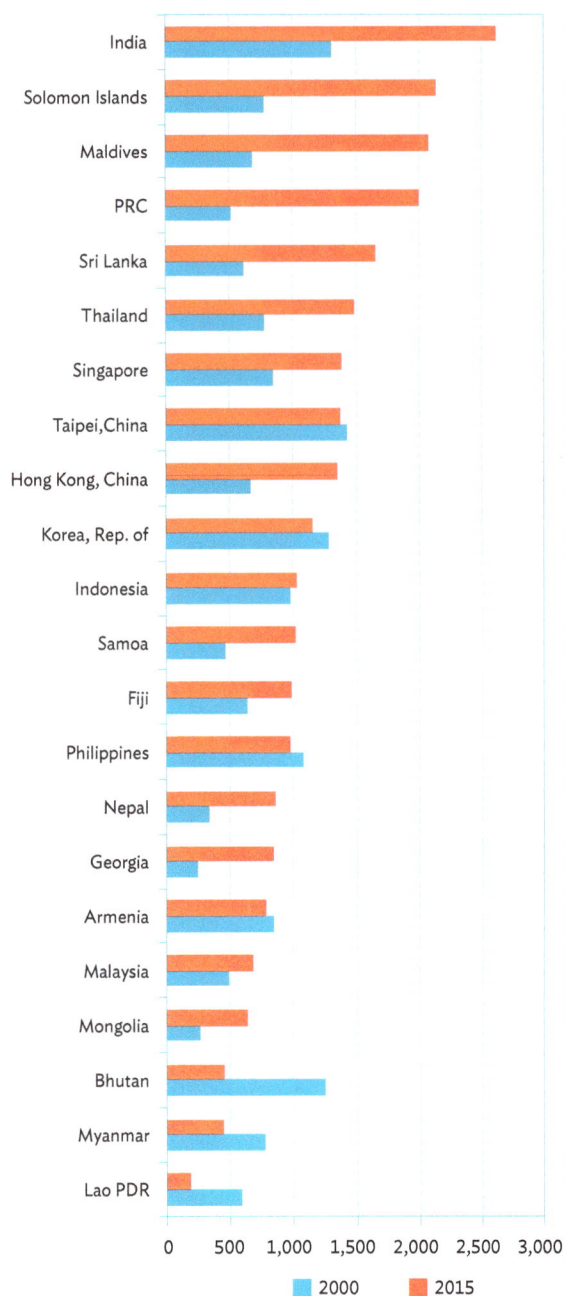

Figure 4.7: International Tourist Arrivals (thousand)

PRC = People's Republic of China.
Source: Table 4.23.

Data Issues and Comparability

Most of the international transactions in this section are taken from balance-of-payments statistics. Countries follow the International Monetary Fund's guidelines when compiling these statistics and meet regularly to discuss methodology, but many countries have difficulty accurately recording nonofficial transactions such as migrant workers' remittances and private capital flows, which is one of the reasons that the Balance of Payments Manual, Fifth Edition (BPM5) was updated to the Balance of Payments and International Investment Position Manual, Sixth Edition (BPM6). Analysis for this section was based on the balance-of-payments data as reported by the economies. A majority of countries use the sixth edition and a few continue to use the fifth or fourth edition. This affects the comparability of data across economies.

International trade statistics are closely monitored by the World Trade Organization and other international agencies. Common definitions are used by all countries, and the larger Asian economies use standard forms and procedures for data processing.

International tourist arrivals and receipts data come from the World Tourism Organization, which serves as a global forum for tourism policy issues and a practical source of information on this topic.

References

Asian Development Bank (ADB). 2015. *Asian Development Outlook 2015*. Manila.

———. 2016. *Asian Development Outlook 2016*. Manila.

DBS Group Research. 2016. *Hong Kong: Cautious Outlook*. Singapore.

Global Knowledge Partnership on Migration and Development. 2016. Migration and Remittances: Recent Developments and Outlook. *Migration and Development Brief* No. 26. Washington, DC: World Bank.

United Nations Conference on Trade and Development (UNCTAD). 2016. *World Investment Report 2016*. Geneva.

P. Vanham. 2015. 14 Charts on the Asian Economy. 16 April. https://www.weforum.org/agenda/2015/04/14-charts-on-the-asian-economy/.

Table 4.1:   **Trade in Goods Balance**
              (% of GDP)

Regional Member	2000	2005	2010	2011	2012	2013	2014	2015
Developing Member Economies								
Central and West Asia								
Afghanistan	−28.4 (2002)	−65.5	−26.3	−28.2	−26.3	−35.6	−27.9	−33.3
Armenia	−24.4	−13.0	−22.3	−20.8	−19.9	−18.8	−17.7	−11.0
Azerbaijan	6.1	24.9	37.3	36.9	32.3	28.0	32.1	11.0
Georgia	−17.5	−19.0	−22.6	−24.2	−26.7	−21.7	−26.0	−30.9
Kazakhstan	11.9	18.1	19.3	22.4	17.7	14.3	16.1	6.9
Kyrgyz Republic	0.3	−17.0	−25.2	−26.2	−39.8	−38.6	−38.1	−30.4
Pakistan	−2.0	−4.1	−6.6	−4.9	−7.3	−7.0	−6.7	−6.5
Tajikistan	−9.5	−14.0	−50.7	−45.6	−46.6	−44.7	−32.5	−28.8
Turkmenistan	15.5	14.1	10.2	21.5	18.6	10.3	9.5	4.1
Uzbekistan	3.6	10.0	7.6	7.3	3.0	4.1	4.4	...
East Asia								
China, People's Rep. of	2.5	5.7	4.1	3.1	3.7	3.8	4.2	5.2
Hong Kong, China	11.9	17.1	1.4	−3.0	−7.2	−10.1	−11.1	−7.4
Korea, Rep. of	2.8	3.6	4.4	2.4	4.0	6.3	6.3	8.7
Mongolia	−6.4	−3.9	−2.5	−9.5	−12.6	−10.5	8.1	10.0
Taipei,China	5.8	6.5	8.3	8.2	10.0	10.7	11.4	13.9
South Asia								
Bangladesh	−4.0	−5.5	−4.5	−7.7	−7.0	−4.7	−3.9	−3.0
Bhutan	−15.6	−30.7	−17.3	−24.5	−20.4	−19.7	−20.2	−19.9
India	−2.7	−6.2	−7.4	−10.4	−10.7	−7.9	−7.1	−6.3
Maldives	−37.4	−44.1	−45.6	−55.8	−50.3	−49.3	−54.3	−49.2
Nepal	−14.4	−14.6	−25.5	−23.4	−24.4	−27.2	−30.4	−31.3
Sri Lanka	−10.8	−10.3	−8.5	−14.9	−13.8	−10.2	−10.4	−10.2
Southeast Asia								
Brunei Darussalam	45.4 (2001)	50.7	45.3	46.6	46.0	38.2	43.4	22.4
Cambodia	−14.7	−16.1	−16.5	−16.7	−17.9	−21.1	−19.1	−19.2
Indonesia	15.2	6.0	4.1	3.8	0.9	0.6	0.8	1.5
Lao PDR	−12.5	−12.1	−4.7	−2.7	−8.6	−7.6	−13.7	−20.0
Malaysia	22.2	23.7	15.1	15.4	11.7	9.5	10.2	9.5
Myanmar	−0.1	0.1	0.1	0.0	1.0	0.2	−3.3	−6.1
Philippines	−7.4	−11.8	−8.4	−9.1	−7.6	−6.5	−6.1	−7.4
Singapore	16.9	37.5	26.6	26.9	24.3	25.2	26.0	28.2
Thailand	4.3	1.8	8.7	4.6	1.7	1.6	6.1	8.7
Viet Nam	1.2	−4.2	−4.4	−0.3	5.6	5.1	6.5	3.8
The Pacific								
Cook Islands	−45.5	−41.6	−33.5	−37.2	−35.2	−35.0	−32.5	−32.8
Fiji	−14.0	−26.0	−23.5	−22.6	−19.4	−27.8	−22.7	...
Kiribati	−52.2	−66.3	−41.7	−43.6	−49.9	−50.4	−56.3	...
Marshall Islands	−54.7	−40.4	−55.5	−30.9	−26.9	−36.2	−37.5	−34.4
Micronesia, Fed. States of	−38.1	−42.7	−43.2	−43.1	−38.4	−40.7	−36.9	−40.6
Nauru	...	...	...	...	...	...	...	...
Palau	−78.4	−50.2	−49.4	−56.0	−57.8	−57.7	−63.1	−49.5
Papua New Guinea	31.4	36.8	15.6	15.0	7.4	2.5	...	...
Samoa	−120.7	−31.5	−31.2	−29.3	−26.6	−29.0	−25.6	−25.1
Solomon Islands	−8.1	−5.6	−19.7	−0.6	7.2	−1.7	−0.5	−1.6
Timor-Leste	...	−3.7 (2006)	−6.6	−6.2	−9.4	−11.0	−14.4	...
Tonga	−27.4	−34.1	−27.6	−28.2	−29.9	−32.6	−31.1	−38.0
Tuvalu	−65.1	−40.4 (2006)	−53.6	−51.2	−46.7	−41.6	...	...
Vanuatu	−18.2	−23.3	−27.1	−23.1	−25.4	−27.9	−24.0	...
Developed Member Economies								
Australia	−1.9	−2.6	−0.7	1.6	0.6	−0.3	0.4	−0.9
Japan	2.5	2.3	2.0	−0.1	−0.9	−1.8	−2.1	−0.1
New Zealand	0.7	−2.1	1.1	0.7	0.2	1.0	−0.2	...

... = data not available at cutoff date, 0.0 = magnitude is less than half of unit employed, GDP = gross domestic product, Lao PDR = Lao People's Democratic Republic.

Source: Economy sources.

Table 4.2:   **Trade in Services Balance**
(% of GDP)

Regional Member	2000	2005	2010	2011	2012	2013	2014	2015
Developing Member Economies								
Central and West Asia								
Afghanistan	...	...	4.6	3.9	−3.9	−4.8	−2.8	...
Armenia	−3.4	−3.0	−2.8	−0.6	−1.0	−1.1	−0.8	−0.6
Azerbaijan	−4.3	−14.5	−2.7	−4.2	−3.8	−5.6	−8.1	−8.0
Georgia	2.4	1.6	4.7	5.2	7.0	8.8	8.0	10.5
Kazakhstan	−5.3	−9.5	−4.9	−3.3	−3.7	−2.9	−2.8	...
Kyrgyz Republic	−6.3	−1.3	−4.2	−1.7	−5.4	−0.9	−4.7	−1.9
Pakistan	−1.1	−3.6	−0.3	−1.4	−0.9	−1.4	−1.1	−0.9
Tajikistan	−2.9 (2002)	−4.5	−1.8	−1.6	−0.9	−3.1	−3.3	−3.1
Turkmenistan[a]	−7.2	−7.9	−21.0	−19.5	−18.5	−17.9	−16.7	−16.4
Uzbekistan[a]	−0.5	−1.1	−1.4	−1.6	−0.1	−0.4	−0.1	...
East Asia								
China, People's Rep. of	3.5	−0.2	−0.4	−0.6	−0.9	−1.3	−1.7	−1.7
Hong Kong, China	−7.5	−4.9	4.4	6.9	8.3	10.7	11.2	9.8
Korea, Rep. of	−0.2	−1.0	−1.3	−1.0	−0.4	−0.5	−0.3	−1.1
Mongolia	−7.5	−2.4	−4.2	−11.2	−9.0	−10.6	−13.0	...
Taipei,China	−3.8	−3.8	−2.5	−2.3	−3.5	−2.7	−1.9	−2.0
South Asia								
Bangladesh	−1.8	−1.5	−1.7	−2.3	−2.2	−2.3	−2.7	−2.4
Bhutan	...	−1.4 (2006)	−4.5	−5.2	−5.2	−3.0	−3.3	−2.9
India	−0.5	0.6	0.1	0.7	0.9	1.2	0.9	...
Maldives	38.2	9.8	58.5	62.2	63.9	67.8	72.5	61.3
Nepal	5.3	−0.7	−1.2	0.4	0.2	1.1	1.0	...
Sri Lanka	−4.1	−2.2	−1.1	−1.4	1.8	1.6	2.3	2.8
Southeast Asia								
Brunei Darussalam	...	−5.2	−5.9	−7.1	−11.3	−13.1	−9.5	...
Cambodia	2.8	7.6	9.4	11.0	11.8	11.3	11.5	...
Indonesia	−6.3	−3.2	−1.3	−1.1	−1.2	−1.3	−1.1	...
Lao PDR	8.1	6.1	3.7	2.7	2.6	2.3	...	...
Malaysia	−2.9	−1.5	0.8	0.2	−0.9	−0.9	−1.0	−1.8
Myanmar	0.2	0.0	0.0	0.0	−0.3	0.9	2.4	...
Philippines	0.5	2.1	2.9	2.9	2.5	2.6	1.6	1.5
Singapore	−4.6	−7.6	−0.2	0.3	−0.7	−2.1	−1.5	−1.3
Thailand	−1.3	−3.6	−3.1	−2.9	−0.8	0.9	0.5	2.6
Viet Nam	−1.8	−0.5	−2.1	−2.2	−1.6	−1.8	−1.9	...
The Pacific								
Cook Islands	...	...	...	...	...	...	...	...
Fiji	6.0	13.2	17.3	16.7	16.3	15.7	...	...
Kiribati	...	−0.0 (2006)	−25.3	−27.5	−30.1	−30.0	−22.4	...
Marshall Islands	...	−28.9	−27.2	−27.6	−27.5	−29.2	−25.9	...
Micronesia, Fed. States of	...	...	−15.1	−14.9	−14.4	−14.6	−12.2	...
Nauru	...	...	...	...	...	...	...	...
Palau	...	21.1	22.3	31.5	33.4	35.8	37.9	...
Papua New Guinea	−15.1	−20.0	−17.2	−14.2	−15.3	−16.4	...	...
Samoa	14.2 (1999)	14.0	13.2	13.0	13.8	14.6	14.7	...
Solomon Islands	−7.1	−3.9	−13.8	−8.4	−9.2	−12.1	−10.8	−7.3
Timor-Leste	...	−7.0 (2006)	−22.6	−23.3	−13.5	−7.8	−9.0	...
Tonga	−4.8 (2001)	−2.4	−0.2	−3.3	−1.4	−4.7	...	...
Tuvalu	−62.2 (2001)	−33.0	−93.6	−100.9	−57.8	−36.2	...	...
Vanuatu	21.8	16.5	21.7	17.5	19.9	25.4	23.2	...
Developed Member Economies								
Australia	0.2	−0.1	−0.4	−0.7	−0.8	−1.0	−0.7	...
Japan	−1.0	−0.8	−0.6	−0.6	−0.8	−0.7	−0.6	−0.3
New Zealand	1.3	1.5	0.9	0.6	0.4	0.4	0.6	...

... = data not available at cutoff date, 0.0 = magnitude is less than half of the unit employed, GDP = gross domestic product, Lao PDR = Lao People's Democratic Republic.

a   Includes other goods and income. Applicable starting 2005 for Uzbekistan.

Sources: International Monetary Fund. June 2016. *International Financial Statistics* (CD-ROM). Washington, DC; for Taipei,China; Turkmenistan; and Uzbekistan: economy sources.

Table 4.3: **Current Account Balance**
(% of GDP)

Regional Member	2000	2005	2010	2011	2012	2013	2014	2015
Developing Member Economies								
Central and West Asia								
Afghanistan	−3.5 (2002)	−2.7	−10.1	−14.9	−20.6	−26.7	−19.0	−25.1
Armenia	−15.8	−2.5	−13.6	−10.4	−10.0	−7.6	−7.3	−2.7
Azerbaijan	−3.2	1.3	28.4	26.0	21.7	16.7	32.1	−0.4
Georgia	−5.8	−10.8	−10.3	−12.8	−11.7	−5.8	−10.6	−12.0
Kazakhstan	2.1	−1.8	0.9	5.1	0.5	0.5	2.8	−3.2
Kyrgyz Republic	−5.5	−1.4	−6.6	−8.1	−15.8	−14.1	−17.3	−11.3
Pakistan	−0.3	−1.4	−2.3	0.1	−2.2	−1.1	−1.3	−1.0
Tajikistan	−7.2	−0.8	−15.9	−2.6	−3.2	−0.7	−2.8	−6.0
Turkmenistan	8.3	6.2	−10.8	2.0	0.0	−7.6	−7.1	−12.3
Uzbekistan	1.6	13.5	6.1	5.7	2.7	3.4	4.1	...
East Asia								
China, People's Rep. of	1.7	5.8	3.9	1.8	2.5	1.6	2.7	3.0
Hong Kong, China	4.4	11.9	7.0	5.6	1.6	1.5	1.3	3.1
Korea, Rep. of	1.9	1.4	2.6	1.6	4.2	6.2	6.0	7.7
Mongolia	−6.1	3.5	−12.3	−26.5	−27.4	−25.4	−11.5	−4.0
Taipei,China	2.5	4.0	8.3	7.8	8.9	10.0	11.7	14.5
South Asia								
Bangladesh	−0.9	−1.0	3.7	−1.3	−0.3	1.6	0.8	0.8
Bhutan	−9.4	−29.0	−20.5	−27.6	−20.1	−24.5	−24.8	−27.6
India	−0.6	−1.2	−2.8	−4.2	−4.8	−1.7	−1.3	−1.1
Maldives	−8.2	−24.4	−15.3	−15.6	−7.4	−4.6	−3.9	−8.8
Nepal	−2.2	2.0	−2.3	−0.9	4.8	3.3	4.5	5.0
Sri Lanka	−6.4	−2.7	−1.9	−7.1	−5.8	−3.4	−2.5	−2.4
Southeast Asia								
Brunei Darussalam	51.5 (2001)	47.3	36.5	34.8	29.8	20.9	30.6	15.9
Cambodia	−2.7	−3.6	−6.0	−6.0	−8.2	−13.0	−9.8	−9.7
Indonesia	4.8	0.1	0.7	0.2	−2.7	−3.2	−3.1	−2.0
Lao PDR	−0.3	−7.1	0.4	2.0	−4.5	−4.1	−10.0	−18.4
Malaysia	9.0	14.4	10.1	10.9	5.2	3.5	4.4	3.0
Myanmar	−0.1	0.0	0.0	0.0	−1.5	−0.8	−2.1	−6.2
Philippines	−2.7	1.9	3.6	2.5	2.8	4.2	3.8	2.9
Singapore	10.8	22.1	23.8	22.8	18.1	17.9	17.5	19.8
Thailand	7.4	−4.0	2.9	2.4	−0.4	−1.2	3.8	8.1
Viet Nam	4.2	−1.0	−3.7	0.2	5.9	4.5	4.9	0.5
The Pacific								
Cook Islands	...	...	...	...	...	...	...	...
Fiji	−1.6	−11.3	−4.7	−5.1	−1.3	−9.8	−7.5	...
Kiribati	−3.2	−34.1	−2.2	−13.4	−4.5	9.3	24.4	...
Marshall Islands	−15.1	5.8	−21.3	1.2	−3.2	−12.0	−3.4	14.8
Micronesia, Fed. States of	−13.3	−9.0	−15.4	−18.8	−13.4	−10.1	1.2	8.6
Nauru	...	...	...	...	...	...	...	...
Palau	−44.1	−18.9	−6.7	−9.2	−8.5	−9.3	−11.8	−0.5
Papua New Guinea	10.1	13.3	−4.5	−1.0	−10.8	−16.4	...	...
Samoa	−3.3	−8.5	−5.4	−5.5	0.1	−4.3	−3.9	−2.5
Solomon Islands	−12.9	−1.9	−20.8	−2.4	2.9	−3.8	−4.8	−3.5
Timor-Leste	...	19.3 (2006)	39.3	39.4	40.2	43.6	26.2	...
Tonga	−5.2	−9.4	−7.4	−9.3	−6.9	−8.7	−5.0	−9.0
Tuvalu	54.7	−1.6 (2006)	−3.7	−26.5	−7.8	−2.8	...	...
Vanuatu	−5.0	−3.5	−5.8	−7.4	−8.8	−0.5	2.2	...
Developed Member Economies								
Australia	−4.9	−6.5	−5.0	−3.1	−3.3	−3.9	−3.3	−3.7
Japan	2.8	3.7	4.0	2.2	1.0	0.9	0.8	3.3
New Zealand	−1.0	−5.4	−2.0	−2.5	−3.0	−2.1	−2.7	...

... = data not available at cutoff date, 0.0 = magnitude is less than half of the unit employed, GDP = gross domestic product, Lao PDR = Lao People's Democratic Republic.

Source: Economy sources.

Table 4.4:   **Workers' Remittances and Compensation of Employees, Receipts**
($ million)

Regional Member	2000	2005	2010	2011	2012	2013	2014	2015
Developing Member Economies								
Central and West Asia								
Afghanistan	...	106 (2008)	342	185	252	314	268	350
Armenia	87	915	1,669	1,799	1,915	2,192	2,079	1,622
Azerbaijan	57	623	1,410	1,893	1,990	1,733	1,846	1,483
Georgia	210	446	1,184	1,547	1,770	1,945	1,986	1,555
Kazakhstan	122	62	226	180	178	207	229	176
Kyrgyz Republic	9	313	1,266	1,709	2,031	2,278	2,243	1,689
Pakistan	1,080	4,280	9,690	12,263	14,007	14,629	17,066	19,255
Tajikistan	79 (2002)	467	2,306	3,060	3,626	4,219	3,384	2,575
Turkmenistan	...	14 (2006)	35	35	37	40	30	16
Uzbekistan	...	898 (2006)	2,858	4,276	5,693	6,689	5,828	3,104
East Asia								
China, People's Rep. of	758	23,626	52,460	61,576	57,987	59,491	62,332	63,938
Hong Kong, China	136	297	340	352	367	360	372	368
Korea, Rep. of	4,862	5,178	5,836	6,582	6,571	6,455	6,551	6,541
Mongolia	12	180	266	279	320	256	255	265
Taipei,China	274	323	500	613	688	792	860	915
South Asia								
Bangladesh	1,969	4,642	10,850	12,071	14,120	13,867	14,983	15,359
Bhutan	...	2 (2006)	8	10	18	12	14	20
India	12,845	22,125	53,480	62,499	68,821	69,970	70,389	68,910
Maldives	2	2	3	3	3	3	3	3
Nepal	112	1,212	3,464	4,217	4,793	5,589	5,770	6,976
Sri Lanka	1,163	1,976	4,123	5,153	6,000	6,422	7,036	6,999
Southeast Asia								
Brunei Darussalam	...	...	...	...	...	...	...	...
Cambodia	121	164	153	160	172	176	377	397
Indonesia	1,190	5,420	6,916	6,924	7,212	7,614	8,551	9,631
Lao PDR	1	1	42	110	59	60	60	60
Malaysia	342	1,117	1,103	1,211	1,294	1,423	1,573	1,623
Myanmar	102	129	115	127	275	1,644	3,103	3,468
Philippines	6,957	13,733	20,563	21,922	23,352	25,369	27,273	28,483
Singapore	...	...	...	...	...	...	...	...
Thailand	1,700	1,187	3,580	4,554	4,713	5,690	5,655	5,217
Viet Nam	1,340	3,150	8,260	8,600	10,000	11,000	12,000	13,200
The Pacific								
Cook Islands	...	...	...	...	...	...	...	...
Fiji	44	204	174	160	191	204	206	222
Kiribati	...	12 (2006)	15	16	17	17	16	16
Marshall Islands	...	24	22	22	23	25	26	27
Micronesia, Fed. States of	...	...	18	19	21	22	23	24
Nauru	...	...	...	...	...	...	...	...
Palau	...	1	2	2	2	2	2	2
Papua New Guinea	7	7	3	17	14	14	10	10
Samoa	45 (1999)	82	139	160	178	165	141	154
Solomon Islands	4	7	14	17	21	21	16	18
Timor-Leste	...	4 (2006)	137	137	120	34	44	64
Tonga	...	69	77	79	118	121	118	118
Tuvalu	...	5	4	5	4	4	4	4
Vanuatu	35	5	12	22	22	24	28	28
Developed Member Economies								
Australia	1,904	940	1,864	2,449	2,441	2,460	2,330	2,266
Japan	1,374	905	1,684	2,132	2,540	2,364	3,733	4,480
New Zealand	236	352	371	455	462	459	462	421
DEVELOPING MEMBER ECONOMIES[a]	35,541	91,971	193,665	224,567	238,993	251,091	262,751	264,885
REGIONAL MEMBERS[a]	39,055	94,169	197,584	229,603	244,435	256,375	269,277	272,053
WORLD	126,750	282,536	460,527	522,934	543,943	571,759	591,968	581,640

... = data not available at cutoff date, Lao PDR = Lao People's Democratic Republic.

a For reporting economies only.

Sources: World Bank. Migration. http://www.worldbank.org/en/topic/migrationremittancesdiasporaissues/brief/migration-remittances-data (accessed June 2016); for Taipei,China: economy source.

Table 4.5: **Workers' Remittances and Compensation of Employees, Receipts**
(% of GDP)

Regional Member	2000	2005	2010	2011	2012	2013	2014	2015
Developing Member Economies								
Central and West Asia								
Afghanistan	...	1.0 (2008)	2.1	1.0	1.2	1.5	1.3	1.7
Armenia	4.6	18.7	18.0	17.7	18.0	19.7	17.9	15.4
Azerbaijan	1.1	4.7	2.7	2.9	2.9	2.3	2.5	2.8
Georgia	6.9	7.0	10.2	10.7	11.2	12.1	12.0	11.1
Kazakhstan	0.7	0.1	0.2	0.1	0.1	0.1	0.1	0.1
Kyrgyz Republic	0.6	12.7	26.4	27.6	30.8	31.1	30.0	25.7
Pakistan	1.5	3.9	5.6	5.8	6.5	6.6	6.9	7.2
Tajikistan	3.8 (2002)	20.2	40.9	46.9	47.5	49.6	36.6	32.8
Turkmenistan	...	0.1 (2006)	0.2	0.1	0.1	0.1	0.1	0.0
Uzbekistan	...	5.2 (2006)	7.2	9.3	11.0	11.6	9.3	4.7
East Asia								
China, People's Rep. of	0.1	1.0	0.9	0.8	0.7	0.6	0.6	0.6
Hong Kong, China	0.1	0.2	0.1	0.1	0.1	0.1	0.1	0.1
Korea, Rep. of	0.9	0.6	0.5	0.5	0.5	0.5	0.5	0.5
Mongolia	1.1	7.1	3.7	2.7	2.6	2.0	2.1	2.2
Taipei,China	0.1	0.1	0.1	0.1	0.1	0.2	0.2	0.2
South Asia								
Bangladesh	4.3	8.1	9.5	9.8	11.0	9.0	8.7	7.9
Bhutan	...	0.2 (2006)	0.5	0.6	1.0	0.7	0.7	1.0
India	2.7	2.6	3.1	3.3	3.7	3.6	3.4	3.3
Maldives	0.4	0.2	0.1	0.1	0.1	0.1	0.1	0.1
Nepal	2.0	14.7	21.3	22.8	26.7	30.7	29.2	33.8
Sri Lanka	7.0	8.1	7.3	7.9	8.8	8.6	8.8	8.5
Southeast Asia								
Brunei Darussalam	...	...	...	...	...	...	...	...
Cambodia	3.3	2.6	1.4	1.3	1.2	1.2	2.2	2.2
Indonesia	0.7	1.9	0.9	0.8	0.8	0.8	1.0	1.1
Lao PDR	0.0	0.0	0.6	1.4	0.6	0.6	0.5	0.5
Malaysia	0.4	0.8	0.4	0.4	0.4	0.4	0.5	0.5
Myanmar	0.0	0.0	0.0	0.0	0.3	2.6	4.7	5.5
Philippines	8.6	13.3	10.3	9.8	9.3	9.3	9.6	9.7
Singapore	...	...	...	...	...	...	...	...
Thailand	1.3	0.6	1.1	1.2	1.2	1.4	1.4	1.3
Viet Nam	4.3	5.5	7.1	6.3	6.4	6.4	6.4	6.8
The Pacific								
Cook Islands	...	...	...	...	...	...	...	...
Fiji	2.6	6.8	5.5	4.2	4.8	4.9	4.5	5.1
Kiribati	...	11.6 (2006)	9.7	9.2	9.0	9.2	8.6	...
Marshall Islands	...	17.2	13.5	12.8	12.6	12.9	14.2	15.0
Micronesia, Fed. States of	...	...	6.1	6.2	6.4	7.0	7.3	7.6
Nauru	...	...	...	...	...	...	...	...
Palau	...	0.8	0.9	1.0	1.1	1.0	0.9	0.8
Papua New Guinea	0.2	0.1	0.0	0.1	0.1	0.1	...	...
Samoa	19.5 (1999)	18.8	20.4	20.3	22.2	20.5	17.0	19.9
Solomon Islands	1.5	1.7	2.1	2.1	2.3	2.0	1.6	1.7
Timor-Leste	...	0.1 (2006)	3.2	2.3	1.8	0.6	1.0	...
Tonga	...	26.0	20.7	17.6	25.3	27.5	27.0	29.8
Tuvalu	...	22.5	12.3	11.7	9.6	10.6	10.8	12.4
Vanuatu	12.7	1.3	1.7	2.7	2.8	3.0	3.5	...
Developed Member Economies								
Australia	0.5	0.1	0.2	0.2	0.2	0.2	0.2	0.2
Japan	0.0	0.0	0.0	0.0	0.0	0.0	0.1	0.1
New Zealand	0.4	0.3	0.3	0.3	0.3	0.2	0.2	...
DEVELOPING MEMBER ECONOMIES[a]	**0.9**	**1.2**	**1.0**	**1.0**	**1.5**	**1.5**	**1.4**	**1.4**
REGIONAL MEMBERS[a]	**0.4**	**0.7**	**0.8**	**0.8**	**1.0**	**1.1**	**1.1**	**1.1**

... = data not available at cutoff date, 0.0 = magnitude is less than half of unit employed, GDP = gross domestic product, Lao PDR = Lao People's Democratic Republic.

a   For reporting economies only.

Sources: World Bank. Migration. http://www.worldbank.org/en/topic/migrationremittancesdiasporaissues/brief/migration-remittances-data (accessed June 2016); for Taipei,China: economy source.

Balance of Payments

Table 4.6:   **Foreign Direct Investment, Net Inflows**
($ million)

Regional Member	2000	2005	2010	2011	2012	2013	2014	2015
Developing Member Economies								
Central and West Asia								
Afghanistan	50 (2002)	271	54	58	62	40	49	169
Armenia	104	292	529	653	497	346	404	178
Azerbaijan	130	4,476	3,353	4,485	5,293	2,619	4,430	4,048
Georgia	131	453	869	1,084	831	956	1,750	1,342
Kazakhstan	1,371	2,546	7,456	13,760	13,648	9,947	7,598	4,021
Kyrgyz Republic	–2	43	420	697	309	633	353	760
Pakistan	308	2,201	2,022	1,326	859	1,333	1,867	979
Tajikistan	24	54	–16	67	198	–54	309	391
Turkmenistan	131	418	3,632	3,391	3,130	3,732	4,170	4,259
Uzbekistan	75	192	1,636	1,635	563	629	626	1,068
East Asia								
China, People's Rep. of	42,095	104,109	243,703	280,072	241,214	290,928	268,097	249,859
Hong Kong, China	70,496	40,963	82,709	96,135	74,887	76,857	129,847	180,844
Korea, Rep. of	11,509	13,643	9,497	9,773	9,496	12,767	9,274	5,042
Mongolia	54	185	1,692	4,713	4,452	2,151	384	196
Taipei,China	4,928	1,625	2,492	–1,957	3,207	3,598	2,839	2,413
South Asia								
Bangladesh	280	761	1,232	1,265	1,584	2,603	2,539	3,380
Bhutan	2 (2002)	6	75	31	24	50	8	34
India	3,584	7,269	27,397	36,499	23,996	28,153	33,871	44,208
Maldives	22	53	216	424	228	361	333	324
Nepal	–0	2	88	94	92	74	30	19
Sri Lanka	173	272	478	956	941	933	894	681
Southeast Asia								
Brunei Darussalam	61 (2001)	175	481	691	865	776	568	173
Cambodia	118	377	735	795	1,441	1,345	1,730	1,701
Indonesia	–4,550	8,336	15,292	20,565	21,201	23,282	26,277	15,508
Lao PDR	34	28	279	301	294	427	913	1,079
Malaysia	3,788	3,925	10,886	15,119	8,896	11,296	10,619	10,963
Myanmar	255	235	901	2,520	1,334	2,255	1,398	3,137
Philippines	1,487	1,664	1,070	2,007	3,215	3,737	5,740	5,724
Singapore	15,515	18,090	55,076	48,329	57,150	66,067	68,496	65,263
Thailand	3,366	8,223	14,715	2,468	12,895	15,822	3,719	7,062
Viet Nam	1,298	1,954	8,000	7,430	8,368	8,900	9,200	11,800
The Pacific								
Cook Islands	...	...	...	...	...	...	...	...
Fiji	1	160	357	417	267	158	343	332
Kiribati	1	3	–7	1	–3	1	8	2
Marshall Islands	0	3	–9	–4	21	33	9	–54
Micronesia, Fed. States of	–0 (2001)	0	1	1	1	1	20	1
Nauru	1	1	1 (2009)	...	...	...	...	...
Palau	3	4	3	8	22	18	40	–9
Papua New Guinea	96	32	29	–310	–64	18	–30	–28
Samoa	–1	4	–1	9	14	24	23	16
Solomon Islands	2	1	166	120	24	53	21	22
Timor-Leste	1 (2002)	1	30	49	40	56	34	43
Tonga	9	7	9	4	2	7	56	13
Tuvalu	–0 (2001)	–0	0	–0	1	0	1	1
Vanuatu	20	13	63	61	60	59	13	29
Developed Member Economies								
Australia	14,893	–25,093	35,211	65,555	57,617	54,554	45,913	36,852
Japan	10,688	5,460	7,441	–851	547	10,648	18,409	–42
New Zealand	–1,508	1,907	286	1,370	3,737	–99	3,245	–547
DEVELOPING MEMBER ECONOMIES[a]	**156,969**	**223,070**	**497,614**	**555,743**	**501,555**	**572,991**	**598,872**	**626,996**
REGIONAL MEMBERS[a]	**181,043**	**205,343**	**540,552**	**621,817**	**563,456**	**638,094**	**666,440**	**663,259**

... = data not available at cutoff date, 0 = magnitude is less than half of unit employed, Lao PDR = Lao People's Democratic Republic.

a   For reporting economies only.

Sources: World Bank. World Development Indicators Online. http://data.worldbank.org/indicator/BX.KLT.DINV.CD.WD (accessed October 2016); for Taipei,China: economy source.

Table 4.7: **Foreign Direct Investment, Net Inflows**
(% of GDP)

Regional Member	2000	2005	2010	2011	2012	2013	2014	2015
Developing Member Economies								
Central and West Asia								
Afghanistan	1.2 (2002)	4.1	0.3	0.3	0.3	0.2	0.2	0.8
Armenia	5.5	6.0	5.7	6.4	4.7	3.1	3.5	1.7
Azerbaijan	2.5	33.8	6.3	6.8	7.6	3.5	5.9	7.6
Georgia	4.3	7.1	7.5	7.5	5.2	5.9	10.6	9.6
Kazakhstan	7.5	4.5	5.0	6.9	6.3	4.1	3.3	2.2
Kyrgyz Republic	−0.2	1.7	8.8	11.3	4.7	8.6	4.7	11.6
Pakistan	0.4	2.0	1.2	0.6	0.4	0.6	0.8	0.4
Tajikistan	2.7	2.4	−0.3	1.0	2.6	−0.6	3.3	5.0
Turkmenistan	2.7	2.9	16.4	11.6	8.9	9.5	9.6	11.9
Uzbekistan	0.5	1.3	4.1	3.5	1.1	1.1	1.0	1.6
East Asia								
China, People's Rep. of	3.5	4.6	4.0	3.7	2.9	3.1	2.6	2.3
Hong Kong, China	41.1	22.6	36.2	38.7	28.5	27.9	44.6	58.5
Korea, Rep. of	2.0	1.5	0.9	0.8	0.8	1.0	0.7	0.4
Mongolia	4.7	7.3	23.5	45.3	36.2	17.1	3.1	1.7
Taipei,China	1.5	0.4	0.6	−0.4	0.6	0.7	0.5	0.5
South Asia								
Bangladesh	0.6	1.3	1.1	1.0	1.2	1.7	1.5	1.7
Bhutan	0.5 (2002)	0.8	4.7	1.7	1.3	2.8	0.4	1.6
India	0.7	0.9	1.6	1.9	1.3	1.5	1.7	2.1
Maldives	3.6	4.7	9.3	17.3	9.1	12.9	10.9	9.6
Nepal	0.0	0.0	0.5	0.5	0.5	0.4	0.2	0.1
Sri Lanka	1.0	1.1	0.8	1.5	1.4	1.3	1.1	0.8
Southeast Asia								
Brunei Darussalam	1.1 (2001)	1.8	3.5	3.7	4.5	4.3	3.3	1.3
Cambodia	3.2	6.0	6.5	6.2	10.3	8.8	10.3	9.4
Indonesia	−2.8	2.9	2.0	2.3	2.3	2.6	3.0	1.8
Lao PDR	2.1	1.0	4.1	3.7	3.2	4.0	7.8	8.8
Malaysia	4.0	2.7	4.3	5.1	2.8	3.5	3.1	3.7
Myanmar	0.1	0.0	0.0	0.0	1.7	3.6	2.1	5.0
Philippines	1.8	1.6	0.5	0.9	1.3	1.4	2.0	2.0
Singapore	16.2	14.2	23.3	17.6	19.8	22.0	22.4	22.3
Thailand	2.7	4.3	4.3	0.7	3.2	3.8	0.9	1.8
Viet Nam	4.2	3.4	6.9	5.5	5.4	5.2	4.9	6.1
The Pacific								
Cook Islands	...	...	...	...	...	...	...	...
Fiji	0.0	5.4	11.4	11.0	6.7	3.8	7.6	7.7
Kiribati	1.1	2.5	−4.3	0.4	−1.8	0.6	4.4	...
Marshall Islands	0.1	2.4	−5.7	−2.5	11.5	17.0	4.9	−29.9
Micronesia, Fed. States of	−0.1 (2001)	0.0	0.3	0.3	0.3	0.3	6.4	0.3
Nauru	...	3.8	2.5 (2009)	...	...	...	...	...
Palau	2.1	2.1	1.5	4.2	10.1	7.9	15.9	−3.1
Papua New Guinea	2.8	0.7	0.2	−1.7	−0.3	0.1	...	...
Samoa	−0.5	0.9	−0.2	1.1	1.7	3.0	2.8	2.0
Solomon Islands	0.7	0.1	23.9	14.6	2.6	5.3	2.0	2.1
Timor-Leste	0.2 (2002)	0.0	0.7	0.8	0.6	1.0	0.8	...
Tonga	4.9	2.7	2.4	0.8	0.4	1.5	12.9	3.2
Tuvalu	−0.1 (2001)	−0.1	1.4	−0.3	3.3	0.9	1.7	1.8
Vanuatu	7.4	3.4	9.0	7.7	7.7	7.4	1.6	...
Developed Member Economies								
Australia	3.9	−3.6	3.0	4.5	3.7	3.7	3.2	3.0
Japan	0.2	0.1	0.1	0.0	0.0	0.2	0.4	0.0
New Zealand	−2.8	1.7	0.2	0.8	2.1	−0.1	1.6	...
DEVELOPING MEMBER ECONOMIES[a]	**4.0**	**2.8**	**2.6**	**2.4**	**3.2**	**3.4**	**3.3**	**3.4**
REGIONAL MEMBERS[a]	**2.0**	**1.5**	**2.1**	**2.0**	**2.4**	**2.7**	**2.7**	**2.8**

... = data not available at cutoff date, 0.0 = magnitude is less than half of the unit employed, GDP = gross domestic product, Lao PDR = Lao People's Democratic Republic.

a For reporting economies only.

Sources: World Bank. World Development Indicators Online. http://data.worldbank.org/indicator/BX.KLT.DINV.CD.WD (accessed October 2016); for Taipei,China: economy source.

Table 4.8:   **Merchandise Exports**
($ million)

Regional Member	2000	2005	2010	2011	2012	2013	2014	2015
Developing Member Economies								
Central and West Asia								
Afghanistan	137	384	388	376	415	515	571	571
Armenia	300	974	1,041	1,334	1,380	1,479	1,547	1,485
Azerbaijan	1,745	7,649	26,374	34,393	32,374	31,703	28,260	15,586
Georgia	323	866	1,677	2,187	2,376	2,910	2,861	2,204
Kazakhstan	8,812	27,849	60,271	84,336	86,449	84,700	78,238	45,726*
Kyrgyz Republic	505	674	1,756	2,242	1,928	2,007	1,884	1,676
Pakistan	8,335	14,453	19,261	24,917	22,797	23,383	25,554	23,329
Tajikistan	784	909	1,195	1,257	1,358	1,162	977	891
Turkmenistan	2,508	4,944	9,679	16,751	19,987	18,854	19,782	20,998*
Uzbekistan	3,265	5,409	13,023	15,021	13,600	14,323	13,546	12,469
East Asia								
China, People's Rep. of	249,203	761,953	1,577,754	1,898,381	2,048,714	2,209,004	2,342,293	2,274,950
Hong Kong, China	201,855	289,325	390,134	428,732	442,775	458,959	473,654	465,092
Korea, Rep. of	172,268	284,419	466,384	555,214	547,870	559,632	572,665	526,757
Mongolia	536	1,064	2,909	4,817	4,385	4,269	5,774	4,669
Taipei,China	151,458	199,807	277,413	312,049	306,267	310,235	318,869	283,469
South Asia								
Bangladesh	4,780	8,259	16,099	22,061	23,508	27,619	30,217	31,106
Bhutan	103	214	535	646	580	511	539	560
India	45,297	103,496	249,951	314,109	305,839	325,099	310,742	267,244
Maldives	109	162	62	115	162	166	145	144
Nepal	701	823	830	869	872	827	924	831
Sri Lanka	5,456	6,351	8,618	10,560	9,761	10,413	11,130	10,495
Southeast Asia								
Brunei Darussalam	3,906	6,247	8,887	12,464	12,980	11,436	10,601	6,338
Cambodia	1,397	2,908	3,906	5,035	5,633	6,530	7,408	8,453
Indonesia	62,124	85,660	157,779	203,497	190,032	182,552	175,981	150,366
Lao PDR	330	553	1,746	2,190	2,271	2,264	2,662	2,769
Malaysia	98,229	141,595	198,325	228,059	227,480	228,503	233,868	199,705
Myanmar	1,961	3,558	8,861	9,136	8,977	11,204	12,524	11,137
Philippines	38,078	41,255	51,498	48,305	52,100	56,698	62,102	58,648
Singapore[a]	137,953	229,832	351,182	408,766	407,258	406,930	405,073	346,432
Thailand	69,152	110,360	192,937	219,994	227,726	224,883	225,157	211,048
Viet Nam	14,483	32,447	72,237	96,906	114,529	132,033	150,217	162,017
The Pacific								
Cook Islands	9	5	5	3	5	11	18	14
Fiji	543	705	837	1,073	1,224	1,137	1,220	895
Kiribati	4	4	4	9	7	7	10	...
Marshall Islands	25	34	34 (2009)	65	...	...	...	...
Micronesia, Fed. States of	17	13	23	43	52	35	...	...
Nauru	68	44	189	242	301	248	168	158
Palau	12	14	16	19	21	21	19	18
Papua New Guinea	2,089	3,311	5,737	6,907	6,326	5,942	8,786	8,353
Samoa	14	12	23	25	31	24	27	34
Solomon Islands	65	105	227	408	488	487	458	401
Timor-Leste	...	43	42	53	77	53	39	...
Tonga	9	10	8	16	16	17	19	...
Tuvalu	0	0	0	0	0	0	...	...
Vanuatu	26	46	48	67	55	39	63	39
Developed Member Economies								
Australia	63,980	106,211	212,027	269,941	256,522	252,894	239,708	187,525
Japan	479,320	595,696	767,825	821,312	798,937	714,931	689,916	624,681
New Zealand	13,292	21,698	31,365	37,685	37,321	39,434	41,541	34,152
DEVELOPING MEMBER ECONOMIES[b]	**1,285,066**	**2,372,498**	**4,171,019**	**4,961,184**	**5,118,003**	**5,347,387**	**5,525,988**	**5,150,741**
REGIONAL MEMBERS[b]	**1,845,565**	**3,102,350**	**5,191,124**	**6,102,585**	**6,223,763**	**6,366,082**	**6,507,754**	**6,003,438**

... = data not available at cutoff date; 0 = magnitude is less than half of unit employed; * = provisional, preliminary, estimate/budget figure; Lao PDR = Lao People's Democratic Republic.

a   Prior to 2003, data exclude Indonesia.
b   For reporting economies only.

Sources: Economy sources; International Monetary Fund. May 2016. *International Financial Statistics* (CD-ROM). Washington, DC.

Table 4.9: **Growth Rates of Merchandise Exports**[a]
(%)

Regional Member	2000	2005	2010	2011	2012	2013	2014	2015
Developing Member Economies								
Central and West Asia								
Afghanistan	-17.4	25.9	-3.7	-3.1	10.4	24.1	10.9	–
Armenia	29.7	34.7	46.6	28.2	3.4	7.1	4.6	-4.0
Azerbaijan	87.7	111.6	25.3	30.4	-5.9	-2.1	-10.9	-44.8
Georgia	35.5	33.8	48.0	30.4	8.7	22.4	-1.7	-22.9
Kazakhstan	50.1	38.6	39.5	39.9	2.5	-2.0	-7.6	-41.6*
Kyrgyz Republic	11.2	-6.5	5.0	27.7	-14.0	4.1	-6.1	-11.0
Pakistan	4.8	14.9	12.0	29.4	-8.5	2.6	9.3	-8.7
Tajikistan	13.9	-0.7	18.3	5.2	8.0	-14.4	-15.9	-8.9
Turkmenistan	115.5	28.3	3.8	73.1	19.3	-5.7	4.9	6.1*
Uzbekistan	0.9	11.5	10.6	15.3	-9.5	5.3	-5.4	-8.0
East Asia								
China, People's Rep. of	27.8	28.4	31.3	20.3	7.9	7.8	6.0	-2.9
Hong Kong, China	16.1	11.6	22.5	9.9	3.3	3.7	3.2	-1.8
Korea, Rep. of	19.9	12.0	28.3	19.0	-1.3	2.1	2.3	-8.0
Mongolia	18.0	22.4	54.3	65.6	-9.0	-2.6	35.3	-19.1
Taipei,China	22.6	8.6	35.1	12.5	-1.9	1.3	2.8	-11.1
South Asia								
Bangladesh	12.5	11.3	3.7	37.0	6.6	17.5	9.4	2.9
Bhutan	-11.3	35.8	6.5	20.7	-10.2	-11.9	5.5	3.9
India	22.2	25.0	43.1	25.7	-2.6	6.3	-4.4	-14.0
Maldives	18.8	-10.5	-63.6	86.5	40.6	2.8	-12.9	-0.6
Nepal	34.0	12.4	-4.9	4.7	0.3	-5.1	11.7	-10.1
Sri Lanka	18.5	10.1	21.7	22.5	-7.6	6.7	6.9	-5.7
Southeast Asia								
Brunei Darussalam	53.1	23.3	23.9	40.2	4.1	-11.9	-7.3	-40.2
Cambodia	23.6	12.3	24.5	28.9	11.9	15.9	13.4	14.1
Indonesia	27.7	19.7	35.4	29.0	-6.6	-3.9	-3.6	-14.6
Lao PDR	9.6	52.2	65.9	25.4	3.7	-0.3	17.6	4.0
Malaysia	16.1	11.8	26.5	15.0	-0.3	0.4	2.3	-14.6
Myanmar	72.3	21.5	16.8	3.1	-1.7	24.8	11.8	-11.1
Philippines	8.7	4.0	34.0	-6.2	7.9	8.8	9.5	-5.6
Singapore[b]	20.3	15.7	30.6	16.4	-0.4	-0.1	-0.5	-14.5
Thailand	18.0	14.6	27.3	14.0	3.5	-1.2	0.1	-6.3
Viet Nam	25.5	22.5	26.5	34.2	18.2	15.3	13.8	7.9
The Pacific								
Cook Islands	154.4	-26.9	88.0	-39.4	69.9	100.6	65.8	-20.3
Fiji	-12.1	1.4	33.0	28.3	14.1	-7.1	7.3	-26.6
Kiribati	-59.1	58.2	-38.0	120.7	-18.3	-4.9	51.9	...
Marshall Islands	48.7	14.0	5.6 (2009)	...	...	...	...	...
Micronesia, Fed. States of	...	-7.3	24.1	88.3	21.8	-33.5	...	...
Nauru	-7.9	-15.3	58.0	27.8	24.3	-17.5	-32.4	-5.8
Palau	65.9	116.9	15.9	16.4	12.2	-0.5	-8.7	-5.3
Papua New Guinea	7.3	26.8	30.9	20.4	-8.4	-6.1	47.9	-4.9
Samoa	-24.9	0.6	114.4	6.3	26.8	-23.2	14.7	23.8
Solomon Islands	-48.1	22.3	37.4	80.0	19.7	-0.3	-5.9	-12.4
Timor-Leste	...	-58.9	20.7	27.8	44.4	-30.7	-26.7	...
Tonga	-27.1	-35.2	7.1	92.0	-1.2	10.2	10.5	...
Tuvalu	-91.5	-54.0	–	0.0	-0.0	–	...	...
Vanuatu	2.8	-6.5	-14.8	38.7	-18.5	-29.4	62.6	-38.0
Developed Member Economies								
Australia	14.1	22.6	38.3	27.3	-5.0	-1.4	-5.2	-21.8
Japan	14.8	5.4	32.6	7.0	-2.7	-10.5	-3.5	-9.5
New Zealand	6.5	6.6	26.6	20.1	-1.0	5.7	5.3	-17.8
DEVELOPING MEMBER ECONOMIES[c]	**20.9**	**18.3**	**30.2**	**18.9**	**3.2**	**4.5**	**3.3**	**-6.8**
REGIONAL MEMBERS[c]	**19.0**	**15.6**	**30.8**	**17.6**	**2.0**	**2.3**	**2.2**	**-7.7**

... = data not available at cutoff date; – = magnitude equals zero; 0.0 or –0.0= magnitude is less than half of unit employed; * = provisional, preliminary, estimate/budget figure;
Lao PDR = Lao People's Democratic Republic.

a Rates are based on US dollar values of exports.
b Prior to 2003, data exclude Indonesia.
c For reporting economies only.

Sources: Economy sources; International Monetary Fund. May 2016. *International Financial Statistics* (CD-ROM). Washington, DC.

External Trade

Table 4.10:   **Merchandise Imports**
($ million)

Regional Member	2000	2005	2010	2011	2012	2013	2014	2015
Developing Member Economies								
Central and West Asia								
Afghanistan	1,176	2,470	5,154	6,390	9,832	8,724	7,729	7,723
Armenia	885	1,802	3,749	4,145	4,261	4,386	4,424	3,239
Azerbaijan	1,172	4,350	6,662	10,056	10,192	10,321	9,332	9,774
Georgia	709	2,490	5,257	7,038	8,037	8,012	8,593	7,729
Kazakhstan	5,040	17,353	31,127	36,906	46,358	48,806	41,296	30,186*
Kyrgyz Republic	554	1,189	3,223	4,261	5,576	5,987	5,735	4,070
Pakistan	9,967	20,630	34,169	40,042	42,960	42,802	45,801	45,190
Tajikistan	675	1,330	2,657	3,206	1,779	4,121	4,297	3,436
Turkmenistan	1,742	2,947	8,204	11,361	14,138	16,090	16,638	18,044*
Uzbekistan	2,947	4,091	9,176	11,345	12,817	...	...	...
East Asia								
China, People's Rep. of	225,094	659,953	1,396,244	1,743,484	1,818,405	1,949,989	1,959,235	1,681,950
Hong Kong, China	212,800	299,520	433,102	483,633	504,377	523,558	544,107	522,001
Korea, Rep. of	160,481	261,238	425,212	524,413	519,584	515,586	525,515	436,499
Mongolia	615	1,177	3,200	6,598	6,738	6,358	5,237	3,797
Taipei,China	140,630	185,245	255,679	287,156	277,268	276,884	280,725	235,580
South Asia								
Bangladesh	8,080	12,575	23,581	34,715	35,219	38,738	41,031	40,564
Bhutan[a]	193	466	810	1,093	952	864	935	965
India	51,372	149,753	368,166	502,558	499,495	463,402	448,486	387,506
Maldives	389	683	909	1,329	1,554	1,728	1,990	1,893
Nepal	1,526	2,094	5,110	5,352	5,419	5,987	7,177	7,547
Sri Lanka	7,198	8,869	13,441	20,273	19,136	17,999	19,417	18,935
Southeast Asia								
Brunei Darussalam	1,107	1,448	2,535	3,600	3,565	3,613	3,596	3,235
Cambodia[a]	1,936	3,918	5,756	7,180	8,139	9,744	10,616	11,920
Indonesia	33,515	57,701	135,663	177,436	191,691	186,629	178,179	142,695
Lao PDR	535	882	2,060	2,404	3,055	3,081	4,271	5,233
Malaysia	81,963	114,302	164,177	187,460	196,412	205,875	208,667	175,494
Myanmar	2,319	1,984	6,413	9,035	9,069	13,760	16,633	16,578
Philippines	33,807	49,487	58,468	64,097	65,839	65,739	65,398	66,686
Singapore[b]	134,675	200,187	310,391	364,496	379,667	373,016	366,030	296,595
Thailand	62,180	118,200	184,834	229,004	250,494	249,214	227,954	201,652
Viet Nam	15,637	36,761	84,839	106,750	113,780	132,033	147,849	165,570
The Pacific								
Cook Islands	51	81	91	110	112	116	121	110
Fiji	856	1,610	1,806	2,182	2,254	2,823	2,656	2,080
Kiribati	39	76	73	92	109	107	107	...
Marshall Islands	116	132	...	176	...	...	...	...
Micronesia, Fed. States of	107	128	168	188	194	188	...	...
Nauru	78	51	42	62	75	280	190	127
Palau	127	108	103	125	136	145	149	156
Papua New Guinea	999	1,519	3,522	4,232	4,757	5,410	4,000	2,260
Samoa	91	187	280	319	308	326	341	298
Solomon Islands	92	185	405	473	497	537	499	467
Timor-Leste	...	109	298	340	670	529	554	...
Tonga	70	121	158	192	199	198	219	...
Tuvalu	5	13	16	25	25	16	...	...
Vanuatu	84	165	284	305	296	314	314	367
Developed Member Economies								
Australia	67,806	118,924	193,081	234,046	250,375	232,450	227,498	200,440
Japan	379,884	516,697	692,242	853,449	885,928	832,440	810,886	647,744
New Zealand	13,963	26,248	30,523	37,048	38,256	39,646	42,523	36,618
DEVELOPING MEMBER ECONOMIES[c]	1,203,634	2,229,583	3,997,211	4,905,635	5,075,441	5,204,032	5,216,041	4,558,148
REGIONAL MEMBERS[c]	1,665,288	2,891,451	4,913,057	6,030,177	6,250,000	6,308,568	6,296,947	5,442,951

... = data not available at cutoff date; * = provisional, preliminary, estimate/budget figure; Lao PDR = Lao People's Democratic Republic.

a   Compilation methodology shifted from cost, insurance, and freight (cif) to free on board (fob) for Bhutan and Cambodia beginning in 2005.
b   Prior to 2003, data exclude Indonesia.
c   For reporting economies only.

Sources: Economy sources; International Monetary Fund. May 2016. *International Financial Statistics* (CD-ROM). Washington, DC.

Table 4.11:   **Growth Rates of Merchandise Imports**[a]
(%)

Regional Member	2000	2005	2010	2011	2012	2013	2014	2015
Developing Member Economies								
Central and West Asia								
Afghanistan	16.2	13.5	54.5	24.0	53.9	–11.3	–11.4	–0.1
Armenia	9.1	33.4	12.9	10.6	2.8	2.9	0.9	–26.8
Azerbaijan	13.1	23.7	6.9	50.9	1.4	1.3	–9.6	4.7
Georgia	21.1	34.9	16.8	33.9	14.2	–0.3	7.3	–10.1
Kazakhstan	37.9	35.8	9.6	18.6	25.6	5.3	–15.4	–26.9*
Kyrgyz Republic	–7.6	25.5	6.0	32.2	30.9	7.4	–4.2	–29.0
Pakistan	5.7	33.7	2.5	17.2	7.3	–0.4	7.0	–1.3
Tajikistan	1.8	11.7	3.4	20.7	–44.5	131.6	4.3	–20.1
Turkmenistan	26.8	–6.4	–8.8	38.5	24.4	13.8	3.4	8.5*
Uzbekistan	–5.2	7.2	–2.8	23.6	13.0	...	...	...
East Asia								
China, People's Rep. of	35.8	17.6	38.8	24.9	4.3	7.2	0.5	–14.2
Hong Kong, China	18.5	10.5	24.7	11.7	4.3	3.8	3.9	–4.1
Korea, Rep. of	34.0	16.4	31.6	23.3	–0.9	–0.8	1.9	–16.9
Mongolia	19.8	15.5	49.7	106.2	2.1	–5.6	–17.6	–27.5
Taipei,China	26.3	7.8	44.3	12.3	–3.4	–0.1	1.4	–16.1
South Asia								
Bangladesh	3.1	16.5	4.4	47.2	1.5	10.0	5.9	–1.1
Bhutan[b]	2.9	77.2	40.7	34.9	–12.9	–9.2	8.2	3.3
India	2.8	35.4	30.7	36.5	–0.6	–7.2	–3.2	–13.6
Maldives	–3.4	21.3	–5.6	46.2	16.9	11.2	15.1	–4.9
Nepal	19.0	13.2	39.3	4.8	1.2	10.5	19.9	5.2
Sri Lanka	20.5	10.7	31.8	50.8	–5.6	–5.9	7.9	–2.5
Southeast Asia								
Brunei Darussalam	–16.7	1.5	5.6	42.0	–1.0	1.4	–0.5	–10.0
Cambodia[b]	21.6	...	18.0	24.7	13.4	19.7	8.9	12.3
Indonesia	39.6	24.0	40.1	30.8	8.0	–2.6	–4.5	–19.9
Lao PDR	–3.4	23.8	41.0	16.7	27.1	0.8	38.6	22.5
Malaysia	25.3	8.7	33.1	14.2	4.8	4.8	1.4	–15.9
Myanmar	–11.0	0.6	53.4	40.9	0.4	51.7	20.9	–0.3
Philippines	3.8	7.3	27.4	9.6	2.7	–0.2	–0.5	2.0
Singapore[c]	21.3	15.3	26.7	17.4	4.2	–1.8	–1.9	–19.0
Thailand	23.3	25.1	37.7	23.9	9.4	–0.5	–8.5	–11.5
Viet Nam	33.2	15.0	21.3	25.8	6.6	16.0	12.0	12.0
The Pacific								
Cook Islands	21.9	7.0	11.2	21.0	1.9	3.9	4.1	–9.3
Fiji	–8.3	11.5	25.8	20.8	3.3	25.3	–5.9	–21.7
Kiribati	–4.2	28.7	5.4	25.5	18.4	–1.2	0.0	...
Marshall Islands	16.7	15.3	...	...	...	...	...	...
Micronesia, Fed. States of	...	–3.2	–1.8	12.0	3.0	–3.1	...	...
Nauru	104.9	52.3	–79.4	48.8	21.2	273.9	–32.2	–33.1
Palau	–5.7	0.7	9.3	21.7	8.4	6.7	3.1	4.4
Papua New Guinea	–7.0	4.5	23.0	20.2	12.4	13.7	–26.1	–43.5
Samoa	–21.7	20.7	36.6	14.1	–3.3	5.6	4.8	–12.7
Solomon Islands	–16.1	52.4	51.2	16.7	5.1	8.1	–7.0	–6.4
Timor-Leste	...	–25.3	1.0	13.9	97.3	–21.1	4.7	...
Tonga	...	15.3	10.3	21.4	3.7	–0.5	10.4	...
Tuvalu	–36.0	13.3	14.3	56.3	0.0	–36.0	...	...
Vanuatu	–12.6	22.4	–2.5	7.3	–2.7	5.8	0.0	17.0
Developed Member Economies								
Australia	3.5	14.5	23.4	21.2	7.0	–7.2	–2.1	–11.9
Japan	22.7	13.6	25.8	23.3	3.8	–6.0	–2.6	–20.1
New Zealand	–2.7	13.4	21.5	21.4	3.3	3.6	7.3	–13.9
DEVELOPING MEMBER ECONOMIES[d]	**24.2**	**16.5**	**26.1**	**22.7**	**3.5**	**2.5**	**0.2**	**–12.6**
REGIONAL MEMBERS[d]	**22.6**	**15.9**	**25.9**	**22.7**	**3.6**	**0.9**	**–0.2**	**–13.6**

... = data not available at cutoff date; 0.0 or –0.0= magnitude is less than half of unit employed; * = provisional, preliminary, estimate/budget figure; Lao PDR = Lao People's Democratic Republic.

a   Rates are based on US dollar values of imports.
b   Compilation methodology shifted from cost, insurance, and freight (cif) to free on board (fob) for Bhutan and Cambodia beginning in 2005.
c   Prior to 2003, data exclude Indonesia.
d   For reporting economies only.

Sources: Economy sources; International Monetary Fund. May 2016. *International Financial Statistics* (CD-ROM). Washington, DC.

External Trade

Table 4.12:   **Trade in Goods**[a]
(% of GDP)

Regional Member	2000	2005	2010	2011	2012	2013	2014	2015
Developing Member Economies								
Central and West Asia								
Afghanistan	...	43.1	34.5	35.3	48.3	42.8	39.3	40.9
Armenia	62.0	56.6	51.7	54.0	53.1	52.7	51.4	44.9
Azerbaijan	55.3	90.6	62.4	67.4	61.1	56.7	50.0	47.8
Georgia	33.8	52.3	59.6	63.9	65.7	67.7	69.4	71.1
Kazakhstan	75.7	79.1	61.7	60.5	61.5	54.8	52.6	41.2*
Kyrgyz Republic	77.3	75.7	103.8	104.9	113.6	109.0	102.0	87.4
Pakistan	25.7	32.1	30.6	30.7	30.6	30.1	28.8	25.7
Tajikistan	169.6	96.8	68.3	68.4	41.1	62.1	57.1	55.1
Turkmenistan	86.2	55.6	80.7	96.2	97.0	89.1	83.8	108.8*
Uzbekistan	45.1	66.0	56.2	57.1	51.2	...	...	...
East Asia								
China, People's Rep. of	39.4	62.7	49.2	48.6	45.7	43.8	41.6	36.4
Hong Kong, China	241.5	324.3	360.1	367.1	360.6	356.4	349.5	319.2
Korea, Rep. of	59.2	60.8	81.5	89.8	87.3	82.4	77.8	69.9
Mongolia	101.2	88.8	85.0	109.7	90.5	84.5	90.1	72.0
Taipei,China	88.1	102.4	119.5	123.4	117.7	114.8	113.1	99.2
South Asia								
Bangladesh	28.3	36.2	34.7	46.0	45.6	43.2	41.2	36.9
Bhutan[b]	67.3	83.1	84.9	95.5	84.0	76.5	75.2	74.8
India	20.0	30.2	36.3	43.6	43.2	41.0	37.1	30.9
Maldives	79.7	75.4	41.8	59.0	68.1	67.8	69.7	60.3
Nepal	38.8	35.3	36.5	33.7	35.1	37.4	41.0	40.6
Sri Lanka	75.7	62.4	38.9	47.2	42.2	38.2	38.2	35.8
Southeast Asia								
Brunei Darussalam	83.5	80.7	83.3	86.7	86.9	83.2	82.9	74.0
Cambodia[b]	90.9	108.5	85.9	95.2	98.1	106.6	107.2	112.7
Indonesia	58.0	50.1	38.9	42.7	41.6	40.5	39.8	34.0
Lao PDR	52.9	52.8	56.5	57.0	58.6	49.7	59.0	64.9
Malaysia	192.1	178.3	142.1	139.5	134.8	134.4	130.9	126.6
Myanmar	1.1	0.3	0.2	0.2	22.6	40.2	44.0	44.3
Philippines	88.7	88.0	55.1	50.1	47.2	45.0	44.8	42.9
Singapore[c]	284.5	337.5	279.8	281.0	272.0	259.7	251.7	219.7
Thailand	103.9	120.7	110.8	121.2	120.4	112.9	112.1	104.4
Viet Nam	96.6	120.1	135.5	150.3	146.5	154.2	160.1	169.5
The Pacific								
Cook Islands	65.3	47.3	37.5	39.4	38.7	42.0	43.6	42.4
Fiji	83.3	77.7	84.2	86.3	87.4	94.4	85.5	68.5
Kiribati	63.6	76.0	50.2	56.6	61.5	60.9	63.1	...
Marshall Islands	127.0	120.1	...	139.6	...	...	...	...
Micronesia, Fed. States of	52.9	56.4	64.2	74.2	75.3	70.3	...	...
Nauru	...	360.0	366.6	351.1	309.1	345.3	...	...
Palau	93.3	63.1	64.6	71.9	73.1	72.4	67.0	60.5
Papua New Guinea	88.3	99.3	65.2	62.0	52.1	53.7	...	...
Samoa	45.1	45.9	44.5	43.6	42.4	43.5	44.7	42.9
Solomon Islands	55.1	68.3	91.1	106.9	108.0	101.4	92.2	83.9
Timor-Leste	...	8.2	7.9	6.6	11.0	10.3	14.2	...
Tonga	41.9	49.6	44.6	46.4	46.2	49.0	54.6	...
Tuvalu	37.4	59.2	51.2	64.4	63.4	42.5	...	...
Vanuatu	40.5	53.5	47.4	46.9	44.9	43.9	46.2	...
Developed Member Economies								
Australia	34.4	32.0	34.1	34.7	32.8	33.0	32.7	32.1
Japan	18.2	24.3	26.6	28.3	28.3	31.5	32.7	30.9
New Zealand	50.1	41.7	42.6	44.4	42.8	41.5	42.0	...
DEVELOPING MEMBER ECONOMIES[d]	**63.0**	**58.0**	**42.5**	**43.1**	**65.1**	**62.0**	**59.1**	**52.1**
REGIONAL MEMBERS[d]	**38.5**	**45.0**	**38.8**	**39.9**	**53.4**	**53.7**	**52.5**	**47.8**

... = data not available at cutoff date; * = provisional, preliminary, estimate/budget figure; Lao PDR = Lao People's Democratic Republic.

a   The sum of merchandise exports and imports.
b   Starting 2005, compilation methodology for imports shifted from cost, insurance, and freight (cif) to free on board (fob).
c   Prior to 2003, data exclude Indonesia.
d   For reporting economies only.

Sources: Economy sources; International Monetary Fund. May 2016. *International Financial Statistics* (CD-ROM). Washington, DC.

Table 4.13: **Direction of Trade: Merchandise Exports**
(% of total merchandise exports)

To From Regional Member	Asia		Europe		North and Central America		Middle East		South America		Africa		Oceania		Rest of the World	
	2000	2015	2000	2015	2000	2015	2000	2015	2000	2015	2000	2015	2000	2015	2000	2015
Developing Member Economies																
Central and West Asia																
Afghanistan	50.1	84.0	40.3	6.3	4.8	3.5	2.3	5.7	2.1	0.1	0.2	0.2	0.1	0.2	0.0	0.0
Armenia	8.5	21.8	55.6	48.5	12.9	11.7	12.5	17.2	0.0	0.0	0.0	0.0	0.0	0.0	10.4	0.8
Azerbaijan	13.4	17.9	75.5	67.9	0.5	4.9	8.6	5.6	0.4	0.0	0.6	2.7	0.0	0.0	1.0	1.0
Georgia	38.9	42.6	52.7	41.9	2.7	8.3	4.0	4.7	0.1	1.4	1.4	0.6	0.0	0.1	0.3	0.4
Kazakhstan	12.8	31.4	48.3	60.4	14.8	3.2	2.5	4.3	0.1	0.5	0.1	0.2	0.0	0.0	21.4	0.2
Kyrgyz Republic	39.4	58.0	58.3	34.5	0.6	0.9	1.7	6.0	0.0	0.0	0.0	0.5	0.0	0.0	0.0	0.0
Pakistan	24.1	29.9	28.6	25.7	28.1	15.0	12.4	17.6	1.2	1.2	3.4	5.8	1.6	1.0	0.5	3.8
Tajikistan	24.5	59.8	73.6	26.0	0.1	3.0	1.7	9.6	0.0	0.0	0.1	0.1	0.0	0.0	0.0	1.4
Turkmenistan	14.1	83.4	71.0	5.8	1.3	2.6	11.9	6.0	0.0	0.0	0.2	0.0	0.0	0.0	1.5	2.1
Uzbekistan	30.0	58.1	63.2	39.4	2.1	0.1	2.2	2.1	1.1	0.1	0.1	0.1	0.0	0.0	1.1	0.0
East Asia																
China, People's Rep. of	48.8	43.4	17.9	17.7	23.6	21.7	2.9	5.5	1.4	3.3	1.7	4.1	1.6	2.1	2.1	2.2
Hong Kong, China	50.0	69.6	16.5	10.9	26.1	10.8	1.4	3.0	1.1	1.1	0.7	1.1	1.5	1.1	2.7	2.5
Korea, Rep. of	43.1	55.6	15.5	11.0	26.4	17.3	4.3	5.5	2.2	2.3	1.5	1.9	1.7	2.4	5.2	4.0
Mongolia	55.5	87.0	17.5	12.1	24.6	0.5	0.1	0.1	0.0	0.0	0.0	0.0	2.3	0.2	0.0	0.0
Taipei,China[a]	52.1	70.2	15.7	9.1	26.1	14.2	1.7	2.5	1.2	1.0	0.9	0.8	1.5	1.4	0.8	0.8
South Asia																
Bangladesh	6.9	11.7	41.0	48.3	33.8	17.0	2.4	2.0	0.2	0.7	0.6	0.5	0.4	2.0	14.6	17.8
Bhutan[b]	82.6	82.6	9.6	16.1	3.4	1.0	0.4	0.0	0.0	0.0	3.9	0.1	0.0	0.1	0.0	0.0
India	25.1	29.8	27.7	18.1	23.7	17.5	12.2	20.1	1.3	2.5	4.5	8.7	1.2	1.4	4.3	1.9
Maldives	35.8	34.3	18.6	50.3	44.4	10.2	0.0	0.3	0.0	0.0	0.0	3.5	0.0	0.3	1.2	1.1
Nepal	45.9	69.7	23.9	13.3	28.1	10.7	0.1	1.4	0.0	0.1	0.0	0.1	0.3	0.7	1.7	4.0
Sri Lanka	13.6	21.9	28.1	31.8	42.2	30.1	7.5	10.1	0.6	1.4	0.6	1.4	1.1	1.9	6.3	1.4
Southeast Asia																
Brunei Darussalam	78.6	80.4	3.7	0.7	12.0	0.4	0.1	0.1	0.0	0.0	0.1	0.1	5.2	10.5	0.3	7.9
Cambodia	27.4	29.5	17.2	36.8	54.4	29.9	0.0	0.5	0.0	0.9	0.0	0.6	0.1	1.1	0.7	0.7
Indonesia	57.8	61.8	14.8	11.4	15.1	12.0	3.4	4.4	0.9	1.3	1.4	2.4	2.7	3.0	3.9	3.7
Lao PDR	47.4	81.2	27.8	5.6	2.6	1.4	0.1	0.0	0.0	0.0	0.2	0.0	0.1	0.1	21.7	11.5
Malaysia	53.5	63.2	14.3	10.3	22.3	13.4	2.0	3.0	0.6	0.8	0.6	2.2	2.9	4.0	3.8	3.0
Myanmar	45.9	87.2	16.9	5.9	24.4	1.2	0.2	0.6	0.2	0.1	0.2	0.5	0.5	0.3	11.8	4.3
Philippines	40.4	62.6	18.3	11.9	31.7	16.9	0.5	1.2	0.2	0.5	0.1	1.5	0.9	0.9	7.9	4.6
Singapore	53.8	68.3	14.5	8.8	19.2	9.4	1.7	2.4	0.4	0.5	1.1	1.6	2.9	4.2	6.4	4.9
Thailand	47.3	57.7	17.3	11.8	23.3	13.7	3.1	4.9	0.6	1.8	1.6	2.6	2.7	5.4	4.0	2.2
Viet Nam	51.8	45.7	22.9	20.6	6.3	23.2	2.9	3.7	0.3	2.1	0.8	0.9	8.9	2.3	5.9	1.5
The Pacific																
Cook Islands	28.1	70.6	0.0	0.0	7.8	0.5	0.0	0.0	0.0	0.0	0.0	0.0	59.0	11.9	5.1	17.0
Fiji	10.3	6.3	16.6	6.4	21.3	14.4	0.1	0.3	0.0	0.0	0.0	0.0	36.9	31.5	14.8	41.1
Kiribati[b]	84.5	85.8	2.8	0.1	6.1	2.2	0.0	0.0	5.4	7.2	0.0	3.0	1.3	1.3	0.1	0.5
Marshall Islands	...	...	...	...	...	...	...	...	...	...	...	...	...	...	...	...
Micronesia, Fed. States of[c]	43.4	4.1	0.0	0.0	23.2	40.3	0.0	0.0	0.0	0.0	0.0	0.0	3.0	4.8	30.5	50.8
Nauru[b]	38.3	12.6	2.0	0.9	7.6	1.5	0.0	0.1	0.1	0.0	6.8	69.9	45.4	15.0	0.1	0.0
Palau[b]	98.4	99.2	0.9	0.7	0.0	0.0	0.0	0.0	0.6	0.1	0.0	0.1	0.1	0.0	0.0	0.0
Papua New Guinea	24.8	37.3	10.2	5.2	1.3	0.6	0.0	0.0	0.0	0.0	0.0	0.0	31.0	16.0	32.7	40.9
Samoa	17.8	2.6	3.0	1.6	10.8	2.9	0.0	0.2	0.1	3.3	0.1	0.1	59.6	24.6	8.7	64.7
Solomon Islands	72.9	76.9	10.6	11.5	0.7	0.5	0.0	0.0	0.0	0.1	0.0	0.1	5.6	3.5	10.2	7.3
Timor-Leste[b]	95.7	95.4	3.6	2.1	0.4	1.8	0.0	0.0	0.0	0.0	0.3	0.2	0.1	0.5	0.0	0.0
Tonga	51.7	29.4	6.6	2.6	31.0	15.3	0.1	0.1	0.0	0.3	0.0	0.3	8.2	42.9	2.5	9.1
Tuvalu[b]	0.6	37.3	75.0	44.4	0.0	2.4	0.0	0.0	4.2	0.1	6.4	5.1	13.7	10.6	0.0	0.1
Vanuatu	78.4	73.9	5.8	9.0	9.9	2.3	0.0	0.0	0.1	0.0	0.2	0.9	3.6	9.4	2.1	4.5
Developed Member Economies																
Australia	52.6	72.0	11.3	5.7	11.6	6.3	5.1	4.0	0.8	0.8	1.8	1.2	7.7	4.4	9.1	5.7
Japan	34.0	47.9	17.7	12.0	34.3	24.3	2.3	4.4	1.2	1.5	0.9	1.1	2.1	2.5	7.6	6.3
New Zealand	33.8	41.1	15.4	10.8	18.0	14.7	2.8	5.3	1.5	1.5	0.9	2.9	22.1	19.0	5.4	4.7
DEVELOPING MEMBER ECONOMIES[d]	47.9	51.2	17.4	15.4	23.6	17.5	2.9	5.4	1.1	2.3	1.2	3.1	2.0	2.4	3.8	2.8
REGIONAL MEMBERS[d]	44.4	51.5	17.3	14.7	25.9	17.8	2.8	5.3	1.1	2.1	1.2	2.8	2.4	2.5	5.0	3.3
WORLD	21.7	30.7	41.6	35.5	25.5	18.8	2.8	5.1	2.2	2.8	1.7	2.7	1.3	1.4	3.3	3.1

... = data not available at cutoff date, 0.0 = magnitude is less than half of unit employed, Lao PDR = Lao People's Democratic Republic.

a Economies are classified following Taipei,China's trade groupings. Data under the heading "Middle East" refer to "Middle and Near East" economies.
b Based on reporting partner-country data. For Palau, data for 2000 refer to 2001; for Timor-Leste, to 2004.
c Data for 2015 refer to 2007.
d For reporting economies only.

Sources: International Monetary Fund. May 2016. *International Financial Statistics* (CD-ROM). Washington, DC; for the Cook Islands; the Federated States of Micronesia; and Taipei,China: economy sources.

External Trade

Table 4.14:   **Direction of Trade: Merchandise Imports**
(% of total merchandise imports)

From / To / Regional Member	Asia 2000	Asia 2015	Europe 2000	Europe 2015	North and Central America 2000	North and Central America 2015	Middle East 2000	Middle East 2015	South America 2000	South America 2015	Africa 2000	Africa 2015	Oceania 2000	Oceania 2015	Rest of the World 2000	Rest of the World 2015
Developing Member Economies																
Central and West Asia																
Afghanistan	78.6	79.9	13.1	8.8	2.0	8.5	0.7	0.5	0.0	0.2	5.6	2.1	0.0	0.0	0.0	0.0
Armenia	8.9	23.1	55.8	59.7	14.6	4.0	15.4	8.2	0.0	2.7	0.0	0.8	0.0	0.5	5.3	1.0
Azerbaijan	24.7	29.1	54.1	61.5	10.5	4.4	7.3	3.4	0.5	0.8	2.1	0.1	0.6	0.5	0.3	0.1
Georgia	32.3	42.6	51.2	46.6	10.2	3.7	4.2	4.9	0.9	1.3	0.1	0.7	0.2	0.1	1.0	0.1
Kazakhstan	14.1	37.6	75.7	58.4	7.0	2.4	1.1	0.8	1.0	0.2	0.5	0.4	0.1	0.1	0.5	0.2
Kyrgyz Republic	44.3	75.7	40.9	23.1	11.8	0.6	2.9	0.4	0.1	0.1	0.0	0.0	0.0	0.0	0.1	0.0
Pakistan	28.8	46.9	19.0	9.5	7.0	4.1	38.3	34.3	1.0	1.0	2.7	1.9	3.0	0.9	0.2	1.3
Tajikistan	57.7	67.5	40.5	24.6	0.1	0.7	1.6	6.7	0.0	0.5	0.1	0.0	0.0	0.0	0.0	0.0
Turkmenistan	31.8	49.4	44.8	32.9	3.5	1.2	13.5	14.7	0.1	0.0	0.0	0.0	0.0	0.0	6.2	1.8
Uzbekistan	38.8	58.2	51.5	40.0	8.9	1.4	0.6	0.2	0.1	0.1	0.0	0.0	0.0	0.0	0.1	0.1
East Asia																
China, People's Rep. of	44.3	34.6	17.5	16.3	11.9	11.0	4.5	6.4	2.1	5.7	2.4	3.2	2.6	4.7	14.7	18.2
Hong Kong, China	72.1	76.2	10.2	9.1	7.6	5.7	0.8	1.4	0.5	0.6	0.3	0.3	1.0	0.4	7.5	6.3
Korea, Rep. of	40.9	43.2	12.5	17.1	19.9	12.1	15.9	15.5	1.6	2.6	1.9	1.5	4.3	4.2	3.1	3.9
Mongolia	46.6	57.8	47.7	38.8	4.8	1.9	0.2	0.9	0.0	0.1	0.0	0.0	0.3	0.4	0.4	0.2
Taipei,China[a]	56.1	58.6	13.6	12.0	19.4	12.7	4.8	10.3	1.0	1.7	2.3	1.4	2.8	3.2	0.0	0.0
South Asia																
Bangladesh	53.5	63.3	12.0	8.7	3.6	4.2	5.1	6.0	1.4	3.4	0.6	2.1	2.1	1.8	21.8	10.5
Bhutan[b]	49.3	86.2	45.9	13.1	3.3	0.5	0.0	0.0	1.2	0.0	0.2	0.0	0.1	0.1	0.0	0.0
India	20.3	34.3	28.8	18.2	7.2	6.9	9.4	21.8	1.4	4.9	6.1	8.1	2.3	2.6	24.5	3.3
Maldives	72.9	59.2	10.5	10.1	3.7	3.4	8.7	22.7	0.1	0.9	0.4	0.7	2.9	2.6	0.8	0.5
Nepal	69.1	85.1	12.6	7.9	2.0	1.1	5.8	3.9	0.8	0.2	0.1	0.0	1.9	0.7	7.7	1.0
Sri Lanka	53.8	69.5	13.8	12.0	4.5	3.1	9.1	10.3	0.5	0.6	0.5	0.2	3.4	2.0	14.4	2.2
Southeast Asia																
Brunei Darussalam	69.3	78.5	16.0	17.2	10.8	2.4	0.2	0.4	0.1	0.1	0.1	0.1	2.2	0.7	1.3	0.6
Cambodia	75.9	88.9	8.2	3.1	2.8	2.4	0.1	0.9	0.1	0.2	0.0	0.0	0.5	0.2	12.4	4.3
Indonesia	50.9	67.7	13.9	9.4	12.3	6.5	8.4	5.0	1.5	2.8	2.4	2.3	6.0	3.9	4.6	2.4
Lao PDR	89.5	96.1	6.8	2.3	0.7	0.4	0.0	0.0	0.0	0.0	0.0	0.0	0.9	0.3	2.0	0.9
Malaysia	57.3	63.1	12.5	10.6	17.3	9.0	2.0	5.3	0.6	2.1	0.4	1.3	2.3	2.7	7.5	5.9
Myanmar	86.5	93.1	4.6	3.6	0.6	1.1	0.2	0.3	0.0	0.2	0.0	0.0	0.6	0.6	7.4	1.1
Philippines	48.9	64.2	10.1	9.9	19.4	10.7	10.5	5.5	0.7	1.0	0.2	0.1	3.0	1.9	7.3	6.7
Singapore	54.5	51.3	14.1	16.2	15.8	12.3	8.2	8.4	0.3	1.3	0.4	0.4	1.9	1.5	4.9	8.5
Thailand	53.2	60.6	12.6	12.4	12.6	7.7	10.2	9.0	1.1	1.6	1.3	0.9	2.3	2.5	6.8	5.2
Viet Nam	68.7	77.9	11.8	6.3	2.6	3.9	1.2	2.1	0.4	2.5	0.3	0.2	2.3	1.5	12.8	5.4
The Pacific																
Cook Islands[c]	1.9	2.8	0.2	0.1	8.6	6.1	0.0	0.0	0.0	0.0	0.0	0.0	85.0	69.1	4.3	21.9
Fiji	26.9	53.2	3.7	9.4	3.7	3.6	0.0	0.3	0.3	0.1	0.1	0.2	64.1	31.1	1.2	2.2
Kiribati[b]	26.1	50.5	3.8	1.8	9.8	3.8	0.0	0.0	0.1	0.1	0.0	0.1	59.2	41.9	1.0	1.7
Marshall Islands[d]	4.9	8.6	0.0	0.0	32.6	24.5	0.0	0.0	0.0	0.0	0.0	0.0	2.2	6.5	60.3	60.3
Micronesia, Fed. States of[c]	31.2	23.6	0.0	0.0	59.9	59.0	0.0	0.0	0.0	0.0	0.0	0.0	6.7	6.4	2.2	11.0
Nauru[b]	6.3	9.1	8.2	5.2	10.7	2.4	0.0	0.0	0.0	0.0	48.2	0.1	26.3	69.7	0.4	13.6
Palau[b]	98.5	91.6	0.9	4.3	0.0	0.0	0.0	0.0	0.3	0.0	0.0	0.0	0.3	4.0	0.0	0.0
Papua New Guinea	37.6	57.0	3.1	3.8	2.3	4.6	0.1	0.1	0.2	0.1	0.9	0.3	53.7	28.6	2.1	5.5
Samoa	15.9	41.0	1.1	0.8	25.9	5.9	0.1	0.3	2.1	0.3	0.0	0.1	52.1	48.5	2.7	3.0
Solomon Islands	38.6	44.4	2.6	1.8	5.2	1.6	0.0	0.1	0.1	0.1	0.5	1.8	39.0	38.7	14.1	11.6
Timor-Leste[b]	90.9	89.2	8.0	5.5	1.0	0.4	0.0	0.0	0.0	1.1	0.0	0.4	0.1	3.4	0.0	0.0
Tonga	31.3	23.2	4.7	2.2	10.3	6.8	0.0	0.0	0.2	0.7	0.0	0.0	52.6	65.9	1.0	1.1
Tuvalu[b]	3.0	50.1	11.9	1.3	0.0	0.6	0.0	0.0	0.0	0.0	0.0	1.1	85.0	46.0	0.0	0.9
Vanuatu	42.5	48.1	6.7	3.8	1.3	1.5	0.0	0.0	0.3	0.1	0.2	1.5	42.1	41.1	6.9	3.8
Developed Member Economies																
Australia	41.1	55.5	22.7	18.7	22.1	13.1	2.8	1.7	0.8	1.0	0.9	1.1	5.5	4.1	4.1	4.8
Japan	37.1	45.6	15.0	15.0	22.2	12.9	13.0	12.2	2.0	2.8	1.3	1.8	4.6	6.2	4.8	3.6
New Zealand	28.5	46.9	18.6	19.6	19.6	13.7	5.6	3.9	1.1	1.2	1.2	0.6	22.5	12.0	2.8	1.9
DEVELOPING MEMBER ECONOMIES[e]	52.3	50.3	14.5	14.5	13.6	9.0	6.7	8.3	1.1	3.3	1.5	2.3	2.6	3.1	7.7	9.2
REGIONAL MEMBERS[e]	48.1	49.9	15.0	14.8	16.0	9.7	7.9	8.5	1.3	3.1	1.4	2.2	3.4	3.5	6.9	8.4
WORLD	25.8	33.5	40.0	36.4	20.3	14.1	4.1	5.1	2.6	3.1	2.1	2.2	1.3	1.5	3.7	4.1

0.0 = magnitude is less than half of unit employed, Lao PDR = Lao People's Democratic Republic.

a Economies are classified following Taipei,China's trade groupings. Data under the heading "Middle East" refer to "Middle and Near East" economies.
b Based on reporting partner-country data. For Timor-Leste, data for 2000 refer to 2004.
c Data for 2015 refer to 2013.
d Data for 2015 refer to 2006.
e For reporting economies only.

Sources: International Monetary Fund. May 2016. *International Financial Statistics* (CD-ROM). Washington, DC; for the Cook Islands; the Federated States of Micronesia; and Taipei,China: economy sources.

Table 4.15:   **International Reserves and Ratio of International Reserves to Imports**

Regional Member	International Reserves[a] (end of year; $ million)				Ratio of International Reserves to Imports[b] (months)			
	2000	2005	2010	2015	2000	2005	2010	2015
Developing Member Economies								
Central and West Asia								
Afghanistan	7 (2002)	0	5,147	6,990	0.0 (2002)	0.0	13.2	11.9
Armenia	314	669	1,866	1,775	4.8	4.8	6.9	7.7
Azerbaijan	680	1,178	6,409	7,910	5.3	3.2	11.5	9.7
Georgia	116	479	2,264	2,521	1.4	2.2	5.4	4.1
Kazakhstan	2,096	7,070	28,275	28,073	3.5	4.7	10.3	10.0
Kyrgyz Republic	262	612	1,720	1,778	6.2	6.6	6.9	5.6
Pakistan	2,056	10,948	17,210	20,045	2.6	6.9	6.6	5.8
Tajikistan	94	189	403	494	1.2	1.6	1.5	2.1
Turkmenistan	1,808	4,457	...	...	12.5	18.1	...	...
Uzbekistan	1,273	2,147 (2004)	...	...	6.3	8.4 (2004)	...	...
East Asia								
China, People's Rep. of	168,855	825,588	2,875,894	3,405,385	10.8	17.5	27.8	25.9
Hong Kong, China	107,560	124,278	268,743	358,773	7.9	6.1	8.4	8.1
Korea, Rep. of	96,198	210,391	291,571	367,944	7.5	10.0	8.4	10.3
Mongolia	202	333	2,288	1,323	4.0	3.4	8.9	4.6
Taipei,China	111,370	257,952	387,207	430,711	9.7	17.0	18.4	19.6
South Asia								
Bangladesh	1,516	2,825	11,178	27,493	2.4	2.9	6.3	9.0
Bhutan	318	467	1,002	1,103	20.6	12.2	15.1	13.3
India	40,155	136,026	297,746	351,551	8.3	10.4	9.3	10.6
Maldives	123	189	364	576	4.3	3.5	3.5	3.6
Nepal	952	1,504	2,939	31	7.3	8.9	7.2	0.0
Sri Lanka	1,147	2,735	7,196	7,304	1.9	3.7	6.4	4.6
Southeast Asia								
Brunei Darussalam	382 (2001)	492	1,563	3,367	4.2 (2001)	4.2	7.3	12.6
Cambodia	611	1,159	3,802	7,376	3.8	3.5	7.9	7.4
Indonesia	29,268	34,731	96,211	105,929	8.7	6.5	9.7	9.4
Lao PDR	140	239	713	1,058	3.1	3.3	4.2	2.4
Malaysia	28,624	70,152	106,525	95,287	4.4	7.8	8.6	7.7
Myanmar	234	782	5,729	2	1.3	5.3	16.0	0.0
Philippines	15,063	18,494	62,373	80,667	4.2	5.9	14.0	14.9
Singapore	80,170	116,172	225,715	247,746	6.9	7.2	8.8	10.1
Thailand	32,661	52,065	172,129	156,514	6.3	5.9	12.8	10.6
Viet Nam	3,510	9,216	12,926	28,616	3.0	3.2	2.0	2.2
The Pacific								
Cook Islands	...	...	...	...	...	...	...	...
Fiji	412	321	721	916 (2014)	6.4	2.6	5.6	4.9 (2014)
Kiribati	0	0	8	7	0.0	0.0	1.4	...
Marshall Islands	...	...	...	...	...	...	...	...
Micronesia, Fed. States of	113	50	56	135	12.4	4.8	4.2	9.7
Nauru	...	...	...	...	...	...	...	...
Palau	0	0	5	4	0.0	0.0	0.5	0.3
Papua New Guinea	296	749	3,092	1,738	3.5	5.9	10.5	9.2
Samoa	64	82	209	139	2.4	5.2	9.0	7.6
Solomon Islands	32	95	266	534	4.2	9.4	8.9	14.6
Timor-Leste	...	84 (2006)	406	438	...	8.9 (2006)	15.9	8.0
Tonga	25	47	105	156	4.7	5.0	11.5	11.9
Tuvalu	...	...	...	...	...	...	...	...
Vanuatu	39	67	161	269	6.1	6.2	8.1	11.2
Developed Member Economies								
Australia	18,817	43,257	42,268	49,267	3.5	4.5	2.6	2.9
Japan	361,639	846,896	1,096,185	1,233,153	12.9	21.9	21.0	23.6
New Zealand	3,952	8,893	16,723	15,861 (2014)	3.7	4.2	6.5	4.7 (2014)
DEVELOPING MEMBER ECONOMIES[c]	728,742	1,895,035	4,902,138	5,752,679	7.2	10.7	15.3	15.3
REGIONAL MEMBERS[c]	1,113,150	2,794,081	6,057,313	7,050,960	8.2	12.3	15.5	15.7

... = data not available at cutoff date, 0 or 0.0 = magnitude is less than half of the unit employed, Lao PDR = Lao People's Democratic Republic.

a   Data refer to international reserves with gold at national valuation unless otherwise specified. For Afghanistan (up to 2007), Kiribati, Palau, Samoa, Solomon Islands, Tonga, Turkmenistan, and Vanuatu, data refer to international reserves without gold.
b   Merchandise imports from the balance of payments were used in the computation.
c   For reporting economies only.

Sources: For international reserves: International Monetary Fund. May 2016. *International Financial Statistics* (CD-ROM). Washington, DC; for Taipei,China: economy source; for the reserves-to-imports ratio: ADB estimates using data from International Monetary Fund. May 2016. *International Financial Statistics* (CD-ROM). Washington, DC; economy sources.

Table 4.16:   **Official Flows[a] from All Sources to Developing Member Economies**
($ million)

Regional Member	2000	2005	2010	2011	2012	2013	2014
Developing Member Economies							
Central and West Asia							
Afghanistan	136	2,838	6,472	6,866	6,667	5,263	4,823
Armenia	216	170	342	397	271	279	265
Azerbaijan	139	217	160	287	285	−73	215
Georgia	169	292	628	588	661	647	563
Kazakhstan	189	229	226	201	129	88	88
Kyrgyz Republic	215	268	382	525	472	536	624
Pakistan	703	1,615	3,020	3,498	2,017	2,192	3,612
Tajikistan	124	252	433	348	393	390	356
Turkmenistan	35	30	46	40	38	36	34
Uzbekistan	186	170	232	204	255	293	324
East Asia							
China, People's Rep. of	1,712	1,814	645	−608	−191	−670	−960
Hong Kong, China	...	...	...	...	...	...	...
Korea, Rep. of	...	...	...	...	...	...	...
Mongolia	217	220	301	350	445	428	315
Taipei,China	...	...	...	...	...	...	...
South Asia							
Bangladesh	1,173	1,319	1,404	1,492	2,149	2,631	2,418
Bhutan	53	90	130	143	161	134	130
India	1,373	1,876	2,812	3,245	1,668	2,436	2,984
Maldives	19	76	111	53	57	21	25
Nepal	386	424	818	887	768	871	880
Sri Lanka	275	1,161	583	610	489	402	488
Southeast Asia							
Brunei Darussalam	...	...	...	...	...	...	...
Cambodia	396	536	733	795	808	806	799
Indonesia	1,653	2,534	1,390	405	66	66	−388
Lao PDR	281	302	414	398	409	421	472
Malaysia	46	26	2	38	16	−120	12
Myanmar	106	145	355	380	505	3,936	1,380
Philippines	572	567	530	−184	−1	193	676
Singapore	...	...	...	...	...	...	...
Thailand	697	−168	−12	−138	−134	27	351
Viet Nam	1,681	1,913	2,939	3,618	4,115	4,084	4,218
The Pacific							
Cook Islands	4	8	13	28	21	16	27
Fiji	29	66	76	79	108	92	92
Kiribati	18	28	23	64	65	65	79
Marshall Islands	57	57	32	83	84	94	56
Micronesia, Fed. States of	102	107	63	134	143	143	116
Nauru	4	9	28	38	36	29	22
Palau	39	24	28	28	16	35	23
Papua New Guinea	275	267	511	611	669	657	577
Samoa	27	44	148	102	121	118	93
Solomon Islands	68	198	340	339	305	289	199
Timor-Leste	231	185	291	279	283	258	247
Tonga	19	32	70	94	78	81	80
Tuvalu	4	9	13	39	25	27	34
Vanuatu	46	39	108	91	102	91	98
DEVELOPING MEMBER ECONOMIES[b]	**13,673**	**19,987**	**26,843**	**26,446**	**24,569**	**27,314**	**26,449**
DEVELOPING ECONOMIES[c]	**49,777**	**108,652**	**131,340**	**141,560**	**132,976**	**151,099**	**161,109**

... = data not available at cutoff date, Lao PDR = Lao People's Democratic Republic.

a Refers to net official development assistance only, i.e., concessional flows to developing economies and multilateral institutions provided by official agencies, including state and local governments, or by their executing agencies, administered with the objective of promoting the economic development and welfare of developing economies, and containing a grant element of at least 25%.

b For reporting economies only.

c Includes data for all developing economies as reported in the Organisation for Economic Co-operation and Development's Geographical Distribution of Financial Flows to Aid Recipients.

Source: Organisation for Economic Co-operation and Development. OECD.Stat Online. http://stats.oecd.org (accessed August 2016).

Table 4.17:   **Net Private Flows**[a] **from All Sources to Developing Member Economies**
($ million)

Regional Member	2000	2005	2010	2011	2012	2013	2014
Developing Member Economies							
Central and West Asia							
Afghanistan	21	–12	–22	7	–11	26	32
Armenia	–21	54	40	19	–90	207	–1
Azerbaijan	467	1,193	724	885	136	927	–143
Georgia	24	–33	27	146	190	48	–75
Kazakhstan	473	2,341	–1,349	1,786	223	3,629	1,958
Kyrgyz Republic	11	2	23	15	15	19	18
Pakistan	–596	883	134	472	533	–550	35
Tajikistan	–8	–1	14	5	14	60	–9
Turkmenistan	93	–69	680	3	–458	156	1,162
Uzbekistan	123	–151	29	–58	119	264	–391
East Asia							
China, People's Rep. of	–308	21,264	46,798	48,961	18,773	53,944	57,192
Hong Kong, China	...	...	...	...	...	...	...
Korea, Rep. of	...	...	...	...	...	...	...
Mongolia	–6	–17	20	65	425	582	480
Taipei,China	...	...	...	...	...	...	...
South Asia							
Bangladesh	63	232	–82	373	805	–17	454
Bhutan	–9	1	26	–5	107	–165	6
India	1,122	5,815	20,931	14,685	15,721	7,659	11,658
Maldives	–5	8	29	–80	–32	25	90
Nepal	–4	–2	–11	–7	78	123	5
Sri Lanka	99	19	213	179	421	654	506
Southeast Asia							
Brunei Darussalam	...	...	...	...	...	...	...
Cambodia	9	2	253	124	271	312	401
Indonesia	43	7,115	3,509	10,242	7,123	6,995	9,740
Lao PDR	6	0	78	26	345	58	45
Malaysia	–189	1,263	6,569	7,001	10,582	10,085	7,366
Myanmar	–70	14	293	499	323	597	–148
Philippines	1,048	3,299	2,296	2,368	4,889	2,067	4,866
Singapore	...	...	...	...	...	...	...
Thailand	–137	11,062	6,109	10,550	5,888	7,074	9,489
Viet Nam	–182	349	3,209	3,751	4,604	8,846	3,614
The Pacific							
Cook Islands	–31	–29	0	8	–1	3	–2
Fiji	1	42	–3	51	163	65	115
Kiribati	0	1	0	3	0	0	3
Marshall Islands	108	2,737	973	2,968	2,122	–1,069	–256
Micronesia, Fed. States of	...	0	3	599	5	92	320
Nauru	–2	2	...	0	...	...	...
Palau	18	1	3	6	22	2	–5
Papua New Guinea	–24	232	4,108	–172	3,062	1,016	–3,311
Samoa	1	29	22	7	7	–32	35
Solomon Islands	–15	–17	3	8	–463	4	23
Timor-Leste	...	0	–4	–1	3	25	2
Tonga	–7	2	–10	–3	0	1	1
Tuvalu	–4	–1	...	1	0	–2	–1
Vanuatu	25	11	31	–23	86	43	15
DEVELOPING MEMBER ECONOMIES[b]	**2,136**	**57,640**	**95,668**	**105,466**	**76,001**	**103,774**	**105,289**
DEVELOPING ECONOMIES[c]	**81,273**	**178,572**	**351,214**	**337,663**	**309,244**	**267,476**	**402,643**

... = data not available at cutoff date, 0 = magnitude is less than half of unit employed, Lao PDR = Lao People's Democratic Republic.

a Refers to the sum of direct investment, portfolio investment, and private net export credits of Development Assistance Committee economies only.
b For reporting economies only.
c Includes data for all developing economies as reported in the Organisation for Economic Co-operation and Development's Geographical Distribution of Financial Flows to Aid Recipients.

Source: Organisation for Economic Co-operation and Development. OECD.Stat Online. http://stats.oecd.org (accessed August 2016).

Capital Flows

Table 4.18:   **Aggregate Net Resource Flows[a] from All Sources to Developing Member Economies**
($ million)

Regional Member	2000	2005	2010	2011	2012	2013	2014
Developing Member Economies							
Central and West Asia							
Afghanistan	157	2,826	6,450	6,873	6,656	5,289	4,855
Armenia	194	224	382	416	181	486	264
Azerbaijan	606	1,409	884	1,172	420	854	73
Georgia	194	260	655	734	851	695	488
Kazakhstan	662	2,570	-1,122	1,988	352	3,718	2,047
Kyrgyz Republic	226	270	405	540	487	555	642
Pakistan	106	2,498	3,155	3,969	2,550	1,643	3,647
Tajikistan	116	250	448	353	407	450	348
Turkmenistan	128	-39	725	44	-420	192	1,196
Uzbekistan	309	18	262	146	374	557	-67
East Asia							
China, People's Rep. of	1,403	23,078	47,443	48,352	18,582	53,273	56,232
Hong Kong, China	...	...	...	...	...	...	...
Korea, Rep. of	...	...	...	...	...	...	...
Mongolia	211	203	321	415	870	1,010	795
Taipei,China	...	...	...	...	...	...	...
South Asia							
Bangladesh	1,236	1,551	1,322	1,865	2,954	2,614	2,872
Bhutan	44	91	156	138	268	-31	136
India	2,495	7,691	23,742	17,930	17,389	10,096	14,641
Maldives	14	84	139	-27	25	46	115
Nepal	382	422	807	880	846	994	885
Sri Lanka	374	1,180	796	788	911	1,056	994
Southeast Asia							
Brunei Darussalam	...	...	...	...	...	...	...
Cambodia	405	537	986	920	1,079	1,118	1,201
Indonesia	1,696	9,649	4,899	10,647	7,189	7,062	9,352
Lao PDR	286	302	492	424	754	479	517
Malaysia	-144	1,289	6,572	7,039	10,597	9,965	7,378
Myanmar	35	158	648	879	828	4,533	1,232
Philippines	1,620	3,866	2,826	2,184	4,888	2,259	5,542
Singapore	...	...	...	...	...	...	...
Thailand	560	10,895	6,096	10,413	5,754	7,100	9,840
Viet Nam	1,499	2,262	6,148	7,369	8,719	12,930	7,832
The Pacific							
Cook Islands	-27	-22	13	36	21	18	24
Fiji	30	108	74	130	271	157	207
Kiribati	18	29	23	67	65	65	82
Marshall Islands	165	2,794	1,006	3,050	2,206	-975	-200
Micronesia, Fed. States of	...	107	67	733	149	235	436
Nauru	2	12	38	...	...	...	...
Palau	57	25	31	34	37	38	18
Papua New Guinea	251	499	4,620	439	3,731	1,673	-2,734
Samoa	28	73	169	109	128	86	128
Solomon Islands	54	182	344	348	-158	292	222
Timor-Leste	...	185	287	278	285	283	249
Tonga	12	34	61	91	78	82	81
Tuvalu	0	9	...	40	25	25	34
Vanuatu	71	51	139	68	188	134	114
DEVELOPING MEMBER ECONOMIES[b]	**15,477**	**77,628**	**122,470**	**131,911**	**100,535**	**131,058**	**131,715**
DEVELOPING ECONOMIES[c]	**131,049**	**287,224**	**482,554**	**479,223**	**442,220**	**418,575**	**563,752**

... = data not available at cutoff date, 0 = magnitude is less than half of unit employed, Lao PDR = Lao People's Democratic Republic.

a   Refers to the sum of official and net private flows.

b   For reporting economies only.

c   Includes data for all developing economies as reported in the Organisation for Economic Co-operation and Development's Geographical Distribution of Financial Flows to Aid Recipients.

Source: Organisation for Economic Co-operation and Development. OECD.Stat Online. http://stats.oecd.org (accessed August 2016).

Table 4.19: **Total External Debt of Developing Member Economies**[a]
($ million)

Regional Member	Total External Debt				External Debt, Public and Publicly Guaranteed			
	2000	2005	2010	2014	2000	2005	2010	2014
Developing Member Economies								
Central and West Asia								
Afghanistan	...	969 (2006)	2,423	2,555	...	911 (2006)	1,966	1,999
Armenia	1,010	1,968	6,304	8,551	675	923	2,557	3,376
Azerbaijan	1,524	2,118	7,029	11,693	734	1,362	3,711	8,094
Georgia	1,825	2,151	9,656	13,912	1,274	1,531	4,141	5,338
Kazakhstan	12,890	43,857	119,145	157,595	3,623	2,177	3,845	15,080
Kyrgyz Republic	1,938	2,257	4,114	7,257	1,220	1,665	2,442	3,222
Pakistan	32,954	34,018	64,003	62,184	27,124	30,089	43,403	45,879
Tajikistan	1,141	1,121	3,082	4,047	755	826	1,806	2,049
Turkmenistan	2,509	1,158	529	441	2,171	878	359	263
Uzbekistan	4,980	4,656	7,796	13,389	3,762	3,626	3,423	5,653
East Asia								
China, People's Rep. of	145,648	281,113	559,772	959,510	94,470	82,015	90,637	83,306
Hong Kong, China[b]	208,260	470,288	879,034	1,303,784 (2015)	...	...	...	...
Korea, Rep. of	135,208	161,956	355,911	395,400 (2015)	52,128	39,665	120,636	158,701 (2015)
Mongolia	960	1,396	5,928	20,826	833	1,267	1,782	3,498
Taipei,China	34,757	86,732	101,581	158,954 (2015)	23	222	8,035	1,116 (2015)
South Asia								
Bangladesh	15,596	18,449	25,752	34,925	14,985	17,385	21,400	26,433
Bhutan	212	657	935	1,840	202	636	919	1,820
India	101,130	121,195	291,651	463,230	81,195	54,726	101,786	164,122
Maldives	206	362	994	1,026	185	300	628	712
Nepal	2,878	3,191	3,789	4,010	2,826	3,112	3,509	3,512
Sri Lanka	9,241	11,297	21,762	43,609	7,936	9,655	16,507	29,502
Southeast Asia								
Brunei Darussalam	...	...	...	...	...	...	...	...
Cambodia	2,648	3,525	3,745	6,811	2,328	3,141	3,335	5,566
Indonesia	143,655	141,820	198,268	293,397	69,649	77,405	103,388	143,068
Lao PDR	2,535	3,277	6,487	10,724	2,474	2,354	3,771	5,631
Malaysia	41,946	64,911	133,800	210,820	19,125	34,387	61,858	66,237
Myanmar	5,875	6,674	8,217	6,351	5,328	5,815	6,646	5,175
Philippines	58,456	58,693	65,304	77,659	33,744	35,364	45,040	38,014
Singapore	...	...	...	...	...	...	...	...
Thailand	79,830	58,464	106,323	135,799	29,462	17,449	21,172	33,420
Viet Nam	12,859	19,039	44,923	71,890	11,558	16,193	32,764	44,818
The Pacific								
Cook Islands	55	71	76	72 (2015)	...	...	...	...
Fiji	182	196	553	864	172	185	388	701
Kiribati	8	11	14	21 (2015)	...	...	...	...
Marshall Islands	105	92	105	95 (2015)	...	...	...	...
Micronesia, Fed. States of	63	62	86	81 (2015)	...	...	...	...
Nauru	...	...	...	...	...	...	...	...
Palau	58	60	67	60 (2015)	...	...	...	...
Papua New Guinea	2,305	1,896	5,965	20,920	1,454	1,264	1,042	1,656
Samoa	139	169	325	450	138	167	299	417
Solomon Islands	156	167	231	187	121	144	125	90
Timor-Leste	...	...	...	...	...	...	...	...
Tonga	74	89	154	196	65	80	144	186
Tuvalu	4	10 (2006)	16	14 (2013)	...	...	...	...
Vanuatu	96	105	173	181	73	72	99	77
DEVELOPING MEMBER ECONOMIES[c]	1,065,919	1,610,241	3,046,021	4,505,331	471,814	446,990	713,562	908,731
DEVELOPING ECONOMIES[d]	2,121,479	2,809,078	5,002,431	7,251,871	1,105,394	1,154,662	1,522,780	2,102,721

... = data not available at cutoff date, Lao PDR = Lao People's Democratic Republic.

a Refers to the sum of public and publicly guaranteed long-term debt, private nonguaranteed long-term debt, use of International Monetary Fund credit, and estimated short-term debt.
b Data in 2000 and 2005 onward are not comparable due to a change in coverage or compilation methodology.
c For reporting economies only.
d Includes data for all developing economies as reported in the World Bank's Global Development Finance Online. For developing member economies not covered by the World Bank, data are from economy sources.

Sources: World Development Indicators and International Debt Statistics. http://data.worldbank.org/data-catalog/world-development-indicators (accessed August 2016); Organisation for Economic Co-operation and Development. *Statistical Compendium 2004/1* (CD-ROM). Paris; economy sources.

Table 4.20: **Total External Debt of Developing Member Economies**
(% of GNI)

Regional Member	Total External Debt				External Debt, Public and Publicly Guaranteed			
	2000	2005	2010	2014	2000	2005	2010	2014
Developing Member Economies								
Central and West Asia								
Afghanistan	...	13.6 (2006)	15.1	12.2	...	12.8 (2006)	12.3	9.6
Armenia	51.4	38.5	64.9	74.8	34.4	18.1	26.3	27.7
Azerbaijan	30.6	18.3	14.2	16.1	14.7	11.7	7.5	11.1
Georgia	57.5	33.2	84.5	85.0	40.1	23.7	36.7	32.6
Kazakhstan	75.7	84.7	92.6	83.3	21.3	4.2	3.0	7.4
Kyrgyz Republic	150.5	95.1	91.7	101.1	94.8	70.2	54.4	44.5
Pakistan	45.1	30.4	34.8	23.9	37.1	26.9	23.6	17.8
Tajikistan	138.4	50.2	55.4	44.3	91.6	37.0	32.5	17.9
Turkmenistan	92.0	15.4	2.6	1.0	79.6	11.6	1.7	0.7
Uzbekistan	36.8	32.6	19.3	20.4	27.8	25.4	8.5	8.6
East Asia								
China, People's Rep. of	12.2	12.5	9.3	9.3	7.9	3.6	1.5	0.8
Hong Kong, China[a]	120.3	257.7	376.5	414.8 (2015)	...	...	...	...
Korea, Rep. of	24.2	18.2	32.5	28.6 (2015)	9.3	4.5	11.0	11.5 (2015)
Mongolia	84.8	56.5	89.9	186.2	73.6	51.2	27.0	31.1
Taipei,China	10.3	22.5	22.1	29.4 (2015)	0.0	0.1	1.7	0.2 (2015)
South Asia								
Bangladesh	28.3	25.4	20.7	18.8	27.2	24.0	17.2	14.3
Bhutan	48.2	81.3	62.4	105.1	46.1	78.7	61.4	99.8
India	21.4	14.6	17.3	22.7	17.2	6.6	6.0	8.1
Maldives	34.7	33.3	49.2	39.1	31.1	27.5	31.2	26.4
Nepal	52.2	39.1	23.5	20.0	51.2	38.2	21.8	17.6
Sri Lanka	57.7	46.9	44.5	59.7	49.6	40.0	29.4	37.7
Southeast Asia								
Brunei Darussalam	...	...	...	...	...	...	...	...
Cambodia	74.9	58.7	35.0	42.9	65.9	52.3	31.1	35.2
Indonesia	95.6	52.1	27.0	34.1	46.3	28.5	14.1	16.6
Lao PDR	152.7	122.7	96.6	95.9	149.0	88.2	56.2	50.6
Malaysia	48.7	47.3	55.9	66.8	22.2	25.1	25.1	20.3
Myanmar	...	...	...	10.2	...	...	...	8.3
Philippines	61.6	45.2	24.6	22.7	35.5	27.2	16.9	11.0
Singapore	...	...	...	...	...	...	...	...
Thailand	66.1	34.8	34.8	38.2	23.8	9.7	6.5	8.7
Viet Nam	38.7	33.7	40.3	40.6	34.8	28.6	29.4	25.3
The Pacific								
Cook Islands[b]	60.1	38.7	29.7	24.6 (2015)	...	...	...	...
Fiji	10.6	6.4	18.2	21.6	10.0	6.1	12.8	16.2
Kiribati	...	7.4	6.4	4.3	...	...	...	...
Marshall Islands	71.2	51.5	53.0	38.6 (2015)	...	...	...	...
Micronesia, Fed. States of	26.4	23.9	27.8	21.9 (2015)	...	...	...	...
Nauru	...	...	...	...	...	...	...	...
Palau[b]	39.2	30.8	36.2	20.8 (2015)	...	...	...	...
Papua New Guinea	69.8	41.9	64.4	147.6 (2013)	44.0	27.9	11.4	10.0
Samoa	51.7	38.3	51.1	58.1	51.2	37.9	46.9	53.9
Solomon Islands	35.9	40.3	46.5	17.0	27.7	34.7	25.2	8.1
Timor-Leste	...	...	...	...	...	...	...	...
Tonga	38.6	34.4	41.1	44.2	34.0	30.7	37.6	42.4
Tuvalu[b]	29.0	45.7 (2006)	49.1	35.6 (2013)	...	...	...	...
Vanuatu	36.9	28.5	25.5	...	28.2	19.5	14.7	9.4

... = data not available at cutoff date, 0.0 = magnitude is less than half of unit employed, GNI = gross national income, Lao PDR = Lao People's Democratic Republic.

a Data in 2000 and 2005 onward are not comparable due to a change in coverage or compilation methodology.
b For total external debt as a percentage of GNI, gross domestic product is used in lieu of GNI.

Sources: World Bank. World Development Indicators and International Debt Statistics. http://data.worldbank.org/data-catalog/world-development-indicators (accessed August 2016); ADB estimates; economy sources.

Table 4.21: **Total External Debt of Developing Member Economies**
(% of exports of goods, services, and primary income)

Regional Member	2000	2005	2010	2011	2012	2013	2014
Developing Member Economies							
Central and West Asia							
Afghanistan	...	...	61.8	61.1	63.9	61.0	...
Armenia	183.4	101.3	193.4	194.5	189.4	196.5	188.7
Azerbaijan	70.1	25.4	24.3	21.2	25.2	27.9	34.2
Georgia	181.3	89.1	210.3	189.3	174.5	169.5	173.5
Kazakhstan	123.0	139.8	174.7	135.5	144.4	164.5	177.6
Kyrgyz Republic	328.5	234.4	170.8	173.7	204.2	217.3	256.5
Pakistan	321.9	172.2	222.7	203.6	194.4	196.6	200.1
Tajikistan	...	88.7	342.8	277.3	221.6	312.2	369.4
Turkmenistan	...	...	...	...	...	...	...
Uzbekistan	...	...	...	...	...	...	...
East Asia							
China, People's Rep. of	49.9	34.7	31.3	33.3	31.9	34.2	34.8
Hong Kong, China[a,b]	76.8	121.2	149.2	148.1	145.6	152.0	168.4 (2015)
Korea, Rep. of[a]	64.6	46.5	62.5	56.7	55.5	56.3	58.6 (2015)
Mongolia	153.2	93.5	173.2	175.6	284.8	375.6	325.1
Taipei,China[a]	19.3	35.9	29.9	32.1	29.2	38.4	39.1 (2015)
South Asia							
Bangladesh	213.9	162.9	108.4	100.1	101.9	105.6	105.2
Bhutan	...	...	154.0	140.6	197.6	223.0	268.2
India	161.9	75.6	81.5	73.8	87.1	89.7	93.1
Maldives	44.1	73.1	49.4	39.6	33.7	28.0	31.2
Nepal	212.5	224.2	212.7	178.0	178.6	162.5	145.9
Sri Lanka	141.6	141.9	190.5	183.5	261.0	264.7	258.2
Southeast Asia							
Brunei Darussalam	...	...	...	...	...	...	...
Cambodia	139.9	86.1	62.2	55.5	64.3	64.2	60.5
Indonesia	196.6	146.2	117.6	101.9	118.2	128.2	146.0
Lao PDR	493.9	429.8	281.1	307.8	280.0	302.3	...
Malaysia	36.7	38.9	55.0	51.4	69.4	77.5	95.2
Myanmar	273.9	173.9	104.7	94.6	80.5	62.9	...
Philippines	132.7	152.4	106.6	102.5	93.1	87.7	95.1
Singapore	...	...	...	...	...	...	...
Thailand	92.8	44.4	46.0	41.1	47.4	47.3	47.3
Viet Nam	73.6	51.5	56.0	50.0	47.5	45.8	44.5
The Pacific							
Cook Islands	...	...	...	...	...	...	...
Fiji	17.8	11.6	29.1	36.9	29.1	34.2	...
Kiribati[a]	16.3	17.6	...	...	...	...	...
Marshall Islands[a]	141.1	98.0	99.0	76.9	70.6	65.9	62.3 (2015)
Micronesia, Fed. States of[a]	100.3	98.2	91.9	88.9	69.3	65.6	52.7 (2015)
Nauru	...	...	...	...	...	...	...
Palau[a]	84.2	68.5	64.8	51.1	48.3	43.6	31.0 (2015)
Papua New Guinea	97.3	52.0	97.8	170.5	218.0	...	...
Samoa	...	114.8	154.5	169.3	168.7	183.1	186.6
Solomon Islands	121.3	108.0	69.2	45.7	35.2	34.0	30.6
Timor-Leste	...	...	...	...	...	...	...
Tonga	...	151.0	220.6	192.2	173.3	...	...
Tuvalu[a]	85.9	54.9 (2006)	65.0	67.6	48.1	47.3	47.3 (2013)
Vanuatu	54.4	51.5	47.4	51.0	89.2	32.4	...

... = data not available at cutoff date, Lao PDR = Lao People's Democratic Republic.

a External debt as a percentage of exports of goods, services, and primary income was derived using balance-of-payments data.
b Data in 2000 and 2005 onward are not comparable due to a change in coverage or compilation methodology.

Sources: World Bank. World Development Indicators and International Debt Statistics. http://data.worldbank.org/data-catalog/world-development-indicators (accessed August 2016); ADB estimates; economy sources.

Table 4.22: **Total Debt Service Paid**

Regional Member	Debt Service Payment ($ million)				Debt Service Payment (% of exports of goods, services, and primary income)			
	2000	2005	2010	2014	2000	2005	2010	2014
Developing Member Economies								
Central and West Asia								
Afghanistan	...	11 (2006)	10	38	...	...	0.3	...
Armenia	51	142	969	1,436	9.2	7.3	29.7	31.7
Azerbaijan	138	222	416	1,791	6.4	2.7	1.4	5.2
Georgia	126	195	803	1,871	12.5	8.1	17.5	23.3
Kazakhstan	3,392	13,158	39,474	31,171	32.4	41.9	57.9	35.1
Kyrgyz Republic	178	143	557	402	30.2	14.8	23.1	14.2
Pakistan	2,871	2,466	4,273	5,948	28.1	12.5	14.9	19.1
Tajikistan	68	73	686	419	...	5.8	76.3	38.2
Turkmenistan	472	310	155	56	...	...	...	...
Uzbekistan	901	795	618	888	...	...	...	...
East Asia								
China, People's Rep. of	26,607	27,404	60,389	51,737	9.1	3.4	3.4	1.9
Hong Kong, China	...	...	...	...	...	...	...	...
Korea, Rep. of[a, b]	22,905	7,224	2,843	...	10.9	2.1	0.5	...
Mongolia	41	45	239	1,361	6.6	3.0	7.0	21.2
Taipei,China[a, b]	45	11,006	3,630	6,150 (2015)	0.0	4.6	1.1	1.5 (2015)
South Asia								
Bangladesh	773	812	1,020	1,741	10.6	7.2	4.3	5.2
Bhutan	7	7	87	83	...	...	14.4	12.1
India	10,667	23,922	24,413	92,519	17.1	14.9	6.8	18.6
Maldives	20	31	81	77	4.2	6.3	4.0	2.3
Nepal	103	120	188	227	7.6	8.5	10.6	8.2
Sri Lanka	791	440	1,396	2,490	12.1	5.5	12.2	14.7
Southeast Asia								
Brunei Darussalam	...	...	...	...	...	...	...	...
Cambodia	32	33	63	165	1.7	0.8	1.0	1.5
Indonesia	16,638	20,258	29,343	46,356	22.8	20.9	17.4	23.1
Lao PDR	41	134	301	357	8.0	17.6	13.0	...
Malaysia	6,441	9,381	5,575	12,948	5.6	5.6	2.3	5.8
Myanmar	9	5	4	62	0.4	0.1	0.0	...
Philippines	7,066	9,528	11,461	6,096	16.0	24.7	18.7	7.5
Singapore	...	...	...	...	...	...	...	...
Thailand	13,996	18,044	10,964	14,975	16.3	13.7	4.7	5.2
Viet Nam	1,310	969	1,873	6,716	7.5	2.6	2.3	4.2
The Pacific								
Cook Islands[a]	1	3	2	5 (2015)	...	...	...	...
Fiji	25	14	24	52	2.4	0.8	1.2	...
Kiribati[b]	1	1	1	1 (2015)	1.7	1.9	...	...
Marshall Islands[b]	22	4	9	7 (2015)	29.8	4.8	8.1	4.6 (2015)
Micronesia, Fed. States of [b]	23	2	5	8 (2015)	36.1	3.9	5.3	5.4 (2015)
Nauru	...	...	...	...	...	...	...	...
Palau	...	...	...	...	...	...	...	...
Papua New Guinea	305	308	812	1,165	12.9	8.4	13.3	...
Samoa	6	6	11	19	...	3.9	5.0	7.9
Solomon Islands	9	14	21	17	7.1	9.1	6.2	2.8
Timor-Leste	...	...	...	...	...	...	...	...
Tonga	5	5	5	7	...	8.8	7.2	...
Tuvalu	...	...	...	...	...	...	...	...
Vanuatu	3	3	6	8	1.6	1.6	1.6	...

... = data not available at cutoff date, 0.0 = magnitude is less than half of unit employed, Lao PDR = Lao People's Democratic Republic.

a   Refers to principal repayments on long-term debts plus interests on short-term and long-term debts.
b   Debt service payment as percent of exports of goods, services, and primary income was derived from the balance-of-payments data.

Sources: World Bank. World Development Indicators and International Debt Statistics. http://data.worldbank.org/data-catalog/world-development-indicators (accessed August 2016); ADB estimates; economy sources.

Table 4.23:   **International Tourist Arrivals**[a]
(thousand)

Regional Member	2000	2005	2010	2011	2012	2013	2014	2015
Developing Member Economies								
Central and West Asia[b]	**3,404**	**6,086**	**8,922**	**11,171**	**12,918**	**16,021**	**14,180**	**5,807**
Afghanistan	...	...	...	...	...	...	...	...
Armenia	45	319	687	758	963	1,082	1,204	1,192
Azerbaijan	576 (2002)	693	1,280	1,562	1,986	2,130	2,160	1,922
Georgia	387	560	1,067	1,319	1,790	2,065	2,229	2,279
Kazakhstan	1,471	3,143	2,991	4,093	4,807	4,926	4,560	...
Kyrgyz Republic	59	319	855	2,278	2,406	3,076	2,849	...
Pakistan	557	798	907	1,161	966	565	965	...
Tajikistan	4	...	160	...	...	208	213	414
Turkmenistan	3	12	...	...	...	...	...	...
Uzbekistan	302	242	975	...	...	1,969	...	...
East Asia	**48,126**	**71,321**	**90,571**	**96,239**	**100,422**	**101,957**	**107,897**	**107,630**
China, People's Rep. of	31,229	46,809	55,665	57,581	57,725	55,686	55,622	56,886
Hong Kong, China	8,814	14,773	20,085	22,316	23,770	25,661	27,770	26,686
Korea, Rep. of	5,322	6,023	8,798	9,795	11,140	12,176	14,202	13,232
Mongolia	137	338	456	460	476	418	393	386
Taipei,China	2,624	3,378	5,567	6,087	7,311	8,016	9,910	10,440
South Asia[b]	**4,187**	**5,460**	**8,169**	**8,898**	**9,575**	**10,430**	**11,459**	**11,769**
Bangladesh	199	208	303	...	125	148	125	...
Bhutan	8	14	41	66	105	116	133	155
India	2,649	3,919	5,776	6,309	6,578	6,968	7,679	8,027
Maldives	467	395	792	931	958	1,125	1,205	1,234
Nepal	464	375	603	736	803	798	790	555
Sri Lanka	400	549	654	856	1,006	1,275	1,527	1,798
Southeast Asia[b]	**35,458**	**48,542**	**70,431**	**77,453**	**84,642**	**94,394**	**97,202**	**104,584**
Brunei Darussalam	...	126	214	242	209	225	201	218
Cambodia	...	1,333	2,508	2,882	3,584	4,210	4,503	4,775
Indonesia	5,064	5,002	7,003	7,650	8,044	8,802	9,435	10,408
Lao PDR	191	672	1,670	1,786	2,140	2,700	3,164	3,543
Malaysia	10,222	16,431	24,577	24,714	25,033	25,715	27,437	25,721
Myanmar	208	232	792	391	1,059	2,044	3,081	4,681
Philippines	1,992	2,623	3,520	3,917	4,273	4,681	4,833	5,361
Singapore	6,062	7,079	9,161	10,390	11,098	11,898	11,864	12,052
Thailand	9,579	11,567	15,936	19,230	22,354	26,547	24,810	29,881
Viet Nam	2,140	3,477	5,050	6,251	6,848	7,572	7,874	7,944
The Pacific[b]	**701**	**1,045**	**1,346**	**1,405**	**1,484**	**1,489**	**1,532**	**1,342**
Cook Islands	73	88	104	113	122	121	121	125
Fiji	294	545	632	675	661	658	693	755
Kiribati	5	4	5	5	5	6	...	...
Marshall Islands	5	9	5	5	5	5	...	...
Micronesia, Fed. States of	21	19	45	...	38	42	35	...
Nauru	...	...	...	...	...	...	...	...
Palau	58	81	86	109	119	105	141	162
Papua New Guinea	58	69	140	163	168	174	182	...
Samoa	88	102	122	121	126	116	120	134
Solomon Islands	5	9	21	23	24	24	20	22
Timor-Leste	...	14 (2006)	40	50	58	79	60	...
Tonga	35	42	47	46	49	48	50	54
Tuvalu	1	1	2	1	1	1	1	...
Vanuatu	58	62	97	94	108	110	109	90
Developed Member Economies[b]	**11,475**	**14,592**	**16,836**	**14,501**	**16,863**	**19,375**	**23,069**	**27,181**
Australia	4,931	5,499	5,790	5,771	6,032	6,382	6,884	7,444
Japan	4,757	6,728	8,611	6,219	8,358	10,364	13,413	19,737
New Zealand	1,787	2,365	2,435	2,511	2,473	2,629	2,772	...
DEVELOPING MEMBER ECONOMIES[b]	**91,876**	**132,454**	**179,439**	**195,166**	**209,041**	**224,291**	**232,270**	**231,132**
REGIONAL MEMBERS[b]	**103,351**	**147,046**	**196,275**	**209,667**	**225,904**	**243,666**	**255,339**	**258,313**

... = data not available at cutoff date, Lao PDR = Lao People's Democratic Republic.

a   For Australia; Japan; the Republic of Korea; the Kyrgyz Republic; Taipei,China; Tajikistan; and Viet Nam, data refer to international visitor arrivals at frontiers (including tourists and same-day visitors). For the rest of the economies, data refer to international tourist arrivals at frontiers (overnight visitors, i.e., excluding same-day visitors).
b   For reporting economies only.

Source: World Tourism Organization (UNWTO). *UNWTO Tourism Highlights, 2016 Edition*. http://mkt.unwto.org/publication/unwto-tourism-highlights-2016-edition (accessed July 2016).

Table 4.24: **International Tourism Receipts**
($ million)

Regional Member	2000	2005	2010	2011	2012	2013	2014	2015
Developing Member Economies								
Central and West Asia[a]	**679**	**1,525**	**3,643**	**4,986**	**6,477**	**7,459**	**7,443**	**7,548**
Afghanistan	...	...	86	71	56	151	84	...
Armenia	38	220	646	448	454	880	966	936
Azerbaijan	63	78	657	1,287	2,433	2,365	2,432	2,309
Georgia	97	241	659	955	1,411	1,720	1,787	1,936
Kazakhstan	356	701	1,005	1,209	1,347	1,522	1,467	1,625
Kyrgyz Republic	15	73	160	640	434	530	423	426
Pakistan	81	182	305	373	339	288	283	315
Tajikistan	2 (2002)	2	4	3	3	3	1	1
Turkmenistan	...	...	...	...	...	...	...	...
Uzbekistan	27	28	121	...	...	...	...	...
East Asia	**32,707**	**50,435**	**87,307**	**100,678**	**108,743**	**117,739**	**176,379**	**180,200**
China, People's Rep. of	16,231	29,296	45,814	48,464	50,028	51,664	105,380	114,109
Hong Kong, China	5,868	10,179	22,200	28,455	33,074	38,934	38,376	36,150
Korea, Rep. of	6,834	5,806	10,328	12,476	13,429	14,629	17,836	15,285
Mongolia	36	177	244	218	442	189	173	250
Taipei,China	3,738	4,977	8,721	11,065	11,770	12,323	14,614	14,406
South Asia	**4,247**	**8,429**	**17,244**	**20,926**	**21,479**	**23,077**	**25,540**	**27,261**
Bangladesh	50	70	87	87	105	129	153	148
Bhutan	10	19	35	48	61	63	73	71
India	3,460	7,493	14,490	17,707	17,971	18,397	19,700	21,013
Maldives	321	287	1,713	1,868	1,951	2,335	2,696	2,567
Nepal	158	131	343	386	352	438	487	481
Sri Lanka	248	429	576	830	1,039	1,715	2,431	2,981
Southeast Asia[a]	**26,902**	**34,953**	**68,422**	**84,594**	**95,823**	**107,854**	**108,059**	**108,132**
Brunei Darussalam	155 (2001)	191	...	...	92	96	79	...
Cambodia	304	840	1,519	2,084	2,462	2,659	2,953	3,130
Indonesia	4,975	4,522	6,958	7,997	8,324	9,119	10,261	10,761
Lao PDR	114	139	382	406	451	596	642	679
Malaysia	5,011	8,846	18,115	19,656	20,250	21,496	22,595	17,597
Myanmar	162	68	72	281	539	959	1,612	2,092
Philippines	2,156	2,265	2,645	3,190	4,061	4,690	5,030	5,276
Singapore	5,142	6,205	14,177	18,086	18,939	19,209	19,134	16,743
Thailand	7,483	9,577	20,104	27,184	33,855	41,780	38,423	44,553
Viet Nam	...	2,300	4,450	5,710	6,850	7,250	7,330	7,301
The Pacific[a]	**416**	**903**	**1,296**	**1,328**	**1,399**	**1,592**	**1,575**	**979**
Cook Islands	36	91	111	...	...	168	175	...
Fiji	189	485	634	724	729	716	744	744
Kiribati	3	3	4	...	3	3	3	...
Marshall Islands	3	6	4	4	4	4	5	...
Micronesia, Fed. States of	17	17	24	...	...	24	25	...
Nauru	...	...	...	...	...	...	...	...
Palau	53	97	73	115	133	113	127	...
Papua New Guinea	7	4	2	5	2	4	3	...
Samoa	41	79	123	134	148	136	146	137
Solomon Islands	4	2	44	71	54	61	55	47
Timor-Leste	...	20 (2006)	31	21	21	29	35	51
Tonga	7	15	27	28	41	45	...	...
Tuvalu	...	...	2	...	3	2	...	...
Vanuatu	56	85	217	226	261	287	257	...
Developed Member Economies[a]	**14,934**	**34,489**	**48,319**	**49,642**	**53,602**	**53,788**	**59,212**	**63,306**
Australia	9,289	16,848	28,598	31,335	31,898	31,261	31,935	29,413
Japan	3,373	12,430	13,199	10,966	14,576	15,131	18,853	24,983
New Zealand	2,272	5,211	6,522	7,341	7,128	7,396	8,424	8,910
DEVELOPING MEMBER ECONOMIES[a]	**64,950**	**96,245**	**177,912**	**212,512**	**233,921**	**257,721**	**318,996**	**324,120**
REGIONAL MEMBERS[a]	**79,884**	**130,734**	**226,231**	**262,154**	**287,523**	**311,509**	**378,208**	**387,426**

... = data not available at cutoff date, Lao PDR = Lao People's Democratic Republic.

a   For reporting economies only.

Source: World Tourism Organization (UNWTO). *UNWTO Tourism Highlights, 2016 Edition.* http://mkt.unwto.org/publication/unwto-tourism-highlights-2016-edition (accessed July 2016).

Transport and Communications

Snapshots

- The average railway density for all reporting member economies in Asia and the Pacific was estimated at 7 kilometers (km) per 1,000 square kilometers (km^2) in 2011, which exceeded Latin America and the Caribbean's average of approximately 5 km per 1,000 km^2, but was far less than Europe's average of 50 km per 1,000 km^2.

- Economies in Asia and the Pacific, led by the People's Republic of China, significantly upgraded the quality of their roads between 2004 and 2015.

- Air carrier departures increased between 2000 and 2015 in 30 out of 37 Asia and Pacific economies for which data are available, while the number of passengers carried increased in 35 out of 37 economies over the same period.

- Mobile phone subscription rates increased in every regional economy between 2000 and 2015 for which data are available, and by at least 10 times in more than two-thirds of these economies.

- The number of internet users per 100 people increased by at least tenfold in more than half of the reporting economies of Asia and the Pacific. However, 58.1% of the region's population remains unconnected to the internet, which slightly exceeds the global average.

Key Trends

The average railway density for all reporting member economies in Asia and the Pacific was estimated at 7 kilometers (km) per 1,000 square kilometers (km^2) in 2011, which exceeded Latin America and the Caribbean's average of approximately 5 km per 1,000 km^2, but was far less than Europe's average of 50 km per 1,000 km^2. The world average stood at 9.5 km per 1,000 km^2 in 2011. A region's average railway density is, of course, largely a function of the total surface area of the region and Asia and the Pacific is significantly larger than Europe.

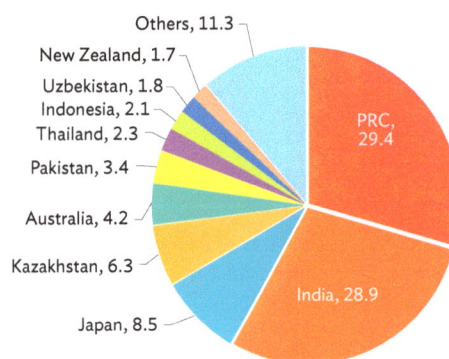

Figure 5.1: Breakdown of Rail Networks in Asia and the Pacific, Latest Year
(%)

Others, 11.3
New Zealand, 1.7
Uzbekistan, 1.8
Indonesia, 2.1
Thailand, 2.3
Pakistan, 3.4
Australia, 4.2
Kazakhstan, 6.3
Japan, 8.5
PRC, 29.4
India, 28.9

PRC = People's Republic of China.
Source: Table 5.4.

The People's Republic of China (PRC) (29.4.%) and India (28.9%) together accounted for 58.3% of Asia and the Pacific's rail network in 2014 (Figure 5.1). Japan had the third-longest rail network, which comprised 8.5% of the regional total.

Malaysia led all regional economies with an average annual increase of 2.4% in rail network density between 2000 and 2014 or the latest year for which data are available (Figure 5.2). The next largest gains were in Taipei,China and Turkmenistan, both with average annual increases of 2.3%. Economies with rail networks that contracted during the review period include Armenia, Azerbaijan, Japan, Indonesia, and Viet Nam.

Figure 5.2: Average Annual Increase in Rail Network Density, 2000–2014
(%)

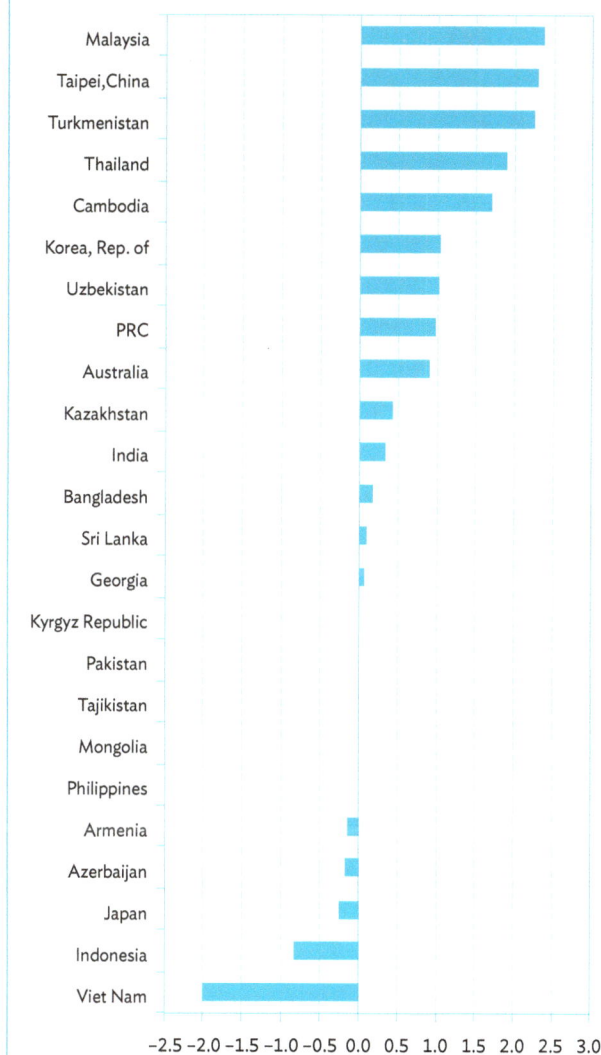

PRC = People's Republic of China.
Note: Data for the Kyrgyz Republic, 2005–2014; for Sri Lanka, 1999–2008; for the Philippines, 2000–2008; and for Turkmenistan, 2005–2011.
Source: Table 5.4.

in 2004 (Figure 5.3).[6] The share of Class II roads as a percentage of the total also jumped from 24.5% to 40.6% between 2004 and 2015. As a result, lower-quality Class III, Below Class III, and Other roads constituted a far smaller share of the region's highway network in 2015 (27.7%) than in 2004 (63.1%).

Figure 5.3: Breakdown of Asian Highways by Class
(%)

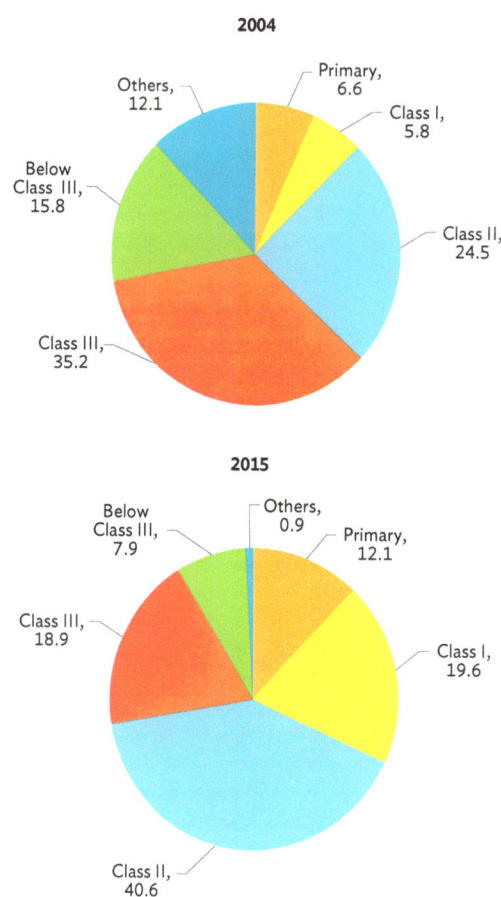

Source: Table 5.1.

Economies in Asia and the Pacific, led by the PRC, significantly upgraded the quality of their roads between 2004 and 2015. Poor transport infrastructure raises production costs, prevents uniform growth across regions, and distorts the relative shares of labor and capital inputs among firms (ADB 2016). In Asia and the Pacific, higher-quality Primary and Class I roads accounted for 31.7% of the region's highway network in 2015, up from only 12.4%

6   Primary class highways are access-controlled motorways used exclusively by automobiles. Class I refers to asphalt, cement, or concrete roads with four or more lanes. Class II refers to double bituminous treated roads with two lanes. Class III is regarded as the minimum desirable standard, usually described as a two-lane (narrow) road. Below Class III refers to road sections below the minimum desirable standard (ESCAP Online Statistical Database).

Road traffic deaths are increasing, as the number of motor vehicles in Asia and the Pacific rises. More than 90.0% of the world's 1.2 million road fatalities each year occur in low-income and middle-income economies, which have only 48.0% of the world's registered vehicles (WHO 2009). The effective enforcement of legislation to curtail excessive speeding and drinking and driving as well as to mandate the use of seat belts, helmets, and child restraints have been shown to reduce road deaths. However, fewer than half of all economies in the world have laws that address all five of these risk factors.

Thailand had the highest prevalence of road deaths within the region with 36 road deaths per 100,000 people in 2013 (Table 5.3). More than 70.0% of these road fatalities involved users of two- or three-wheeled vehicles (Figure 5.4). Viet Nam had the next highest rate of road deaths with 25 per 100,000 people, followed by the Cook Islands, Kazakhstan, and Malaysia with 24 each. By type of vehicle, four-wheeled vehicles comprised the plurality of road traffic deaths in 15 of the 32 economies for which 2013 data are available. Two- or three-wheeled vehicles comprised a plurality of road deaths in 11 economies, pedestrians in 8, and other vehicles in 1.

Figure 5.4: Distribution of Road Deaths by Type of Vehicle, 2013
(%)

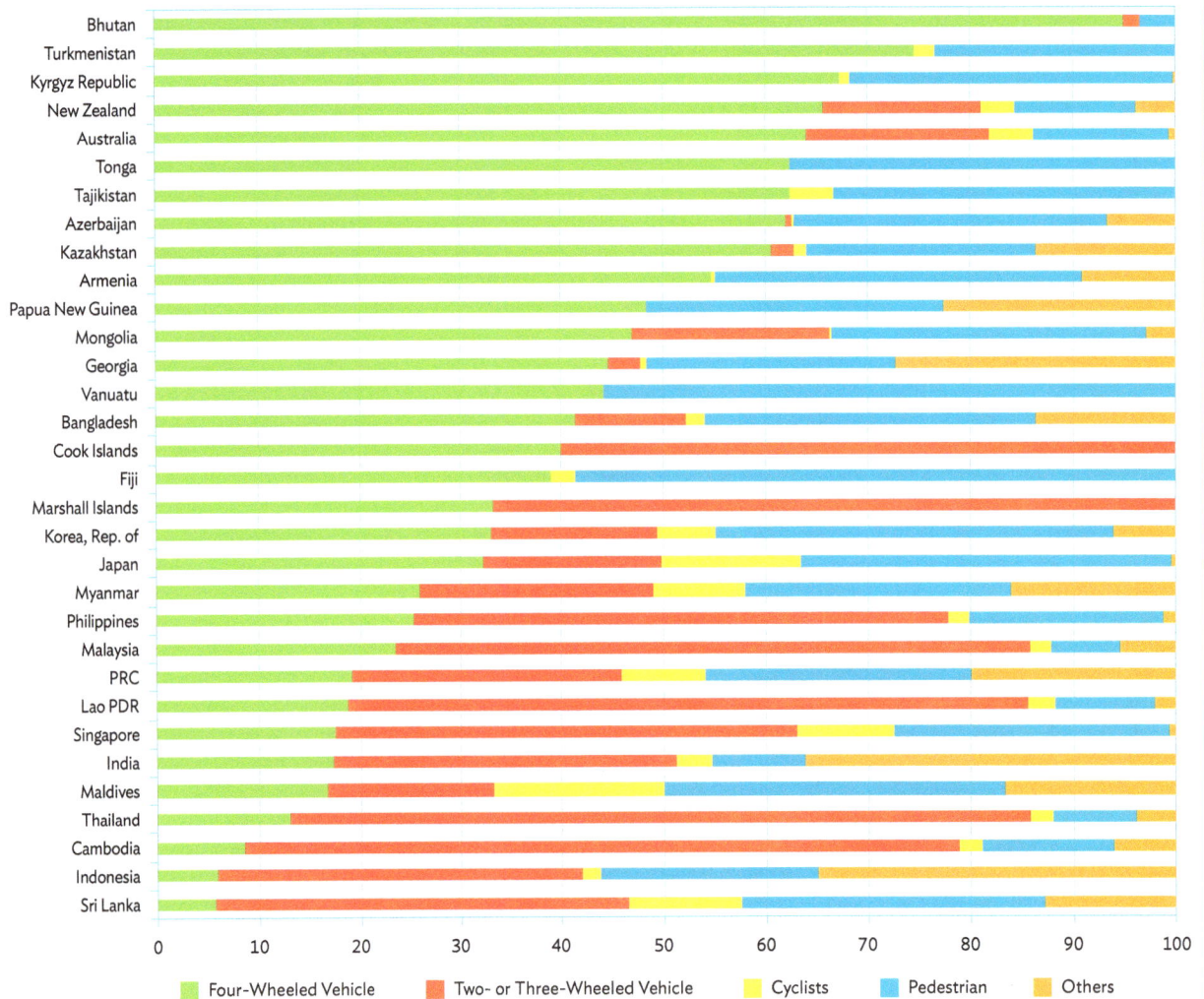

Lao PDR = Lao People's Democratic Republic, PRC = People's Republic of China.
Source: Table 5.3.

Air carrier departures increased between 2000 and 2015 in 30 out of 37 economies of Asia and the Pacific for which data are available, while the number of passengers carried increased in 35 out of 37 economies over the same period. Between 2000 and 2015 (or 2010 in cases when this was the most recent year available), air carrier departures increased in 30 out of 37 regional economies for which data are available (Table 5.6). The largest percentage increases were seen in Kazakhstan (801.5%), Viet Nam (607.7%), and Afghanistan (590.3%). Between 2000 and 2015 (or 2010), the number of passengers carried increased in 35 out of 37 regional economies. The largest percentage increases in number of passengers carried during the review period occurred in Afghanistan (1,189.1%), Kazakhstan (1,001.6%), and Viet Nam (940.5%). The only declines in air passengers carried during the review period were in Nepal (–20.7%) and Taipei,China (–18.4%). The observed decline in Nepal may in fact be caused by other contextual factors such as the reduction in air traffic following the April 2015 earthquake. If 2010 is used as the last year for which data are available, then the number of Nepal's passengers carried would have increased 42.7% during the review period.

Mobile phone subscription rates increased in every regional economy between 2000 and 2015 for which data are available, and by at least 10 times in more than two-thirds of these economies. By the end of 2015, about 95.0% of the global population lived in an area with mobile-cellular network coverage (ITU 2016). In Asia and the Pacific, 28 of 45 reporting economies had a mobile phone subscription rates exceeding 95 subscriptions per 100 people while 26 economies had mobile phone subscription rates that are

higher than 100 subscriptions per 100 people in 2015 or the latest year for which data are available (Table 5.9). The highest mobile phone subscription rates per 100 people in 2015 were observed in Hong Kong, China (228.8); the Maldives (206.7); and Kazakhstan (187.2). The lowest rates were found in the Federated States of Micronesia (26.7), the Marshall Islands (29.2), and Kiribati (38.8). Growth rates in mobile phone subscriptions were extremely robust throughout the region between 2000 and 2015, with 31 economies experiencing increases in mobile phone subscription rate per 100 people of more than ten times during the review period.

The number of internet users per 100 people increased by at least tenfold in more than half of the reporting economies of Asia and the Pacific. The number of internet users per 100 people increased in all reporting economies of Asia and the Pacific. Significant gains were observed in developing economies like Azerbaijan; Kazakhstan; Japan; Brunei Darussalam; and Taipei,China. In 30 economies, the number of internet users per 100 people increased tenfold between 2000 and 2015.

Although internet penetration rates surged across the region between 2000 and 2015, a majority of the population in Asia and the Pacific (58.1%) was still not connected to the internet in 2016. This compares negatively with the global average of about 53.0% but positively with the regional average for Africa of about 75.0%. Furthermore, there is a digital divide in the internet penetration rates of men and women in Asia and the Pacific: only 39.5% of women in the region are connected to the internet compared with 47.5% of men. This is roughly comparable with the developing world averages of 37.4% for men and 45.0% for women (ITU 2016).[7]

---

[7] The numbers provided in this paragraph are based on ICT Facts in Figures: The World in 2016 published by ITU. The list of economies of Asia and the Pacific covered by ITU is not exactly the same as that of ADB. Details of ITU's coverage are provided here: http://www.itu.int/en/ITU-D/Pages/Contact/Bangkok.aspx.

Figure 5.5: Number of Internet Users
(per 100 people)

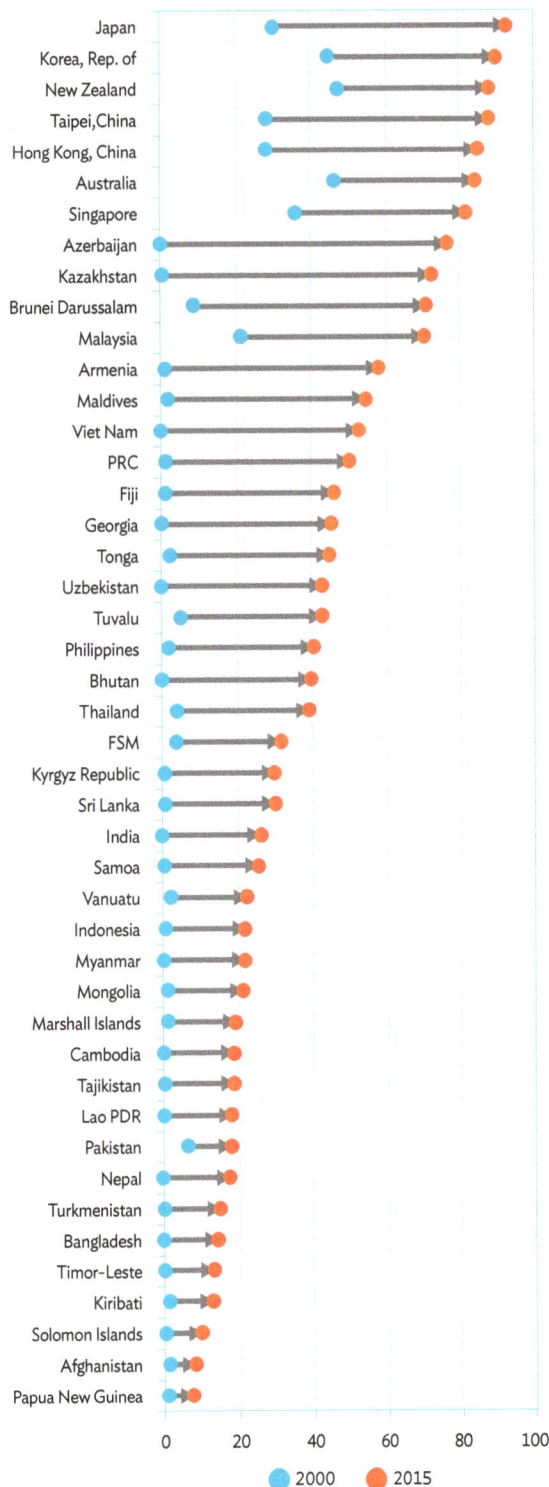

FSM = Federated States of Micronesia, Lao PDR = Lao People's Democratic Republic, PRC = People's Republic of China.
Note: Data for Afghanistan, Pakistan, Myanmar, and Nauru, 2001–2015; for Palau 2002–2015; for Timor-Leste, 2005–2015.
Source: Table 5.8.

Data Issues and Comparability

Recent and complete data for all types of road indicators are scarce. Consequently, writers can describe but not draw analytical results that may be needed to convince policy makers to adopt corrective measures. The most recent data are usually 2–3 years lagged. Some subregions, especially the Pacific, have incomplete or no data. The problems with the data organization, collection, compilation, and dissemination pose a continuing challenge and affect the availability, quality, and timeliness of road statistics.

Most data on telephone and internet subscriptions come from questionnaires that the International Telecommunication Union sent to participating economies. Other information and reports are sourced from the ministries in charge of telecommunications and staff estimates.

References

Asian Development Bank (ADB). 2016. *Asian Development Outlook 2016*. Manila.

International Telecommunication Union (ITU). 2016. *ICT Facts in Figures: The World in 2016*. http://www.itu.int/en/ITU-D/Statistics/Documents/facts/ICTFactsFigures2016.pdf

United Nations Economic and Social Commission for Asia and the Pacific (ESCAP). ESCAP Online Statistical Database. http://www.unescap.org/ stat/data/statdb/DataExplorer.aspx (accessed 7 June 2016).

World Health Organization (WHO). 2009. *Global Status Report on Road Safety*. Geneva.

Transport

Table 5.1: Road Indicators—Network[a]
(kilometers)

Regional Member	Primary 2004	Primary 2015	Class I 2004	Class I 2015	Class II 2004	Class II 2015	Class III 2004	Class III 2015	Below III 2004	Below III 2015	Other 2004	Other 2015	Total[b] 2004	Total[b] 2015
Developing Member Economies														
Central and West Asia														
Afghanistan	...	...	...	10	621	2,549	77	...	3,549	1,461	...	...	4,247	4,020
Armenia	...	...	142	147	377	721	479	58	...	40	...	...	998	966
Azerbaijan	...	...	82	290	1,012	1,174	348	...	...	...	228	...	1,670	1,464
Georgia	...	...	8	74	788	897	358	182	...	...	...	...	1,154	1,153
Kazakhstan	...	...	72	557	767	5,407	10,004	6,389	2,346	475	...	...	13,189	12,828
Kyrgyz Republic	...	...	...	...	464	303	511	1,324	720	136	...	...	1,695	1,763
Pakistan	358	357	1,116	1,116	160	275	2,569	2,442	1,174	1,138	...	...	5,377	5,328
Tajikistan	...	...	...	20	289	978	603	...	1,033	914	...	...	1,925	1,912
Turkmenistan	...	...	...	60	...	...	2,180	2,120	24	24	...	...	2,204	2,204
Uzbekistan	...	...	255	1,195	765	1,101	1,618	670	328	...	...	...	2,966	2,966
East Asia														
China, People's Rep. of	4,140	16,554 (2012)	189	2,659 (2012)	2,749	6,689 (2012)	2,008	1,482 (2012)	1,443	4 (2012)	15,400	...	25,929	27,389 (2012)
Hong Kong, China	...	...	...	...	...	...	...	...	...	...	...	...	...	...
Korea, Rep. of	466	457	197	423	244	40	...	...	...	...	...	...	907	920
Mongolia	...	...	...	8	440	1,702	345	158	3,501	2,450	...	...	4,286	4,318
Taipei,China	...	...	...	...	...	...	...	...	...	...	...	...	...	...
South Asia														
Bangladesh	...	...	20	311	441	1,400	476	44	868	5	...	...	1,805	1,760
Bhutan	...	...	...	7	6	116	...	...	161	47	...	...	167	170
India	...	90	484	4,738	...	5,984	10,869	782	105	96	...	...	11,458	11,690
Maldives	...	...	...	...	...	...	...	...	...	...	...	...	...	...
Nepal	...	...	...	...	311	218	1,003	1,082	12	13	...	...	1,326	1,313
Sri Lanka	...	...	...	60	269	519	190	71	191	...	...	...	650	650
Southeast Asia														
Brunei Darussalam	...	...	...	...	...	...	...	...	...	...	...	...	...	...
Cambodia	...	...	...	...	398	610	743	1,346	199	...	...	...	1,340	1,958
Indonesia	335	409	18	603	1,600	3,045	1,965	...	...	...	34	34	3,952	4,091
Lao PDR	...	...	...	...	...	244	2,375	2,307	...	306	3	...	2,378	2,857
Malaysia	795	795	67	61	733	817	...	...	...	...	...	...	1,595	1,673
Myanmar	...	...	147	320	144	575	983	1,702	1,729	1,928	...	...	3,003	4,525
Philippines	...	...	17	380	27	2,310	2,872	691	451	...	150	...	3,517	3,381
Singapore	11	13	8	6	...	...	...	...	...	...	...	...	19	19
Thailand	182	617	2,572	4,123	1,226	598	1,128	202	...	...	4	...	5,112	5,540
Viet Nam	–	–	408	343	1,915	1,829	104	337	251	76	...	...	2,678	2,585
The Pacific														
Cook Islands	...	...	...	...	...	...	...	...	...	...	...	...	...	...
Fiji	...	...	...	...	...	...	...	...	...	...	...	...	...	...
Kiribati	...	...	...	...	...	...	...	...	...	...	...	...	...	...
Marshall Islands	...	...	...	...	...	...	...	...	...	...	...	...	...	...
Micronesia, Fed. States of	...	...	...	...	...	...	...	...	...	...	...	...	...	...
Nauru	...	...	...	...	...	...	...	...	...	...	...	...	...	...
Palau	...	...	...	...	...	...	...	...	...	...	...	...	...	...
Papua New Guinea	...	...	...	...	...	...	...	...	...	...	...	...	...	...
Samoa	...	...	...	...	...	...	...	...	...	...	...	...	...	...
Solomon Islands	...	...	...	...	...	...	...	...	...	...	...	...	...	...
Timor-Leste	...	...	...	...	...	...	...	...	...	...	...	...	...	...
Tonga	...	...	...	...	...	...	...	...	...	...	...	...	...	...
Tuvalu	...	...	...	...	...	...	...	...	...	...	...	...	...	...
Vanuatu	...	...	...	...	...	...	...	...	...	...	...	...	...	...
Developed Member Economies														
Australia	...	...	...	...	...	...	...	...	...	...	...	...	...	...
Japan	1,111	1,138	...	...	...	...	...	...	...	...	...	...	1,111	1,138
New Zealand	...	...	...	...	...	...	...	...	...	...	...	...	...	...

... = data not available at cutoff date, – = magnitude equals zero, Lao PDR = Lao People's Democratic Republic.

a The road network refers to the Asian Highway that consists of highway routes of international importance within Asia, including highway routes substantially crossing more than one subregion; highway routes within subregions that connected neighboring subregions; and highway routes located within member states that provide access to (a) capital cities; (b) main industrial and agricultural centers; (c) major air, sea, and river ports; (d) major container terminals and depots; and (e) major tourist attractions. "Primary" class in the classification is access-controlled motorways. Access-controlled motorways are used exclusively by automobiles. Motorcycles, bicycles, and pedestrians are not allowed to enter the motorway to ensure traffic safety and the high running speed of automobiles.
Class I refers to asphalt, cement, or concrete roads with four or more lanes.
Class II refers to double bituminous treated roads with two lanes.
Class III is also regarded as the minimum desirable standard usually described as a two-lane (narrow) road.
Roads classified below class III are road sections below the minimum desirable standard.
b Sum of reported available data.

Source: United Nations Economic and Social Commission for Asia and the Pacific. ESCAP Online Statistical Database. http://www.unescap.org/stat/data/statdb/DataExplorer.aspx (accessed 7 June 2016).

Table 5.2:   **Road Indicators—Vehicles**

Regional Member	Total		By Type[a]				
	(thousand)	(per 1,000 people)[b]	Cars and Four-Wheeled	Two- or Three-Wheeled	Heavy Trucks	Buses	Others
Developing Member Economies							
Central and West Asia							
Afghanistan	655.4	23.8	407,608	68,090	81,416	20,589	77,654
Armenia	300.1 (2010)	92.3	247,723	28	40,924	11,396	20
Azerbaijan	1,135.9 (2012)	122.3	958,594	2,067	130,019	29,647	15,609
Georgia	951.6	212.2	774,453	4,830	151,057	21,309	–
Kazakhstan	3,926.5	230.5	3,190,057	74,762	398,753	94,417	168,498
Kyrgyz Republic	958.2	169.2	777,847	21,696	114,853	34,561	9,230
Pakistan	9,080.4 (2011)	51.3	3,095,900	5,560,218	223,152	201,167	–
Tajikistan	411.5	50.4	353,919	4,925	36,942	15,762	–
Turkmenistan	847.9 (2014)	159.7	676,622	37,275	114,004	19,973	–
Uzbekistan	...	...	...	...	...	...	...
East Asia							
China, People's Rep. of[c]	250,138.2	183.8	137,406,846	95,326,138	5,069,292	...	12,335,936
Hong Kong, China	...	...	...	...	...	...	...
Korea, Rep. of	23,150.6	461.0	15,078,354	2,117,035	970,805	4,984,425	–
Mongolia	675.1	232.9	491,771	25,771	151,530	5,992	–
Taipei,China[d]	21,290.3 (2014)	909.7	6,405,778	13,735,994	1,054,149	32,928	61,464
South Asia							
Bangladesh	2,088.6 (2014)	13.4	547,423	1,336,339	141,850	59,500	3,454
Bhutan	68.2 (2014)	91.5	46,575	9,758	9,397	475	1,968
India	159,490.6 (2012)	129.1	38,338,015	115,419,175	4,056,885	1,676,503	–
Maldives	61.4	141.3	10,256	50,775	145	140	96
Nepal	1,178.9 (2011)	44.3	133,992	891,018	47,930	35,100	70,871
Sri Lanka	5,203.7	252.9	832,840	3,566,184	329,648	93,428	381,578
Southeast Asia							
Brunei Darussalam	349.3 (2010)	903.0	...	...	...	...	...
Cambodia	2,457.6	164.9	67,645	2,068,937	45,625	4,473	270,889
Indonesia	104,211.1	418.8	10,838,592	86,253,257	5,156,362	1,962,921	–
Lao PDR	1,439.5	215.5	276,493	1,120,673	38,454	3,861	–
Malaysia	23,819.3	796.1	10,689,450	11,087,878	1,116,167	62,784	862,977
Myanmar	4,310.1 (2014)	83.7	386,049	3,712,220	127,947	22,253	61,643
Philippines	7,690.0	79.0	3,009,116	4,250,667	358,445	31,665	40,145
Singapore	974.2	180.4	763,008	144,934	48,719	17,065	444
Thailand	32,477.0 (2012)	488.4	11,829,221	19,169,418	901,014	137,609	439,715
Viet Nam	40,790.8	454.7	798,592	38,643,091	696,316	111,030	541,812
The Pacific							
Cook Islands	12.5	669.5	5,085	6,846	491	31	–
Fiji	86.5	100.4	...	...	...	...	...
Kiribati	3.5	31.4	1,926	701	536	289	–
Marshall Islands	2.1	39.5	1,917	52	26	63	58
Micronesia, Fed. States of	8.3 (2010)	81.1	7,356	96	747	138	–
Nauru	...	...	...	...	...	...	...
Palau	7.1	405.1	...	...	...	...	...
Papua New Guinea	94.3 (2014)	12.4	61,255	1,155	21,075	10,812	–
Samoa	17.4	91.5	16,243	97	873	236	–
Solomon Islands	45.0	79.5	...	...	...	...	...
Timor-Leste[e]	63.6	53.9	14,621	48,143	651	138	–
Tonga	8.2	78.8	6,039	184	1,882	49	–
Tuvalu	...	...	...	...	...	...	...
Vanuatu	14.0	52.9	...	...	...	...	...
Developed Member Economies							
Australia	17,180.6	742.9	15,871,827	744,732	416,902	93,034	54,101
Japan	91,377.3	717.6	76,137,715	11,948,432	...	...	3,291,072
New Zealand	3,250.1 (2012)	737.3	2,643,624	114,930	112,856	8,286	370,370

... = data not available at cutoff date, – = magnitude equals zero, Lao PDR = Lao People's Democratic Republic.

a   Figures refer to the same year indicated in the column for "Total" unless otherwise specified.
b   Computed by dividing the total number of registered vehicles by the midyear population in thousands.
c   Per 1,000 people computation used end-year population data instead of midyear data.
d   Combination of trucks and wagons in the category "Heavy Trucks."
e   There is no renewal process for vehicles in Timor-Leste; hence, 2013 data refer to the total number of vehicles from 2006 to 2013.

Sources: All economies except Armenia and Brunei Darussalam: World Health Organization. 2015. *Global Status Report on Road Safety 2015*. Geneva; for Armenia and Brunei Darussalam: World Health Organization. 2013. *Global Status Report on Road Safety 2013*. Geneva; ADB estimates; for Taipei,China: National Development Council. 2015.

Transport

Table 5.3:   **Road Indicators—Safety**

Regional Members	Estimated Road Traffic Deaths in 2013		Road Users Deaths in 2013 (%)				
	Total	Death Rate (per 100,000 population)	Four-Wheeled Vehicle	Two- or Three-Wheeled Vehicle	Cyclists	Pedestrian	Others
Developing Member Economies							
Central and West Asia							
Afghanistan	4,734	16	...	...	...	...	...
Armenia	546	18	54.7	–	0.3	35.8	9.2
Azerbaijan	943	10	62.1	0.5	0.3	30.5	6.7
Georgia	514	12	44.7	3.1	0.6	24.3	27.2
Kazakhstan	3,983	24	60.5	2.3	1.1	22.5	13.5
Kyrgyz Republic	1,220	22	67.3	–	1.1	31.6	0.1
Pakistan	25,781	14	...	...	...	...	...
Tajikistan	1,543	19	62.5	–	4.2	33.3	–
Turkmenistan	914	17	74.7	–	1.9	23.4	–
Uzbekistan	3,240	11	...	...	...	...	...
East Asia							
China, People's Rep. of	261,367	19	19.2	26.8	8.1	26.1	19.8
Hong Kong, China	...	...	...	...	...	...	...
Korea, Rep. of	5,931	12	33.2	16.3	5.5	38.9	6.1
Mongolia	597	21	47.0	19.3	0.2	30.6	2.9
Taipei,China	...	...	...	...	...	...	...
South Asia							
Bangladesh	21,316	14	41.5	10.8	1.8	32.2	13.7
Bhutan	114	15	94.9	1.7	–	3.4	–
India	207,551	17	17.2	33.9	3.5	9.1	36.2
Maldives	12	4	16.7	16.7	16.7	33.3	16.7
Nepal	4,713	17	...	...	...	...	...
Sri Lanka	3,691	17	5.7	40.8	11.0	29.8	12.7
Southeast Asia							
Brunei Darussalam	...	...	...	...	...	...	...
Cambodia	2,635	17	8.5	70.4	2.3	12.7	6.1
Indonesia	38,279	15	6.0	36.0	2.0	21.0	35.0
Lao PDR	971	14	18.7	66.9	2.7	9.6	2.1
Malaysia	7,129	24	23.7	62.1	2.2	6.6	5.5
Myanmar	10,809	20	26.0	23.0	9.0	26.0	16.0
Philippines	10,379	11	25.3	52.5	2.0	19.0	1.1
Singapore	197	4	17.5	45.6	9.4	26.9	0.6
Thailand	24,237	36	13.0	72.8	2.3	8.1	3.8
Viet Nam	22,419	25	...	...	...	...	...
The Pacific							
Cook Islands	5	24	40.0	60.0	–	–	–
Fiji	51	6	39.0	–	2.4	58.5	–
Kiribati	3	3	–	–	33.3	66.7	–
Marshall Islands	3	6	33.3	66.7	–	–	–
Micronesia, Fed. States of	2	2	...	...	...	...	...
Nauru	...	...	...	...	...	...	...
Palau	1	5	–	–	–	100.0	–
Papua New Guinea	1,232	17	48.4	–	–	29.0	22.6
Samoa	30	16	–	–	–	76.5	23.5
Solomon Islands	108	19	...	...	...	...	...
Timor-Leste	188	17	...	...	...	...	...
Tonga	8	8	62.5	–	–	37.5	–
Tuvalu	...	...	...	...	...	...	...
Vanuatu	42	17	44.4	–	–	55.6	–
Developed Member Economies							
Australia	1,252	5	64.2	17.9	4.2	13.2	0.6
Japan	5,971	5	32.4	17.4	13.7	36.2	0.3
New Zealand	272	6	65.7	15.4	3.1	11.8	3.9

... = data not available at cutoff date, – = magnitude equals zero, Lao PDR = Lao People's Democratic Republic.

Source: World Health Organization. 2015. *Global Status Report on Road Safety 2015*. Geneva.

Table 5.4:   **Rail Indicators**

Regional Member	Rail Lines (total route, kilometers)				Rail Network, Length per Land Area (kilometers per thousand square kilometers)			
	2000	2005	2010	2014	2000	2005	2010	2014
Developing Member Economies								
Central and West Asia								
Afghanistan	...	...	...	...	...	...	...	...
Armenia	842	732	826	826	29.6	25.7	29.0	29.0
Azerbaijan	2,116	2,122	2,079	2,068	25.6	25.7	25.2	25.0
Georgia	1,562	1,336	1,566	1,578	22.5	19.2	22.5	22.7
Kazakhstan	13,545	14,204	14,202	14,329	5.0	5.3	5.3	5.3
Kyrgyz Republic	...	417 (2006)	417	417	...	2.2 (2006)	2.2	2.2
Pakistan	7,791	7,791	7,791	7,791	10.1	10.1	10.1	10.1
Tajikistan	...	616	621	621	...	4.4	4.4	4.4
Turkmenistan	...	2,529	3,115	3,115	...	5.4	6.6	6.6
Uzbekistan	3,645	4,014	4,227	4,192	8.6	9.4	9.9	9.9
East Asia								
China, People's Rep. of	58,656	62,200	66,239	66,989	6.2	6.6	7.1	7.1
Hong Kong, China	...	...	...	...	...	...	...	...
Korea, Rep. of	3,123	3,392	3,379	3,648	32.4	35.0	34.8	37.4
Mongolia	1,810	1,810	1,814	1,818	1.2	1.2	1.2	1.2
Taipei,China	1,190	1,336	1,743	1766	79.5	87.0	108.9	109
South Asia								
Bangladesh	2,768	2,855	2,835	2,835	21.3	21.9	21.8	21.8
Bhutan	...	...	...	...	...	...	...	...
India	62,759	63,465	63,974	65,808	21.1	21.3	21.5	22.1
Maldives	...	...	...	...	...	...	...	...
Nepal	...	...	...	...	...	...	...	...
Sri Lanka	1,447 (1999)	1,449 (2004)	1,463 (2008)	...	23.1 (1999)	23.1 (2004)	23.3 (2008)	...
Southeast Asia								
Brunei Darussalam	...	...	...	...	...	...	...	...
Cambodia	601	650	...	...	3.4	3.7	...	...
Indonesia	5,324 (1998)	3,370 (2008)	4,684 (2011)	4684	2.9 (1998)	1.9 (2008)	2.6 (2011)	2.6
Lao PDR	...	...	...	...	...	...	...	...
Malaysia	1,622	1,657	1,665	2,250	4.9	5.0	5.1	6.8
Myanmar	...	...	...	...	...	...	...	...
Philippines	491	491 (2004)	479 (2008)	...	1.6	1.6 (2004)	1.6 (2008)	...
Singapore	...	...	...	...	...	...	...	...
Thailand	4,103	4,044 (2004)	4,429	5,327	8.0	7.9 (2004)	8.7	10.4
Viet Nam	3,142	2,671	2,347	2,347	10.1	8.6	7.6	7.6
The Pacific								
Cook Islands	...	...	...	...	...	...	...	...
Fiji	...	...	...	...	...	...	...	...
Kiribati	...	...	...	...	...	...	...	...
Marshall Islands	...	...	...	...	...	...	...	...
Micronesia, Fed. States of	...	...	...	...	...	...	...	...
Nauru	...	...	...	...	...	...	...	...
Palau	...	...	...	...	...	...	...	...
Papua New Guinea	...	...	...	...	...	...	...	...
Samoa	...	...	...	...	...	...	...	...
Solomon Islands	...	...	...	...	...	...	...	...
Timor-Leste	...	...	...	...	...	...	...	...
Tonga	...	...	...	...	...	...	...	...
Tuvalu	...	...	...	...	...	...	...	...
Vanuatu	...	...	...	...	...	...	...	...
Developed Member Economies								
Australia	9,499	9,528	9,674 (2009)	...	1.2	1.2	1.3 (2009)	...
Japan	20,165	20,096	20,035	19,470	55.3	55.1	55.0	53.4
New Zealand	3,913 (1999)	...	...	...	14.9 (1999)	...	...	...

... = data not available at cutoff date, Lao PDR = Lao People's Democratic Republic.

Sources: World Bank. World Development Indicators. http://data.worldbank.org/indicator (accessed 14 September 2016); ADB estimates; for Taipei,China: National Development Council. 2015.

Table 5.5:   **Railways, Passengers Carried, and Goods Transported**

Regional Member	Passenger Carried (million passenger-km)				Goods Transported (million ton-km)			
	2000	2005	2010	2014	2000	2005	2010	2014
Developing Member Economies								
Central and West Asia								
Afghanistan	...	...	...	...	...	...	...	...
Armenia	47	30	50	50	354	654	346	345
Azerbaijan	493	789	917	591	5,770	11,059 (2006)	8,250	8,212
Georgia	453	720	655	625	3,912	6,127	6,228	5,976
Kazakhstan	10,215	12,129	15,448	18,498	124,983	171,855	213,174	235,845
Kyrgyz Republic	...	45 (2006)	99	75	...	715 (2006)	738	922
Pakistan	18,495	23,045	24,731	20,619	3,754	4,796	6,187	1,757
Tajikistan	...	50	33	24	1,326	1,220 (2006)	808	554
Turkmenistan	...	1,286	1,811	1,811	...	8,670	11,992	11,992
Uzbekistan	2,163	2,012	2,905	3,437	15,441	18,007	22,282	22,686
East Asia								
China, People's Rep. of	441,468	583,320	791,158	807,065	1,333,606	1,934,612	2,451,185	2,308,669
Hong Kong, China	...	...	...	...	...	...	...	...
Korea, Rep. of	28,097	31,004	33,027	22,626	10,803	10,108	9,452	10,459
Mongolia	1,070	1,228	1,220	1,399	4,293	9,219 (2006)	10,287	11,418
Taipei,China	12,624	12,255	20,931	26,340	1,179	982	873	683
South Asia								
Bangladesh	3,941	4,340	7,305	7,305	777	896	710	710
Bhutan	...	...	...	...	...	...	...	...
India	430,666	575,702	903,465	1,158,742	305,201	407,398	600,548	665,810
Maldives	...	...	...	...	...	...	...	...
Nepal	...	...	...	...	...	...	...	...
Sri Lanka	4,627 (2003)	4,682	...	...	88	138	...	...
Southeast Asia								
Brunei Darussalam	...	...	...	...	...	...	...	...
Cambodia	45	45	...	...	92	92	...	...
Indonesia	...	25,535	20,283 (2011)	20,283	...	4,698	7,166 (2011)	7,166
Lao PDR	...	...	...	...	...	...	...	...
Malaysia	1,312	1,181	1,527	3,293	907	1,178	1,384	3,071
Myanmar	...	4,163 (2006)	...	...	...	885 (2006)	...	...
Philippines	171	83 (2006)	...	...	1 (2003)	...	...	...
Singapore	...	...	...	...	...	...	...	...
Thailand	9,935	9,195	8,037	7,504	3,384	4,037	3,161	2,455
Viet Nam	3,200	4,558	4,378	4,558	1,902	2,928	3,901	3,959
The Pacific								
Cook Islands	...	...	...	...	...	...	...	...
Fiji	...	...	...	...	...	...	...	...
Kiribati	...	...	...	...	...	...	...	...
Marshall Islands	...	...	...	...	...	...	...	...
Micronesia, Fed. States of	...	...	...	...	...	...	...	...
Nauru	...	...	...	...	...	...	...	...
Palau	...	...	...	...	...	...	...	...
Papua New Guinea	...	...	...	...	...	...	...	...
Samoa	...	...	...	...	...	...	...	...
Solomon Islands	...	...	...	...	...	...	...	...
Timor-Leste	...	...	...	...	...	...	...	...
Tonga	...	...	...	...	...	...	...	...
Tuvalu	...	...	...	...	...	...	...	...
Vanuatu	...	...	...	...	...	...	...	...
Developed Member Economies								
Australia	1,265	1,290	1,500	...	34,050	46,164	64,172	59,649
Japan	240,793	239,246	244,235	260,014	22,313	21,900	20,432	20,255
New Zealand	...	...	...	...	4,078	...	...	...

... = data not available at cutoff date, km = kilometer, Lao PDR = Lao People's Democratic Republic.

Sources: World Bank. World Development Indicators. http://data.worldbank.org/indicator (accessed 17 August 2016); for Taipei,China: Directorate-General of Budget, Accounting and Statistics. 2015. *Statistical Yearbook 2014*. Nantou City.

Table 5.6:   **Air Transport**

Regional Member	Carrier Departure Worldwide (number of takeoffs)				Freight (million ton-km)				Passenger Carried (thousand)			
	2000	2005	2010	2015	2000	2005	2010	2015	2000	2005	2010	2015
Developing Member Economies												
Central and West Asia												
Afghanistan	3,409	...	21,677	23,533	7.8	...	108.0	33.1	150	...	1,999	1,930
Armenia	4,406	5,939	8,761	852 (2013)	8.8	7.0	6.0	1.0 (2013)	298	556	705	45 (2013)
Azerbaijan	8,012	12,470	9,885	18,199	47.2	11.9	7.8	42.0	546	1,134	797	1,803
Georgia	1,906	4,673	2,803	3,959	2.0	2.8	0.9	0.2	118	249	164	232
Kazakhstan	8,041	17,302	33,483	72,485	11.8	15.8	42.4	37.7	461	1,160	3,098	5,082
Kyrgyz Republic	6,051	5,228	7,371	16,826	3.7	2.0	1.3	0.1	241	226	376	625
Pakistan	63,956	48,905	64,932	65,750	340.3	407.9	333.0	183.2	5,294	5,364	6,588	8,468
Tajikistan	3,953	6,987	5,710	6,288	2.0	3.7	1.0	0.1	168	479	617	802
Turkmenistan	21,858	14,094	3,221	12,219	11.9	10.1	6.2	2.8 (2012)	1,284	1,654	301	2,138
Uzbekistan	30,075	22,183	22,924	22,579	79.6	71.6	153.7	114.3	1,745	1,639	2,114	2,487
East Asia												
China, People's Rep. of	572,921	1,349,269	2,377,789	3,616,026	3,900.1	7,579.4	17,193.9	19,805.6	61,892	136,722	266,293	436,184
Hong Kong, China	79,182	122,705	158,255	228,582	5,111.5	7,763.9	10,373.4	11,294.3	14,378	20,230	28,348	41,867
Korea, Rep. of	226,910	221,424	280,427	392,926	7,651.3	7,432.6	12,942.7	11,297.0	34,331	33,888	36,988	65,482
Mongolia	6,200	5,332	6,528	5,285	8.4	6.1	3.9	7.1	254	295	391	541
Taipei,China	586,560	479,499	360,409	454,911 (2014)	1.2	1.3	1.2	1.2 (2014)	46,430	41,779	40,839	54,954 (2014)
South Asia												
Bangladesh	6,313	7,399	19,300	37,219	193.9	183.5	164.4	182.7	1,331	1,634	1,819	2,907
Bhutan	1,138	2,467	3,053	4,640	–	0.3	0.4	0.5	34	49	182	163
India	198,426	330,484	623,197	787,998	547.7	774.0	1,631.0	1,833.8	17,299	27,879	64,374	98,928
Maldives	5,970	4,520	...	...	13.2	0.0	...	...	315	82	...	...
Nepal	12,130	6,255	45,990	19,395	17.0	6.9	6.5	4.5	643	480	918	510
Sri Lanka	5,206	19,712	20,921	30,927	255.7	310.4	339.0	381.4	1,756	2,818	3,008	4,912
Southeast Asia												
Brunei Darussalam	12,739	11,808	12,333	11,624	140.2	134.1	148.5	115.1	864	978	1,263	1,150
Cambodia	4,648	3,207	5,105	12,983	4.1	1.2	0.0	2.3	125	169	278	1,104
Indonesia	159,027	320,724	520,932	639,389	408.5	439.8	665.7	747.5	9,916	26,836	59,384	88,686
Lao PDR	6,411	9,002	11,374	9,772	1.7	2.5	0.1	1.4	211	293	444	1,181
Malaysia	169,263	176,152	302,185	475,933	1,863.8	2,577.6	2,564.7	2,006.0	16,561	20,369	34,239	50,347
Myanmar	10,329	26,460	20,485	49,506	0.8	2.7	2.1	3.4	438	1,504	924	2,029
Philippines	44,547	58,944	205,318	278,835	289.9	322.7	460.2	484.2	5,756	8,057	22,575	32,231
Singapore	71,042	77,119	131,722	176,912	6,004.9	7,571.3	7,121.4	6,154.4	16,704	17,744	24,860	33,291
Thailand	101,591	124,347	201,306	381,918	1,712.9	2,002.4	2,938.7	2,134.1	17,392	18,903	28,781	54,260
Viet Nam	28,999	54,415	109,176	205,217	117.3	230.2	426.9	384.5	2,878	5,454	14,378	29,945
The Pacific												
Cook Islands	...	...	...	...	...	...	...	...	...	...	...	...
Fiji	57,776	41,886	26,127	19,487	90.8	92.1	77.1	83.7	586	871	1,259	1,337
Kiribati	...	...	...	...	...	...	...	...	...	...	...	...
Marshall Islands	2,324	3,083	...	...	0.2	0.3	...	...	16	26	...	...
Micronesia, Fed. States of	...	...	...	...	...	...	...	...	...	...	...	...
Nauru	...	...	...	...	...	...	...	...	...	...	...	...
Palau	...	...	...	...	...	...	...	...	...	...	...	...
Papua New Guinea	27,512	19,606	32,741	33,261	22.3	21.1	28.5	34.8	1,100	819	1,405	2,063
Samoa	10,877	11,439	...	...	2.2	1.8	...	...	164	267	...	...
Solomon Islands	11,481	12,318	7,388	13,107	1.0	0.8	2.5	3.7	75	91	143	374
Timor-Leste	...	...	...	...	...	...	...	...	...	...	...	...
Tonga	3,814	...	...	...	0.0	...	...	...	52	...	...	...
Tuvalu	...	...	...	...	...	...	...	...	...	...	...	...
Vanuatu	1,402	1,580	17,212	9,347	1.8	1.8	0.2	1.5	102	112	248	288
Developed Member Economies												
Australia	382,514	342,509	572,906	658,699	1,730.7	2,444.6	2,938.3	1,887.3	32,578	44,657	60,641	69,294
Japan	645,087	651,858	934,487	953,258	8,672.0	8,549.2	7,698.8	8,868.7	109,123	102,279	109,617	113,762
New Zealand	240,046	209,469	207,872	210,449	817.1	781.5	468.6	999.4	10,781	11,952	13,295	15,304

... = data not available at cutoff date, – = magnitude equals zero, 0.0 = magnitude is less than half of unit employed, Lao PDR = Lao People's Democratic Republic.

Sources: World Bank. World Development Indicators. http://databank.worldbank.org/data/views/reports/tableview.aspx# (accessed 15 August 2016); for Taipei,China: Directorate-General of Budget, Accounting and Statistics. 2015. *Statistical Yearbook 2014*. Nantou City.

Transport

Table 5.7: **Container Port Traffic**
(thousand teu)

Regional Member	Container Port Traffic										
	2000	2005	2006	2007	2008	2009	2010	2011	2012	2013	2014
Developing Member Economies											
Central and West Asia											
Afghanistan	...	...	...	...	...	...	...	...	...	...	...
Armenia	...	...	...	...	...	...	...	...	...	...	...
Azerbaijan	...	...	...	...	...	...	...	...	...	...	...
Georgia	...	...	...	185	254	182	226	239	257	277	291
Kazakhstan	...	...	...								
Kyrgyz Republic	...				...				...		
Pakistan	...	1,686	1,777	1,936	1,938	2,058	2,149	2,193	2,375	2,485	2,597
Tajikistan	...	...	...	...	...	...	...	...	...	...	...
Turkmenistan	...	...	...	...	...	...	...	...	...	...	...
Uzbekistan	...	...	...	...	...	...	...	...	...	...	...
East Asia											
China, People's Rep. of	41,000	67,245	84,811	103,823	115,942	108,800	130,290	144,642	161,319	170,859	181,635
Hong Kong, China	...	22,602	23,539	23,998	24,494	21,040	23,699	24,384	23,117	22,352	22,300
Korea, Rep. of	9,030	15,113	15,514	17,086	17,418	15,700	18,543	20,834	21,610	22,588	23,797
Mongolia	...			...					...		
Taipei,China	...	12,791	13,102	13,720	12,971	11,352	12,737	14,076	14,976	15,353	16,431
South Asia											
Bangladesh	456	809	902	978	1,091	1,182	1,356	1,432	1,436	1,500	1,655
Bhutan	...		...		...		...		...		...
India	2,451	4,982	6,141	7,398	7,672	8,014	9,753	10,285	10,279	10,883	11,656
Maldives	...	...	...	48	54	56	65	69	74	80	84
Nepal	...		...		...		...		...		...
Sri Lanka	1,733	2,455	3,079	3,687	3,687	3,464	4,000	4,263	4,321	4,306	4,908
Southeast Asia											
Brunei Darussalam	...	...	...	...	90	86	99	105	113	122	128
Cambodia	...	...	...	253	259	208	224	237	255	275	289
Indonesia	3,798	5,503	4,316	6,583	7,405	7,255	8,483	8,966	9,639	11,273	11,901
Lao PDR	...		...		...		...		...		...
Malaysia	4,642	12,198	13,419	14,829	16,094	15,923	18,267	20,139	20,873	21,169	22,719
Myanmar	...		...	170	180	164	190	201	216	233	245
Philippines	3,032	3,634	3,676	4,351	4,471	4,307	4,947	5,289	5,686	5,860	5,869
Singapore	17,100	23,192	24,792	28,768	30,891	26,593	29,179	30,728	32,499	33,516	34,832
Thailand	3,179	5,115	5,574	6,339	6,726	5,898	6,649	7,171	7,469	7,702	8,284
Viet Nam	1,190	2,537	3,000	4,009	4,394	4,937	5,984	6,930	7,548	9,137	9,531
The Pacific											
Cook Islands	...	...	...	...	...	...	...	...	...	...	...
Fiji	...	...	...	...	...	...	...	...	...	...	...
Kiribati	...	...	...	...	...	...	...	...	...	...	...
Marshall Islands	...	...	...	...	...	...	...	...	...	...	...
Micronesia, Fed. States of	...	...	...	...	...	...	...	...	...	...	...
Nauru	...	...	...	...	...	...	...	...	...	...	...
Palau	...	...	...	...	...	...	...	...	...	...	...
Papua New Guinea	...	...	...	282	255	262	295	314	337	364	382
Samoa	...	...	...	...	...	...	...	...	...	...	...
Solomon Islands	...	...	...	...	...	...	...	...	...	...	...
Timor-Leste	...	...	...	...	...	...	...	...	...	...	...
Tonga	...	...	...	...	...	...	...	...	...	...	...
Tuvalu	...	...	...	...	...	...	...	...	...	...	...
Vanuatu	...	...	...	...	...	...	...	...	...	...	...
Developed Member Economies											
Australia	3,543	5,191	5,742	6,290	6,102	6,200	6,668	7,012	7,155	7,313	7,524
Japan	13,100	17,055	18,470	19,165	18,944	16,286	18,098	19,422	20,115	20,486	20,744
New Zealand	1,067	1,603	1,807	2,312	2,318	2,325	2,463	2,517	2,867	3,093	3,251

... = data not available at cutoff date, teu = twenty-foot equivalent unit, Lao PDR = Lao People's Democratic Republic.

Sources: World Bank. World Development Indicators. http://data.worldbank.org/indicator (accessed 8 June 2016); for Taipei,China from 2005–2007: United Nations Conference on Trade and Development (UNCTAD). 2008 and 2010. *Review of Maritime Transport*. New York, NY: United Nations Publications; from 2008–2013: UNCTAD. UNCTADstat. http://unctadstat.unctad.org/EN/ (accessed 15 August 2016).

Table 5.8:   **Telephone and Internet Subscriptions**
(thousand)

Regional Member	Telephone Subscribers		Mobile Phone Subscribers		Fixed Broadband Subscribers		Internet Users	
	2000	2015	2000	2015	2000	2015	2000	2015
Developing Member Economies								
Central and West Asia								
Afghanistan	29.0	110.0	25.0 (2002)	19,709.0	0.2 (2004)	1.5	1.0 (2001)	2,643.8
Armenia	533.4	551.4	17.5	3,442.2	0.0 (2001)	286.3	40.0	1,741.3
Azerbaijan	801.2	1,796.0	420.4	10,697.1	1.0 (2002)	1,899.5	12.0	7,401.7
Georgia	508.8	950.2	194.7	5,550.7	0.4 (2001)	630.0	23.0	1,943.9
Kazakhstan	1,834.2	4,143.1	197.3	31,389.9	1.0 (2003)	2,188.4	97.5	12,220.0
Kyrgyz Republic	376.1	408.0	9.0	7,579.4	0.0 (2002)	211.5	51.6	1,726.4
Pakistan	3,053.5	2,991.0	306.5	125,899.6	14.6 (2005)	1,793.2	1,936.4 (2001)	33,865.9
Tajikistan	218.5	457.0	1.2	8,489.0	0.0 (2003)	6.0	3.0	1,634.3
Turkmenistan	364.4	648.0	7.5	7,842.0	0.1 (2008)	3.0	6.0	805.8
Uzbekistan	1,655.0	2,507.7	53.1	21,783.3	2.8 (2003)	1,059.4	120.3	12,715.9
East Asia								
China, People's Rep. of	144,829.0	230,996.0	85,260.0	1,305,738.0	22.7	260,145.0	22,739.3	704,998.1
Hong Kong, China	3,925.8	4,327.3	5,447.3	16,735.7	444.5	2,335.7	1,902.1	6,212.7
Korea, Rep. of	25,863.0	28,882.8	26,816.4	58,935.1	3,870.0	20,024.4	20,551.8	44,723.6
Mongolia	117.5	255.6	154.6	3,068.2	0.0 (2001)	208.0	30.1	626.6
Taipei,China	12,642.2	13,916.3	17,873.8	29,681.5	229.0	5,656.3	6,164.3	20,513.3
South Asia								
Bangladesh	491.3	830.8	279.0	133,720.4	43.7 (2007)	3,866.5	94.0	23,099.2
Bhutan	14.1	21.8	–	676.4	2.1 (2008)	27.6	2.3	309.0
India	32,436.1	25,518.0	3,577.1	1,011,054.0	50.0 (2001)	17,120.0	5,498.3	333,421.5
Maldives	24.4	21.9	7.6	739.8	0.2 (2002)	23.2	6.0	195.0
Nepal	266.9	846.9	10.2	27,516.1	1.0 (2006)	302.7	47.4	5,000.3
Sri Lanka	767.4	2,601.2	430.2	24,384.5	0.3 (2001)	670.0	122.0	6,481.1
Southeast Asia								
Brunei Darussalam	80.5	38.4	95.0	463.4	1.9 (2001)	34.3	29.8	305.1
Cambodia	30.9	256.4	130.5	20,850.5	0.1 (2002)	83.5	5.7	2,978.6
Indonesia	6,662.6	22,386.0	3,669.3	338,426.0	4.0	2,785.0	1,933.9	56,194.7
Lao PDR	40.9	962.5	12.7	3,727.2	0.0 (2003)	36.4	6.0	1,277.6
Malaysia	4,628.0	4,394.6	5,121.7	44,111.0	4.0 (2001)	2,743.3	5,008.5	21,782.0
Myanmar	271.4	523.7	13.4	41,529.3	0.2 (2005)	189.5	0.1 (2001)	11,807.8
Philippines	3,061.4	3,039.0	6,454.4	120,255.0	10.0 (2001)	3,460.0	1,539.3	41,433.7
Singapore	1,946.0	2,021.5	2,747.4	8,211.4	69.0	1,486.2	1,410.5	4,613.3
Thailand	5,591.1	5,309.0	3,056.0	84,797.0	1.6 (2001)	6,229.0	2,299.9	26,499.4
Viet Nam	2,542.7	5,900.0	788.6	122,000.0	1.1 (2002)	7,600.0	205.7	49,233.4
The Pacific								
Cook Islands	...	...	...	...	...	...	...	...
Fiji	86.4	72.6	55.1	966.0	7.0 (2005)	12.7	12.1	413.6
Kiribati	3.4	1.5	0.3	41.0	0.3 (2005)	0.1	1.5	13.7
Marshall Islands	4.0	2.4 (2014)	0.4	15.5	1.3 (2013)	1.0	0.8	10.2
Micronesia, Fed. States of	9.6	6.8	–	31.4 (2013)	0.0 (2003)	3.3	4.0	32.9
Nauru	1.8	1.9 (2009)	1.2	6.8 (2012)	...	1.0 (2010)	0.3 (2001)	5.4 (2011)
Palau	6.9 (2002)	7.2	2.5 (2002)	23.7	0.1 (2004)	1.2	4.0 (2002)	5.3 (2004)
Papua New Guinea	64.8	150.0	8.6	3,560.0	3.0 (2008)	15.0	44.9	602.9
Samoa	8.5	10.9	2.5	113.1	0.0 (2004)	2.1	1.0	49.1
Solomon Islands	7.7	7.4	1.2	424.7	0.2 (2004)	1.4	2.0	58.5
Timor-Leste	2.0 (2003)	2.7	20.1 (2003)	1,376.7	0.0 (2003)	1.0	1.0 (2005)	157.1
Tonga	9.7	13.2	0.2	69.8	0.0 (2002)	2.0	2.4	47.9
Tuvalu	0.7	2.0	0.5 (2004)	4.0	0.1 (2004)	1.0	0.5	4.2
Vanuatu	6.6	4.8	0.4	174.8	0.0 (2003)	4.3	3.9	59.0
Developed Member Economies								
Australia	10,050.0	9,080.0	8,562.0	31,770.0	122.8 (2001)	6,663.0	9,004.9	20,229.5
Japan	61,957.1	63,633.1	66,784.4	158,590.7	854.7	38,662.5	37,702.8	118,358.5
New Zealand	1,831.0	1,850.0	1,542.0	5,600.0	4.7	1,450.0	1,827.9	4,055.1

...= data not available at cutoff date, 0.0 = magnitude is less than half of unit employed, – = magnitude equals zero, Lao PDR = Lao People's Democratic Republic.

Sources: International Telecommunication Union. World Telecommunication/ICT Indicators Database. http://www.itu.int/en/ITU-D/Statistics/Pages/stat/default.aspx
(accessed 6 June 2016); ADB estimates.

Communications

Table 5.9:   Telephone and Internet Subscriptions
(per 100 people)

Regional Member	Telephone Subscribers				Mobile Phone Subscribers				Fixed Broadband Subscribers				Internet Users			
	2000	2005	2010	2015	2000	2005	2010	2015	2000	2005	2010	2015	2000	2005	2010	2015
Developing Member Economies																
Central and West Asia																
Afghanistan	0.1	...	0.1	0.3	–	4.8	36.0	61.6	...	0.0	0.0	0.0	...	1.2	4.0	8.3
Armenia	17.3	19.7	20.0	18.4	0.6	10.5	130.4	115.1	...	0.1	3.2	9.6	1.3	5.3	25.0	58.2
Azerbaijan	9.9	12.8	16.6	18.7	5.2	26.2	100.1	111.3	...	0.0	5.2	19.8	0.1	8.0	46.0	77.0
Georgia	10.7	12.7	25.3	22.1	4.1	26.2	90.6	129.0	...	0.1	4.2	14.6	0.5	6.1	26.9	45.2
Kazakhstan	12.6	18.0	25.5	24.7	1.4	35.8	121.9	187.2	...	0.0	5.5	13.0	0.7	3.0	31.6	72.9
Kyrgyz Republic	7.6	8.7	9.2	7.1	0.2	10.7	98.9	132.8	...	0.0	0.4	3.7	1.0	10.5	16.3	30.2
Pakistan	2.1	3.3	3.5	1.6	0.2	8.1	57.3	66.9	...	0.0	0.5	1.0	...	6.3	8.0	18.0
Tajikistan	3.5	4.1	4.8	5.3	0.0	3.9	77.9	98.6	...	...	0.1	0.1	0.0	0.3	11.6	19.0
Turkmenistan	8.1	8.4	10.3	12.1	0.2	2.2	63.4	145.9	...	...	0.0	0.1	0.1	1.0	3.0	15.0
Uzbekistan	6.7	6.9	6.8	8.4	0.2	2.8	75.5	73.3	...	0.0	0.4	3.6	0.5	3.3	15.9	42.8
East Asia																
China, People's Rep. of	11.3	26.6	21.6	16.5	6.7	29.8	63.2	93.2	0.0	2.8	9.3	18.6	1.8	8.5	34.3	50.3
Hong Kong, China	57.4	55.0	61.9	59.2	79.7	123.9	195.7	228.8	6.5	24.1	30.7	31.9	27.8	56.9	72.0	84.9
Korea, Rep. of	56.3	50.8	58.9	58.1	58.3	81.5	104.8	118.5	8.4	25.9	35.5	40.2	44.7	73.5	83.7	89.9
Mongolia	4.9	6.2	7.1	8.7	6.4	22.1	92.5	105.0	...	0.1	2.8	7.1	1.3	...	10.2	21.4
Taipei,China	57.6	63.7	70.8	59.7	81.5	97.5	119.9	127.3	1.0	19.1	22.9	24.3	28.1	58.0	71.5	88.0
South Asia																
Bangladesh	0.4	0.7	0.8	0.5	0.2	6.3	44.9	83.4	...	...	0.3	2.4	0.1	0.2	3.7	14.4
Bhutan	2.5	5.1	3.7	2.8	–	5.5	55.0	87.1	...	...	1.2	3.6	0.4	3.8	13.6	39.8
India	3.1	4.5	2.9	2.0	0.3	8.0	62.4	78.8	...	0.1	0.9	1.3	0.5	2.4	7.5	26.0
Maldives	9.0	10.9	8.7	6.1	2.8	68.4	151.8	206.7	...	1.1	4.8	6.5	2.2	6.9	26.5	54.5
Nepal	1.2	1.9	3.1	3.0	0.0	0.9	34.3	96.7	...	...	0.2	1.1	0.2	0.8	7.9	17.6
Sri Lanka	4.1	6.2	17.2	12.0	2.3	16.8	83.6	112.8	...	0.1	1.1	3.1	0.6	1.8	12.0	30.0
Southeast Asia																
Brunei Darussalam	24.3	22.8	19.9	9.0	28.6	63.3	108.6	108.1	...	2.2	5.4	8.0	9.0	36.5	53.0	71.2
Cambodia	0.3	0.2	2.5	1.6	1.1	8.0	56.7	133.0	...	0.0	0.2	0.5	0.0	0.3	1.3	19.0
Indonesia	3.2	6.0	17.0	8.8	1.8	20.9	87.8	132.3	0.0	0.0	0.9	1.1	0.9	3.6	10.9	22.0
Lao PDR	0.8	1.6	1.6	13.7	0.2	11.4	62.6	53.1	...	0.0	0.1	0.5	0.1	0.9	7.0	18.2
Malaysia	19.8	16.9	16.3	14.3	21.9	75.6	119.7	143.9	...	1.9	7.4	9.0	21.4	48.6	56.3	71.1
Myanmar	0.6	1.0	0.9	1.0	0.0	0.3	1.1	76.7	...	0.0	0.0	0.3	...	0.1	0.3	21.8
Philippines	3.9	3.9	3.6	3.0	8.3	40.5	89.0	118.1	...	0.1	...	3.4	2.0	5.4	25.0	40.7
Singapore	49.7	41.0	39.3	36.0	70.1	97.5	145.4	146.1	1.8	14.6	26.4	26.5	36.0	61.0	71.0	82.1
Thailand	9.0	10.7	10.3	7.9	4.9	46.5	108.0	125.8	...	0.8	4.9	9.2	3.7	15.0	22.4	39.3
Viet Nam	3.1	...	16.1	6.3	1.0	11.3	...	...	...	0.2	4.1	8.1	0.3	12.7	30.7	52.7
The Pacific																
Cook Islands	...	...	...	...	...	...	...	...	...	...	...	...	...	...	...	...
Fiji	10.6	13.7	15.1	8.1	6.8	24.9	81.1	108.2	...	0.9	2.7	1.4	1.5	8.5	20.0	46.3
Kiribati	4.1	4.6	8.6	1.4	0.4	0.7	10.8	38.8	...	0.4	0.9	0.1	1.8	4.0	9.1	13.0
Marshall Islands	7.7	...	...	...	0.9	1.3	...	29.2	...	...	...	1.9	1.5	3.9	7.0	19.3
Micronesia, Fed. States of	9.0	11.7	8.2	6.5	–	13.3	26.6	...	...	0.0	1.0	3.1	3.7	11.9	20.0	31.5
Nauru	17.9	17.8	–	...	11.9	...	61.8	...	...	...	9.5	...	...	...	...	...
Palau	...	40.1	34.1	33.8	...	30.4	70.9	111.5	...	0.5	1.2	5.7	...	...	...	...
Papua New Guinea	1.2	1.0	1.8	2.0	0.2	1.2	27.8	46.6	...	...	0.1	0.2	0.8	1.7	1.3	7.9
Samoa	4.9	10.8	4.3	5.6	1.4	13.3	48.4	58.5	...	0.0	0.1	1.1	0.6	3.4	7.0	25.4
Solomon Islands	1.9	1.6	1.6	1.3	0.3	1.3	21.9	72.7	...	0.1	0.5	0.2	0.5	0.8	5.0	10.0
Timor-Leste	...	0.2	0.3	0.2	...	3.3	43.8	117.4	...	0.0	0.0	0.1	...	0.1	0.2	13.4
Tonga	9.9	13.6	29.8	12.4	0.2	29.6	52.2	65.6	...	0.6	1.1	1.9	2.4	4.9	16.0	45.0
Tuvalu	7.0	9.2	12.2	20.2	–	13.4	16.3	40.3	...	1.5	2.4	10.1	5.2	...	25.0	42.7
Vanuatu	3.6	3.3	3.0	1.8	0.2	6.1	71.9	66.2	...	0.0	0.2	1.6	2.1	5.1	8.0	22.4
Developed Member Economies																
Australia	52.2	49.3	47.4	38.0	44.5	89.8	100.4	132.8	...	9.8	24.6	27.9	46.8	63.0	76.0	84.6
Japan	49.3	45.7	51.5	50.2	53.1	76.0	96.8	125.1	0.7	18.4	26.8	30.0	30.0	66.9	78.2	93.3
New Zealand	47.5	41.8	43.0	40.2	40.0	85.4	107.8	121.8	0.1	7.8	25.0	31.5	47.4	62.7	80.5	88.2

... = data not available at cutoff date, 0.0 = magnitude is less than half of unit employed, – = magnitude equals zero, Lao PDR = Lao People's Democratic Republic.

Source: International Telecommunication Union. World Telecommunication/ICT Indicators Database. http://www.itu.int/en/ITU-D/Statistics/Pages/stat/default. aspx (accessed 12 August 2016).

Energy and Electricity

Snapshots

- Asia and the Pacific accounts for 43.4% of the global energy use according to latest available data and leads all regions in terms of global energy use.

- Since 2000, per capita electricity consumption has increased by at least 50% in 20 out of the 41 developing member economies.

- Asia and the Pacific's energy production and use are rapidly expanding along with economic growth, but sustaining the growth momentum may require further expansion of the region's energy endowment.

- While Asia and the Pacific in general remains a net energy importer, 12 developing member economies were net exporters of energy in 2013 and seven of them exported more energy than they consumed.

- More than three-quarters of economies in Asia and the Pacific for which data are available increased their energy efficiency levels between 2000 and 2013.

- Across Asia and the Pacific, coal, oil, and natural gas are the predominant sources of electricity production; renewables and nuclear energy comprise a smaller share.

Key Trends

Asia and the Pacific accounts for more than 43% of the global energy use according to latest data available and leads all regions in terms of global energy use. In 2013, the People's Republic of China (PRC) comprised more than half of all energy demand in Asia and the Pacific and 22.8% of the world total (Figure 6.1). This was followed by India (5.9%) and Japan (3.4%). Asia and the Pacific's share of global energy use is expected to rise to between 51% and 56% by 2035, depending on trends in energy use per capita and on energy intensity measured by changes in the physical energy required to generate each

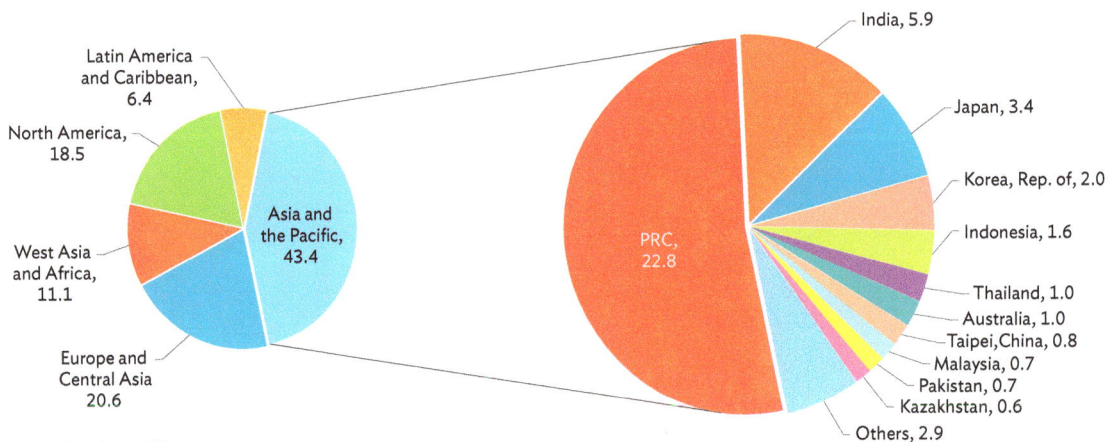

Figure 6.1: Energy Use by Global Region and by Economy in Asia and the Pacific, 2013
(kilotons of oil equivalent, %)

Latin America and Caribbean, 6.4
North America, 18.5
West Asia and Africa, 11.1
Europe and Central Asia 20.6
Asia and the Pacific, 43.4

India, 5.9
Japan, 3.4
Korea, Rep. of, 2.0
Indonesia, 1.6
Thailand, 1.0
Australia, 1.0
Taipei,China, 0.8
Malaysia, 0.7
Pakistan, 0.7
Kazakhstan, 0.6
Others, 2.9
PRC, 22.8

PRC = People's Republic of China.
Sources: Table 6.3 and International Energy Agency.

unit of gross domestic product (GDP). The region's energy consumption will continue to grow despite substantial improvements in energy intensity because of rapid gains in GDP per capita, which is associated with behavior marked by increased use of energy-consuming goods such as cars and air-conditioning units (ADB 2013).

Since 2000, per capita electricity consumption rose by at least 50% in 20 out of the 41 developing member economies. Per capita electricity consumption increased throughout the region during the review period with the exception of Vanuatu (–5.4%), Uzbekistan (–7.9%), Solomon Islands (–16.3%), and Tajikistan (–23.5%), as well as all three developed member economies—Australia (–1.4%), Japan (–1.8%), and New Zealand (–3.4%) (Figure 6.2). At the same time, per capita electricity consumption more than tripled in Bhutan (273.2%), the PRC (277.0%), Timor-Leste (280.7%), Viet Nam (336.7%), Afghanistan (403.4%), and Cambodia (633.3%).

In terms of kilowatt-hours (kWh), the highest levels of per capita electricity consumption in 2013 were found in Australia (10,070 kWh); the Republic of Korea (10,430 kWh); and Taipei,China (10,460 kWh) (Table 6.2). The economies with the lowest per capita electricity consumption were Timor-Leste (103 kWh), Afghanistan (104 kWh), and Solomon Islands (112 kWh).

Asia and the Pacific's energy production and use are rapidly expanding along with economic growth, but sustaining the growth momentum may require further expansion of the region's energy endowment. Figure 6.3 shows the average annual percentage growth of energy production and use for regional economies between 2000 and 2013. The largest average annual growth rates in energy use during the review period were seen in Afghanistan (21.7%); the PRC (7.6%), which has also experienced a significant GDP expansion since 2000; and the Maldives (7.3%). Afghanistan and the Maldives saw gains that were driven by low base effects.

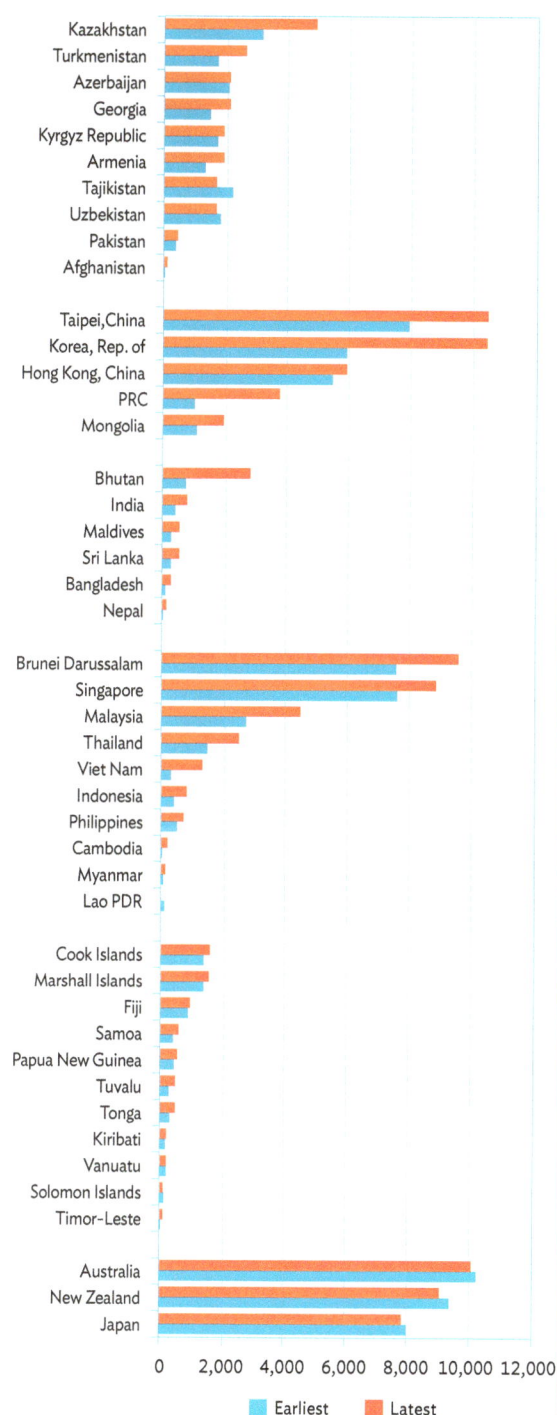

Figure 6.2: Per Capita Electric Power Consumption
(kWh)

kWh = kilowatt-hour, Lao PDR = Lao People's Democratic Republic, PRC = People's Republic of China.
Notes: The earliest year is 2000 except for Afghanistan (2001), the Lao PDR (1997), and Timor-Leste (2006). The latest year is 2015 for Afghanistan, the Cook Islands, Samoa, and Vanuatu; 2014 for Bhutan, Fiji, the Maldives, Solomon Islands, Timor-Leste, and Tonga; 2012 for Kiribati; 2011 for Tuvalu; 2006 for the Marshall Islands; and 2013 for the rest of the economies.
Source: Table 6.2.

Figure 6.3: Average Annual Growth of Energy Production and Energy Use, 2000–2013
(kilotons of oil equivalent, %)

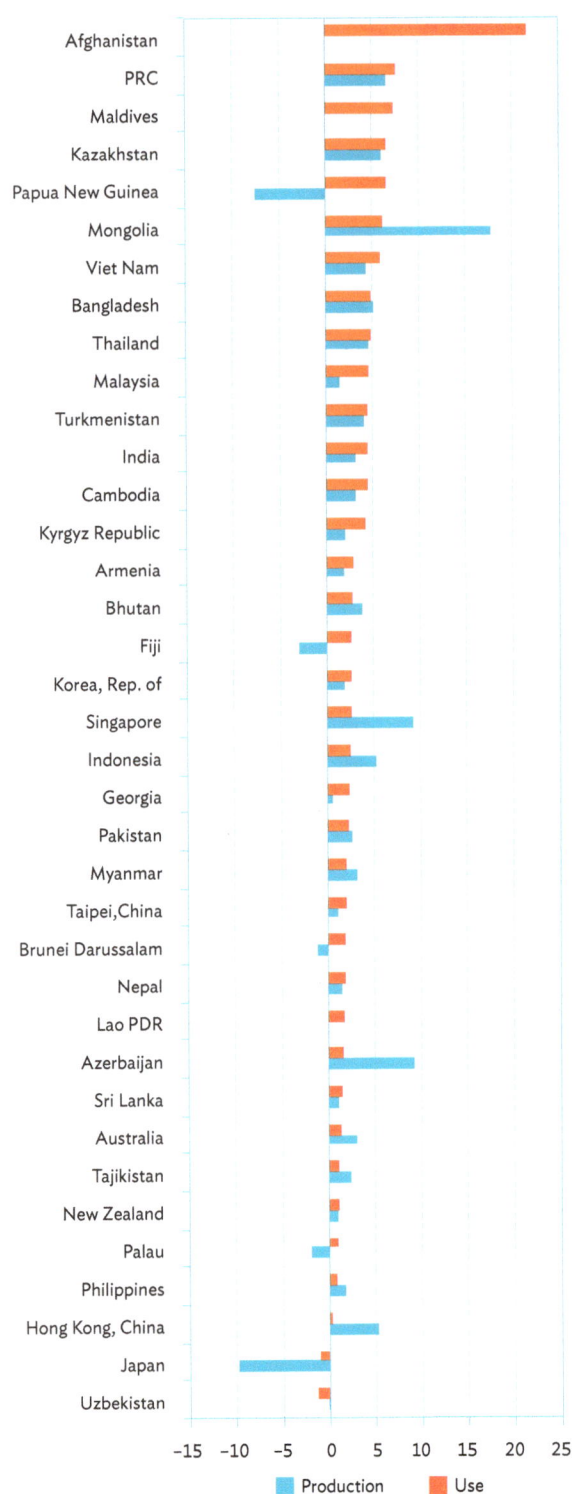

PRC = People's Republic of China.
Note: Growth rates are computed only for economies with complete annual data from 2000 to 2013.
Sources: Tables 6.3 and 6.4.

The PRC was the largest energy consumer in 2013 with energy use (measured as kilotons of oil equivalent, ktoe) that was nearly four times higher (at 3.01 million ktoe) than that of the next largest energy consumer, India (0.78 million ktoe) (Table 6.3). The region's two most populous economies were followed in terms of energy use by Japan (0.45 million ktoe) and the Republic of Korea (0.26 million ktoe).

In terms of average annual growth in energy production, the region's leader was Mongolia (17.8%), followed by Singapore (9.3%) and Azerbaijan (9.2%). Mongolia is a major producer and exporter of coal, Singapore is almost wholly dependent upon natural gas imports, and Azerbaijan is a major exporter of oil and natural gas (ADB 2015). Japan and Papua New Guinea experienced notable declines in energy production during the review period, with average annual contractions of 9.7% and 7.5%, respectively.

In terms of energy production, the PRC again led all economies in the region by a wide margin with production equivalent to 2.57 million ktoe (Table 6.4). This was followed by India (0.52 million ktoe) and Indonesia (0.46 million ktoe).

While Asia and the Pacific in general remains a net energy importer, 12 developing member economies were net exporters of energy in 2013 and seven of them exported more energy than they consumed. Led by oil- and gas-rich Brunei Darussalam and Timor-Leste, a dozen Asia and Pacific economies were net energy exporters in 2013. While Timor-Leste's energy export data in 2000 are not available, in 2013 its energy exports were the equivalent of 2,300% of domestic energy use. Brunei Darussalam's exports as a share of total energy use[8] fell from 725.6% to 453.1% between 2000 and 2013. Meanwhile, Azerbaijan's energy exports increased from 65.9% to 322.4% and Mongolia switched from a net importer (–19.7%) to a net exporter (225.6%) during the review period.

---

8   Net energy exports is computed as negative of net imports, plus stock changes, minus fuels supplied to ships and aircraft engaged in international transport.

According to an ADB (2013) assessment, Asia and the Pacific's energy needs are expected to expand in tandem with its growing GDP and the region will remain heavily dependent on energy imports, particularly oil, as the region's own energy production is insufficient to meet present and future needs. The assessment estimates that by 2035 most regional economies will produce less than half the energy they need.

More than three-quarters of economies in Asia and the Pacific for which data are available increased their level of energy efficiency between 2000 and 2013. The region has realized widespread efficiency gains with regard to energy use since 2000. Out of 39 regional economies for which data are available, 30 increased their level of GDP per unit use of energy between 2000 and 2013 (Figure 6.4). Among the most energy-efficient economies were some of those with the highest income levels in the region, including Singapore and Hong Kong, China; as well as lower-middle-income economies such as the Lao People's Democratic Republic, the Philippines, and Sri Lanka.

The largest efficiency gains during the review period were realized in Azerbaijan, Uzbekistan, and Tajikistan, with average annual growth rates for GDP per unit use of energy of 11.1%, 9.4%, and 7.5%, respectively.

ADB projections show every Asian subregion will see a decline in electricity expenditure as a fraction of GDP between 2012 and 2035, suggesting that on average energy will become more affordable (ADB 2013).

Across Asia and the Pacific, coal, oil, and natural gas are the predominant sources of electricity production, while renewables and nuclear energy comprise a smaller share. At the same time, there are some unique characteristics within subregions. Coal plays a larger role in East Asia than anywhere else in the region. Natural gas

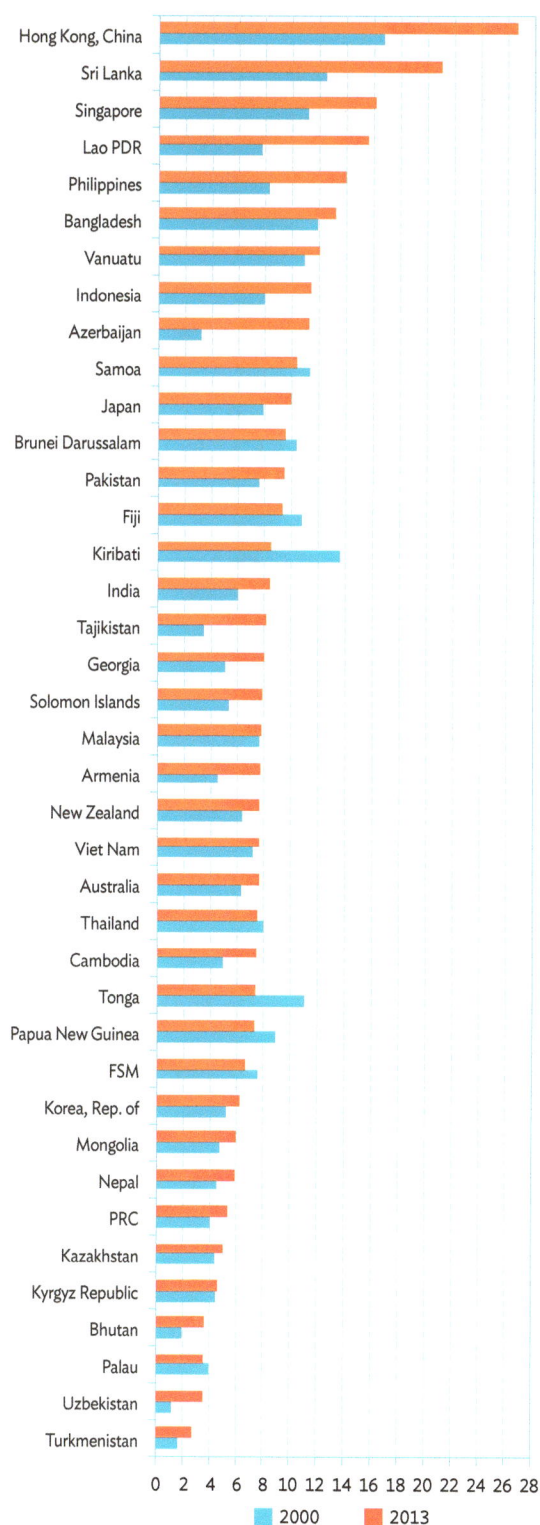

Figure 6.4: Gross Domestic Product per Unit Use of Energy
(constant 2011 PPP $ per kilogram of oil equivalent)

FSM = Federated States of Micronesia, Lao PDR = Lao People's Democratic Republic, PPP = purchasing power parity, PRC = People's Republic of China.
Source: Table 6.3.

is a far larger source of electricity production in Central and West Asia and Southeast Asia than in East Asia and South Asia. Among the region's top energy producers, coal is the dominant source of energy in the PRC, India, and Australia, accounting for 75.5%, 72.8%, and 64.7% of electricity production, respectively (Figure 6.5). Coal also plays the most significant role in energy production in Indonesia (51.2%); Taipei,China (48.8%); and the Republic of Korea (41.1%). Natural gas is the biggest contributor to energy production in Thailand (70.6%), Malaysia (49.0%), and Japan (38.4%). In Viet Nam, the hydropower sector is the primary source of electricity generation, accounting for 45.0% of the total.

Data Issues and Comparability

Most of the energy data are compiled by the International Energy Agency using standard procedures and conversion factors. Data for the indicator on the household electrification rate are lacking. Rather than having data for uniform starting and ending years across all economies, data for each are posted over a different range of years depending on data availability; thus, the data may not be comparable. This could indicate infrequent or irregular timing in the generation of data, making data inconsistent and limiting possibilities for analysis.

Similarly, data on the sources of electricity are incomplete. For the Pacific island economies, which have limited resources for power generation, data on the source of their electricity generated are not available.

References

Asian Development Bank. 2013. *Asian Development Outlook 2013*. Manila.

Asian Development Bank. 2015. *Key Indicators for Asia and the Pacific 2015*. Manila.

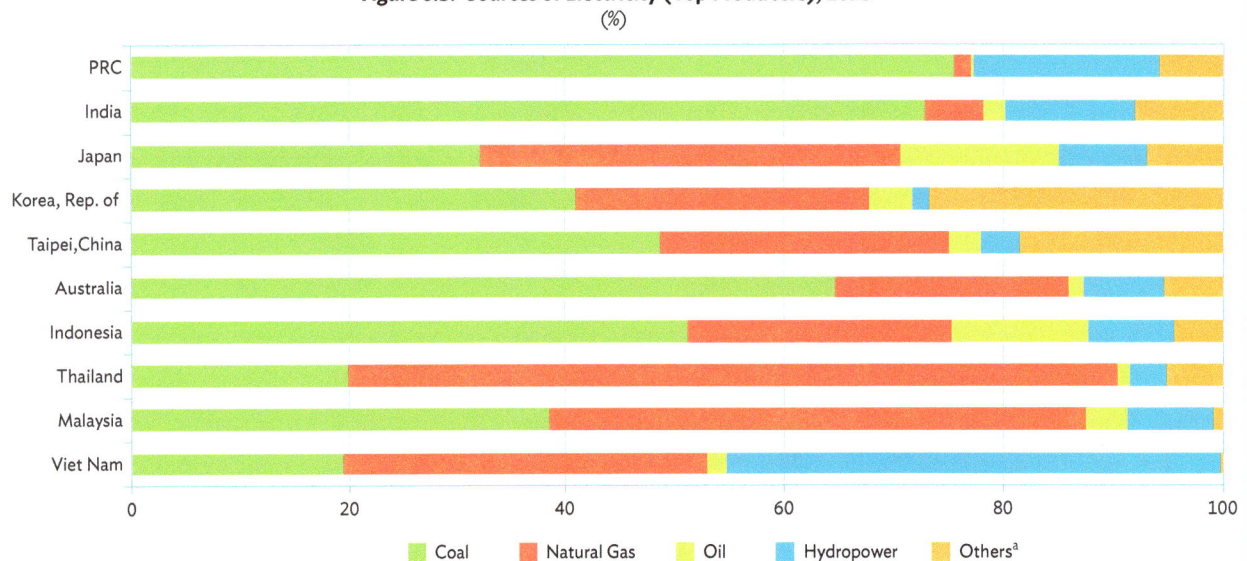

Figure 6.5: Sources of Electricity (Top Producers), 2013 (%)

PRC = People's Republic of China.
a Computed as residual that includes combustible renewables and waste; and generation by nuclear power, geothermal, solar, wind, and tide and wave energy.
Source: Table 6.1.

Table 6.1:   **Electricity Production and Sources**

Regional Member	Total Electricity Production (billion kWh)		Sources of Electricity (% of total)									
			Coal		Natural Gas		Oil		Hydropower		Others[a]	
	2000	2013	2000	2013	2000	2013	2000	2013	2000	2013	2000	2013
Developing Member Economies												
Central and West Asia												
Afghanistan	0.7	1.0 (2015)	...	...	...	...	...	...	...	...	...	...
Armenia	6.0	7.7	–	–	45.2	41.2	–	–	21.2	28.2	33.7	30.7
Azerbaijan	18.7	23.4	–	–	19.8	93.0	72.0	0.1	8.2	6.4	–	0.6
Georgia	7.4	10.1	–	–	17.4	17.8	3.7	–	78.9	82.2	–	–
Kazakhstan	51.3	95.4	69.5	81.3	10.7	10.0	5.2	0.6	14.7	8.1	–	–
Kyrgyz Republic	14.9	14.0	4.3	5.6	9.8	0.2	–	0.7	85.9	93.5	–	–
Pakistan	68.1	97.8	0.4	0.1	32.0	26.3	39.5	36.9	25.2	31.9	2.9	4.9
Tajikistan	14.2	17.1	–	–	1.6	0.3	–	–	98.4	99.7	–	0.0
Turkmenistan	9.8	18.9	–	–	100.0	100.0	–	–	–	–	–	–
Uzbekistan	46.9	54.2	4.1	4.1	73.3	74.1	10.1	0.5	12.5	21.3	–	–
East Asia												
China, People's Rep. of	1,356.4	5,447.2	78.2	75.5	0.4	1.7	3.5	0.1	16.4	16.9	1.5	5.9
Hong Kong, China	31.3	39.2	98.2	74.8	–	24.5	1.8	0.4	–	–	–	0.2
Korea, Rep. of	290.1	542.0	38.4	41.1	10.2	26.7	11.9	4.0	1.9	1.5	37.6	26.7
Mongolia	2.9	5.0	97.0	92.9	–	–	3.0	5.4	–	–	–	1.7
Taipei,China	184.9	252.0	47.8	48.8	9.5	26.2	16.2	3.0	4.8	3.4	21.7	18.6
South Asia												
Bangladesh	15.8	53.0	–	2.3	88.8	83.1	6.4	12.6	4.7	1.7	–	0.3
Bhutan	2.1	7.2 (2014)	...	...	...	...	...	...	...	...	...	...
India	569.7	1,193.5	68.5	72.8	9.8	5.5	5.1	1.9	13.1	11.9	3.5	7.9
Maldives	0.1	0.3 (2014)	...	...	...	...	...	...	...	...	...	...
Nepal	1.7	3.6	–	–	–	–	1.6	0.3	98.4	99.7	–	–
Sri Lanka	7.0	12.0	–	12.2	–	–	54.2	27.9	45.6	57.5	0.2	2.3
Southeast Asia												
Brunei Darussalam	2.5	4.4	–	–	99.1	99.0	0.9	0.9	–	–	–	0.0
Cambodia	0.2	1.8	–	9.5	–	–	100.0	32.6	–	57.1	–	0.8
Indonesia	93.3	215.6	36.4	51.2	28.0	24.0	19.7	12.4	10.7	7.9	5.2	4.5
Lao PDR	3.7	14.9 (2014)	...	...	...	...	...	...	...	...	...	...
Malaysia	69.3	138.3	11.1	38.6	73.6	49.0	5.2	3.9	10.1	7.7	–	0.9
Myanmar	5.1	11.9	–	4.3	49.5	20.5	13.5	0.5	37.0	74.7	–	–
Philippines	45.3	75.3	36.8	42.6	0.0	25.0	20.3	6.0	17.2	13.3	25.7	13.1
Singapore	31.7	48.0	–	0.8	18.5	91.5	80.0	4.9	–	–	1.5	2.9
Thailand	96.0	165.7	18.5	19.9	64.2	70.6	10.4	1.0	6.3	3.5	0.5	5.0
Viet Nam	26.6	127.0	11.8	19.5	16.4	33.6	17.0	1.8	54.8	45.0	–	0.1
The Pacific												
Cook Islands	0.0	0.0 (2015)	...	...	...	...	...	...	...	...	...	...
Fiji	0.7	0.8 (2014)	...	...	...	...	...	...	...	...	...	...
Kiribati	0.0	0.0 (2012)	...	...	...	...	...	...	...	...	...	...
Marshall Islands	0.1	0.1 (2006)	...	...	...	...	...	...	...	...	...	...
Micronesia, Fed. States of	0.1	0.1 (2011)	...	...	...	...	...	...	...	...	...	...
Nauru	0.0	0.0 (2007)	...	...	...	...	...	...	...	...	...	...
Palau	0.1	0.1 (2011)	...	...	...	...	...	...	...	...	...	...
Papua New Guinea	2.3	4.1	...	...	...	...	...	...	...	...	...	...
Samoa	0.1	0.1 (2015)	...	...	...	...	...	...	...	...	...	...
Solomon Islands	0.1	0.1 (2014)	...	...	...	...	...	...	...	...	...	...
Timor-Leste	0.1 (2006)	0.3 (2014)	...	...	...	...	...	...	...	...	...	...
Tonga	0.0	0.1 (2014)	...	...	...	...	...	...	...	...	...	...
Tuvalu	...	...	...	...	...	...	...	...	...	...	...	...
Vanuatu	0.0	0.1 (2015)	...	...	...	...	...	...	...	...	...	...
Developed Member Economies												
Australia	210.2	249.1	82.9	64.7	7.7	21.3	0.8	1.4	8.0	7.3	0.6	5.3
Japan	1,058.5	1,045.3	21.6	32.2	24.2	38.4	12.8	14.3	9.1	8.1	32.2	6.9
New Zealand	39.2	43.3	3.9	5.5	24.4	20.1	–	0.0	62.3	53.3	9.4	21.1

... = data not available at cutoff date, – = magnitude equals zero, 0.0 = magnitude is less than half of unit employed, kWh = kilowatt-hour, Lao PDR = Lao People's Democratic Republic.

a   Computed as residual that includes combustible renewables and waste; and generation by nuclear power, geothermal, solar, wind, and tide and wave energy.

Sources: International Energy Agency; economy sources for Afghanistan, Bhutan, the Lao PDR, the Maldives, and the Pacific economies.

Table 6.2:   **Electric Power Consumption and Electrification**

Regional Member	Electric Power Consumption (per capita kWh)		Household Electrification Rate (% of households)	
	2000	**2013**	**Earliest Year**	**Latest Year**
Developing Member Economies				
Central and West Asia				
Afghanistan	21 (2001)	104 (2015)	...	25.0 (2005)
Armenia	1,290	1,880	98.9 (2000)	99.8 (2010)
Azerbaijan	2,040	2,090	99.5 (2006)	...
Georgia	1,450	2,070	...	...
Kazakhstan	3,170	4,890	97.0 (1999)	...
Kyrgyz Republic	1,700	1,890	100.0 (2002)	99.8 (2012)
Pakistan	360	450	89.2 (2006)	93.6 (2012)
Tajikistan	2,170	1,660	99.0 (2002)	99.1 (2012)
Turkmenistan	1,700	2,600	99.6 (2000)	...
Uzbekistan	1,780	1,640	99.7 (2002)	...
East Asia				
China, People's Rep. of	1,000	3,770	...	...
Hong Kong, China	5,450	5,930	...	...
Korea, Rep. of	5,910	10,430	...	...
Mongolia	1,050	1,920	67.3 (2000)	86.2 (2005)
Taipei,China	7,910	10,460	...	...
South Asia				
Bangladesh	100	290	32.0 (2000)	59.6 (2011)
Bhutan	748	2,793 (2014)	41.1 (2003)	72.0 (2007)
India	400	780	60.1 (1999)	67.9 (2006)
Maldives	273	531 (2014)	83.8 (2000)	99.8 (2009)
Nepal	60	130	24.6 (2001)	76.3 (2011)
Sri Lanka	290	530	80.7 (2002)	...
Southeast Asia				
Brunei Darussalam	7,570	9,550	...	...
Cambodia	30	220	16.6 (2000)	31.1 (2010)
Indonesia	400	790	90.7 (2003)	96.0 (2012)
Lao PDR	103 (1997)	...	46.3 (2002)	...
Malaysia	2,720	4,470	...	...
Myanmar	70	160	47.0 (2002)	...
Philippines	500	690	76.6 (2003)	87.5 (2013)
Singapore	7,580	8,840	...	...
Thailand	1,460	2,490	...	...
Viet Nam	300	1,310	89.1 (2002)	96.1 (2005)
The Pacific				
Cook Islands	1,372	1,566 (2015)	97.0 (2006)	99.0 (2010)
Fiji	858	917 (2014)	84.0 (2008)	...
Kiribati	169	211 (2012)	...	62.0 (2010)
Marshall Islands	1,352	1,516 (2006)	72.0 (2007)	90.0 (2011)
Micronesia, Fed. States of	...	...	46.0 (2000)	65.0 (2010)
Nauru	...	...	100.0 (2002)	100.0 (2011)
Palau	...	...	98.9 (2005)	98.0 (2012)
Papua New Guinea	438	525	12.0 (2006)	19.5 (2010)
Samoa	400	588 (2015)	98.0 (2006)	96.4 (2011)
Solomon Islands	134	112 (2014)	14.0 (2005)	21.0 (2009)
Timor-Leste	27 (2006)	103 (2014)	27.0 (2002)	38.0 (2009)
Tonga	324	461 (2014)	89.0 (2006)	97.0 (2011)
Tuvalu	289	472 (2011)	94.0 (2005)	98.0 (2012)
Vanuatu	214	202 (2015)	...	33.0 (2009)
Developed Member Economies				
Australia	10,210	10,070	...	...
Japan	7,980	7,840	...	...
New Zealand	9,370	9,050	...	...

... = data not available at cutoff date, kWh = kilowatt-hour, Lao PDR = Lao People's Democratic Republic.

Sources: For electric power consumption: International Energy Agency; economy sources for Afghanistan, Bhutan, the Lao PDR, the Maldives, and the Pacific economies. For household electrification rate: International Development Association (IDA). Results Measurement System (RMS) Online. http://data.worldbank.org/data-catalog/IDA-results-measurement (accessed 15 August 2016); United States Agency for International Development, Demographic and Health Surveys (DHS) Program. The DHS Program STAT compiler. http://www.statcompiler.com/ (accessed 21 June 2016); Secretariat of the Pacific Community, Pacific Regional Information System (PRISM). National Minimum Development Indicators. http://www.spc.int/nmdi/MdiHome.aspx (accessed 16 August 2016).

Energy

Table 6.3:   **Use of Energy**

Regional Member	GDP per Unit Use of Energy (constant 2011 PPP $ per kilogram of oil equivalent)				Energy Use (kilotons of oil equivalent)			
	2000	2005	2010	2013	2000	2005	2010	2013
Developing Member Economies								
Central and West Asia								
Afghanistan	...	33.1	14.2	7.5	597	860	3,272	7,667
Armenia	4.5	6.4	7.8	7.7	2,015	2,512	2,483	2,900
Azerbaijan	3.2	5.0	12.5	11.3	11,296	13,427	11,585	13,880
Georgia	5.0	7.2	8.5	8.0	2,869	2,841	3,122	3,897
Kazakhstan	4.3	5.0	4.9	5.0	35,679	50,878	69,121	81,542
Kyrgyz Republic	4.4	4.8	5.5	4.5	2,319	2,574	2,753	3,949
Pakistan	7.6	8.1	8.7	9.4	64,069	76,255	84,400	86,041
Tajikistan	3.4	5.0	7.4	8.1	2,149	2,340	2,176	2,456
Turkmenistan	1.6	1.6	2.2	2.7	14,880	19,175	22,685	26,261
Uzbekistan	1.2	1.7	2.8	3.5	50,868	47,085	43,210	42,930
East Asia								
China, People's Rep. of	4.0	4.2	5.1	5.3	1,160,776	1,775,266	2,469,052	3,009,472
Hong Kong, China	16.7	21.7	24.7	26.6	13,553	12,843	13,675	13,932
Korea, Rep. of	5.2	5.8	6.0	6.2	188,158	210,288	250,025	263,828
Mongolia	4.7	5.1	5.3	5.9	2,397	2,996	3,941	5,222
Taipei,China	...	...	...	...	84,840	102,370	111,445	108,631
South Asia								
Bangladesh	11.8	12.2	12.2	13.2	18,253	22,767	30,422	33,870
Bhutan	1.9	2.6	3.3	3.6	1,051	1,146	1,403	1,504
India	6.0	7.1	7.8	8.4	441,327	517,655	692,676	775,445
Maldives	...	11.9	10.5	12.5	143	215	366	359
Nepal	4.5	4.7	5.3	5.9	8,108	9,132	10,211	10,290
Sri Lanka	12.5	14.0	17.7	21.0	8,326	9,001	9,741	10,033
Southeast Asia								
Brunei Darussalam	10.4	12.3	8.7	9.5	2,385	2,218	3,240	3,042
Cambodia	4.9	7.6	6.8	7.5	3,412	3,436	5,299	5,974
Indonesia	7.9	8.6	9.8	11.4	155,643	179,801	209,437	213,641
Lao PDR	7.7	9.6	13.8	15.6	1,624	1,767	1,810	2,028
Malaysia	7.6	7.2	8.0	7.8	49,499	66,567	74,475	88,980
Myanmar	...	...	...	...	12,842	14,832	13,965	16,571
Philippines	8.2	10.6	13.0	13.9	39,990	38,854	40,397	44,603
Singapore	11.1	12.2	14.4	16.1	18,668	21,568	25,417	26,097
Thailand	8.0	7.6	7.7	7.5	72,285	99,005	117,840	134,065
Viet Nam	7.2	7.0	6.6	7.7	28,736	41,252	58,912	59,928
The Pacific								
Cook Islands	...	...	...	...	9	20	...	24
Fiji	10.7	8.3	10.0	9.3	534	776	669	750
Kiribati	13.6	20.3	...	8.5	11	8	...	22
Marshall Islands	...	...	7.7	8.1	...	...	24	24
Micronesia, Fed. States of	7.6	9.2	...	6.6	45	38	...	52
Nauru	...	...	...	...	44	46	...	52
Palau	3.9	4.5	3.4	3.5	67	66	74	76
Papua New Guinea	8.9	6.2	11.9	7.3	1,123	1,797	1,249	2,560
Samoa	11.3	13.0	...	10.3	67	74	...	101
Solomon Islands	5.3	5.4	...	7.9	134	138	...	145
Timor-Leste	...	...	21.0	14.0	...	...	96	172
Tonga	11.0	8.7	...	7.4	41	58	...	70
Tuvalu	...	...	...	...	...	...	...	...
Vanuatu	10.9	14.0	...	12.0	48	39	...	61
Developed Member Economies								
Australia	6.2	7.0	7.3	7.7	108,101	113,478	124,451	129,141
Japan	7.9	8.3	8.8	10.0	519,132	520,531	498,920	454,655
New Zealand	6.4	7.8	7.6	7.7	17,090	16,929	18,382	19,508
WORLD	**6.2**	**6.6**	**7.1**	**7.4**	**10,056,562**	**11,480,903**	**12,788,992**	**13,541,283**

... = data not available at cutoff date, GDP = gross domestic product, Lao PDR = Lao People's Democratic Republic, PPP = purchasing power parity.

Sources: For GDP per unit use of energy: ADB estimates; for energy use: International Energy Agency. Statistics. http://www.iea.org/statistics/statisticssearch/ (accessed 20 June 2016); for Papua New Guinea: Asia-Pacific Economic Cooperation. Energy Database. http://www.ieej.or.jp/egeda/database/database-top.html (accessed 21 June 2016); for Afghanistan, Bhutan, the Lao PDR, the Maldives, and the Pacific economies except Papua New Guinea: ADB. *Energy Statistics in Asia and the Pacific 1990–2009*. Manila; United Nations (UN) Statistics Division. 2011 and 2013. *Energy Balances*. New York; UN Statistics Division. 2010, 2011, and 2013. *Energy Statistics Yearbook*. New York.

Table 6.4: **Energy Production and Imports**

Regional Member	Production (kiloton of oil equivalent)				Energy Imports, Net (% of energy use)			
	2000	2005	2010	2013	2000	2005	2010	2013
Developing Member Economies								
Central and West Asia								
Afghanistan	...	...	1,064	1,405	...	...	68.1	81.7
Armenia	643	869	878	811	68.0	65.4	64.7	72.1
Azerbaijan	18,808	27,253	65,514	59,353	−66.5	−103.0	−465.5	−327.6
Georgia	1,324	980	1,312	1,428	53.9	65.5	58.0	63.4
Kazakhstan	78,575	118,644	156,875	169,071	−120.2	−133.2	−127.0	−107.3
Kyrgyz Republic	1,369	1,324	1,270	1,759	40.9	48.6	53.9	55.5
Pakistan	46,896	60,735	64,369	65,156	26.8	20.4	23.7	24.3
Tajikistan	1,264	1,546	1,542	1,724	41.1	34.0	29.1	29.8
Turkmenistan	45,968	61,602	47,247	76,537	−208.9	−221.3	−108.3	−191.4
Uzbekistan	55,085	56,535	55,133	54,127	−8.3	−20.1	−27.6	−26.1
East Asia								
China, People's Rep. of	1,129,135	1,701,092	2,203,943	2,565,674	2.7	4.2	10.7	14.7
Hong Kong, China	50	51	96	97	99.6	99.6	99.3	99.3
Korea, Rep. of	34,445	42,982	44,955	43,603	81.7	79.6	82.0	83.5
Mongolia	1,949	3,848	15,674	16,336	18.7	−28.4	−297.7	−212.8
Taipei,China	11,793	12,485	12,957	13,514	86.1	87.8	88.4	87.6
South Asia								
Bangladesh	15,148	19,298	25,969	28,727	17.0	15.2	14.6	15.2
Bhutan	1,115	1,284	1,749	1,797	−4.6	−4.1	−24.7	−19.4
India	351,182	403,878	496,169	523,339	20.4	22.0	28.4	32.5
Maldives	–	–	...	3	100.0	100.0	...	99.0
Nepal	7,138	8,152	8,877	8,618	12.0	10.7	13.1	16.2
Sri Lanka	4,748	4,920	5,544	5,430	43.0	45.3	43.1	45.9
Southeast Asia								
Brunei Darussalam	19,684	21,060	18,573	16,987	−725.4	−849.5	−473.2	−458.4
Cambodia	2,718	2,496	3,621	4,087	20.3	27.4	31.7	31.6
Indonesia	237,465	280,317	379,864	459,987	−52.6	−55.9	−81.4	−115.3
Lao PDR	...	...	1,878	2,022	...	...	−3.8	0.3
Malaysia	78,469	96,797	90,869	94,631	−58.5	−45.4	−22.0	−6.3
Myanmar	15,418	22,214	22,503	23,189	−20.1	−49.8	−61.1	−39.9
Philippines	19,549	21,396	23,548	24,492	51.1	44.9	41.7	45.1
Singapore	202	394	588	644	98.9	98.2	97.7	97.5
Thailand	43,948	55,188	70,578	78,073	39.2	44.3	40.1	41.8
Viet Nam	39,919	60,759	66,388	69,276	−38.9	−47.3	−12.7	−15.6
The Pacific								
Cook Islands	–	–	–	–	100.0	100.0	100.0	100.0
Fiji	269	250	143	180	49.6	67.8	78.6	76.0
Kiribati	–	–	...	1	100.0	100.0	...	96.9
Marshall Islands	...	–	–	–	...	100.0	100.0	100.0
Micronesia, Fed. States of	–	–	...	1	100.0	100.0	...	97.3
Nauru	–	–	–	–	100.0	100.0	100.0	100.0
Palau	2	2	2	2	97.0	97.0	97.3	98.0
Papua New Guinea	3,866	2,775	1,458	1,394	−244.3	−54.4	−16.7	45.5
Samoa	21	21	...	21	68.7	71.6	...	79.7
Solomon Islands	79	79	...	77	41.0	42.8	...	47.1
Timor-Leste	...	...	4,443	4,013	...	...	−4,550.0	−2,300.0
Tonga	–	1	...	0	100.0	98.3	...	99.4
Tuvalu	...	...	...	...	...	...	...	...
Vanuatu	20	20	...	23	58.3	48.7	...	62.9
Developed Member Economies								
Australia	233,552	265,161	310,734	343,903	−116.1	−133.7	−149.7	−166.3
Japan	105,696	100,395	99,237	27,958	79.6	80.7	80.1	93.9
New Zealand	14,291	12,862	16,885	16,200	16.4	24.0	8.1	17.0

... = data not available at cutoff date, – = magnitude equals zero, Lao PDR = Lao People's Democratic Republic.

Sources: For production: International Energy Agency. Statistics. http://www.iea.org/statistics/statisticssearch/ (accessed 20 June 2016); for Papua New Guinea: Asia-Pacific Economic Cooperation. Energy Database. http://www.ieej.or.jp/egeda/database/database-top.html (accessed 21 June 2016); for Afghanistan, Bhutan, the Lao PDR, the Maldives, and the Pacific economies except Papua New Guinea: Asian Development Bank (ADB). *Energy Statistics in Asia and the Pacific 1990–2009*. Manila; United Nations (UN) Statistics Division. 2011 and 2013. *Energy Balances*. New York; UN Statistics Division. 2010 and 2013. *Energy Statistics Yearbook*. New York; for net energy imports as % of energy use: ADB estimates.

Table 6.5:   **Retail Prices of Fuel Energy**
           ($ per liter)

Regional Member	Gasoline Premium				Diesel			
	2000	2005[a]	2010[b]	2015[c]	2000	2005[d]	2010[e]	2015[f]
Developing Member Economies								
Central and West Asia								
Afghanistan	...	...	...	...	...	...	...	...
Armenia	0.51	0.73	1.01	0.90	0.34	0.60	0.92	0.89
Azerbaijan	...	...	...	...	...	...	...	...
Georgia	...	...	...	...	...	...	...	...
Kazakhstan	0.35	0.47	0.58	0.56	0.30	0.39	0.53	0.44
Kyrgyz Republic	...	...	...	...	...	...	...	...
Pakistan	0.48	0.82	0.80	0.68	0.22	0.54	0.83	0.78
Tajikistan	...	...	...	...	...	...	...	...
Turkmenistan	...	...	...	...	...	...	...	...
Uzbekistan	0.44	0.33	...	...	...	...	...	...
East Asia								
China, People's Rep. of	...	...	...	...	...	...	...	...
Hong Kong, China	1.32	1.60	1.75	1.77	0.80	1.00	1.25	1.41
Korea, Rep. of	1.10	1.40	1.48	1.33	0.54	1.05	1.30	1.15
Mongolia	0.33	0.56	1.01	0.85	0.38	0.81	0.96	0.98
Taipei,China	0.57	0.73	0.94	0.75	0.44	0.60	0.82	0.68
South Asia								
Bangladesh	...	...	...	...	...	...	...	...
Bhutan	...	...	...	...	...	...	...	...
India	0.58	0.86	1.05	1.18	0.32	0.64	0.83	0.91
Maldives	...	...	...	...	...	...	...	...
Nepal	0.58	0.87	1.22	1.30	0.33	0.58	0.95	1.08
Sri Lanka	0.65	0.80	1.02	0.86	0.32	0.50	0.65	0.70
Southeast Asia								
Brunei Darussalam	...	...	...	...	...	...	...	...
Cambodia	...	...	...	...	...	...	...	...
Indonesia	0.14	0.46	0.62	...	0.07	0.53	0.66	...
Lao PDR	...	...	...	...	...	...	...	...
Malaysia	0.29	0.40	0.67	0.60	0.18	0.29	0.57	0.49
Myanmar	...	1.84	1.41	0.76	...	1.62	1.37	0.80
Philippines	0.37	0.57	0.96	0.88	0.28	0.51	0.76	0.61
Singapore	0.81	0.83	...	...	0.33	0.56	0.89	0.85
Thailand	0.39	0.59	1.12	...	0.32	0.50	0.90	0.73
Viet Nam	...	...	0.99	0.85	...	...	0.93	0.68
The Pacific								
Cook Islands	...	...	...	...	...	...	...	...
Fiji	...	...	...	...	...	...	...	...
Kiribati	...	...	...	...	...	...	...	...
Marshall Islands	...	...	...	...	...	...	...	...
Micronesia, Fed. States of	...	...	...	...	...	...	...	...
Nauru	...	...	...	...	...	...	...	...
Palau	...	...	...	...	...	...	...	...
Papua New Guinea	...	...	...	...	...	...	...	...
Samoa	...	...	...	...	...	...	...	...
Solomon Islands	...	...	...	...	...	...	...	...
Timor-Leste	...	...	...	...	...	...	...	...
Tonga	...	...	...	...	...	...	...	...
Tuvalu	...	...	...	...	...	...	...	...
Vanuatu	0.78	1.23	1.50	1.84	...	...	...	...
Developed Member Economies								
Australia	0.49	0.82	1.09	0.89	...	0.87	1.09	0.87
Japan	1.05	1.23	1.64	1.23	0.76	0.91	1.28	0.97
New Zealand	0.51	0.97	1.34	1.41	0.33	0.64	0.85	0.80

... = data not available at cutoff date, Lao PDR = Lao People's Democratic Republic.

a   Refers to (i) 2004 data for Uzbekistan and Singapore and (ii) 2007 data for Myanmar.
b   Refers to (i) 2008 data for Indonesia, (ii) 2009 data for Thailand, and (iii) 2011 data for Viet Nam.
c   Refers to (i) 2014 data for India, Mongolia, and Nepal and (ii) 2013 data for Vanuatu.
d   Refers to (i) 2006 data for Mongolia and (ii) 2007 data for Myanmar.
e   Refers to (i) 2011 data for Viet Nam and (ii) 2008 data for Indonesia.
f   Refers to 2014 data for India, Mongolia, and Nepal.

Source: Economy sources.

Environment

Snapshots

- Asia and the Pacific's total greenhouse gas emissions grew faster than the global average over the past decade, largely reflecting the region's rapid development and the resultant use of fossil fuels for electricity generation, transport, and industrial and residential uses.

- Less than half of the region's economies for which data are available experienced an increase in total forested land in 2013.

- Between 2000 and 2013, less than half of the economies in the region experienced an increase in the percent share of total land devoted to agriculture.

- While Asia and the Pacific accounts for more than 50% of the global population, the region accounts for less than a third of the world's internal renewable freshwater resources.

Key Trends

Asia and the Pacific's total greenhouse gas (GHG) emissions grew faster than the global average over the past decade, largely reflecting the region's rapid development and the resultant use of fossil fuels for electricity generation, transport, and industrial and residential uses. If global GHG emissions continue to grow, climate change could threaten access to water, food production, health, use of land, and physical and natural capital, potentially resulting in large-scale, irreversible, and catastrophic damage (Marchal et al. 2011).

In 2012, Brunei Darussalam (36.6 tons) led all economies in Asia and the Pacific in per capita emissions of carbon dioxide, methane, nitrous oxide, and other GHGs, followed by Australia (24.1 tons), Kazakhstan (20.9 tons), Turkmenistan (17.2 tons), and New Zealand (16.3 tons) (Figure 7.1). This compares with the region's list of economies with the highest per capita emissions which includes Brunei Darussalam (32.0 tons), Australia (28.0 tons), New Zealand (18.4 tons), Singapore (14.2 tons), and Turkmenistan (13.3 tons).

The largest percentage increases in per capita emissions of carbon dioxide, methane, nitrous oxide, and other GHGs between 2000 and 2012 occurred in Cambodia (142.4%), the People's Republic of China (PRC) (118.7%), Viet Nam (87.5%), the Lao People's Democratic Republic (Lao PDR) (80.0%), and Kazakhstan (71.5%). The largest percentage reductions during the review period were observed in Singapore (–64.7%), Nauru (–48.3%), Vanuatu (–19.3%), Solomon Islands (–18.2%), Australia (–13.8%), and New Zealand (–11.6%).

More than one-third of the region's economies for which data are available experienced an increase in total forested land in 2013. Asia's total forest area has shown a continuous overall increase since 2000, albeit with subregional variations. In 2013, 16 regional economies for which data are available expanded their forested area (Figure 7.2). The largest annual increases in 2013 occurred in the Philippines (3.3%), Azerbaijan (2.5%), the Lao PDR (1.0%), and Viet Nam (0.9%). Meanwhile, the highest annual deforestation rates were observed in Pakistan (2.7%), Myanmar (1.8%), and Timor-Leste (1.6%). In 2000, 18 out of 46 regional economies for which data are available increased their forested area, led by Samoa (2.5%), Viet Nam (2.1%), and Thailand (1.8%). The highest annual deforestation rates in 2000 were observed in Nepal (2.3%), Pakistan (1.9%), and Indonesia (1.9%).

Figure 7.1: Per Capita Emissions of Carbon Dioxide, Methane, Nitrous Oxide, and Other Greenhouse Gases
(tons)

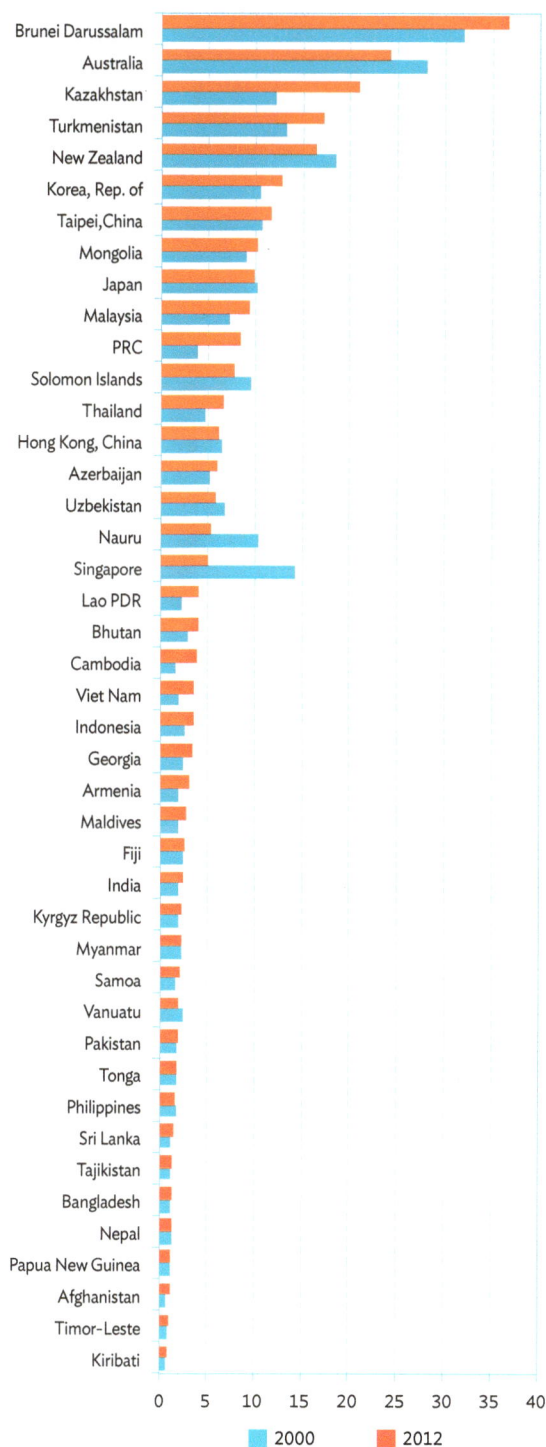

Brunei Darussalam
Australia
Kazakhstan
Turkmenistan
New Zealand
Korea, Rep. of
Taipei,China
Mongolia
Japan
Malaysia
PRC
Solomon Islands
Thailand
Hong Kong, China
Azerbaijan
Uzbekistan
Nauru
Singapore
Lao PDR
Bhutan
Cambodia
Viet Nam
Indonesia
Georgia
Armenia
Maldives
Fiji
India
Kyrgyz Republic
Myanmar
Samoa
Vanuatu
Pakistan
Tonga
Philippines
Sri Lanka
Tajikistan
Bangladesh
Nepal
Papua New Guinea
Afghanistan
Timor-Leste
Kiribati

0 5 10 15 20 25 30 35 40

■ 2000   ■ 2012

Lao PDR = Lao People's Democratic Republic, PRC = People's Republic of China.
Note: Data for carbon dioxide emissions for 2012 refer to 2011.
Sources: Table 1.1; Table 7.2; United Nations. *Millennium Development Goals Indicators.* http://mdgs.un.org/unsd/mdg/Data.aspx; for Taipei,China, Directorate General of Budget, Accounting, and Statistics. *Statistical Yearbook 2014.* http://eng.dgbas.gov.tw; and economy sources.

Figure 7.2: Deforestation Rates
(%)

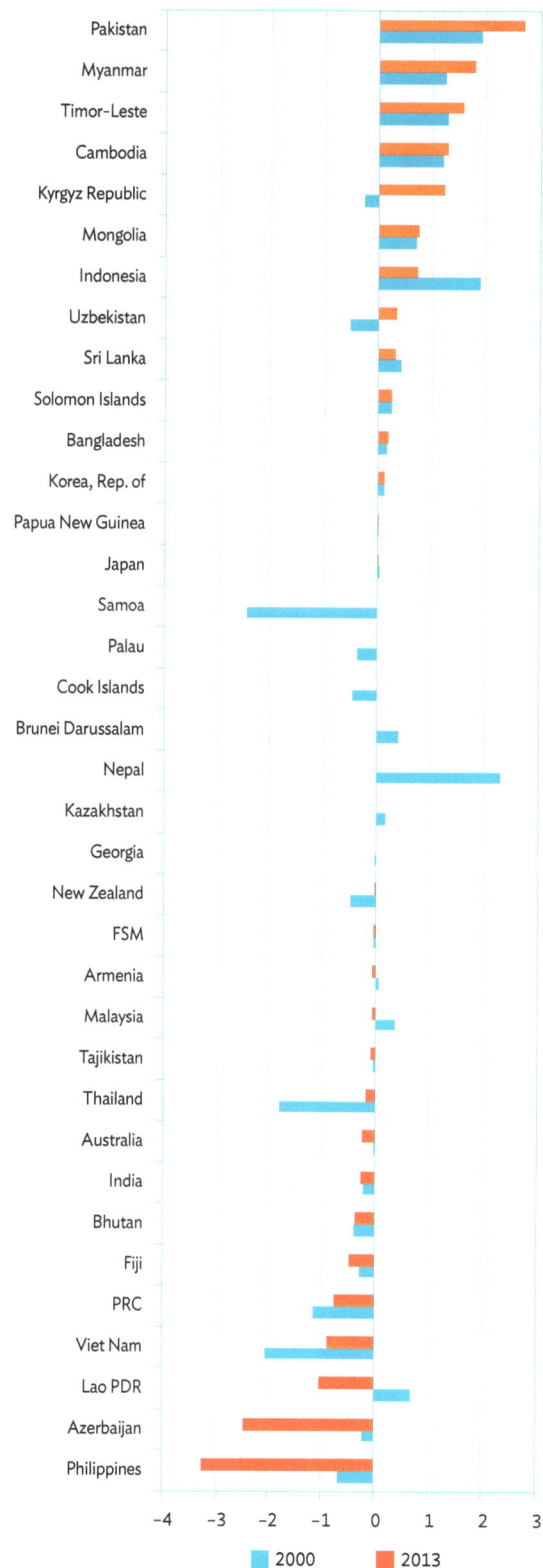

Pakistan
Myanmar
Timor-Leste
Cambodia
Kyrgyz Republic
Mongolia
Indonesia
Uzbekistan
Sri Lanka
Solomon Islands
Bangladesh
Korea, Rep. of
Papua New Guinea
Japan
Samoa
Palau
Cook Islands
Brunei Darussalam
Nepal
Kazakhstan
Georgia
New Zealand
FSM
Armenia
Malaysia
Tajikistan
Thailand
Australia
India
Bhutan
Fiji
PRC
Viet Nam
Lao PDR
Azerbaijan
Philippines

-4 -3 -2 -1 0 1 2 3

■ 2000   ■ 2013

FSM = Federated States of Micronesia, Lao PDR = Lao People's Democratic Republic, PRC = People's Republic of China.
Source: Table 7.2.

Between 2000 and 2013, less than half of the region's economies experienced an increase in the percent share of total land devoted to agriculture. The need to feed an expanding population as well as changing dietary preferences (e.g., increased meat consumption) can contribute to the expansion of agricultural land as a percentage of total land area in an economy (Chakravorty, Moreaux, and Nostbakken 2010). On the other hand, urbanization and the development of formerly rural areas can reduce the amount of agricultural land (UNEP 2016). Out of all 48 regional economies, 21 saw an increase in the percentage of land devoted to agriculture between 2000 and 2013, 24 experienced a decline, and three had no change (Figure 7.3). The largest gains occurred in Brunei Darussalam where the amount of agricultural land as a share of total land rose 44.0% during the review period. This was followed by Solomon Islands (42.1%) and the Lao PDR (29.3%). The most significant declines were observed in the Cook Islands (–68.8%), Singapore (–47.1%), and New Zealand (–27.9%).

On a subregional basis, none of the member economies in East Asia experienced an increase in the percentage of agricultural land as a share of total land during the review period, compared with five out of 10 economies in Central and West Asia, two out of six economies in South Asia, nine out of 10 economies in Southeast Asia, five out of 14 economies in the Pacific, and none of the three developed member economies (Table 7.1).

Nearly half of the economies of Asia and the Pacific for which data are available experienced a decrease in the amount of arable land as a share of total land between 2000 and 2013. While agricultural output has intensified substantially in the region in recent decades, the overall expansion of arable land has been minimal due to the increased use of chemical fertilizers and pesticides (UNEP 2016). The percentage of arable land, (or land that can be used to grow crops) as a share of a country's total land area decreased in 23 out of 48 regional

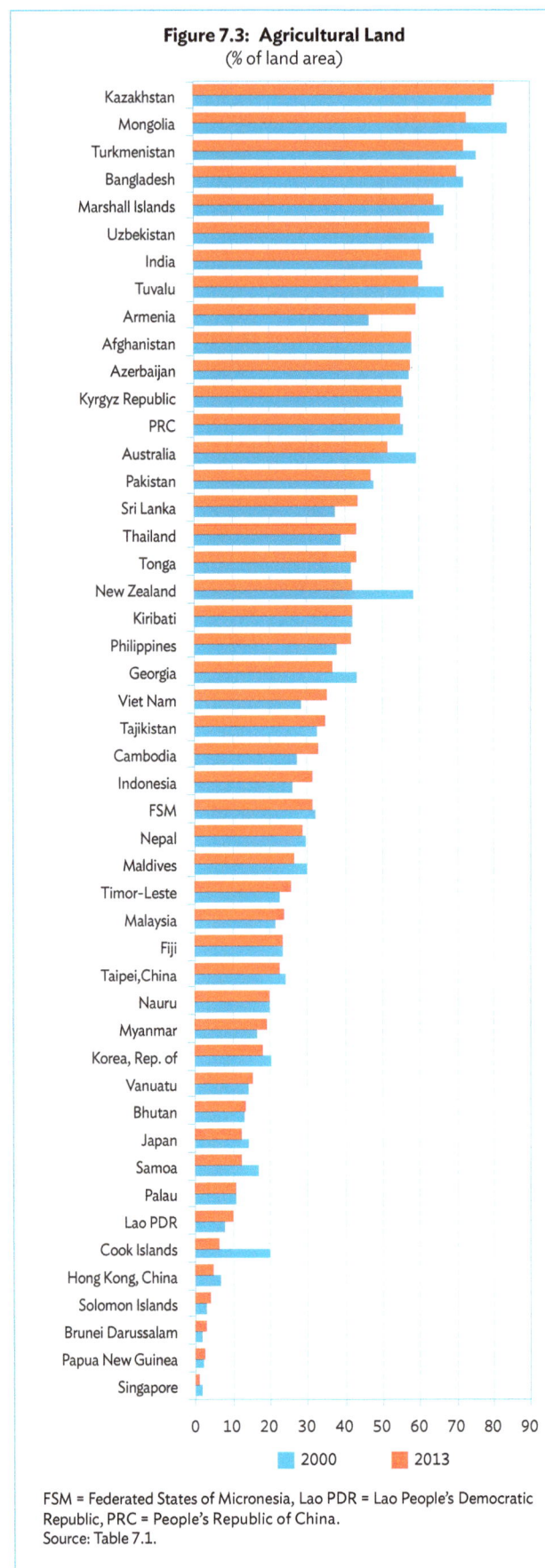

Figure 7.3: Agricultural Land
(% of land area)

Kazakhstan, Mongolia, Turkmenistan, Bangladesh, Marshall Islands, Uzbekistan, India, Tuvalu, Armenia, Afghanistan, Azerbaijan, Kyrgyz Republic, PRC, Australia, Pakistan, Sri Lanka, Thailand, Tonga, New Zealand, Kiribati, Philippines, Georgia, Viet Nam, Tajikistan, Cambodia, Indonesia, FSM, Nepal, Maldives, Timor-Leste, Malaysia, Fiji, Taipei,China, Nauru, Myanmar, Korea, Rep. of, Vanuatu, Bhutan, Japan, Samoa, Palau, Lao PDR, Cook Islands, Hong Kong, China, Solomon Islands, Brunei Darussalam, Papua New Guinea, Singapore

■ 2000   ■ 2013

FSM = Federated States of Micronesia, Lao PDR = Lao People's Democratic Republic, PRC = People's Republic of China.
Source: Table 7.1.

economies between 2000 and 2013, increased in 18 economies, and remained unchanged in seven economies (Figure 7.4). The most notable increases during the review period occurred in Brunei Darussalam (150.0%), the Marshall Islands (100.0%), and the Lao PDR (61.8%). The largest decreases were in New Zealand (–63.5%), Mongolia (–51.8%), and Singapore (–46.0%).

The amount of permanent cropland available as a share of total land increased or remained unchanged in three-quarters of the region's economies between 2000 and 2013. As a share of total land, the amount of cropland increased in 27 economies, remained unchanged in nine economies, and decreased in 12 economies in Asia and the Pacific between 2000 and 2013 (Figure 7.5). The largest increase during the review period was in Myanmar where the percentage of permanent cropland as a share of the total increased 156.4%. This was followed by Mongolia (150.0%) and the Lao PDR (108.6%). The largest decreases in the shares of permanent cropland occurred in the Cook Islands (–83.3%), Singapore (–52.6%), and Georgia (–40.5%).

While Asia and the Pacific accounts for more than 50% of the global population, the region accounts for less than a third of the world's internal renewable freshwater resources (UNEP 2016). Water is critical for human survival, agriculture, industrial production, and the maintenance of ecosystems. The preservation of freshwater resources is of paramount importance in many regional economies, especially given the extreme subregional variation in the per capita availability of freshwater resources, which ranges from 1,210 cubic meters in Central and West Asia to 79,857 cubic meters in the Pacific.

Between 2002 and 2014, the internal renewable freshwater resources of economies in Asia and the Pacific declined on a per capita basis in all but two economies for which data are available (Figure 7.6). Armenia and Georgia were the only two

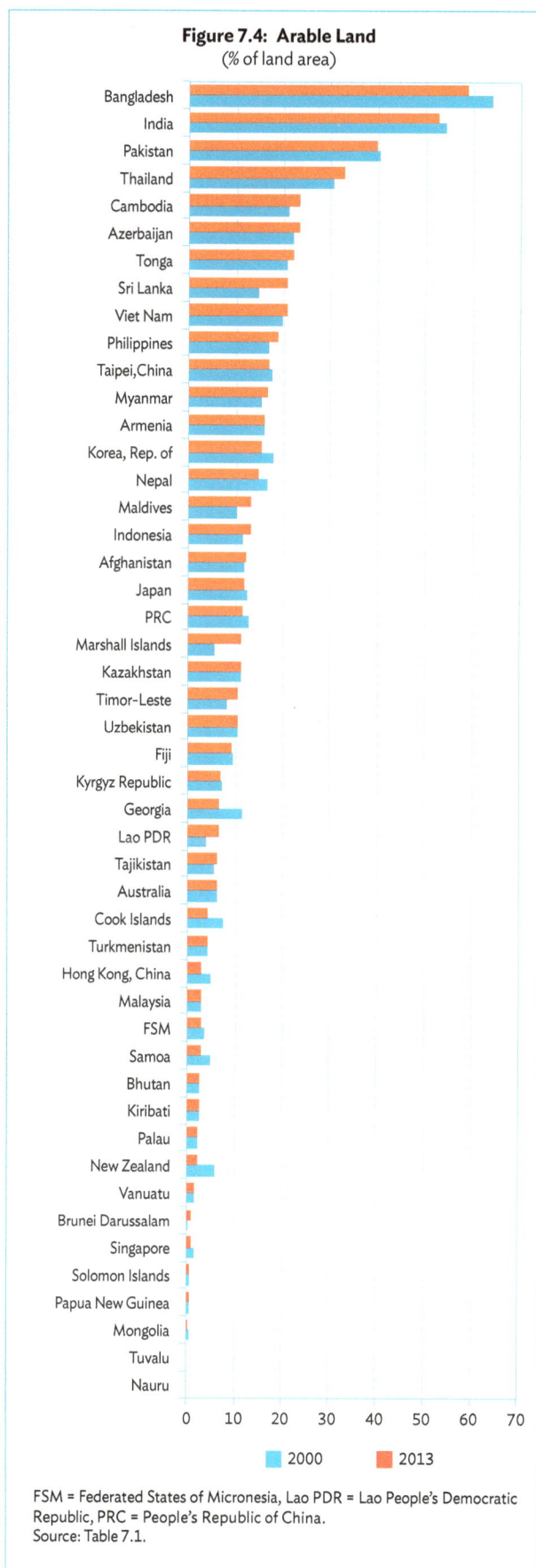

Figure 7.4: **Arable Land**
(% of land area)

FSM = Federated States of Micronesia, Lao PDR = Lao People's Democratic Republic, PRC = People's Republic of China.
Source: Table 7.1.

Figure 7.5: Permanent Cropland
(% of land area)

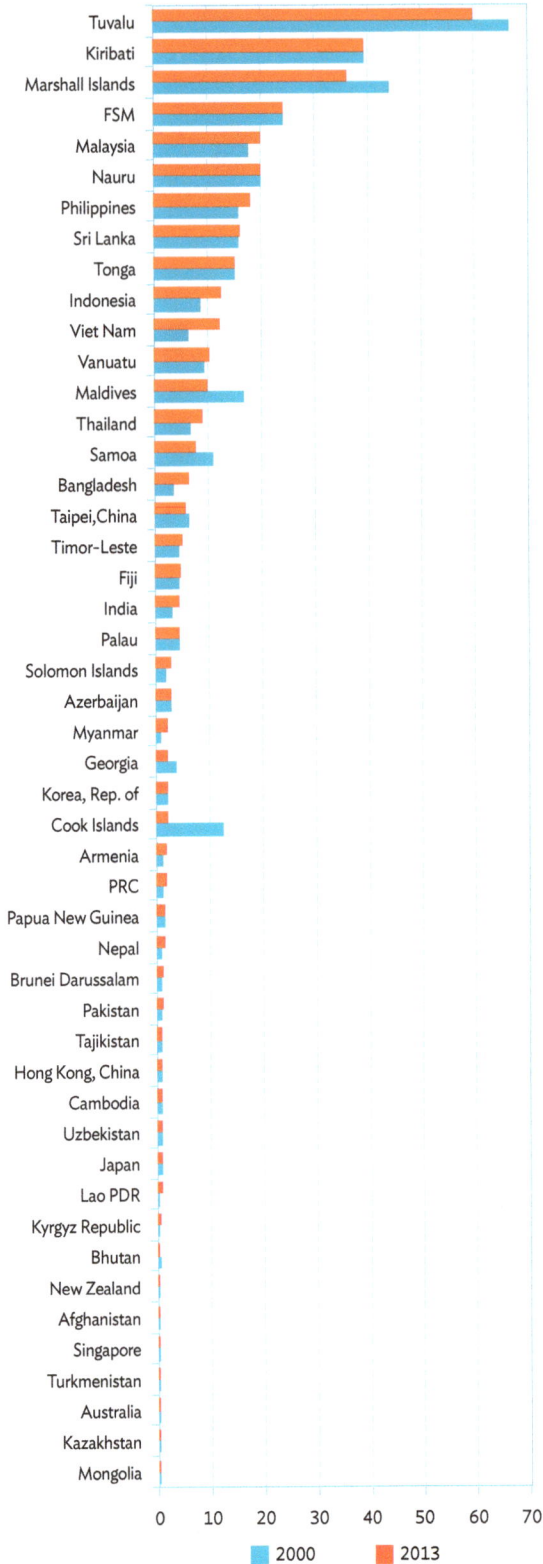

Tuvalu
Kiribati
Marshall Islands
FSM
Malaysia
Nauru
Philippines
Sri Lanka
Tonga
Indonesia
Viet Nam
Vanuatu
Maldives
Thailand
Samoa
Bangladesh
Taipei,China
Timor-Leste
Fiji
India
Palau
Solomon Islands
Azerbaijan
Myanmar
Georgia
Korea, Rep. of
Cook Islands
Armenia
PRC
Papua New Guinea
Nepal
Brunei Darussalam
Pakistan
Tajikistan
Hong Kong, China
Cambodia
Uzbekistan
Japan
Lao PDR
Kyrgyz Republic
Bhutan
New Zealand
Afghanistan
Singapore
Turkmenistan
Australia
Kazakhstan
Mongolia

0 10 20 30 40 50 60 70

■ 2000   ■ 2013

FSM = Federated States of Micronesia, Lao PDR = Lao People's Democratic Republic, PRC = People's Republic of China.
Source: Table 7.1.

Figure 7.6: Internal Renewable Freshwater Resources Per Capita
(thousand m³/year per inhabitant)

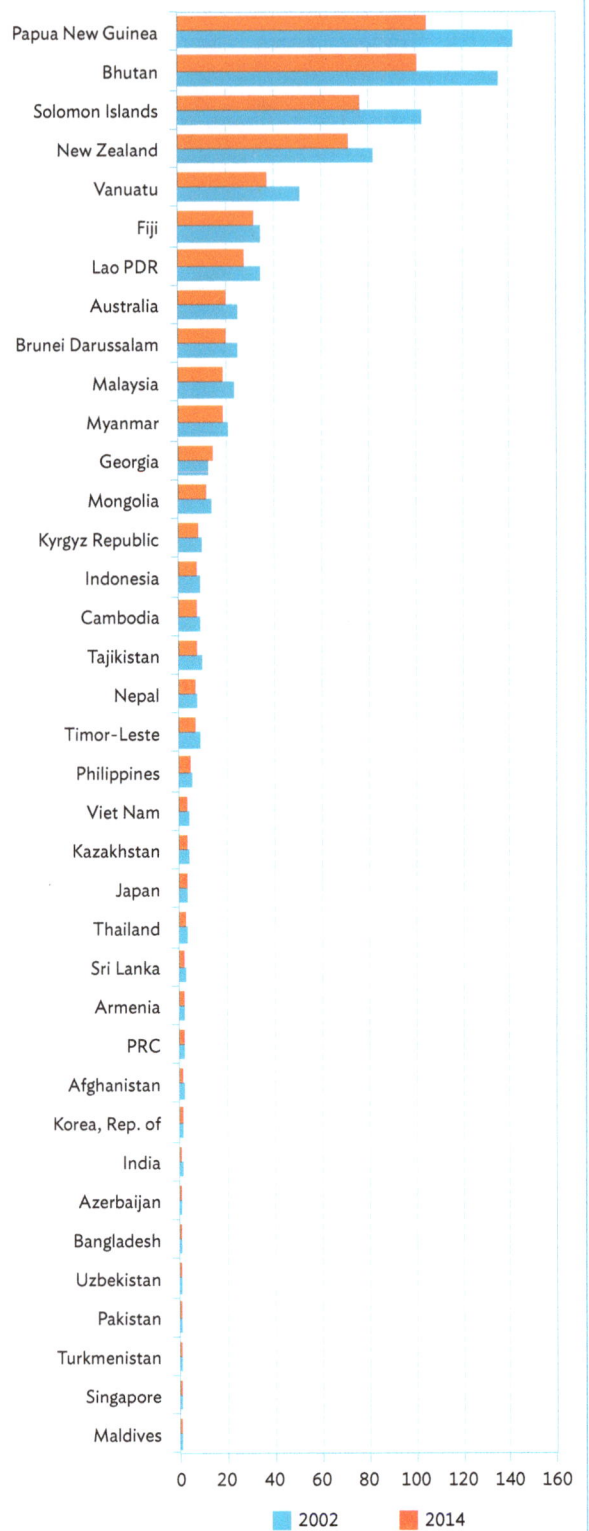

Papua New Guinea
Bhutan
Solomon Islands
New Zealand
Vanuatu
Fiji
Lao PDR
Australia
Brunei Darussalam
Malaysia
Myanmar
Georgia
Mongolia
Kyrgyz Republic
Indonesia
Cambodia
Tajikistan
Nepal
Timor-Leste
Philippines
Viet Nam
Kazakhstan
Japan
Thailand
Sri Lanka
Armenia
PRC
Afghanistan
Korea, Rep. of
India
Azerbaijan
Bangladesh
Uzbekistan
Pakistan
Turkmenistan
Singapore
Maldives

0 20 40 60 80 100 120 140 160

■ 2002   ■ 2014

m³ = cubic meter, Lao PDR = Lao People's Democratic Republic, PRC = People's Republic of China.
Source: Table 7.3.

economies in the region to experience an increase. Both economies underwent population declines during the review period (Table 1.1). Among the region's economies experiencing a decrease in per capita internal renewable freshwater resources between 2002 and 2014, Afghanistan's was the most significant at (–33.9%), followed by that of Vanuatu (–26.7%) and Singapore (–26.2%).

Box 7.1: Trends in Carbon Dioxide Emissions, 1960–Present

Asia and the Pacific's carbon dioxide (CO_2) emissions increased at a declining rate between the 1960s and 1990s before accelerating again in the 2000s. In 1965, the region's CO_2 emissions totaled 1,424.8 million metric tons; by 2015, the total had climbed to 16,066.8 million metric tons with an average annual growth of 5.01% (Box Figure). For comparison, total global emissions experienced an average annual growth of 2.21% between 1965 and 2015. By decade, the region's average annual growth rates in CO_2 emissions were 8.31% in the 1960s, 6.13% in the 1970s, 3.94% in the 1980s, 3.74% in the 1990s, 5.97% in the 2000s, and 3.23% in the 2010s.

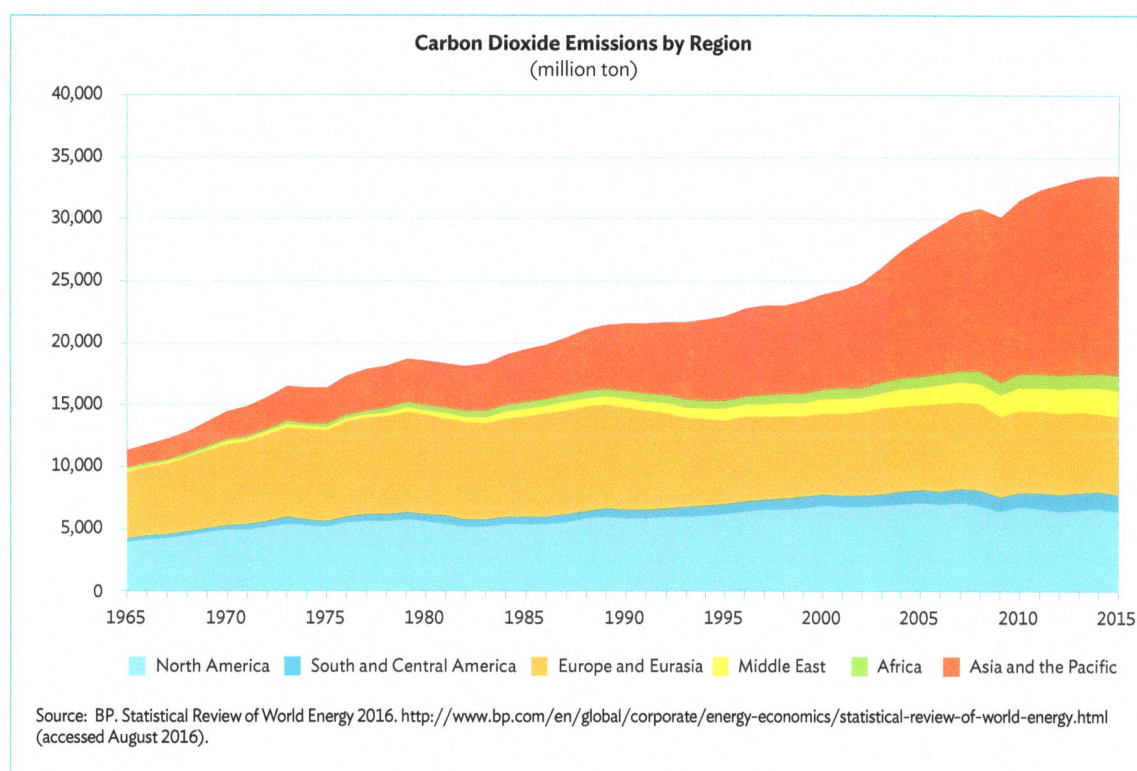

Carbon Dioxide Emissions by Region
(million ton)

Source: BP. Statistical Review of World Energy 2016. http://www.bp.com/en/global/corporate/energy-economics/statistical-review-of-world-energy.html (accessed August 2016).

On a per capita basis, Asia and the Pacific's CO_2 emissions rose from 0.81 metric tons in 1965 to 3.99 in 2015 at an average annual growth of 3.28%. This compares with the world average of 3.43 metric tons in 1965 and 4.58 metric tons in 2015, which reflects an average annual growth of 0.60%. By decade, the region's average annual growth rates in CO_2 emissions per capita were 5.69% in the 1960s, 3.87% in the 1970s, 1.97% in the 1980s, 2.17% in the 1990s, 4.80% in the 2000s, and 2.22% in the 2010s.

Asia and the Pacific's share of the world's CO_2 emissions advanced steadily between 1965 and 2015, comprising nearly half of the global total at the end of the review period. The region accounted for 12.6% of the world's CO_2 emissions in 1965. At the midpoint of each subsequent decade, the region's shares of total global emissions were 17.8% in 1975, 21.5% in 1985, 30.5% in 1995, 39.2% in 2005, and 48.0% in 2015. For comparison, the other regions of the world experienced the following changes in their respective shares of total global emissions between 1965 and 2015: North America (from 34.9% to 19.4%), South and Central America (from 2.6% to 4.1%), Europe and Eurasia (from 47.0% to 18.5%), Middle East (from 1.2% to 6.5%), and Africa (from 1.7% to 3.6%).

Source: BP. Statistical Review of World Energy 2016. http://www.bp.com/en/global/corporate/energy-economics/statistical-review-of-world-energy.html (accessed August 2016).

Data Issues and Comparability

Data on greenhouse gas emissions are sourced from World Bank's World Development Indicators (WDI). In previous issues of the Key Indicators, WDI data for these indicators were compiled from International Energy Agency. Starting this year, WDI data were compiled from European Commission Joint Research Centre's Emissions Database for Global Atmospheric Research.

The Food and Agriculture Organization of the United Nations monitors land use and forestry data using country reports and satellite imagery.

References

U. Chakravorty, M. Moreaux, and L. Nostbakken. 2010. Will Biofuel Mandates Raise Food Prices. *TSE Working Papers* 10-212. Toulouse, France: Toulouse School of Economics.

V. Marchal, R. Dellink, D. van Vuuren, C. Clapp, J. Château, E. Lanzi, B. Magné, and J. van Vliet. 2011. *OECD Environmental Outlook to 2050*. Paris: Organisation for Economic Co-operation and Development.

United Nations Environment Programme (UNEP). 2016. *Global Environment Outlook: GEO-6 Regional Assessment for Asia and the Pacific*. Nairobi.

Table 7.1: **Agriculture Land Use**
(% of land area)

Regional Member	Agricultural Land				Arable Land				Permanent Cropland			
	2000	2005	2010	2013	2000	2005	2010	2013	2000	2005	2010	2013
Developing Member Economies												
Central and West Asia												
Afghanistan	57.8	58.1	58.1	58.1	11.8	12.0	11.9	11.9	0.1	0.2	0.2	0.2
Armenia	46.5	56.4	60.9	59.1	15.8	16.0	15.8	15.7	1.3	1.8	1.9	2.0
Azerbaijan	57.4	57.6	57.7	57.7	22.1	22.3	22.8	23.3	2.9	2.7	2.8	2.8
Georgia	43.2	36.3	35.7	36.7	11.4	6.8	6.0	6.5	3.9	1.6	1.8	2.3
Kazakhstan	79.8	78.6	80.4	80.4	11.2	10.6	10.6	10.9	0.1	0.0	0.0	0.0
Kyrgyz Republic	55.9	56.0	55.3	55.2	7.1	6.7	6.7	6.7	0.3	0.4	0.4	0.4
Pakistan	47.6	46.7	45.7	47.1	40.3	39.1	38.1	39.5	0.9	1.0	1.1	1.1
Tajikistan	32.7	33.4	34.6	34.8	5.6	5.4	6.0	6.1	0.7	0.8	0.9	1.0
Turkmenistan	75.5	74.2	72.4	72.0	4.1	4.3	4.1	4.1	0.1	0.1	0.1	0.1
Uzbekistan	64.2	62.9	62.7	62.9	10.5	10.3	10.2	10.3	0.8	0.8	0.8	0.9
East Asia												
China, People's Rep. of	55.6	55.1	54.8	54.8	12.6	12.0	11.4	11.3	1.2	1.3	1.5	1.7
Hong Kong, China	6.7	6.7	5.2	4.9	4.8	4.8	3.3	3.0	1.0	1.0	1.0	1.0
Korea, Rep. of	20.5	19.4	18.2	18.1	17.8	17.0	15.5	15.3	2.1	1.9	2.1	2.2
Mongolia	84.0	73.0	73.1	72.9	0.8	0.4	0.4	0.4	0.0	0.0	0.0	0.0
Taipei,China	24.0	23.5	23.0	22.6	17.5	17.0	16.9	16.8	6.5	6.5	6.1	5.8
South Asia												
Bangladesh	72.2	71.5	71.0	70.0	64.1	60.8	59.9	59.0	3.5	6.1	6.5	6.4
Bhutan	13.3	15.6	13.6	13.6	2.7	4.4	2.6	2.6	0.5	0.5	0.3	0.3
India	60.9	60.6	60.4	60.6	54.1	53.6	52.8	52.8	3.1	3.4	4.1	4.4
Maldives	30.0	30.0	26.3	26.3	10.0	10.0	13.0	13.0	16.7	16.7	10.0	10.0
Nepal	29.6	29.3	28.8	28.7	16.4	15.9	15.2	14.7	0.8	0.9	1.1	1.5
Sri Lanka	37.5	40.0	41.8	43.7	14.6	17.5	19.1	20.7	15.9	15.5	15.6	15.9
Southeast Asia												
Brunei Darussalam	1.9	2.1	2.5	2.7	0.4	0.4	0.8	0.9	0.8	0.9	1.1	1.1
Cambodia	27.0	30.3	32.0	32.9	21.0	21.0	22.7	23.5	0.8	0.9	0.9	0.9
Indonesia	26.0	28.6	30.7	31.5	11.3	12.7	13.0	13.0	8.6	9.9	11.6	12.4
Lao PDR	7.8	8.6	9.6	10.1	4.0	5.0	6.1	6.5	0.4	0.4	0.6	0.7
Malaysia	21.4	21.7	22.7	23.9	2.9	2.9	2.8	2.9	17.6	18.0	19.0	20.1
Myanmar	16.5	17.2	19.2	19.3	15.2	15.4	16.5	16.5	0.9	1.4	2.2	2.3
Philippines	37.7	38.1	40.6	41.7	16.9	16.8	17.8	18.7	15.8	16.3	17.8	17.9
Singapore	1.8	1.1	1.1	0.9	1.5	1.0	0.9	0.8	0.3	0.1	0.1	0.1
Thailand	38.8	38.4	41.2	43.3	30.6	29.8	30.8	32.9	6.6	7.1	8.8	8.8
Viet Nam	28.2	32.4	34.7	35.1	19.9	20.5	20.8	20.7	6.2	9.8	11.9	12.3
The Pacific												
Cook Islands	20.0	11.4	5.6	6.3	7.5	5.2	2.9	4.2	12.5	6.2	2.7	2.1
Fiji	23.4	23.4	23.3	23.3	9.3	9.3	9.0	9.0	4.5	4.5	4.7	4.7
Kiribati	42.0	42.0	42.0	42.0	2.5	2.5	2.5	2.5	39.5	39.5	39.5	39.5
Marshall Islands	66.7	72.2	72.2	63.9	5.6	11.1	11.1	11.1	44.4	44.4	44.4	36.1
Micronesia, Fed. States of	32.1	32.1	31.4	31.4	3.6	3.6	2.9	2.9	24.3	24.3	24.3	24.3
Nauru	20.0	20.0	20.0	20.0	–	–	–	–	20.0	20.0	20.0	20.0
Palau	10.9	10.9	10.9	10.9	2.2	2.2	2.2	2.2	4.3	4.3	4.3	4.3
Papua New Guinea	2.2	2.3	2.6	2.6	0.5	0.5	0.7	0.7	1.4	1.3	1.5	1.5
Samoa	17.0	14.8	12.4	12.4	4.9	3.9	2.8	2.8	11.0	9.5	7.8	7.8
Solomon Islands	2.7	3.2	3.8	3.9	0.5	0.6	0.7	0.7	2.0	2.3	2.9	2.9
Timor-Leste	22.7	25.9	25.0	25.6	8.1	11.4	10.1	10.4	4.5	4.4	4.8	5.0
Tonga	41.7	41.7	43.1	43.1	20.8	20.8	22.2	22.2	15.3	15.3	15.3	15.3
Tuvalu	66.7	56.7	60.0	60.0	–	–	–	–	66.7	56.7	60.0	60.0
Vanuatu	14.4	15.0	15.3	15.3	1.6	1.6	1.6	1.6	9.3	9.9	10.3	10.3
Developed Member Economies												
Australia	59.3	57.9	51.9	51.6	6.2	6.4	5.5	6.0	0.0	0.0	0.1	0.1
Japan	14.4	12.9	12.6	12.4	12.3	12.0	11.7	11.6	1.0	0.9	0.9	0.8
New Zealand	58.5	44.5	43.3	42.2	5.7	1.6	1.9	2.1	0.2	0.2	0.3	0.3

– = magnitude equals zero, 0.0 = magnitude is less than half of unit employed, Lao PDR = Lao People's Democratic Republic.

Source: Food and Agriculture Organization of the United Nations. FAOSTAT Database. http://faostat3.fao.org (accessed 12 August 2016).

Table 7.2:   **Deforestation and Pollution**

Regional Member	Deforestation Rate[a] (average % change)		Nitrous Oxide Emissions (thousand metric tons CO_2 equivalent)		Agricultural Nitrous Oxide Emissions (percent of total)	
	2000	2013	2000	2012	2000	2008
Developing Member Economies						
Central and West Asia						
Afghanistan	–	–	3,317	3,424	72.4	71.3
Armenia	0.06	−0.06	462	1,023	77.1	81.1
Azerbaijan	−0.23	−2.47	2,030	2,673	77.9	80.0
Georgia	−0.03	–	2,437	2,352	46.7	53.7
Kazakhstan	0.17	–	14,865	17,822	66.2	73.4
Kyrgyz Republic	−0.26	1.21	1,452	1,567	80.1	82.3
Pakistan	1.91	2.69	26,350	30,651	67.5	75.3
Tajikistan	−0.05	−0.10	1,110	1,848	83.4	87.7
Turkmenistan	–	–	3,046	4,924	68.1	75.8
Uzbekistan	−0.52	0.34	9,610	13,192	77.9	85.5
East Asia						
China, People's Rep. of	−1.13	−0.76	414,138	587,166	73.3	74.7
Hong Kong, China	...	...	513	476	–	–
Korea, Rep. of	0.13	0.12	18,576	14,979	25.6	42.2
Mongolia	0.69	0.76	5,058	3,548	90.5	93.5
Taipei,China	–	–	4,289	4,116	...	...
South Asia						
Bangladesh	0.18	0.18	20,770	26,683	78.2	82.9
Bhutan	−0.38	−0.36	281	555	34.6	42.1
India	−0.22	−0.25	207,700	239,755	72.2	73.8
Maldives	–	–	12	27	6.0	8.3
Nepal	2.30	–	4,232	4,598	76.7	76.4
Sri Lanka	0.42	0.32	2,044	2,174	66.8	64.5
Southeast Asia						
Brunei Darussalam	0.40	–	395	342	20.9	27.9
Cambodia	1.20	1.29	3,295	16,685	80.3	51.9
Indonesia	1.89	0.74	94,933	93,139	63.1	65.5
Lao PDR	0.67	−1.04	3,265	8,987	72.7	66.7
Malaysia	0.36	−0.06	13,822	15,310	60.8	68.8
Myanmar	1.23	1.78	31,300	26,783	31.9	53.4
Philippines	−0.68	−3.28	12,365	12,762	71.7	76.4
Singapore	–	–	6,635	1,909	0.6	1.8
Thailand	−1.80	−0.18	18,677	30,833	72.2	69.8
Viet Nam	−2.06	−0.90	19,746	34,494	84.1	83.8
The Pacific						
Cook Islands	−0.47	–	...	...	...	...
Fiji	−0.28	−0.48	343	344	92.6	91.4
Kiribati	–	–	3	4	44.9	47.2
Marshall Islands	–	–	0	0	–	–
Micronesia, Fed. States of	−0.05	−0.05	11	11	98.1	98.2
Nauru	...	...	0	0	91.5	91.3
Palau	−0.38	–	0	0	–	–
Papua New Guinea	0.01	0.01	1,613	1,234	13.3	19.6
Samoa	−2.46	–	37	40	79.6	82.7
Solomon Islands	0.25	0.25	2,425	2,656	99.3	99.3
Timor-Leste	1.29	1.56	164	226	89.7	88.0
Tonga	–	–	22	22	93.5	95.8
Tuvalu	–	–	1	1	98.2	98.5
Vanuatu	–	–	118	109	96.0	95.7
Developed Member Economies						
Australia	−0.02	−0.25	75,581	54,247	74.9	81.0
Japan	0.03	0.01	30,411	24,911	28.5	30.1
New Zealand	−0.48	−0.00	11,549	11,880	93.4	95.1

continued

Pollution

Table 7.2:   **Deforestation and Pollution** (continued)

Regional Member	Methane Emissions (thousand metric tons CO$_2$ equivalent)		Agricultural Methane Emissions (percent of total)		Other Greenhouse Gases[b] (thousand metric tons CO$_2$ equivalent)	
	2000	2012	2000	2008	2000	2012
Developing Member Economies						
Central and West Asia						
Afghanistan	9,384	13,763	71.2	62.7	126	349
Armenia	2,565	3,426	35.2	35.9	112	710
Azerbaijan	9,955	19,955	41.4	32.1	464	1,142
Georgia	4,137	5,019	51.9	50.0	3	227
Kazakhstan	38,779	71,350	24.3	21.9	14,065	30,363
Kyrgyz Republic	3,486	4,291	71.4	73.9	93	68
Pakistan	117,125	158,337	65.7	62.3	757	1,159
Tajikistan	3,304	5,408	65.0	71.3	798	367
Turkmenistan	21,241	22,009	19.7	20.5	124	595
Uzbekistan	37,233	47,333	29.6	32.8	298	989
East Asia						
China, People's Rep. of	1,043,400	1,752,290	46.6	37.6	104,677	251,254
Hong Kong, China	2,695	3,147	–	–	155	150
Korea, Rep. of	30,916	32,625	40.6	40.6	14,934	8,968
Mongolia	9,218	6,257	92.2	87.5	26,233	2,216
Taipei,China	11,315	2,924	...	...	1,833	3,212
South Asia						
Bangladesh	89,247	105,142	73.6	68.9	686	1,329
Bhutan	1,032	1,770	29.6	42.8	644	488
India	561,733	636,396	66.9	62.7	56,626	153,658
Maldives	34	52	0.6	1.2	0	–0
Nepal	21,206	23,982	83.0	82.1	2,443	7,995
Sri Lanka	9,606	11,864	64.1	67.1	441	91
Southeast Asia						
Brunei Darussalam	3,882	4,539	0.4	0.3	101	427
Cambodia	14,985	35,915	83.1	63.2	23,021	73,300
Indonesia	170,032	223,316	46.4	41.1	63,048	2,556
Lao PDR	7,219	15,011	80.6	77.0	13,588	136,841
Malaysia	29,309	34,271	19.0	15.2	5,144	3,866
Myanmar	66,942	80,637	66.1	77.0	78,176	406,274
Philippines	49,911	57,170	63.1	62.7	12,487	3,891
Singapore	1,684	2,386	1.4	1.4	1,410	3,299
Thailand	83,564	106,499	65.3	62.4	8,756	45,556
Viet Nam	75,430	113,564	68.1	54.2	5,782	25,707
The Pacific						
Cook Islands	...	...	...	...	...	...
Fiji	705	715	81.7	78.4	9	52
Kiribati	13	16	6.8	7.1	–	–0
Marshall Islands	6	8	–	–	...	...
Micronesia, Fed. States of	28	30	67.3	64.0	...	...
Nauru	3	3	9.1	7.7	–0	–0
Palau	1	1	–	–	...	...
Papua New Guinea	2,001	2,143	13.5	15.0	1,949	2,188
Samoa	116	133	69.8	70.5	–0	0
Solomon Islands	1,394	1,449	97.3	96.8	0	0
Timor-Leste	450	732	83.2	86.4	–	–0
Tonga	58	61	72.8	70.7	–0	0
Tuvalu	3	3	34.8	35.2	–0	0
Vanuatu	267	254	88.4	85.4	0	–0
Developed Member Economies						
Australia	128,133	125,588	61.3	56.8	520,911	174,653
Japan	47,496	38,957	67.0	72.5	51,527	71,746
New Zealand	26,584	28,658	88.5	91.0	1,506	1,764

... = data not available at cutoff date, – = magnitude equals zero, CO$_2$ = carbon dioxide, Lao PDR = Lao People's Democratic Republic.

a   Rate refers to percentage change over previous year. A negative value indicates that the deforestation rate is decreasing (i.e., reforestation).
b   Other greenhouse gas emissions refer to hydrofluorocarbons, perfluorocarbons, and sulfur hexafluoride.

Sources: Food and Agriculture Organization of the United Nations. FAOSTAT Database. http://faostat3.fao.org/download/R/RL/E (accessed 8 June 2016); World Bank. World Development Indicators Online. http://data.worldbank.org/indicator (accessed 12 August 2016); for Taipei,China: Directorate General of Budget, Accounting and Statistics. *Statistical Yearbook 2014*. http://eng.dgbas.gov.tw/lp.asp?ctNode=2351&CtUnit=1072&BaseDSD=36&MP=2 (accessed 8 June 2016).

Table 7.3: **Freshwater Resources**

Regional Member	Internal Renewable Freshwater Resources				Annual Freshwater Withdrawals	Water Productivity[a]
	(billion cubic meters per year)	(cubic meters per inhabitant per year)				
	2014	2002	2012	2014	(billion cubic meters)	2014
Developing Member Economies	**11,040**	**3,228**	**2,894**	**2,808**		
Central and West Asia	**370**	**1,554**	**1,285**	**1,210**		
Afghanistan	47	2,194	1,586	1,450	20 (2000)	1
Armenia	7	2,251	2,303	2,273	3 (2012)	4
Azerbaijan	8	980	867	832	12 (2012)	5
Georgia	58	12,555	14,044	14,532	2 (2008)	8
Kazakhstan	64	4,287	3,826	3,651	20 (2010)	9
Kyrgyz Republic	49	9,732	8,663	8,237	8 (2006)	1
Pakistan	55	381	310	291	184 (2008)	1
Tajikistan	63	9,905	8,002	7,482	11 (2006)	1
Turkmenistan	1	305	272	261	28 (2004)	1
Uzbekistan	16	651	572	547	49 (2005)	1
East Asia	**2,913**	**2,137**	**2,024**	**1,994**		
China, People's Rep. of	2,813	2,141	2,029	1,999	554 (2005)	15
Hong Kong, China	...	...	...	...	...	...
Korea, Rep. of	65	1,387	1,307	1,289	29 (2005)	42
Mongolia	35	14,239	12,393	11,761	1 (2009)	21
Taipei,China	...	...	...	...		...
South Asia	**1,880**	**1,482**	**1,281**	**1,235**		
Bangladesh	105	771	676	652	36 (2008)	4
Bhutan	78	135,361	104,881	100,671	0 (2008)	6
India	1,446	1,326	1,144	1,103	648 (2010)	3
Maldives	0	103	87	82	0 (2008)	489
Nepal	198	8,084	7,207	6,951	9 (2006)	2
Sri Lanka	53	2,770	2,585	2,549	13 (2005)	6
Southeast Asia	**4,985**	**9,223**	**8,170**	**7,884**		
Brunei Darussalam	9	24,752	20,962	20,085	...	135
Cambodia	121	9,510	8,131	7,742	2 (2006)	7
Indonesia	2,019	9,288	8,140	7,839	113 (2000)	8
Lao PDR	190	34,606	29,414	27,992	3 (2005)	3
Malaysia	580	23,769	19,985	19,122	11 (2005)	28
Myanmar	1,003	20,600	19,089	18,610	33 (2000)	...
Philippines	479	5,892	4,989	4,757	82 (2009)	3
Singapore	1	145	113	107	...	...
Thailand	225	3,500	3,343	3,303	57 (2007)	7
Viet Nam	359	4,387	3,978	3,846	82 (2005)	2
The Pacific	**892**	**104,114**	**84,629**	**79,857**		
Cook Islands	...	...	...	...	...	...
Fiji	29	35,001	32,658	32,003	0 (2005)	43
Kiribati	...	...	...	...	...	...
Marshall Islands	...	...	...	...	...	...
Micronesia, Fed. States of	...	...	...	...	...	...
Nauru	...	...	...	...	...	...
Palau	...	...	...	...	...	...
Papua New Guinea	801	141,695	111,950	105,132	0 (2005)	34
Samoa	...	...	...	...	...	...
Solomon Islands	45	102,782	81,391	76,594	...	...
Timor-Leste	8	9,181	7,455	6,932	1 (2004)	1
Tonga	...	...	...	...	...	...
Tuvalu	...	...	...	...	...	...
Vanuatu	10	51,546	40,404	37,793	...	...
Developed Member Economies	**1,249**	**8,342**	**8,085**	**8,054**		
Australia	492	25,213	21,474	20,527	19 (2013)	64
Japan	430	3,406	3,382	3,397	81 (2009)	69
New Zealand	327	82,534	73,715	72,201	5 (2010)	31

... = data not available at cutoff date, 0 = magnitude is less than half of unit employed, Lao PDR = Lao People's Democratic Republic.

a Gross domestic product in constant 2010 US dollars per cubic meter of total freshwater withdrawal.

Sources: Food and Agriculture Organization of the United Nations. AQUASTAT Main Database. http://www.fao.org/nr/water/aquastat/data/query/index.html (accessed 15 June 2016); World Bank. World Development Indicators Online. http://data.worldbank.org/indicator (accessed 2 September 2016).

Government and Governance

Snapshots

- In 2015, the majority of the economies in Asia and the Pacific had fiscal deficits amounting to 1%–7% of their respective gross domestic product (GDP).

- Total government revenue as a percentage of GDP increased by at least 1 percentage point in eight economies between 2014 and 2015. Tax revenue as a percentage of GDP, on the other hand, dropped in a majority of the economies in the region.

- Government spending on health as a percentage of GDP has increased in about two-thirds of the region's economies since 2000.

- The (arithmetic) average number of days required to start up a business in developing economies of Asia and the Pacific declined from 45 days in 2005 to 20 days in 2015. The (arithmetic) average cost of starting up a business as a percentage of gross national income per capita among developing economies went down from 41.4% in 2005 to 17.9% in 2015.

- Ten out of 34 economies in Asia and the Pacific scored 50 or higher on a scale of 0 (highly corrupt) to 100 (very clean) in Transparency International's 2015 Corruption Perceptions Index.

Key Trends

In 2015, the majority of the economies in Asia and the Pacific had fiscal deficits amounting to 1%–7% of their respective gross domestic product (GDP). Figure 8.1 shows fiscal balances—the difference between total government revenue and expenditure as a percentage of GDP. Of the 36 reporting economies in 2015, nine ran fiscal surpluses while the rest had government expenditure exceeding their revenues. The largest fiscal surpluses as a percentage of GDP were recorded in the Federated States of Micronesia (10.5%), Palau (5.9%), and the Marshall Islands (2.8%) while the largest deficits were in Brunei Darussalam (–14.0%), Sri Lanka (–7.4%), and the Maldives (–6.9%). The (simple) average fiscal balance among the economies with data in 2015 is approximately –2.08% of GDP.

Continued low oil prices are exerting fiscal pressures in resource-exporting economies such as Brunei Darussalam, whose deficit position in 2015 is in stark contrast with 2000 when it enjoyed one of the region's largest fiscal surplus as a percentage of GDP at 10.9% (ADB 2016) while the next largest fiscal surpluses in 2000 were in the Marshall Islands (8.1%) and New Zealand (2.0%). The largest deficits as a percentage of GDP were in Palau (–12.8%) and Sri Lanka (–9.3%).

Figure 8.1: Fiscal Balance, 2015
(% of GDP)

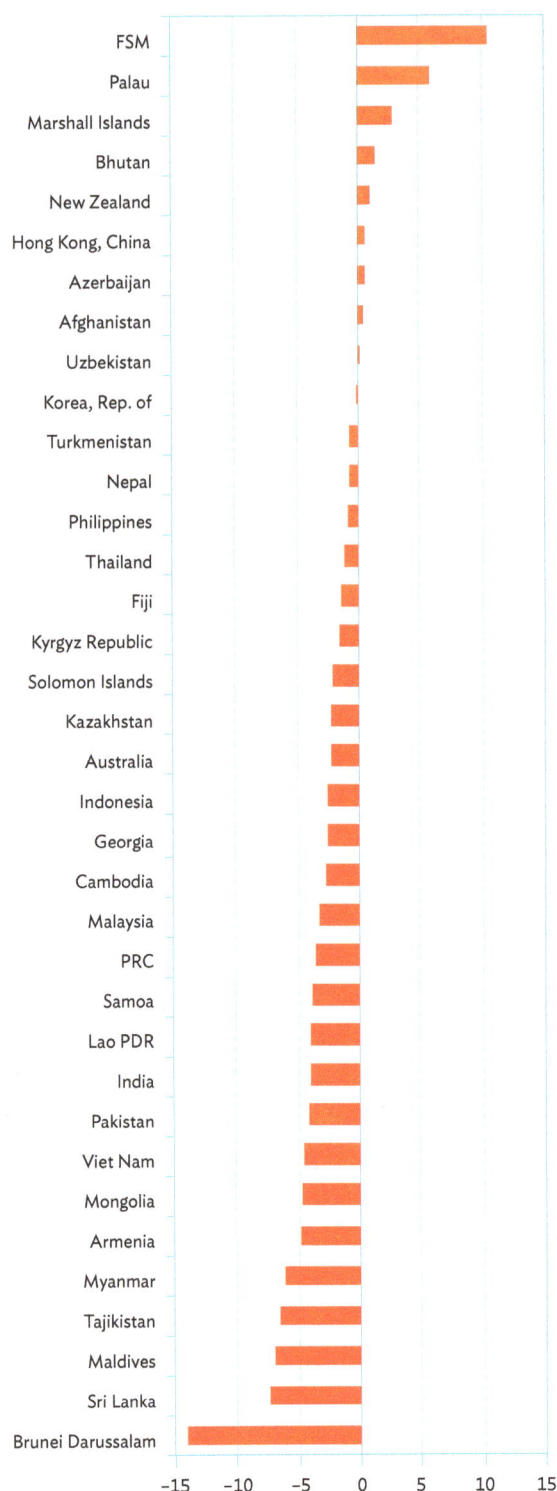

FSM = Federated States of Micronesia, GDP = gross domestic product,
Lao PDR = Lao People's Democratic Republic, PRC = People's Republic
of China.
Source: Table 8.1.

Total government revenue as a percentage to GDP increased by at least 1 percentage point in eight economies between 2014 and 2015.[9] Relative to GDP, average government revenue among member economies with data from 2014 to 2015 rose by approximately 1 percentage point. Among developing economies of Asia and the Pacific, noticeable increases were seen in Fiji (from 27.6% to 31.1%) and the Marshall Islands (from 23.8% to 27.1%). The largest declines in the ratio of government revenue-to-GDP in developing member economies were in Brunei Darussalam (from 31.0% to 20.3%), Solomon Islands (from 41.6% to 37.3%), and Myanmar (from 25.1% to 22.5%). Among developed member economies, government revenue increased from 23.6% to 23.7% in Australia and from 34.1% to 34.7% in New Zealand. Figure 8.2 summarizes the results.

Tax revenue relative to GDP dropped in the majority of the regional economies between 2014 and 2015. Figure 8.3 shows tax revenues as a percentage of GDP over the past 2 years. In 2015, the economies with the highest tax revenue-to-GDP ratios were Solomon Islands (32.4%), New Zealand (28.9%), Fiji (25.9%), and Georgia (25.3%) while those with the lowest ratios included India (7.0%), Afghanistan (7.2%), and Myanmar (8.8%).

About 17 economies noted a reduced tax revenue-to-GDP ratio from 2014 to 2015. The list of economies with the largest reduction in tax revenue relative to GDP (at least 2 percentage points) includes the Federated States of Micronesia (19.0% to 12.4%) and Solomon Islands (from 35.0% to 32.4%). On the other hand, the highest increases in tax revenue relative to GDP were recorded in Sri Lanka (from 10.1% to 12.1%), the Marshall Islands (from 15.9% to 17.2%), and Fiji (from 24.8% to 25.9%).

Figure 8.2: Total Government Revenue
(% of GDP)

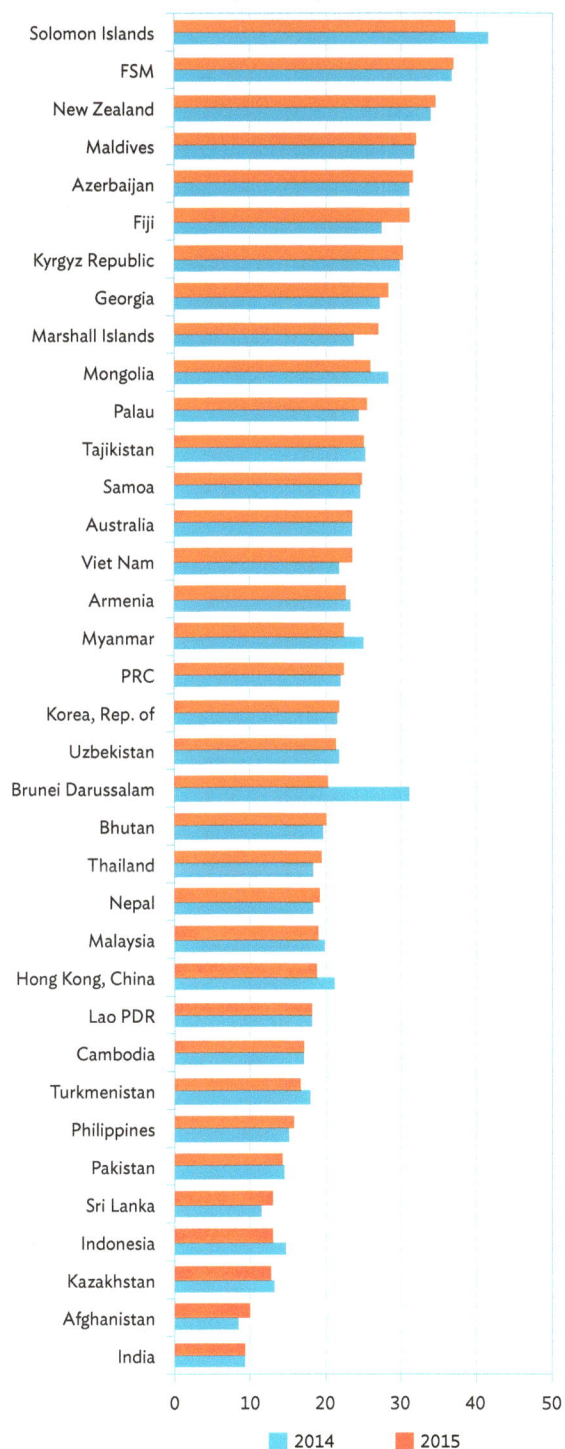

FSM = Federated States of Micronesia, GDP = gross domestic product,
Lao PDR = Lao People's Democratic Republic, PRC = People's Republic
of China.
Notes: The coverage of the budget data is not standard throughout the
region. Data for some economies refer only to central government while
others refer to consolidated government or general government.
For details, please see section on Data Issues and Comparability.
Source: Table 8.3.

Figure 8.3: Tax Revenue
(% of GDP)

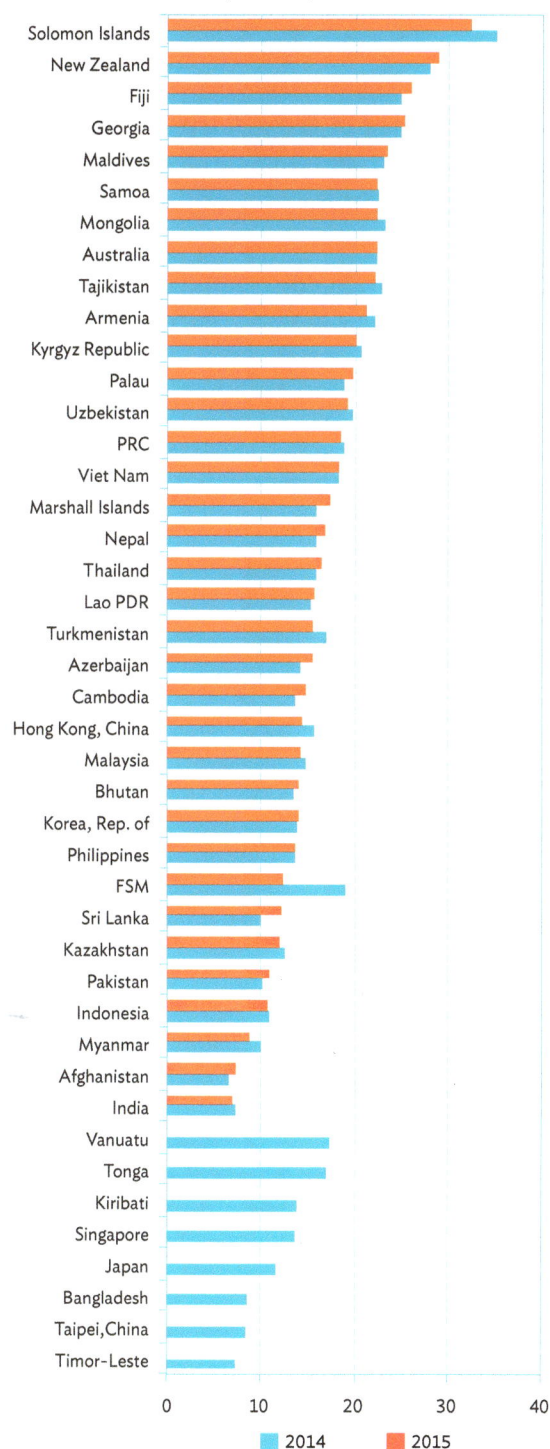

FSM = Federated States of Micronesia, GDP = gross domestic product,
Lao PDR = Lao People's Democratic Republic, PRC = People's Republic
of China.
Notes: The coverage of the budget data is not standard throughout the
region. Data for some economies refer only to central government while
others refer to consolidated government or general government.
For details, please see section on Data Issues and Comparability.
Source: Table 8.2.

Regional Trends and Tables

Government expenditure relative to GDP decreased in more than half of the economies in the majority of economies in East Asia, South Asia, and Southeast Asia between 2014 and 2015, and it increased in the majority of economies in the Pacific and all but one economy in Central and West Asia. Figure 8.4 shows the government expenditure for each economy as a percentage of GDP. Among developing member economies, public spending as a percentage of GDP declined most notably in Palau (from 39.8% to 34.5%), Samoa (from 34.1% to 30.8%), and Solomon Islands (from 43.9% to 41.9%). The largest increases occurred in the Maldives (from 35.1% to 41.0%), the Marshall Islands (from 50.0% to 55.8%), Tajikistan (29.0% to 32.4%), and Sri Lanka (from 17.1% to 20.5%). Among developed member economies, New Zealand experienced the most significant drop in public spending as a percentage of GDP between 2014 and 2015 (from 34.0% to 33.7%). Between 2000 and 2015, government expenditure as a percentage of GDP increased in approximately 60% of the region's economies (Table 8.4).

Government spending on health as a percentage of GDP has increased in about two-thirds of the region's economies since 2000. During the period 2000–2015, health spending as a percentage of GDP increased steadily in many of the region's developing economies, led by Georgia (from 0.6% to 2.9%), Samoa (from 4.0% to 5.2%), and Tajikistan (from 0.9% to 2.0%) (Table 8.5). In 2015 or the latest year for which data are available, spending on health was equivalent to 2.0% or less of GDP in 60.0% of the region's developing economies (Figure 8.5). For comparison, health spending as a percentage of GDP was 4.1% in Australia (2015), 7.4% in Japan (2014), and 7.0% in New Zealand (2015). The higher ratios in developed economies, particularly with respect to Japan, are partially a function of the additional health care requirements of an older population.

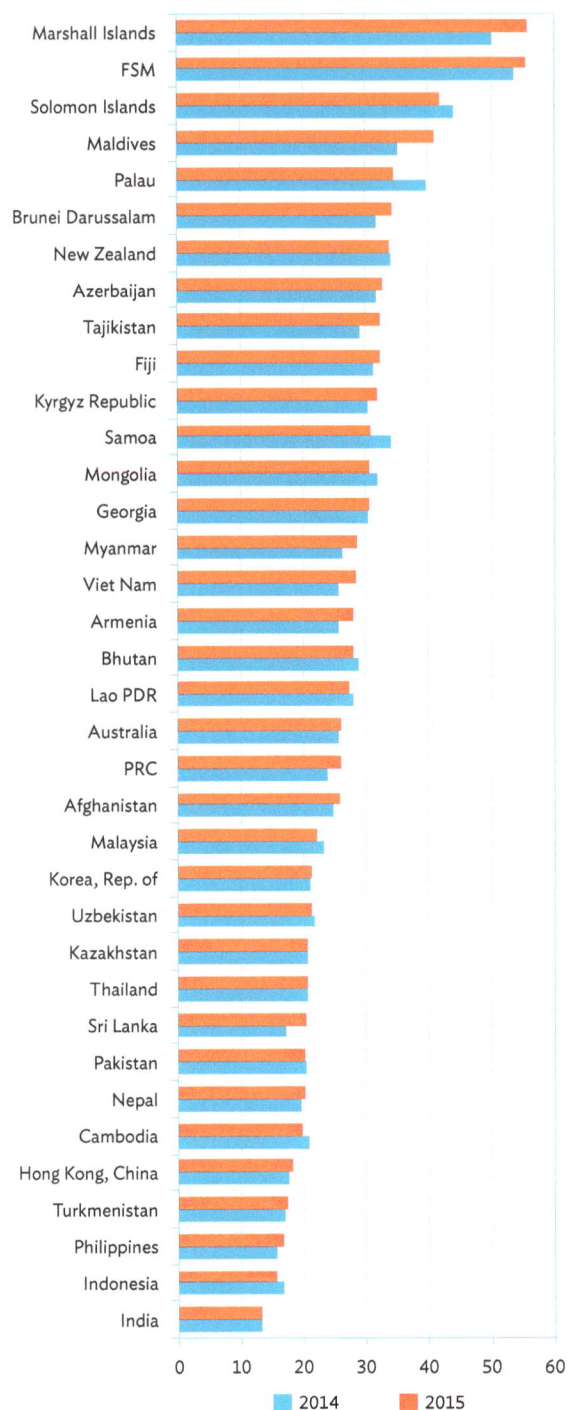

Figure 8.4: Total Government Expenditure
(% of GDP)

FSM = Federated States of Micronesia, GDP = gross domestic product, Lao PDR = Lao People's Democratic Republic, PRC = People's Republic of China.
Notes: The coverage of the budget data is not standard throughout the region. Data for some economies refer only to central government while others refer to consolidated government or general government. For details, please see section on Data Issues and Comparability.
Source: Table 8.4.

Figure 8.5: Government Expenditure on Health, 2015 or Latest Year
(% of GDP)

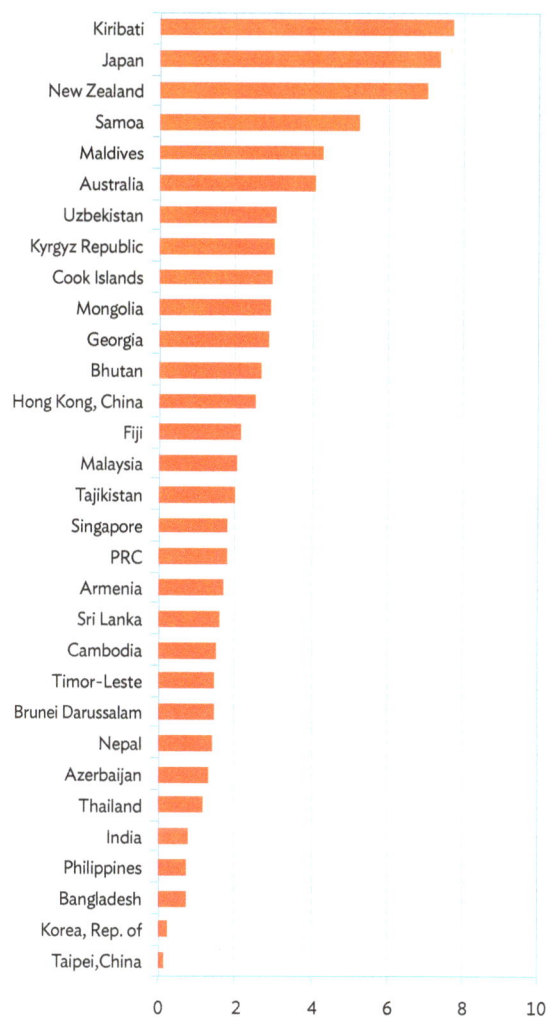

GDP = gross domestic product, PRC = People's Republic of China.
Notes: The coverage of the budget data is not standard throughout the region. Data for some economies refer only to central government while others refer to consolidated government or general government. For details, please see section on Data Issues and Comparability.
Source: Table 8.5.

Government expenditure on social security and welfare continues to expand in most developing economies of Asia and the Pacific. Increases in spending on social security and welfare between 2010 and 2015, or the latest year for which data are available, were observed in about two-thirds of the developing economies, continuing a trend in place in

most economies in the region since 2000 (Table 8.5). In 2015, the majority of developing economies allocated between 0.1% to 10.3% of their GDP to social safety nets. On the other hand, in developed economies where the share of the older population is higher, government expenditure on social security and welfare ranges between 9% and 18%.

Figure 8.6: Government Expenditure on Social Security and Welfare, 2015 or Latest Year
(% of GDP)

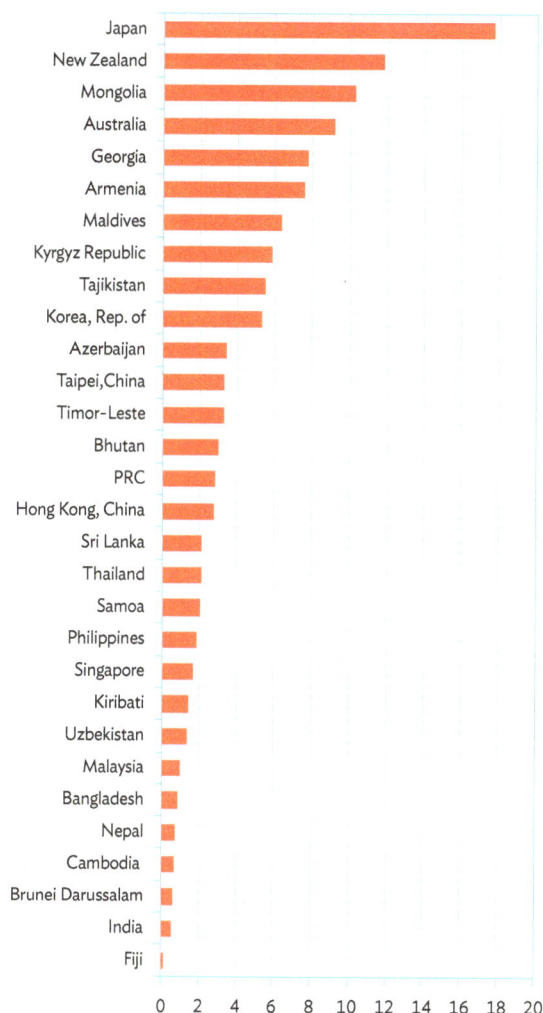

GDP = gross domestic product, PRC = People's Republic of China.
Notes: The coverage of the budget data is not standard throughout the region. Data for some economies refer only to central government while others refer to consolidated government or general government. For details, please see section on Data Issues and Comparability.
Source: Table 8.5.

Governments in the region generally spend more on education than on health. Spending on education by governments exceeded 2.0% of GDP in almost all of the region's developing economies in 2015 or the latest year for which data are available, except for Taipei,China (1.5%) and Cambodia (1.8%) (Figure 8.7). Furthermore, the governments of many developing economies spent more on education relative to GDP than those of developed members Australia (1.9%) and Japan (3.1%). Since 2000, about 44% of the region's governments have increased spending on education as a share of GDP, while about 52% have reduced their ratio of education spending to GDP (Table 8.5).

The average number of days required to start up a business in developing economies declined from 45 days in 2005 to 20 days in 2015. Between 2005 and 2015, the time required to start up a business was shortened in 27, rose in three, and remained unchanged in five economies (Figure 8.8). In terms of the reduction in the number of days required to start up a business, the economies with the most notable improvement are Timor-Leste, Azerbaijan, and Brunei Darussalam. On the other hand, all three economies that experienced an increase in the time required to start a business during the review period were in the Pacific: Fiji 14 days, Palau 4 days, and Papua New Guinea 1 day.

The average cost of starting up a business as a share of gross national income (GNI) per capita among developing economies went down from 41.4% in 2005 to 17.9% in 2015 (Table 8.6). The largest percentage point declines were in Cambodia (from 276.1% to 78.7%), Timor-Leste (from 125.4% to 0.3%), and Solomon Islands (from 135.5% to 31.4%). While starting a business is becoming less expensive in the majority of the developing member economies, the cost still exceeds 100% of GNI per capita in the Federated States of Micronesia (141.1%).

Ten out of 34 economies of Asia and the Pacific scored 50 or higher on a scale of 0 (highly corrupt) to 100 (very clean) in Transparency International's 2015 Corruption Perceptions Index. Australia; Bhutan; Hong Kong, China; Japan; New Zealand; and Singapore had the highest scores in the 2015 Corruption Perceptions Index within the region. On the other hand, the economies in Asia and the Pacific with the lowest scores in the 2015 Corruption Perceptions Index were Afghanistan, Turkmenistan, and Uzbekistan.

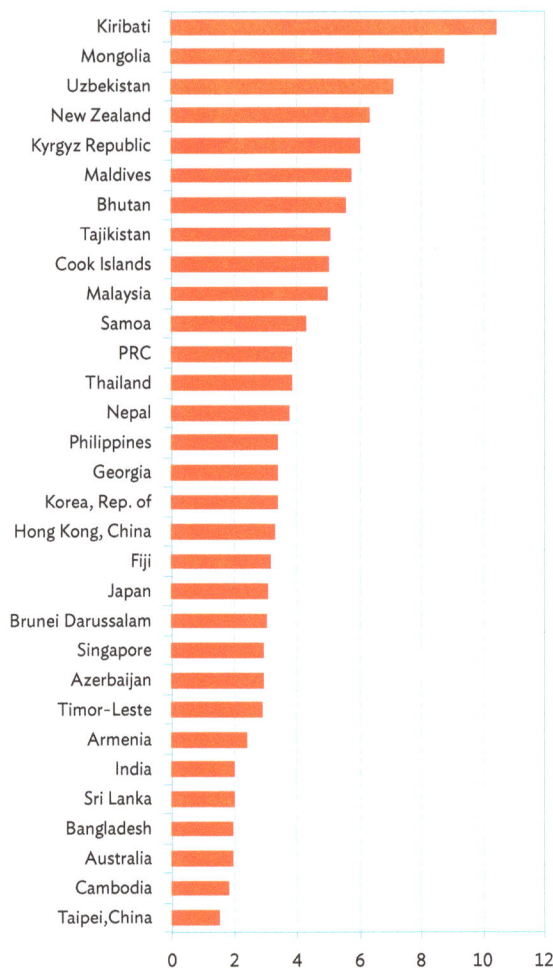

Figure 8.7: Government Expenditure on Education, 2015 or Latest Year
(% of GDP)

GDP = gross domestic product, PRC = People's Republic of China.
Notes: The coverage of the budget data is not standard throughout the region. Data for some economies refer only to central government while others refer to consolidated government or general government.
For details, please see section on Data Issues and Comparability.
Source: Table 8.5.

Figure 8.8: Number of Days Required to Start Up a Business

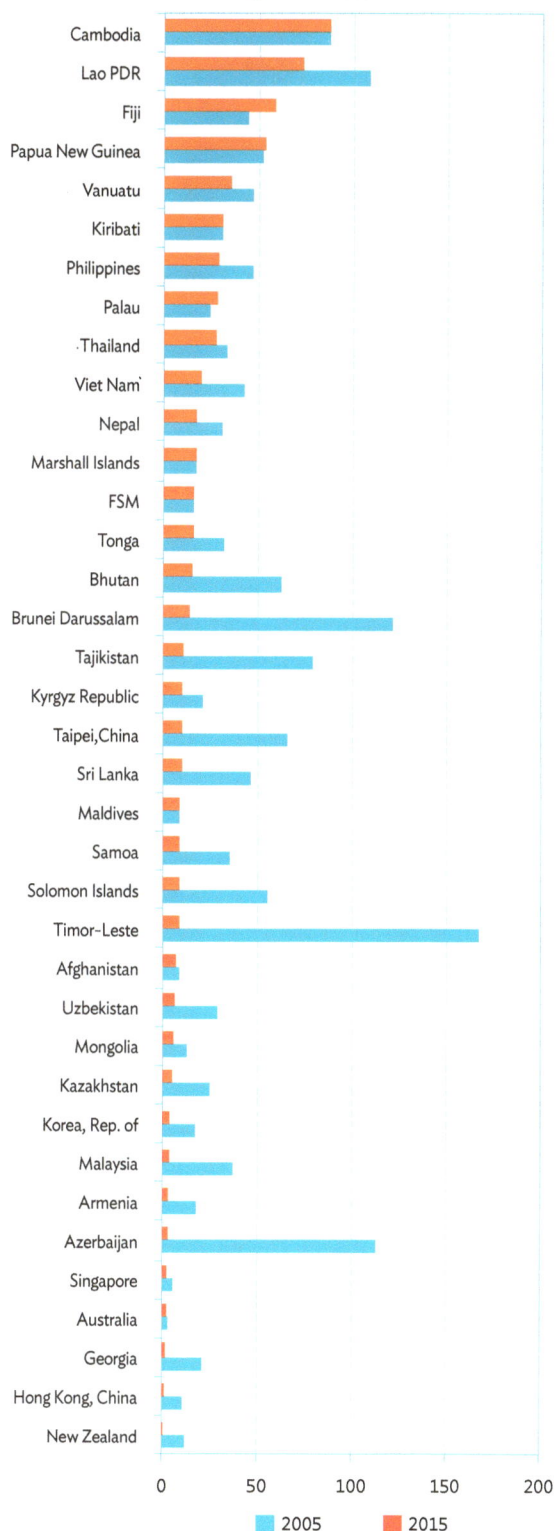

FSM = Federated States of Micronesia, Lao PDR = Lao People's Democratic Republic.
Note: For Brunei Darussalam, figure for 2005 refers to 2006.
Source: Table 8.7.

Data Issues and Comparability

Data on government expenditure and revenue are from economy sources. The coverage of the budget data is not standard throughout the region. Data from different economies refer only to the central government, except for Bangladesh, Georgia, Kiribati, the Kyrgyz Republic, Mongolia, Pakistan, and Tajikistan, where data refer to consolidated government or general government. For the People's Republic of China, data refer to consolidated central, provincial, and local governments. For Australia, data refer to the Commonwealth government. For Viet Nam, data refer to state budget or expenditure. Most economies try to follow the International Monetary Fund's Government Finance Statistics guidelines; some economies are still using the 1986 version while others have switched to the 2001 guidelines. Most economies record their transactions on a cash basis; and a few on accrual.

Statistics on the time and cost for registering new businesses and on perceived corruption are taken from nonofficial sources. Common procedures are used in all economies and the researchers producing these data have refined their procedures over several surveys. However, because of the subjective nature of much of the data, they can only be used to give a broad idea of trends, levels, and rankings and small changes from one year to the next should be taken with caution.

Reference

Asian Development Bank. 2016. *Asian Development Outlook 2016*. Manila.

Table 8.1: **Fiscal Balance**[a]
(% of GDP)

Regional Member	2000	2005	2010	2011	2012	2013	2014	2015
Developing Member Economies								
Central and West Asia								
Afghanistan[b]	−1.2 (2002)	−4.5	2.5	−0.2	−0.5	2.3	−1.7	0.4
Armenia	−4.9	−1.9	−5.0	−2.8	−1.4	−1.6	−1.9	−4.8
Azerbaijan	−1.0	−0.7	−0.9	0.6	−0.2	0.6	0.5	0.5
Georgia	−1.3	1.2	−5.6	−2.1	−1.7	−2.1	−2.8	−2.6
Kazakhstan	−0.1	0.6	−2.4	−1.9	−2.8	−1.9	−2.7	−2.2
Kyrgyz Republic	−2.2	0.2	−4.9	−4.8	−6.5	−0.7	−0.5	−1.5
Pakistan[c]	−5.4	−3.0	−5.9	−6.3	−8.6	−8.1	−4.2	−4.1
Tajikistan	−0.6	0.2	−7.1	−5.8	−3.1	−4.8	−3.7	−6.5
Turkmenistan	−0.3	0.8	2.0	3.5	6.4	1.5	0.9	−0.7
Uzbekistan	−1.0	0.1	0.3	0.4	0.4	0.3	0.2	0.1
East Asia								
China, People's Rep. of	−2.8	−1.2	−1.7	−1.1	−1.6	−1.9	−1.8	−3.5
Hong Kong, China[d]	−0.6	1.0	4.2	3.8	3.2	1.0	3.7	0.6
Korea, Rep. of	1.0	0.4	1.3	1.4	1.3	1.0	0.6	−0.0
Mongolia	−5.7	2.4	0.4	−6.4	−6.8	−1.2	−3.8	−4.6
Taipei,China	−4.5	−0.3	−2.6	−1.5	−2.8	−1.0	−0.8	...
South Asia								
Bangladesh[c]	−4.5	−3.7	−2.8	−3.6	−3.2	−3.3	−3.1	...
Bhutan[c]	−3.9	−6.6	1.5	−2.0	−1.1	−4.0	3.6	1.4
India[d]	−5.5	−4.0	−4.8	−5.9	−4.9	−4.5	−4.1	−3.9
Maldives	−4.4	−7.3	−14.4	−6.6	−7.7	−4.1	−2.9	−6.9
Nepal[e]	−4.7	−2.4	−1.9	−2.4	−2.0	0.6	0.9	−0.7
Sri Lanka	−9.3	−7.0	−7.0	−6.2	−5.6	−5.4	−5.7	−7.4
Southeast Asia								
Brunei Darussalam[f]	10.9	21.1	15.6	25.6	15.7	10.1	−0.7	−14.0
Cambodia	−2.1	−0.7	−8.8	−7.6	−6.8	−7.1	−3.8	−2.6
Indonesia	−1.1	−0.5	−0.7	−1.1	−1.8	−2.2	−2.1	−2.5
Lao PDR[g]	−4.6	−4.5	−2.2	−1.6	−1.2	−5.8	−3.6	−3.9
Malaysia	−5.5	−3.4	−5.3	−4.7	−4.3	−3.8	−3.4	−3.2
Myanmar[d]	0.7	−4.3 (2006)	−4.6	−3.8	−4.7	−5.4	−1.1	−6.1
Philippines	−3.7	−2.6	−3.5	−2.0	−2.3	−1.4	−0.6	−0.9
Singapore[d]	9.7	6.4	7.4	9.1	8.5	8.1	7.2	...
Thailand[g]	−2.8	0.1	−2.9	−1.6	−2.2	−0.9	−2.1	−1.2
Viet Nam[h]	−4.3	−1.0	−2.1	−0.5	−3.4	−5.0	−4.4	−4.6
The Pacific								
Cook Islands[c]	−1.5	2.1	6.4	3.7	4.1	2.6	...	...
Fiji	−3.1	−3.4	−2.2	−1.4	−1.1	−0.5	−4.0	−1.4
Kiribati	42.3	7.3	17.5 (2008)	...	...	...	...	...
Marshall Islands[g]	8.1	−22.3	3.4	2.1	−0.7	−0.2	3.2	2.8
Micronesia, Fed. States of	−3.5	−5.6	0.5	−0.6	0.9	2.9	11.2	10.5
Nauru[c]	...	4.3	0.1	...	...	...	...	...
Palau[g]	−12.8	1.5	−1.0	1.3	1.0	0.7	1.3	5.9
Papua New Guinea	−2.0	0.1	0.5	−0.2	−3.1	−5.6	...	...
Samoa[c]	−0.7	2.0	−5.6	−5.1	−7.2	−3.7	−5.1	−3.8
Solomon Islands	−0.6	−0.9	8.3	6.4	2.4	5.6	1.8	−2.1
Timor-Leste	...	3.9	3.5	−11.1	−30.9	−29.5	−53.1	...
Tonga[c]	−0.3	3.0	−2.7	−7.6	−7.1	−0.8	1.9	...
Tuvalu	−2.0	−7.7	−0.1	0.1	0.1	17.6	...	...
Vanuatu	−6.2	2.9	−2.0	−2.3	1.6	0.9	0.7	...
Developed Member Economies								
Australia[c]	1.8	1.5	−3.5	−3.3	−2.7	−1.4	−2.0	−2.3
Japan[d]	−6.3	−4.1	−6.7	−8.2	−7.8	−7.3	−5.5	...
New Zealand[i]	2.0	6.1	0.9	1.1	0.5	0.6	0.8	0.9

... = data not available at cutoff date, 0.0 = magnitude is less than half of unit employed, GDP = gross domestic product, Lao PDR = Lao People's Democratic Republic.

a Data refer to central government, except for Bangladesh, Georgia, Kiribati, the Kyrgyz Republic, Mongolia, Pakistan, and Tajikistan, where data refer to consolidated government or general government. For the People's Republic of China, data refer to consolidated central, provincial, and local governments. For Australia, data refer to the Commonwealth government. For Viet Nam, data refer to state budget and/or expenditure.

b Data for 2000–2011 are based on fiscal year beginning 21 March. For 2012, government finance covers 9 months only (21 March–20 December) due to the change of Afghanistan's fiscal year (FY) effective 2012 (FY1391). From 2013, the fiscal year begins on 21 December and ends on 20 December.

c Data are based on fiscal year ending 30 June.

d Data are based on fiscal year beginning 1 April.

e Data are based on fiscal year ending 15 July.

f Data for 2005 onward are based on fiscal year beginning 1 April.

g Data are based on fiscal year ending 30 September.

h Tax revenue includes local government taxes.

i Data for 2000–2005 are based on fiscal year ending 31 March, while data for 2010 onward are based on fiscal year ending 30 June.

Source: Economy sources.

Table 8.2: **Tax Revenue**[a]
(% of GDP)

Regional Member	2000	2005	2010	2011	2012	2013	2014	2015
Developing Member Economies								
Central and West Asia								
Afghanistan[b]	...	3.8	8.9	8.4	5.5	6.7	6.5	7.2
Armenia	14.8	14.3	20.2	20.6	20.6	22.0	22.0	21.2
Azerbaijan	12.2	14.0	12.4	12.3	12.7	13.3	14.2	15.5
Georgia	14.6	20.8	23.5	25.2	25.5	24.8	24.8	25.3
Kazakhstan	20.2	26.3	13.4	13.6	12.7	12.9	12.6	11.9
Kyrgyz Republic	11.7	16.2	17.9	18.5	20.6	20.5	20.6	20.0
Pakistan[c]	10.6	10.1	9.9	9.3	10.2	9.8	10.2	11.0
Tajikistan	13.1	16.5	18.0	19.5	19.9	21.0	22.8	22.0
Turkmenistan	23.0	20.9 (2004)	...	17.5	20.2	17.7	17.0	15.5
Uzbekistan	23.4 (2001)	21.5	20.0	19.5	19.6	19.6	19.7	19.1
East Asia								
China, People's Rep. of	12.6	15.5	17.9	18.5	18.8	18.8	18.7	18.5
Hong Kong, China[d]	9.7	12.3	13.6	14.2	13.7	13.5	15.7	14.4
Korea, Rep. of	17.0	13.9	14.0	14.4	14.7	14.1	13.8	14.0
Mongolia	22.4	22.8	27.6	27.6	25.0	26.5	23.2	22.2
Taipei,China	13.1	8.8	7.6	8.4	8.4	8.0	8.4	...
South Asia								
Bangladesh[c]	6.8	8.6	7.8	8.7	9.0	9.0	8.6	...
Bhutan[c]	10.0	9.4	13.3	13.6	15.1	14.6	13.5	14.1
India[d]	6.3	7.3	7.3	7.2	7.5	7.2	7.2	7.0
Maldives	13.8	12.0	9.9	13.7	17.8	20.7	23.0	23.4
Nepal[e]	8.7	9.2	13.4	13.0	13.9	15.3	15.9	16.8
Sri Lanka	14.2	13.7	11.3	11.7	10.4	10.5	10.1	12.1
Southeast Asia								
Brunei Darussalam[f]	23.4	33.1	24.0 (2009)	...	...	...	...	...
Cambodia	7.3	7.7	10.1	10.2	11.4	11.7	13.8	14.8
Indonesia	8.3	12.5	11.2	11.2	11.4	11.3	10.9	10.7
Lao PDR[g]	10.6	9.7	13.5	14.1	15.0	15.0	15.4	15.6
Malaysia	13.2	14.8	13.3	14.8	15.6	15.3	14.8	14.3
Myanmar[d]	2.0	4.3 (2006)	3.2	3.7	3.8	6.3	10.0	8.8
Philippines	12.8	12.4	12.1	12.4	12.9	13.3	13.6	13.6
Singapore[d]	14.9	11.6	12.6	13.1	13.7	13.4	13.8	...
Thailand[g]	12.8	15.2	14.6	15.9	15.1	16.9	15.8	16.4
Viet Nam[h]	18.0	21.0	22.4	22.3	19.0	19.1	18.2	18.2
The Pacific								
Cook Islands[c]	22.3	25.3	25.5	25.1	23.6	25.5	...	...
Fiji	20.0	21.1	21.6	23.5	24.2	24.3	24.8	25.9
Kiribati	21.5	22.0	17.1	18.0	15.1	15.3	13.8	...
Marshall Islands[g]	15.4	18.3	17.1	16.8	15.8	15.9	15.9	17.2
Micronesia, Fed. States of	11.9	11.7	12.0	12.0	11.6	12.1	19.0	12.4
Nauru	...	...	...	...	...	...	...	...
Palau[g]	16.1	16.4	16.9	17.7	18.0	18.1	18.8	19.8
Papua New Guinea	23.8	24.8	16.7	18.6	18.4	18.1	...	...
Samoa[c]	20.6	20.6	20.9	18.8	19.7	21.8	22.4	22.3
Solomon Islands	19.1	24.3	34.0	36.9	37.3	37.2	35.0	32.4
Timor-Leste	...	1.5	1.2	2.0	3.4	4.7	7.2	...
Tonga[c]	15.8	19.2	16.1	17.0	15.9	17.0	17.0	...
Tuvalu	21.6	21.3	16.2	18.9	19.3	19.0	...	...
Vanuatu	15.7	16.4	16.0	16.3	16.6	17.2	17.4	...
Developed Member Economies								
Australia[c]	23.2	24.9	20.7	20.6	21.4	22.3	22.3	22.2
Japan[d]	10.4	10.2	8.9	9.4	9.8	10.6	11.7	...
New Zealand[i]	30.9	33.9	27.0	26.5	27.1	28.2	27.9	28.9

... = data not available at cutoff date, GDP = gross domestic product, Lao PDR = Lao People's Democratic Republic.

a Data refer to central government, except for Bangladesh, Georgia, Kiribati, the Kyrgyz Republic, Mongolia, Pakistan, and Tajikistan, where data refer to consolidated government or general government. For the People's Republic of China, data refer to consolidated central, provincial, and local governments. For Australia, data refer to the Commonwealth government. For Viet Nam, data refer to state budget and/or expenditure.
b Data for 2000–2011 are based on fiscal year beginning 21 March. For 2012, government finance covers 9 months only (21 March–20 December) due to the change of Afghanistan's fiscal year (FY) effective 2012 (FY1391). From 2013, the fiscal year begins on 21 December and ends on 20 December.
c Data are based on fiscal year ending 30 June.
d Data are based on fiscal year beginning 1 April.
e Data are based on fiscal year ending 15 July.
f Data for 2005 onward are based on fiscal year beginning 1 April.
g Data are based on fiscal year ending 30 September.
h Tax revenue includes local government taxes.
i Data for 2000–2005 are based on fiscal year ending 31 March, while data for 2010 onward are based on fiscal year ending 30 June.

Source: Economy sources.

Table 8.3:   **Total Government Revenue**[a]
(% of GDP)

Regional Member	2000	2005	2010	2011	2012	2013	2014	2015
Developing Member Economies								
Central and West Asia								
Afghanistan[b]	2.9 (2002)	6.9	10.8	11.1	7.5	9.2	8.3	9.8
Armenia	15.9	16.2	21.7	21.8	21.8	23.3	23.4	22.7
Azerbaijan	14.7	16.3	26.8	30.1	31.6	33.8	31.2	31.6
Georgia	15.5	27.1	27.1	28.9	28.9	27.3	27.3	28.4
Kazakhstan	22.9	27.6	14.2	14.2	13.8	13.4	13.2	12.7
Kyrgyz Republic	14.2	19.8	23.1	24.2	26.2	26.1	29.8	30.3
Pakistan[c]	13.4	13.8	14.0	12.3	12.8	13.3	14.5	14.4
Tajikistan	14.1	19.2	19.3	21.1	21.7	23.0	25.3	25.0
Turkmenistan	23.5	20.5	16.1	18.1	21.0	18.4	17.9	16.6
Uzbekistan	28.0	22.6	21.8	21.7	21.7	21.7	21.9	21.3
East Asia								
China, People's Rep. of	13.4	17.0	20.3	21.5	22.0	22.0	22.1	22.5
Hong Kong, China[d]	16.8	17.5	21.2	22.6	21.7	21.3	21.2	18.8
Korea, Rep. of	21.4	20.8	21.4	21.9	22.6	22.0	21.6	21.8
Mongolia	27.8	27.4	31.6	31.6	29.0	31.0	28.4	26.0
Taipei,China	17.7	14.3	10.7	11.8	11.0	11.5	10.9	...
South Asia								
Bangladesh[c]	8.5	10.6	9.5	10.2	10.9	10.7	10.4	...
Bhutan[c]	23.2	17.0	27.4	20.8	20.7	20.0	19.7	20.1
India[d]	9.5	9.7	10.6	9.0	9.2	9.4	9.2	9.2
Maldives	30.0	26.4	21.5	25.6	25.3	27.4	31.8	32.0
Nepal[e]	11.3	11.9	14.9	14.5	16.0	17.6	18.5	19.1
Sri Lanka	16.4	15.5	12.7	13.4	12.0	11.9	11.4	13.0
Southeast Asia								
Brunei Darussalam[f]	49.1	53.2	49.0	55.3	46.8	37.9	31.0	20.3
Cambodia	10.0	10.6	12.6	12.4	14.4	13.5	17.1	17.1
Indonesia	14.7	17.8	15.4	15.4	15.5	15.0	14.6	12.9
Lao PDR[g]	13.1	11.7	15.3	15.7	17.1	17.4	18.2	18.1
Malaysia	17.4	19.6	19.4	20.3	21.4	20.9	19.9	18.9
Myanmar[d]	4.2	17.6 (2006)	14.2	14.7	22.9	24.4	25.1	22.5
Philippines	14.3	14.4	13.4	14.0	14.5	14.9	15.1	15.8
Singapore[d]	29.3	20.9	21.5	23.6	22.7	21.9	22.1	...
Thailand[g]	14.7	17.3	16.8	17.8	17.1	19.4	18.4	19.4
Viet Nam[h]	20.1	25.7	26.7	25.5	22.3	22.8	21.8	23.5
The Pacific								
Cook Islands[c]	27.0	29.3	34.1	35.1	33.4	35.3	...	...
Fiji	25.5	24.2	25.4	26.6	27.0	27.0	27.6	31.1
Kiribati	94.4	68.8	83.3 (2008)	...	...	...	...	...
Marshall Islands[g]	22.0	22.0	19.9	20.0	19.2	21.4	23.8	27.1
Micronesia, Fed. States of	22.5	19.7	21.4	20.6	22.8	26.7	36.9	37.1
Nauru[c]	...	33.1	39.2	...	...	...	...	...
Palau[g]	22.8	19.6	20.4	21.5	22.7	22.7	24.4	25.5
Papua New Guinea	25.7	26.8	17.8	19.5	19.5	18.9	...	...
Samoa[c]	25.6	24.1	23.6	21.9	22.7	23.8	24.7	24.9
Solomon Islands	21.6	26.7	37.0	40.4	42.4	43.7	41.6	37.3
Timor-Leste	...	9.5	21.2	16.1	5.2	6.5	9.8	...
Tonga[c]	21.1	22.8	20.1	19.6	18.1	19.7	20.1	...
Tuvalu	216.4	55.1	51.9	56.3	59.6	74.3	...	...
Vanuatu	18.7	18.5	17.6	18.0	18.8	19.2	19.3	...
Developed Member Economies								
Australia[c]	25.3	26.3	22.6	22.0	22.7	23.8	23.6	23.7
Japan[d]	12.0	11.9	11.2	11.3	11.2	12.1	13.2	...
New Zealand[i]	37.6	41.9	33.5	35.1	33.5	34.4	34.1	34.7

... = data not available at cutoff date, GDP = gross domestic product, Lao PDR = Lao People's Democratic Republic.

a Data refer to central government, except for Bangladesh, Georgia, Kiribati, the Kyrgyz Republic, Mongolia, Pakistan, and Tajikistan, where data refer to consolidated government or general government. For the People's Republic of China, data refer to consolidated central, provincial, and local governments. For Australia, data refer to the Commonwealth government. For Viet Nam, data refer to state budget and/or expenditure.
b Data for 2000–2011 are based on fiscal year beginning 21 March. For 2012, government finance covers 9 months only (21 March–20 December) due to the change of Afghanistan's fiscal year (FY) effective 2012 (FY1391). From 2013, the fiscal year begins on 21 December and ends on 20 December.
c Data are based on fiscal year ending 30 June.
d Data are based on fiscal year beginning 1 April.
e Data are based on fiscal year ending 15 July.
f Data for 2005 onward are based on fiscal year beginning 1 April.
g Data are based on fiscal year ending 30 September.
h Tax revenue includes local government taxes.
i Data for 2000–2005 are based on fiscal year ending 31 March, while data for 2010 onward are based on fiscal year ending 30 June.

Source: Economy sources.

Table 8.4:   **Total Government Expenditure**[a]
(% of GDP)

Regional Member	2000	2005	2010	2011	2012	2013	2014	2015
Developing Member Economies								
Central and West Asia								
Afghanistan[b]	7.7 (2002)	16.5	20.6	22.3	17.4	23.2	24.8	25.9
Armenia	20.1	18.0	27.6	26.2	23.6	25.1	25.6	28.0
Azerbaijan	16.2	16.8	27.6	29.2	31.6	31.6	31.7	32.7
Georgia	16.3	26.6	34.0	30.7	30.6	29.4	30.3	30.6
Kazakhstan	22.2	25.6	22.0	20.0	20.7	19.0	20.5	20.7
Kyrgyz Republic	18.0	20.4	31.2	32.0	34.5	29.3	30.3	31.8
Pakistan[c]	18.9	18.0	20.2	18.6	21.2	19.8	20.5	20.2
Tajikistan	14.7	19.4	25.1	27.4	25.1	28.0	29.0	32.4
Turkmenistan	23.9	19.7	14.1	14.6	14.7	16.9	17.0	17.3
Uzbekistan	28.9	22.5	21.5	21.2	21.3	21.4	21.7	21.2
East Asia								
China, People's Rep. of	16.2	18.3	22.0	22.6	23.6	23.8	23.9	26.0
Hong Kong, China[d]	17.4	16.5	17.0	18.8	18.5	20.3	17.5	18.2
Korea, Rep. of	17.2	20.1	19.8	20.2	20.8	21.1	21.0	21.2
Mongolia	28.6	22.7	29.2	34.3	35.5	31.5	31.8	30.6
Taipei,China	22.2	14.6	13.3	13.3	13.7	12.5	11.7	...
South Asia								
Bangladesh[c]	14.5	15.0	12.7	13.0	13.0	13.1	13.7	...
Bhutan[c]	42.2	35.4	35.6	34.8	35.8	34.7	29.0	27.9
India[d]	15.0	13.7	15.4	14.9	14.2	13.8	13.3	13.2
Maldives	37.3	40.3	37.0	35.4	34.1	31.8	35.1	41.0
Nepal[e]	17.5	15.3	19.0	18.8	19.3	17.8	19.6	20.2
Sri Lanka	25.0	23.8	19.3	19.4	17.5	17.3	17.1	20.5
Southeast Asia								
Brunei Darussalam[f]	40.6	32.1	33.3	29.7	31.0	27.8	31.7	34.3
Cambodia	14.8	13.2	21.4	20.0	21.2	20.6	20.9	19.7
Indonesia	15.8	18.4	16.2	16.5	17.3	17.3	16.8	15.6
Lao PDR[g]	20.8	18.4	24.2	23.3	24.8	29.2	28.0	27.4
Malaysia	22.9	23.0	24.7	25.0	25.7	24.7	23.3	22.1
Myanmar[d]	3.5	19.2	18.9	18.5	27.6	29.8	26.2	28.6
Philippines	18.1	16.9	16.8	15.9	16.6	16.1	15.6	16.7
Singapore[d]	18.2	14.5	14.1	14.5	14.2	13.8	14.9	...
Thailand[g]	16.8	17.2	19.7	19.4	19.4	20.3	20.5	20.6
Viet Nam[h]	22.6	25.1	27.2	25.4	28.2	28.8	25.6	28.5
The Pacific								
Cook Islands[c]	31.0	33.3	33.0	39.7	36.5	41.2	...	...
Fiji	28.6	27.6	27.7	28.0	28.3	27.6	31.3	32.3
Kiribati	87.4	105.8	86.9	91.8	107.2	96.4	105.6	...
Marshall Islands[g]	58.6	85.3	57.9	55.8	52.0	53.7	50.0	55.8
Micronesia, Fed. States of	67.2	59.1	67.0	65.2	65.0	59.1	53.6	55.5
Nauru[c]	...	28.5	83.6	...	...	...	...	...
Palau[g]	56.8	39.2	48.4	43.3	44.2	40.3	39.8	34.5
Papua New Guinea	32.9	35.2	21.0	22.0	24.7	26.3	...	...
Samoa[c]	31.2	32.7	30.0	33.0	32.6	30.2	34.1	30.8
Solomon Islands	31.6	34.6	39.7	41.2	47.1	43.8	43.9	41.9
Timor-Leste	...	5.6	17.7	27.2	36.2	35.9	63.0	...
Tonga[c]	22.2	21.2	28.0	32.4	29.5	25.5	26.7	...
Tuvalu	186.9	77.9	104.1	93.3	79.8	81.3	...	...
Vanuatu	26.0	18.4	26.3	23.7	23.4	20.7	21.3	...
Developed Member Economies								
Australia[c]	23.5	24.8	26.1	25.3	25.4	25.2	25.6	26.0
Japan[d]	18.3	16.0	18.0	19.5	19.0	19.4	18.7	...
New Zealand[i]	35.7	35.8	35.9	42.8	35.5	35.3	34.0	33.7

... = data not available at cutoff date, GDP = gross domestic product, Lao PDR = Lao People's Democratic Republic.

a Data refer to central government, except for Bangladesh, Georgia, Kiribati, the Kyrgyz Republic, Mongolia, Pakistan, and Tajikistan, where data refer to consolidated government or general government. For the People's Republic of China, data refer to consolidated central, provincial, and local governments. For Australia, data refer to the Commonwealth government. For Viet Nam, data refer to state budget and/or expenditure.

b Data for 2000–2011 are based on fiscal year beginning 21 March. For 2012, government finance covers nine months only (21 March–20 December) due to the change of Afghanistan's fiscal year (FY) effective 2012 (FY1391). From 2013, the fiscal year begins on 21 December and ends on 20 December.

c Data are based on fiscal year ending 30 June.

d Data are based on fiscal year beginning 1 April.

e Data are based on fiscal year ending 15 July.

f Data for 2005 onward are based on fiscal year beginning 1 April.

g Data are based on fiscal year ending 30 September.

h Total expenditure includes local government expenditure.

i Data for 1990–2005 are based on fiscal year ending 31 March, while data for 2010 onward are based on fiscal year ending 30 June.

Source: Economy sources.

Table 8.5:   **Government Expenditure by Economic Activity**[a]
(% of GDP)

Regional Member	Health			Education			Social Security and Welfare		
	2000	2010	2015	2000	2010	2015	2000	2010	2015
Developing Member Economies									
Central and West Asia									
Afghanistan	...	...	...	...	...	2.4	...	...	...
Armenia	1.0	1.6	1.7	2.8	2.8	2.4	2.1	7.1	7.6
Azerbaijan	0.9	1.0	1.3	3.9	2.8	3.0	3.0	2.6	3.4
Georgia	0.6	2.2	2.9	2.2	2.9	3.4	4.3	6.9	7.8
Kazakhstan	...	...	...	...	...	...	...	...	...
Kyrgyz Republic	2.0	3.1	3.0	3.5	5.8	6.0	1.7	5.0	5.9
Pakistan	...	...	...	...	...	...	...	...	...
Tajikistan[b]	0.9	1.4	2.0	2.3	4.0	5.1	1.8	3.5	5.6
Turkmenistan	...	...	...	...	...	...	...	...	...
Uzbekistan	...	2.8	3.0	...	7.2	7.1	...	2.2	1.3
East Asia									
China, People's Rep. of[c]	...	1.2	1.8	3.3 (2002)	3.1	3.9	0.7	2.2	2.8
Hong Kong, China[d]	2.4	2.2	2.5	3.9	3.4	3.3	2.1	2.3	2.7
Korea, Rep. of	0.1	0.2	0.2 (2014)	3.1	3.0	3.4 (2014)	3.0	4.5	5.3 (2014)
Mongolia	3.8	2.5	2.9 (2014)	6.7	5.1	8.8 (2014)	6.2	11.1	10.3 (2014)
Taipei,China	0.2	0.2	0.1 (2014)	2.3	1.7	1.5 (2014)	5.6	3.1	3.3 (2014)
South Asia									
Bangladesh[e]	1.0	0.8	0.7 (2014)	2.0	2.0	2.0 (2014)	0.1	0.9	0.9 (2014)
Bhutan[e]	4.4 (2002)	3.0	2.6	5.5 (2002)	6.7	5.6	1.8 (2002)	1.8	3.0
India[d]	0.7	0.7	0.8 (2013)	3.2	1.9	2.0 (2013)	0.8	0.4	0.6 (2013)
Maldives	4.1	3.3	4.3	7.4	5.5	5.7	1.0	1.9	6.4
Nepal[f]	0.9	1.5	1.4	2.4	3.9	3.8	0.9	0.8	0.7
Sri Lanka	1.6	1.2	1.6	2.4	1.6	2.0	2.8	1.7	2.1
Southeast Asia									
Brunei Darussalam[g]	2.1	1.8	1.5 (2012)	4.2	3.6	3.0 (2012)	1.2	0.8	0.6 (2012)
Cambodia	0.9	1.3	1.5 (2013)	1.3	1.6	1.8 (2013)	0.2	0.5	0.7 (2013)
Indonesia	0.3 (2001)	...	...	0.8 (2001)	...	...	...	...	...
Lao PDR[h]	1.0	...	...	1.0	...	...	...	...	...
Malaysia	1.5	2.0	2.0	5.6	6.1	5.0	0.9	1.2	1.0
Myanmar	...	...	...	...	...	...	...	...	...
Philippines	0.4	0.3	0.7	3.3	2.5	3.4	0.7	0.5	1.9
Singapore[d]	0.9	1.1	1.8 (2014)	3.9	3.0	3.0 (2014)	0.6	1.1	1.6 (2014)
Thailand[h]	1.3	1.9	1.2	3.9	4.1	3.8	0.9	1.7	2.1
Viet Nam	...	...	...	...	...	...	...	...	...
The Pacific									
Cook Islands[e]	3.1	3.3	3.0 (2013)	3.2	4.9	5.0 (2013)	...	...	...
Fiji	2.3	2.1	2.1	4.3	3.5	3.2	0.1	0.1	0.1
Kiribati	7.6	8.6	7.7 (2012)	11.0	10.1	10.4 (2012)	0.9	1.6	1.4 (2012)
Marshall Islands	...	...	...	...	...	...	...	...	...
Micronesia, Fed. States of	...	...	...	...	...	...	...	...	...
Nauru	...	...	...	...	...	...	...	...	...
Palau	...	...	...	...	...	...	...	...	...
Papua New Guinea	1.6	...	...	5.1	...	...	...	...	...
Samoa[e]	4.0	3.7	5.2	4.9	4.3	4.3	1.1	1.2	2.0
Solomon Islands	...	...	...	...	...	...	...	...	...
Timor-Leste	0.8 (2004)	0.8	1.5 (2014)	1.3 (2004)	1.6	2.9 (2014)	– (2004)	3.3	3.3 (2014)
Tonga[e]	4.8	...	...	4.4	...	...	...	...	...
Tuvalu	...	...	...	...	...	...	...	...	...
Vanuatu	2.4	2.0 (2007)	...	4.9	4.7 (2007)	...	0.0	...	...
Developed Member Economies									
Australia[e]	3.9	4.0	4.1	1.6	2.8	1.9	8.6	8.4	9.1
Japan[d]	6.3	6.8	7.4 (2014)	3.9	3.1	3.1 (2014)	10.6	17.0	17.7 (2014)
New Zealand[i]	5.6	7.1	7.0	5.2	6.8	6.3	12.4	12.6	11.8

... = data not available at cutoff date, 0.0 = magnitude is less than half of unit employed, GDP = gross domestic product, Lao PDR = Lao People's Democratic Republic.

a Data refer to central government, except for Georgia, Japan, the Kyrgyz Republic, Mongolia, and Tajikistan, where data refer to consolidated government or general government. For the People's Republic of China, data refer to consolidated central, provincial, and local governments. For Australia, data refer to the Commonwealth government.
b Data for social security and welfare include defense.
c Prior to 2010, education expenditure data include health and education expenditures.
d Data are based on fiscal year beginning 1 April.
e Data are based on fiscal year ending 30 June.
f Data are based on fiscal year ending 15 July.
g Data for 2005 onward are based on fiscal year beginning 1 April.
h Data are based on fiscal year ending 30 September.
i Data for 2000–2005 are based on fiscal year ending 31 March, while data for 2010 onward are based on fiscal year ending 30 June.

Source: Economy sources.

Table 8.6:   **Doing Business Start-Up Indicators**

Regional Member	Cost of Business Start-Up Procedure (% of GNI per capita)			Time Required to Start Up Business (days)		
	2005	2010	2015	2005	2010	2015
Developing Member Economies						
Central and West Asia[a]	**27.9**	**11.3**	**6.8**	**39**	**12**	**7**
Afghanistan	75.2	26.7	19.0	9	7	7
Armenia	6.1	3.1	1.0	18	14	3
Azerbaijan	12.3	3.1	1.2	113	8	3
Georgia	13.7	5.0	3.1	21	3	2
Kazakhstan	8.6	1.0	0.1	25	19	5
Kyrgyz Republic	10.4	3.7	2.1	21	14	10
Pakistan	...	...	9.4	...	...	19
Tajikistan	85.1	36.9	21.5	79	16	11
Turkmenistan	...	...	...	...	...	...
Uzbekistan	11.5	10.8	3.4	29	15	7
East Asia[a]	**8.3**	**6.0**	**4.0**	**27**	**12**	**11**
China, People's Rep. of	...	...	0.7	...	...	31
Hong Kong, China	3.4	2.0	1.2	11	6	2
Korea, Rep. of	15.7	14.7	14.5	17	14	4
Mongolia	9.6	3.2	1.5	13	13	6
Taipei,China	4.4	4.0	2.1	65	15	10
South Asia[a]	**37.1**	**24.0**	**13.9**	**37**	**31**	**17**
Bangladesh	...	...	13.9	...	...	20
Bhutan	16.9	6.1	4.0	62	46	15
India	...	...	13.5	...	...	29
Maldives	11.5	9.4	4.9	9	9	9
Nepal	69.9	46.6	28.4	31	31	17
Sri Lanka	50.0	33.9	18.7	46	38	10
Southeast Asia[a]	**48.7**	**40.8**	**23.7**	**60**	**52**	**32**
Brunei Darussalam	8.9 (2006)	13.7	1.2	121 (2006)	108	14
Cambodia	276.1	127.5	78.7	87	102	87
Indonesia	...	...	19.9	...	...	48
Lao PDR	17.4	8.9	4.9	108	63	73
Malaysia	26.6	17.5	6.7	37	17	4
Myanmar	...	157.7 (2012)	97.1	...	74 (2012)	13
Philippines	23.9	22.1	16.1	47	37	29
Singapore	0.9	0.7	0.6	6	3	3
Thailand	8.1	6.9	6.4	33	32	28
Viet Nam	27.6	12.1	4.9	42	36	20
The Pacific[a]	**59.4**	**37.1**	**30.3**	**47**	**39**	**26**
Cook Islands	...	...	...	...	...	...
Fiji	28.4	23.8	21.3	44	44	58
Kiribati	40.3	47.1	46.0	31	31	31
Marshall Islands	22.4	17.6	12.7	17	17	17
Micronesia, Fed. States of	127.6	137.8	141.1	16	16	16
Nauru	...	...	...	...	...	...
Palau	4.7	5.7	3.3	24	28	28
Papua New Guinea	27.7	27.0	17.3	52	52	53
Samoa	46.4	9.8	8.0	35	9	9
Solomon Islands	135.5	78.5	31.4	55	55	9
Timor-Leste	125.4	5.7	0.3	167	110	9
Tonga	11.7	7.0	7.8	32	25	16
Tuvalu	...	...	...	...	...	...
Vanuatu	83.5	48.2	44.2	47	47	35
Developed Member Economies[a]	**1.1**	**0.6**	**2.8**	**8**	**2**	**4**
Australia	1.9	0.7	0.7	3	3	3
Japan	...	...	7.5	...	...	10
New Zealand	0.2	0.4	0.3	12	1	1
DEVELOPING MEMBER ECONOMIES[a]	**41.4**	**27.4**	**17.9**	**45**	**33**	**20**
REGIONAL MEMBERS[a]	**39.2**	**26.0**	**16.9**	**43**	**31**	**19**
WORLD	**82.7**	**44.4**	**26.1**	**50**	**34**	**20**

... = data not available at cutoff date, GNI = gross national income, Lao PDR = Lao People's Democratic Republic.

a   Arithmetic average of reporting economies only.

Source: World Bank. Doing Business Online. http://data.worldbank.org/indicator (accessed 8 June 2016).

Table 8.7:   **Corruption Perceptions Index**[a]

Regional Member	2000	2005	2010	2011	2012	2013	2014	2015	Rank in 2014[b]	Rank in 2015[b]
Developing Member Economies										
Central and West Asia										
Afghanistan	...	2.5	1.4	1.5	8	8	12	11	172	166
Armenia	2.5	2.9	2.6	2.6	34	36	37	35	94	95
Azerbaijan	1.5	2.2	2.4	2.4	27	28	29	29	126	119
Georgia	2.4 (2002)	2.3	3.8	4.1	52	49	52	52	50	48
Kazakhstan	3.0	2.6	2.9	2.7	28	26	29	28	126	123
Kyrgyz Republic	...	2.3	2.0	2.1	24	24	27	28	136	123
Pakistan	2.3 (2001)	2.1	2.3	2.5	27	28	29	30	126	117
Tajikistan	...	2.1	2.1	2.3	22	22	23	26	152	136
Turkmenistan	...	1.8	1.6	1.6	17	17	17	18	169	154
Uzbekistan	2.4	2.2	1.6	1.6	17	17	18	19	166	153
East Asia										
China, People's Rep. of	3.1	3.2	3.5	3.6	39	40	36	37	100	83
Hong Kong, China	7.7	8.3	8.4	8.4	77	75	74	75	17	18
Korea, Rep. of	4.0	5.0	5.4	5.4	56	55	55	56	43	37
Mongolia	...	3.0	2.7	2.7	36	38	39	39	80	72
Taipei,China	5.5	5.9	5.8	6.1	61	61	61	62	35	30
South Asia										
Bangladesh	0.4 (2001)	1.7	2.4	2.7	26	27	25	25	145	139
Bhutan	...	6.0 (2006)	5.7	5.7	63	63	65	65	30	27
India	2.8	2.9	3.3	3.1	36	36	38	38	85	76
Maldives	...	3.3 (2007)	2.3	2.5	...	...	...	...	...	...
Nepal	...	2.5	2.2	2.2	27	31	29	27	126	130
Sri Lanka	3.7 (2002)	3.2	3.2	3.3	40	37	38	37	85	83
Southeast Asia										
Brunei Darussalam	...	...	5.5	5.2	55	60	...	...	...	...
Cambodia	...	2.3	2.1	2.1	22	20	21	21	156	150
Indonesia	1.7	2.2	2.8	3.0	32	32	34	36	107	88
Lao PDR	...	3.3	2.1	2.2	21	26	25	25	145	139
Malaysia	4.8	5.1	4.4	4.3	49	50	52	50	50	54
Myanmar	...	1.8	1.4	1.5	15	21	21	22	156	147
Philippines	2.8	2.5	2.4	2.6	34	36	38	35	85	95
Singapore	9.1	9.4	9.3	9.2	87	86	84	85	7	8
Thailand	3.2	3.8	3.5	3.4	37	35	38	38	85	76
Viet Nam	2.5	2.6	2.7	2.9	31	31	31	31	119	112
The Pacific										
Cook Islands	...	...	...	...	...	...	...	...	...	...
Fiji	...	4.0	...	...	...	...	...	...	...	...
Kiribati	...	3.3 (2007)	3.2	3.1	...	...	...	...	...	...
Marshall Islands	...	...	...	...	...	...	...	...	...	...
Micronesia, Fed. States of	...	...	...	...	...	...	...	...	...	...
Nauru	...	...	...	...	...	...	...	...	...	...
Palau	...	...	...	...	...	...	...	...	...	...
Papua New Guinea	...	2.3	2.1	2.2	25	25	25	25	145	139
Samoa	...	4.5 (2007)	4.1	3.9	...	...	52	...	50	...
Solomon Islands	...	2.8 (2007)	2.8	2.7	...	...	...	...	...	...
Timor-Leste	...	2.6 (2006)	2.5	2.4	33	30	28	28	133	123
Tonga	...	1.7 (2007)	3.0	3.1	...	...	...	...	...	...
Tuvalu	...	...	...	...	...	...	...	...	...	...
Vanuatu	...	3.1 (2007)	3.6	3.5	...	...	...	...	...	...
Developed Member Economies										
Australia	8.3	8.8	8.7	8.8	85	81	80	79	11	13
Japan	6.4	7.3	7.8	8.0	74	74	76	75	15	18
New Zealand	9.4	9.6	9.3	9.5	90	91	91	88	2	4

... = data not available at cutoff date, Lao PDR = Lao People's Democratic Republic.

a For 2000–2011, score relates to perceptions of the degree of corruption as seen by business people and country analysts, and ranges from 10 (highly clean) to 0 (highly corrupt). From 2012 onward, computation of the score used an updated methodology and is now presented on a scale from 100 (very clean) to 0 (highly corrupt). Scores from 2011 and previous editions should not be compared with scores from 2012 onward.

b The highest rank is the most clean, while the lowest rank is the most corrupt; 2014 is based on 175 economies and 2015 is based on 168 economies.

Source: Transparency International. Corruption Perceptions Index 2015. https://www.transparency.org/cpi2015/#results-table (accessed 2 June 2016).

PART III
Global Value Chains

Asia's Evolving Role in International Production-Sharing Arrangements: Reemergence of the Local Market

In 2015, international trade declined significantly across the globe, particularly in value terms, raising concerns about stagnant economic growth. However, the gross domestic product (GDP) in developing Asia grew steadily, except in a number of commodity-dependent economies, due to strong domestic consumption and investment, possibly indicating a trend toward localization of the market. Data on international production-sharing arrangements studied through the internationally articulated input–output (IO) economics framework point to the development and maturation of local value chains (LVCs). Further, the local role in global value chains (GVCs) progressed notably, with economies in developing Asia increasingly engaging in more value-adding activities. With technological advancements continuing to bridge the time–space gap and economic growth propelling higher-valued demand, the geographic orientation and product orientation of economic activities are also evolving. The statistics and analysis presented in this chapter provide greater insights into the evolving dynamics of global production sharing. The study covers 13 Asian economies: Bangladesh, the People's Republic of China (PRC); India; Indonesia; Japan; the Republic of Korea; Malaysia; Mongolia; the Philippines; Sri Lanka; Taipei,China; Thailand; and Viet Nam. [1]

Value-added Exports of Selected Asian Economies

Domestic value added in gross exports, principally measured as the unduplicated domestic value added embedded in an economy's export that remains abroad—termed VAX_G by Wang, Wei, and Zhu

(2014)—increased in 11 of the 13 economies during 2011–2015 (Table 3.2f), Malaysia and Viet Nam being the exceptions to the trend due to specific economic factors.[2] The PRC augmented its value-added share in the exports of all the five aggregate sectors (primary, low-technology manufacturing, medium- and high-technology manufacturing, business services, and personal services). The trends over 2000–2015 are indicative of the PRC's evolving role in the world economy. From the turn of the 21st century, domestic shares declined steadily (from 82% in 2000 to 75% in 2008) as the economy's productive processes increasingly integrated, directly or indirectly, into various GVCs. However, the 2008 global financial crisis (GFC) had a nearly universal reversal effect on the international sharing and geographical dispersion of production activities. Consequently, the PRC has gradually been increasing its value added in the exports of every sector since 2008, with the overall share surpassing 81% in 2015. The trend is indicative of the economy deepening and enhancing its involvement in various GVCs by localizing additional, often higher-value-adding, stages of globally shared production processes. Of particular interest for economic policy making is the trend in the medium- and high-technology manufacturing sector where the expanding domestic share of value added in exports, from 65% in 2005 to 76% in 2015, was due to the economy moving up the value chains by engaging in greater value-adding activities requiring higher-skilled labor.

The economies of Indonesia, Malaysia, and Thailand exhibited very similar movements over the 2000–2015 period with domestic value added steadily increasing in the exports of the primary and manufacturing sectors (Tables 3.2a–3.2c). The 1997 Asian financial crisis set in motion a series of public and private sector reactions and decisions that resulted in greater localization of productive activities. In addition, the PRC's entry into

[1] The data presented in this chapter are not official statistics. Production and trade data from varied sources were integrated into the input–output economic framework and adjusted as required to respect specific macroeconomic concepts. As such, data and statistics presented herein could differ from relevant official statistics.

[2] For a detailed exposition on the trade in value-added concepts and methods, refer to ADB (2015).

international production networks led to a major realignment in the location of production processes participating in GVCs due to specific relative factor endowment advantages such as lower-cost labor and easier access to markets. Consequently, in these economies the movement toward localization seems to have commenced as early as in 2000, especially in the industries in the medium- and high-technology manufacturing sector, the GVCs of which already had significant local components. Although Malaysia's value-added share in the exports of the low-tech manufacturing sector was increasing up to 2011 (from 62% in 2000 to 71%), it declined to pre-2000 levels (61%) by 2015 largely due to relocation of segments of the production processes to the PRC.

In these three economies, as well as in the PRC, services exports (Tables 3.2d and 3.2e) continue to be concentrated around traditional sectors such as distributive trades, transportation, hotels, and restaurants, which tend to have high domestic value-added shares, despite increasing orientation toward business processing and information and communication technology (ICT) services that are components of GVCs. However, of particular interest is the strong growth seen in the exports of services such as health care (e.g., from $1 billion in 2011 to $6 billion in 2015 in the PRC, and $2.5 billion to $5.6 billion in Thailand) and education ($0.9 billion to $2 billion in the PRC and $0.2 billion to $0.6 billion in Thailand). Although these services conventionally require very high levels of domestic inputs, and are hence less amenable to be readily integrated into global production networks, the growth in gross exports points to greater globalization of the consumption of the products which often is a precursor to the development of particular GVCs with the entry or greater integration of the concerned economy into international supply chains.

The advanced economies—Japan; the Republic of Korea; and Taipei,China—have exhibited comparable movements in all the sectors since 2000. The economies' share of value added in exports

declined until the GFC period (2008–2009), but the trend has reversed since then. In the manufacturing sectors, Japan's value-added share has always been relatively high (above 80%) due to its well established industrial ecosystem that enables the economy to participate in specific GVCs in multiple interlinked and consecutive stages. The shares of the other two economies are comparatively low (generally below 70%) since they specialize in specific segments of select GVCs (e.g., electronic integrated circuit manufacturing). Whether the shares were increasing due to the economies localizing additional stages of given GVCs or due to changes in relative prices of various components of the exported products needs to be studied further especially in light of the declining trend in the producer price index (PPI) in recent years.

The same frame of analysis can be extended to the industries in the primary sector of the advanced economies since the observed trends are similar to those seen in the manufacturing sector. Domestic value added in service sector exports too followed the same trend path, although the year-over-year differences were less stark in nonbusiness services (categorized as "personal services") that generally had high domestic value-added shares (above 85%) over the years. Data also show that the Republic of Korea and Taipei,China enlarged not only their exports of business services but also the domestic content therein. The trend is notable especially in transportation (the Republic of Korea) and ICT (Taipei,China). Given that Japan's domestic value-added shares in exports have been among the highest in the world in almost all the sectors (at least 80%) over the years, the contention whether Japan's industries have already reached their potential in benefiting from participating in GVCs in the current global supply and demand environment, and technological paradigm, needs to be studied further.

The primary sector in Bangladesh, India, and Sri Lanka remain heavily localized with the pure domestic content accounting for well over 85% of the exports; indeed, in almost all years, the shares were higher than 90% in India and Bangladesh. Input–output analysis shows that the industries in the primary sector of these economies tend to be upstream in value chains, whether GVCs or LVCs. In India, the record GDP growth experienced over the last 5 years despite a generally declining trend in exports indicates that the outputs of the primary industries are increasingly being channeled to meet growing local consumption and investment demand, and that the economy is effectively getting insulated from variations in the external environment due to a robust domestic demand market. Bangladesh bucked the global trend by increasing its primary sector exports (from $0.64 billion in 2011 to $1.07 billion in 2015) while decreasing its value-added share (from 90% to 88%), indicating a definite movement toward the sector's integration into certain GVCs.

The domestic value-added shares in manufacturing exports have been increasing steadily in all the three South Asian economies. That Indian manufacturing industries are broadening and deepening their role in GVCs is evidenced by the magnitude of the increase in the domestic value-added share (through multiple intermediate inputs) in exports, from 68% in 2008 to 83% in the low-tech sectors and from 74% to 85% in the medium- and high-technology sector. However, data show that manufacturing exports declined between 2014 and 2015 and domestic content in exports increased at a time when GDP growth was strong, signifying a trend toward the development of technology LVCs. A comprehensive analysis is required to determine whether these movements in India's manufacturing are the results of the natural maturation of the sector in a robust economy or the consequences of major policy initiatives.

Bangladesh saw similar trends in the low-tech manufacturing sector largely due to its textile industry's gradually deepening involvement in the garment GVCs. The country's value-added share in its medium- and high-technology sector exports increased markedly from 57% in 2008 to 81% in 2015 signifying the sector's movement up the GVCs by localizing higher-value-adding activities. Input–output economic analysis shows that the high-tech sector, albeit relatively nascent and small, could play a significant role in the country's export diversification and economic diversification initiatives. Likewise, the 23-percentage-point increase (from 42% to 65%) realized in Sri Lanka's value-added share in its rising medium- and high-technology sector exports since 2008 indicates the sector's potential in catalyzing future economic growth in the country. Input–output data show that the production of services exports of the South Asian economies is highly localized and is becoming more entrenched domestically. Even India's ICT sector exports included only less than 10%, in value terms, foreign-produced components at any point in time since 2000.

Even as Viet Nam's exports increased, its economy wide value-added share has declined notably since 2011 (from 69% to 66%, in 2015). In particular, the shares in the primary and low-tech manufacturing sectors, which account for most of Viet Nam's exports, have been declining since 2000. As discussed earlier, the simultaneous occurrence of these two trends signifies the gradual integration into GVCs of the sectors, or their specific subsectors. Even in the medium- and high-technology manufacturing sector, the economy's value-added share remained relatively low (about 60% or less) throughout 2000–2015 while sector exports increased rather dramatically. Input–output economic analysis reveals that initially, even though the PRC was a major trading partner, participation of businesses in Viet Nam in international production-sharing arrangements was heavily oriented toward developed-economy-centric GVCs. Gradually, as the principal developing economies of the region (the PRC, India, Indonesia, Thailand, etc.) expanded, Viet Nam became an important link in a number of Asia-centric regional and subregional value chains.

The country's value-added share remained high (generally above 80%) in services exports, which increased remarkably between 2000 and 2015 (from $3 billion to $26 billion). Although most of the services exports were attributable to traditional sectors such as distributive trades, tourism, and transportation, modern services such as information and communication, finance, and business processing are emerging as important export sectors that hold the potential for greater involvement in various GVCs and contribute further to the economy's growth. Analysis indicates that Viet Nam's relative factor endowment advantages in labor, access to markets, economic infrastructure, technical capacity, etc. are likely to propel its participation in international production-sharing arrangements.

Mongolia's primary sector, essentially the mining and quarrying industry, has accounted for most of its exports since 2000 (45% in 2000 and 70% in 2015). Among the manufacturing sectors, commodity-processing industries and textiles contributed notably to the country's exports. Distributive trades, tourism, land transportation, and equipment rentals were the major contributing services industries. Although Mongolia's value-added shares in the primary and manufacturing sector exports are generally less than 80%, the country's industries are quite upstream in every GVC that they are part of. Intermediates and machinery were imported mainly to support the production processes in Mongolia rather than to be incorporated into any product as components. Services exports were generally aligned with the primary and manufacturing sector outputs in that they were provided to foreign sectors in order to get the outputs to the intermediate product markets or the transportation hubs. Analysis indicates that moving up the value chains would require the concerned sectors to develop the appropriate economic infrastructure to localize more higher-value-adding components of the GVCs.

Exports from the Philippines grew significantly until the onset of the 2008 GFC while the country's value-added share declined from 80% (2000) to about 67% (2008) indicating increasing participation in certain major GVCs. The trends were driven primarily by the electrical and optical equipment manufacturing industry in the medium- and high-technology sector. In fact, in almost every other industry, the value-added share was notably high (above 80% or even 90%) and generally stable between 2000 and 2015. The medium- and high-technology manufacturing sector's share decreased from 77% to 48% between 2000 and 2008 while its exports grew from $17 billion to $32 billion. Since then, this sector's exports notably declined, reaching $19 billion in 2015 while the value-added share grew to 75%, definitely scaling back the country's participation in the relevant GVCs. Input–output economic analysis suggests that during the period of export growth and increasing participation in high-tech GVCs, at a certain level in the production processes, spillover effects in terms of the development of local supply chains to systematically support the GVCs were not realized to any significant degree. However, the effect of the lack of industrial agglomeration on the observed trend needs to be studied further.

Growth in the Philippines' business services exports has been quite strong since 2000. Propelled by the expanding business processing, tourism, and transportation industries, services exports reached $25 billion in 2015. The country's value-added share has been quite high (over 90%) in services exports, underlining the highly localized nature of the production processes. The ICT and finance services, although relatively small, display the potential to participate in certain GVCs. It should be noted that while the Philippines' exports have slowed in recent years, its GDP has grown at a healthy rate of about 6%, averaged annually, since 2010, underlining the significance of the local demand market in the expansion of the economy.

As noted earlier, the decline in exports and GVC participation even as the developing economies continue to post strong growth should indicate the development and strengthening of LVCs, an eventuality that can also be evidenced by strong domestic inter-sectoral backward and forward linkages—from the primary industries to the final consumer markets discernible through the input–output economics framework. From a value-added trade or trade in value added (TiVA) perspective, the strengthening local linkages should also result in higher indirect exports through forward and backward linkage measures (Box 3.1). The next section discusses the indicators of the evolution of domestic inter-sectoral linkages that facilitate the formation of sustainable LVCs.

Direct and Indirect Value-added Exports and the Localization of Production Processes

The PRC's primary sector has been in a relatively upstream segment of the value chains with the backward-linked indirect exports accounting for 26%–30% of the sector's total during 2000–2015 (Table 3.3a)[3]. However, the magnitude of the indicator points to a certain degree of sophistication with the sector using intermediates from manufacturing industries such as chemicals, fuels, electricity, and low- and high-tech equipment. The sector also made considerable use of the distributive trades, transportation, and even ICT services. The high (nearly 90%) proportion of forward-linked indirect exports not only underlines the centrality of the sector to various value chains emanating or passing through the PRC but also provides a quantitative depiction of the economy's relatively strong involvement in those value chains at multiple levels. Generally similar trends were seen in the Republic of Korea and, to a lesser extent, in Thailand and the Philippines.

Data show that Mongolia, Sri Lanka, and Viet Nam exported their primary products more or less directly indicating that the subsequent components of the value chains were not localized.

---

[3]   The summary analysis in this section is mainly focused on the primary sector. However, detailed statistics and economic analysis can be produced for any of the industries using the IO economics framework and the export decomposition framework of Wang, Wei, and Zhu (2014).

Box 3.1: Indicators of Localization

Gross measures of exports include all the constituent components of the exported product, including imported intermediates, the benefits (or "income" or "value") of producing which accrues to where it originated. Any value received by the exporting economy that is attributable and apportionable to such imported components is countered by a value equal in magnitude paid by the economy to their producers. Thus, the import contents of exports are excluded in the value-added measures. For further exposition, these newer estimation methods view exports of value from two angles: the total value produced in an economy embedded in a given exported product (backward linkage approach), and the total domestically generated value attributable to a product that is also used in the economy's production of other exported goods and services (forward linkage method).

In the backward linkage approach, the values attributable to domestic intermediates embedded in the exported product are treated as indirect exports whereas in the forward linkage method the domestically produced value of a product embedded in other goods and services produced and exported by the economy is counted as indirect exports. In both the approaches, the value added (income accruing to labor, capital, government, and the entrepreneurial input) to the economy exclusively by its undertaking the processes to produce the specific good or service is defined as direct exports.

For any given sector, the magnitude of the proportion of backward-linked indirect value-added exports provides a reasonable proxy measure of the sophistication or complexity of the local supply chains supporting its production processes. Similarly, the proportion of indirect exports via forward linkages serves to quantify the criticality of the sector to the production processes of the economy. Taken together these measures provide an indication of the degree of localization or strength of the local value chains, or the local segment of the global value chains that include the sector. This type of analysis is meaningful only at the sector level since the total indirect exports estimated using both the approaches will be equal at the economy level. It should be noted that given the highly aggregated data used, only broad and qualified inferences can be made through the current analysis.

Forward-linked export trends indicate that over the years India and Indonesia have domesticated certain processes that principally use primary products. The respective primary sector in these two economies was also less reliant on other sectors, as depicted by the relatively low backward-linked export proportions. Meanwhile, the higher figures (50%) seen in Japan over the years point to the complexity and sophistication of the production processes in its primary sector with intermediates provisioned from multiple manufacturing and services industries.

Analyzing together the high forward- and backward-linked proportions, it can be discerned that Japan's primary sector has been part of a number of complex and higher-value GVCs, significant portions of which are highly localized. The declining backward-linked export proportion in Taipei,China is indicative of possible offshoring of certain stages of the value chains, perhaps due to changes in the relative factor endowment advantages of the economies in the region. Data indicate that Malaysia has increasingly been localizing productive processes using its primary outputs. The relatively high forward-linked proportion in Bangladesh is due to the primary sector's intermediate contribution to the country's export-oriented textile industry, and the increases in the backward-linked exports are largely due to the sector's increasing reliance on distributive trade and transportation services.

With the statistics presented in Tables 3.3a–3.3f, the preceding analysis can be extended to other sectors in the economies being analyzed. In the low-tech manufacturing sector, the proportion of backward-linked indirect exports has generally been growing since 2000 in every economy except Bangladesh and Mongolia, suggesting increasing localization of upstream activities. The forward-linked indirect export proportion was also rising in all the economies except for Bangladesh, Japan, and the PRC—the decline in the latter two could possibly be attributed to offshoring of certain downstream processes to other emerging economies in the region. The trends in Bangladesh were driven by the increasing concentration of resources in the textile sector.

Data suggest that as far as the medium- and high-technology manufacturing sector is concerned, many of the economies have progressively been

localizing both upstream and downstream activities. Relevant proportions for Sri Lanka, however, have been fairly stagnant since 2005, denoting the medium- and high-technology sector as a possibly focus area in future economic reform and growth strategies. In the business services sector, a gradual localization of upstream and downstream processes is distinctly evident from the data related to Bangladesh; the PRC; Indonesia; the Republic of Korea; Mongolia; Sri Lanka; Taipei,China; and Viet Nam; while the trends in India, Japan, Malaysia, the Philippines, and Thailand point to the increasing concentration on specific subsectors (such as ICT in India and business processing in the Philippines). An inclination toward gradual localization is discernible from the data on the PRC's personal services sector; however, Japan; the Republic of Korea; and Taipei,China displayed an indication of offshoring of productive processes in the sector.

While localizing additional consecutive productive processes in a value chain increases an economy's income, it could lead to reduced participation (based on standard conventional measures) in GVCs, unless, in consequence, the products enter the economy more than once for processing. The vertical specialization (VS) index and its components related to the various industries of an economy provide additional information to sketch their evolving roles in international production-sharing arrangements. The ensuing section discusses the relevant statistics.

Indicators of Global Value Chain Participation and Trends in Localization

The vertical specialization index is composed of the foreign value added (FVA) embedded in an industry's or a sector's output for final or intermediate consumption and the domestic and FVA portions double-counted due to a product entering an economy more than once for processing (Tables 3.5a–3.5e show the vertical specialization index by economy–industry for the years 2000, 2005, 2008, 2011, and

2015; and the vertical specialization disaggregated by principal components for select industries are given in Tables 3.6a–3.6m. Tables 3.7a–3.7d show the changes in the index over the years).

Data show that between 2000 and 2005, GVC entry or participation of many industries in Bangladesh; the PRC; India; Japan; the Republic of Korea; Taipei,China; and Thailand increased notably. In fact, the participation of almost all the major industries in the PRC; Japan; Taipei,China; and Thailand showed rather significant increases. Indonesia's primary and manufacturing industries (except fuel production) and transportation services; certain manufacturing industries in Malaysia and the Philippines; agriculture, food production, and wood products in Viet Nam; and several industries in Sri Lanka also increased their GVC participation. Analysis of input–output and value-decomposed export data show that the trend was primarily, if not almost entirely, caused by increased import contents (FVA_INT-FVA in intermediate exports, FVA_FIN – FVA in exports for final consumption, and FDC – FVA double counted in exports as the products enter the economy more than once for processing; see Tables 3.6a–3.6m) in the exports of these sectors. Since 2005 and up until the GFC, many economic sectors continued to increase their participation.

It is noteworthy that while Viet Nam's industries increased their participation during this period, the sectors in the PRC and, to a lesser extent, Indonesia started to scale back, indicating the onset of a trend toward localizing certain production stages. The fallout of the GFC on GVC participation is quite evident in Table 3.7c. The patterns seen in Mongolia are largely reflective of an economy growing at a healthy rate and the consequent development of local industries gradually reducing their reliance on imports.

Since the GFC, all the developing economies studied as well as the Republic of Korea and Taipei,China have seen steady GDP growth. However,

as shown in Table 3.7d, industries in many of the economies analyzed have continued to scale down their participation in GVCs, in effect reducing the import content in their exports. The trends in vertical specialization statistics and the data from the input–output tables corroborate the analysis presented above on the increasing localization of productive processes in many economies in Asia. The deduction is further strengthened by the increases seen in the revealed comparative advantage (RCA) index, derived through the forward-linked value-added approach (Table 3.4), in certain sectors of a number of economies since 2000. Besides the traditional interpretation, an increasing revealed comparative advantage index (especially as measured by the value-added method) for any given sector of an economy could also indicate that the economy is increasing its value-added export of the sector relative to that of the rest of the world by domesticating or localizing additional value-creating production processes at the cost of the rest of the world.

Summary

A comprehensive analysis of the international production and trade data, using the input–output economics framework and the Wang, Wei, and Zhu (2014) export decomposition framework, points to a strong tendency in many Asian economies to utilize domestic markets for growth. The uncertainty created by the 2008 GFC followed by the increasing domestic demand for goods and services due to robust growth and rising domestic income could be deduced as the catalyzing factors for this phenomenon. Consequently, local production processes and resources in many economies were channeled toward meeting increasing local demand. Further, economies started to localize additional stages of the production processes both upstream and downstream, thereby increasing their domestic value added and, therefore, their income. These developments related to both the intermediate and final products have led to the decline in gross trade, as well as value-added trade, experienced internationally in recent years.

Consequently, economies' participation in various GVCs has decreased rather significantly.

The increase in demand propelled by local consumption and local investment decisions and the diversion of domestic resources to meet domestic demand have been creating LVCs with the result that the supply and demand chains have been showing a tendency to gravitate toward, and converge in, local markets. Further, the evolving relative factor endowment among the economies in the region is also causing a geographic realignment of the production chains, resulting in very dynamic global trade and supply patterns that have direct implication for the growth of developing Asia. Thus, the evolution of value chains in the dynamic modern local and global environment needs to be studied systematically and comprehensively to make effective and efficient economic and policy decisions.

References

Asian Development Bank (ADB). 2015. Part IV - Global Value Chains: Indicators for International Production Sharing. In *Key Indicators for Asia and the Pacific 2015*. Manila.

Z. Wang, S. Wei, and K. Zhu. 2014. Quantifying International Production Sharing at the Bilateral and Sector Levels. *NBER Working Paper*. No. 19677. Cambridge, MA: National Bureau of Economic Research.

Table 3.1a: Value-Added Decomposition of Exports – Primary Sector

		Exports	VAX_G	RDV_B	FVA	PDC	VAX_G	RDV_B	FVA	PDC
			($ million)				(% share in exports)			
PRC	2000	10,913.96	9,946.62	128.73	650.69	187.92	91.14	1.18	5.96	1.72
	2005	20,989.37	18,111.95	464.92	1,583.78	828.72	86.29	2.22	7.55	3.95
	2008	25,091.04	21,687.91	534.51	1,901.69	966.93	86.44	2.13	7.58	3.85
	2011	34,237.15	29,729.82	967.05	2,410.87	1,129.41	86.83	2.82	7.04	3.30
	2015	44,928.07	40,781.84	804.36	2,472.07	869.80	90.77	1.79	5.50	1.94
Indonesia	2000	10,794.33	10,287.98	51.94	327.13	127.29	95.31	0.48	3.03	1.18
	2005	21,998.21	20,432.30	122.97	921.95	520.99	92.88	0.56	4.19	2.37
	2008	36,871.59	34,642.99	212.69	1,226.35	789.55	93.96	0.58	3.33	2.14
	2011	65,323.49	61,875.07	615.20	1,787.21	1,046.02	94.72	0.94	2.74	1.60
	2015	39,882.12	38,398.16	340.34	724.94	418.68	96.28	0.85	1.82	1.05
India	2000	8,241.66	7,943.73	10.14	233.39	54.39	96.39	0.12	2.83	0.66
	2005	14,571.58	13,866.36	55.83	458.66	190.73	95.16	0.38	3.15	1.31
	2008	21,706.11	20,494.45	117.89	720.65	373.12	94.42	0.54	3.32	1.72
	2011	28,737.83	27,503.22	171.00	753.22	310.38	95.70	0.60	2.62	1.08
	2015	21,172.38	20,030.89	176.76	730.52	234.21	94.61	0.83	3.45	1.11
Japan	2000	2,242.99	1,872.27	57.42	222.37	90.93	83.47	2.56	9.91	4.05
	2005	2,957.53	2,133.47	51.59	518.49	253.97	72.14	1.74	17.53	8.59
	2008	4,797.37	2,702.73	74.15	1,263.04	757.45	56.34	1.55	26.33	15.79
	2011	5,467.05	3,155.54	67.97	1,556.38	687.17	57.72	1.24	28.47	12.57
	2015	3,133.70	2,629.77	62.44	333.59	107.90	83.92	1.99	10.65	3.44
Republic of Korea	2000	481.62	427.23	1.20	47.84	5.35	88.71	0.25	9.93	1.11
	2005	627.11	549.61	1.61	67.98	7.92	87.64	0.26	10.84	1.26
	2008	518.92	412.58	1.52	90.28	14.54	79.51	0.29	17.40	2.80
	2011	770.65	607.87	2.84	137.06	22.89	78.88	0.37	17.78	2.97
	2015	1,218.63	1,024.04	4.37	166.23	23.99	84.03	0.36	13.64	1.97
Taipei,China	2000	1,829.67	1,525.06	1.66	288.68	14.26	83.35	0.09	15.78	0.78
	2005	2,136.96	1,652.75	2.18	452.35	29.68	77.34	0.10	21.17	1.39
	2008	2,609.74	1,886.16	2.19	671.77	49.63	72.27	0.08	25.74	1.90
	2011	4,804.99	3,562.72	4.00	1,158.98	79.29	74.15	0.08	24.12	1.65
	2015	5,542.35	4,268.90	4.77	1,180.32	88.35	77.02	0.09	21.30	1.59
Bangladesh	2000	390.28	377.47	0.51	8.62	3.68	96.72	0.13	2.21	0.94
	2005	368.79	353.38	0.65	10.16	4.60	95.82	0.18	2.75	1.25
	2008	465.26	437.28	0.67	19.23	8.07	93.99	0.15	4.13	1.73
	2011	636.99	573.94	0.27	39.45	23.34	90.10	0.04	6.19	3.66
	2015	1,069.47	938.40	0.48	79.11	51.49	87.74	0.04	7.40	4.81

continued on next page

Table 3.1a: continued

Table 3.1a: Value-Added Decomposition of Exports – Primary Sector

		Exports	VAX_G	RDV_B	FVA	PDC	VAX_G	RDV_B	FVA	PDC
			($ million)				(% share in exports)			
Malaysia	2000	9,555.73	8,233.91	24.97	886.24	410.61	86.17	0.26	9.27	4.30
	2005	15,801.93	13,791.36	64.51	1,250.33	695.73	87.28	0.41	7.91	4.40
	2008	38,694.02	33,974.25	123.07	3,163.33	1,433.37	87.80	0.32	8.18	3.70
	2011	17,811.43	15,969.60	57.31	1,236.14	548.38	89.66	0.32	6.94	3.08
	2015	10,597.02	9,161.75	44.85	1,015.93	374.49	86.46	0.42	9.59	3.53
Philippines	2000	697.59	649.35	0.47	41.34	6.43	93.09	0.07	5.93	0.92
	2005	925.27	850.97	1.02	62.07	11.21	91.97	0.11	6.71	1.21
	2008	2,153.04	1,969.22	2.51	146.07	35.25	91.46	0.12	6.78	1.64
	2011	1,467.88	1,357.64	2.00	85.27	22.97	92.49	0.14	5.81	1.56
	2015	1,622.13	1,484.56	3.28	109.93	24.36	91.52	0.20	6.78	1.50
Thailand	2000	1,515.61	1,309.84	17.73	135.11	52.93	86.42	1.17	8.91	3.49
	2005	2,494.81	2,111.82	12.76	250.40	119.83	84.65	0.51	10.04	4.80
	2008	4,591.39	3,893.91	18.96	455.22	223.30	84.81	0.41	9.91	4.86
	2011	7,073.21	6,089.28	22.79	702.76	258.37	86.09	0.32	9.94	3.65
	2015	7,393.86	6,221.76	31.88	826.78	313.44	84.15	0.43	11.18	4.24
Viet Nam	2000	5,953.49	5,183.53	7.66	599.96	162.34	87.07	0.13	10.08	2.73
	2005	10,704.56	9,024.99	13.68	1,270.05	395.85	84.31	0.13	11.86	3.70
	2008	25,345.58	19,168.64	71.51	4,667.85	1,437.58	75.63	0.28	18.42	5.67
	2011	26,068.80	21,419.60	46.48	3,654.89	947.83	82.17	0.18	14.02	3.64
	2015	41,929.01	32,681.60	76.36	7,805.68	1,365.37	77.95	0.18	18.62	3.26
Mongolia	2000	184.31	139.78	0.01	32.80	11.73	75.84	0.00	17.80	6.36
	2005	708.22	549.46	0.02	106.88	51.86	77.58	0.00	15.09	7.32
	2008	1,460.71	1,157.27	0.11	193.43	109.90	79.23	0.01	13.24	7.52
	2011	3,637.57	2,333.74	0.42	872.58	430.83	64.16	0.01	23.99	11.84
	2015	3,986.99	2,856.89	0.33	775.49	354.28	71.66	0.01	19.45	8.89
Sri Lanka	2000	1,227.42	1,035.59	0.35	162.78	28.70	84.37	0.03	13.26	2.34
	2005	1,699.18	1,462.35	0.78	203.64	32.40	86.06	0.05	11.98	1.91
	2008	2,698.11	2,281.86	1.46	324.16	90.62	84.57	0.05	12.01	3.36
	2011	2,870.23	2,545.93	1.69	264.65	57.96	88.70	0.06	9.22	2.02
	2015	2,705.12	2,351.91	2.73	298.97	51.52	86.94	0.10	11.05	1.90

FVA = foreign value added, PDC = pure double counted terms, PRC = People's Republic of China, RDV_B = domestic value added first exported then returned home, VAX_G = domestic value added absorbed abroad.

Source: ADB Multi Region Input–Output Tables Database.

Table 3.1b: Value-Added Decomposition of Exports – Low-Technology Manufacturing Sector

		Exports	VAX_G	RDV_B	FVA	PDC	VAX_G	RDV_B	FVA	PDC
			($ million)				(% share in exports)			
PRC	2000	94,579.86	78,750.98	373.83	13,368.60	2,086.45	83.26	0.40	14.13	2.21
	2005	215,067.98	173,438.84	891.91	34,622.24	6,114.99	80.64	0.41	16.10	2.84
	2008	374,045.07	311,230.07	1,824.14	51,719.41	9,271.44	83.21	0.49	13.83	2.48
	2011	515,989.76	430,535.65	3,996.67	68,478.51	12,978.93	83.44	0.77	13.27	2.52
	2015	621,467.80	536,511.21	4,443.12	71,184.38	9,329.09	86.33	0.71	11.45	1.50
Indonesia	2000	25,158.01	19,788.42	24.12	4,327.26	1,018.21	78.66	0.10	17.20	4.05
	2005	29,989.11	23,450.92	40.75	5,075.61	1,421.83	78.20	0.14	16.92	4.74
	2008	49,037.44	39,148.53	96.25	7,578.07	2,214.58	79.83	0.20	15.45	4.52
	2011	64,744.94	52,009.46	157.98	9,909.58	2,667.93	80.33	0.24	15.31	4.12
	2015	72,541.82	63,891.59	175.10	7,018.26	1,456.87	88.08	0.24	9.67	2.01
India	2000	29,631.28	25,538.88	30.15	3,594.60	467.66	86.19	0.10	12.13	1.58
	2005	56,477.49	40,422.34	104.92	14,519.87	1,430.36	71.57	0.19	25.71	2.53
	2008	83,437.14	56,829.67	194.33	23,711.89	2,701.25	68.11	0.23	28.42	3.24
	2011	110,565.11	71,406.03	227.34	36,095.42	2,836.33	64.58	0.21	32.65	2.57
	2015	134,634.27	112,270.47	316.27	20,486.66	1,560.87	83.39	0.23	15.22	1.16
Japan	2000	26,831.00	24,125.38	705.94	1,418.67	581.01	89.92	2.63	5.29	2.17
	2005	37,772.16	32,816.28	864.84	2,714.53	1,376.50	86.88	2.29	7.19	3.64
	2008	48,171.52	39,357.30	836.62	5,260.78	2,716.82	81.70	1.74	10.92	5.64
	2011	59,620.72	49,198.36	942.89	6,426.33	3,053.15	82.52	1.58	10.78	5.12
	2015	53,403.95	44,357.02	711.51	6,050.96	2,284.46	83.06	1.33	11.33	4.28
Republic of Korea	2000	30,447.23	22,853.66	82.18	5,841.13	1,670.27	75.06	0.27	19.18	5.49
	2005	28,354.23	21,081.59	105.28	5,316.09	1,851.27	74.35	0.37	18.75	6.53
	2008	33,486.87	22,152.98	132.65	8,103.43	3,097.81	66.15	0.40	24.20	9.25
	2011	39,838.06	26,242.83	156.07	9,994.29	3,444.89	65.87	0.39	25.09	8.65
	2015	38,994.24	29,317.40	136.74	7,744.46	1,795.64	75.18	0.35	19.86	4.60
Taipei,China	2000	31,315.20	22,732.57	65.75	6,649.25	1,867.63	72.59	0.21	21.23	5.96
	2005	28,325.89	18,936.50	53.03	6,698.39	2,637.97	66.85	0.19	23.65	9.31
	2008	29,726.10	17,817.95	40.55	8,387.53	3,480.06	59.94	0.14	28.22	11.71
	2011	35,854.34	21,441.80	47.27	10,653.44	3,711.83	59.80	0.13	29.71	10.35
	2015	48,755.75	32,215.86	58.91	12,999.38	3,481.59	66.08	0.12	26.66	7.14
Bangladesh	2000	4,701.33	3,961.19	0.78	648.86	90.50	84.26	0.02	13.80	1.92
	2005	6,958.69	5,593.05	1.62	1,168.14	195.87	80.38	0.02	16.79	2.81
	2008	12,615.07	9,316.33	3.39	2,802.59	492.75	73.85	0.03	22.22	3.91
	2011	19,607.53	16,666.58	5.11	2,286.59	649.24	85.00	0.03	11.66	3.31
	2015	30,510.52	26,324.96	8.61	3,365.39	811.57	86.28	0.03	11.03	2.66

continued on next page

Table 3.1b: continued

Table 3.1b: Value-Added Decomposition of Exports – Low-Technology Manufacturing Sector

		Exports	VAX_G	RDV_B	FVA	PDC	VAX_G	RDV_B	FVA	PDC
			($ million)				(% share in exports)			
Malaysia	2000	16,805.50	10,375.30	14.55	5,382.34	1,033.30	61.74	0.09	32.03	6.15
	2005	20,517.30	13,448.36	20.97	5,581.00	1,466.96	65.55	0.10	27.20	7.15
	2008	21,322.33	14,212.20	23.12	5,707.24	1,379.77	66.65	0.11	26.77	6.47
	2011	46,869.96	33,454.32	45.12	10,775.36	2,595.16	71.38	0.10	22.99	5.54
	2015	45,356.51	27,736.37	48.97	14,454.02	3,117.14	61.15	0.11	31.87	6.87
Philippines	2000	5,490.79	4,605.12	1.60	806.80	77.27	83.87	0.03	14.69	1.41
	2005	8,045.10	6,732.33	3.87	1,162.48	146.42	83.68	0.05	14.45	1.82
	2008	13,948.90	11,356.21	6.52	2,289.42	296.76	81.41	0.05	16.41	2.13
	2011	10,773.78	9,365.95	5.80	1,213.13	188.91	86.93	0.05	11.26	1.75
	2015	13,682.74	11,235.74	12.04	2,133.30	301.66	82.12	0.09	15.59	2.20
Thailand	2000	26,465.20	19,096.81	44.03	6,418.15	906.21	72.16	0.17	24.25	3.42
	2005	36,019.68	24,547.81	59.98	9,494.36	1,917.54	68.15	0.17	26.36	5.32
	2008	54,289.37	38,511.34	86.24	13,179.51	2,512.28	70.94	0.16	24.28	4.63
	2011	63,118.28	46,886.88	110.32	12,893.26	3,227.82	74.28	0.17	20.43	5.11
	2015	64,780.50	46,022.94	133.81	15,090.95	3,532.79	71.04	0.21	23.30	5.45
Viet Nam	2000	4,343.19	2,697.92	0.81	1,475.08	169.38	62.12	0.02	33.96	3.90
	2005	8,645.75	5,608.67	2.40	2,635.87	398.81	64.87	0.03	30.49	4.61
	2008	15,745.78	8,441.75	13.99	6,112.63	1,177.42	53.61	0.09	38.82	7.48
	2011	29,208.94	15,966.54	20.04	11,731.22	1,491.14	54.66	0.07	40.16	5.11
	2015	46,279.82	23,039.12	29.99	21,694.44	1,516.28	49.78	0.06	46.88	3.28
Mongolia	2000	67.84	49.18	0.00	16.17	2.49	72.49	0.00	23.84	3.67
	2005	107.62	81.79	0.00	20.40	5.43	76.00	0.00	18.96	5.04
	2008	215.06	166.34	0.01	37.76	10.95	77.35	0.00	17.56	5.09
	2011	373.66	290.77	0.04	68.71	14.15	77.82	0.01	18.39	3.79
	2015	421.98	345.86	0.04	63.86	12.22	81.96	0.01	15.13	2.90
Sri Lanka	2000	3,672.90	2,651.00	0.59	890.41	130.90	72.18	0.02	24.24	3.56
	2005	4,113.75	2,582.65	0.31	1,352.59	178.19	62.78	0.01	32.88	4.33
	2008	4,818.02	4,002.94	1.31	692.33	121.44	83.08	0.03	14.37	2.52
	2011	6,363.32	5,335.08	1.11	911.04	116.09	83.84	0.02	14.32	1.82
	2015	6,826.02	6,115.95	0.62	641.81	67.65	89.60	0.01	9.40	0.99

FVA = foreign value added, PDC = pure double counted terms, PRC = People's Republic of China, RDV_B = domestic value added first exported then returned home, VAX_G = domestic value added absorbed abroad.

Source: ADB Multi Region Input–Output Tables Database.

Table 3.1c: Value-Added Decomposition of Exports – Medium- and High-Technology Manufacturing Sector

		Exports	VAX_G	RDV_B	FVA	PDC	VAX_G	RDV_B	FVA	PDC
			($ million)				(% share in exports)			
PRC	2000	126,982.80	97,604.76	1,295.32	20,919.92	7,162.80	76.86	1.02	16.47	5.64
	2005	477,551.66	310,627.16	7,351.96	116,407.32	43,165.22	65.05	1.54	24.38	9.04
	2008	972,567.61	676,699.92	17,577.00	199,616.33	78,674.36	69.58	1.81	20.52	8.09
	2011	1,252,597.72	872,687.13	30,005.43	256,930.81	92,974.35	69.67	2.40	20.51	7.42
	2015	1,269,026.06	966,810.53	34,125.23	212,349.42	55,740.88	76.19	2.69	16.73	4.39
Indonesia	2000	23,470.31	17,351.40	46.77	4,426.01	1,646.13	73.93	0.20	18.86	7.01
	2005	31,683.76	22,959.31	93.58	5,538.67	3,092.21	72.46	0.30	17.48	9.76
	2008	48,348.79	36,100.72	206.13	7,893.42	4,148.51	74.67	0.43	16.33	8.58
	2011	66,413.42	51,292.95	298.15	10,741.83	4,080.50	77.23	0.45	16.17	6.14
	2015	63,909.21	57,299.75	258.26	4,741.27	1,609.93	89.66	0.40	7.42	2.52
India	2000	21,265.62	16,259.89	49.96	3,677.46	1,278.31	76.46	0.23	17.29	6.01
	2005	47,602.78	35,856.83	313.49	7,933.64	3,498.82	75.33	0.66	16.67	7.35
	2008	89,317.52	65,590.34	549.50	16,235.85	6,941.83	73.44	0.62	18.18	7.77
	2011	121,677.35	94,578.53	490.54	20,193.02	6,415.26	77.73	0.40	16.60	5.27
	2015	138,550.42	115,745.36	576.12	18,104.65	4,124.29	83.54	0.42	13.07	2.98
Japan	2000	393,877.43	348,647.34	7,259.28	27,641.63	10,329.18	88.52	1.84	7.02	2.62
	2005	494,688.44	419,450.58	8,837.25	45,864.71	20,535.90	84.79	1.79	9.27	4.15
	2008	635,730.79	495,346.76	8,275.44	90,110.87	41,997.72	77.92	1.30	14.17	6.61
	2011	660,244.56	524,716.21	8,020.24	90,634.60	36,873.50	79.47	1.21	13.73	5.58
	2015	510,603.33	417,417.31	4,528.42	68,925.78	19,731.83	81.75	0.89	13.50	3.86
Republic of Korea	2000	133,867.89	86,674.53	482.38	34,823.05	11,887.93	64.75	0.36	26.01	8.88
	2005	251,877.04	161,539.31	1,152.59	60,639.76	28,545.38	64.13	0.46	24.08	11.33
	2008	388,734.61	211,965.47	1,385.69	118,814.17	56,569.27	54.53	0.36	30.56	14.55
	2011	488,539.74	274,717.32	1,649.84	154,916.43	57,256.15	56.23	0.34	31.71	11.72
	2015	445,103.76	310,992.07	1,432.42	103,243.54	29,435.73	69.87	0.32	23.20	6.61
Taipei,China	2000	122,063.97	71,497.08	435.72	36,558.58	13,572.59	58.57	0.36	29.95	11.12
	2005	177,663.57	92,580.17	530.67	50,803.07	33,749.67	52.11	0.30	28.60	19.00
	2008	232,829.75	111,209.78	457.56	72,620.58	48,541.82	47.76	0.20	31.19	20.85
	2011	276,000.22	136,001.98	489.35	90,456.51	49,052.38	49.28	0.18	32.77	17.77
	2015	311,002.41	199,796.21	601.43	77,934.94	32,669.84	64.24	0.19	25.06	10.50
Bangladesh	2000	117.41	98.86	0.09	12.74	5.71	84.21	0.08	10.85	4.86
	2005	136.66	116.79	0.10	11.53	8.23	85.46	0.08	8.44	6.02
	2008	531.64	304.49	0.50	174.27	52.38	57.27	0.09	32.78	9.85
	2011	431.00	304.23	0.09	83.91	42.76	70.59	0.02	19.47	9.92
	2015	609.56	496.36	0.16	80.58	32.46	81.43	0.03	13.22	5.32

continued on next page

Table 3.1c: continued

Table 3.1c: Value-Added Decomposition of Exports – Medium- and High-Technology Manufacturing Sector

		Exports	VAX_G	RDV_B	FVA	PDC	VAX_G	RDV_B	FVA	PDC
			($ million)					(% share in exports)		
Malaysia	2000	72,457.29	25,671.31	82.55	35,294.21	11,409.23	35.43	0.11	48.71	15.75
	2005	94,215.18	38,966.35	125.30	39,768.73	15,354.79	41.36	0.13	42.21	16.30
	2008	127,923.18	60,973.38	225.06	44,896.41	21,828.33	47.66	0.18	35.10	17.06
	2011	91,019.86	54,835.88	189.85	24,894.01	11,100.12	60.25	0.21	27.35	12.20
	2015	84,312.00	54,666.27	175.39	22,430.90	7,039.44	64.84	0.21	26.60	8.35
Philippines	2000	16,752.49	12,878.05	21.34	2,413.42	1,439.68	76.87	0.13	14.41	8.59
	2005	17,065.30	10,054.47	21.16	4,722.01	2,267.66	58.92	0.12	27.67	13.29
	2008	32,083.97	15,484.77	23.08	12,381.09	4,195.04	48.26	0.07	38.59	13.08
	2011	22,002.25	13,346.69	17.31	6,427.56	2,210.69	60.66	0.08	29.21	10.05
	2015	19,057.91	14,386.77	20.65	3,545.65	1,104.84	75.49	0.11	18.60	5.80
Thailand	2000	38,470.04	15,355.00	109.52	18,663.81	4,341.71	39.91	0.28	48.52	11.29
	2005	62,344.90	25,524.78	93.16	28,387.36	8,339.61	40.94	0.15	45.53	13.38
	2008	116,318.96	54,355.85	149.79	49,755.36	12,057.95	46.73	0.13	42.77	10.37
	2011	71,412.57	36,465.42	111.19	28,876.47	5,959.50	51.06	0.16	40.44	8.35
	2015	70,430.15	43,623.02	105.78	23,484.45	3,216.90	61.94	0.15	33.34	4.57
Viet Nam	2000	594.18	291.77	0.36	199.98	102.07	49.11	0.06	33.66	17.18
	2005	3,340.36	2,121.49	2.27	821.52	395.07	63.51	0.07	24.59	11.83
	2008	16,132.98	7,058.29	25.00	6,150.81	2,898.88	43.75	0.15	38.13	17.97
	2011	11,758.61	6,665.92	12.55	3,870.79	1,209.35	56.69	0.11	32.92	10.28
	2015	15,926.87	8,525.36	17.46	6,111.60	1,272.45	53.53	0.11	38.37	7.99
Mongolia	2000	29.19	14.98	0.00	11.04	3.18	51.30	0.00	37.81	10.88
	2005	39.87	22.49	0.00	12.41	4.96	56.42	0.00	31.13	12.45
	2008	149.70	102.24	0.01	32.80	14.65	68.30	0.00	21.91	9.79
	2011	112.24	62.66	0.01	37.35	12.22	55.82	0.01	33.28	10.89
	2015	130.76	86.38	0.00	34.73	9.64	66.06	0.00	26.56	7.37
Sri Lanka	2000	332.83	223.49	0.11	83.76	25.47	67.15	0.03	25.17	7.65
	2005	359.47	225.92	0.11	108.43	25.01	62.85	0.03	30.16	6.96
	2008	660.75	277.17	0.05	345.45	38.08	41.95	0.01	52.28	5.76
	2011	776.86	478.07	0.29	222.57	75.93	61.54	0.04	28.65	9.77
	2015	921.90	599.87	0.46	254.97	66.60	65.07	0.05	27.66	7.22

FVA = foreign value added, PDC = pure double counted terms, PRC = People's Republic of China, RDV_B = domestic value added first exported then returned home, VAX_G = domestic value added absorbed abroad.

Source: ADB Multi Region Input–Output Tables Database.

Table 3.1d: Value-Added Decomposition of Exports – Business Services Sector

		Exports	VAX_G	RDV_B	FVA	PDC	VAX_G	RDV_B	FVA	PDC
			($ million)				(% share in exports)			
PRC	2000	39,280.26	35,011.02	307.50	3,125.54	836.20	89.13	0.78	7.96	2.13
	2005	114,129.50	96,200.87	1,465.64	12,349.60	4,113.39	84.29	1.28	10.82	3.60
	2008	195,098.77	165,391.99	2,701.22	20,274.38	6,731.18	84.77	1.38	10.39	3.45
	2011	274,229.73	232,429.91	5,678.59	25,961.88	10,159.34	84.76	2.07	9.47	3.70
	2015	316,773.96	283,621.84	5,706.45	21,151.43	6,294.23	89.53	1.80	6.68	1.99
Indonesia	2000	4,895.61	4,107.59	11.28	611.27	165.47	83.90	0.23	12.49	3.38
	2005	8,419.52	7,105.67	25.95	911.91	375.99	84.40	0.31	10.83	4.47
	2008	13,760.94	11,786.47	29.62	1,375.89	568.96	85.65	0.22	10.00	4.13
	2011	19,033.93	16,560.18	32.36	1,744.64	696.75	87.00	0.17	9.17	3.66
	2015	18,889.07	17,229.57	31.61	1,245.72	382.17	91.21	0.17	6.59	2.02
India	2000	6,790.81	6,221.66	14.63	434.01	120.51	91.62	0.22	6.39	1.77
	2005	36,703.32	33,276.66	151.08	2,528.84	746.73	90.66	0.41	6.89	2.03
	2008	60,546.61	54,617.73	150.00	4,585.33	1,193.55	90.21	0.25	7.57	1.97
	2011	70,365.61	64,297.99	136.38	4,832.26	1,098.98	91.38	0.19	6.87	1.56
	2015	67,737.70	62,851.01	195.23	3,820.22	871.24	92.79	0.29	5.64	1.29
Japan	2000	88,511.38	80,955.55	1,675.22	4,411.31	1,469.30	91.46	1.89	4.98	1.66
	2005	112,836.20	101,247.45	2,062.97	6,656.23	2,869.55	89.73	1.83	5.90	2.54
	2008	170,126.24	147,769.17	2,673.18	13,790.07	5,893.82	86.86	1.57	8.11	3.46
	2011	171,220.37	151,141.37	2,091.38	14,688.69	3,298.93	88.27	1.22	8.58	1.93
	2015	162,662.46	146,575.41	1,694.28	11,514.08	2,878.69	90.11	1.04	7.08	1.77
Republic of Korea	2000	31,860.20	25,954.80	118.71	4,466.29	1,320.39	81.46	0.37	14.02	4.14
	2005	45,505.39	34,863.04	214.66	7,556.71	2,870.98	76.61	0.47	16.61	6.31
	2008	71,505.37	48,992.16	273.76	16,764.66	5,474.78	68.52	0.38	23.45	7.66
	2011	81,102.07	57,721.22	264.28	16,199.04	6,917.53	71.17	0.33	19.97	8.53
	2015	92,446.09	76,827.63	333.22	11,741.56	3,543.69	83.11	0.36	12.70	3.83
Taipei,China	2000	17,096.91	13,707.79	44.91	2,662.98	681.23	80.18	0.26	15.58	3.98
	2005	17,611.01	12,823.48	35.13	3,523.87	1,228.53	72.82	0.20	20.01	6.98
	2008	21,675.29	14,817.24	36.07	4,764.57	2,057.40	68.36	0.17	21.98	9.49
	2011	21,953.51	15,579.85	28.98	4,600.84	1,743.83	70.97	0.13	20.96	7.94
	2015	22,317.02	17,255.00	33.68	3,997.28	1,031.06	77.32	0.15	17.91	4.62
Bangladesh	2000	753.99	730.80	0.17	20.70	2.31	96.93	0.02	2.75	0.31
	2005	858.38	826.44	0.19	28.00	3.76	96.28	0.02	3.26	0.44
	2008	1,233.00	900.88	0.36	271.15	60.61	73.06	0.03	21.99	4.92
	2011	1,363.01	1,133.93	0.20	161.89	66.99	83.19	0.01	11.88	4.91
	2015	2,586.16	2,325.54	0.45	197.09	63.08	89.92	0.02	7.62	2.44

continued on next page

Table 3.1d: continued

Table 3.1d: Value-Added Decomposition of Exports – Business Services Sector

		VAX_G	RDV_B	FVA	PDC	VAX_G	RDV_B	FVA	PDC
	Exports	($ million)				(% share in exports)			
Malaysia									
2000	11,891.12	8,145.86	18.80	3,085.19	641.27	68.50	0.16	25.95	5.39
2005	15,512.30	12,497.24	18.71	2,342.79	653.56	80.56	0.12	15.10	4.21
2008	29,524.14	22,613.72	63.91	5,250.17	1,596.34	76.59	0.22	17.78	5.41
2011	33,085.50	27,414.85	46.37	4,597.24	1,027.04	82.86	0.14	13.90	3.10
2015	43,170.10	33,880.99	73.99	7,709.89	1,505.23	78.48	0.17	17.86	3.49
Philippines									
2000	3,803.04	3,287.21	2.46	437.84	75.53	86.44	0.06	11.51	1.99
2005	5,904.56	5,313.99	4.44	490.71	95.42	90.00	0.08	8.31	1.62
2008	13,057.53	11,755.53	13.11	1,027.75	261.14	90.03	0.10	7.87	2.00
2011	17,910.80	16,492.43	17.53	1,088.17	312.66	92.08	0.10	6.08	1.75
2015	25,078.69	22,574.02	35.74	1,951.26	517.67	90.01	0.14	7.78	2.06
Thailand									
2000	13,479.87	11,294.17	28.70	1,847.32	309.68	83.79	0.21	13.70	2.30
2005	19,306.47	15,334.21	49.18	3,246.89	676.20	79.43	0.25	16.82	3.50
2008	27,511.36	22,239.06	77.99	4,102.55	1,091.77	80.84	0.28	14.91	3.97
2011	42,776.54	36,031.89	97.85	5,463.59	1,183.21	84.23	0.23	12.77	2.77
2015	58,739.86	46,572.43	126.00	10,293.38	1,748.05	79.29	0.21	17.52	2.98
Viet Nam									
2000	2,843.63	2,183.02	1.10	543.50	116.01	76.77	0.04	19.11	4.08
2005	4,127.91	3,545.32	1.35	520.57	60.66	85.89	0.03	12.61	1.47
2008	11,937.75	10,285.80	12.15	1,416.26	223.54	86.16	0.10	11.86	1.87
2011	15,159.56	12,627.86	11.00	2,273.77	246.93	83.30	0.07	15.00	1.63
2015	21,775.52	17,691.00	19.60	3,725.89	339.04	81.24	0.09	17.11	1.56
Mongolia									
2000	140.71	90.04	0.01	41.13	9.53	63.99	0.01	29.23	6.77
2005	260.26	177.47	0.02	66.90	15.87	68.19	0.01	25.71	6.10
2008	569.71	382.13	0.07	149.22	38.29	67.07	0.01	26.19	6.72
2011	1,141.58	843.93	0.35	246.27	51.04	73.93	0.03	21.57	4.47
2015	872.28	593.21	0.10	234.62	44.36	68.01	0.01	26.90	5.09
Sri Lanka									
2000	923.80	761.28	0.21	132.42	29.88	82.41	0.02	14.33	3.23
2005	970.13	828.64	0.21	114.02	27.26	85.41	0.02	11.75	2.81
2008	1,254.50	971.45	0.34	220.30	62.41	77.44	0.03	17.56	4.97
2011	1,649.47	1,443.21	0.45	162.17	43.64	87.50	0.03	9.83	2.65
2015	2,078.59	1,792.67	0.54	232.75	52.64	86.24	0.03	11.20	2.53

FVA = foreign value added, PDC = pure double counted terms, PRC = People's Republic of China, RDV_B = domestic value added first exported then returned home, VAX_G = domestic value added absorbed abroad.

Source: ADB Multi Region Input–Output Tables Database.

Table 3.1e: Value-Added Decomposition of Exports – Personal Services Sector

		VAX_G	RDV_B ($ million)	FVA	PDC	VAX_G	RDV_B (% share in exports)	FVA	PDC
PRC	2000	6,698.46	47.24	559.49	283.84	88.27	0.62	7.37	3.74
	2005	9,227.45	111.44	1,109.53	434.00	84.79	1.02	10.20	3.99
	2008	11,088.96	124.31	1,239.32	403.90	86.25	0.97	9.64	3.14
	2011	14,391.49	272.82	1,515.81	530.62	86.12	1.63	9.07	3.18
	2015	33,323.01	129.66	2,412.36	276.41	92.20	0.36	6.67	0.76
Indonesia	2000	802.75	0.71	107.93	16.79	86.49	0.08	11.63	1.81
	2005	1,661.32	1.91	270.99	42.61	84.04	0.10	13.71	2.16
	2008	2,732.70	2.76	407.58	59.49	85.33	0.09	12.73	1.86
	2011	3,662.83	3.23	515.31	56.89	86.42	0.08	12.16	1.34
	2015	12,344.37	4.43	1,180.73	40.80	90.97	0.03	8.70	0.30
India	2000	1,936.15	3.97	109.79	46.48	91.72	0.21	5.67	2.40
	2005	3,539.36	7.63	320.30	114.25	87.51	0.22	9.05	3.23
	2008	4,779.73	13.29	331.50	131.91	90.93	0.25	6.31	2.51
	2011	5,518.88	14.52	387.74	165.97	90.66	0.24	6.37	2.73
	2015	7,283.29	21.13	179.74	45.06	96.73	0.28	2.39	0.60
Japan	2000	1,712.86	18.15	42.50	9.63	96.06	1.02	2.38	0.54
	2005	2,789.95	20.37	103.43	16.69	95.21	0.70	3.53	0.57
	2008	3,842.06	24.40	204.59	40.87	93.44	0.59	4.98	0.99
	2011	3,549.89	25.09	161.47	35.96	94.10	0.67	4.28	0.95
	2015	9,599.29	33.00	623.43	53.23	93.12	0.32	6.05	0.52
Republic of Korea	2000	2,552.72	6.56	254.76	38.89	89.48	0.23	8.93	1.36
	2005	2,522.84	10.58	252.71	43.48	89.16	0.37	8.93	1.54
	2008	3,853.14	12.37	576.77	92.04	84.98	0.27	12.72	2.03
	2011	4,299.13	13.72	643.98	92.75	85.14	0.27	12.75	1.84
	2015	12,424.64	9.85	1,360.02	50.32	89.74	0.07	9.82	0.36
Taipei,China	2000	858.56	2.01	109.01	15.48	87.16	0.20	11.07	1.57
	2005	903.83	0.86	96.60	10.23	89.35	0.08	9.55	1.01
	2008	1,311.65	1.51	144.76	24.13	88.50	0.10	9.77	1.63
	2011	1,427.72	1.73	153.18	23.43	88.90	0.11	9.54	1.46
	2015	5,913.64	3.09	746.27	41.39	88.21	0.05	11.13	0.62
Bangladesh	2000	470.91	0.20	16.10	1.17	96.42	0.04	3.30	0.24
	2005	510.01	0.21	20.02	1.48	95.92	0.04	3.76	0.28
	2008	792.22	0.28	58.91	11.68	91.79	0.03	6.83	1.35
	2011	704.72	0.18	40.82	16.47	92.46	0.02	5.36	2.16
	2015	1,894.63	0.41	108.91	33.06	93.01	0.02	5.35	1.62

continued on next page

Table 3.1e: continued

Table 3.1e: Value-Added Decomposition of Exports – Personal Services Sector

		Exports	VAX_G	RDV_B	FVA	PDC	VAX_G	RDV_B	FVA	PDC
				($ million)				(% share in exports)		
Malaysia	2000	1,122.44	846.99	0.19	269.91	5.33	75.46	0.02	24.05	0.47
	2005	1,216.76	921.78	0.79	268.27	25.92	75.76	0.06	22.05	2.13
	2008	5,466.21	3,932.16	4.90	1,368.67	160.49	71.94	0.09	25.04	2.94
	2011	3,015.96	2,504.26	2.92	468.46	40.31	83.03	0.10	15.53	1.34
	2015	5,982.16	4,793.68	2.57	1,131.61	54.30	80.13	0.04	18.92	0.91
Philippines	2000	93.75	83.73	0.07	8.77	1.17	89.31	0.08	9.36	1.25
	2005	418.20	376.24	0.22	34.63	7.11	89.97	0.05	8.28	1.70
	2008	761.14	658.50	0.68	76.30	25.65	86.52	0.09	10.03	3.37
	2011	746.97	685.12	0.40	44.70	16.75	91.72	0.05	5.98	2.24
	2015	1,039.64	941.76	0.70	79.07	18.11	90.59	0.07	7.61	1.74
Thailand	2000	1,584.36	1,224.29	1.40	323.97	34.69	77.27	0.09	20.45	2.19
	2005	2,459.96	1,883.96	2.28	519.85	53.87	76.58	0.09	21.13	2.19
	2008	2,717.34	2,040.60	4.10	577.14	95.50	75.10	0.15	21.24	3.51
	2011	4,018.31	3,101.02	4.50	825.33	87.47	77.17	0.11	20.54	2.18
	2015	8,170.86	6,501.62	6.37	1,541.32	121.55	79.57	0.08	18.86	1.49
Viet Nam	2000	284.38	237.59	0.09	41.52	5.18	83.55	0.03	14.60	1.82
	2005	225.56	194.11	0.10	28.96	2.38	86.06	0.04	12.84	1.06
	2008	389.50	309.06	0.30	72.37	7.76	79.35	0.08	18.58	1.99
	2011	2,383.64	1,990.97	2.64	348.87	41.17	83.53	0.11	14.64	1.73
	2015	4,457.52	3,682.27	5.42	703.00	66.84	82.61	0.12	15.77	1.50
Mongolia	2000	4.44	2.91	0.00	1.13	0.41	65.45	0.00	25.40	9.15
	2005	5.32	3.74	0.00	1.12	0.46	70.24	0.00	21.11	8.64
	2008	6.25	4.60	0.00	1.22	0.42	73.69	0.00	19.56	6.75
	2011	17.92	13.96	0.00	3.55	0.42	77.88	0.01	19.79	2.33
	2015	20.87	18.19	0.00	2.39	0.28	87.19	0.00	11.45	1.36
Sri Lanka	2000	242.79	195.90	0.03	41.04	5.82	80.69	0.01	16.90	2.40
	2005	277.23	238.33	0.04	34.38	4.49	85.97	0.01	12.40	1.62
	2008	314.57	254.49	0.05	50.63	9.40	80.90	0.01	16.10	2.99
	2011	421.83	372.11	0.07	42.15	7.50	88.21	0.02	9.99	1.78
	2015	563.78	489.90	0.09	64.94	8.85	86.89	0.02	11.52	1.57

FVA = foreign value added, PDC = pure double counted terms, PRC = People's Republic of China, RDV_B = domestic value added first exported then returned home, VAX_G = domestic value added absorbed abroad.

Source: ADB Multi Region Input–Output Tables Database.

Table 3.1f: Value-Added Decomposition of Exports – Total Economy

		Exports	VAX_G	RDV_B	FVA	PDC	VAX_G	RDV_B	FVA	PDC
			($ million)				(% share in exports)			
PRC	2000	279,346	228,012	2,153	38,624	10,557	81.62	0.77	13.83	3.78
	2005	838,621	607,606	10,286	166,072	54,656	72.45	1.23	19.80	6.52
	2008	1,579,659	1,186,099	22,761	274,751	96,048	75.09	1.44	17.39	6.08
	2011	2,093,765	1,579,774	40,921	355,298	117,773	75.45	1.95	16.97	5.62
	2015	2,288,337	1,861,048	45,209	309,570	72,510	81.33	1.98	13.53	3.17
Indonesia	2000	65,246	52,338	135	9,800	2,974	80.22	0.21	15.02	4.56
	2005	94,067	75,610	285	12,719	5,454	80.38	0.30	13.52	5.80
	2008	151,221	124,411	547	18,481	7,781	82.27	0.36	12.22	5.15
	2011	219,754	185,400	1,107	24,699	8,548	84.37	0.50	11.24	3.89
	2015	208,793	189,163	810	14,911	3,908	90.60	0.39	7.14	1.87
India	2000	67,866	57,740	109	8,049	1,967	85.08	0.16	11.86	2.90
	2005	158,895	126,519	633	25,761	5,981	79.62	0.40	16.21	3.76
	2008	260,264	202,312	1,025	45,585	11,342	77.73	0.39	17.52	4.36
	2011	337,433	263,305	1,040	62,262	10,827	78.03	0.31	18.45	3.21
	2015	369,624	318,181	1,286	43,322	6,836	86.08	0.35	11.72	1.85
Japan	2000	513,246	457,313	9,716	33,736	12,480	89.10	1.89	6.57	2.43
	2005	651,185	558,438	11,837	55,857	25,053	85.76	1.82	8.58	3.85
	2008	862,938	689,018	11,884	110,629	51,407	79.85	1.38	12.82	5.96
	2011	900,325	731,761	11,148	113,467	43,949	81.28	1.24	12.60	4.88
	2015	740,112	620,579	7,030	87,448	25,056	83.85	0.95	11.82	3.39
Republic of Korea	2000	199,510	138,463	691	45,433	14,923	69.40	0.35	22.77	7.48
	2005	329,193	220,556	1,485	73,833	33,319	67.00	0.45	22.43	10.12
	2008	498,780	287,376	1,806	144,349	65,248	57.62	0.36	28.94	13.08
	2011	615,300	363,588	2,087	181,891	67,734	59.09	0.34	29.56	11.01
	2015	591,608	430,586	1,917	124,256	34,849	72.78	0.32	21.00	5.89
Taipei,China	2000	173,291	110,321	550	46,269	16,151	63.66	0.32	26.70	9.32
	2005	226,749	126,897	622	61,574	37,656	55.96	0.27	27.16	16.61
	2008	288,323	147,043	538	86,589	54,153	51.00	0.19	30.03	18.78
	2011	340,219	178,014	571	107,023	54,611	52.32	0.17	31.46	16.05
	2015	394,322	259,450	702	96,858	37,312	65.80	0.18	24.56	9.46
Bangladesh	2000	6,451	5,639	2	707	103	87.41	0.03	10.96	1.60
	2005	8,854	7,400	3	1,238	214	83.57	0.03	13.98	2.42
	2008	15,708	11,751	5	3,326	625	74.81	0.03	21.17	3.98
	2011	22,801	19,383	6	2,613	799	85.01	0.03	11.46	3.50
	2015	36,813	31,980	10	3,831	992	86.87	0.03	10.41	2.69

continued on next page

Table 3.1f: continued

Table 3.1f: Value-Added Decomposition of Exports – Total Economy

		Exports	VAX_G	RDV_B	FVA	PDC	VAX_G	RDV_B	FVA	PDC
			($ million)					(% share in exports)		
Malaysia	2000	111,832	53,273	141	44,918	13,500	47.64	0.13	40.17	12.07
	2005	147,263	79,625	230	49,211	18,197	54.07	0.16	33.42	12.36
	2008	222,930	135,706	440	60,386	26,398	60.87	0.20	27.09	11.84
	2011	191,803	134,179	342	41,971	15,311	69.96	0.18	21.88	7.98
	2015	189,418	130,239	346	46,742	12,091	68.76	0.18	24.68	6.38
Philippines	2000	26,838	21,503	26	3,708	1,600	80.12	0.10	13.82	5.96
	2005	32,358	23,328	31	6,472	2,528	72.09	0.09	20.00	7.81
	2008	62,005	41,224	46	15,921	4,814	66.49	0.07	25.68	7.76
	2011	52,902	41,248	43	8,859	2,752	77.97	0.08	16.75	5.20
	2015	60,481	50,623	72	7,819	1,967	83.70	0.12	12.93	3.25
Thailand	2000	81,515	48,280	201	27,388	5,645	59.23	0.25	33.60	6.93
	2005	122,626	69,403	217	41,899	11,107	56.60	0.18	34.17	9.06
	2008	205,428	121,041	337	68,070	15,981	58.92	0.16	33.14	7.78
	2011	188,399	128,574	347	48,761	10,716	68.25	0.18	25.88	5.69
	2015	209,515	148,942	404	51,237	8,933	71.09	0.19	24.45	4.26
Viet Nam	2000	14,019	10,594	10	2,860	555	75.57	0.07	20.40	3.96
	2005	27,044	20,495	20	5,277	1,253	75.78	0.07	19.51	4.63
	2008	69,552	45,264	123	18,420	5,745	65.08	0.18	26.48	8.26
	2011	84,580	58,671	93	21,880	3,936	69.37	0.11	25.87	4.65
	2015	130,369	85,619	149	40,041	4,560	65.67	0.11	30.71	3.50
Mongolia	2000	426	297	0	102	27	69.61	0.00	23.98	6.41
	2005	1,121	835	0	208	79	74.46	0.00	18.52	7.01
	2008	2,401	1,813	0	414	174	75.48	0.01	17.26	7.25
	2011	5,283	3,545	1	1,228	509	67.10	0.02	23.25	9.63
	2015	5,433	3,901	0	1,111	421	71.79	0.01	20.45	7.75
Sri Lanka	2000	6,400	4,867	1	1,310	221	76.05	0.02	20.48	3.45
	2005	7,420	5,338	1	1,813	267	71.94	0.02	24.44	3.60
	2008	9,746	7,788	3	1,633	322	79.91	0.03	16.75	3.30
	2011	12,082	10,174	4	1,603	301	84.21	0.03	13.26	2.49
	2015	13,095	11,350	4	1,493	247	86.67	0.03	11.40	1.89

FVA = foreign value added, PDC = pure double counted terms, PRC = People's Republic of China, RDV_B = domestic value added first exported then returned home, VAX_G = domestic value added absorbed abroad.

Source: ADB Multi Region Input–Output Tables Database.

Table 3.2a: Value-Added Exports by Various Measures – Primary Sector

		Exports	VAX_G	DVA_B	DVA_F	VAX_B	VAX_F	VAX_G	DVA_B	DVA_F	VAX_B	VAX_F
		($ million)						Value–Added Export Measure to Gross Exports Ratio (%)				
PRC	2000	10,913.96	9,946.62	10,093.33	32,223.68	9,946.62	31,931.10	91.14	92.48	295.25	91.14	292.57
	2005	20,989.37	18,111.95	18,677.96	89,744.95	18,111.95	88,383.75	86.29	88.99	427.57	86.29	421.09
	2008	25,091.04	21,687.91	22,322.48	160,047.95	21,687.91	157,316.85	86.44	88.97	637.87	86.44	626.98
	2011	34,237.15	29,729.82	30,806.61	209,830.83	29,729.82	205,033.31	86.83	89.98	612.87	86.83	598.86
	2015	44,928.07	40,781.84	41,651.18	263,775.77	40,781.84	258,648.15	90.77	92.71	587.11	90.77	575.69
Indonesia	2000	10,794.33	10,287.98	10,346.05	19,570.16	10,287.98	19,496.69	95.31	95.85	181.30	95.31	180.62
	2005	21,998.21	20,432.30	20,565.25	29,845.77	20,432.30	29,691.93	92.88	93.49	135.67	92.88	134.97
	2008	36,871.59	34,642.99	34,869.47	52,549.54	34,642.99	52,263.01	93.96	94.57	142.52	93.96	141.74
	2011	65,323.49	61,875.07	62,521.50	88,996.00	61,875.07	88,261.98	94.72	95.71	136.24	94.72	135.12
	2015	39,882.12	38,398.16	38,752.17	74,937.66	38,398.16	74,457.95	96.28	97.17	187.90	96.28	186.70
India	2000	8,241.66	7,943.73	7,954.48	13,476.17	7,943.73	13,456.93	96.39	96.52	163.51	96.39	163.28
	2005	14,571.58	13,866.36	13,927.97	22,619.62	13,866.36	22,521.46	95.16	95.58	155.23	95.16	154.56
	2008	21,706.11	20,494.45	20,624.76	33,240.08	20,494.45	33,056.84	94.42	95.02	153.14	94.42	152.29
	2011	28,737.83	27,503.22	27,694.39	43,930.71	27,503.22	43,710.87	95.70	96.37	152.87	95.70	152.10
	2015	21,172.38	20,030.89	20,218.37	44,026.51	20,030.89	43,763.54	94.61	95.49	207.94	94.61	206.70
Japan	2000	2,242.99	1,872.27	1,933.05	4,414.35	1,872.27	4,310.84	83.47	86.18	196.81	83.47	192.19
	2005	2,957.53	2,133.47	2,185.93	5,071.18	2,133.47	4,960.76	72.14	73.91	171.47	72.14	167.73
	2008	4,797.37	2,702.73	2,780.65	5,503.16	2,702.73	5,396.25	56.34	57.96	114.71	56.34	112.48
	2011	5,467.05	3,155.54	3,225.76	6,877.72	3,155.54	6,759.52	57.72	59.00	125.80	57.72	123.64
	2015	3,133.70	2,629.77	2,694.14	5,649.17	2,629.77	5,563.90	83.92	85.97	180.27	83.92	177.55
Republic of Korea	2000	481.62	427.23	428.57	3,027.15	427.23	3,018.25	88.71	88.99	628.54	88.71	626.69
	2005	627.11	549.61	551.25	3,733.03	549.61	3,715.91	87.64	87.90	595.27	87.64	592.54
	2008	518.92	412.58	414.17	3,809.66	412.58	3,791.16	79.51	79.81	734.15	79.51	730.59
	2011	770.65	607.87	610.85	4,797.86	607.87	4,778.19	78.88	79.26	622.57	78.88	620.02
	2015	1,218.63	1,024.04	1,028.48	6,876.58	1,024.04	6,853.96	84.03	84.40	564.29	84.03	562.43
Taipei,China	2000	1,829.67	1,525.06	1,526.54	1,635.37	1,525.06	1,631.61	83.35	83.43	89.38	83.35	89.17
	2005	2,136.96	1,652.75	1,654.55	1,704.39	1,652.75	1,700.35	77.34	77.43	79.76	77.34	79.57
	2008	2,609.74	1,886.16	1,888.04	2,224.03	1,886.16	2,219.08	72.27	72.35	85.22	72.27	85.03
	2011	4,804.99	3,562.72	3,566.19	3,774.76	3,562.72	3,768.22	74.15	74.22	78.56	74.15	78.42
	2015	5,542.35	4,268.90	4,272.78	3,755.20	4,268.90	3,750.36	77.02	77.09	67.75	77.02	67.67
Bangladesh	2000	390.28	377.47	378.11	797.75	377.47	797.19	96.72	96.88	204.41	96.72	204.26
	2005	368.79	353.38	354.21	932.77	353.38	932.00	95.82	96.05	252.93	95.82	252.72
	2008	465.26	437.28	438.14	728.95	437.28	728.37	93.99	94.17	156.68	93.99	156.55
	2011	636.99	573.94	574.26	1,280.16	573.94	1,279.73	90.10	90.15	200.97	90.10	200.90
	2015	1,069.47	938.40	938.96	2,044.52	938.40	2,043.78	87.74	87.80	191.17	87.74	191.10

continued on next page

Table 3.2a: continued

Table 3.2a: Value-Added Exports by Various Measures – Primary Sector

		Exports	VAX_G	DVA_F	DVA_B	VAX_B	VAX_F	VAX_G	DVA_B	DVA_F	VAX_B	VAX_F
		($ million)						Value-Added Export Measure to Gross Exports Ratio (%)				
Malaysia	2000	9,555.73	8,233.91	8,279.01	12,455.76	8,233.91	12,423.16	86.17	86.64	130.35	86.17	130.01
	2005	15,801.93	13,791.36	13,889.03	21,642.76	13,791.36	21,563.96	87.28	87.89	136.96	87.28	136.46
	2008	38,694.02	33,974.25	34,138.40	47,995.97	33,974.25	47,830.68	87.80	88.23	124.04	87.80	123.61
	2011	17,811.43	15,969.60	16,038.82	39,164.23	15,969.60	39,056.95	89.66	90.05	219.88	89.66	219.28
	2015	10,597.02	9,161.75	9,215.24	28,353.11	9,161.75	28,256.83	86.46	86.96	267.56	86.46	266.65
Philippines	2000	697.59	649.35	649.86	1,783.26	649.35	1,782.05	93.09	93.16	255.63	93.09	255.46
	2005	925.27	850.97	852.06	3,002.89	850.97	2,999.96	91.97	92.09	324.54	91.97	324.22
	2008	2,153.04	1,969.22	1,971.97	5,585.36	1,969.22	5,579.95	91.46	91.59	259.42	91.46	259.17
	2011	1,467.88	1,357.64	1,359.73	5,315.53	1,357.64	5,310.72	92.49	92.63	362.12	92.49	361.79
	2015	1,622.13	1,484.56	1,487.94	4,903.08	1,484.56	4,896.03	91.52	91.73	302.26	91.52	301.83
Thailand	2000	1,515.61	1,309.84	1,329.45	5,444.64	1,309.84	5,417.87	86.42	87.72	359.24	86.42	357.47
	2005	2,494.81	2,111.82	2,128.28	7,896.53	2,111.82	7,868.43	84.65	85.31	316.52	84.65	315.39
	2008	4,591.39	3,893.91	3,919.63	16,981.46	3,893.91	16,927.42	84.81	85.37	369.85	84.81	368.68
	2011	7,073.21	6,089.28	6,116.66	22,300.27	6,089.28	22,236.25	86.09	86.48	315.28	86.09	314.37
	2015	7,393.86	6,221.76	6,259.82	21,563.17	6,221.76	21,490.30	84.15	84.66	291.64	84.15	290.65
Viet Nam	2000	5,953.49	5,183.53	5,192.37	5,059.92	5,183.53	5,053.30	87.07	87.22	84.99	87.07	84.88
	2005	10,704.56	9,024.99	9,041.10	9,236.41	9,024.99	9,223.93	84.31	84.46	86.28	84.31	86.17
	2008	25,345.58	19,168.64	19,254.65	19,441.03	19,168.64	19,373.83	75.63	75.97	76.70	75.63	76.44
	2011	26,068.80	21,419.60	21,474.80	23,381.54	21,419.60	23,336.35	82.17	82.38	89.69	82.17	89.52
	2015	41,929.01	32,681.60	32,775.96	35,354.16	32,681.60	35,278.64	77.95	78.17	84.32	77.95	84.14
Mongolia	2000	184.31	139.78	139.78	154.37	139.78	154.36	75.84	75.84	83.75	75.84	83.75
	2005	708.22	549.46	549.48	523.17	549.46	523.15	77.58	77.59	73.87	77.58	73.87
	2008	1,460.71	1,157.27	1,157.38	1,144.27	1,157.27	1,144.16	79.23	79.23	78.34	79.23	78.33
	2011	3,637.57	2,333.74	2,334.17	1,965.37	2,333.74	1,965.02	64.16	64.17	54.03	64.16	54.02
	2015	3,986.99	2,856.89	2,857.23	2,207.91	2,856.89	2,207.66	71.66	71.66	55.38	71.66	55.37
Sri Lanka	2000	288.80	243.67	243.76	349.17	243.67	349.06	84.37	84.40	120.90	84.37	120.86
	2005	471.99	406.21	406.43	426.97	406.21	426.76	86.06	86.11	90.46	86.06	90.42
	2008	1,218.66	1,030.65	1,031.33	1,333.87	1,030.65	1,333.12	84.57	84.63	109.45	84.57	109.39
	2011	484.84	430.06	430.35	1,010.55	430.06	1,010.11	88.70	88.76	208.43	88.70	208.34
	2015	751.42	653.31	654.12	1,326.55	653.31	1,325.76	86.94	87.05	176.54	86.94	176.43

DVA_B = domestic value added exports by backward industrial linkages, DVA_F = domestic value added exports by forward industrial linkages, PRC = People's Republic of China, VAX_B = value added exports by backward industrial linkages, VAX_F = value added exports by forward industrial linkages, VAX_G = domestic value added absorbed abroad.

Source: ADB Multi Region Input–Output Tables Database.

Table 3.2b: Value-Added Exports by Various Measures – Low-Technology Manufacturing Sector

		Exports	VAX_G	DVA_B	DVA_F	VAX_B	VAX_F	VAX_G	DVA_B	DVA_F	VAX_B	VAX_F
			($ million)					Value–Added Export Measure to Gross Exports Ratio (%)				
PRC	2000	94,579.86	78,750.98	79,065.60	56,742.70	78,750.98	56,369.37	83.26	83.60	59.99	83.26	59.60
	2005	215,067.98	173,438.84	174,075.02	135,191.49	173,438.84	133,765.08	80.64	80.94	62.86	80.64	62.20
	2008	374,045.07	311,230.07	312,563.02	245,340.87	311,230.07	242,360.65	83.21	83.56	65.59	83.21	64.79
	2011	515,989.76	430,535.65	433,937.24	334,830.82	430,535.65	329,226.24	83.44	84.10	64.89	83.44	63.80
	2015	621,467.80	536,511.21	540,294.94	334,587.00	536,511.21	329,883.33	86.33	86.94	53.84	86.33	53.08
Indonesia	2000	25,158.01	19,788.42	19,805.23	12,378.06	19,788.42	12,362.34	78.66	78.72	49.20	78.66	49.14
	2005	29,989.11	23,450.92	23,481.64	15,111.78	23,450.92	15,084.93	78.20	78.30	50.39	78.20	50.30
	2008	49,037.44	39,148.53	39,233.30	23,716.57	39,148.53	23,657.41	79.83	80.01	48.36	79.83	48.24
	2011	64,744.94	52,009.46	52,147.07	31,639.16	52,009.46	31,542.13	80.33	80.54	48.87	80.33	48.72
	2015	72,541.82	63,891.59	64,056.92	36,594.74	63,891.59	36,497.74	88.08	88.30	50.45	88.08	50.31
India	2000	29,631.28	25,538.88	25,565.60	13,471.89	25,538.88	13,452.64	86.19	86.28	45.47	86.19	45.40
	2005	56,477.49	40,422.34	40,488.42	23,190.72	40,422.34	23,114.74	71.57	71.69	41.06	71.57	40.93
	2008	83,437.14	56,829.67	56,974.07	32,776.47	56,829.67	32,646.27	68.11	68.28	39.28	68.11	39.13
	2011	110,565.11	71,406.03	71,568.45	40,842.00	71,406.03	40,698.56	64.58	64.73	36.94	64.58	36.81
	2015	134,634.27	112,270.47	112,555.84	53,427.48	112,270.47	53,260.52	83.39	83.60	39.68	83.39	39.56
Japan	2000	26,831.00	24,125.38	24,844.40	47,022.90	24,125.38	45,938.27	89.92	92.60	175.26	89.92	171.21
	2005	37,772.16	32,816.28	33,701.83	54,940.11	32,816.28	53,715.70	86.88	89.22	145.45	86.88	142.21
	2008	48,171.52	39,357.30	40,223.14	59,695.48	39,357.30	58,606.46	81.70	83.50	123.92	81.70	121.66
	2011	59,620.72	49,198.36	50,171.77	71,365.54	49,198.36	70,188.67	82.52	84.15	119.70	82.52	117.73
	2015	53,403.95	44,357.02	45,090.87	62,572.87	44,357.02	61,765.80	83.06	84.43	117.17	83.06	115.66
Republic of Korea	2000	30,447.23	22,853.66	22,929.70	21,206.92	22,853.66	21,119.65	75.06	75.31	69.65	75.06	69.36
	2005	28,354.23	21,081.59	21,180.92	24,668.00	21,081.59	24,526.27	74.35	74.70	87.00	74.35	86.50
	2008	33,486.87	22,152.98	22,283.22	26,954.52	22,152.98	26,792.29	66.15	66.54	80.49	66.15	80.01
	2011	39,838.06	26,242.83	26,398.87	34,798.81	26,242.83	34,596.61	65.87	66.27	87.35	65.87	86.84
	2015	38,994.24	29,317.40	29,440.52	40,572.10	29,317.40	40,378.15	75.18	75.50	104.05	75.18	103.55
Taipei,China	2000	31,315.20	22,732.57	22,798.70	14,921.57	22,732.57	14,868.75	72.59	72.80	47.65	72.59	47.48
	2005	28,325.89	18,936.50	18,985.48	12,992.53	18,936.50	12,946.94	66.85	67.03	45.87	66.85	45.71
	2008	29,726.10	17,817.95	17,852.09	11,438.93	17,817.95	11,408.23	59.94	60.06	38.48	59.94	38.38
	2011	35,854.34	21,441.80	21,481.80	13,602.95	21,441.80	13,568.72	59.80	59.91	37.94	59.80	37.84
	2015	48,755.75	32,215.86	32,259.74	27,144.84	32,215.86	27,082.07	66.08	66.17	55.68	66.08	55.55
Bangladesh	2000	4,701.33	3,961.19	3,961.77	1,993.73	3,961.19	1,993.32	84.26	84.27	42.41	84.26	42.40
	2005	6,958.69	5,593.05	5,594.42	2,730.39	5,593.05	2,729.58	80.38	80.39	39.24	80.38	39.23
	2008	12,615.07	9,316.33	9,319.47	5,324.25	9,316.33	5,322.29	73.85	73.88	42.21	73.85	42.19
	2011	19,607.53	16,666.58	16,671.62	8,994.25	16,666.58	8,991.49	85.00	85.03	45.87	85.00	45.86
	2015	30,510.52	26,324.96	26,333.46	15,345.15	26,324.96	15,340.13	86.28	86.31	50.29	86.28	50.28

continued on next page

Table 3.2b: continued

Table 3.2b: Value-Added Exports by Various Measures – Low-Technology Manufacturing Sector

		Exports	VAX_G	DVA_B	DVA_F	VAX_B	VAX_F	VAX_G	DVA_B	DVA_F	VAX_B	VAX_F
			\(\$ million)					Value–Added Export Measure to Gross Exports Ratio (%)				
Malaysia	2000	16,805.50	10,375.30	10,390.25	7,640.78	10,375.30	7,626.70	61.74	61.83	45.47	61.74	45.38
	2005	20,517.30	13,448.36	13,468.70	10,827.01	13,448.36	10,803.52	65.55	65.65	52.77	65.55	52.66
	2008	21,322.33	14,212.20	14,226.98	11,593.45	14,212.20	11,566.61	66.65	66.72	54.37	66.65	54.25
	2011	46,869.96	33,454.32	33,492.06	14,602.88	33,454.32	14,577.05	71.38	71.46	31.16	71.38	31.10
	2015	45,356.51	27,736.37	27,777.15	14,582.61	27,736.37	14,553.02	61.15	61.24	32.15	61.15	32.09
Philippines	2000	5,490.79	4,605.12	4,606.48	4,309.53	4,605.12	4,307.21	83.87	83.89	78.49	83.87	78.44
	2005	8,045.10	6,732.33	6,735.98	4,933.57	6,732.33	4,929.97	83.68	83.73	61.32	83.68	61.28
	2008	13,948.90	11,356.21	11,362.20	8,508.20	11,356.21	8,502.54	81.41	81.46	61.00	81.41	60.95
	2011	10,773.78	9,365.95	9,371.57	7,367.52	9,365.95	7,362.25	86.93	86.99	68.38	86.93	68.33
	2015	13,682.74	11,235.74	11,247.13	10,763.56	11,235.74	10,751.15	82.12	82.20	78.67	82.12	78.57
Thailand	2000	26,465.20	19,096.81	19,139.14	13,336.28	19,096.81	13,301.04	72.16	72.32	50.39	72.16	50.26
	2005	36,019.68	24,547.81	24,603.87	16,114.35	24,547.81	16,075.04	68.15	68.31	44.74	68.15	44.63
	2008	54,289.37	38,511.34	38,588.54	24,554.07	38,511.34	24,498.45	70.94	71.08	45.23	70.94	45.13
	2011	63,118.28	46,886.88	46,996.85	28,207.62	46,886.88	28,142.51	74.28	74.46	44.69	74.28	44.59
	2015	64,780.50	46,022.94	46,155.80	30,696.05	46,022.94	30,613.26	71.04	71.25	47.38	71.04	47.26
Viet Nam	2000	4,343.19	2,697.92	2,697.71	1,830.15	2,697.92	1,829.37	62.12	62.11	42.14	62.12	42.12
	2005	8,645.75	5,608.67	5,608.84	3,563.22	5,608.67	3,561.33	64.87	64.87	41.21	64.87	41.19
	2008	15,745.78	8,441.75	8,443.44	6,312.24	8,441.75	6,298.89	53.61	53.62	40.09	53.61	40.00
	2011	29,208.94	15,966.54	15,978.92	9,690.60	15,966.54	9,676.92	54.66	54.71	33.18	54.66	33.13
	2015	46,279.82	23,039.12	23,052.45	14,525.77	23,039.12	14,504.54	49.78	49.81	31.39	49.78	31.34
Mongolia	2000	67.84	49.18	49.18	28.01	49.18	28.01	72.49	72.49	41.29	72.49	41.29
	2005	107.62	81.79	81.79	59.36	81.79	59.36	76.00	76.00	55.16	76.00	55.16
	2008	215.06	166.34	166.35	89.79	166.34	89.79	77.35	77.35	41.75	77.35	41.75
	2011	373.66	290.77	290.81	204.50	290.77	204.47	77.82	77.83	54.73	77.82	54.72
	2015	421.98	345.86	345.89	338.96	345.86	338.92	81.96	81.97	80.33	81.96	80.32
Sri Lanka	2000	1,469.16	1,059.28	1,059.51	856.85	1,059.28	856.67	72.10	72.12	58.32	72.10	58.31
	2005	462.22	313.88	313.90	277.35	313.88	277.31	67.91	67.91	60.00	67.91	59.99
	2008	3,599.57	2,697.06	2,698.04	1,881.41	2,697.06	1,880.73	74.93	74.95	52.27	74.93	52.25
	2011	5,080.50	4,229.70	4,230.55	3,155.29	4,229.70	3,154.63	83.25	83.27	62.11	83.25	62.09
	2015	8,142.57	7,068.41	7,069.07	5,557.55	7,068.41	5,556.92	86.81	86.82	68.25	86.81	68.25

DVA_B = domestic value added exports by backward industrial linkages, DVA_F = domestic value added exports by forward industrial linkages, PRC = People's Republic of China, VAX_B = value added exports by backward industrial linkages, VAX_F = value added exports by forward industrial linkages, VAX_G = domestic value added absorbed abroad.

Source: ADB Multi Region Input–Output Tables Database.

Table 3.2c: Value-Added Exports by Various Measures – Medium- and High-Technology Manufacturing Sector

		Exports	VAX_G	DVA_B	DVA_F	VAX_B	VAX_F	VAX_G	DVA_B	DVA_F	VAX_B	VAX_F
				($ million)				Value-Added Export Measure to Gross Exports Ratio (%)				
PRC	2000	126,982.80	97,604.76	98,907.35	72,801.41	97,604.76	71,949.62	76.86	77.89	57.33	76.86	56.66
	2005	477,551.66	310,627.16	317,840.15	213,045.37	310,627.16	208,545.62	65.05	66.56	44.61	65.05	43.67
	2008	972,567.61	676,699.92	694,191.31	440,254.87	676,699.92	430,057.68	69.58	71.38	45.27	69.58	44.22
	2011	1,252,597.72	872,687.13	902,449.80	572,878.65	872,687.13	555,341.65	69.67	72.05	45.74	69.67	44.34
	2015	1,269,026.06	966,810.53	1,000,989.81	585,754.45	966,810.53	567,563.84	76.19	78.88	46.16	76.19	44.72
Indonesia	2000	23,470.31	17,351.40	17,398.95	10,838.27	17,351.40	10,810.75	73.93	74.13	46.18	73.93	46.06
	2005	31,683.76	22,959.31	23,053.05	15,565.75	22,959.31	15,504.93	72.46	72.76	49.13	72.46	48.94
	2008	48,348.79	36,100.72	36,305.98	25,187.58	36,100.72	25,055.18	74.67	75.09	52.10	74.67	51.82
	2011	66,413.42	51,292.95	51,585.05	32,189.44	51,292.95	32,014.83	77.23	77.67	48.47	77.23	48.21
	2015	63,909.21	57,299.75	57,560.45	32,700.33	57,299.75	32,565.53	89.66	90.07	51.17	89.66	50.96
India	2000	21,265.62	16,259.89	16,311.78	11,290.24	16,259.89	11,259.69	76.46	76.70	53.09	76.46	52.95
	2005	47,602.78	35,856.83	36,189.21	22,876.24	35,856.83	22,702.69	75.33	76.02	48.06	75.33	47.69
	2008	89,317.52	65,590.34	66,169.05	41,107.85	65,590.34	40,800.62	73.44	74.08	46.02	73.44	45.68
	2011	121,677.35	94,578.53	95,104.61	54,571.34	94,578.53	54,301.26	77.73	78.16	44.85	77.73	44.63
	2015	138,550.42	115,745.36	116,335.16	76,684.87	115,745.36	76,339.85	83.54	83.97	55.35	83.54	55.10
Japan	2000	393,877.43	348,647.34	355,814.07	229,594.60	348,647.34	224,923.51	88.52	90.34	58.29	88.52	57.10
	2005	494,688.44	419,450.58	428,154.19	279,995.35	419,450.58	274,254.21	84.79	86.55	56.60	84.79	55.44
	2008	635,730.79	495,346.76	503,403.71	316,468.59	495,346.76	311,292.57	77.92	79.19	49.78	77.92	48.97
	2011	660,244.56	524,716.21	532,653.70	342,285.01	524,716.21	337,125.02	79.47	80.68	51.84	79.47	51.06
	2015	510,603.33	417,417.31	421,874.72	260,673.35	417,417.31	257,888.83	81.75	82.62	51.05	81.75	50.51
Republic of Korea	2000	133,867.89	86,674.53	87,142.19	66,735.39	86,674.53	66,371.02	64.75	65.10	49.85	64.75	49.58
	2005	251,877.04	161,539.31	162,665.22	120,426.20	161,539.31	119,577.19	64.13	64.58	47.81	64.13	47.47
	2008	388,734.61	211,965.47	213,309.16	157,914.70	211,965.47	156,898.77	54.53	54.87	40.62	54.53	40.36
	2011	488,539.74	274,717.32	276,332.07	207,169.92	274,717.32	205,938.56	56.23	56.56	42.41	56.23	42.15
	2015	445,103.76	310,992.07	312,402.71	221,465.61	310,992.07	220,473.26	69.87	70.19	49.76	69.87	49.53
Taipei,China	2000	122,063.97	71,497.08	71,924.05	47,130.06	71,497.08	46,850.66	58.57	58.92	38.61	58.57	38.38
	2005	177,663.57	92,580.17	93,110.35	59,571.80	92,580.17	59,240.25	52.11	52.41	33.53	52.11	33.34
	2008	232,829.75	111,209.78	111,668.22	67,484.09	111,209.78	67,209.56	47.76	47.96	28.98	47.76	28.87
	2011	276,000.22	136,001.98	136,495.73	84,019.93	136,001.98	83,722.62	49.28	49.45	30.44	49.28	30.33
	2015	311,002.41	199,796.21	200,412.27	120,422.75	199,796.21	120,068.82	64.24	64.44	38.72	64.24	38.61
Bangladesh	2000	117.41	98.86	98.96	172.31	98.86	172.23	84.21	84.29	146.76	84.21	146.70
	2005	136.66	116.79	116.91	266.11	116.79	265.99	85.46	85.55	194.73	85.46	194.64
	2008	531.64	304.49	305.02	325.60	304.49	325.20	57.27	57.37	61.25	57.27	61.17
	2011	431.00	304.23	304.33	505.95	304.23	505.80	70.59	70.61	117.39	70.59	117.35
	2015	609.56	496.36	496.52	446.29	496.36	446.16	81.43	81.46	73.22	81.43	73.19

continued on next page

Global Value Chains

Table 3.2c: continued

Table 3.2c: Value-Added Exports by Various Measures – Medium- and High-Technology Manufacturing Sector

		Exports	VAX_G	DVA_B	DVA_F	VAX_B	VAX_F	VAX_G	DVA_B	DVA_F	VAX_B	VAX_F
		($ million)						Value-Added Export Measure to Gross Exports Ratio (%)				
Malaysia	2000	72,457.29	25,671.31	25,721.76	18,188.71	25,671.31	18,131.55	35.43	35.50	25.10	35.43	25.02
	2005	94,215.18	38,966.35	39,052.50	23,035.80	38,966.35	22,962.68	41.36	41.45	24.45	41.36	24.37
	2008	127,923.18	60,973.38	61,153.71	29,270.53	60,973.38	29,164.16	47.66	47.81	22.88	47.66	22.80
	2011	91,019.86	54,835.88	55,019.27	35,549.52	54,835.88	35,434.02	60.25	60.45	39.06	60.25	38.93
	2015	84,312.00	54,666.27	54,839.80	33,695.63	54,666.27	33,595.06	64.84	65.04	39.97	64.84	39.85
Philippines	2000	16,752.49	12,878.05	12,899.61	9,990.31	12,878.05	9,974.30	76.87	77.00	59.63	76.87	59.54
	2005	17,065.30	10,054.47	10,075.43	6,310.12	10,054.47	6,297.97	58.92	59.04	36.98	58.92	36.91
	2008	32,083.97	15,484.77	15,507.25	9,928.05	15,484.77	9,914.71	48.26	48.33	30.94	48.26	30.90
	2011	22,002.25	13,346.69	13,361.39	8,389.50	13,346.69	8,379.20	60.66	60.73	38.13	60.66	38.08
	2015	19,057.91	14,386.77	14,406.92	10,004.60	14,386.77	9,990.58	75.49	75.60	52.50	75.49	52.42
Thailand	2000	38,470.04	15,355.00	15,458.53	11,664.29	15,355.00	11,585.70	39.91	40.18	30.32	39.91	30.12
	2005	62,344.90	25,524.78	25,608.41	18,869.43	25,524.78	18,801.64	40.94	41.08	30.27	40.94	30.16
	2008	116,318.96	54,355.85	54,487.17	35,599.56	54,355.85	35,502.36	46.73	46.84	30.61	46.73	30.52
	2011	71,412.57	36,465.42	36,560.69	28,422.65	36,465.42	28,339.74	51.06	51.20	39.80	51.06	39.68
	2015	70,430.15	43,623.02	43,715.94	29,772.03	43,623.02	29,699.01	61.94	62.07	42.27	61.94	42.17
Viet Nam	2000	594.18	291.77	292.10	462.71	291.77	462.28	49.11	49.16	77.87	49.11	77.80
	2005	3,340.36	2,121.49	2,123.72	1,618.71	2,121.49	1,617.14	63.51	63.58	48.46	63.51	48.41
	2008	16,132.98	7,058.29	7,081.55	5,077.48	7,058.29	5,060.31	43.75	43.89	31.47	43.75	31.37
	2011	11,758.61	6,665.92	6,678.57	5,172.73	6,665.92	5,163.66	56.69	56.80	43.99	56.69	43.91
	2015	15,926.87	8,525.36	8,542.08	6,808.28	8,525.36	6,795.39	53.53	53.63	42.75	53.53	42.67
Mongolia	2000	29.19	14.98	14.98	9.57	14.98	9.57	51.30	51.30	32.77	51.30	32.77
	2005	39.87	22.49	22.49	17.08	22.49	17.08	56.42	56.42	42.86	56.42	42.85
	2008	149.70	102.24	102.25	45.93	102.24	45.92	68.30	68.30	30.68	68.30	30.68
	2011	112.24	62.66	62.66	76.40	62.66	76.38	55.82	55.83	68.06	55.82	68.05
	2015	130.76	86.38	86.38	119.51	86.38	119.50	66.06	66.07	91.40	66.06	91.39
Sri Lanka	2000	9.51	6.39	6.39	15.26	6.39	15.26	67.15	67.18	160.51	67.15	160.46
	2005	7.99	5.02	5.02	5.98	5.02	5.98	62.85	62.88	74.92	62.85	74.89
	2008	16.00	6.71	6.71	55.22	6.71	55.20	41.95	41.95	345.13	41.95	345.00
	2011	374.93	230.73	230.87	209.48	230.73	209.38	61.54	61.58	55.87	61.54	55.85
	2015	222.14	144.55	144.66	248.83	144.55	248.71	65.07	65.12	112.01	65.07	111.96

DVA_B = domestic value added exports by backward industrial linkages, DVA_F = domestic value added exports by forward industrial linkages, PRC = People's Republic of China, VAX_B = value added exports by backward industrial linkages, VAX_F = value added exports by forward industrial linkages, VAX_G = domestic value added absorbed abroad.

Source: ADB Multi Region Input–Output Tables Database.

Table 3.2d: Value-Added Exports by Various Measures – Business Services Sector

		Exports	VAX_G	DVA_B	DVA_F	VAX_B	VAX_F	VAX_G	DVA_B	DVA_F	VAX_B	VAX_F
			($ million)					Value–Added Export Measure to Gross Exports Ratio (%)				
PRC	2000	39,280.26	35,011.02	35,351.52	62,899.99	35,011.02	62,308.83	89.13	90.00	160.13	89.13	158.63
	2005	114,129.50	96,200.87	97,954.39	166,099.38	96,200.87	163,309.60	84.29	85.83	145.54	84.29	143.09
	2008	195,098.77	165,391.99	168,567.60	337,574.05	165,391.99	331,169.96	84.77	86.40	173.03	84.77	169.74
	2011	274,229.73	232,429.91	238,825.28	470,367.32	232,429.91	458,182.21	84.76	87.09	171.52	84.76	167.08
	2015	316,773.96	283,621.84	289,905.18	633,157.56	283,621.84	617,890.42	89.53	91.52	199.88	89.53	195.06
Indonesia	2000	4,895.61	4,107.59	4,119.34	8,914.98	4,107.59	8,897.76	83.90	84.14	182.10	83.90	181.75
	2005	8,419.52	7,105.67	7,131.82	13,061.91	7,105.67	13,023.05	84.40	84.71	155.14	84.40	154.68
	2008	13,760.94	11,786.47	11,815.51	19,827.02	11,786.47	19,766.09	85.65	85.86	144.08	85.65	143.64
	2011	19,033.93	16,560.18	16,589.45	28,083.49	16,560.18	27,996.91	87.00	87.16	147.54	87.00	147.09
	2015	18,889.07	17,229.57	17,259.52	34,121.62	17,229.57	34,036.98	91.21	91.37	180.64	91.21	180.19
India	2000	6,790.81	6,221.66	6,237.02	17,686.17	6,221.66	17,650.46	91.62	91.85	260.44	91.62	259.92
	2005	36,703.32	33,276.66	33,441.75	53,892.06	33,276.66	53,621.69	90.66	91.11	146.83	90.66	146.09
	2008	60,546.61	54,617.73	54,775.51	88,831.24	54,617.73	88,450.85	90.21	90.47	146.72	90.21	146.09
	2011	70,365.61	64,297.99	64,442.56	115,674.58	64,297.99	115,295.19	91.38	91.58	164.39	91.38	163.85
	2015	67,737.70	62,851.01	63,051.95	134,827.29	62,851.01	134,348.75	92.79	93.08	199.04	92.79	198.34
Japan	2000	88,511.38	80,955.55	82,706.15	173,351.94	80,955.55	169,750.64	91.46	93.44	195.85	91.46	191.78
	2005	112,836.20	101,247.45	103,422.15	214,827.13	101,247.45	210,372.49	89.73	91.66	190.39	89.73	186.44
	2008	170,126.24	147,769.17	150,627.35	297,497.19	147,769.17	292,335.24	86.86	88.54	174.87	86.86	171.83
	2011	171,220.37	151,141.37	153,281.63	299,703.42	151,141.37	295,340.39	88.27	89.52	175.04	88.27	172.49
	2015	162,662.46	146,575.41	148,318.72	272,559.91	146,575.41	269,452.61	90.11	91.18	167.56	90.11	165.65
Republic of Korea	2000	31,860.20	25,954.80	26,093.72	45,348.33	25,954.80	45,127.25	81.46	81.90	142.34	81.46	141.64
	2005	45,505.39	34,863.04	35,109.47	69,533.67	34,863.04	69,076.52	76.61	77.15	152.80	76.61	151.80
	2008	71,505.37	48,992.16	49,309.72	94,958.61	48,992.16	94,375.37	68.52	68.96	132.80	68.52	131.98
	2011	81,102.07	57,721.22	58,019.60	112,655.16	57,721.22	112,049.42	71.17	71.54	138.91	71.17	138.16
	2015	92,446.09	76,827.63	77,201.45	150,113.16	76,827.63	149,431.47	83.11	83.51	162.38	83.11	161.64
Taipei,China	2000	17,096.91	13,707.79	13,760.98	45,777.65	13,707.79	45,568.95	80.18	80.49	267.75	80.18	266.53
	2005	17,611.01	12,823.48	12,863.57	51,296.11	12,823.48	51,062.31	72.82	73.04	291.27	72.82	289.95
	2008	21,675.29	14,817.24	14,859.15	63,773.23	14,817.24	63,552.87	68.36	68.55	294.22	68.36	293.20
	2011	21,953.51	15,579.85	15,612.19	74,103.11	15,579.85	73,877.72	70.97	71.11	337.55	70.97	336.52
	2015	22,317.02	17,255.00	17,291.74	99,549.50	17,255.00	99,283.90	77.32	77.48	446.07	77.32	444.88
Bangladesh	2000	753.99	730.80	731.00	1,767.72	730.80	1,767.32	96.93	96.95	234.45	96.93	234.40
	2005	858.38	826.44	826.65	2,346.61	826.44	2,345.95	96.28	96.30	273.38	96.28	273.30
	2008	1,233.00	900.88	901.23	4,193.76	900.88	4,191.98	73.06	73.09	340.13	73.06	339.98
	2011	1,363.01	1,133.93	1,134.14	6,931.28	1,133.93	6,929.25	83.19	83.21	508.53	83.19	508.38
	2015	2,586.16	2,325.54	2,326.00	10,622.85	2,325.54	10,619.62	89.92	89.94	410.76	89.92	410.63

continued on next page

Global Value Chains Indicators 28

Table 3.2d: continued

Table 3.2d: Value-Added Exports by Various Measures – Business Services Sector

		Exports	VAX_G	DVA_B	DVA_F	VAX_B	VAX_F	VAX_G	DVA_B	DVA_F	VAX_B	VAX_F
			($ million)					Value-Added Export Measure to Gross Exports Ratio (%)				
Malaysia	2000	11,891.12	8,145.86	8,177.08	14,400.10	8,145.86	14,363.23	68.50	68.77	121.10	68.50	120.79
	2005	15,512.30	12,497.24	12,522.87	23,503.30	12,497.24	23,449.57	80.56	80.73	151.51	80.56	151.17
	2008	29,524.14	22,613.72	22,691.55	43,931.61	22,613.72	43,795.50	76.59	76.86	148.80	76.59	148.34
	2011	33,085.50	27,414.85	27,463.62	42,070.46	27,414.85	41,982.80	82.86	83.01	127.16	82.86	126.89
	2015	43,170.10	33,880.99	33,958.30	49,025.48	33,880.99	48,911.76	78.48	78.66	113.56	78.48	113.30
Philippines	2000	3,803.04	3,287.21	3,289.67	5,281.37	3,287.21	5,275.17	86.44	86.50	138.87	86.44	138.71
	2005	5,904.56	5,313.99	5,318.78	8,741.98	5,313.99	8,730.20	90.00	90.08	148.05	90.00	147.86
	2008	13,057.53	11,755.53	11,769.47	16,552.43	11,755.53	16,531.74	90.03	90.14	126.77	90.03	126.61
	2011	17,910.80	16,492.43	16,512.64	19,354.50	16,492.43	19,332.59	92.08	92.19	108.06	92.08	107.94
	2015	25,078.69	22,574.02	22,610.81	24,026.10	22,574.02	23,988.17	90.01	90.16	95.80	90.01	95.65
Thailand	2000	13,479.87	11,294.17	11,328.43	16,870.27	11,294.17	16,811.91	83.79	84.04	125.15	83.79	124.72
	2005	19,306.47	15,334.21	15,393.41	24,861.92	15,334.21	24,783.46	79.43	79.73	128.78	79.43	128.37
	2008	27,511.36	22,239.06	22,337.26	41,669.71	22,239.06	41,545.94	80.84	81.19	151.46	80.84	151.01
	2011	42,776.54	36,031.89	36,141.85	46,480.66	36,031.89	46,354.02	84.23	84.49	108.66	84.23	108.36
	2015	58,739.86	46,572.43	46,707.28	61,219.99	46,572.43	61,055.07	79.29	79.52	104.22	79.29	103.94
Viet Nam	2000	2,843.63	2,183.02	2,184.01	3,021.09	2,183.02	3,019.01	76.77	76.80	106.24	76.77	106.17
	2005	4,127.91	3,545.32	3,546.52	5,852.59	3,545.32	5,848.88	85.89	85.92	141.78	85.89	141.69
	2008	11,937.75	10,285.80	10,297.57	14,164.77	10,285.80	14,140.16	86.16	86.26	118.66	86.16	118.45
	2011	15,159.56	12,627.86	12,637.53	18,683.48	12,627.86	18,661.18	83.30	83.36	123.25	83.30	123.10
	2015	21,775.52	17,691.00	17,709.67	25,653.66	17,691.00	25,619.59	81.24	81.33	117.81	81.24	117.65
Mongolia	2000	140.71	90.04	90.05	102.52	90.04	102.51	63.99	64.00	72.86	63.99	72.86
	2005	260.26	177.47	177.49	230.93	177.47	230.91	68.19	68.20	88.73	68.19	88.72
	2008	569.71	382.13	382.20	488.44	382.13	488.37	67.07	67.09	85.73	67.07	85.72
	2011	1,141.58	843.93	844.27	1,265.61	843.93	1,265.20	73.93	73.96	110.86	73.93	110.83
	2015	872.28	593.21	593.30	1,180.20	593.21	1,180.03	68.01	68.02	135.30	68.01	135.28
Sri Lanka	2000	1,847.60	1,522.56	1,523.00	1,755.75	1,522.56	1,755.27	82.41	82.43	95.03	82.41	95.00
	2005	1,616.89	1,381.06	1,381.42	1,386.15	1,381.06	1,385.81	85.41	85.44	85.73	85.41	85.71
	2008	2,509.01	1,942.90	1,943.57	2,331.60	1,942.90	2,330.76	77.44	77.46	92.93	77.44	92.90
	2011	3,665.50	3,207.13	3,208.17	3,651.18	3,207.13	3,650.08	87.50	87.52	99.61	87.50	99.58
	2015	4,619.09	3,983.70	3,984.92	4,626.89	3,983.70	4,625.66	86.24	86.27	100.17	86.24	100.14

DVA_B = domestic value added exports by backward industrial linkages, DVA_F = domestic value added exports by forward industrial linkages, PRC = People's Republic of China, VAX_B = value added exports by backward industrial linkages, VAX_F = value added exports by forward industrial linkages, VAX_G = domestic value added absorbed abroad.

Source: ADB Multi Region Input–Output Tables Database.

Table 3.2e: Value-Added Exports by Various Measures – Personal Services Sector

		Exports	VAX_G	DVA_B	DVA_F	VAX_B	VAX_F	VAX_G	DVA_B	DVA_F	VAX_B	VAX_F
			($ million)					Value–Added Export Measure to Gross Exports Ratio (%)				
PRC	2000	7,589.02	6,698.46	6,746.66	5,496.68	6,698.46	5,452.91	88.27	88.90	72.43	88.27	71.85
	2005	10,882.42	9,227.45	9,344.62	13,810.94	9,227.45	13,602.22	84.79	85.87	126.91	84.79	124.99
	2008	12,856.49	11,088.96	11,215.63	25,642.29	11,088.96	25,193.71	86.25	87.24	199.45	86.25	195.96
	2011	16,710.74	14,391.49	14,675.63	32,786.95	14,391.49	31,990.60	86.12	87.82	196.20	86.12	191.44
	2015	36,141.44	33,323.01	33,416.16	88,982.47	33,323.01	87,062.69	92.20	92.46	246.21	92.20	240.89
Indonesia	2000	928.18	802.75	803.40	771.50	802.75	770.60	86.49	86.56	83.12	86.49	83.02
	2005	1,976.84	1,661.32	1,662.92	2,309.46	1,661.32	2,304.68	84.04	84.12	116.83	84.04	116.58
	2008	3,202.53	2,732.70	2,734.61	3,678.16	2,732.70	3,669.73	85.33	85.39	114.85	85.33	114.59
	2011	4,238.25	3,662.83	3,664.32	5,599.30	3,662.83	5,584.64	86.42	86.46	132.11	86.42	131.77
	2015	13,570.33	12,344.37	12,344.11	11,618.82	12,344.37	11,605.23	90.97	90.96	85.62	90.97	85.52
India	2000	1,936.15	1,775.91	1,780.05	1,924.45	1,775.91	1,920.35	91.72	91.94	99.40	91.72	99.18
	2005	3,539.36	3,097.18	3,104.98	4,573.68	3,097.18	4,558.79	87.51	87.73	129.22	87.51	128.80
	2008	5,256.43	4,779.73	4,793.54	7,381.29	4,779.73	7,357.35	90.93	91.19	140.42	90.93	139.97
	2011	6,087.11	5,518.88	5,534.42	9,325.80	5,518.88	9,298.77	90.66	90.92	153.21	90.66	152.76
	2015	7,529.22	7,283.29	7,305.21	10,500.38	7,283.29	10,468.37	96.73	97.02	139.46	96.73	139.04
Japan	2000	1,783.14	1,712.86	1,731.75	12,645.63	1,712.86	12,390.14	96.06	97.12	709.18	96.06	694.85
	2005	2,930.43	2,789.95	2,810.65	15,440.98	2,789.95	15,134.57	95.21	95.91	526.92	95.21	516.46
	2008	4,111.91	3,842.06	3,866.96	21,737.39	3,842.06	21,387.51	93.44	94.04	528.64	93.44	520.14
	2011	3,772.42	3,549.89	3,576.08	22,677.23	3,549.89	22,347.76	94.10	94.80	601.13	94.10	592.40
	2015	10,308.95	9,599.29	9,629.99	26,153.14	9,599.29	25,907.65	93.12	93.41	253.69	93.12	251.31
Republic of Korea	2000	2,852.93	2,552.72	2,559.78	2,836.19	2,552.72	2,826.76	89.48	89.72	99.41	89.48	99.08
	2005	2,829.61	2,522.84	2,534.25	3,680.20	2,522.84	3,660.52	89.16	89.56	130.06	89.16	129.36
	2008	4,534.32	3,853.14	3,866.05	5,544.83	3,853.14	5,518.74	84.98	85.26	122.29	84.98	121.71
	2011	5,049.59	4,299.13	4,313.71	6,253.37	4,299.13	6,225.57	85.14	85.43	123.84	85.14	123.29
	2015	13,844.82	12,424.64	12,429.23	13,474.93	12,424.64	13,448.93	89.74	89.78	97.33	89.74	97.14
Taipei,China	2000	985.06	858.56	860.83	1,406.46	858.56	1,401.09	87.16	87.39	142.78	87.16	142.23
	2005	1,011.52	903.83	904.64	1,953.76	903.83	1,946.88	89.35	89.43	193.15	89.35	192.47
	2008	1,482.05	1,311.65	1,313.17	2,660.39	1,311.65	2,653.05	88.50	88.61	179.51	88.50	179.01
	2011	1,606.08	1,427.72	1,429.50	3,084.65	1,427.72	3,076.81	88.90	89.01	192.06	88.90	191.57
	2015	6,704.39	5,913.64	5,914.96	9,279.20	5,913.64	9,264.45	88.21	88.23	138.40	88.21	138.18
Bangladesh	2000	488.38	470.91	471.14	909.47	470.91	909.17	96.42	96.47	186.22	96.42	186.16
	2005	531.71	510.01	510.26	1,126.56	510.01	1,126.16	95.92	95.97	211.87	95.92	211.80
	2008	863.09	792.22	792.52	1,183.82	792.22	1,183.37	91.79	91.82	137.16	91.79	137.11
	2011	762.18	704.72	704.91	1,677.62	704.72	1,677.14	92.46	92.49	220.11	92.46	220.04
	2015	2,037.02	1,894.63	1,895.05	3,531.18	1,894.63	3,530.20	93.01	93.03	173.35	93.01	173.30

continued on next page

Table 3.2e: continued

Table 3.2e: Value–Added Exports by Various Measures – Personal Services Sector

		Exports	VAX_G	DVA_B	DVA_F	VAX_B	VAX_F	VAX_G	DVA_B	DVA_F	VAX_B	VAX_F
		($ million)						Value–Added Export Measure to Gross Exports Ratio (%)				
Malaysia	2000	1,122.44	846.99	846.32	729.07	846.99	728.73	75.46	75.40	64.95	75.46	64.92
	2005	1,216.76	921.78	922.27	846.50	921.78	845.37	75.76	75.80	69.57	75.76	69.48
	2008	5,466.21	3,932.16	3,935.13	3,354.22	3,932.16	3,348.76	71.94	71.99	61.36	71.94	61.26
	2011	3,015.96	2,504.26	2,506.72	3,133.40	2,504.26	3,128.10	83.03	83.12	103.89	83.03	103.72
	2015	5,982.16	4,793.68	4,794.35	4,928.01	4,793.68	4,922.40	80.13	80.14	82.38	80.13	82.28
Philippines	2000	93.75	83.73	83.80	164.95	83.73	164.74	89.31	89.39	175.95	89.31	175.73
	2005	418.20	376.24	376.47	370.15	376.24	369.90	89.97	90.02	88.51	89.97	88.45
	2008	761.14	658.50	659.24	696.09	658.50	695.29	86.52	86.61	91.45	86.52	91.35
	2011	746.97	685.12	685.53	863.81	685.12	863.07	91.72	91.77	115.64	91.72	115.54
	2015	1,039.64	941.76	942.46	997.92	941.76	996.92	90.59	90.65	95.99	90.59	95.89
Thailand	2000	1,584.36	1,224.29	1,225.93	1,166.01	1,224.29	1,163.60	77.27	77.38	73.60	77.27	73.44
	2005	2,459.96	1,883.96	1,885.94	1,877.68	1,883.96	1,874.00	76.58	76.67	76.33	76.58	76.18
	2008	2,717.34	2,040.60	2,045.25	2,573.05	2,040.60	2,566.60	75.10	75.27	94.69	75.10	94.45
	2011	4,018.31	3,101.02	3,105.08	3,509.95	3,101.02	3,501.96	77.17	77.27	87.35	77.17	87.15
	2015	8,170.86	6,501.62	6,506.76	6,094.36	6,501.62	6,084.11	79.57	79.63	74.59	79.57	74.46
Viet Nam	2000	284.38	237.59	237.67	229.98	237.59	229.89	83.55	83.57	80.87	83.55	80.84
	2005	225.56	194.11	194.21	243.46	194.11	243.30	86.06	86.10	107.94	86.06	107.87
	2008	389.50	309.06	309.29	390.97	309.06	390.34	79.35	79.41	100.38	79.35	100.22
	2011	2,383.64	1,990.97	1,993.78	1,835.25	1,990.97	1,832.78	83.53	83.64	76.99	83.53	76.89
	2015	4,457.52	3,682.27	3,688.01	3,426.31	3,682.27	3,421.18	82.61	82.74	76.87	82.61	76.75
Mongolia	2000	4.44	2.91	2.91	2.42	2.91	2.42	65.45	65.45	54.53	65.45	54.53
	2005	5.32	3.74	3.74	4.45	3.74	4.44	70.24	70.24	83.48	70.24	83.47
	2008	6.25	4.60	4.60	44.35	4.60	44.34	73.69	73.69	710.13	73.69	710.05
	2011	17.92	13.96	13.96	33.99	13.96	33.98	77.88	77.88	189.62	77.88	189.59
	2015	20.87	18.19	18.19	54.42	18.19	54.41	87.19	87.19	260.80	87.19	260.77
Sri Lanka	2000	971.17	783.59	783.71	639.34	783.59	639.23	80.69	80.70	65.83	80.69	65.82
	2005	138.62	119.16	119.18	129.50	119.16	129.48	85.97	85.98	93.43	85.97	93.41
	2008	62.91	50.90	50.91	128.46	50.90	128.42	80.90	80.91	204.19	80.90	204.12
	2011	337.47	297.68	297.74	371.19	297.68	371.11	88.21	88.23	109.99	88.21	109.97
	2015	451.02	391.92	391.98	484.94	391.92	484.84	86.89	86.91	107.52	86.89	107.50

DVA_B = domestic value added exports by backward industrial linkages, DVA_F = domestic value added exports by forward industrial linkages, PRC = People's Republic of China, VAX_B = value added exports by backward industrial linkages, VAX_F = value added exports by forward industrial linkages, VAX_G = domestic value added absorbed abroad.

Source: ADB Multi Region Input–Output Tables Database.

Table 3.2f: Value-Added Exports by Various Measures – All Sectors

		Exports	VAX_G	DVA_B	DVA_F	VAX_B	VAX_F	VAX_G	DVA_B	DVA_F	VAX_B	VAX_F
		($ million)						Value–Added Export Measure to Gross Exports Ratio (%)				
PRC	2000	279,345.90	228,011.83	230,164.46	230,164.46	228,011.83	228,011.83	81.62	82.39	82.39	81.62	81.62
	2005	838,620.93	607,606.26	617,892.13	617,892.13	607,606.26	607,606.26	72.45	73.68	73.68	72.45	72.45
	2008	1,579,658.98	1,186,098.86	1,208,860.03	1,208,860.03	1,186,098.86	1,186,098.86	75.09	76.53	76.53	75.09	75.09
	2011	2,093,765.10	1,579,774.00	1,620,694.56	1,620,694.56	1,579,774.00	1,579,774.00	75.45	77.41	77.41	75.45	75.45
	2015	2,288,337.32	1,861,048.43	1,906,257.26	1,906,257.26	1,861,048.43	1,861,048.43	81.33	83.30	83.30	81.33	81.33
Indonesia	2000	65,246.45	52,338.15	52,472.96	52,472.96	52,338.15	52,338.15	80.22	80.42	80.42	80.22	80.22
	2005	94,067.44	75,609.51	75,894.67	75,894.67	75,609.51	75,609.51	80.38	80.68	80.68	80.38	80.38
	2008	151,221.29	124,411.41	124,958.87	124,958.87	124,411.41	124,411.41	82.27	82.63	82.63	82.27	82.27
	2011	219,754.04	185,400.49	186,507.40	186,507.40	185,400.49	185,400.49	84.37	84.87	84.87	84.37	84.37
	2015	208,792.55	189,163.43	189,973.18	189,973.18	189,163.43	189,163.43	90.60	90.99	90.99	90.60	90.60
India	2000	67,865.51	57,740.07	57,848.92	57,848.92	57,740.07	57,740.07	85.08	85.24	85.24	85.08	85.08
	2005	158,894.54	126,519.38	127,152.33	127,152.33	126,519.38	126,519.38	79.62	80.02	80.02	79.62	79.62
	2008	260,263.80	202,311.92	203,336.93	203,336.93	202,311.92	202,311.92	77.73	78.13	78.13	77.73	77.73
	2011	337,433.02	263,304.65	264,344.43	264,344.43	263,304.65	263,304.65	78.03	78.34	78.34	78.03	78.03
	2015	369,623.98	318,181.02	319,466.53	319,466.53	318,181.02	318,181.02	86.08	86.43	86.43	86.08	86.08
Japan	2000	513,245.95	457,313.40	467,029.42	467,029.42	457,313.40	457,313.40	89.10	91.00	91.00	89.10	89.10
	2005	651,184.76	558,437.73	570,274.75	570,274.75	558,437.73	558,437.73	85.76	87.57	87.57	85.76	85.76
	2008	862,937.83	689,018.02	700,901.80	700,901.80	689,018.02	689,018.02	79.85	81.22	81.22	79.85	79.85
	2011	900,325.12	731,761.37	742,908.93	742,908.93	731,761.37	731,761.37	81.28	82.52	82.52	81.28	81.28
	2015	740,112.40	620,578.79	627,608.44	627,608.44	620,578.79	620,578.79	83.85	84.80	84.80	83.85	83.85
Republic of Korea	2000	199,509.87	138,462.93	139,153.96	139,153.96	138,462.93	138,462.93	69.40	69.75	69.75	69.40	69.40
	2005	329,193.38	220,556.40	222,041.11	222,041.11	220,556.40	220,556.40	67.00	67.45	67.45	67.00	67.00
	2008	498,780.09	287,376.34	289,182.32	289,182.32	287,376.34	287,376.34	57.62	57.98	57.98	57.62	57.62
	2011	615,300.11	363,588.36	365,675.11	365,675.11	363,588.36	363,588.36	59.09	59.43	59.43	59.09	59.09
	2015	591,607.55	430,585.78	432,502.37	432,502.37	430,585.78	430,585.78	72.78	73.11	73.11	72.78	72.78
Taipei,China	2000	173,290.82	110,321.06	110,871.11	110,871.11	110,321.06	110,321.06	63.66	63.98	63.98	63.66	63.66
	2005	226,748.95	126,896.72	127,518.59	127,518.59	126,896.72	126,896.72	55.96	56.24	56.24	55.96	55.96
	2008	288,322.92	147,042.79	147,580.67	147,580.67	147,042.79	147,042.79	51.00	51.19	51.19	51.00	51.00
	2011	340,219.14	178,014.08	178,585.41	178,585.41	178,014.08	178,014.08	52.32	52.49	52.49	52.32	52.32
	2015	394,321.92	259,449.60	260,151.49	260,151.49	259,449.60	259,449.60	65.80	65.97	65.97	65.80	65.80
Bangladesh	2000	6,451.39	5,639.23	5,640.98	5,640.98	5,639.23	5,639.23	87.41	87.44	87.44	87.41	87.41
	2005	8,854.23	7,399.67	7,402.45	7,402.45	7,399.67	7,399.67	83.57	83.60	83.60	83.57	83.57
	2008	15,708.05	11,751.19	11,756.39	11,756.39	11,751.19	11,751.19	74.81	74.84	74.84	74.81	74.81
	2011	22,800.71	19,383.40	19,389.26	19,389.26	19,383.40	19,383.40	85.01	85.04	85.04	85.01	85.01
	2015	36,812.72	31,979.89	31,989.99	31,989.99	31,979.89	31,979.89	86.87	86.90	86.90	86.87	86.87

continued on next page

Table 3.2f continued

Table 3.2f: Value-Added Exports by Various Measures – All Sectors

		Exports	VAX_G	DVA_B	DVA_F	VAX_B	VAX_F	VAX_G	DVA_B	DVA_F	VAX_B	VAX_F
			($ million)					Value–Added Export Measure to Gross Exports Ratio (%)				
Malaysia	2000	111,832.08	53,273.37	53,414.43	53,414.43	53,273.37	53,273.37	47.64	47.76	47.76	47.64	47.64
	2005	147,263.47	79,625.09	79,855.38	79,855.38	79,625.09	79,625.09	54.07	54.23	54.23	54.07	54.07
	2008	222,929.88	135,705.71	136,145.77	136,145.77	135,705.71	135,705.71	60.87	61.07	61.07	60.87	60.87
	2011	191,802.71	134,178.91	134,520.49	134,520.49	134,178.91	134,178.91	69.96	70.13	70.13	69.96	69.96
	2015	189,417.80	130,239.06	130,584.83	130,584.83	130,239.06	130,239.06	68.76	68.94	68.94	68.76	68.76
Philippines	2000	26,837.67	21,503.47	21,529.42	21,529.42	21,503.47	21,503.47	80.12	80.22	80.22	80.12	80.12
	2005	32,358.42	23,327.99	23,358.72	23,358.72	23,327.99	23,327.99	72.09	72.19	72.19	72.09	72.09
	2008	62,004.58	41,224.23	41,270.13	41,270.13	41,224.23	41,224.23	66.49	66.56	66.56	66.49	66.49
	2011	52,901.69	41,247.83	41,290.86	41,290.86	41,247.83	41,247.83	77.97	78.05	78.05	77.97	77.97
	2015	60,481.11	50,622.85	50,695.26	50,695.26	50,622.85	50,622.85	83.70	83.82	83.82	83.70	83.70
Thailand	2000	81,515.09	48,280.11	48,481.49	48,481.49	48,280.11	48,280.11	59.23	59.48	59.48	59.23	59.23
	2005	122,625.82	69,402.57	69,619.92	69,619.92	69,402.57	69,402.57	56.60	56.77	56.77	56.60	56.60
	2008	205,428.43	121,040.76	121,377.84	121,377.84	121,040.76	121,040.76	58.92	59.09	59.09	58.92	58.92
	2011	188,398.91	128,574.48	128,921.14	128,921.14	128,574.48	128,574.48	68.25	68.43	68.43	68.25	68.25
	2015	209,515.22	148,941.76	149,345.60	149,345.60	148,941.76	148,941.76	71.09	71.28	71.28	71.09	71.09
Viet Nam	2000	14,018.88	10,593.84	10,603.85	10,603.85	10,593.84	10,593.84	75.57	75.64	75.64	75.57	75.57
	2005	27,044.14	20,494.58	20,514.38	20,514.38	20,494.58	20,494.58	75.78	75.86	75.86	75.78	75.78
	2008	69,551.59	45,263.54	45,386.49	45,386.49	45,263.54	45,263.54	65.08	65.26	65.26	65.08	65.08
	2011	84,579.55	58,670.89	58,763.60	58,763.60	58,670.89	58,670.89	69.37	69.48	69.48	69.37	69.37
	2015	130,368.75	85,619.34	85,768.17	85,768.17	85,619.34	85,619.34	65.67	65.79	65.79	65.67	65.67
Mongolia	2000	426.49	296.87	296.89	296.89	296.87	296.87	69.61	69.61	69.61	69.61	69.61
	2005	1,121.30	834.95	835.00	835.00	834.95	834.95	74.46	74.47	74.47	74.46	74.46
	2008	2,401.43	1,812.58	1,812.78	1,812.78	1,812.58	1,812.58	75.48	75.49	75.49	75.48	75.48
	2011	5,282.98	3,545.05	3,545.87	3,545.87	3,545.05	3,545.05	67.10	67.12	67.12	67.10	67.10
	2015	5,432.88	3,900.53	3,901.00	3,901.00	3,900.53	3,900.53	71.79	71.80	71.80	71.79	71.79
Sri Lanka	2000	4,586.24	3,615.49	3,616.37	3,616.37	3,615.49	3,615.49	78.83	78.85	78.85	78.83	78.83
	2005	2,697.70	2,225.33	2,225.96	2,225.96	2,225.33	2,225.33	82.49	82.51	82.51	82.49	82.49
	2008	7,406.15	5,728.22	5,730.56	5,730.56	5,728.22	5,728.22	77.34	77.38	77.38	77.34	77.34
	2011	9,943.23	8,395.31	8,397.69	8,397.69	8,395.31	8,395.31	84.43	84.46	84.46	84.43	84.43
	2015	14,186.26	12,241.88	12,244.75	12,244.75	12,241.88	12,241.88	86.29	86.31	86.31	86.29	86.29

DVA_B = domestic value added exports by backward industrial linkages, DVA_F = domestic value added exports by forward industrial linkages, PRC = People's Republic of China, VAX_B = value added exports by backward industrial linkages, VAX_F = value added exports by forward industrial linkages, VAX_G = domestic value added absorbed abroad.

Source: ADB Multi Region Input–Output Tables Database.

Table 3.3a: Direct and Indirect Value-Added Exports – Primary Sector

		Gross Exports	VAX_F	VAX_B	Direct Exports	Indirect Exports (Forward Linkages)	Indirect Exports (Backward Linkages)	Share of Direct Exports in VAX_F	Share of Indirect Exports in VAX_F	Share of Direct Exports in VAX_B	Share of Indirect Exports in VAX_B
		($ million)						(percentage)			
PRC	2000	10,913.96	31,931.10	9,946.62	7,099.72	24,831.38	2,846.90	22.23	77.77	71.38	28.62
	2005	20,989.37	88,383.75	18,111.95	13,168.96	75,214.79	4,942.99	14.90	85.10	72.71	27.29
	2008	25,091.04	157,316.85	21,687.91	15,202.79	142,114.07	6,485.12	9.66	90.34	70.10	29.90
	2011	34,237.15	205,033.31	29,729.82	21,634.36	183,398.95	8,095.46	10.55	89.45	72.77	27.23
	2015	44,928.07	258,648.15	40,781.84	30,100.34	228,547.81	10,681.50	11.64	88.36	73.81	26.19
Indonesia	2000	10,794.33	19,496.69	10,287.98	10,007.89	9,488.81	280.09	51.33	48.67	97.28	2.72
	2005	21,998.21	29,691.93	20,432.30	19,646.52	10,045.42	785.78	66.17	33.83	96.15	3.85
	2008	36,871.59	52,263.01	34,642.99	33,048.76	19,214.25	1,594.23	63.24	36.76	95.40	4.60
	2011	65,323.49	88,261.98	61,875.07	59,224.11	29,037.87	2,650.96	67.10	32.90	95.72	4.28
	2015	39,882.12	74,457.95	38,398.16	36,542.81	37,915.13	1,855.35	49.08	50.92	95.17	4.83
India	2000	8,241.66	13,456.93	7,943.73	7,007.94	6,448.99	935.79	52.08	47.92	88.22	11.78
	2005	14,571.58	22,521.46	13,866.36	11,938.18	10,583.29	1,928.19	53.01	46.99	86.09	13.91
	2008	21,706.11	33,056.84	20,494.45	17,781.64	15,275.20	2,712.81	53.79	46.21	86.76	13.24
	2011	28,737.83	43,710.87	27,503.22	23,899.57	19,811.30	3,603.66	54.68	45.32	86.90	13.10
	2015	21,172.38	43,763.54	20,030.89	17,706.22	26,057.32	2,324.67	40.46	59.54	88.39	11.61
Japan	2000	2,242.99	4,310.84	1,872.27	1,074.96	3,235.88	797.31	24.94	75.06	57.41	42.59
	2005	2,957.53	4,960.76	2,133.47	1,114.78	3,845.98	1,018.69	22.47	77.53	52.25	47.75
	2008	4,797.37	5,396.25	2,702.73	1,298.01	4,098.25	1,404.72	24.05	75.95	48.03	51.97
	2011	5,467.05	6,759.52	3,155.54	1,567.20	5,192.32	1,588.34	23.19	76.81	49.66	50.34
	2015	3,133.70	5,563.90	2,629.77	1,251.20	4,312.70	1,378.57	22.49	77.51	47.58	52.42
Republic of Korea	2000	481.62	3,018.25	427.23	361.54	2,656.71	65.69	11.98	88.02	84.62	15.38
	2005	627.11	3,715.91	549.61	433.63	3,282.28	115.98	11.67	88.33	78.90	21.10
	2008	518.92	3,791.16	412.58	312.84	3,478.33	99.74	8.25	91.75	75.82	24.18
	2011	770.65	4,778.19	607.87	457.96	4,320.23	149.91	9.58	90.42	75.34	24.66
	2015	1,218.63	6,853.96	1,024.04	747.36	6,106.60	276.68	10.90	89.10	72.98	27.02
Taipei,China	2000	1,829.67	1,631.61	1,525.06	960.30	671.30	564.76	58.86	41.14	62.97	37.03
	2005	2,136.96	1,700.35	1,652.75	1,041.05	659.29	611.70	61.23	38.77	62.99	37.01
	2008	2,609.74	2,219.08	1,886.16	1,298.65	920.42	587.51	58.52	41.48	68.85	31.15
	2011	4,804.99	3,768.22	3,562.72	2,477.77	1,290.45	1,084.95	65.75	34.25	69.55	30.45
	2015	5,542.35	3,750.36	4,268.90	2,852.40	897.96	1,416.50	76.06	23.94	66.82	33.18
Bangladesh	2000	390.28	797.19	377.47	342.88	454.30	34.58	43.01	56.99	90.84	9.16
	2005	368.79	932.00	353.38	318.47	613.53	34.92	34.17	65.83	90.12	9.88
	2008	465.26	728.37	437.28	268.75	459.62	168.53	36.90	63.10	61.46	38.54
	2011	636.99	1,279.73	573.94	348.75	930.98	225.18	27.25	72.75	60.76	39.24
	2015	1,069.47	2,043.78	938.40	572.18	1,471.60	366.22	28.00	72.00	60.97	39.03

continued on next page

Table 3.3a: continued

Table 3.3a: Direct and Indirect Value-Added Exports – Primary Sector

		Gross Exports	VAX_F	VAX_B	Direct Exports	Indirect Exports (Forward Linkages)	Indirect Exports (Backward Linkages)	Share of Direct Exports in VAX_F	Share of Indirect Exports in VAX_F	Share of Direct Exports in VAX_B	Share of Indirect Exports in VAX_B
		($ million)						(percentage)			
Malaysia	2000	9,555.73	12,423.16	8,233.91	7,708.97	4,714.18	524.93	62.05	37.95	93.62	6.38
	2005	15,801.93	21,563.96	13,791.36	12,126.45	9,437.51	1,664.91	56.23	43.77	87.93	12.07
	2008	38,694.02	47,830.68	33,974.25	30,352.29	17,478.39	3,621.96	63.46	36.54	89.34	10.66
	2011	17,811.43	39,056.95	15,969.60	13,743.32	25,313.62	2,226.27	35.19	64.81	86.06	13.94
	2015	10,597.02	28,256.83	9,161.75	7,810.22	20,446.61	1,351.53	27.64	72.36	85.25	14.75
Philippines	2000	697.59	1,782.05	649.35	572.11	1,209.94	77.24	32.10	67.90	88.10	11.90
	2005	925.27	2,999.96	850.97	712.96	2,287.00	138.01	23.77	76.23	83.78	16.22
	2008	2,153.04	5,579.95	1,969.22	1,652.01	3,927.94	317.21	29.61	70.39	83.89	16.11
	2011	1,467.88	5,310.72	1,357.64	1,127.90	4,182.82	229.74	21.24	78.76	83.08	16.92
	2015	1,622.13	4,896.03	1,484.56	1,219.55	3,676.49	265.01	24.91	75.09	82.15	17.85
Thailand	2000	1,515.61	5,417.87	1,309.84	1,070.76	4,347.11	239.09	19.76	80.24	81.75	18.25
	2005	2,494.81	7,868.43	2,111.82	1,691.32	6,177.11	420.50	21.49	78.51	80.09	19.91
	2008	4,591.39	16,927.42	3,893.91	3,118.60	13,808.82	775.31	18.42	81.58	80.09	19.91
	2011	7,073.21	22,236.25	6,089.28	4,808.90	17,427.34	1,280.38	21.63	78.37	78.97	21.03
	2015	7,393.86	21,490.30	6,221.76	4,928.73	16,561.57	1,293.03	22.93	77.07	79.22	20.78
Viet Nam	2000	5,953.49	5,053.30	5,183.53	4,389.60	663.70	793.93	86.87	13.13	84.68	15.32
	2005	10,704.56	9,223.93	9,024.99	7,414.15	1,809.78	1,610.83	80.38	19.62	82.15	17.85
	2008	25,345.58	19,373.83	19,168.64	16,370.40	3,003.43	2,798.24	84.50	15.50	85.40	14.60
	2011	26,068.80	23,336.35	21,419.60	18,125.78	5,210.57	3,293.83	77.67	22.33	84.62	15.38
	2015	41,929.01	35,278.64	32,681.60	27,910.19	7,368.45	4,771.41	79.11	20.89	85.40	14.60
Mongolia	2000	184.31	154.36	139.78	125.55	28.82	14.23	81.33	18.67	89.82	10.18
	2005	708.22	523.15	549.46	478.32	44.83	71.14	91.43	8.57	87.05	12.95
	2008	1,460.71	1,144.16	1,157.27	1,018.14	126.02	139.12	88.99	11.01	87.98	12.02
	2011	3,637.57	1,965.02	2,333.74	1,844.58	120.44	489.16	93.87	6.13	79.04	20.96
	2015	3,986.99	2,207.66	2,856.89	2,076.67	130.99	780.22	94.07	5.93	72.69	27.31
Sri Lanka	2000	1,227.42	1,307.93	1,035.59	944.79	363.14	90.80	72.24	27.76	91.23	8.77
	2005	1,699.18	1,535.04	1,381.11	1,246.81	288.23	134.30	81.22	18.78	90.28	9.72
	2008	2,698.11	2,666.24	2,396.27	2,081.30	584.94	314.97	78.06	21.94	86.86	13.14
	2011	2,870.23	2,929.31	2,623.34	2,254.17	675.13	369.16	76.95	23.05	85.93	14.07
	2015	2,705.12	2,717.81	2,449.91	2,074.90	642.91	375.00	76.34	23.66	84.69	15.31

PRC = People's Republic of China, VAX_B = value added exports by backward industrial linkages, VAX_F = value added exports by forward industrial linkages.

Source: ADB Multi Region Input–Output Tables Database.

Table 3.3b: Direct and Indirect Value-Added Exports – Low Technology Manufacturing Sector

		Gross Exports	VAX_F	VAX_B	Direct Exports	Indirect Exports (Forward Linkages)	Indirect Exports (Backward Linkages)	Share of Direct Exports in VAX_F	Share of Indirect Exports in VAX_F	Share of Direct Exports in VAX_B	Share of Indirect Exports in VAX_B
		($ million)						(percentage)			
PRC	2000	94,579.86	56,369.37	78,750.98	35,512.38	20,856.99	43,238.60	63.00	37.00	45.09	54.91
	2005	215,067.98	133,765.08	173,438.84	72,594.06	61,171.02	100,844.77	54.27	45.73	41.86	58.14
	2008	374,045.07	242,360.65	311,230.07	125,625.09	116,735.56	185,604.98	51.83	48.17	40.36	59.64
	2011	515,989.76	329,226.24	430,535.65	174,726.86	154,499.37	255,808.79	53.07	46.93	40.58	59.42
	2015	621,467.80	329,883.33	536,511.21	193,876.33	136,007.00	342,634.88	58.77	41.23	36.14	63.86
Indonesia	2000	25,158.01	12,362.34	19,788.42	10,876.88	1,485.46	8,911.54	87.98	12.02	54.97	45.03
	2005	29,989.11	15,084.93	23,450.92	13,073.19	2,011.74	10,377.73	86.66	13.34	55.75	44.25
	2008	49,037.44	23,657.41	39,148.53	20,633.58	3,023.83	18,514.95	87.22	12.78	52.71	47.29
	2011	64,744.94	31,542.13	52,009.46	27,220.37	4,321.76	24,789.09	86.30	13.70	52.34	47.66
	2015	72,541.82	36,497.74	63,891.59	30,576.56	5,921.18	33,315.03	83.78	16.22	47.86	52.14
India	2000	29,631.28	13,452.64	25,538.88	9,567.35	3,885.29	15,971.53	71.12	28.88	37.46	62.54
	2005	56,477.49	23,114.74	40,422.34	16,671.35	6,443.38	23,750.98	72.12	27.88	41.24	58.76
	2008	83,437.14	32,646.27	56,829.67	22,785.14	9,861.13	34,044.53	69.79	30.21	40.09	59.91
	2011	110,565.11	40,698.56	71,406.03	28,359.98	12,338.57	43,046.04	69.68	30.32	39.72	60.28
	2015	134,634.27	53,260.52	112,270.47	35,137.28	18,123.23	77,133.19	65.97	34.03	31.30	68.70
Japan	2000	26,831.00	45,938.27	24,125.38	11,600.64	34,337.63	12,524.74	25.25	74.75	48.08	51.92
	2005	37,772.16	53,715.70	32,816.28	15,545.32	38,170.38	17,270.97	28.94	71.06	47.37	52.63
	2008	48,171.52	58,606.46	39,357.30	16,789.08	41,817.38	22,568.23	28.65	71.35	42.66	57.34
	2011	59,620.72	70,188.67	49,198.36	20,736.07	49,452.61	28,462.29	29.54	70.46	42.15	57.85
	2015	53,403.95	61,765.80	44,357.02	18,502.12	43,263.68	25,854.90	29.96	70.04	41.71	58.29
Republic of Korea	2000	30,447.23	21,119.65	22,853.66	12,780.51	8,339.14	10,073.15	60.51	39.49	55.92	44.08
	2005	28,354.23	24,526.27	21,081.59	10,835.72	13,690.54	10,245.87	44.18	55.82	51.40	48.60
	2008	33,486.87	26,792.29	22,152.98	11,745.93	15,046.36	10,407.05	43.84	56.16	53.02	46.98
	2011	39,838.06	34,596.61	26,242.83	13,548.45	21,048.16	12,694.38	39.16	60.84	51.63	48.37
	2015	38,994.24	40,378.15	29,317.40	14,139.31	26,238.84	15,178.09	35.02	64.98	48.23	51.77
Taipei,China	2000	31,315.20	14,868.75	22,732.57	10,526.75	4,342.00	12,205.83	70.80	29.20	46.31	53.69
	2005	28,325.89	12,946.94	18,936.50	8,599.32	4,347.62	10,337.18	66.42	33.58	45.41	54.59
	2008	29,726.10	11,408.23	17,817.95	8,026.64	3,381.59	9,791.32	70.36	29.64	45.05	54.95
	2011	35,854.34	13,568.72	21,441.80	9,517.01	4,051.70	11,924.79	70.14	29.86	44.39	55.61
	2015	48,755.75	27,082.07	32,215.86	13,350.20	13,731.87	18,865.66	49.30	50.70	41.44	58.56
Bangladesh	2000	4,701.33	1,993.32	3,961.19	1,774.64	218.68	2,186.55	89.03	10.97	44.80	55.20
	2005	6,958.69	2,729.58	5,593.05	2,433.06	296.52	3,159.99	89.14	10.86	43.50	56.50
	2008	12,615.07	5,322.29	9,316.33	5,075.92	246.37	4,240.41	95.37	4.63	54.48	45.52
	2011	19,607.53	8,991.49	16,666.58	8,493.89	497.60	8,172.69	94.47	5.53	50.96	49.04
	2015	30,510.52	15,340.13	26,324.96	14,396.50	943.63	11,928.46	93.85	6.15	54.69	45.31

continued on next page

Table 3.3b: continued

Table 3.3b: Direct and Indirect Value-Added Exports – Low Technology Manufacturing Sector

		Gross Exports	VAX_F	VAX_B	Direct Exports	Indirect Exports (Forward Linkages)	Indirect Exports (Backward Linkages)	Share of Direct Exports in VAX_F	Share of Indirect Exports in VAX_F	Share of Direct Exports in VAX_B	Share of Indirect Exports in VAX_B
		($ million)						(percentage)			
Malaysia	2000	16,805.50	7,626.70	10,375.30	5,190.60	2,436.10	5,184.70	68.06	31.94	50.03	49.97
	2005	20,517.30	10,803.52	13,448.36	6,297.99	4,505.53	7,150.37	58.30	41.70	46.83	53.17
	2008	21,322.33	11,566.61	14,212.20	6,181.88	5,384.73	8,030.33	53.45	46.55	43.50	56.50
	2011	46,869.96	14,577.05	33,454.32	8,949.94	5,627.11	24,504.39	61.40	38.60	26.75	73.25
	2015	45,356.51	14,553.02	27,736.37	8,479.61	6,073.41	19,256.76	58.27	41.73	30.57	69.43
Philippines	2000	5,490.79	4,307.21	4,605.12	2,926.30	1,380.90	1,678.82	67.94	32.06	63.54	36.46
	2005	8,045.10	4,929.97	6,732.33	3,380.38	1,549.59	3,351.96	68.57	31.43	50.21	49.79
	2008	13,948.90	8,502.54	11,356.21	5,715.70	2,786.84	5,640.50	67.22	32.78	50.33	49.67
	2011	10,773.78	7,362.25	9,365.95	4,332.44	3,029.81	5,033.51	58.85	41.15	46.26	53.74
	2015	13,682.74	10,751.15	11,235.74	5,808.13	4,943.02	5,427.61	54.02	45.98	51.69	48.31
Thailand	2000	26,465.20	13,301.04	19,096.81	10,370.72	2,930.32	8,726.09	77.97	22.03	54.31	45.69
	2005	36,019.68	16,075.04	24,547.81	11,942.59	4,132.45	12,605.21	74.29	25.71	48.65	51.35
	2008	54,289.37	24,498.45	38,511.34	18,165.02	6,333.42	20,346.32	74.15	25.85	47.17	52.83
	2011	63,118.28	28,142.51	46,886.88	20,647.47	7,495.04	26,239.40	73.37	26.63	44.04	55.96
	2015	64,780.50	30,613.26	46,022.94	21,178.47	9,434.79	24,844.46	69.18	30.82	46.02	53.98
Viet Nam	2000	4,343.19	1,829.37	2,697.92	1,295.08	534.28	1,402.84	70.79	29.21	48.00	52.00
	2005	8,645.75	3,561.33	5,608.67	2,187.07	1,374.26	3,421.59	61.41	38.59	38.99	61.01
	2008	15,745.78	6,298.89	8,441.75	3,677.31	2,621.58	4,764.43	58.38	41.62	43.56	56.44
	2011	29,208.94	9,676.92	15,966.54	5,710.65	3,966.27	10,255.89	59.01	40.99	35.77	64.23
	2015	46,279.82	14,504.54	23,039.12	8,335.09	6,169.44	14,704.03	57.47	42.53	36.18	63.82
Mongolia	2000	67.84	28.01	49.18	17.64	10.37	31.53	62.99	37.01	35.88	64.12
	2005	107.62	59.36	81.79	30.07	29.29	51.72	50.66	49.34	36.77	63.23
	2008	215.06	89.79	166.34	47.62	42.16	118.72	53.04	46.96	28.63	71.37
	2011	373.66	204.47	290.77	118.83	85.64	171.94	58.12	41.88	40.87	59.13
	2015	421.98	338.92	345.86	156.54	182.38	189.32	46.19	53.81	45.26	54.74
Sri Lanka	2000	3,672.90	2,056.00	2,648.19	1,898.83	157.17	749.37	92.36	7.64	71.70	28.30
	2005	4,113.75	2,468.03	2,730.73	1,940.10	527.93	790.63	78.61	21.39	71.05	28.95
	2008	4,818.02	3,065.60	3,611.37	2,385.07	680.52	1,226.29	77.80	22.20	66.04	33.96
	2011	6,363.32	4,648.66	5,329.43	3,527.56	1,121.10	1,801.87	75.88	24.12	66.19	33.81
	2015	6,826.02	5,105.13	5,906.02	3,894.37	1,210.76	2,011.65	76.28	23.72	65.94	34.06

PRC = People's Republic of China, VAX_B = value added exports by backward industrial linkages, VAX_F = value added exports by forward industrial linkages.

Source: ADB Multi Region Input–Output Tables Database.

Table 3.3c: Direct and Indirect Value-Added Exports – Medium- and High-Technology Manufacturing Sector

		Gross Exports	VAX_F	VAX_B	Direct Exports	Indirect Exports (Forward Linkages)	Indirect Exports (Backward Linkages)	Share of Direct Exports in VAX_F	Share of Indirect Exports in VAX_F	Share of Direct Exports in VAX_B	Share of Indirect Exports in VAX_B
		($ million)						(percentage)			
PRC	2000	126,982.80	71,949.62	97,604.76	42,435.53	29,514.08	55,169.23	58.98	41.02	43.48	56.52
	2005	477,551.66	208,545.62	310,627.16	128,126.35	80,419.27	182,500.81	61.44	38.56	41.25	58.75
	2008	972,567.61	430,057.68	676,699.92	254,741.56	175,316.12	421,958.37	59.23	40.77	37.64	62.36
	2011	1,252,597.72	555,341.65	872,687.13	328,935.98	226,405.67	543,751.15	59.23	40.77	37.69	62.31
	2015	1,269,026.06	567,563.84	966,810.53	311,066.26	256,497.58	655,744.27	54.81	45.19	32.17	67.83
Indonesia	2000	23,470.31	10,810.75	17,351.40	9,124.28	1,686.48	8,227.12	84.40	15.60	52.59	47.41
	2005	31,683.76	15,504.93	22,959.31	13,592.69	1,912.24	9,366.62	87.67	12.33	59.20	40.80
	2008	48,348.79	25,055.18	36,100.72	21,395.84	3,659.34	14,704.88	85.39	14.61	59.27	40.73
	2011	66,413.42	32,014.83	51,292.95	28,633.96	3,380.87	22,658.99	89.44	10.56	55.82	44.18
	2015	63,909.21	32,565.53	57,299.75	27,559.33	5,006.21	29,740.42	84.63	15.37	48.10	51.90
India	2000	21,265.62	11,259.69	16,259.89	7,417.78	3,841.91	8,842.11	65.88	34.12	45.62	54.38
	2005	47,602.78	22,702.69	35,856.83	15,637.14	7,065.55	20,219.69	68.88	31.12	43.61	56.39
	2008	89,317.52	40,800.62	65,590.34	28,609.36	12,191.26	36,980.99	70.12	29.88	43.62	56.38
	2011	121,677.35	54,301.26	94,578.53	39,128.78	15,172.48	55,449.75	72.06	27.94	41.37	58.63
	2015	138,550.42	76,339.85	115,745.36	49,007.02	27,332.82	66,738.33	64.20	35.80	42.34	57.66
Japan	2000	393,877.43	224,923.51	348,647.34	179,368.40	45,555.11	169,278.94	79.75	20.25	51.45	48.55
	2005	494,688.44	274,254.21	419,450.58	218,479.70	55,774.51	200,970.88	79.66	20.34	52.09	47.91
	2008	635,730.79	311,292.57	495,346.76	242,308.56	68,984.01	253,038.20	77.84	22.16	48.92	51.08
	2011	660,244.56	337,125.02	524,716.21	266,534.89	70,590.14	258,181.33	79.06	20.94	50.80	49.20
	2015	510,603.33	257,888.83	417,417.31	201,506.13	56,382.70	215,911.17	78.14	21.86	48.27	51.73
Republic of Korea	2000	133,867.89	66,371.02	86,674.53	52,810.25	13,560.77	33,864.28	79.57	20.43	60.93	39.07
	2005	251,877.04	119,577.19	161,539.31	93,724.56	25,852.62	67,814.75	78.38	21.62	58.02	41.98
	2008	388,734.61	156,898.77	211,965.47	124,830.59	32,068.18	87,134.88	79.56	20.44	58.89	41.11
	2011	488,539.74	205,938.56	274,717.32	164,277.92	41,660.64	110,439.40	79.77	20.23	59.80	40.20
	2015	445,103.76	220,473.26	310,992.07	169,357.44	51,115.82	141,634.64	76.82	23.18	54.46	45.54
Taipei,China	2000	122,063.97	46,850.66	71,497.08	38,927.26	7,923.40	32,569.81	83.09	16.91	54.45	45.55
	2005	177,663.57	59,240.25	92,580.17	49,491.47	9,748.77	43,088.69	83.54	16.46	53.46	46.54
	2008	232,829.75	67,209.56	111,209.78	57,558.35	9,651.21	53,651.43	85.64	14.36	51.76	48.24
	2011	276,000.22	83,722.62	136,001.98	71,391.12	12,331.49	64,610.86	85.27	14.73	52.49	47.51
	2015	311,002.41	120,068.82	199,796.21	83,044.30	37,024.53	116,751.91	69.16	30.84	41.56	58.44
Bangladesh	2000	117.41	172.23	98.86	53.29	118.94	45.58	30.94	69.06	53.90	46.10
	2005	136.66	265.99	116.79	62.88	203.11	53.91	23.64	76.36	53.84	46.16
	2008	531.64	325.20	304.49	209.51	115.69	94.98	64.42	35.58	68.81	31.19
	2011	431.00	505.80	304.23	146.72	359.08	157.52	29.01	70.99	48.23	51.77
	2015	609.56	446.16	496.36	117.86	328.30	378.50	26.42	73.58	23.74	76.26

continued on next page

Table 3.3c: continued

Table 3.3c: Direct and Indirect Value-Added Exports – Medium- and High-Technology Manufacturing Sector

		Gross Exports	VAX_F	VAX_B	Direct Exports	Indirect Exports (Forward Linkages)	Indirect Exports (Backward Linkages)	Share of Direct Exports in VAX_F	Share of Indirect Exports in VAX_F	Share of Direct Exports in VAX_B	Share of Indirect Exports in VAX_B
		($ million)						(percentage)			
Malaysia	2000	72,457.29	18,131.55	25,671.31	16,149.80	1,981.75	9,521.51	89.07	10.93	62.91	37.09
	2005	94,215.18	22,962.68	38,966.35	18,817.50	4,145.18	20,148.86	81.95	18.05	48.29	51.71
	2008	127,923.18	29,164.16	60,973.38	22,287.91	6,876.26	38,685.47	76.42	23.58	36.55	63.45
	2011	91,019.86	35,434.02	54,835.88	26,048.84	9,385.17	28,787.03	73.51	26.49	47.50	52.50
	2015	84,312.00	33,595.06	54,666.27	24,346.48	9,248.58	30,319.79	72.47	27.53	44.54	55.46
Philippines	2000	16,752.49	9,974.30	12,878.05	8,329.13	1,645.17	4,548.92	83.51	16.49	64.68	35.32
	2005	17,065.30	6,297.97	10,054.47	5,411.34	886.63	4,643.13	85.92	14.08	53.82	46.18
	2008	32,083.97	9,914.71	15,484.77	8,488.97	1,425.74	6,995.80	85.62	14.38	54.82	45.18
	2011	22,002.25	8,379.20	13,346.69	6,899.59	1,479.61	6,447.10	82.34	17.66	51.70	48.30
	2015	19,057.91	9,990.58	14,386.77	7,697.40	2,293.18	6,689.36	77.05	22.95	53.50	46.50
Thailand	2000	38,470.04	11,585.70	15,355.00	9,378.27	2,207.42	5,976.72	80.95	19.05	61.08	38.92
	2005	62,344.90	18,801.64	25,524.78	15,172.99	3,628.65	10,351.79	80.70	19.30	59.44	40.56
	2008	116,318.96	35,502.36	54,355.85	29,383.89	6,118.47	24,971.96	82.77	17.23	54.06	45.94
	2011	71,412.57	28,339.74	36,465.42	20,217.69	8,122.05	16,247.73	71.34	28.66	55.44	44.56
	2015	70,430.15	29,699.01	43,623.02	20,520.57	9,178.45	23,102.45	69.10	30.90	47.04	52.96
Viet Nam	2000	594.18	462.28	291.77	179.23	283.05	112.54	38.77	61.23	61.43	38.57
	2005	3,340.36	1,617.14	2,121.49	662.20	954.94	1,459.29	40.95	59.05	31.21	68.79
	2008	16,132.98	5,060.31	7,058.29	3,451.92	1,608.40	3,606.37	68.22	31.78	48.91	51.09
	2011	11,758.61	5,163.66	6,665.92	2,317.22	2,846.44	4,348.70	44.88	55.12	34.76	65.24
	2015	15,926.87	6,795.39	8,525.36	3,115.81	3,679.58	5,409.55	45.85	54.15	36.55	63.45
Mongolia	2000	29.19	9.57	14.98	7.07	2.50	7.91	73.88	26.12	47.20	52.80
	2005	39.87	17.08	22.49	10.13	6.95	12.36	59.30	40.70	45.04	54.96
	2008	149.70	45.92	102.24	31.38	14.54	70.86	68.33	31.67	30.69	69.31
	2011	112.24	76.38	62.66	43.03	33.35	19.62	56.34	43.66	68.68	31.32
	2015	130.76	119.50	86.38	56.09	63.41	30.29	46.94	53.06	64.93	35.07
Sri Lanka	2000	332.83	465.38	226.30	203.56	261.82	22.73	43.74	56.26	89.95	10.05
	2005	359.47	257.25	220.90	144.48	112.77	76.42	56.16	43.84	65.40	34.60
	2008	660.75	569.89	554.34	302.47	267.42	251.86	53.08	46.92	54.57	45.43
	2011	776.86	435.51	438.38	239.07	196.45	199.32	54.89	45.11	54.53	45.47
	2015	921.90	770.99	751.64	415.04	355.95	336.60	53.83	46.17	55.22	44.78

PRC = People's Republic of China, VAX_B = value added exports by backward industrial linkages, VAX_F = value added exports by forward industrial linkages.

Source: ADB Multi Region Input–Output Tables Database.

Table 3.3d: Direct and Indirect Value-Added Exports – Business Services Sector

		Gross Exports	VAX_F	VAX_B	Direct Exports	Indirect Exports (Forward Linkages)	Indirect Exports (Backward Linkages)	Share of Direct Exports in VAX_F	Share of Indirect Exports in VAX_F	Share of Direct Exports in VAX_B	Share of Indirect Exports in VAX_B
		($ million)						(percentage)			
PRC	2000	39,280.26	62,308.83	35,011.02	19,628.16	42,680.68	15,382.86	31.50	68.50	56.06	43.94
	2005	114,129.50	163,309.60	96,200.87	55,936.33	107,373.27	40,264.54	34.25	65.75	58.15	41.85
	2008	195,098.77	331,169.96	165,391.99	94,053.40	237,116.56	71,338.59	28.40	71.60	56.87	43.13
	2011	274,229.73	458,182.21	232,429.91	132,256.62	325,925.58	100,173.28	28.87	71.13	56.90	43.10
	2015	316,773.96	617,890.42	283,621.84	157,056.16	460,834.26	126,565.68	25.42	74.58	55.38	44.62
Indonesia	2000	4,895.61	8,897.76	4,107.59	2,583.47	6,314.28	1,524.12	29.04	70.96	62.89	37.11
	2005	8,419.52	13,023.05	7,105.67	4,701.95	8,321.11	2,403.72	36.10	63.90	66.17	33.83
	2008	13,760.94	19,766.09	11,786.47	7,676.05	12,090.04	4,110.43	38.83	61.17	65.13	34.87
	2011	19,033.93	27,996.91	16,560.18	10,644.03	17,352.88	5,916.15	38.02	61.98	64.27	35.73
	2015	18,889.07	34,036.98	17,229.57	10,612.33	23,424.65	6,617.24	31.18	68.82	61.59	38.41
India	2000	6,790.81	17,650.46	6,221.66	4,162.92	13,487.54	2,058.74	23.59	76.41	66.91	33.09
	2005	36,703.32	53,621.69	33,276.66	24,522.35	29,099.34	8,754.32	45.73	54.27	73.69	26.31
	2008	60,546.61	88,450.85	54,617.73	40,596.74	47,854.11	14,020.99	45.90	54.10	74.33	25.67
	2011	70,365.61	115,295.19	64,297.99	47,916.89	67,378.30	16,381.10	41.56	58.44	74.52	25.48
	2015	67,737.70	134,348.75	62,851.01	48,436.69	85,912.06	14,414.32	36.05	63.95	77.07	22.93
Japan	2000	88,511.38	169,750.64	80,955.55	51,889.71	117,860.92	29,065.84	30.57	69.43	64.10	35.90
	2005	112,836.20	210,372.49	101,247.45	66,765.77	143,606.73	34,481.69	31.74	68.26	65.94	34.06
	2008	170,126.24	292,335.24	147,769.17	99,460.19	192,875.04	48,308.98	34.02	65.98	67.31	32.69
	2011	171,220.37	295,340.39	151,141.37	102,375.18	192,965.21	48,766.19	34.66	65.34	67.73	32.27
	2015	162,662.46	269,452.61	146,575.41	97,744.65	171,707.96	48,830.76	36.28	63.72	66.69	33.31
Republic of Korea	2000	31,860.20	45,127.25	25,954.80	18,132.42	26,994.82	7,822.37	40.18	59.82	69.86	30.14
	2005	45,505.39	69,076.52	34,863.04	26,107.85	42,968.67	8,755.20	37.80	62.20	74.89	25.11
	2008	71,505.37	94,375.37	48,992.16	36,390.57	57,984.80	12,601.59	38.56	61.44	74.28	25.72
	2011	81,102.07	112,049.42	57,721.22	42,581.61	69,467.82	15,139.61	38.00	62.00	73.77	26.23
	2015	92,446.09	149,431.47	76,827.63	50,738.56	98,692.91	26,089.07	33.95	66.05	66.04	33.96
Taipei,China	2000	17,096.91	45,568.95	13,707.79	8,694.41	36,874.54	5,013.37	19.08	80.92	63.43	36.57
	2005	17,611.01	51,062.31	12,823.48	8,043.41	43,018.90	4,780.06	15.75	84.25	62.72	37.28
	2008	21,675.29	63,552.87	14,817.24	10,210.90	53,341.97	4,606.34	16.07	83.93	68.91	31.09
	2011	21,953.51	73,877.72	15,579.85	10,950.30	62,927.42	4,629.55	14.82	85.18	70.29	29.71
	2015	22,317.02	99,283.90	17,255.00	11,291.12	87,992.78	5,963.88	11.37	88.63	65.44	34.56
Bangladesh	2000	753.99	1,767.32	730.80	621.98	1,145.34	108.82	35.19	64.81	85.11	14.89
	2005	858.38	2,345.95	826.44	689.75	1,656.20	136.69	29.40	70.60	83.46	16.54
	2008	1,233.00	4,191.98	900.88	619.18	3,572.80	281.70	14.77	85.23	68.73	31.27
	2011	1,363.01	6,929.25	1,133.93	704.85	6,224.40	429.08	10.17	89.83	62.16	37.84
	2015	2,586.16	10,619.62	2,325.54	1,370.77	9,248.85	954.77	12.91	87.09	58.94	41.06

continued on next page

Table 3.3d: continued

Table 3.3d: Direct and Indirect Value-Added Exports – Business Services Sector

		Gross Exports	VAX_F	VAX_B	Direct Exports	Indirect Exports (Forward Linkages)	Indirect Exports (Backward Linkages)	Share of Direct Exports in VAX_F	Share of Indirect Exports in VAX_F	Share of Direct Exports in VAX_B	Share of Indirect Exports in VAX_B
		($ million)						(percentage)			
Malaysia	2000	11,891.12	14,363.23	8,145.86	6,034.01	8,329.22	2,111.86	42.01	57.99	74.07	25.93
	2005	15,512.30	23,449.57	12,497.24	8,327.58	15,121.99	4,169.66	35.51	64.49	66.64	33.36
	2008	29,524.14	43,795.50	22,613.72	17,647.91	26,147.58	4,965.81	40.30	59.70	78.04	21.96
	2011	33,085.50	41,982.80	27,414.85	19,205.72	22,777.07	8,209.12	45.75	54.25	70.06	29.94
	2015	43,170.10	48,911.76	33,880.99	24,644.49	24,267.27	9,236.51	50.39	49.61	72.74	27.26
Philippines	2000	3,803.04	5,275.17	3,287.21	1,931.40	3,343.77	1,355.81	36.61	63.39	58.75	41.25
	2005	5,904.56	8,730.20	5,313.99	3,515.97	5,214.23	1,798.02	40.27	59.73	66.16	33.84
	2008	13,057.53	16,531.74	11,755.53	7,850.16	8,681.57	3,905.36	47.49	52.51	66.78	33.22
	2011	17,910.80	19,332.59	16,492.43	11,296.87	8,035.72	5,195.55	58.43	41.57	68.50	31.50
	2015	25,078.69	23,988.17	22,574.02	16,009.52	7,978.65	6,564.51	66.74	33.26	70.92	29.08
Thailand	2000	13,479.87	16,811.91	11,294.17	7,966.93	8,844.98	3,327.23	47.39	52.61	70.54	29.46
	2005	19,306.47	24,783.46	15,334.21	10,452.70	14,330.76	4,881.51	42.18	57.82	68.17	31.83
	2008	27,511.36	41,545.94	22,239.06	16,109.69	25,436.25	6,129.37	38.78	61.22	72.44	27.56
	2011	42,776.54	46,354.02	36,031.89	22,542.19	23,811.84	13,489.70	48.63	51.37	62.56	37.44
	2015	58,739.86	61,055.07	46,572.43	30,443.57	30,611.51	16,128.86	49.86	50.14	65.37	34.63
Viet Nam	2000	2,843.63	3,019.01	2,183.02	1,618.17	1,400.84	564.85	53.60	46.40	74.13	25.87
	2005	4,127.91	5,848.88	3,545.32	2,571.18	3,277.69	974.14	43.96	56.04	72.52	27.48
	2008	11,937.75	14,140.16	10,285.80	8,643.32	5,496.83	1,642.48	61.13	38.87	84.03	15.97
	2011	15,159.56	18,661.18	12,627.86	9,581.88	9,079.31	3,045.98	51.35	48.65	75.88	24.12
	2015	21,775.52	25,619.59	17,691.00	13,567.11	12,052.49	4,123.89	52.96	47.04	76.69	23.31
Mongolia	2000	140.71	102.51	90.04	68.07	34.44	21.96	66.40	33.60	75.61	24.39
	2005	260.26	230.91	177.47	131.51	99.40	45.96	56.95	43.05	74.10	25.90
	2008	569.71	488.37	382.13	263.51	224.85	118.62	53.96	46.04	68.96	31.04
	2011	1,141.58	1,265.20	843.93	681.89	583.31	162.04	53.90	46.10	80.80	19.20
	2015	872.28	1,180.03	593.21	408.10	771.93	185.11	34.58	65.42	68.80	31.20
Sri Lanka	2000	923.80	877.64	761.28	665.30	212.34	95.98	75.81	24.19	87.39	12.61
	2005	970.13	831.48	790.66	632.39	199.09	158.27	76.06	23.94	79.98	20.02
	2008	1,254.50	1,165.38	971.45	778.45	386.93	193.00	66.80	33.20	80.13	19.87
	2011	1,649.47	1,697.29	1,411.14	1,101.88	595.41	309.26	64.92	35.08	78.08	21.92
	2015	2,078.59	2,150.93	1,752.83	1,359.04	791.89	393.79	63.18	36.82	77.53	22.47

PRC = People's Republic of China, VAX_B = value added exports by backward industrial linkages, VAX_F = value added exports by forward industrial linkages.

Source: ADB Multi Region Input–Output Tables Database.

Table 3.3e: Direct and Indirect Value–Added Exports – Personal Services Sector

		Gross Exports	VAX_F	VAX_B	Direct Exports	Indirect Exports (Forward Linkages)	Indirect Exports (Backward Linkages)	Share of Direct Exports in VAX_F	Share of Indirect Exports in VAX_F	Share of Direct Exports in VAX_B	Share of Indirect Exports in VAX_B
		($ million)						(percentage)			
PRC	2000	7,589.02	5,452.91	6,698.46	3,622.69	1,830.22	3,075.77	66.44	33.56	54.08	45.92
	2005	10,882.42	13,602.22	9,227.45	5,267.95	8,334.27	3,959.50	38.73	61.27	57.09	42.91
	2008	12,856.49	25,193.71	11,088.96	6,152.63	19,041.08	4,936.33	24.42	75.58	55.48	44.52
	2011	16,710.74	31,990.60	14,391.49	7,938.80	24,051.80	6,452.70	24.82	75.18	55.16	44.84
	2015	36,141.44	87,062.69	33,323.01	18,376.30	68,686.38	14,946.70	21.11	78.89	55.15	44.85
Indonesia	2000	928.18	770.60	802.75	608.64	161.96	194.11	78.98	21.02	75.82	24.18
	2005	1,976.84	2,304.68	1,661.32	1,091.82	1,212.86	569.50	47.37	52.63	65.72	34.28
	2008	3,202.53	3,669.73	2,732.70	1,755.08	1,914.65	977.62	47.83	52.17	64.23	35.77
	2011	4,238.25	5,584.64	3,662.83	2,351.86	3,232.77	1,310.96	42.11	57.89	64.21	35.79
	2015	13,570.33	11,605.23	12,344.37	7,655.78	3,949.45	4,688.58	65.97	34.03	62.02	37.98
India	2000	1,936.15	1,920.35	1,775.91	1,385.64	534.71	390.28	72.16	27.84	78.02	21.98
	2005	3,539.36	4,558.79	3,097.18	2,776.73	1,782.07	320.46	60.91	39.09	89.65	10.35
	2008	5,256.43	7,357.35	4,779.73	4,434.72	2,922.63	345.01	60.28	39.72	92.78	7.22
	2011	6,087.11	9,298.77	5,518.88	5,153.08	4,145.69	365.80	55.42	44.58	93.37	6.63
	2015	7,529.22	10,468.37	7,283.29	6,485.60	3,982.77	797.70	61.95	38.05	89.05	10.95
Japan	2000	1,783.14	12,390.14	1,712.86	1,163.00	11,227.14	549.86	9.39	90.61	67.90	32.10
	2005	2,930.43	15,134.57	2,789.95	1,897.25	13,237.32	892.50	12.54	87.46	68.00	32.00
	2008	4,111.91	21,387.51	3,842.06	2,723.64	18,663.87	1,118.42	12.73	87.27	70.89	29.11
	2011	3,772.42	22,347.76	3,549.89	2,513.74	19,834.02	1,036.15	11.25	88.75	70.81	29.19
	2015	10,308.95	25,907.65	9,599.29	6,981.19	18,926.46	2,618.09	26.95	73.05	72.73	27.27
Republic of Korea	2000	2,852.93	2,826.76	2,552.72	1,899.42	927.34	653.30	67.19	32.81	74.41	25.59
	2005	2,829.61	3,660.52	2,522.84	1,873.21	1,787.31	649.63	51.17	48.83	74.25	25.75
	2008	4,534.32	5,518.74	3,853.14	2,937.65	2,581.09	915.49	53.23	46.77	76.24	23.76
	2011	5,049.59	6,225.57	4,299.13	3,255.20	2,970.37	1,043.92	52.29	47.71	75.72	24.28
	2015	13,844.82	13,448.93	12,424.64	9,475.20	3,973.73	2,949.43	70.45	29.55	76.26	23.74
Taipei,China	2000	985.06	1,401.09	858.56	567.06	834.03	291.50	40.47	59.53	66.05	33.95
	2005	1,011.52	1,946.88	903.83	629.75	1,317.13	274.07	32.35	67.65	69.68	30.32
	2008	1,482.05	2,653.05	1,311.65	941.45	1,711.60	370.20	35.49	64.51	71.78	28.22
	2011	1,606.08	3,076.81	1,427.72	1,028.44	2,048.37	399.28	33.43	66.57	72.03	27.97
	2015	6,704.39	9,264.45	5,913.64	4,736.82	4,527.63	1,176.82	51.13	48.87	80.10	19.90
Bangladesh	2000	488.38	909.17	470.91	382.12	527.05	88.78	42.03	57.97	81.15	18.85
	2005	531.71	1,126.16	510.01	412.89	713.26	97.11	36.66	63.34	80.96	19.04
	2008	863.09	1,183.37	792.22	519.44	663.92	272.78	43.90	56.10	65.57	34.43
	2011	762.18	1,677.14	704.72	492.40	1,184.74	212.32	29.36	70.64	69.87	30.13
	2015	2,037.02	3,530.20	1,894.63	1,255.22	2,274.98	639.41	35.56	64.44	66.25	33.75

continued on next page

Table 3.3e: continued

Table 3.3e: Direct and Indirect Value-Added Exports – Personal Services Sector

		Gross Exports	VAX_F	VAX_B	Direct Exports	Indirect Exports (Forward Linkages)	Indirect Exports (Backward Linkages)	Share of Direct Exports in VAX_F	Share of Indirect Exports in VAX_F	Share of Direct Exports in VAX_B	Share of Indirect Exports in VAX_B
		($ million)						(percentage)			
Malaysia	2000	1,122.44	728.73	846.99	654.56	74.17	192.43	89.82	10.18	77.28	22.72
	2005	1,216.76	845.37	921.78	549.27	296.10	372.51	64.97	35.03	59.59	40.41
	2008	5,466.21	3,348.76	3,932.16	2,633.80	714.96	1,298.35	78.65	21.35	66.98	33.02
	2011	3,015.96	3,128.10	2,504.26	1,689.62	1,438.47	814.64	54.01	45.99	67.47	32.53
	2015	5,982.16	4,922.40	4,793.68	3,328.26	1,594.14	1,465.42	67.61	32.39	69.43	30.57
Philippines	2000	93.75	164.74	83.73	63.51	101.23	20.22	38.55	61.45	75.85	24.15
	2005	418.20	369.90	376.24	281.60	88.29	94.63	76.13	23.87	74.85	25.15
	2008	761.14	695.29	658.50	490.79	204.49	167.71	70.59	29.41	74.53	25.47
	2011	746.97	863.07	685.12	499.69	363.38	185.43	57.90	42.10	72.93	27.07
	2015	1,039.64	996.92	941.76	687.51	309.41	254.25	68.96	31.04	73.00	27.00
Thailand	2000	1,584.36	1,163.60	1,224.29	801.65	361.95	422.64	68.89	31.11	65.48	34.52
	2005	2,459.96	1,874.00	1,883.96	1,180.52	693.48	703.44	62.99	37.01	62.66	37.34
	2008	2,717.34	2,566.60	2,040.60	1,446.66	1,119.94	593.95	56.36	43.64	70.89	29.11
	2011	4,018.31	3,501.96	3,101.02	1,850.84	1,651.12	1,250.18	52.85	47.15	59.68	40.32
	2015	8,170.86	6,084.11	6,501.62	4,127.85	1,956.26	2,373.77	67.85	32.15	63.49	36.51
Viet Nam	2000	284.38	229.89	237.59	203.36	26.52	34.23	88.46	11.54	85.59	14.41
	2005	225.56	243.30	194.11	144.12	99.19	50.00	59.23	40.77	74.24	25.76
	2008	389.50	390.34	309.06	237.29	153.05	71.77	60.79	39.21	76.78	23.22
	2011	2,383.64	1,832.78	1,990.97	1,553.25	279.53	437.72	84.75	15.25	78.01	21.99
	2015	4,457.52	3,421.18	3,682.27	2,904.09	517.09	778.18	84.89	15.11	78.87	21.13
Mongolia	2000	4.44	2.42	2.91	2.02	0.41	0.89	83.25	16.75	69.36	30.64
	2005	5.32	4.44	3.74	2.28	2.16	1.46	51.38	48.62	61.06	38.94
	2008	6.25	44.34	4.60	3.07	41.28	1.53	6.92	93.08	66.67	33.33
	2011	17.92	33.98	13.96	9.54	24.45	4.42	28.07	71.93	68.32	31.68
	2015	20.87	54.41	18.19	13.68	40.73	4.51	25.14	74.86	75.20	24.80
Sri Lanka	2000	242.79	159.81	195.90	149.46	10.35	46.44	93.53	6.47	76.30	23.70
	2005	277.23	246.01	214.49	146.93	99.08	67.57	59.72	40.28	68.50	31.50
	2008	314.57	321.05	254.49	184.97	136.07	69.52	57.62	42.38	72.68	27.32
	2011	421.83	463.88	372.11	263.62	200.27	108.49	56.83	43.17	70.85	29.15
	2015	563.78	606.05	489.90	338.36	267.69	151.54	55.83	44.17	69.07	30.93

PRC = People's Republic of China, VAX_B = value added exports by backward industrial linkages, VAX_F = value added exports by forward industrial linkages.

Source: ADB Multi Region Input–Output Tables Database.

Table 3.3f: Direct and Indirect Value-Added Exports – Total Economy

		Gross Exports	VAX_F	VAX_B	Direct Exports	Indirect Exports (Forward Linkages)	Indirect Exports (Backward Linkages)	Share of Direct Exports in VAX_F	Share of Indirect Exports in VAX_F	Share of Direct Exports in VAX_B	Share of Indirect Exports in VAX_B
		($ million)						(percentage)			
PRC	2000	279,345.90	228,011.83	228,011.83	108,298.48	119,713.35	119,713.35	47.50	52.50	47.50	52.50
	2005	838,620.93	607,606.26	607,606.26	275,093.64	332,512.62	332,512.62	45.27	54.73	45.27	54.73
	2008	1,579,658.98	1,186,098.86	1,186,098.86	495,775.47	690,323.39	690,323.39	41.80	58.20	41.80	58.20
	2011	2,093,765.10	1,579,774.00	1,579,774.00	665,492.62	914,281.38	914,281.38	42.13	57.87	42.13	57.87
	2015	2,288,337.32	1,861,048.43	1,861,048.43	710,475.40	1,150,573.03	1,150,573.03	38.18	61.82	38.18	61.82
Indonesia	2000	65,246.45	52,338.15	52,338.15	33,201.16	19,136.99	19,136.99	63.44	36.56	63.44	36.56
	2005	94,067.44	75,609.51	75,609.51	52,106.16	23,503.35	23,503.35	68.91	31.09	68.91	31.09
	2008	151,221.29	124,411.41	124,411.41	84,509.30	39,902.11	39,902.11	67.93	32.07	67.93	32.07
	2011	219,754.04	185,400.49	185,400.49	128,074.33	57,326.16	57,326.16	69.08	30.92	69.08	30.92
	2015	208,792.55	189,163.43	189,163.43	112,946.81	76,216.62	76,216.62	59.71	40.29	59.71	40.29
India	2000	67,865.51	57,740.07	57,740.07	29,541.63	28,198.45	28,198.45	51.16	48.84	51.16	48.84
	2005	158,894.54	126,519.38	126,519.38	71,545.74	54,973.63	54,973.63	56.55	43.45	56.55	43.45
	2008	260,263.80	202,311.92	202,311.92	114,207.60	88,104.32	88,104.32	56.45	43.55	56.45	43.55
	2011	337,433.02	263,304.65	263,304.65	144,458.30	118,846.35	118,846.35	54.86	45.14	54.86	45.14
	2015	369,623.98	318,181.02	318,181.02	156,772.82	161,408.20	161,408.20	49.27	50.73	49.27	50.73
Japan	2000	513,245.95	457,313.40	457,313.40	245,096.72	212,216.68	212,216.68	53.59	46.41	53.59	46.41
	2005	651,184.76	558,437.73	558,437.73	303,802.81	254,634.92	254,634.92	54.40	45.60	54.40	45.60
	2008	862,937.83	689,018.02	689,018.02	362,579.48	326,438.55	326,438.55	52.62	47.38	52.62	47.38
	2011	900,325.12	731,761.37	731,761.37	393,727.07	338,034.30	338,034.30	53.81	46.19	53.81	46.19
	2015	740,112.40	620,578.79	620,578.79	325,985.30	294,593.49	294,593.49	52.53	47.47	52.53	47.47
Republic of Korea	2000	199,509.87	138,462.93	138,462.93	85,984.14	52,478.79	52,478.79	62.10	37.90	62.10	37.90
	2005	329,193.38	220,556.40	220,556.40	132,974.97	87,581.42	87,581.42	60.29	39.71	60.29	39.71
	2008	498,780.09	287,376.34	287,376.34	176,217.58	111,158.75	111,158.75	61.32	38.68	61.32	38.68
	2011	615,300.11	363,588.36	363,588.36	224,121.14	139,467.21	139,467.21	61.64	38.36	61.64	38.36
	2015	591,607.55	430,585.78	430,585.78	244,457.87	186,127.91	186,127.91	56.77	43.23	56.77	43.23
Taipei,China	2000	173,290.82	110,321.06	110,321.06	59,675.79	50,645.27	50,645.27	54.09	45.91	54.09	45.91
	2005	226,748.95	126,896.72	126,896.72	67,805.01	59,091.71	59,091.71	53.43	46.57	53.43	46.57
	2008	288,322.92	147,042.79	147,042.79	78,035.99	69,006.80	69,006.80	53.07	46.93	53.07	46.93
	2011	340,219.14	178,014.08	178,014.08	95,364.65	82,649.43	82,649.43	53.57	46.43	53.57	46.43
	2015	394,321.92	259,449.60	259,449.60	115,274.84	144,174.77	144,174.77	44.43	55.57	44.43	55.57
Bangladesh	2000	6,451.39	5,639.23	5,639.23	3,174.91	2,464.32	2,464.32	56.30	43.70	56.30	43.70
	2005	8,854.23	7,399.67	7,399.67	3,917.05	3,482.62	3,482.62	52.94	47.06	52.94	47.06
	2008	15,708.05	11,751.19	11,751.19	6,692.80	5,058.39	5,058.39	56.95	43.05	56.95	43.05
	2011	22,800.71	19,383.40	19,383.40	10,186.61	9,196.80	9,196.80	52.55	47.45	52.55	47.45
	2015	36,812.72	31,979.89	31,979.89	17,712.53	14,267.36	14,267.36	55.39	44.61	55.39	44.61

continued on next page

Table 3.3f: continued

Table 3.3f: Direct and Indirect Value-Added Exports – Total Economy

		Gross Exports	VAX_F	VAX_B	Direct Exports	Indirect Exports (Forward Linkages)	Indirect Exports (Backward Linkages)	Share of Direct Exports in VAX_F	Share of Indirect Exports in VAX_F	Share of Direct Exports in VAX_B	Share of Indirect Exports in VAX_B
		($ million)						(percentage)			
Malaysia	2000	111,832.08	53,273.37	53,273.37	35,737.95	17,535.42	17,535.42	67.08	32.92	67.08	32.92
	2005	147,263.47	79,625.09	79,625.09	46,118.78	33,506.31	33,506.31	57.92	42.08	57.92	42.08
	2008	222,929.88	135,705.71	135,705.71	79,103.79	56,601.92	56,601.92	58.29	41.71	58.29	41.71
	2011	191,802.71	134,178.91	134,178.91	69,637.45	64,541.46	64,541.46	51.90	48.10	51.90	48.10
	2015	189,417.80	130,239.06	130,239.06	68,609.05	61,630.01	61,630.01	52.68	47.32	52.68	47.32
Philippines	2000	26,837.67	21,503.47	21,503.47	13,822.45	7,681.02	7,681.02	64.28	35.72	64.28	35.72
	2005	32,358.42	23,327.99	23,327.99	13,302.25	10,025.75	10,025.75	57.02	42.98	57.02	42.98
	2008	62,004.58	41,224.23	41,224.23	24,197.64	17,026.59	17,026.59	58.70	41.30	58.70	41.30
	2011	52,901.69	41,247.83	41,247.83	24,156.50	17,091.33	17,091.33	58.56	41.44	58.56	41.44
	2015	60,481.11	50,622.85	50,622.85	31,422.11	19,200.74	19,200.74	62.07	37.93	62.07	37.93
Thailand	2000	81,515.09	48,280.11	48,280.11	29,588.33	18,691.78	18,691.78	61.28	38.72	61.28	38.72
	2005	122,625.82	69,402.57	69,402.57	40,440.11	28,962.46	28,962.46	58.27	41.73	58.27	41.73
	2008	205,428.43	121,040.76	121,040.76	68,223.86	52,816.91	52,816.91	56.36	43.64	56.36	43.64
	2011	188,398.91	128,574.48	128,574.48	70,067.09	58,507.39	58,507.39	54.50	45.50	54.50	45.50
	2015	209,515.22	148,941.76	148,941.76	81,199.18	67,742.58	67,742.58	54.52	45.48	54.52	45.48
Viet Nam	2000	14,018.88	10,593.84	10,593.84	7,685.45	2,908.39	2,908.39	72.55	27.45	72.55	27.45
	2005	27,044.14	20,494.58	20,494.58	12,978.73	7,515.85	7,515.85	63.33	36.67	63.33	36.67
	2008	69,551.59	45,263.54	45,263.54	32,380.25	12,883.29	12,883.29	71.54	28.46	71.54	28.46
	2011	84,579.55	58,670.89	58,670.89	37,288.77	21,382.12	21,382.12	63.56	36.44	63.56	36.44
	2015	130,368.75	85,619.34	85,619.34	55,832.29	29,787.05	29,787.05	65.21	34.79	65.21	34.79
Mongolia	2000	426.49	296.87	296.87	220.35	76.53	76.53	74.22	25.78	74.22	25.78
	2005	1,121.30	834.95	834.95	652.32	182.63	182.63	78.13	21.87	78.13	21.87
	2008	2,401.43	1,812.58	1,812.58	1,363.73	448.85	448.85	75.24	24.76	75.24	24.76
	2011	5,282.98	3,545.05	3,545.05	2,697.88	847.18	847.18	76.10	23.90	76.10	23.90
	2015	5,432.88	3,900.53	3,900.53	2,711.08	1,189.45	1,189.45	69.51	30.49	69.51	30.49
Sri Lanka	2000	6,399.74	4,866.76	4,867.26	3,861.95	1,004.81	1,005.31	79.35	20.65	79.35	20.65
	2005	7,419.76	5,337.81	5,337.88	4,110.71	1,227.11	1,227.18	77.01	22.99	77.01	22.99
	2008	9,745.95	7,788.15	7,787.91	5,732.27	2,055.88	2,055.64	73.60	26.40	73.60	26.40
	2011	12,081.72	10,174.65	10,174.39	7,386.29	2,788.36	2,788.10	72.60	27.40	72.60	27.40
	2015	13,095.41	11,350.92	11,350.29	8,081.71	3,269.21	3,268.58	71.20	28.80	71.20	28.80

PRC = People's Republic of China, VAX_B = value added exports by backward industrial linkages, VAX_F = value added exports by forward industrial linkages.

Source: ADB Multi Region Input–Output Tables Database.

Table 3.4: Revealed Comparative Advantage by Aggregate Sector

		RCA Calculated through Traditional Method (ratio)					RCA Calculated through Value-Added Export Method (ratio)				
		2000	2005	2008	2011	2015	2000	2005	2008	2011	2015
PRC	Primary	0.45	0.25	0.13	0.14	0.23	1.17	1.00	0.77	0.74	0.93
	Low Technology Manufacturing	1.86	1.47	1.45	1.41	1.40	1.72	1.59	1.54	1.54	1.27
	Medium- and High-Technology Manufacturing	0.85	1.08	1.18	1.17	1.12	0.99	1.13	1.27	1.22	1.13
	Business Services	0.78	0.74	0.67	0.71	0.71	0.70	0.70	0.74	0.78	0.85
	Personal Services	2.10	0.99	0.64	0.61	0.49	0.84	0.76	0.73	0.71	0.94
Indonesia	Primary	1.92	2.35	2.04	2.55	2.23	3.10	2.71	2.45	2.74	2.65
	Low Technology Manufacturing	2.11	1.83	1.99	1.69	1.80	1.65	1.44	1.44	1.26	1.40
	Medium- and High-Technology Manufacturing	0.67	0.64	0.62	0.59	0.62	0.65	0.67	0.70	0.60	0.64
	Business Services	0.41	0.49	0.49	0.47	0.46	0.44	0.45	0.42	0.40	0.46
	Personal Services	1.10	1.60	1.65	1.48	2.03	0.52	1.03	1.01	1.05	1.23
India	Primary	1.41	0.92	0.70	0.73	0.67	1.94	1.23	0.95	0.95	0.93
	Low Technology Manufacturing	2.39	2.04	1.97	1.88	1.88	1.63	1.32	1.22	1.15	1.21
	Medium- and High-Technology Manufacturing	0.58	0.57	0.66	0.71	0.76	0.61	0.59	0.70	0.71	0.89
	Business Services	0.55	1.26	1.26	1.13	0.94	0.79	1.11	1.15	1.17	1.07
	Personal Services	2.21	1.70	1.58	1.39	0.64	1.17	1.22	1.24	1.23	0.66
Japan	Primary	0.05	0.05	0.05	0.05	0.05	0.08	0.06	0.05	0.05	0.06
	Low Technology Manufacturing	0.29	0.33	0.34	0.38	0.37	0.70	0.70	0.65	0.72	0.72
	Medium- and High-Technology Manufacturing	1.43	1.43	1.42	1.44	1.40	1.54	1.61	1.57	1.59	1.53
	Business Services	0.95	0.94	1.06	1.03	1.12	0.96	0.99	1.12	1.08	1.11
	Personal Services	0.27	0.34	0.37	0.32	0.44	0.95	0.92	1.06	1.07	0.84
Republic of Korea	Primary	0.03	0.02	0.01	0.01	0.02	0.18	0.12	0.08	0.08	0.11
	Low Technology Manufacturing	0.84	0.50	0.41	0.37	0.34	1.06	0.81	0.71	0.71	0.68
	Medium- and High-Technology Manufacturing	1.25	1.45	1.50	1.55	1.53	1.50	1.78	1.90	1.96	1.89
	Business Services	0.88	0.75	0.77	0.71	0.80	0.84	0.82	0.87	0.82	0.88
	Personal Services	1.11	0.66	0.71	0.63	0.73	0.71	0.56	0.66	0.60	0.63

continued on next page

Table 3.4: continued

Table 3.4: Revealed Comparative Advantage by Aggregate Sector

		RCA Calculated through Traditional Method (ratio)					RCA Calculated through Value-Added Export Method (ratio)				
		2000	2005	2008	2011	2015	2000	2005	2008	2011	2015
Taipei,China	Primary	0.12	0.09	0.08	0.12	0.16	0.12	0.09	0.09	0.12	0.10
	Low Technology Manufacturing	0.99	0.72	0.63	0.60	0.64	0.94	0.74	0.59	0.57	0.76
	Medium- and High-Technology Manufacturing	1.31	1.48	1.55	1.59	1.60	1.33	1.53	1.59	1.63	1.71
	Business Services	0.54	0.42	0.41	0.35	0.29	1.06	1.05	1.14	1.11	0.97
	Personal Services	0.44	0.34	0.40	0.36	0.53	0.44	0.52	0.62	0.60	0.72
Bangladesh	Primary	0.70	0.42	0.25	0.24	0.34	1.18	0.87	0.36	0.38	0.43
	Low Technology Manufacturing	4.00	4.52	4.93	4.93	4.28	2.47	2.68	3.44	3.46	3.48
	Medium- and High-Technology Manufacturing	0.03	0.03	0.07	0.04	0.03	0.10	0.12	0.10	0.09	0.05
	Business Services	0.65	0.53	0.42	0.32	0.36	0.81	0.83	0.94	0.96	0.85
	Personal Services	5.86	4.58	4.29	2.57	1.73	5.65	5.14	3.45	3.02	2.22
Malaysia	Primary	0.99	1.08	1.45	0.80	0.65	1.94	1.87	2.05	1.67	1.46
	Low Technology Manufacturing	0.82	0.80	0.59	1.40	1.24	1.00	0.98	0.65	0.81	0.81
	Medium- and High-Technology Manufacturing	1.21	1.21	1.10	0.93	0.90	1.07	0.95	0.75	0.91	0.95
	Business Services	0.59	0.57	0.72	0.93	1.16	0.69	0.77	0.85	0.84	0.96
	Personal Services	0.78	0.63	1.92	1.21	0.99	0.48	0.36	0.84	0.81	0.76
Philippines	Primary	0.30	0.29	0.29	0.24	0.31	0.69	0.89	0.79	0.74	0.65
	Low Technology Manufacturing	1.12	1.43	1.38	1.17	1.17	1.40	1.53	1.56	1.33	1.54
	Medium- and High-Technology Manufacturing	1.16	1.00	1.00	0.81	0.64	1.45	0.89	0.84	0.70	0.73
	Business Services	0.78	0.99	1.14	1.83	2.12	0.63	0.98	1.06	1.25	1.21
	Personal Services	0.27	0.98	0.96	1.09	0.54	0.27	0.54	0.58	0.73	0.40
Thailand	Primary	0.22	0.20	0.19	0.32	0.41	0.93	0.78	0.81	0.99	0.97
	Low Technology Manufacturing	1.78	1.69	1.62	1.92	1.60	1.92	1.68	1.53	1.63	1.49
	Medium- and High-Technology Manufacturing	0.88	0.96	1.09	0.74	0.68	0.75	0.89	1.02	0.76	0.74
	Business Services	0.91	0.86	0.72	1.23	1.43	0.90	0.93	0.90	0.96	1.04
	Personal Services	1.50	1.53	1.03	1.64	1.22	0.84	0.91	0.73	0.95	0.82

continued on next page

Table 3.4: continued

Table 3.4: Revealed Comparative Advantage by Aggregate Sector

		RCA Calculated through Traditional Method					RCA Calculated through Value-Added Export Method				
		2000	2005	2008	2011	2015	2000	2005	2008	2011	2015
			(ratio)					(ratio)			
Viet Nam	Primary	4.92	3.98	3.05	2.65	3.75	3.97	3.10	2.49	2.28	2.77
	Low Technology Manufacturing	1.70	1.84	1.39	1.98	1.83	1.21	1.26	1.06	1.23	1.23
	Medium- and High-Technology Manufacturing	0.08	0.23	0.45	0.27	0.25	0.14	0.26	0.39	0.30	0.29
	Business Services	1.12	0.83	0.93	0.97	0.85	0.73	0.75	0.82	0.85	0.76
	Personal Services	1.57	0.64	0.44	2.17	1.07	0.76	0.40	0.29	1.09	0.80
Mongolia	Primary	5.01	6.35	5.10	5.91	8.56	4.33	4.32	3.67	3.18	3.80
	Low Technology Manufacturing	0.87	0.55	0.55	0.41	0.40	0.66	0.52	0.38	0.43	0.63
	Medium- and High-Technology Manufacturing	0.13	0.07	0.12	0.04	0.05	0.10	0.07	0.09	0.07	0.11
	Business Services	1.82	1.26	1.28	1.17	0.82	0.89	0.72	0.71	0.95	0.77
	Personal Services	0.81	0.36	0.20	0.26	0.12	0.29	0.18	0.84	0.33	0.28
Sri Lanka	Primary	2.22	2.30	2.32	2.04	2.49	2.38	1.98	1.80	2.75	2.49
	Low Technology Manufacturing	3.15	3.19	3.03	3.02	2.78	2.88	3.34	2.00	2.36	2.62
	Medium- and High-Technology Manufacturing	0.10	0.09	0.13	0.13	0.15	0.32	0.16	0.83	0.12	0.30
	Business Services	0.80	0.71	0.69	0.74	0.84	0.43	0.41	0.32	0.35	0.41
	Personal Services	2.94	2.85	2.52	2.69	1.39	1.08	1.63	2.30	1.30	0.95

PRC = People's Republic of China

Source: ADB Multi Region Input–Output Tables Database.

Table 3.5a: Vertical Specialization by Sector, 2000
(% of gross exports)

	PRC	Indonesia	India	Japan	Republic of Korea	Taipei,China	Bangladesh	Malaysia	Philippines	Thailand	Viet Nam	Mongolia	Sri Lanka
Agriculture, Hunting, Forestry and Fishing	6.22	5.79	2.96	5.21	10.86	16.57	3.15	14.64	6.43	13.26	16.25	15.46	17.09
Mining and Quarrying	9.07	3.99	5.24	18.21	10.31	16.29	2.66	13.21	13.46	10.85	10.43	25.80	9.96
Food, Beverages and Tobacco	7.97	12.29	9.29	5.60	19.05	22.48	11.92	34.75	11.85	20.07	24.26	30.25	15.57
Textiles and Textile Products	18.22	25.84	10.78	7.69	25.98	26.96	15.81	50.98	16.89	27.15	47.99	26.69	35.14
Leather, Leather Products and Footwear	17.50	19.42	10.85	6.22	23.69	19.78	15.60	42.92	19.30	29.52	47.08	23.16	2.84
Wood and Products of Wood and Cork	13.96	15.21	11.83	12.55	31.66	38.89	13.23	28.49	14.45	32.74	24.43	33.64	16.23
Pulp, Paper, Paper Products, Printing and Publishing	14.55	28.40	17.55	5.85	21.51	29.20	13.85	44.99	23.94	40.14	40.22	40.88	12.28
Coke, Refined Petroleum and Nuclear Fuel	28.85	18.63	58.70	32.87	70.51	49.36	11.47	36.26	55.50	68.10	49.91	94.45	63.45
Chemicals and Chemical Products	18.01	19.35	20.91	9.34	33.05	40.90	9.10	38.03	21.48	39.86	42.68	64.61	35.59
Rubber and Plastics	18.68	25.45	16.95	7.51	25.90	33.76	12.84	41.86	22.33	30.46	42.19	85.55	42.47
Other Non-Metallic Mineral	12.32	18.63	21.15	10.55	20.91	27.06	31.25	30.40	24.98	25.00	35.57	40.96	16.72
Basic Metals and Fabricated Metal	16.51	23.84	18.48	10.52	32.91	31.72	25.97	60.37	28.20	42.96	55.95	46.05	23.34
Machinery, Nec	15.91	45.91	17.70	8.72	25.45	33.31	24.44	48.55	20.61	47.61	50.39	69.52	10.63
Electrical and Optical Equipment	26.25	30.49	18.27	10.40	35.54	44.80	20.04	70.29	22.02	66.37	54.54	62.20	38.35
Transport Equipment	16.09	28.21	16.88	8.08	25.18	30.31	10.68	52.60	26.96	52.45	50.17	45.90	27.95
Manufacturing, Nec; Recycling	13.72	17.90	22.79	7.83	23.21	22.50	14.09	46.32	17.42	39.42	48.24	52.42	30.89
Electricity, Gas and Water Supply	9.63	13.88	11.72	9.20	25.73	25.53	7.82	17.37	14.13	11.01	20.13	28.23	26.77
Construction	14.35	23.36	16.45	7.35	19.59	28.66	13.18	38.51	17.99	30.58	43.00	50.32	28.13
Sale, Maintenance and Repair of Motor Vehicles and Motorcycles; Retail Sale of Fuel	…	…	2.95	6.80	11.22	20.44	1.23	42.78	14.90	…	36.08	41.23	7.01
Wholesale Trade and Commission Trade, Except of Motor Vehicles and Motorcycles	8.26	13.28	2.97	2.65	8.17	6.75	1.09	14.07	11.12	4.64	23.14	22.70	4.92
Retail Trade, Except of Motor Vehicles and Motorcycles; Repair of Household Goods	8.53	13.52	2.92	2.17	8.59	4.90	1.30	14.09	11.12	4.13	22.45	13.61	8.63
Hotels and Restaurants	6.55	11.17	7.63	4.00	14.10	5.38	13.19	31.29	12.55	14.27	20.61	30.10	21.15
Inland Transport	8.45	20.62	16.59	4.12	24.27	16.50	5.74	43.92	22.94	35.89	23.55	40.79	24.61
Water Transport	13.22	29.60	10.17	17.64	26.71	32.51	7.12	27.43	17.97	24.10	38.55	45.13	12.80
Air Transport	12.83	44.27	15.48	10.12	25.58	29.28	13.87	38.89	30.85	28.24	38.35	51.38	51.99
Other Supporting and Auxiliary Transport Activities; Activities of Travel Agencies	8.35	14.79	10.16	3.96	15.29	12.50	6.06	40.11	18.56	9.45	18.00	44.51	15.52
Post and Telecommunications	12.40	8.42	6.29	2.52	14.91	11.19	6.72	25.44	12.91	4.62	16.60	36.56	35.34
Financial Intermediation	5.69	8.16	2.92	1.89	7.41	3.25	4.10	31.82	10.01	4.69	16.15	17.44	8.78
Real Estate Activities	3.81	5.89	1.89	0.78	4.31	3.71	0.88	2.85	2.79	1.49	15.50	15.59	8.47
Renting of Machinery and Equipment and Other Business Activities	13.89	19.59	6.12	2.47	8.09	18.58	3.76	34.32	11.73	17.36	22.91	37.34	18.32
Public Admin and Defense; Compulsory Social Security	7.81	14.89	0.00	3.01	10.16	9.32	5.22	26.12	7.92	0.01	24.02	34.64	3.38

continued on next page

Table 3.5a: continued

Table 3.5a: Vertical Specialization by Sector, 2000

	PRC	Indonesia	India	Japan	Republic of Korea	Taipei,China	Bangladesh	Malaysia	Philippines	Thailand	Viet Nam	Mongolia	Sri Lanka
						(% of gross exports)							
Education	7.44	16.11	1.89	1.37	5.69	9.66	1.53	11.45	9.93	4.95	16.31	...	1.02
Health and Social Work	15.22	15.92	11.02	4.36	15.42	15.64	5.46	33.86	12.46	21.58	23.43	33.71	6.36
Other Community, Social and Personal Services	11.23	13.14	8.08	2.97	10.61	12.75	1.72	13.46	14.94	19.07	15.09	26.26	19.30
Private Households with Employed Persons	...	...	...	...	...	...	...	...	...	...	...	...	...

... = data not available, PRC = People's Republic of China.

Source: ADB Multi Region Input–Output Tables Database.

Global Value Chains

Table 3.5b: Vertical Specialization by Sector, 2005
(% of gross exports)

	PRC	Indonesia	India	Japan	Republic of Korea	Taipei;China	Bangladesh	Malaysia	Philippines	Thailand	Viet Nam	Mongolia	Sri Lanka
Agriculture, Hunting, Forestry and Fishing	8.19	7.34	3.40	7.99	11.93	22.69	4.01	16.04	7.57	15.06	21.51	13.37	14.63
Mining and Quarrying	14.75	6.48	5.73	32.39	14.73	19.16	3.49	11.55	11.20	14.65	9.84	22.81	11.95
Food, Beverages and Tobacco	11.14	13.28	11.08	7.94	20.19	27.27	11.71	34.43	11.42	23.03	34.03	25.85	20.89
Textiles and Textile Products	19.26	26.11	16.10	11.27	25.96	30.09	20.18	32.75	21.38	28.84	36.92	24.14	35.25
Leather, Leather Products and Footwear	18.85	20.23	12.20	8.63	24.27	31.74	15.30	35.04	25.86	32.29	36.95	19.40	14.85
Wood and Products of Wood and Cork	18.03	15.31	16.26	15.41	32.57	39.47	14.49	24.79	14.11	19.25	33.23	26.94	19.31
Pulp, Paper, Paper Products, Printing and Publishing	19.06	25.90	18.26	7.25	21.41	32.31	17.40	35.71	21.30	40.79	33.28	38.20	45.08
Coke, Refined Petroleum and Nuclear Fuel	35.06	22.61	38.85	45.66	71.60	65.82	12.71	39.40	29.77	77.41	32.69	70.13	44.06
Chemicals and Chemical Products	25.13	26.53	22.63	15.88	36.73	47.70	8.53	40.32	26.07	40.15	31.67	49.08	30.98
Rubber and Plastics	25.62	31.23	20.55	11.36	28.24	39.58	11.58	43.55	26.03	32.74	35.77	74.59	26.56
Other Non-Metallic Mineral	17.40	18.93	18.90	12.91	24.50	33.20	19.89	39.36	22.28	28.31	31.70	36.59	33.14
Basic Metals and Fabricated Metal	25.54	25.05	22.75	15.88	35.74	41.76	26.07	53.21	30.63	53.70	42.04	41.75	39.95
Machinery, Nec	25.38	45.94	21.46	11.91	28.59	38.38	25.75	51.32	30.25	50.40	42.02	53.02	41.71
Electrical and Optical Equipment	38.26	29.75	20.69	12.74	35.01	49.76	21.18	63.60	45.82	64.47	42.04	47.25	46.49
Transport Equipment	25.20	23.81	20.87	11.29	27.08	38.18	11.42	51.92	26.62	54.48	38.08	96.39	38.74
Manufacturing, Nec; Recycling	17.43	20.23	46.10	10.87	25.50	30.98	17.71	25.12	23.17	48.68	31.68	37.51	26.44
Electricity, Gas and Water Supply	15.98	22.03	16.28	14.89	33.52	43.58	7.15	25.27	6.87	23.07	15.67	26.70	44.08
Construction	19.80	21.96	17.42	9.49	20.84	36.27	14.77	41.35	17.81	37.43	29.36	42.19	25.77
Sale, Maintenance and Repair of Motor Vehicles and Motorcycles; Retail Sale of Fuel	...	...	2.78	9.72	12.23	29.94	1.66	11.49	10.41	...	19.55	30.35	5.32
Wholesale Trade and Commission Trade, Except of Motor Vehicles and Motorcycles	9.96	10.12	2.84	3.44	9.90	4.65	1.23	11.53	4.64	5.36	19.56	19.32	7.15
Retail Trade, Except of Motor Vehicles and Motorcycles; Repair of Household Goods	9.81	10.41	2.68	3.17	10.07	6.32	1.48	11.52	4.28	4.77	9.79	11.61	5.21
Hotels and Restaurants	9.45	11.05	9.68	5.80	14.73	8.32	12.94	16.40	13.64	16.53	22.31	26.11	14.65
Inland Transport	12.44	22.88	18.45	5.91	23.16	21.22	6.18	13.55	18.18	41.05	16.76	34.23	19.66
Water Transport	16.87	27.23	11.99	23.20	38.69	38.69	7.59	28.16	16.39	38.01	22.31	29.16	8.01
Air Transport	22.14	14.86	23.08	12.57	24.57	42.84	15.37	35.63	24.17	33.07	28.83	42.92	49.79
Other Supporting and Auxiliary Transport Activities; Activities of Travel Agencies	14.75	7.63	9.30	4.81	15.04	14.08	6.90	21.06	13.03	12.74	15.06	37.80	17.20
Post and Telecommunications	14.79	7.87	7.35	3.37	12.54	11.17	6.65	12.72	11.48	7.54	14.60	30.32	38.11
Financial Intermediation	7.75	6.02	4.05	2.15	5.55	3.51	3.73	7.98	5.82	6.38	5.64	14.44	12.28
Real Estate Activities	5.40	16.46	1.44	0.91	4.62	4.90	1.06	12.15	3.66	2.77	7.29	12.87	4.45
Renting of Machinery and Equipment and Other Business Activities	18.93	13.46	8.13	3.14	9.63	19.72	4.58	28.91	6.87	19.80	15.34	31.66	17.31
Public Admin and Defense; Compulsory Social Security	10.09	15.06	0.00	4.01	9.61	6.66	6.42	28.90	4.56	0.59	11.88	30.04	4.66

continued on next page

Table 3.5b: continued

Table 3.5b: Vertical Specialization by Sector, 2005

	PRC	Indonesia	India	Japan	Republic of Korea	Taipei,China	Bangladesh	Malaysia	Philippines	Thailand	Viet Nam	Mongolia	Sri Lanka
							(% of gross exports)						
Education	10.67	16.46	2.52	1.95	5.33	10.20	1.69	15.08	5.56	7.99	9.68	...	...
Health and Social Work	19.20	11.47	11.26	6.33	15.31	17.29	6.18	30.47	11.59	24.68	21.38	29.20	7.24
Other Community, Social and Personal Services	14.46	15.99	12.39	4.17	11.84	11.22	1.82	6.08	12.96	21.72	13.44	20.68	14.03
Private Households with Employed Persons	...	...	...	...	...	...	...	...	...	...	...	...	...

... = data not available, PRC = People's Republic of China.

Source: ADB Multi Region Input–Output Tables Database.

Table 3.5c: Vertical Specialization by Sector, 2008
(% of gross exports)

	PRC	Indonesia	India	Japan	Republic of Korea	Taipei,China	Bangladesh	Malaysia	Philippines	Thailand	Viet Nam	Mongolia	Sri Lanka
Agriculture, Hunting, Forestry and Fishing	7.79	6.24	3.91	12.12	20.09	28.59	5.72	17.11	7.85	14.77	28.79	15.99	17.91
Mining and Quarrying	14.90	5.37	6.60	49.51	19.08	17.94	17.36	8.63	13.68	14.80	16.38	21.02	10.29
Food, Beverages and Tobacco	11.51	11.37	12.38	12.83	31.08	34.74	10.31	34.20	10.62	19.75	38.95	21.06	34.44
Textiles and Textile Products	15.51	32.88	18.29	14.50	32.42	36.40	25.37	27.80	26.97	33.57	46.98	23.20	45.17
Leather, Leather Products and Footwear	15.83	21.17	14.23	11.88	31.35	34.86	26.75	33.46	32.49	31.39	46.99	19.93	50.45
Wood and Products of Wood and Cork	17.43	12.81	16.10	23.68	50.02	41.62	10.90	29.61	17.01	19.42	44.75	22.41	32.31
Pulp, Paper, Paper Products, Printing and Publishing	19.28	24.15	20.19	12.32	29.67	37.87	39.86	35.56	24.88	31.20	44.79	28.29	61.23
Coke, Refined Petroleum and Nuclear Fuel	41.96	18.91	43.19	58.00	81.69	81.60	54.76	43.91	50.64	38.27	50.33	45.08	66.80
Chemicals and Chemical Products	24.82	20.88	26.45	24.85	48.23	57.73	54.92	39.36	32.97	34.17	50.42	33.68	40.39
Rubber and Plastics	23.64	27.65	24.59	17.45	37.61	45.86	14.86	40.92	30.75	25.60	55.45	51.40	43.11
Other Non–Metallic Mineral	17.02	15.82	19.84	21.07	33.38	44.49	44.59	42.02	33.29	28.89	50.42	26.77	45.80
Basic Metals and Fabricated Metal	25.98	21.84	23.50	25.53	48.68	49.84	36.09	52.09	43.18	55.24	60.03	31.14	50.72
Machinery, Nec	21.88	43.65	21.71	16.24	37.07	42.92	28.52	49.38	35.21	49.35	59.99	37.45	54.48
Electrical and Optical Equipment	32.00	31.14	21.30	17.51	41.15	49.30	14.26	58.70	55.83	58.70	60.00	34.30	61.19
Transport Equipment	22.09	21.03	23.02	17.61	34.41	38.23	21.20	58.19	29.49	49.78	58.33	25.94	59.04
Manufacturing, Nec; Recycling	15.49	17.61	47.46	17.69	34.44	39.50	42.89	27.09	31.29	44.19	50.33	27.92	39.71
Electricity, Gas and Water Supply	17.44	19.74	18.62	28.24	55.65	72.34	8.86	28.59	9.91	21.90	19.79	22.48	27.77
Construction	18.10	20.25	18.22	14.20	29.08	39.96	13.28	45.20	22.46	42.68	45.66	52.12	24.08
Sale, Maintenance and Repair of Motor Vehicles and Motorcycles; Retail Sale of Fuel	...	...	2.37	13.45	15.32	33.62	8.95	19.36	12.34	7.05	25.53	40.10	8.79
Wholesale Trade and Commission Trade, Except of Motor Vehicles and Motorcycles	8.28	9.06	2.39	5.18	13.16	2.79	3.01	15.92	5.80	7.07	25.54	25.01	7.77
Retail Trade, Except of Motor Vehicles and Motorcycles; Repair of Household Goods	8.41	9.23	2.37	4.59	13.63	8.29	15.83	15.86	5.37	12.27	12.26	14.77	10.30
Hotels and Restaurants	9.69	9.91	10.45	8.45	21.96	10.31	4.54	25.32	12.13	17.56	26.23	21.23	22.51
Inland Transport	12.35	21.09	21.28	8.35	34.73	30.39	6.04	16.27	22.60	36.52	27.99	43.36	25.35
Water Transport	16.63	26.04	14.39	28.98	52.27	41.55	44.85	30.76	21.55	27.20	37.91	24.86	2.10
Air Transport	23.61	14.97	26.81	18.09	37.17	54.47	75.26	40.73	29.93	33.86	40.40	52.89	54.86
Other Supporting and Auxiliary Transport Activities; Activities of Travel Agencies	14.29	7.72	10.58	6.62	23.06	16.46	4.01	27.52	15.27	18.14	18.57	37.02	20.55
Post and Telecommunications	11.46	6.56	8.51	4.72	18.35	12.48	5.32	20.95	13.79	18.49	14.66	21.32	37.07
Financial Intermediation	6.16	5.17	4.51	3.89	8.91	4.19	10.89	15.39	6.52	9.87	5.67	14.73	8.45
Real Estate Activities	4.31	15.13	1.49	1.40	6.41	5.43	3.14	16.77	4.25	4.43	7.37	7.98	8.13
Renting of Machinery and Equipment and Other Business Activities	16.73	12.43	8.12	4.78	12.09	20.23	6.42	28.79	7.79	34.41	18.28	23.97	19.14
Public Admin and Defense; Compulsory Social Security	9.37	14.08	0.01	5.51	13.99	7.79	12.50	30.91	5.00	0.05	13.26	39.18	3.26
Education	10.11	14.41	2.88	2.87	7.52	11.54	6.27	16.19	6.32	9.30	10.99	10.12	...

continued on next page

Table 3.5c: continued

Table 3.5c: Vertical Specialization by Sector, 2008
(% of gross exports)

	PRC	Indonesia	India	Japan	Republic of Korea	Taipei,China	Bangladesh	Malaysia	Philippines	Thailand	Viet Nam	Mongolia	Sri Lanka
Health and Social Work	17.59	9.88	12.76	8.62	19.18	19.09	4.21	22.33	12.31	21.33	34.46	18.62	6.31
Other Community, Social and Personal Services	12.72	14.87	8.90	6.19	16.36	12.10	6.44	10.88	15.49	28.82	20.05	19.99	19.23
Private Households with Employed Persons	…	…	…	…	…	…	…	…	…	…	…	…	…

… = data not available, PRC = People's Republic of China.

Source: ADB Multi Region Input–Output Tables Database.

Table 3.5d: Vertical Specialization by Sector, 2011

	PRC	Indonesia	India	Japan	Republic of Korea	Taipei,China	Bangladesh	Malaysia	Philippines	Thailand	Viet Nam	Mongolia	Sri Lanka
							(% of gross exports)						
Agriculture, Hunting, Forestry and Fishing	7.66	5.68	2.95	10.76	20.69	26.36	9.71	13.79	6.92	13.89	24.69	13.20	11.99
Mining and Quarrying	15.51	4.18	5.00	49.59	20.19	7.25	11.59	7.28	10.49	11.85	11.38	36.87	7.13
Food, Beverages and Tobacco	11.22	10.54	11.50	11.39	31.18	33.81	18.58	25.55	10.01	20.09	39.89	21.17	10.93
Textiles and Textile Products	14.57	34.05	16.05	13.07	33.29	36.75	13.66	30.86	19.84	23.63	55.43	19.48	19.14
Leather, Leather Products and Footwear	14.47	21.46	11.53	11.69	30.52	36.44	11.66	26.53	22.89	26.18	55.82	15.98	16.07
Wood and Products of Wood and Cork	17.24	12.61	13.04	18.96	45.98	41.70	11.20	24.79	13.99	17.12	43.98	30.32	11.99
Pulp, Paper, Paper Products, Printing and Publishing	19.31	22.07	16.39	9.80	28.20	36.28	22.21	31.24	18.96	24.78	40.78	44.05	26.17
Coke, Refined Petroleum and Nuclear Fuel	43.75	14.26	33.40	51.49	81.99	78.21	30.77	21.65	31.56	30.64	37.33	56.16	46.17
Chemicals and Chemical Products	25.00	17.97	19.65	20.94	47.92	50.45	22.88	34.93	27.69	31.60	37.37	39.97	31.95
Rubber and Plastics	23.60	26.54	19.96	17.50	37.95	45.32	18.89	35.37	25.33	29.96	42.64	60.53	17.67
Other Non-Metallic Mineral	17.23	15.24	16.74	22.65	31.90	43.96	16.20	31.87	22.11	24.93	37.30	30.39	22.68
Basic Metals and Fabricated Metal	27.66	16.89	20.77	24.89	46.03	49.79	22.20	45.47	30.71	54.46	51.55	42.70	41.34
Machinery, Nec	23.18	43.27	19.44	15.68	35.57	42.92	21.79	45.77	28.02	49.08	49.18	46.62	27.27
Electrical and Optical Equipment	30.18	30.50	19.90	16.51	37.64	48.80	40.84	44.51	45.05	54.26	49.22	46.94	33.55
Transport Equipment	22.85	19.30	19.86	15.91	32.64	40.89	50.76	49.38	24.67	43.54	45.19	36.68	34.10
Manufacturing, Nec; Recycling	15.37	16.28	52.90	16.34	33.34	41.34	55.58	25.97	19.49	37.70	38.64	30.75	19.82
Electricity, Gas and Water Supply	17.90	18.48	15.86	24.39	49.46	66.86	11.04	20.94	6.93	17.19	18.41	26.91	19.71
Construction	18.21	17.99	16.45	13.15	28.48	38.29	16.61	30.75	15.66	37.18	36.44	48.04	21.38
Sale, Maintenance and Repair of Motor Vehicles and Motorcycles; Retail Sale of Fuel	...	...	2.09	12.69	15.59	35.75	17.36	18.01	9.87	18.32	24.03	29.68	5.58
Wholesale Trade and Commission Trade, Except of Motor Vehicles and Motorcycles	7.90	8.20	2.11	4.27	13.45	2.80	2.91	12.73	4.72	5.50	28.95	17.97	4.84
Retail Trade, Except of Motor Vehicles and Motorcycles; Repair of Household Goods	8.07	8.55	2.10	3.72	13.95	8.13	6.93	13.51	4.51	5.46	11.86	9.51	6.20
Hotels and Restaurants	9.23	9.18	10.78	7.36	22.28	10.02	12.33	18.65	11.67	15.63	26.04	32.73	11.05
Inland Transport	12.31	19.59	17.39	7.35	33.34	28.03	6.94	24.28	18.18	27.37	20.45	37.91	17.18
Water Transport	16.82	24.08	11.19	25.34	48.81	46.59	27.18	22.28	17.17	19.24	27.10	3.26	1.48
Air Transport	23.56	12.37	25.59	16.39	36.23	44.58	43.67	32.60	22.52	19.87	35.43	53.39	34.16
Other Supporting and Auxiliary Transport Activities; Activities of Travel Agencies	14.18	7.17	8.61	6.43	22.48	17.20	9.88	23.24	11.45	11.58	18.00	49.00	8.88
Post and Telecommunications	10.51	5.54	8.79	3.67	18.04	12.94	4.04	18.97	10.96	9.99	21.40	22.13	29.85
Financial Intermediation	5.72	4.61	3.78	3.51	8.28	4.30	7.68	10.11	4.72	7.08	7.53	17.49	4.35
Real Estate Activities	4.13	13.61	1.29	1.28	6.15	4.89	2.86	7.67	2.99	2.99	8.98	6.49	4.99
Renting of Machinery and Equipment and Other Business Activities	15.49	11.03	6.85	5.08	12.14	19.87	7.00	14.37	6.09	19.54	18.67	30.00	13.28
Public Admin and Defense; Compulsory Social Security	9.07	12.49	0.01	5.22	13.46	7.72	13.68	17.23	4.05	0.02	14.98	...	1.90

continued on next page

Table 3.5d: continued

Table 3.5d: Vertical Specialization by Sector, 2011

	PRC	Indonesia	India	Japan	Republic of Korea	Taipei,China	Bangladesh	Malaysia	Philippines	Thailand	Viet Nam	Mongolia	Sri Lanka
						(% of gross exports)							
Education	9.72	13.17	2.67	2.18	7.51	11.42	...	8.30	4.72	6.84	12.32	11.92	...
Health and Social Work	17.43	8.93	10.51	7.62	19.47	18.92	4.46	26.41	11.07	20.82	26.45	24.28	5.08
Other Community, Social and Personal Services	12.22	13.92	9.19	5.31	16.66	11.63	5.98	17.52	11.44	21.20	16.39	26.21	11.78
Private Households with Employed Persons	...	...	...	...	...	...	...	...	...	...	...	...	...

... = data not available, PRC = People's Republic of China.

Source: ADB Multi Region Input–Output Tables Database.

Table 3.5e: Vertical Specialization by Sector, 2015

(% of gross exports)

	PRC	Indonesia	India	Japan	Republic of Korea	Taipei,China	Bangladesh	Malaysia	Philippines	Thailand	Viet Nam	Mongolia	Sri Lanka
Agriculture, Hunting, Forestry and Fishing	6.11	4.24	4.46	10.20	15.66	22.91	12.71	17.56	8.37	15.60	29.17	6.86	14.41
Mining and Quarrying	11.10	2.53	4.85	19.45	14.52	4.75	8.60	7.77	6.18	14.14	11.66	29.17	7.30
Food, Beverages and Tobacco	8.38	10.54	15.96	12.33	25.14	31.00	17.96	39.53	17.18	26.88	47.17	14.76	7.84
Textiles and Textile Products	10.41	13.51	16.04	13.45	23.51	34.04	13.67	30.61	19.48	29.47	57.48	12.94	16.59
Leather, Leather Products and Footwear	10.60	12.24	15.25	14.38	26.24	31.16	14.18	26.64	20.57	26.07	60.33	10.56	16.23
Wood and Products of Wood and Cork	16.65	10.57	11.30	14.47	27.30	28.52	14.39	35.09	21.19	23.48	56.97	21.93	13.37
Pulp, Paper, Paper Products, Printing and Publishing	21.47	12.69	15.55	11.10	23.15	32.63	13.68	31.12	23.86	27.60	45.06	32.93	32.78
Coke, Refined Petroleum and Nuclear Fuel	28.29	5.80	17.35	18.08	35.04	46.94	19.91	26.00	26.25	33.46	40.11	45.90	33.43
Chemicals and Chemical Products	17.97	10.08	16.03	16.84	29.64	37.88	19.12	36.35	20.05	27.85	39.64	30.60	31.21
Rubber and Plastics	21.83	12.50	18.77	17.59	23.92	35.03	8.23	43.45	22.61	32.01	41.37	46.28	18.13
Other Non-Metallic Mineral	14.20	9.46	14.46	15.34	23.78	41.05	16.08	34.52	8.70	26.56	39.62	22.98	32.67
Basic Metals and Fabricated Metal	23.74	9.60	16.67	18.09	34.63	40.29	16.57	39.22	25.62	33.73	52.65	32.54	41.58
Machinery, Nec	26.47	13.91	15.21	14.43	28.59	36.59	23.70	35.91	23.96	32.41	52.63	35.95	39.13
Electrical and Optical Equipment	20.34	13.27	15.58	16.14	28.21	34.04	18.87	34.77	26.69	41.35	52.53	36.36	44.02
Transport Equipment	20.47	12.14	15.52	19.55	29.32	33.33	19.74	40.05	31.14	34.14	48.25	30.06	45.48
Manufacturing, Nec; Recycling	15.92	11.58	16.63	16.91	27.17	34.14	13.74	23.53	19.39	30.36	40.52	24.59	23.70
Electricity, Gas and Water Supply	14.61	11.32	14.20	12.47	25.92	43.64	7.77	21.04	5.69	23.17	17.58	22.93	24.45
Construction	13.88	10.78	13.11	11.67	23.64	34.50	13.30	31.66	6.63	32.75	36.76	41.27	21.31
Sale, Maintenance and Repair of Motor Vehicles and Motorcycles; Retail Sale of Fuel	…	…	2.21	13.50	14.71	28.28	12.94	19.50	6.68	23.02	25.62	20.73	5.73
Wholesale Trade and Commission Trade, Except of Motor Vehicles and Motorcycles	4.14	7.27	2.22	5.56	11.25	3.16	4.13	13.74	8.91	7.56	27.36	13.72	4.78
Retail Trade, Except of Motor Vehicles and Motorcycles; Repair of Household Goods	4.09	7.46	2.21	5.28	12.26	15.86	4.83	14.61	8.00	6.83	12.68	8.65	6.19
Hotels and Restaurants	6.05	8.28	11.87	9.95	20.03	11.38	16.46	26.50	16.09	23.60	30.22	20.40	11.55
Inland Transport	9.97	11.80	12.47	7.76	21.42	23.68	7.20	30.15	13.81	31.40	21.78	38.22	18.11
Water Transport	15.08	12.60	8.92	15.02	22.34	30.56	13.71	27.45	16.16	24.99	28.48	21.30	1.48
Air Transport	18.95	8.37	11.42	11.79	21.26	31.64	19.43	37.54	19.38	28.17	36.35	52.27	41.46
Other Supporting and Auxiliary Transport Activities; Activities of Travel Agencies	12.67	4.37	10.07	8.88	18.37	14.10	8.12	29.90	7.34	16.55	18.38	50.58	8.64
Post and Telecommunications	6.80	6.09	6.68	6.43	16.25	13.25	6.60	23.76	9.73	13.51	19.68	23.57	28.39
Financial Intermediation	3.79	4.05	4.47	6.88	10.95	8.59	7.64	18.91	6.96	10.19	7.51	9.98	5.54
Real Estate Activities	3.30	8.44	1.77	2.39	7.70	7.45	4.14	13.79	3.03	4.93	9.39	6.84	5.23
Renting of Machinery and Equipment and Other Business Activities	9.67	8.37	5.36	8.87	11.73	18.36	9.10	14.76	8.30	25.44	19.80	26.69	14.12
Public Admin and Defense; Compulsory Social Security	4.74	8.74	0.00	6.22	9.83	7.90	8.74	20.46	7.60	0.01	14.66	…	2.23

continued on next page

Table 3.5e: continued

Table 3.5e: Vertical Specialization by Sector, 2015

	PRC	Indonesia	India	Japan	Republic of Korea	Taipei,China	Bangladesh	Malaysia	Philippines	Thailand	Viet Nam	Mongolia	Sri Lanka
						(% of gross exports)							
Education	5.06	9.69	2.10	2.49	5.99	10.67	...	9.10	4.39	8.75	12.31	9.42	...
Health and Social Work	12.73	8.51	7.81	7.89	13.55	16.36	7.22	24.55	11.87	19.92	27.08	20.29	4.61
Other Community, Social and Personal Services	6.81	9.11	3.03	7.31	12.53	16.39	5.75	20.75	11.54	21.31	17.12	12.32	13.10
Private Households with Employed Persons	...	...	...	...	...	...	...	...	...	...	...	...	...

... = data not available, PRC = People's Republic of China.

Source: ADB Multi Region Input–Output Tables Database.

Table 3.6a: Vertical Specialization Disaggregated (People's Republic of China)

		Gross Export	VS	FVA_FIN	FVA_INT	DDC	FDC	VS	FVA_FIN	FVA_INT	DDC	FDC
				($ million)				(% of gross export)	(% of VS)			
Textiles and Textile Products	2000	46,204	8,418	5,657	1,395	145	1,221	18	67	17	2	15
	2005	109,093	21,013	13,953	3,431	330	3,299	19	66	16	2	16
	2008	180,061	27,921	19,494	4,005	432	3,989	16	70	14	2	14
	2011	240,164	35,002	23,382	5,950	615	5,054	15	67	17	2	14
	2015	252,903	26,334	19,201	3,667	506	2,960	10	73	14	2	11
Chemicals and Chemical Products	2000	12,498	2,250	520	1,048	51	632	18	23	47	2	28
	2005	37,160	9,339	2,270	3,948	352	2,769	25	24	42	4	30
	2008	83,168	20,642	3,999	8,911	941	6,790	25	19	43	5	33
	2011	117,855	29,469	5,385	13,511	1,385	9,187	25	18	46	5	31
	2015	132,962	23,898	8,501	8,867	971	5,558	18	36	37	4	23
Electrical and Optical Equipment	2000	70,263	18,444	9,531	4,085	233	4,596	26	52	22	1	25
	2005	298,552	114,220	56,637	26,103	3,616	27,864	38	50	23	3	24
	2008	556,821	178,196	88,035	41,001	7,298	41,861	32	49	23	4	23
	2011	719,587	217,137	105,470	55,452	9,109	47,105	30	49	26	4	22
	2015	715,925	145,609	80,201	35,371	5,451	24,585	20	55	24	4	17
Post and Telecommunications	2000	1,483	184	30	118	4	31	12	16	64	2	17
	2005	4,565	675	114	409	30	122	15	17	61	4	18
	2008	8,487	973	168	555	55	195	11	17	57	6	20
	2011	11,551	1,214	196	710	73	235	11	16	58	6	19
	2015	15,324	1,042	197	583	54	208	7	19	56	5	20
Renting of Machinery and Equipment and Other Business Activities	2000	7,339	1,019	74	770	16	159	14	7	76	2	16
	2005	24,975	4,728	335	3,331	174	887	19	7	70	4	19
	2008	50,839	8,506	596	5,749	398	1,762	17	7	68	5	21
	2011	67,201	10,410	733	7,360	486	1,830	15	7	71	5	18
	2015	97,061	9,386	1,016	6,677	356	1,337	10	11	71	4	14

DDC = domestic value added double counted in exports, FDC = foreign value added double counted in exports, FVA_FIN = foreign value added in exports for final consumption, FVA_INT = foreign value added in exports in intermediate exports, VS = vertical specialization.

Source: ADB Multi Region Input–Output Tables Database.

Table 3.6b: Vertical Specialization Disaggregated (Indonesia)

		Gross Export	VS	FVA_FIN	FVA_INT	DDC	FDC	VS	FVA_FIN	FVA_INT	DDC	FDC
				($ million)				(% of gross export)	(% of VS)			
Mining and Quarrying	2000	9,485	379	0	266	7	105	4	0	70	2	28
	2005	19,868	1,287	2	800	14	471	6	0	62	1	37
	2008	32,605	1,750	3	1,025	18	703	5	0	59	1	40
	2011	58,303	2,434	1	1,490	40	904	4	0	61	2	37
	2015	31,983	808	1	483	15	311	3	0	60	2	38
Food, Beverages and Tobacco	2000	4,271	525	268	200	1	56	12	51	38	0	11
	2005	7,794	1,035	294	564	4	173	13	28	54	0	17
	2008	20,252	2,302	400	1,425	11	466	11	17	62	0	20
	2011	27,640	2,914	521	1,875	17	500	11	18	64	1	17
	2015	33,141	3,495	825	2,086	18	566	11	24	60	1	16
Coke, Refined Petroleum and Nuclear Fuel	2000	7,037	1,311	326	704	6	275	19	25	54	0	21
	2005	9,373	2,120	280	1,163	9	667	23	13	55	0	31
	2008	14,347	2,713	329	1,400	13	971	19	12	52	0	36
	2011	19,995	2,851	490	1,529	16	816	14	17	54	1	29
	2015	20,162	1,170	274	592	9	295	6	23	51	1	25
Electrical and Optical Equipment	2000	7,682	2,342	1,125	481	6	730	30	48	21	0	31
	2005	8,805	2,620	903	613	9	1,095	30	34	23	0	42
	2008	9,717	3,026	1,015	857	11	1,143	31	34	28	0	38
	2011	12,440	3,794	1,696	1,086	14	998	30	45	29	0	26
	2015	11,565	1,535	797	406	4	329	13	52	26	0	21
Hotels and Restaurants	2000	1,867	208	64	108	1	36	11	31	52	0	17
	2005	1,836	203	75	97	1	31	11	37	48	0	15
	2008	3,047	302	120	137	1	44	10	40	45	0	15
	2011	4,087	375	161	163	2	50	9	43	43	0	13
	2015	3,860	320	167	114	1	38	8	52	36	0	12

DDC = domestic value added double counted in exports, FDC = foreign value added double counted in exports, FVA_FIN = foreign value added in exports for final consumption, FVA_INT = foreign value added in intermediate exports, VS = vertical specialization.

Source: ADB Multi Region Input–Output Tables Database.

Table 3.6c: Vertical Specialization Disaggregated (India)

		Gross Export	VS	FVA_FIN	FVA_INT	DDC	FDC	VS	FVA_FIN	FVA_INT	DDC	FDC
				($ million)				(% of gross export)	(% of VS)			
Textiles and Textile Products	2000	14,713	1,585	1,176	214	2	193	11	74	13	0	12
	2005	19,596	3,155	2,571	303	6	276	16	81	10	0	9
	2008	22,744	4,159	3,407	383	6	364	18	82	9	0	9
	2011	26,085	4,187	3,334	510	8	335	16	80	12	0	8
	2015	28,421	4,558	3,799	434	4	321	16	83	10	0	7
Electrical and Optical Equipment	2000	2,026	370	139	106	1	124	18	38	29	0	34
	2005	6,717	1,390	559	385	7	439	21	40	28	1	32
	2008	15,168	3,231	1,544	869	14	804	21	48	27	0	25
	2011	28,851	5,741	3,063	1,399	21	1,259	20	53	24	0	22
	2015	34,250	5,336	3,434	1,044	11	847	16	64	20	0	16
Transport Equipment	2000	1,610	272	106	112	0	53	17	39	41	0	20
	2005	5,395	1,126	460	453	5	208	21	41	40	0	18
	2008	12,593	2,898	1,307	996	11	584	23	45	34	0	20
	2011	19,677	3,908	2,090	1,168	12	637	20	53	30	0	16
	2015	23,416	3,634	2,215	934	8	477	16	61	26	0	13
Manufacturing, Nec; Recycling	2000	6,482	1,477	918	444	2	113	23	62	30	0	8
	2005	23,821	10,981	7,512	2,681	23	765	46	68	24	0	7
	2008	40,150	19,055	12,783	4,572	42	1,658	47	67	24	0	9
	2011	59,235	31,334	22,550	6,847	54	1,883	53	72	22	0	6
	2015	74,562	12,402	9,699	2,166	17	520	17	78	17	0	4
Renting of Machinery and Equipment and Other Business Activities	2000	3,080	188	62	88	1	39	6	33	46	0	21
	2005	25,868	2,102	543	1,057	20	482	8	26	50	1	23
	2008	39,683	3,222	1,379	1,236	20	587	8	43	38	1	18
	2011	45,749	3,133	1,592	1,051	15	474	7	51	34	0	15
	2015	46,845	2,510	1,138	920	12	440	5	45	37	0	18

DDC = domestic value added double counted in exports, FDC = foreign value added double counted in exports, FVA_FIN = foreign value added in exports for final consumption, FVA_INT = foreign value added in intermediate exports, VS = vertical specialization.

Source: ADB Multi Region Input–Output Tables Database.

Tables 3.6d: Vertical Specialization Disaggregated (Japan)

			FVA_FIN	FVA_INT	DDC	FDC	VS	FVA_FIN	FVA_INT	DDC	FDC
		Gross Export	VS	($ million)				(% of gross export)	(% of VS)		

		Gross Export	VS	FVA_FIN	FVA_INT	DDC	FDC	VS	FVA_FIN	FVA_INT	DDC	FDC
				($ million)				(% of gross export)	(% of VS)			
Basic Metals and Fabricated Metal	2000	45,368	4,774	350	2,582	219	1,623	11	7	54	5	34
	2005	69,092	10,973	668	5,605	401	4,299	16	6	51	4	39
	2008	105,932	27,047	1,746	13,211	708	11,383	26	6	49	3	42
	2011	121,211	30,174	1,746	16,841	591	10,995	25	6	56	2	36
	2015	81,589	14,758	1,003	8,255	281	5,219	18	7	56	2	35
Machinery, Nec	2000	66,471	5,793	3,997	1,038	107	651	9	69	18	2	11
	2005	75,407	8,984	5,477	2,021	179	1,307	12	61	22	2	15
	2008	86,785	14,091	8,638	2,992	211	2,250	16	61	21	1	16
	2011	96,028	15,062	7,600	4,630	233	2,599	16	50	31	2	17
	2015	70,850	10,221	5,859	2,782	107	1,473	14	57	27	1	14
Electrical and Optical Equipment	2000	141,463	14,714	5,850	3,761	742	4,360	10	40	26	5	30
	2005	153,124	19,514	6,325	5,355	896	6,938	13	32	27	5	36
	2008	170,014	29,766	9,430	9,081	921	10,334	18	32	31	3	35
	2011	169,372	27,959	9,128	9,938	657	8,236	17	33	36	2	29
	2015	127,707	20,616	7,931	7,595	334	4,758	16	38	37	2	23
Transport Equipment	2000	99,941	8,078	4,783	2,190	158	948	8	59	27	2	12
	2005	137,503	15,522	9,307	3,975	274	1,967	11	60	26	2	13
	2008	186,824	32,908	19,201	8,487	484	4,737	18	58	26	1	14
	2011	178,915	28,457	15,638	8,229	363	4,226	16	55	29	1	15
	2015	155,394	30,375	19,666	7,049	225	3,435	20	65	23	1	11
Wholesale Trade and Commission Trade, Except of Motor Vehicles and Motorcycles	2000	31,859	845	164	424	45	212	3	19	50	5	25
	2005	40,958	1,407	244	718	56	388	3	17	51	4	28
	2008	58,904	3,053	432	1,629	120	871	5	14	53	4	29
	2011	59,672	2,549	1,342	478	26	703	4	53	19	1	28
	2015	52,045	2,896	1,506	562	24	804	6	52	19	1	28

DDC = domestic value added double counted in exports, FDC = foreign value added double counted in exports, FVA_FIN = foreign value added in exports for final consumption, FVA_INT = foreign value added in intermediate exports, VS = vertical specialization.

Source: ADB Multi Region Input–Output Tables Database.

Table 3.6e: Vertical Specialization Disaggregated (Republic of Korea)

		Gross Export	VS	FVA_FIN	FVA_INT	DDC	FDC	VS	FVA_FIN	FVA_INT	DDC	FDC
				($ million)				(% of gross export)		(% of VS)		
Chemicals and Chemical Products	2000	13,642	4,509	295	2,703	34	1,477	33	7	60	1	33
	2005	27,515	10,105	529	5,692	87	3,797	37	5	56	1	38
	2008	42,121	20,315	1,100	11,415	142	7,658	48	5	56	1	38
	2011	56,223	26,943	1,609	15,902	176	9,256	48	6	59	1	34
	2015	67,420	19,983	2,895	10,910	181	5,997	30	14	55	1	30
Basic Metals and Fabricated Metal	2000	11,918	3,923	251	2,398	35	1,238	33	6	61	1	32
	2005	24,966	8,922	346	5,169	101	3,305	36	4	58	1	37
	2008	47,677	23,209	640	12,385	214	9,970	49	3	53	1	43
	2011	60,669	27,927	765	16,912	233	10,016	46	3	61	1	36
	2015	40,679	14,088	580	8,544	125	4,840	35	4	61	1	34
Electrical and Optical Equipment	2000	61,163	21,737	8,542	6,251	239	6,705	36	39	29	1	31
	2005	105,745	37,016	10,802	10,785	647	14,782	35	29	29	2	40
	2008	129,372	53,235	14,128	18,040	734	20,332	41	27	34	1	38
	2011	158,301	59,582	15,891	23,213	797	19,681	38	27	39	1	33
	2015	157,440	44,420	14,399	18,559	487	10,974	28	32	42	1	25
Transport Equipment	2000	25,288	6,367	4,884	950	13	521	25	77	15	0	8
	2005	54,721	14,817	9,764	3,348	59	1,645	27	66	23	0	11
	2008	92,711	31,905	19,194	8,022	131	4,557	34	60	25	0	14
	2011	114,777	37,463	22,895	9,959	155	4,453	33	61	27	0	12
	2015	111,288	32,629	21,607	7,483	111	3,427	29	66	23	0	11
Water Transport	2000	10,212	2,728	574	1,413	16	724	27	21	52	1	27
	2005	17,639	6,825	1,257	3,469	123	1,976	39	18	51	2	29
	2008	27,249	14,244	3,005	7,583	101	3,555	52	21	53	1	25
	2011	27,918	13,627	3,280	5,499	69	4,779	49	24	40	1	35
	2015	30,254	6,760	2,209	2,724	42	1,784	22	33	40	1	26

DDC = domestic value added double counted in exports, FDC = foreign value added double counted in exports, FVA_FIN = foreign value added in exports for final consumption, FVA_INT = foreign value added in intermediate exports, VS = vertical specialization.

Source: ADB Multi Region Input–Output Tables Database.

Table 3.6f: Vertical Specialization Disaggregated (Taipei,China)

		Gross Export	VS	FVA_FIN	FVA_INT	DDC	FDC	VS	FVA_FIN	FVA_INT	DDC	FDC
				($ million)				(% of gross export)		(% of VS)		
Chemicals and Chemical Products	2000	10,299	4,213	535	2,488	22	1,168	41	13	59	1	28
	2005	22,502	10,734	1,538	5,635	45	3,515	48	14	52	0	33
	2008	31,091	17,947	1,466	9,972	60	6,449	58	8	56	0	36
	2011	38,082	19,212	2,159	11,089	69	5,895	50	11	58	0	31
	2015	27,619	10,461	1,618	5,798	48	2,997	38	15	55	0	29
Basic Metals and Fabricated Metal	2000	14,448	4,582	597	2,661	37	1,288	32	13	58	1	28
	2005	22,070	9,217	816	5,264	55	3,081	42	9	57	1	33
	2008	30,415	15,159	1,140	8,251	67	5,702	50	8	54	0	38
	2011	33,716	16,787	1,281	9,863	62	5,581	50	8	59	0	33
	2015	24,097	9,709	655	5,922	42	3,090	40	7	61	0	32
Electrical and Optical Equipment	2000	77,494	34,714	14,405	10,284	379	9,646	45	41	30	1	28
	2005	100,948	50,237	10,672	15,921	779	22,865	50	21	32	2	46
	2008	122,305	60,300	10,313	21,626	674	27,687	49	17	36	1	46
	2011	147,897	72,172	12,600	29,387	785	29,400	49	17	41	1	41
	2015	210,302	71,582	18,494	30,340	723	22,025	34	26	42	1	31
Air Transport	2000	2,404	704	232	382	2	87	29	33	54	0	12
	2005	3,392	1,453	510	799	2	142	43	35	55	0	10
	2008	4,340	2,364	831	1,247	3	284	54	35	53	0	12
	2011	3,909	1,743	588	929	2	223	45	34	53	0	13
	2015	5,312	1,681	649	846	3	182	32	39	50	0	11
Renting of Machinery and Equipment and Other Business Activities	2000	3,431	637	100	445	5	88	19	16	70	1	14
	2005	2,887	569	50	436	5	79	20	9	77	1	14
	2008	3,748	758	58	525	5	170	20	8	69	1	22
	2011	4,033	801	65	567	5	165	20	8	71	1	21
	2015	2,330	428	38	306	3	81	18	9	72	1	19

DDC = domestic value added double counted in exports, FDC = foreign value added double counted in exports, FVA_FIN = foreign value added in exports for final consumption, FVA_INT = foreign value added in intermediate exports, VS = vertical specialization.

Source: ADB Multi Region Input–Output Tables Database.

Table 3.6g: Vertical Specialization Disaggregated (Bangladesh)

		Gross Export	VS	FVA_FIN	FVA_INT	DDC	FDC	VS	FVA_FIN	FVA_INT	DDC	FDC
				($ million)				(% of gross export)	(% of VS)			
Textiles and Textile Products	2000	4,337	686	510	93	0	83	16	74	13	0	12
	2005	6,197	1,251	889	182	1	179	20	71	15	0	14
	2008	11,368	2,884	2,022	428	3	431	25	70	15	0	15
	2011	18,077	2,469	1,544	435	2	488	14	63	18	0	20
	2015	28,465	3,891	2,590	550	4	747	14	67	14	0	19
Leather, Leather Products and Footwear	2000	256	40	30	5	0	5	16	75	13	0	12
	2005	627	96	71	13	0	13	15	73	13	0	13
	2008	364	97	78	10	0	10	27	80	10	0	10
	2011	617	72	52	11	0	9	12	72	15	0	13
	2015	657	93	65	14	0	14	14	70	15	0	15
Manufacturing, Nec; Recycling	2000	3	0	0	0	0	0	14	24	49	0	28
	2005	5	1	0	1	0	0	18	26	53	0	21
	2008	668	286	167	76	0	43	43	58	27	0	15
	2011	609	339	42	166	0	131	56	12	49	0	39
	2015	918	126	58	37	0	31	14	46	30	0	24
Water Transport	2000	26	2	1	1	0	0	7	51	35	0	14
	2005	41	3	2	1	0	1	8	51	32	0	17
	2008	432	194	89	66	0	38	45	46	34	0	20
	2011	475	129	3	78	0	48	27	3	60	0	37
	2015	781	107	2	66	0	38	14	2	62	0	36
Post and Telecommunications	2000	29	2	1	1	0	0	7	51	40	0	9
	2005	33	2	1	1	0	0	7	50	40	0	10
	2008	568	30	3	19	0	8	5	11	64	0	25
	2011	639	26	12	9	0	5	4	45	35	0	20
	2015	1,151	76	40	24	0	12	7	53	31	0	16

DDC = domestic value added double counted in exports, FDC = foreign value added double counted in exports, FVA_FIN = foreign value added in exports for final consumption, FVA_INT = foreign value added in intermediate exports, VS = vertical specialization.

Source: ADB Multi Region Input–Output Tables Database.

Table 3.6h: Vertical Specialization Disaggregated (Malaysia)

		Gross Export	VS	FVA_FIN	FVA_INT	DDC	FDC	VS	FVA_FIN	FVA_INT	DDC	FDC
				($ million)				(% of gross export)		(% of VS)		
Agriculture, Hunting, Forestry and Fishing	2000	2,430	356	75	227	3	51	15	21	64	1	14
	2005	2,686	431	67	280	4	80	16	16	65	1	19
	2008	14,839	2,539	441	1,551	20	527	17	17	61	1	21
	2011	7,496	1,034	178	651	5	200	14	17	63	1	19
	2015	5,795	1,017	244	560	4	209	18	24	55	0	21
Coke, Refined Petroleum and Nuclear Fuel	2000	2,472	896	157	482	6	251	36	18	54	1	28
	2005	4,875	1,920	191	1,045	12	673	39	10	54	1	35
	2008	39,296	17,256	1,007	7,985	187	8,077	44	6	46	1	47
	2011	17,445	3,778	378	2,039	24	1,336	22	10	54	1	35
	2015	15,551	4,043	841	1,917	19	1,267	26	21	47	0	31
Electrical and Optical Equipment	2000	55,097	38,729	21,638	7,780	184	9,127	70	56	20	0	24
	2005	68,042	43,274	21,573	10,823	183	10,696	64	50	25	0	25
	2008	49,307	28,943	12,107	8,690	145	8,000	59	42	30	0	28
	2011	31,532	14,034	4,270	4,474	70	5,221	45	30	32	0	37
	2015	25,153	8,746	2,893	2,948	32	2,873	35	33	34	0	33
Post and Telecommunications	2000	818	208	100	85	1	22	25	48	41	1	11
	2005	797	101	14	70	1	17	13	14	69	1	17
	2008	1,604	336	30	242	2	62	21	9	72	1	18
	2011	3,452	655	43	509	3	100	19	7	78	0	15
	2015	6,740	1,602	281	1,075	6	240	24	18	67	0	15
Financial Intermediation	2000	781	249	68	141	1	38	32	27	57	0	15
	2005	2,888	231	54	128	3	45	8	23	56	1	20
	2008	5,693	876	154	502	7	213	15	18	57	1	24
	2011	3,450	349	61	209	2	77	10	18	60	1	22
	2015	4,158	786	150	470	3	164	19	19	60	0	21

DDC = domestic value added double counted in exports, FDC = foreign value added double counted in exports, FVA_FIN = foreign value added in exports for final consumption, FVA_INT = foreign value added in intermediate exports, VS = vertical specialization.

Source: ADB Multi Region Input–Output Tables Database.

Table 3.6i: Vertical Specialization Disaggregated (Philippines)

		Gross Export	VS	FVA_FIN	FVA_INT	DDC	FDC	VS	FVA_FIN	FVA_INT	DDC	FDC
				($ million)				(% of gross export)	(% of VS)			
Food, Beverages and Tobacco	2000	1,144	136	64	59	0	12	12	47	44	0	9
	2005	4,260	486	207	220	0	59	11	43	45	0	12
	2008	7,435	790	343	328	1	118	11	43	42	0	15
	2011	7,494	750	359	287	0	104	10	48	38	0	14
	2015	10,300	1,770	940	605	1	224	17	53	34	0	13
Textiles and Textile Products	2000	2,333	394	312	64	0	18	17	79	16	0	5
	2005	1,703	364	276	68	0	20	21	76	19	0	5
	2008	2,513	678	576	59	0	42	27	85	9	0	6
	2011	1,136	225	189	21	0	16	20	84	9	0	7
	2015	1,130	220	190	16	0	15	19	86	7	0	7
Basic Metals and Fabricated Metal	2000	606	171	24	95	0	52	28	14	56	0	31
	2005	1,036	317	35	177	0	105	31	11	56	0	33
	2008	3,377	1,458	166	809	1	483	43	11	55	0	33
	2011	1,855	569	67	316	0	186	31	12	56	0	33
	2015	1,869	479	86	261	0	131	26	18	54	0	27
Electrical and Optical Equipment	2000	9,879	2,175	446	761	9	960	22	21	35	0	44
	2005	12,346	5,657	1,750	2,047	12	1,848	46	31	36	0	33
	2008	23,582	13,166	4,300	5,784	5	3,077	56	33	44	0	23
	2011	14,903	6,713	2,429	2,599	10	1,675	45	36	39	0	25
	2015	11,317	3,021	931	1,332	4	754	27	31	44	0	25
Renting of Machinery and Equipment and Other Business Activities	2000	352	41	1	32	0	8	12	2	79	0	20
	2005	2,047	141	3	101	0	36	7	2	72	0	25
	2008	5,667	441	34	275	1	132	8	8	62	0	30
	2011	10,128	616	47	379	3	188	6	8	61	0	31
	2015	7,187	597	55	364	1	175	8	9	61	0	29

DDC = domestic value added double counted in exports, FDC = foreign value added double counted in exports, FVA_FIN = foreign value added in exports for final consumption, FVA_INT = foreign value added in intermediate exports, VS = vertical specialization.

Source: ADB Multi Region Input–Output Tables Database.

Table 3.6j: Vertical Specialization Disaggregated (Thailand)

		($ million)						(% of gross export)			(% of VS)	
		Gross Export	VS	FVA_FIN	FVA_INT	DDC	FDC	VS	FVA_FIN	FVA_INT	DDC	FDC
Food, Beverages and Tobacco	2000	9,563	1,919	1,083	693	3	140	20	56	36	0	7
	2005	11,970	2,757	1,482	987	6	282	23	54	36	0	10
	2008	20,070	3,964	2,129	1,282	11	542	20	54	32	0	14
	2011	25,990	5,221	2,980	1,657	9	574	20	57	32	0	11
	2015	29,438	7,912	4,485	2,420	14	992	27	57	31	0	13
Textiles and Textile Products	2000	5,947	1,615	1,029	357	3	226	27	64	22	0	14
	2005	7,434	2,144	1,318	463	4	358	29	61	22	0	17
	2008	8,619	2,893	2,000	429	5	459	34	69	15	0	16
	2011	8,907	2,105	1,387	356	3	358	24	66	17	0	17
	2015	8,350	2,461	1,661	355	3	441	29	68	14	0	18
Electrical and Optical Equipment	2000	25,037	16,617	9,885	4,163	27	2,542	66	59	25	0	15
	2005	34,311	22,120	12,031	6,102	54	3,933	64	54	28	0	18
	2008	65,888	38,674	22,316	11,503	84	4,771	59	58	30	0	12
	2011	41,128	22,317	13,789	6,029	34	2,464	54	62	27	0	11
	2015	43,170	17,852	14,062	2,674	15	1,101	41	79	15	0	6
Post and Telecommunications	2000	500	23	3	16	0	4	5	13	67	1	18
	2005	895	67	9	44	1	14	8	13	65	1	21
	2008	2,069	383	47	254	3	79	18	12	66	1	21
	2011	1,178	118	17	78	1	22	10	14	66	1	18
	2015	1,667	225	42	137	1	45	14	19	61	1	20
Renting of Machinery and Equipment and Other Business Activities	2000	131	23	1	16	0	5	17	4	72	1	24
	2005	298	59	3	39	0	17	20	5	65	1	29
	2008	1,386	477	70	230	3	173	34	15	48	1	36
	2011	5,395	1,054	201	570	5	278	20	19	54	1	26
	2015	6,255	1,592	419	762	6	405	25	26	48	0	25

DDC = domestic value added double counted in exports, FDC = foreign value added double counted in exports, FVA_FIN = foreign value added in exports for final consumption, FVA_INT = foreign value added in intermediate exports, VS = vertical specialization.

Source: ADB Multi Region Input–Output Tables Database.

Table 3.6k: Vertical Specialization Disaggregated (Viet Nam)

	Gross Export	VS	FVA_FIN	FVA_INT	DDC	FDC	VS	FVA_FIN	FVA_INT	DDC	FDC
			($ million)				(% of gross export)		(% of VS)		
Agriculture, Hunting, Forestry and Fishing											
2000	2,426	394	125	201	1	67	16	32	51	0	17
2005	5,248	1,129	358	568	2	201	22	32	50	0	18
2008	15,737	4,531	1,464	2,177	16	874	29	32	48	0	19
2011	12,294	3,036	883	1,671	8	475	25	29	55	0	16
2015	24,452	7,133	2,899	3,446	15	774	29	41	48	0	11
Textiles and Textile Products											
2000	1,221	586	435	78	0	73	48	74	13	0	12
2005	3,910	1,444	1,091	168	1	184	37	76	12	0	13
2008	9,064	4,259	3,311	427	7	514	47	78	10	0	12
2011	6,926	3,839	2,870	539	4	426	55	75	14	0	11
2015	13,657	7,850	7,102	454	4	290	57	90	6	0	4
Leather, Leather Products and Footwear											
2000	1,055	497	408	65	0	23	47	82	13	0	5
2005	248	92	64	18	0	10	37	70	19	0	11
2008	933	439	334	47	1	57	47	76	11	0	13
2011	4,467	2,494	1,880	341	3	270	56	75	14	0	11
2015	7,825	4,721	4,312	248	2	159	60	91	5	0	3
Hotels and Restaurants											
2000	819	169	128	28	0	13	21	76	16	0	8
2005	1,093	244	197	30	0	17	22	81	12	0	7
2008	685	180	138	27	0	15	26	77	15	0	8
2011	4,643	1,209	876	243	1	89	26	72	20	0	7
2015	7,361	2,224	1,710	373	2	139	30	77	17	0	6
Financial Intermediation											
2000	195	31	2	22	0	7	16	6	71	0	23
2005	711	40	11	20	0	9	6	28	49	0	23
2008	3,432	195	93	71	1	29	6	48	37	0	15
2011	3,106	234	53	133	1	47	8	23	57	1	20
2015	5,475	411	101	242	3	66	8	25	59	1	16

DDC = domestic value added double counted in exports, FDC = foreign value added double counted in exports, FVA__FIN = foreign value added in exports for final consumption, FVA__INT = foreign value added in intermediate exports, VS = vertical specialization.

Source: ADB Multi Region Input–Output Tables Database.

Table 3.6i: Vertical Specialization Disaggregated (Mongolia)

		Gross Export	VS	FVA_FIN	FVA_INT	DDC	FDC	VS	FVA_FIN	FVA_INT	DDC	FDC
				($ million)				(% of gross export)		(% of VS)		
Mining and Quarrying	2000	155	40	0	29	0	11	26	0	72	0	28
	2005	678	155	0	103	0	51	23	0	67	0	33
	2008	1,386	291	1	182	0	108	21	0	63	0	37
	2011	3,478	1,282	3	851	0	428	37	0	66	0	33
	2015	3,838	1,120	2	764	0	353	29	0	68	0	32
Food, Beverages and Tobacco	2000	15	4	2	2	0	0	30	44	46	0	10
	2005	22	6	3	2	0	0	26	57	37	0	6
	2008	11	2	1	1	0	0	21	58	37	0	5
	2011	115	24	14	9	0	1	21	58	37	0	5
	2015	105	16	9	6	0	1	15	59	36	0	6
Textiles and Textile Products	2000	41	11	7	2	0	1	27	68	20	0	12
	2005	66	16	9	3	0	4	24	59	19	0	22
	2008	141	33	19	7	0	7	23	60	20	0	20
	2011	161	31	17	8	0	7	19	54	25	0	21
	2015	170	22	12	6	0	5	13	53	26	0	21
Basic Metals and Fabricated Metal	2000	26	12	0	9	0	3	46	2	76	0	22
	2005	36	15	0	10	0	4	42	1	69	0	30
	2008	140	44	1	29	0	14	31	1	68	0	31
	2011	78	33	0	25	0	8	43	1	74	0	25
	2015	92	30	0	24	0	6	33	1	79	0	20
Renting of Machinery and Equipment and Other Business Activities	2000	0	0	0	0	0	0	37	20	64	0	16
	2005	1	0	0	0	0	0	32	27	51	0	22
	2008	28	7	2	4	0	1	24	23	56	0	21
	2011	85	26	2	17	0	7	30	7	66	0	26
	2015	193	52	4	32	0	16	27	7	62	0	31

DDC = domestic value added double counted in exports, FDC = foreign value added double counted in exports, FVA_FIN = foreign value added in exports for final consumption, FVA_INT = foreign value added in intermediate exports, VS = vertical specialization.

Source: ADB Multi Region Input–Output Tables Database.

Global Value Chains

Table 3.6m: Vertical Specialization Disaggregated (Sri Lanka)

		Gross Export	VS	FVA_FIN	FVA_INT	DDC	FDC	VS	FVA_FIN	FVA_INT	DDC	FDC
				($ million)				(% of gross export)	(% of VS)			
Food, Beverages and Tobacco	2000	90	14	12	2	0	1	16	83	13	0	4
	2005	64	13	10	3	0	1	21	75	19	0	6
	2008	133	46	39	4	0	2	34	86	9	0	5
	2011	1,502	164	120	32	0	12	11	73	19	0	8
	2015	3,649	286	208	57	0	21	8	73	20	0	7
Textiles and Textile Products	2000	112	39	37	2	0	1	35	94	4	0	2
	2005	339	119	103	10	0	6	35	86	9	0	5
	2008	91	41	40	1	0	0	45	98	1	0	1
	2011	2,503	479	404	41	0	33	19	84	9	0	7
	2015	3,872	642	538	61	0	43	17	84	10	0	7
Manufacturing, Nec; Recycling	2000	11	4	3	0	0	0	31	88	7	0	5
	2005	12	3	2	0	0	0	26	77	15	0	7
	2008	5	2	2	0	0	0	40	92	4	0	4
	2011	381	76	54	13	0	9	20	71	17	0	12
	2015	419	99	77	14	0	8	24	78	14	0	8
Hotels and Restaurants	2000	158	33	20	9	0	4	21	61	26	0	13
	2005	125	18	13	3	0	1	15	73	19	0	8
	2008	254	57	35	13	0	9	23	61	23	0	16
	2011	310	34	21	8	0	5	11	61	24	0	15
	2015	415	48	35	9	0	4	12	73	18	0	8
Inland Transport	2000	718	177	63	89	0	24	25	36	50	0	14
	2005	559	110	36	59	0	15	20	33	54	0	13
	2008	1,185	300	90	153	0	57	25	30	51	0	19
	2011	1,416	243	83	119	0	42	17	34	49	0	17
	2015	1,887	342	127	167	0	48	18	37	49	0	14

DDC = domestic value added double counted in exports, FDC = foreign value added double counted in exports, FVA__FIN = foreign value added in exports for final consumption, FVA__INT = foreign value added in intermediate exports, VS = vertical specialization.

Source: ADB Multi Region Input–Output Tables Database.

Table 3.7a: Vertical Specialization Index: Difference between 2000 and 2005 (percentage points)

Industries	PRC	INO	IND	JPN	KOR	TAP	BAN	MAL	PHI	THA	VIE	MON	SRI
Agriculture, Hunting, Forestry, and Fishing	2	2	0	3	1	6	1	1	1	2	5	(2)	(2)
Mining and Quarrying	6	2	0	14	4	3	1	(2)	(2)	4	(1)	(3)	2
Food, Beverages, and Tobacco	3	1	2	2	1	5	(0)	(0)	(0)	3	10	(4)	5
Textiles and Textile Products	1	0	5	4	(0)	3	4	(18)	4	2	(11)	(3)	0
Leather, Leather products and Footwear	1	1	1	2	1	12	(0)	(8)	7	3	(10)	(4)	12
Wood and Products of Wood and Cork	4	0	4	3	1	1	1	(4)	(0)	(13)	9	(7)	3
Pulp, Paper, Paper Products, Printing and Publishing	5	(2)	1	1	(0)	3	4	(9)	(3)	1	(7)	(3)	33
Coke, Refined Petroleum, and Nuclear Fuel	6	4	(20)	13	1	16	1	3	(26)	9	(17)	(24)	(19)
Chemicals and Chemical Products	7	7	2	7	4	7	(1)	2	5	0	(11)	(16)	(5)
Rubber and Plastics	7	6	4	4	2	6	(1)	2	4	2	(6)	(11)	(16)
Other Nonmetallic Mineral	5	0	(2)	2	4	6	(11)	9	(3)	3	(4)	(4)	16
Basic Metals and Fabricated Metal	9	1	4	5	3	10	0	(7)	2	11	(14)	(4)	17
Machinery, Not Elsewhere Classified	9	0	4	3	3	5	1	3	10	3	(8)	(17)	31
Electrical and Optical Equipment	12	(1)	2	2	(1)	5	1	(7)	24	(2)	(13)	(15)	8
Transport Equipment	9	(4)	4	3	2	8	1	(1)	(0)	2	(12)	50	11
Manufacturing, Not Elsewhere Classified; Recycling	4	2	23	3	2	8	4	(21)	6	9	(17)	(15)	(4)
Electricity, Gas, and Water Supply	6	8	5	6	8	18	(1)	8	(7)	12	(4)	2	17
Construction	5	(1)	1	2	1	8	2	3	(0)	7	(14)	(8)	(2)
Sale, Maintenance, and Repair of Motor Vehicles and Motorcycles; Retail Sale of Fuel	...	...	(0)	3	1	9	0	(31)	(4)	...	(17)	(11)	(2)
Wholesale Trade and Commission Trade, Except of Motor Vehicles and Motorcycles	2	(3)	(0)	1	2	(2)	0	(3)	(6)	1	(4)	3	2
Retail Trade, Except of Motor Vehicles and Motorcycles; Repair of Household Goods	1	(3)	(0)	1	1	1	0	(3)	(7)	1	(13)	(2)	(3)
Hotels and Restaurants	3	(0)	2	2	1	3	(0)	(15)	1	2	2	(4)	(6)
Inland Transport	4	2	2	2	(1)	5	0	(30)	(5)	5	(7)	(7)	(5)
Water Transport	4	(2)	2	6	12	6	0	1	(2)	14	(16)	(16)	(5)
Air Transport	9	(29)	8	2	(1)	14	2	(3)	(7)	5	(10)	(8)	(2)
Other Supporting and Auxiliary Transport Activities; Activities of Travel Agencies	6	(7)	(1)	1	(0)	2	1	(19)	(6)	3	(3)	(7)	2
Post and Telecommunications	2	(1)	1	1	(2)	(0)	(0)	(13)	(1)	3	(2)	(6)	3
Financial Intermediation	2	(2)	1	0	(2)	0	(0)	(24)	(4)	2	(11)	(3)	3
Real Estate Activities	2	11	(0)	0	0	1	0	9	1	1	(8)	(3)	(4)
Renting of Machinery and Equipment and Other Business Activities	5	(6)	2	1	2	1	1	(5)	(5)	2	(8)	(6)	(1)
Public Administration and Defense; Compulsory Social Security	2	0	(0)	1	(1)	(3)	1	3	(3)	1	(12)	(5)	1
Education	3	0	1	1	(0)	1	0	4	(4)	3	(7)	-	(1)
Health and Social Work	4	(4)	0	2	(0)	2	1	(3)	(1)	3	(2)	(5)	1
Other Community, Social, and Personal Services	3	3	4	1	1	(2)	0	(7)	(2)	3	(2)	(6)	(5)
Private Households with Employed Persons	...	...	...	...	...	...	...	...	...	...	...	...	...

... = data not available, ( ) = indicates negative number.

BAN = Bangladesh; IND = India; INO = Indonesia; JAP = Japan; KOR = Republic of Korea; MAL = Malaysia; MON = Mongolia; PHI = Philippines; PRC = People's Republic of China; SRI = Sri Lanka; TAP = Taipei,China; THA = Thailand; VIE = Viet Nam.

Source: ADB Multi Region Input–Output Tables Database.

Table 3.7b: Vertical Specialization Index: Difference between 2005 and 2008 (percentage points)

Industries	PRC	INO	IND	JPN	KOR	TAP	BAN	MAL	PHI	THA	VIE	MON	SRI
Agriculture, Hunting, Forestry, and Fishing	(0)	(1)	1	4	8	6	2	1	0	(0)	7	3	3
Mining and Quarrying	0	(1)	1	17	4	(1)	14	(3)	2	0	7	(2)	(2)
Food, Beverages, and Tobacco	0	(2)	1	5	11	7	(1)	(0)	(1)	(3)	5	(5)	14
Textiles and Textile Products	(4)	7	2	3	6	6	5	(5)	6	5	10	(1)	10
Leather, Leather products and Footwear	(3)	1	2	3	7	3	11	(2)	7	(1)	10	1	36
Wood and Products of Wood and Cork	(1)	(3)	(0)	8	17	2	(4)	5	3	0	12	(5)	13
Pulp, Paper, Paper Products, Printing and Publishing	0	(2)	2	5	8	6	22	(0)	4	(10)	12	(10)	16
Coke, Refined Petroleum, and Nuclear Fuel	7	(4)	4	12	10	16	42	5	21	(39)	18	(25)	23
Chemicals and Chemical Products	(0)	(6)	4	9	12	10	46	(1)	7	(6)	19	(15)	9
Rubber and Plastics	(2)	(4)	4	6	9	6	3	(3)	5	(7)	20	(23)	17
Other Nonmetallic Mineral	(0)	(3)	1	8	9	11	25	3	11	1	19	(10)	13
Basic Metals and Fabricated Metal	0	(3)	1	10	13	8	10	(1)	13	2	18	(11)	11
Machinery, Not Elsewhere Classified	(4)	(2)	0	4	8	5	3	(2)	5	(1)	18	(16)	13
Electrical and Optical Equipment	(6)	1	1	5	6	(0)	(7)	(5)	10	(6)	18	(13)	15
Transport Equipment	(3)	(3)	2	6	7	0	10	6	3	(5)	20	(70)	20
Manufacturing, Not Elsewhere Classified; Recycling	(2)	(3)	1	7	9	9	25	2	8	(4)	19	(10)	13
Electricity, Gas, and Water Supply	1	(2)	2	13	22	29	2	3	3	(1)	4	(4)	(16)
Construction	(2)	(2)	1	5	8	4	(1)	4	5	5	16	10	(2)
Sale, Maintenance, and Repair of Motor Vehicles and Motorcycles; Retail Sale of Fuel	...	...	(0)	4	3	4	7	8	2	7	6	10	3
Wholesale Trade and Commission Trade, Except of Motor Vehicles and Motorcycles	(2)	(1)	(0)	2	3	(2)	2	4	1	2	6	6	1
Retail Trade, Except of Motor Vehicles and Motorcycles; Repair of Household Goods	(1)	(1)	(0)	1	4	2	14	4	1	7	2	3	5
Hotels and Restaurants	0	(1)	1	3	7	2	(8)	9	(2)	1	4	(5)	8
Inland Transport	(0)	(2)	3	2	12	9	(0)	3	4	(5)	11	9	6
Water Transport	(0)	(1)	2	6	14	3	37	3	5	(11)	16	(4)	(6)
Air Transport	1	0	4	6	13	12	60	5	6	1	12	10	5
Other Supporting and Auxiliary Transport Activities; Activities of Travel Agencies	(0)	0	1	2	8	2	(3)	6	2	5	4	(1)	3
Post and Telecommunications	(3)	(1)	1	1	6	1	(1)	8	2	11	0	(9)	(1)
Financial Intermediation	(2)	(1)	0	2	3	1	7	7	1	3	0	0	(4)
Real Estate Activities	(1)	(1)	0	0	2	1	2	5	1	2	0	(5)	4
Renting of Machinery and Equipment and Other Business Activities	(2)	(1)	(0)	2	2	1	2	(0)	1	15	3	(8)	2
Public Administration and Defense; Compulsory Social Security	(1)	(1)	0	2	4	1	6	2	0	(1)	1	9	(1)
Education	(1)	(2)	0	1	2	1	5	1	1	1	1	10	–
Health and Social Work	(2)	(2)	2	2	4	2	(2)	(8)	1	(3)	13	(11)	(1)
Other Community, Social, and Personal Services	(2)	(1)	(3)	2	5	1	5	5	3	7	7	(1)	5
Private Households with Employed Persons	...	...	...	...	...	...	...	...	...	...	...	...	...

... = data not available, ( ) = indicates negative number.

BAN = Bangladesh; IND = India; INO = Indonesia; JAP = Japan; KOR = Republic of Korea; MAL = Malaysia; MON = Mongolia; PHI = Philippines; PRC = People's Republic of China; SRI = Sri Lanka; TAP = Taipei,China; THA = Thailand; VIE = Viet Nam.

Source: ADB Multi Region Input–Output Tables Database.

Table 3.7c: Vertical Specialization Index: Difference between 2008 and 2011 (percentage points)

Industries	PRC	INO	IND	JPN	KOR	TAP	BAN	MAL	PHI	THA	VIE	MON	SRI
Agriculture, Hunting, Forestry, and Fishing	(0)	(1)	(1)	(1)	1	(2)	4	(3)	(1)	(1)	(4)	(3)	(6)
Mining and Quarrying	1	(1)	(2)	0	1	(11)	(6)	(1)	(3)	(3)	(5)	16	(3)
Food, Beverages, and Tobacco	(0)	(1)	(1)	(1)	0	(1)	8	(9)	(1)	0	1	0	(24)
Textiles and Textile Products	(1)	1	(2)	(1)	1	0	(12)	3	(7)	(10)	8	(4)	(26)
Leather, Leather Products and Footwear	(1)	0	(3)	(0)	(1)	2	(15)	(7)	(10)	(5)	9	(4)	(34)
Wood and Products of Wood and Cork	(0)	(0)	(3)	(5)	(4)	0	0	(5)	(3)	(2)	(1)	8	(20)
Pulp, Paper, Paper Products, Printing and Publishing	0	(2)	(4)	(3)	(1)	(2)	(18)	(4)	(6)	(6)	(4)	16	(35)
Coke, Refined Petroleum, and Nuclear Fuel	2	(5)	(10)	(7)	0	(3)	(24)	(22)	(19)	(8)	(13)	11	(21)
Chemicals and Chemical Products	0	(3)	(7)	(4)	(0)	(7)	(32)	(4)	(5)	(3)	(13)	6	(8)
Rubber and Plastics	(0)	(1)	(5)	0	0	(1)	4	(6)	(5)	4	(13)	9	(25)
Other Nonmetallic Mineral	0	(1)	(3)	2	(1)	(1)	(28)	(10)	(11)	(4)	(13)	4	(23)
Basic Metals and Fabricated Metal	2	(5)	(3)	(1)	(3)	(0)	(14)	(7)	(12)	(1)	(8)	12	(9)
Machinery, Not Elsewhere Classified	1	(0)	(2)	(1)	(2)	0	(7)	(4)	(7)	(0)	(11)	9	(27)
Electrical and Optical Equipment	(2)	(1)	(1)	(1)	(4)	(1)	27	(14)	(11)	(4)	(11)	13	(28)
Transport Equipment	1	(2)	(3)	(2)	(2)	3	30	(9)	(5)	(6)	(13)	11	(25)
Manufacturing, Not Elsewhere Classified; Recycling	(0)	(1)	5	(1)	(1)	2	13	(1)	(12)	(6)	(12)	3	(20)
Electricity, Gas, and Water Supply	0	(1)	(3)	(4)	(6)	(5)	2	(8)	(3)	(5)	(1)	4	(8)
Construction	0	(2)	(2)	(1)	(1)	(2)	3	(14)	(7)	(5)	(9)	(4)	(3)
Sale, Maintenance, and Repair of Motor Vehicles and Motorcycles; Retail Sale of Fuel	...	...	(0)	(1)	0	2	8	(1)	(2)	11	(2)	(10)	(3)
Wholesale Trade and Commission Trade, Except of Motor Vehicles and Motorcycles	(0)	(1)	(0)	(1)	0	0	(0)	3	(1)	(2)	3	(7)	3
Retail Trade, Except of Motor Vehicles and Motorcycles; Repair of Household Goods	(0)	(1)	(0)	(1)	0	(0)	(9)	(2)	(1)	(7)	(0)	(5)	(4)
Hotels and Restaurants	(0)	(1)	0	(1)	0	(0)	8	(7)	(0)	(2)	(0)	12	(11)
Inland Transport	(0)	(2)	(4)	(1)	(1)	(2)	1	8	(4)	(9)	(8)	(5)	(8)
Water Transport	0	(2)	(3)	(4)	(3)	5	(18)	(8)	(4)	(8)	(11)	(22)	(1)
Air Transport	(0)	(3)	(1)	(2)	(1)	(10)	(32)	(8)	(7)	(14)	(5)	0	(21)
Other Supporting and Auxiliary Transport Activities; Activities of Travel Agencies													
Post and Telecommunications	(0)	(1)	(2)	(0)	(1)	1	6	(4)	(4)	(7)	(1)	12	(12)
Financial Intermediation	(1)	(1)	0	(1)	(0)	0	(1)	(2)	(3)	(9)	7	1	(7)
Real Estate Activities	(0)	(1)	(1)	(0)	(1)	0	(3)	(5)	(2)	(3)	2	3	(4)
Renting of Machinery and Equipment and Other Business Activities	(0)	(2)	0	(0)	(0)	(1)	(0)	(9)	(1)	(1)	2	(1)	(3)
Public Administration and Defense; Compulsory Social Security	(1)	(1)	(1)	0	0	(0)	1	(14)	(2)	(15)	0	6	(6)
Education	(0)	(1)	(0)	(0)	(1)	(0)	1	(14)	(1)	(0)	2	(39)	(1)
Health and Social Work	(0)	(1)	(0)	(1)	(0)	(0)	(6)	(8)	(2)	(2)	1	2	...
Other Community, Social, and Personal Services	(0)	(1)	(2)	(1)	0	(0)	0	4	(1)	(1)	(8)	6	(1)
Private Households with Employed Persons	(1)	(1)	0	(1)	0	(0)	(0)	7	(4)	(8)	(4)	6	(7)

... = data not available, ( ) = indicates negative number.

BAN = Bangladesh; IND = India; INO = Indonesia; JAP = Japan; KOR = Republic of Korea; MAL = Malaysia; MON = Mongolia; PHI = Philippines; PRC = People's Republic of China; SRI = Sri Lanka; TAP = Taipei,China; THA = Thailand; VIE = Viet Nam.

Source: ADB Multi Region Input–Output Tables Database.

Table 3.7d: Vertical Specialization Index: Difference between 2011 and 2015 (percentage points)

Industries	PRC	INO	IND	JPN	KOR	TAP	BAN	MAL	PHI	THA	VIE	MON	SRI
Agriculture, Hunting, Forestry, and Fishing	(2)	(1)	2	(1)	(5)	(3)	3	4	1	2	4	(6)	2
Mining and Quarrying	(4)	(2)	(0)	(30)	(6)	(2)	(3)	0	(4)	2	0	(8)	0
Food, Beverages, and Tobacco	(3)	0	4	1	(6)	(3)	(1)	14	7	7	7	(6)	(3)
Textiles and Textile Products	(4)	(21)	(0)	0	(10)	(3)	0	(0)	(0)	6	2	(7)	(3)
Leather, Leather Products and Footwear	(4)	(9)	4	3	(4)	(5)	3	0	(2)	(0)	5	(5)	0
Wood and Products of Wood and Cork	(1)	(2)	(2)	(4)	(19)	(13)	3	10	7	6	13	(8)	1
Pulp, Paper, Paper Products, Printing and Publishing	2	(9)	(1)	1	(5)	(4)	(9)	(0)	5	3	4	(11)	7
Coke, Refined Petroleum, and Nuclear Fuel	(15)	(8)	(16)	(33)	(47)	(31)	(11)	4	(5)	3	3	(10)	(13)
Chemicals and Chemical Products	(7)	(8)	(4)	(4)	(18)	(13)	(4)	1	(8)	(4)	2	(9)	(1)
Rubber and Plastics	(2)	(14)	(1)	0	(14)	(10)	(11)	8	(3)	2	(1)	(14)	0
Other Nonmetallic Mineral	(3)	(6)	(2)	(7)	(8)	(3)	(0)	3	(13)	2	2	(7)	10
Basic Metals and Fabricated Metal	(4)	(7)	(4)	(7)	(11)	(10)	(6)	(6)	(5)	(21)	1	(10)	0
Machinery, Not Elsewhere Classified	3	(29)	(4)	(1)	(7)	(6)	2	(10)	(4)	(17)	3	(11)	12
Electrical and Optical Equipment	(10)	(17)	(4)	(0)	(9)	(15)	(22)	(10)	(18)	(13)	3	(11)	10
Transport Equipment	(2)	(7)	(4)	4	(3)	(8)	(31)	(9)	6	(9)	3	(7)	11
Manufacturing, Not Elsewhere Classified; Recycling	1	(5)	(36)	1	(6)	(7)	(42)	(2)	(0)	(7)	2	(6)	4
Electricity, Gas, and Water Supply	(3)	(7)	(2)	(12)	(24)	(23)	(3)	0	(1)	6	(1)	(4)	5
Construction	(4)	(7)	(3)	(1)	(5)	(4)	(3)	1	(9)	(4)	0	(7)	(0)
Sale, Maintenance, and Repair of Motor Vehicles and Motorcycles; Retail Sale of Fuel	...	...	0	1	(1)	(7)	(4)	1	(3)	5	2	(9)	0
Wholesale Trade and Commission Trade, Except of Motor Vehicles and Motorcycles	(4)	(1)	0	1	(2)	0	1	1	4	2	(2)	(4)	(0)
Retail Trade, Except of Motor Vehicles and Motorcycles; Repair of Household Goods	(4)	(1)	0	2	(2)	8	(2)	1	3	1	1	(1)	(0)
Hotels and Restaurants	(3)	(1)	1	3	(2)	1	4	8	4	8	4	(12)	1
Inland Transport	(2)	(8)	(5)	0	(12)	(4)	0	6	(4)	4	1	0	1
Water Transport	(2)	(11)	(2)	(10)	(26)	(16)	(13)	5	(1)	6	1	18	0
Air Transport	(5)	(4)	(14)	(5)	(15)	(13)	(24)	5	(3)	8	1	(1)	7
Other Supporting and Auxiliary Transport Activities; Activities of Travel Agencies	(2)	(3)	1	2	(4)	(3)	(2)	7	(4)	5	0	2	(0)
Post and Telecommunications	(4)	1	(2)	3	(2)	0	3	5	(1)	4	(2)	1	(1)
Financial Intermediation	(2)	(1)	1	3	3	4	(0)	9	2	3	(0)	(8)	1
Real Estate Activities	(1)	(5)	0	1	2	3	1	6	0	2	0	0	0
Renting of Machinery and Equipment and Other Business Activities	(6)	(3)	(1)	4	(0)	(2)	2	0	2	6	1	(3)	1
Public Administration and Defense; Compulsory Social Security	(4)	(4)	(0)	1	(4)	0	(5)	3	4	(0)	(0)	...	0
Education	(5)	(3)	(1)	0	(2)	(1)	...	1	(0)	2	(0)	(2)	...
Health and Social Work	(5)	(0)	(3)	0	(6)	(3)	3	(2)	1	(1)	1	(4)	(0)
Other Community, Social, and Personal Services	(5)	(5)	(6)	2	(4)	5	(0)	3	0	0	1	(14)	1
Private Households with Employed Persons													

... = data not available, ( ) = indicates negative number.

BAN = Bangladesh; IND = India; INO = Indonesia; JAP = Japan; KOR = Republic of Korea; MAL = Malaysia; MON = Mongolia; PHI = Philippines; PRC = People's Republic of China; SRI = Sri Lanka; TAP = Taipei,China; THA = Thailand; VIE = Viet Nam.

Source: ADB Multi Region Input–Output Tables Database.

PART IV
Definitions

This part contains the definitions of statistical indicators that are covered in Part 1 - Sustainable Development Goals (SDGs) and Part 2 - Regional Trends and Tables. The definitions are taken mostly from the Asian Development Bank's Development Indicators Reference Manual, including websites and publications of international and private organizations such as the Food and Agriculture Organization of the United Nations (FAO); International Labour Organization (ILO); International Monetary Fund (IMF); International Telecommunication Union (ITU); Organisation for Economic Co-operation and Development (OECD); Transparency International; United Nations Children's Fund (UNICEF); United Nations Educational, Scientific and Cultural Organization (UNESCO); United Nations Population Division (UNPD); United Nations Statistics Division (UNSD); World Bank; World Health Organization (WHO); and United Nations World Tourism Organization (UNWTO). The SDG indicators are arranged according to their respective goals and targets before they are defined, while the indicators for the Regional Trends and Tables are grouped according to their themes and subtopics before they are defined. In many instances, the indicators themselves, rather than their growth rates or ratios to another indicator, are defined.

Sustainable Development Goals

Goals and Targets	Statistical Indicators	Definition
Goal 1: End poverty in all its forms everywhere		
Target 1.1: By 2030, eradicate extreme poverty for all people everywhere, currently measured as people living on less than $1.25 a day.	1.1.1 Proportion of population below the international poverty line, by sex, age, employment status and geographical location (urban/rural)	Proportion of the population living on less than $1.90 a day, measured at 2011 international prices, adjusted for purchasing power parity (PPP). Note: PPP conversion factor for private consumption is the number of units of a country's currency required to buy the same amount of goods and services in the domestic market as a US dollar would buy in the United States.
		The working poor refers to the proportion of employed population living in households with consumption or income per capita that is less than $1.9 (2011 PPP) per day. Note: The proportion of working poor in total employment (also known as the working poverty rate) combines data on household income or consumption with labor force variables measured at the individual level.
Target 1.2: By 2030, reduce at least by half the proportion of men, women and children of all ages living in poverty in all its dimensions according to national definitions.	1.2.1 Proportion of population living below the national poverty line, by sex and age	Proportion of population living below the national poverty line. Note: National poverty rate is defined at country-specific poverty lines in local currencies, which are different in real terms across countries and different from the $1.90-a-day international poverty line. Thus, national poverty rates cannot be compared across countries or with the $1.90-a-day poverty rate.
Target 1.3: Implement nationally appropriate social protection systems and measures for all, including floors, and by 2030 achieve substantial coverage of the poor and the vulnerable.	1.3.1 Proportion of population covered by social protection floors/systems, by sex, distinguishing children, unemployed persons, older persons, persons with disabilities, pregnant women, newborns, work-injury victims and the poor and the vulnerable	Proportion of the population covered by social protection floors or systems and includes the component proportion of unemployed who receive unemployment benefits, which is defined as the number of unemployed persons receiving unemployment benefits divided by the total number of unemployment persons times 100. Note: Social protection floors are nationally defined sets of basic social security guarantees that should ensure, as a minimum, that over the life cycle, all in need have access to essential health care and to basic income security which, together, secure effective access to goods and services defined as necessary at the national level. This should include at least access to essential health care, including maternity care; basic income security for children; basic income security for persons of working age who are unable to earn sufficient income, in particular in cases of sickness, unemployment, maternity and disability; and basic income security for older persons.

continued.

Goals and Targets	Statistical Indicators	Definition
Goal 2: End hunger, achieve food security and improved nutrition and promote sustainable agriculture		
Target 2.1: By 2030, end hunger and ensure access by all people, in particular the poor and people in vulnerable situations, including infants, to safe, nutritious and sufficient food all year round.	2.1.1 Prevalence of undernourishment	Proportion of the population whose habitual food consumption is insufficient to provide the dietary energy levels that are required to maintain a normal active and healthy life. Note: Undernourishment is defined as the condition by which a person has access, on a regular basis, to amounts of food that are insufficient to provide the energy required for conducting a normal, healthy and active life, given his or her own dietary energy requirements.
Target 2.2: By 2030, end all forms of malnutrition, including achieving, by 2025, the internationally agreed targets on stunting and wasting in children under 5 years of age, and address the nutritional needs of adolescent girls, pregnant and lactating women and older persons.	2.2.1 Prevalence of stunting (height for age <–2 standard deviation from the median of the World Health Organization (WHO) Child Growth Standards) among children under 5 years of age	Percentage of children aged 0–59 months who are below minus two standard deviations from median height-for-age of the WHO Child Growth Standards.
	2.2.2.a Prevalence of malnutrition (weight for height <–2 standard deviation from the median of the WHO Child Growth Standards) among children under 5 years of age (wasting)	Percentage of children aged 0–59 months who are below minus two standard deviations from median weight-for-height of the WHO Child Growth Standards.
	2.2.2.b Prevalence of malnutrition (weight for height >+2 standard deviation from the median of the WHO Child Growth Standards) among children under 5 years of age (overweight)	Percentage of children aged 0–59 months who are above two standard deviations from median weight-for-height of the WHO Child Growth Standards.
Target 2.a: Increase investment, including through enhanced international cooperation, in rural infrastructure, agricultural research and extension services, technology development and plant and livestock gene banks in order to enhance agricultural productive capacity in developing countries, in particular least developed countries.	2.a.2 Total official flows (official development assistance plus other official flows) to the agriculture sector	Gross disbursements of total Official Development Assistance (ODA) and Other Official Flows (OOF) from all donors to the agriculture sector. Note: Total ODA and OOF to developing countries quantify the public effort (excluding export credits) that donors provide to developing countries for agriculture.
Goal 3: Ensure healthy lives and promote well-being for all at all ages		
Target 3.1: By 2030, reduce the global maternal mortality ratio to less than 70 per 100,000 live births.	3.1.1 Maternal mortality ratio	Number of maternal deaths during a given time period per 100,000 live births during the same time period. Note: The term maternal deaths refers to the annual number of female deaths from any cause related to or aggravated by pregnancy or its management (excluding accidental or incidental causes) during pregnancy and childbirth or within 42 days of termination of pregnancy, irrespective of the duration and site of the pregnancy, expressed per 100,000 live births, for a specified time period.
	3.1.2 Proportion of births attended by skilled health personnel	Percentage of live births attended by skilled health personnel during a specified time period, generally up to the past 5 years. Note: The proportion of birth attended by skilled health personnel provides an indicator of access by pregnant women to appropriate delivery care that can provide quality management of labor and delivery, assess obstetric risks, treat, and refer appropriately.

continued.

Goals and Targets	Statistical Indicators	Definition
Target 3.2: By 2030, end preventable deaths of newborns and children under 5 years of age, with all countries aiming to reduce neonatal mortality to at least as low as 12 per 1,000 live births and under-5 mortality to at least as low as 25 per 1,000 live births.	3.2.1 Under-five mortality rate	The probability of a child born in a specific year or period dying before reaching the age of 5 years, if subject to age specific mortality rates of that period, expressed per 1,000 live births. Note: The under-five mortality rate as defined here is, strictly speaking, not a rate (i.e., the number of deaths divided by the number of population at risk during a certain period of time) but a probability of death derived from a life table and expressed as a rate per 1,000 live births.
	3.2.2 Neonatal mortality rate	Probability that a child born in a specific year or period will die during the first 28 completed days of life if subject to age-specific mortality rates of that period, expressed per 1,000 live births. Note: Neonatal deaths (deaths among live births during the first 28 completed days of life) may be subdivided into early neonatal deaths, occurring during the first 7 days of life, and late neonatal deaths, occurring after the 7th day but before the 28th completed day of life.
Target 3.3: By 2030, end the epidemics of AIDS, tuberculosis, malaria and neglected tropical diseases and combat hepatitis, water-borne diseases, and other communicable diseases.	3.3.1 Number of new HIV infections per 1,000 uninfected population, by sex, age, and key populations	The number of new HIV infections per 1,000 person-years among the uninfected population.
	3.3.2 Tuberculosis incidence per 100,000 population	The estimated number of new and relapse TB cases (all forms of TB, including cases in people living with HIV) arising in a given year, expressed as a rate per 100,000 population.
	3.3.3 Malaria incidence per 1,000 population	Number of reported new cases of malaria per 1,000 people each year.
Target 3.4: By 2030, reduce by one third premature mortality from noncommunicable diseases through prevention and treatment and promote mental health and well-being.	3.4.1 Mortality rate attributed to cardiovascular disease, cancer, diabetes or chronic respiratory disease	Probability of dying between the ages of 30 and 70 years from cardiovascular diseases, cancer, diabetes or chronic respiratory diseases, defined as the per cent of 30-year-old people who would die before their 70th birthday from cardiovascular disease, cancer, diabetes, or chronic respiratory disease, assuming that s/he would experience current mortality rates at every age and s/he would not die from any other cause of death (e.g., injuries or HIV/AIDS).
Target 3.6: By 2020, halve the number of global deaths and injuries from road traffic accidents.	3.6.1 Death rate due to road traffic injuries	The number of road traffic fatal injury deaths per 100,000 population.
Target 3.7: By 2030, ensure universal access to sexual and reproductive health-care services, including for family planning, information and education, and the integration of reproductive health into national strategies and programmes.	3.7.2 Adolescent birth rate (aged 10–14 years; aged 15–19 years) per 1,000 women in that age group	Annual number of births to females aged 10–14 or 15–19 years per 1,000 females in the respective age group. Note: The adolescent birth rate among women aged 10–14 or 15–19 years is also referred to as the age-specific fertility rate for women aged 10–14 or 15–19.
Goal 4: Ensure inclusive and equitable quality education and promote lifelong learning opportunities for all		
Target 4.1: By 2030, ensure that all girls and boys complete free, equitable and quality primary and secondary education leading to relevant and effective learning outcomes.	4.1.1 Proportion of children at the end of primary achieving at least a minimum proficiency level in mathematics, by sex	Percentage of children at the end of primary education achieving at least a minimum proficiency level in mathematics. Note: The minimum proficiency level will be measured relative to new common mathematics scales currently in development. The actual SDG indicator is the proportion of children and young people: (a) in grades 2/3; (b) at the end or primary; and (c) at the end of lower secondary school achieving at least a minimum proficiency level in (i) reading and (ii) mathematics. This indicator is calculated as the percentage of children and/or young people at the relevant stage of education achieving or exceeding a pre-defined proficiency level in a given subject.

continued.

Goals and Targets	Statistical Indicators	Definition
Target 4.2: By 2030, ensure that all girls and boys have access to quality early childhood development, care and pre-primary education so that they are ready for primary education.	4.2.2 Participation rate in organized learning (one year before the official primary entry age), by sex	Percentage of children in the given age range who participate in one or more organized learning programs, including programs that offer a combination of education and care. Note: An organized learning program is one that consists of a coherent set or sequence of educational activities designed with the intention of achieving pre-determined learning outcomes or the accomplishment of a specific set of educational tasks. Early childhood and primary education programs are examples of organized learning programmes. The official primary entry age is the age at which children are obliged to start primary education according to national legislation or policies.
Target 4.c: By 2030, substantially increase the supply of qualified teachers, including through international cooperation for teacher training in developing countries, especially least developed countries and small island developing States.	4.c.1.a Proportion of teachers in preprimary education who have received at least the minimum organized teacher training	The percentage of teachers by level of education taught (pre-primary, primary, lower secondary and upper secondary) who have received at least the minimum organized pedagogical teacher training pre-service and in-service required for teaching at the relevant level in a given country. Note: The indicator should be calculated separately for public and private institutions.
	4.c.1.b Proportion of teachers in primary education who have received at least the minimum organized teacher training	
	4.c.1.c Proportion of teachers in lower secondary education who have received at least the minimum organized teacher training	
	4.c.1.d Proportion of teachers in upper secondary education who have received at least the minimum organized teacher training	
Goal 5: Achieve gender equality and empower all women and girls		
Target 5.3: Eliminate all harmful practices, such as child, early and forced marriage and female genital mutilation.	5.3.1 Proportion of women aged 20–24 years who were married or in a union before age 15 and before age 18	Proportion of women aged 20–24 years who were married or in a union by age 15 and by age 18. Note: Both formal (i.e., marriages) and informal unions are covered under this indicator. Informal unions are generally defined as those in which a couple lives together for some time, intends to have a lasting relationship, but for which there has been no formal civil or religious ceremony (i.e., cohabitation).
Target 5.5: Ensure women's full and effective participation and equal opportunities for leadership at all levels of decision-making in political, economic and public life.	5.5.1 Proportion of seats held by women in national parliaments and local governments	The percentage of parliamentary seats in a single or lower chamber held by women. Note: The data available for the countries may vary with suspensions and dissolutions of parliaments.
Goal 6: Ensure availability and sustainable management of water and sanitation for all		
Target 6.1: By 2030, achieve universal and equitable access to safe and affordable drinking water for all.	6.1.1 Proportion of population using safely managed drinking water services	Proportion of population using an improved basic drinking water source that is located on premises and available when needed and free of faecal (and priority chemical) contamination. Note: Improved drinking water sources include the following: piped water into dwelling, yard or plot; public taps or standpipes; boreholes or tubewells; protected dug wells; and protected springs and rainwater. Packaged drinking water is considered improved if households use an improved water source for other domestic purposes. The WHO/UNICEF Joint Monitoring Programme for Water Supply and Sanitation (JMP) estimates access to basic services for each country, separately in urban and rural areas, by fitting a regression line to a series of data points from household surveys and censuses. This approach was used to report on use of "improved water" sources for MDG monitoring. The JMP is evaluating the use of alternative statistical estimation methods as more data become available.

continued.

Goals and Targets	Statistical Indicators	Definition
Target 6.2: By 2030, achieve access to adequate and equitable sanitation and hygiene for all and end open defecation, paying special attention to the needs of women and girls and those in vulnerable situations.	6.2.1 Proportion of population using safely managed sanitation services, including a hand-washing facility with soap and water	The proportion of the population using an improved basic sanitation facility at the household level which is not shared with other households and where excreta is safely disposed in situ or treated off-site. Note: "Improved" source includes flush or pour flush toilets to sewer systems, septic tanks or pit latrines, ventilated improved pit latrines, pit latrines with a slab, and composting toilets. A handwashing facility pertains to a device that serves to contain, transport or regulate the flow of water to facilitate handwashing with soap and water.
Target 6.4: By 2030, substantially increase water-use efficiency across all sectors and ensure sustainable withdrawals and supply of freshwater to address water scarcity and substantially reduce the number of people suffering from water scarcity.	6.4.2 Level of water stress: freshwater withdrawal as a proportion of available freshwater resources	The ratio between total freshwater withdrawn by all major sectors and total renewable freshwater resources, after taking into account environmental water requirements. Note: Total freshwater withdrawal (TWW) is the volume of freshwater extracted from its source (rivers, lakes, aquifers) for agriculture, industries and municipalities. Freshwater withdrawal includes primary freshwater (not withdrawn before), secondary freshwater (previously withdrawn and returned to rivers and groundwater, such as discharged wastewater and agricultural drainage water) and fossil groundwater. Main sectors, as defined by ISIC standards, include agriculture; forestry and fishing; manufacturing; electricity industry; and services. Environmental water requirements are the quantities of water required to sustain freshwater and estuarine ecosystems. This indicator is also known as water withdrawal intensity.
Target 6.a: By 2030, expand international cooperation and capacity-building support to developing countries in water- and sanitation-related activities and programmes, including water harvesting, desalination, water efficiency, wastewater treatment, recycling and reuse technologies.	6.a.1 - Amount of water- and sanitation-related official development assistance that is part of a government-coordinated spending plan	The proportion of total water and sanitation-related official development assistance (ODA) disbursements that are included in the government budget. Note: The amount of water and sanitation-related ODA is a quantifiable measurement as a proxy for "international cooperation and capacity development support" in financial terms. A low value of this indicator (near 0%) would suggest that international donors are investing in water-and sanitation-related activities and programs in the country outside the purview of the national government. A high value (near 100%) would indicate that donors are aligned with national government and national policies and plans for water and sanitation.
Goal 7: Ensure access to affordable, reliable, sustainable and modern energy for all		
Target 7.1: By 2030, ensure universal access to affordable, reliable and modern energy services.	7.1.1 Proportion of population with access to electricity	Percentage of the population that has access to electricity. Access to electricity addresses major critical issues in all the dimensions of sustainable development. The target has a wide range of social and economic impacts, including facilitating development of household-based income generating activities and lightening the burden of household tasks.
Target 7.2: By 2030, increase substantially the share of renewable energy in the global energy mix.	7.2.1 Renewable energy share in the total final energy consumption	The percentage of final consumption of energy that is derived from renewable resources. Note: Renewable energy consumption includes consumption of energy derived from hydro, solid biofuels, wind, solar, liquid biofuels, biogas, geothermal, marine, and waste. Total final energy consumption is calculated from national balances and statistics as total final consumption minus non-energy use.
Target 7.3: By 2030, double the global rate of improvement in energy efficiency.	7.3.1 Energy intensity measured in terms of primary energy and GDP	The energy supplied to the economy per unit value of economic output. Note: Total energy supply, as defined by the International Recommendations for Energy Statistics, as made up of production plus net imports minus international marine and aviation bunkers plus stock changes. For international comparison purposes, gross domestic product (GDP) is measured in constant terms at purchasing power parity.

continued.

Goals and Targets	Statistical Indicators	Definition
Goal 8: Promote sustained, inclusive and sustainable economic growth, full and productive employment and decent work for all		
Target 8.1: Sustain per capita economic growth in accordance with national circumstances and, in particular, at least 7 percent gross domestic product growth per annum in the least developed countries.	8.1.1 Annual growth rate of real GDP per capita	Percentage change in the real GDP per capita between two consecutive years. Note: Real GDP per capita is calculated by dividing GDP at constant prices by the population of a country or area. The data for real GDP are measured in constant US dollars to facilitate the calculation of country growth rates and aggregation of the country data.
Target 8.2: Achieve higher levels of economic productivity through diversification, technological upgrading and innovation, including through a focus on high-value added and labour-intensive sectors.	8.2.1 Annual growth rate of real GDP per employed person	Annual growth rate of real GDP per employed person conveys the annual percentage change in real GDP per employed person.
Target 8.5: By 2030, achieve full and productive employment and decent work for all women and men, including for young people and persons with disabilities, and equal pay for work of equal value.	8.5.2 Unemployment rate, by sex	Percentage of number of unemployed in the labor force.
Target 8.6: By 2020, substantially reduce the proportion of youth not in employment, education or training.	8.6.1 Proportion of youth (aged 15–24 years) not in education, employment or training	Percentage of youth (15–24 years old) who are not in employment and not in education or training (Not in Education, Employment or Training [NEET]).
Target 8.7: Take immediate and effective measures to eradicate forced labour, end modern slavery and human trafficking and secure the prohibition and elimination of the worst forms of child labour, including recruitment and use of child soldiers, and by 2025 end child labour in all its forms.	8.7.1 Proportion and number of children aged 5–17 years engaged in child labor	The number of children aged 5–17 years who are reported to have been engaged in child labour in the past week divided by the total number of children aged 5–17 in the population.
Target 8.10: Strengthen the capacity of domestic financial institutions to encourage and expand access to banking, insurance and financial services for all.	8.10.1 Number of commercial bank branches and automated teller machines (ATMs) per 100,000 adults	The number of ATMs per 100,000 adults is calculated by dividing the product of the number of ATMs and 100,000 to total adult population in the reporting country. The number of commercial bank branches is calculated by dividing the product of number of institutions plus number of branches and 100,000 to total adult population in the reporting country. Note: The number of commercial bank branches is calculated for commercial banks, credit unions and financial cooperatives, and all multilateral financing institutions.
	8.10.2 Proportion of adults (15 years and older) with an account at a bank or other financial institution or with a mobile- money-service provider	The percentage of adults (ages 15+) who report having an account (by themselves or together with someone else) at a bank or another type of financial institution or personally using a mobile money service in the past 12 months.

continued.

Goals and Targets	Statistical Indicators	Definition
Target 8.a: Increase Aid for Trade support for developing countries, in particular least developed countries, including through the Enhanced Integrated Framework for Trade-related Technical Assistance to Least Developed Countries.	8.a.1 Aid for Trade commitments and disbursements	Gross disbursements and commitments of total ODA from all donors for aid for trade.
Goal 9: Build resilient infrastructure, promote inclusive and sustainable industrialization and foster innovation		
Target 9.1: Develop quality, reliable, sustainable and resilient infrastructure, including regional and transborder infrastructure, to support economic development and human well-being, with a focus on affordable and equitable access for all.	9.1.2 Freight volume, by air transport (thousand metric tons)	Passenger and freight volumes is the sum of the passenger and freight volumes reported for the air carriers in terms of number of people and metric tons of cargo respectively.
	9.1.2 Passenger volume, by air transport (number of units)	
Target 9.2: Promote inclusive and sustainable industrialization and, by 2030, significantly raise industry's share of employment and gross domestic product, in line with national circumstances, and double its share in least developed countries.	9.2.1 Manufacturing value added as a proportion of GDP and per capita	Total value of goods and services net of intermediate consumption. It is generally compiled as the sum of the value added of all manufacturing activity units in operation in the reference period. Note: For the purpose of comparing over time and across countries, manufacturing value added is estimated in terms of constant prices in US dollars. The current series are given at constant prices of 2010.
	9.2.2 Manufacturing employment as a proportion of total employment	The proportion of employed population who are engaged in manufacturing activities
Target 9.5: Enhance scientific research, upgrade the technological capabilities of industrial sectors in all countries, in particular developing countries, including, by 2030, encouraging innovation and substantially increasing the number of research and development workers per 1 million people and public and private research and development spending.	9.5.1 Research and development expenditure as a proportion of GDP	Amount of research and development (R&D) expenditure divided by the total output of the economy.
	9.5.2 Researchers (in full-time equivalent) per million inhabitants	Number of research and development workers (in full-time equivalent) per 1 million people.
Target 9.a: Facilitate sustainable and resilient infrastructure development in developing countries through enhanced financial, technological and technical support to African countries, least developed countries, landlocked developing countries and small island developing States.	9.a.1 Total official international support (official development assistance plus other official flows) to infrastructure	Gross disbursements of total ODA and other official flows (OOF) from all donors in support of infrastructure.

continued.

Goals and Targets	Statistical Indicators	Definition
Target 9.b: Support domestic technology development, research and innovation in developing countries, including by ensuring a conducive policy environment for, inter alia, industrial diversification and value addition to commodities.	9.b.1 Proportion of medium and high-tech industry value added in total value added	Proportion of medium and high-technology industry value added in total value added shows the level of technological intensity of manufacturing in an economy. Note: It is based on classification of industry into high, high-medium, low-medium, and low technology sectors. Designation of an industry to high or medium level of technology is determined by R&D intake in manufacturing value added. A higher share of R&D expenditure means a higher level of technological intensity.
Goal 10: Reduce inequality within and among countries		
Target 10.1: By 2030, progressively achieve and sustain income growth of the bottom 40 percent of the population at a rate higher than the national average.	10.1.1.a Growth rates of household expenditure or income per capita among the bottom 40% of the population (%)	The growth rate in the welfare aggregate of bottom 40% is computed as the annualized average growth rate in per capita real consumption or income of the bottom 40% of the income distribution in a country from household surveys over a roughly 5-year period.
	10.1.1.b Growth rates of household expenditure or income per capita (%)	The national average growth rate in the welfare aggregate is computed as the annualized average growth rate in per capita real consumption or income of the total population in a country from household surveys over a roughly 5-year period.
Goal 11: Make cities and human settlements inclusive, safe, resilient and sustainable		
Target 11.1: By 2030, ensure access for all to adequate, safe and affordable housing and basic services and upgrade slums	11.1.1: Proportion of urban population living in slums, informal settlements or inadequate housing	Proportion of urban population living in slums, informal settlements or inadequate housing is currently being measured by the proportion of urban population living in slums. This indicator integrates the component of the slums and informal settlements that has been monitored for the last 15 years by UN-Habitat in mostly developing countries with a new component—inadequate housing—that applies largely to the developed countries. By integrating these two components, the indicator is now universal and can be monitored in both developing and developed regions. The inadequate housing component allows capturing housing informality in more developed countries and wealthier urban contexts.
Target 11.6: By 2030, reduce the adverse per capita environmental impact of cities, including by paying special attention to air quality and municipal and other waste management.	11.6.2.a PM2.5 air pollution, mean annual exposure (micrograms per cubic meter)	The mean annual concentration of fine suspended particles of less than 2.5 microns in diameters (PM2.5) is a common measure of air pollution. Note: The mean is a population-weighted average for urban population in a country.
	11.6.2.b PM2.5 air pollution, population exposed to levels exceeding WHO guideline value (% of total)	Percent of population exposed to ambient concentrations of PM2.5 that exceed the World Health Organization (WHO) guideline value is defined as the portion of a country's population living in places where mean annual concentrations of PM2.5 are greater than 10 micrograms per cubic meter, the guideline value recommended by WHO as the lower end of the range of concentrations over which adverse health effects due to PM2.5 exposure have been observed.
Goal 14: Conserve and sustainably use the oceans, seas and marine resources for sustainable development		
Target 14.5: By 2020, conserve at least 10 per cent of coastal and marine areas, consistent with national and international law and based on the best available scientific information.	14.5.1 Coverage of protected areas in relation to marine areas	The indicator coverage of protected areas in relation to marine areas shows temporal trends in the percentage of important sites for marine biodiversity (i.e., those that contribute significantly to the global persistence of biodiversity) that are wholly covered by designated protected areas.

continued.

Goals and Targets	Statistical Indicators	Definition
Goal 15: Protect, restore and promote sustainable use of terrestrial ecosystems, sustainably manage forests, combat desertification, and halt and reverse land degradation and halt biodiversity loss		
Target 15.1: By 2020, ensure the conservation, restoration and sustainable use of terrestrial and inland freshwater ecosystems and their services, in particular forests, wetlands, mountains and drylands, in line with obligations under international agreements.	15.1.1 Forest area as a proportion of total land area	Forest area as a proportion of total land area.
Target 15.5: Take urgent and significant action to reduce the degradation of natural habitats, halt the loss of biodiversity and, by 2020, protect and prevent the extinction of threatened species.	15.5.1 Red List Index	The Red List Index measures change in aggregate extinction risk across groups of species. It is based on genuine changes in the number of species in each category of extinction risk on The IUCN Red List of Threatened Species (IUCN 2015), which is expressed as changes in an index ranging from 0 to 1. Note: The Red List Index value ranges from 1 (all species are categorized as "Least Concern") to 0 (all species are categorized as "Extinct"), and so indicates how far the set of species has moved overall toward extinction.
Goal 16: Promote peaceful and inclusive societies for sustainable development, provide access to justice for all and build effective, accountable and inclusive institutions at all levels		
Targets 16.1: Significantly reduce all forms of violence and related death rates everywhere.	16.1.1 Number of victims of intentional homicide (per 100,000 population)	The total count of victims of intentional homicide divided by the total population, expressed per 100,000 population. Intentional homicide is defined as the unlawful death inflicted upon a person with the intent to cause death or serious injury (International Classification of Crime for Statistical Purposes); population refers to total resident population in a given country in a given year. This indicator is widely used at national and international levels to measure the most extreme form of violent crime, and it also provides a direct indication of lack of security.
	16.1.3 Proportion of population subjected to physical, psychological, or sexual violence in the previous 12 months	The total number of persons who have been victim of physical, psychological, or sexual violence in the previous 12 months, as a share of the total population.
Target 16.9: By 2030, provide legal identity for all, including birth registration.	16.9.1 Proportion of children under 5 years of age whose births have been registered with a civil authority	Proportion of children under 5 years of age whose births have been registered with a civil authority.
Goal 17: Strengthen the means of implementation and revitalize the Global Partnership for Sustainable Development		
Target 17.3: Mobilize additional financial resources for developing countries from multiple sources.	17.3.2 Volume of remittances (in United States dollars) as a proportion of total GDP	Inflow of personal remittances expressed as a percentage of GDP. Note: Personal remittances comprise of personal transfers and compensation of employees. Personal transfers consist of all current transfers in cash or in kind made or received by resident households to or from nonresident households. Personal transfers thus include all current transfers between resident and nonresident individuals. Compensation of employees refers to the income of border, seasonal, and other short-term workers who are employed in an economy where they are not residents, and of residents employed by nonresident entities.

continued.

Goals and Targets	Statistical Indicators	Definition
Target 17.4: Assist developing countries in attaining long-term debt sustainability through coordinated policies aimed at fostering debt financing, debt relief and debt restructuring, as appropriate, and address the external debt of highly indebted poor countries to reduce debt distress.	17.4.1 Debt service as a proportion of exports of goods and services	Percentage of debt services (principal and interest payments) to the exports of goods and services. Note: Debt services covered in this indicator refer only to public and publicly guaranteed debt.
Target 17.6: Enhance North-South, South-South and triangular regional and international cooperation on and access to science, technology and innovation and enhance knowledge sharing on mutually agreed terms, including through improved coordination among existing mechanisms, in particular at the United Nations level, and through a global technology facilitation mechanism.	17.6.2 Fixed Internet broadband subscriptions per 100 inhabitants, by speed	Number of fixed-broadband subscriptions to the public Internet, split by advertised download speed. Note: The indicator is currently broken down by the following subscription speeds: - 256 kbit/s to less than 2 Mbit/s subscriptions: Refers to all fixed broadband internet subscriptions with advertised downstream speeds equal to, or greater than, 256 kbit/s and less than 2 Mbit/s. - 2 Mbit/s to less than 10 Mbit/s subscriptions: Refers to all fixed -broadband internet subscriptions with advertised downstream speeds equal to, or greater than, 2 Mbit/s and less than 10 Mbit/s. - Equal to or above 10 Mbit/s subscriptions (4213_G10). Refers to all fixed -broadband Internet subscriptions with advertised downstream speeds equal to, or greater than, 10 Mbit/s.

Source: United Nations Statistics Division Sustainable Development Goals Indicators. http://unstats.un.org/sdgs/metadata/

Regional Trends and Tables

Indicator	Definition
PEOPLE	
Population	
Midyear Population	Estimates of the midyear de facto population. De facto population includes all persons physically present in the country during the census day, including foreign, military, and diplomatic personnel and their accompanying household members; and transient foreign visitors in the country or in harbors.
Growth Rates in Population	Number of people added to (or subtracted from) a population over a given period of time because of natural increase and net migration expressed as a percentage of the population at the given period of time.
Net International Migration Rate	Number of immigrants minus the specified number of emigrants over a period, divided by the person-years lived by the population of the receiving country over that period. It is expressed as net number of migrants per 1,000 population.
Urban Population	Population living in urban areas, defined in accordance with the national definition or as used in the most recent population census. Because of national differences in the characteristics that distinguish urban from rural areas, the distinction between urban and rural populations is not amenable to a single definition that would be applicable to all countries. National definitions are most commonly based on size of locality. Population that is not urban is considered rural.
Urban population (as % of total population)	The estimated population living in urban areas at midyear as a percentage of the total midyear population in a country.
Age Dependency Ratio	Ratio of the nonworking-age population to the working-age population. Since countries define working age differently, a straightforward application of the definition will lead to noncomparable data. ADB therefore uses the following UN definition that can be computed directly from an age distribution: $$\frac{\text{Population aged } (0-14) + (65 \text{ and over}) \text{ years} \times 100}{\text{Population aged } (15-64) \text{ years}}$$
Labor Force and Employment	
Labor Force Participation Rate	Percentage of the labor force to the working-age population. The labor force is the sum of those employed and unemployed seeking work. The labor force participation rate measures the extent of economically active working-age population in an economy. It provides an indication of the relative size of the supply of labor available for the production of goods and services in the economy. It must be noted that definition of working-age population varies across countries.
Unemployment Rate	Percentage of unemployed to the labor force. Unemployed are persons without work but available and actively seeking it. This is probably the best known labor market measure. Together with the employment rate, it provides the broadest indicator of the status of the country's labor market. It must be noted that definition of unemployed varies across countries for some of them do not consider availability to work as part of the definition.
Unemployment Rate of 15–24-Year-Olds	Number of unemployed people aged 15–24 years divided by the labor force of the same age group.
Employment in Agriculture, Forestry, and Fishing	Employment in agriculture, forestry, and fishing that corresponds to division 1 (International Standard of Industrial Classification [ISIC] revision 2), tabulation categories A and B (ISIC revision 3), and category A of ISIC revision 4.
Employment in Mining and Quarrying	Employment in mining and quarrying that corresponds to division 2 (ISIC revision 2), tabulation category C (ISIC revision 3), and category B of ISIC revision 4.
Employment in Manufacturing	Employment in manufacturing that corresponds to division 3 (ISIC revision 2), tabulation category D (ISIC revision 3), and category C of ISIC revision 4.
Employment in Electricity, gas, steam and air conditioning supply; water supply, sewerage, waste management and remediation activities	Employment in electricity, gas, steam and air conditioning supply; water supply, sewerage, waste management and remediation activities that corresponds to division 4 (ISIC revision 2), tabulation category E (ISIC revision 3), and categories D and E of ISIC revision 4.

continued.

Indicator	Definition
Employment in Construction	Employment in construction that corresponds to division 5 (ISIC revision 2), tabulation category F (ISIC revisions 3), and category F of ISIC revision 4.
Employment in Wholesale and Retail Trade; Repair of Motor Vehicles and Motorcycles	Employment in wholesale and retail trade; repair of motor vehicles and motorcycles that corresponds to division 6 (subdivisions 61 and 62, ISIC revision 2); tabulation category G (ISIC revision 3); and category G of ISIC revision 4.
Employment in Accommodation and Food Service Activities	Employment in accommodation and food service activities that corresponds to division 6 (subdivision 63, ISIC revision 2); tabulation category H (ISIC revision 3); and category I of ISIC revision 4.
Employment in Transportation and Storage	Employment in transport and storage that corresponds to division 7 (subdivision 71, ISIC revision 2); tabulation category I (sub-categories 60–63, ISIC revision 3); and category H of ISIC revision 4.
Employment in Information and communication	Employment in information and communication that corresponds to division 7 (subdivision 72, ISIC revision 2); tabulation category I (subcategory 64, ISIC revision 3); and category J of ISIC revision 4.
Employment in Financial and Insurance Activities	Employment in financial and insurance activities that corresponds to division 8 (subdivisions 81–82, ISIC revision 2), tabulation category J (ISIC revision 3), and category K of ISIC revision 4.
Employment in Real Estate Activities	Employment in real estate activities that corresponds to division 8 (subdivision 83, ISIC revision 2); tabulation category K (subcategory 70, ISIC revision 3); and category L of ISIC revision 4.
Employment in Other Services	Employment in other services that corresponds to divisions 9 and 0 (ISIC revision 2), tabulation categories L to Q (ISIC revision 3), and categories M to U of ISIC revision 4.
Poverty Indicators	
Proportion of Population below $1.90-a-day (2011 international prices)	Percentage of the population living on less than $1.90 a day at 2011 international prices.
Income Ratio of Highest 20% to Lowest 20%	Income or consumption share that accrues to the richest 20% of the population divided by the income share of the lowest 20% of the population.
Gini Coefficient or Index	Measure of the degree to which an economy's income distribution diverges from perfect equal distribution. A value of zero (0) implies perfect equality while a value of one (1) implies perfect inequality.
Human Development Index	Composite index of longevity (measured by life expectancy at birth), knowledge (measured by expected years of schooling and mean years of schooling), and decent standard of living (measured by the adjusted per capita income in purchasing power parity [PPP] US dollars).
Social Indicators	
Life Expectancy at Birth	Number of years that a newborn is expected to live if prevailing patterns of mortality at the time of his/her birth are to stay the same throughout his/her life.
Crude Birth Rate	Ratio of the total number of live births in a given period to the midyear total population of the same period, expressed per 1,000 people.
Crude Death Rate	Ratio of the number of deaths occurring within a given period to the midyear total population of the same period, expressed per 1,000 people.
Total Fertility Rate	Number of children that would be born to a woman if she were to live to the end of her childbearing years and bear children in accordance with current age-specific fertility rates.
Primary Education Completion Rate	Total number of new entrants in the last grade of primary education, regardless of age, expressed as percentage of the total population of the theoretical entrance age to the last grade of primary. This indicator is also known as "gross intake rate to the last grade of primary." The ratio can exceed 100% due to over aged and under aged children who enter primary school late, early, and/or repeat grades.
Adult Literacy Rate	The percentage of population aged 15 years and over who can both read and write with understanding a short simple statement on his/her everyday life. Generally, literacy also encompasses numeracy, the ability to make simple arithmetic calculations.
Primary Pupil–Teacher Ratio	Average number of pupils (students) per teacher at the primary level of education in a given school year. This indicator is used to measure the level of human resources input in terms of number of teachers in relation to the size of the primary pupil population.

continued.

Indicator	Definition
Secondary Pupil–Teacher Ratio	Average number of pupils (students) per teacher at the secondary level of education in a given school year. This indicator is used to measure the level of human resources input in terms of number of teachers in relation to the size of the secondary pupil population.
Physicians	Physicians, including generalist and specialist medical practitioners, expressed in terms of 1,000 people.
Hospital Beds	In-patient beds for both acute and chronic care available in public, private, general, and specialized hospitals and rehabilitation centers expressed in terms of 1,000 people.
Number of Adults Living with HIV	All adults, defined as men and women aged 15 and over years old, with HIV infection, whether or not they have developed symptoms of AIDS.
ECONOMY AND OUTPUT	
National Accounts	
Gross Domestic Product	Unduplicated market value of the total production activity of all resident producer units within the economic territory of a country during a given period. It is calculated without making deductions for depreciation of fabricated assets or for depletion and degradation of natural resources. Transfer payments are excluded from the calculation of gross domestic product (GDP). GDP can be computed using the production, expenditure, and income approaches. Production-based GDP is the sum of the gross value added by all resident producers in the economy plus any taxes and minus any subsidies not included in the value of the products. Gross value added is the net output of an industry after adding up all outputs and subtracting intermediate inputs. Income-based GDP is the sum of the compensation of employees, mixed income, operating surplus, consumption of fixed capital, and taxes less subsidies on production and imports. Expenditure-based GDP is the sum of final consumption expenditure of households, nonprofit institutions serving households, and the government; gross capital formation; and exports minus imports of goods and services. GDP can be measured at current prices (the prices of the current reporting period), and constant prices (obtained by expressing values in terms of a base period and chain volume measure).
GDP at PPP	Measures obtained by using PPP to convert the GDP into a common currency, and by valuing them at a uniform price level. They are the spatial equivalent of a time series of GDP for a single country expressed at constant prices. At the level of GDP, they are used to compare the economic size of countries.
GDP per Capita at PPP	GDP at PPP divided by the midyear population.
GNI per Capita, Atlas Method	The gross national income (GNI) converted to US dollars using the World Bank Atlas method, divided by the midyear population. GNI is the sum of value added by all resident producers plus any product taxes (less subsidies) not included in the valuation of output plus net receipts of primary income (compensation of employees and property income) from abroad. GNI, calculated in national currency, is usually converted to US dollars at official exchange rates for comparisons across economies, although an alternative rate is used when the official exchange rate is judged to diverge by an exceptionally large margin from the rate actually applied in international transactions. To smooth fluctuations in prices and exchange rates, a special Atlas method of conversion is used by the World Bank. This applies a conversion factor that averages the exchange rate for a given year and the two preceding years, adjusted for differences in rates of inflation between the country, and the G-5 countries (France, Germany, Japan, the United Kingdom, and the United States).
Agriculture Value Added	The gross output of agriculture less the corresponding value of intermediate consumption. The industrial origin of value added is determined by ISIC revision 4 where agriculture corresponds to ISIC Section A and includes agriculture, forestry, and fishing.
Industry Value Added	The gross output of industry sectors less the corresponding value of intermediate consumption. The industrial origin of value added is determined by ISIC revision 4 where industry corresponds to ISIC Sections B-F and includes mining and quarrying (B); manufacturing (C); electricity, gas steam and air conditioning supply (D); water supply, sewage waste management, and remediation activities (E); and construction (F).

continued.

Indicator	Definition
Services Value Added	The gross output of services sectors less the corresponding value of intermediate consumption. The industrial origin of value added is determined by ISIC revision 4. Services corresponds to ISIC Sections G–U and includes wholesale and retail trade, repair of motor vehicles and motorcycles (G); transport and storage (H); accommodation and food service activities (I); information and communication (J); financial and insurance activities (K); real estate activities (L); professional, scientific and technical activities (M); administrative and support service activities (N); public administration and defense, compulsory social security (O); education (P); human health and social work activities (Q); arts, entertainment, and recreation (R); other service activities (S); activities of households as employers, undifferentiated goods and services-producing activities of households for own use (T); and activities of extraterritorial organizations and bodies (U).
Household Consumption Expenditure	Market value of all goods and services, including durable products (such as cars, washing machines, and home computers), purchased or received as income in kind by households. It excludes purchases of dwellings but includes imputed rent for owner-occupied dwellings. It also includes payments and fees to governments to obtain permits and licenses. The expenditure of nonprofit institutions serving households is generally recorded as the consumption of households for most economies.
Government Consumption Expenditure	Includes all current outlays on purchases of goods and services (including wages and salaries). It also includes most expenditure on national defense and security, but excludes government military expenditures that are part of public investment.
Gross Capital Formation	Total value of gross fixed capital formation, changes in inventories, and acquisitions less disposals of valuables. Gross fixed capital formation is the value of acquisitions less disposals of tangible goods such as buildings and intangible goods such as computer software that are intended for use in production during several accounting periods. Changes in inventories are changes in stocks of produced goods and goods for intermediate consumption, and the net increase in the value of work in progress. Valuables are goods such as precious metals and works of art that are acquired in the expectation that they will retain or increase their value over time.
Exports of Goods and Services	Consist of sales, barter, or gifts or grants, of goods and services from residents to nonresidents. The treatment of exports in the System of National Accounts (SNA) is generally identical with that in the balance of payments accounts as described in the Balance of Payments Manual.
Imports of Goods and Services	Consist of purchases, barter, or receipts of gifts or grants, of goods and services by residents from nonresidents. The treatment of imports in the SNA is generally identical with that in the balance of payments accounts as described in the Balance of Payments Manual.
Gross Domestic Saving	Difference between GDP and final consumption expenditure, where final consumption expenditure is the sum of the final consumption of household, nonprofit institutions serving households, and the government.

Production

Indicator	Definition
Agriculture Production Index	Relative level of the aggregate volume of agricultural production for each year in comparison with the base period. It is based on the sum of price-weighted quantities of different agricultural commodities produced after deductions of quantities used as seed and feed weighted in a similar manner. The resulting aggregate represents, therefore, disposable production for any use except as seed and feed.
Manufacturing Production Index	An index covering production in manufacturing. The exact coverage, the weighting system, and the methods of calculation vary from country to country but the divergences are less important than, for example, in the case of price and wage indexes.

MONEY, FINANCE, AND PRICES

Prices

Indicator	Definition
Consumer Price Index	An index that measures changes in prices against a reference period of a basket of goods and services purchased by households. Based on the purpose of the consumer price index, different basket of goods and services can be selected. For macroeconomic purposes, a broad-based basket is used to represent the relative price movement of household final consumption expenditure.
Food Consumer Price Index	An index that measures the change over time in the general level of prices of food and nonalcoholic beverage items that households acquire, use, or pay for consumption. This is done by measuring the cost of purchasing a fixed basket of consumer food and beverage of constant quality and similar characteristics, with the products in the basket being selected to be representative of households' expenditure during a specified period.

continued.

Indicator	Definition
Nonfood Consumer Price Index	An index that measures the change over time, in general level, the prices of nonfood items that household acquire, use, or pay for consumption. Nonfood index includes items such as clothing, housing and repairs, water, electricity, fuel, services and miscellaneous goods or all items in the basket of goods and services other than food and nonalcoholic beverages.
Wholesale Price Index	A measure that reflects changes in the prices paid for goods at various stages of distribution up to the point of retail. It can include prices of raw materials for intermediate and final consumption, prices of intermediate or unfinished goods, and prices of finished goods. The goods are usually valued at purchasers' prices.
Producer Price Index	A measure of the change in the prices of goods and services either as they leave their place of production or as they enter the production process. A measure of the change in the prices received by domestic producers for their outputs or of the change in the prices paid by domestic producers for their intermediate inputs.
GDP Deflator	A measure of the annual rate of price change in the economy as a whole for the period shown obtained by dividing GDP at current prices by GDP at constant prices.
Money and Finance	
Money Supply	Refers to total amount of money in circulation in a specific country.
	Money supply can be measured in different ways:
	M1 (Narrow Money) is a measure of money supply that includes all coins and notes (M0) as well as personal money in current accounts. M2 (Intermediate Money) is the sum of M1 and personal money in deposit accounts. M3 (Broad Money) is the sum of M2 and government and other deposits. According to the Organisation for Economic Co-operation and Development, M3 includes currency, deposits with an agreed maturity of up to two years, deposits redeemable at notice of up to 3 months and repurchase agreements, money market fund shares or units and debt securities up to two years.
	Not all countries publish the same types of aggregates, and even when aggregates have the same name (e.g., M1, M2, M3, etc.) their asset composition often differs significantly. Cross-country differences in national definitions of lowered-ordered aggregates also arise from differences in the maturity categories of nontransferable deposits included in a particular money aggregate. For example, the definition of M2 in one country may include time deposits with maturities of 1 year or less, whereas another country's M2 definition may include time deposits with maturities of 2 years or less.
	When the monetary policy strategy consists of monetary aggregate targeting, the choice of the definition of the targeted aggregate is guided mainly by two considerations. The aggregate should be sufficiently sensitive to interest rate changes for the central bank to be able to control it and display a stable relationship over time to the movement of the overall price level.
Interest Rate on Savings Deposits	Rate paid by commercial and similar banks for savings deposits.
Interest Rate on Time Deposits	Rate paid by commercial and similar banks for time deposits.
Lending Interest Rate	Bank rate that usually meets the short- and medium-term financing needs of the private sector. This rate is normally differentiated according to creditworthiness of borrowers and objectives of financing.
Yield on Short-Term Treasury Bills	Rate at which short-term securities are issued or traded in the market.
Domestic Credit Provided by Banking Sector	Includes all credits to various sectors on a gross basis, except credit to the central government, which is net. The banking sector includes monetary authorities, deposit money banks, and other banking institutions for which data are available (including institutions that do not accept transferable deposits but do incur such liabilities as time and savings deposits). Examples of other banking institutions are savings and mortgage loan institutions and building and loan associations.
Ratio of Bank Nonperforming Loans to Total Gross Loans	Value of nonperforming loans divided by the total value of the loan portfolio (including nonperforming loans before the deduction of loan loss provisions). The amount recorded as nonperforming should be the gross value of the loan as recorded in the balance sheet, not just the amount that is overdue.
Stock Market Price Index	Index that measures changes in the prices of stocks traded in the stock exchange. The price changes of the stocks are usually weighted by their market capitalization.
Stock Market Capitalization	The share price times the number of shares outstanding (also known as market value).

continued.

Indicator	Definition
Exchange Rates	
Official Exchange Rate	The exchange rate determined by national authorities or the rate determined in the legally sanctioned exchange market. It is calculated as an annual average based on the monthly averages (local currency units relative to the US dollar).
Purchasing Power Parity Conversion Factor	Number of units of country B's currency that are needed in country B to purchase the same quantity of an individual good or service, which one unit of country A's currency can purchase in country A.
Price Level Index	Ratio of the relevant PPP to the exchange rate. It is expressed as an index on a base of 100. A price level index (PLI) greater than 100 means that, when the national average prices are converted at exchange rates, the resulting prices tend to be higher on average than prices in the base country (or countries) of the region (and vice versa). At the level of GDP, PLIs provide a measure of the differences in the general price levels of countries. PLIs are also referred to as comparative price levels.
GLOBALIZATION	
Balance of Payments	
Trade in Goods Balance	Difference between exports and imports of goods.
Trade in Services Balance	Difference between exports and imports of services.
Current Account Balance	Sum of net exports of goods, services, net income, and net current transfers.
Workers' Remittances and Compensation of Employees, Receipts	Consist of: (1) Current transfers from migrant workers who are residents of the host country to recipients in their country of origin. To count as resident, the workers must have been living in the host country for more than a year. (2) Compensation of employees of migrants who have lived in the host country for less than a year. (3) Migrants' transfers defined as the net worth of migrants who are expected to remain in the host country for more than 1 year that is transferred from one country to another at the time of migration.
Foreign Direct Investment	Refers to net inflows of investment to acquire a lasting management interest (10% or more of voting stock) in an enterprise operating in an economy other than that of the investor. It is the sum of equity capital, reinvestment of earnings, other long-term capital, and short-term capital as shown in the balance of payments.
External Trade	
Merchandise Exports or Imports	Covers all movable goods, with a few specified exceptions, the ownership of which changes between a resident and a foreigner. For merchandise exports, it represents the value of the goods and related distributive services at the customs frontier of the exporting economy, i.e., the free-on-board value. Merchandise imports, on the other hand, are reported in cost, insurance, and freight values.
Trade in Goods	Sum of merchandise exports and merchandise imports.
International Reserves	
International Reserves	External assets that are readily available to and controlled by monetary authorities for meeting balance of payments financing needs, for intervention in exchange markets to affect the currency exchange rate, and for other related purposes (such as maintaining confidence in the currency and the economy, and serving as a basis for foreign borrowing). Consist of monetary gold, special drawing rights (SDR) holdings, reserve position in the International Monetary Fund (IMF), currency and deposits, securities (including debt and equity securities), financial derivatives, and other claims (loans and other financial instruments).
Ratio of International Reserves to Imports	International reserves outstanding at the end of the year as a ratio to imports of goods from the balance of payments during the year, where imports of goods are expressed in terms of monthly average. It is a useful measure for reserve needs of countries with limited access to capital markets.

continued.

Indicator	Definition
Capital Flows	
Official Flows	Flows of official financing administered with the promotion of the economic development and welfare of developing countries as the main objective, and which are concessional in character with a grant element of at least 25% (using a fixed 10% rate of discount). By convention, ODA flows comprise contributions of donor government agencies, at all levels, to developing countries ("bilateral ODA") and to multilateral institutions. ODA receipts comprise disbursements by bilateral donors and multilateral institutions. Lending by export credit agencies—with the pure purpose of export promotion—is excluded.
Net Private Flows	Sum of direct investment, portfolio investment, and private net export credits of Development Assistance Committee economies only. Direct investment is a category of international investment made by a resident entity in one economy (direct investor) with the objective of establishing a lasting interest in an enterprise resident in an economy other than that of the investor (direct investment enterprise). "Lasting interest" implies the existence of a long-term relationship between the direct investor and the enterprise and a significant degree of influence by the direct investor on the management of the direct investment enterprise. Direct investment involves both the initial transaction between the two entities and all subsequent capital transactions between them and among affiliated enterprises, both incorporated and unincorporated. Portfolio investment is the category of international investment that covers investment in equity and debt securities, excluding any such instruments that are classified as direct investment or reserve assets.
Aggregate Net Resource Flows	Sum of net official and private capital flows. Net flow is disbursements less principal repayments.
External Indebtedness	
Total External Debt	Debt owed to nonresidents repayable in currency, goods, or services. It is the sum of public, publicly guaranteed, and private nonguaranteed long-term debt, use of IMF credit, and short-term debt. Short-term debt includes all debt having an original maturity of 1 year or less and interest in arrears on long-term debt.
Public and Publicly Guaranteed Debt	Public and publicly guaranteed debt comprises long-term external obligations of public debtors, including the national government, political subdivisions (or an agency of either), and autonomous public bodies, and external obligations of private debtors that are guaranteed for repayment by a public entity
External Debt as Percent of Gross National Income	Total external debt as a percentage of gross national income (GNI). GNI is the sum of value added by all resident producers plus any product taxes (less subsidies) not included in the valuation of output plus net receipts of primary income (compensation of employees and property income) from abroad.
External Debt as Percent of Exports of Goods and Services and Primary Income	Total external debt as a percentage of exports of goods, services, and income. Exports of goods, services, and primary income constitute the total value of exports of goods and services, receipts of compensation of nonresident workers, and investment income from abroad.
Total Debt Service Paid	The sum of principal repayments and interest actually paid in currency, goods, or services on long-term debt, interest paid on short-term debt, and repayments (repurchases and charges) to the IMF.
Total Debt Service Paid as Percent of Exports of Goods and Services and Primary Income	Total debt service as a percentage of exports of goods, services, and primary income.
Tourism	
International Tourist Arrivals	The number of tourists (overnight visitors) who travel to a country other than in which they usually reside, and outside their usual environment, for a period not exceeding 12 months and whose main purpose of visit is other than the activity remunerated from within the country visited. In some cases, data may also include same day visitors when data on overnight visitors are not available separately. Data refer to the number of arrivals and not to the number of persons.

continued.

Indicator	Definition
International Tourism, Receipts	The receipts earned by a destination country from inbound tourism and covering all tourism receipts resulting from expenditures made by visitors from abroad. These include lodging, food and drinks, fuel, transport in the country, entertainment, shopping, etc. This concept includes receipts generated by overnight as well as by same-day trips. It excludes, however, the receipts related to international transport contracted by residents of the other countries (for instance ticket receipts from foreigners travelling with a national company).
TRANSPORT AND COMMUNICATIONS	
Transport	
Road Traffic Deaths	Death caused by a road traffic crash within 24 hours (Azerbaijan, the Federated States of Micronesia, Solomon Islands, Timor-Leste, Vanuatu); 7 days (Afghanistan, the People's Republic of China, Kiribati, Tajikistan, Viet Nam); 30 days (Australia, Bhutan, Brunei Darussalam, Cambodia, Georgia, Indonesia, Kazakhstan, the Republic of Korea, Malaysia, the Maldives, the Marshall Islands, Myanmar, New Zealand, Pakistan, Singapore, Sri Lanka); 35 days in Nepal; 1 year (Japan, the Kyrgyz Republic, the Lao People's Democratic Republic, Mongolia, Tonga); unlimited time period (Armenia, Bangladesh, the Cook Islands, India, Palau, the Philippines, Thailand); no definition for other countries.
Road Network	The road network refers to the Asian Highway that consists of highway routes of international importance within Asia, including highway routes substantially crossing more than one subregion; highway routes within subregions that connect neighboring subregions; and highway routes located within member states that provide access to: (a) capital cities; (b) main industrial and agricultural centers; (c) major air, sea, and river ports; (d) major container terminals and depots; and (e) major tourist attractions.
Motor Vehicles	Include cars, buses, freight vehicles, and two- and three-wheeled vehicles.
Container Port Traffic	Port container traffic measures the flow of containers from land to sea transport modes., and vice versa, in twenty-foot equivalent units (TEUs), a standard-size container. Data refer to coastal shipping as well as international journeys. Transshipment traffic is counted as two lifts at the intermediate port (once to off-load and again as an outbound lift) and includes empty units.
Air Transport, Passengers Carried	Air passengers carried include both domestic and international aircraft passengers of air carriers registered in the country.
Air Transport, Carrier Departures Worldwide	Registered carrier departures worldwide are domestic takeoffs and takeoffs abroad of air carriers registered in the country.
Air Transport, Freight	Air freight is the volume of freight, express, and diplomatic bags carried on each flight stage (operation of an aircraft from takeoff to its next landing), measured in metric tons times kilometers traveled.
Rail Lines	Rail lines are the length of railway route available for train service, irrespective of the number of parallel tracks.
Rail Network	Length of rail lines divided by the land area (in square kilometers).
Railways, Passengers Carried	Passengers carried by railway are the number of passengers transported by rail times kilometers traveled.
Railways, Goods Transported	Goods transported by railway are the volume of goods transported by railway, measured in metric tons times kilometers traveled.
Communications	
Telephone Subscribers	Fixed telephone subscriptions refers to the sum of active number of analogue fixed telephone lines, voice-over-IP subscriptions, fixed wireless local loop subscriptions, ISDN voice-channel equivalents, and fixed public payphones.
Mobile Phone Subscribers	This is the proportion of individuals who used a mobile telephone in the last 3 months. A mobile (cellular) telephone refers to a portable telephone subscribing to a public mobile telephone service using cellular technology, which provides access to the PSTN. This includes analogue and digital cellular systems and technologies such as IMT-2000 (3G) and IMT-Advanced. Users of both postpaid subscriptions and prepaid accounts are included.
Fixed-broadband Subscribers	Fixed broadband subscriptions refers to fixed subscriptions to high-speed access to the public internet (a TCP/IP connection), at downstream speeds equal to, or greater than, 256 kbit/s. This includes cable modem, DSL, fiber-to-the-home/building, other fixed (wired)-broadband subscriptions, satellite broadband and terrestrial fixed wireless broadband. This total is measured irrespective of the method of payment. It excludes subscriptions that have access to data communications (including the Internet) via mobile-cellular networks. It should include fixed WiMAX and any other fixed wireless technologies. It includes both residential subscriptions and subscriptions for organizations.

continued.

Indicator	Definition
Internet Users	This is the frequency of internet use by individuals who used the internet from any location in the last 3 months. The internet is a worldwide public computer network. It provides access to a number of communication services including the World Wide Web and carries e-mail, news, entertainment and data files, irrespective of the device used (not assumed to be only via a computer—it may also be by mobile telephone, tablet, PDA, games machine, digital TV etc.). Access can be via a fixed or mobile network.

ENERGY AND ELECTRICITY

Energy

Indicator	Definition
GDP per Unit of Energy Use	The ratio of GDP to total energy use (measured in terms of per kilogram of oil equivalent) with GDP converted to 2011 constant international dollars using PPP rates. An international dollar has the same purchasing power over GDP as a US dollar has in the United States.
Energy Production	Forms of primary energy—petroleum (crude oil, natural gas liquids, and oil from nonconventional sources); natural gas; solid fuels (coal, lignite, and other derived fuels); and combustible renewables and waste—and primary electricity, all converted into oil equivalents. Primary electricity is electricity generated by nuclear, hydro, wind, and solar power.
Energy Use	Usage of primary energy before its transformation to other end-use fuels, which is equal to indigenous production plus imports and stock changes, minus exports and fuels supplied to ships and aircraft engaged in international transport.
Energy Exports, Net	Estimated as energy exports less imports, both measured in oil equivalents.
Energy Imports, Net	Energy imports, net estimated as energy use less production, both measured in oil equivalents.

Electricity

Indicator	Definition
Electricity Production	Total amount of electricity generated by a power plant. It includes own-use electricity, as well as transmission and distribution losses.
Sources of Electricity	Electricity is produced as primary as well as secondary energy. Primary electricity is obtained from natural sources such as hydro, wind, solar, tide, and wave power. Secondary electricity is produced from the heat of nuclear fission of nuclear fuels, from geothermal heat and solar thermal heat, and by burning primary combustible fuels such as coal, natural gas, oil and renewables and wastes. After electricity is produced, it is distributed to final consumers through national or international transmission and distribution grids.
Electric Power Consumption Per Capita	Measure of the production of power plants and combined heat and power plants less transmission, distribution, and transformation losses and own use by heat and power plants, divided by midyear population.
Household Electrification Rate	Percentage of households with an electricity connection.

ENVIRONMENT

Land

Indicator	Definition
Agricultural Land or Area	Land area that is arable, under permanent crops, and under permanent meadows and pastures.
Arable Land	Land under temporary agricultural crops (multiple-cropped areas are counted only once), temporary meadows for mowing or pasture, land under market and kitchen gardens and land temporarily fallow (less than 5 years). The abandoned land resulting from shifting cultivation is not included. Data for arable land are not meant to indicate the amount of land that are potentially cultivable.
Permanent Cropland	Land cultivated with long-term crops that do not have to be replanted for several years (such as cocoa and coffee); land under trees and shrubs producing flowers, such as roses and jasmine; and nurseries (except those for forest trees, which should be classified under "forest"). Permanent meadows and pastures are excluded from land under permanent crops.
Deforestation Rate	Rate of permanent conversion of natural forest area into other uses, including shifting cultivation, permanent agriculture, ranching, settlements, and infrastructure development. Deforested areas do not include areas logged but intended for regeneration or areas degraded by fuelwood gathering, acid precipitation, or forest fires. A negative rate indicates reforestation or increase in forest area.

continued.

Indicator	Definition
Pollution	
Nitrous Oxide Emissions	Nitrous oxide emissions are mainly from fossil fuel combustion, fertilizers, rainforest fires, and animal waste. Nitrous oxide is a powerful greenhouse gas, with an estimated atmospheric lifetime of 114 years, compared with 12 years for methane. The per kilogram global warming potential of nitrous oxide is nearly 310 times that of carbon dioxide within 100 years.
Methane Emissions	Methane omissions are those stemming from human activities such as agriculture and from industrial methane production. A kilogram of methane is 21 times as effective at trapping heat in the earth's atmosphere as a kilogram of carbon dioxide within 100 years.
Other Greenhouse Gases	By-product emissions of hydrofluorocarbons, perfluorocarbons, and sulfur hexafluoride.
Agricultural Nitrous Oxide Emissions	Emissions produced through fertilizer use (synthetic and animal manure), animal waste management, agricultural waste burning (nonenergy, on-site), and savannah burning.
Agricultural Methane Emissions	Emissions from animals, animal waste, rice production, agricultural waste burning (nonenergy, on-site), and savannah burning.
Freshwater	
Internal renewable water resources	Internal renewable water resources (IRWR) refer to long-term average annual flow of rivers and recharge of aquifers generated from endogenous precipitation. Double counting of surface water and groundwater resources is avoided by deducting the overlap from the sum of the surface water and groundwater resources. IRWR in billion cubic meters per year refers to surface water produced internally plus groundwater produced internally deducted by the overlap between surface water and groundwater. IRWR in cubic meter per inhabitant per year is calculated as total annual internal renewable water resources divided by total population.
Annual freshwater withdrawals	Sum of surface water withdrawal and groundwater withdrawal. Total water withdrawal summed by sector deducted by: desalinated water produced, direct use of treated wastewater, and direct use of agricultural drainage water.
Water productivity	Water productivity is the ratio of the net benefits from crop, forestry, fishery, livestock, and mixed agricultural systems to the amount of water used to produce those benefits. It is calculated as GDP in constant US dollar prices divided by annual total water withdrawal.
GOVERNMENT AND GOVERNANCE	
Government Finance	
Fiscal Balance	Difference between total revenue (including grants) and total expenditure (including net lending). This provides a picture of the overall financial position of the government. When the difference is positive, then the fiscal position is in surplus; otherwise, it is in deficit.
Tax Revenue	Compulsory transfers to the central government for public purposes. Certain compulsory transfers such as fines, penalties, and most social security contributions are excluded. Refunds and corrections of erroneously collected tax revenue are treated as negative revenue.
Total Government Revenue	Includes current and capital revenues. Current revenue is the revenue accruing from taxes, as well as all current nontax revenues except transfers received from foreign governments and international institutions. Major items of nontax revenue include receipts from government enterprises, rents and royalties, fees and fines, forfeits, private donations, and repayments of loans properly defined as components of net lending. Capital revenue constitutes the proceeds from the sale of nonfinancial capital assets.

continued.

Indicator	Definition
Total Government Expenditure	Sum of current and capital expenditures. Current expenditure comprises purchases of goods and services by the central government, transfers to noncentral government units and to households, subsidies to producers, and interest on public debt. Capital expenditure, on the other hand, covers outlays for the acquisition or construction of capital assets and for the purchase of intangible assets, as well as capital transfers to domestic and foreign recipients. Loans and advances for capital purposes are also included.
Government Expenditure on Education	Consists of expenditure by government to provide education services at all levels.
Government Expenditure on Health	Consists of expenditure by government to provide medical products, appliances, and equipment; outpatient services; hospital services; public health services; among others.
Government Expenditure on Social Security and Welfare	Consists of expenditure by government to provide benefits in cash or in kind to persons who are sick, fully or partially disabled, of old age, survivors, or unemployed, among others.
Governance	
Cost of Business Start-Up Procedure	Cost to register a business normalized by presenting it as a percentage of GNI per capita. It includes all official fees and fees for legal or professional services if such services are required by law. Fees for purchasing and legalizing company books are included if these transactions are required by law. Although value added tax registration can be counted as a separate procedure, value added tax is not part of the incorporation cost. The company law, the commercial code, and specific regulations and fee schedules are used as sources for calculating costs. In the absence of fee schedules, a government officer's estimate is taken as an official source. In the absence of a government officer's estimate, estimates of incorporation lawyers are used. If several incorporation lawyers provide different estimates, the median reported value is applied. In all cases, the cost excludes bribes.
Time Required to Start Up a Business	Number of calendar days needed to complete the procedures to legally operate a business. If a procedure can be speeded up at additional cost, the fastest procedure, independent of cost, is chosen.
Corruption Perceptions Index	The Corruptions Perception Index ranks countries and territories based on how corrupt their public sector is perceived to be. It is a composite index—a combination of polls—drawing on corruption—related data collected by a variety of reputable institutions. The index reflects the views of observers from around the world, including experts living and working in the countries and territories evaluated. The scores range between 0 (highly corrupt) and 100 (very clean). A country's rank indicates its position relative to the other countries or territories included in the index. It is important to keep in mind that a country's rank can change simply because new countries enter the index or others drop out.

Global Value Chains

Global Value Chains (GVCs): A network of interlinked stages of production for goods and services that straddles international borders. Typically, a GVC involves combining imported and domestically produced goods and services into products that are then exported for use as intermediates in the subsequent stage of production or as final consumption products.

Domestic Value Added (DVA): Domestic inputs of goods and services in the overall exports of an economy.

Foreign Value Added (FVA): Imported inputs of goods and services in the overall exports of an economy.

Pure Double-Counted Terms (PDC): In a GVC, some goods or services may cross the same national border for three or more times. For example, the United States (US) may first export cellphone parts for assembly in the People's Republic of China (PRC); then the PRC exports the assembled cellphones to the US for further enhancement; finally, the US exports the enhanced cellphones to the PRC for final consumption. In this process, the parts produced by the US are counted as its export twice. The double-counted value added of these parts is referred to as the "pure double-counted terms."

GVC participation: There are various ways to measure economies' participation in GVCs. A simple metric is the share of foreign value added in total exports. It reflects the extent to which an economy uses foreign inputs in producing for exports. A more rigorous measure is **Vertical Specialization (VS)**, which is the share of foreign value added and pure double counted terms in total exports.

Revealed Comparative Advantage (RCA): It is an index, introduced by Bela Balassa, to calculate the relative advantage an economy has in the export of any given good or service. An economy is said to have an RCA in a product if it exports more than its "fair share," or a share that is equal to or greater than the share of total world trade that the product represents.

Domestic Value Added Absorbed Abroad (VAX_G): All domestic value added embodied in the gross exports and ultimately absorbed abroad.

Domestic Value Added First Exported then Returned Home (RDV_B): Domestic value added that are exported first, but then return to the home economy for domestic consumption. This would happen, for example, when the Philippines export electronic parts to the PRC for final assembly of laptops, which then return to the Philippines for final consumption.

Value Added Exports by Forward Industrial Linkages (VAX_F): Domestic value added that is originated from a particular sector and ultimately absorbed abroad via the exports of all sectors in the source economy. For example, besides direct export, the value added of German business services sector may be exported as an input to German automobiles. This indicator is useful in understanding the contribution of a given sector to the economy's aggregate exports.

Value Added Exports by Backward Industrial Linkages (VAX_B): Value added that is originated from all domestic sectors and ultimately absorbed abroad via the export of a particular sector in the source economy. For example, the domestic value added of German automobile exports includes that of all German sectors (e.g., business service, computers) used as inputs.

www.ingramcontent.com/pod-product-compliance
Lightning Source LLC
Chambersburg PA
CBHW041428270326
41932CB00031B/3492